A
CHECKLIST OF
AMERICAN IMPRINTS
for
1845

Items 45-1–45-7137

compiled by

CAROL RINDERKNECHT
and
SCOTT BRUNTJEN

The Scarecrow Press, Inc.
Lanham, Md., and London

SCARECROW PRESS, INC.

Published in the United States of America
by Scarecrow Press, Inc.
4720 Boston Way
Lanham, Maryland 20706

4 Pleydell Gardens, Folkestone
Kent CT20 2DN, England

ISBN 0–8108–3109–0 (cloth : alk. paper)

ISSN 0361–7920

⊖™ The paper used in this publication meets the minimum requirements of
American National Standard for Information Sciences—Permanence of
Paper for Printed Library Materials, ANSI Z39.48–1984.
Manufactured in the United States of America.

PREFACE TO 1845

These volumes continue to incorporate the ideas presented by reviewers of earlier editions of *The Checklist*.

Beginning with the volume for 1840, the entry numbers have taken a new form. Prior to the 1840s, each entry was numbered sequentially. The numbers had no meaning. One review of the indexes for the 1830s noted that it would be helpful to know which volume to examine after finding the entry in the index. In these volumes the entry number has as a prefix two digits representing the year. Thus 42-1 is the first item for the 1842 volume and 43-2 is the second item in the 1843 *Checklist*. When the indexes are compiled for the decade of the 1840s, the user will not have to examine the entry numbers on the spines of the individual *Checklists* to find the correct volume.

One reviewer questioned how the location symbols were constructed and where one could find a table listing the library represented by the symbol. The *Checklist* uses the National Union Catalog (NUC) symbol for the library. This system was developed by Frank Petersen in the 1920s. Petersen's system was expanded by Douglas C. McMurtrie, the primary leader of the American Imprints Inventory; the governmental agency which listed most of the raw material that the compilers use in identifying the items for each volume of the *Checklist*. A further discussion of McMurtrie, The American Imprints Inventory, and the NUC symbols can be found in *Douglas C. McMurtrie, Bibliographer and Historian of Printing* by Scott Bruntjen and Melissa L. Young published by Scarecrow Press in 1979. A fairly complete list of NUC symbols is appended to volume 200 of *The National Union Catalog, pre-1956 Imprints* published by Mansell in 1972.

Previous editions of the *Checklist* used "dash-on entries" for representing the same author in the second and subsequent items in the same volume. This technique is well documented for use in bibliographies but the compilers found it confusing when one author, such as the City of New York, might have fifty entries in a volume. The reader was forced to look back to the first entry to determine the author of the item. Beginning with 1840, the author is provided in full for each entry. As this is a reference work to be used one item at a time, this change should make it easier for the reader.

Carol R. Rinderknecht and Scott Bruntjen

Eldora, Colorado

November, 1995

A

A'Beckett, Gilbert Abbott, 1811-1856. The comic blackstone. Philadelphia: Carey and Hart, printer, 1845-1846. 3 v. in 1. MB. 45-1

A'Beckett, Gilbert Abbott, 1811-1856. The comic blackstone. Philadelphia: Carey and Hart, printer, 1845. 52 p. LU. 45-2

A'Beckett, Gilbert Abbott, 1811-1856. George Cruikshank's table book. Philadelphia: Carey, 1845. 70 p. DLC. 45-3

A'Beckett, Gilbert Abbott, 1811-1856. Heathen mythology, by "Punch." Philadelphia: Carey and Hart, 1845. 71 p. CaLU; MB; MH; PHi; PP. 45-4

Abbot, Anne Wales. Kate and Lizzie, or six months out of school. New York: C.S. Francis and company, etc., etc., 1845. MH; NN; NNC; PPULC. 45-5

Abbot, Anne Wales. The tamed and the untamed, and other stories. By the author of Willie Rogers. Boston: S.G. Simpkins, 1845. [9]-96 p. DLC; MH; MHi; PPULC; ViU. 45-6

Abbot, Anne Wales. Willie Rogers; or temper improved. Second edition. Boston. 1845. MH. 45-7

Abbot, Theodore. Endless amusements; or the art of legerdemain made easy to young persons. Second edition. Boston: T. Abbott, 1845. 108 p. CtY. 45-8

Abbot Academy, Andover, Massachusetts. Catalogue. Andover, 1845-1871. MHi. 45-9

Abbott, Austin. Religious bigotry. Being a statement of facts, in relation to the death and burial of Mr. Stephen Marlbe. Also, a funeral sermon by Rev. A. Abbott. Also, a letter by Rev. John Boyden. Boston: A. Tompkins, 1845. 28 p. ICMe; MiD-B; MMeT; MWHi; RPB. 45-10

Abbott, Gorham Dummer. The death of the righteous. A discourse delivered... on the occasion of the funeral services of Dr. Matson Smith... New York: Printed for the family, 1845. 32 p. InHi; MeLew-B; MH-AH; MHi; MWA. 45-11

Abbott, Jacob, 1803-1879. The corner stone, or a familiar illustration of the principles of Christian truth... Cooperstown: H. and E. Phinney, 1845. 360 p. DLC; GEU-T; MeB; NbOP; ViRU. 45-12

Abbott, Jacob, 1803-1879. Cousin Lucy on the seashore. Boston: B.B. Mussey, 1845. 180 p. NN; RJa. 45-13

Abbott, Jacob, 1803-1879. Cousin Lucy's conversations. By the author of Rollo books. Boston: B.B. Mussey, 1845. 180 p. RJa. 45-14

Abbott, Jacob, 1803-1879. Jonas, a judge; or law among the boys. By the author of the Rollo books. Boston: W.D. Ticknor and company, 1845. 179 p. Ct; MBC; MH; OO; PWaybu. 45-15

Abbott, Jacob, 1803-1879. Jonas on a farm in winter, by the author of the Rollo books. Boston: Ticknor, 1845. 180 p. MH; OClW. 45-16

Abbott, Jacob, 1803-1879. Marco Paul's adventures in pursuit of knowledge. City of Boston. Boston: B.B. Mussey, 1845. 144 p. MB; MH; Nh-Hi; NN. 45-17

Abbott, Jacob, 1803-1879. Marco Paul's adventures in pursuit of knowledge. Forests of Maine. Boston: Benjamin Mussey, 1845. ViU. 45-18

Abbott, Jacob, 1803-1879. Marco Paul's travels and adventures in the pursuit of knowledge. City of New York. Fifth edition. Boston: T.H. Carter and company, 1845. 144 p. CoD; DLC; MH; Nh-Hi; NN. 45-19

Abbott, Jacob, 1803-1879. Marco Paul's travels and adventures in the pursuit of knowledge. State of Vermont. Fifth edition. Boston: T.H. Carter, 1845. 144 p. MiD. 45-20

Abbott, Jacob, 1803-1879. Marco Paul's travels and adventures in the pursuit of knowledge on the Erie Canal. Fifth edition. Boston: T.H. Carter and company, 1845. 144 p. MWA; NN. 45-21

Abbott, Jacob, 1803-1879. Rollo at play; or safe amusements. Fifth edition. Philadelphia: Hogan and Thompson; Boston: Gould, Kendall and Lincoln, 1845. 191 p. DLC; MH; ScCliTO. 45-22

Abbott, Jacob, 1803-1879. Rollo at school. Philadelphia: Hogan and Thompson, etc., etc., 1845. 194 p. MDux; MH; RJa. 45-23

Abbott, Jacob, 1803-1879. Rollo at work; or the way for a boy to learn to be industrious. Fifth edition. Philadelphia: Hogan and Thompson, etc., etc., 1845. DLC; MH; NN. 45-24

Abbott, Jacob, 1803-1879. Rollo learning to read, or easy stories for young children. Philadelphia: Hogan and Thompson; etc., etc., 1845. MH; PU. 45-25

Abbott, Jacob, 1803-1879. Rollo learning to talk. New edition. Philadelphia: Hogan and Thompson; Boston: Gould, Kendall and Lincoln, 1845. 179 p. MDux. 45-26

Abbott, Jacob, 1803-1879. Rollo philosophy. Part 1-4. Philadelphia: Hogan and Thompson, etc., etc., 1845. 4 v. M; MDux; MeB; MH; PPF. 45-27

Abbott, Jacob, 1803-1879. Rollo's correspondence. Philadelphia: Hogan and Thompson; Boston: Gould, Kendall and Lincoln, 1845. 189 p. CtY; MDux; MH. 45-28

Abbott, Jacob, 1803-1879. Rollo's experiments. Philadelphia: Hogan and Thompson, etc., etc., 1845. MH. 45-29

Abbott, Jacob, 1803-1879. Rollo's Museum. Philadelphia: Hogan and Thompson, etc., etc., 1845. 187 p. ICU; MH; NjN. 45-30

Abbott, Jacob, 1803-1879. Rollo's travels. Philadelphia: Hogan and

Thompson, etc., etc., 1845. 189 p. CtY; MH. 45-31

Abbott, Jacob, 1803-1879. Rollo's vacation. Philadelphia: Hogan and Thompson, etc., etc., 1845. 191 p. MH; ViU. 45-32

Abbott, Jacob, 1803-1879. The way to do good: or the Christian character mature. The sequel to "The young christian and cornerstone." Cooperstown: H. and E. Phinney, 1845. [13]-348 p. ICU; IG; MWA; MeB; TN. 45-33

Abbott, Jacob, 1803-1879. The young Christian; or a familiar illustration of the principles of Christian duty. Third edition. Cooperstown: H. and E. Phinney, 1845. 372 p. MeB; N. 45-34

Abbott, Lyman. That unknown country, the whole field explored. Springfield, Massachusetts: C.A. Nichols and company, 1845. 960 p. ODaB. 45-35

Abercrombie, John, 1780-1844. The contest and the armour, to which is added, "Think on these things." New York: Robert Carter; Pittsburg: Thomas Carter, 1845. 107 p. MH; MLow. 45-36

Abercrombie, John, 1780-1844. Essays... from the nineteenth Edinburgh edition. New York: Harper and brothers, 1845. 295 p. DLC; LNP; MeB; PAtM; ViU. 45-37

Abercrombie, John, 1780-1844. Inquiries concerning the intellectual powers, and the investigation of truth. With additions and explanations to adapt the work to the use of schools and academies. Boston: Otis, Broaders and

company, 1845. 284 p. MB; MMeT-Hi; OClW; PU; TNT. 45-38

Abercrombie, John, 1780-1844. Miscellaneous essays. New York, 1845. NN-As. 45-39

Abercrombie, John, 1780-1844. Pathological and practical researches on the diseases of the stomach, the intestinal canal, the liver and other viscera of the abdomen. Fourth American from the last London edition. Philadelphia: Lea and Blanchard, 1845. 259 p. CtY; GU-M; MNBedf; NNN; TxU-M. 45-40

Abercrombie, John, 1780-1844. The philosophy of the moral feelings... An introductory chapter with additions and explanations... By Jacob Abbott. Boston: Otis Broaders, and company, 1845. 250 p. ArCH; GGaB; LN; PAtM; ScGaL. 45-41

Abert, James William, 1820-1897. Map showing the route pursued by the exploring expedition to New Mexico and the Southern Rocky Mountains, made under the orders of Captain J.C. Fremont during the year 1845. Washington, D.C.: Government printers, 1845. CoD. 45-42

Abolition Tract Number One. [New York, 1845] CtY; MB. 45-43

Abrege de geographie. Nouvelle Orleans, Impr. par H. Meridier, 1845. 78, [3] p. DLC. 45-44

Ackerman, Abraham. First book of natural history. Twelfth edition. New York: Cady and Burgess, 1845. OMC. 45-45

Acton, Eliza, 1799-1859. Modern cookery in all its branches reduced to a system of easy practice... revised... by Mrs. S.J. Hale. From the second London edition. Philadelphia: Lea and Blanchard, 1845. 418 p. DLC; KyLx; PP; NN; WaS. 45-46

Adam, Adolphe Charles, 1803-1856. Music from the Postillon of Lonjumeau. New York, [1845] 10 p. MH. 45-47

Adam, Adolphe Charles, 1803-1856. Music from the Postillon of Lonjumeau, embracing three of the most popular songs in the opera; together with a souvenir of the whole opera, consisting of eight of the most celebrated airs, beautifully arranged by K.A. Ritter. New York: E. Ferrett and company, [1845] 16 p. MH. 45-48

Adam, Alexander, 1741-1809. A grammar of the Latin language on the basis of the grammar of Dr. Adam. Third edition. Philadelphia: Thomas, Cowperthwait and company, 1845. 320 p. CtY; DLC; MB; MH; OTifH. 45-49

Adam, Alexander, 1741-1809. Rudiments of Latin and English grammar. Third edition. Philadelphia, 1845. DLC. 45-50

Adams, Aaron Chester, b. 1815. Waiting upon God, the way to secure our country's welfare. A sermon preached upon the day of public fast, April 17, 1845. By A.C. Adams, pastor of the First Congregational Church, Gorham. Portland: Thurston, Ilsley and company, 1845. 30 p. CBPSR; MeBaT; MiD-B; NjR; PPPrHi. 45-51

Adams, Charles A. Collection of sacred hymns, for the Church of Jesus Christ of Latter Day Saints. Bellows Falls: C.A.

Adams, 1845. 160 p. CtY; MH; RPB. 45-52

Adams, Charles Baker, 1814-1853. Synopsis conchliorum jamaicensium specierum novarum conchyliorum in Jamaica reportorum synopsis. Bostoniae, 1845. 17 p. DLC; PPAN. 45-53

Adams, Daniel, 1773-1864. Arithmetic, in which the principles of operating by numbers are analytically explained and synthetically applied. Revised edition. Keene, New Hampshire: J.W. Prentiss and company, 1845. 306 p. CtHT-W; DLC; MH; MiKT; VtStjA. 45-54

Adams, Daniel, 1773-1864. The monitorial reader designed for the use of academies and schools, and as a monitor to youth. Concord, New Hampshire: L. Roby, 1845. 288 p. CtHWatk; MH; NhU; NNC. 45-55

Adams, Henry W. Christ's kingdom: a sermon delivered at the dedication of the Methodist Episcopal Church at Great Falls, New Hampshire, September 14, 1845. Worcester, [Massachusetts] P.L. Cox, printer, 1845. 32 p. CtMW; ICN; MBNMHi; Nh; NNUT; RPB. 45-56

Adams, John Milton. An address before the Independent Order of Rechabites, delivered February 19, 1845. Portland: Thurston, 1845. MeWC; PPPrHi. 45-57

Adams, John Quincy, 1767-1848. Address to his constituents, April 3, 1845. [n.p.: n.p., 1845] 16 p. CtY; MH; MHi; WHi. 45-58

Adams, John Quincy, 1767-1848. Oration on the life and character of Gilbert

Motier de Lafayette before Congress. Washington, 1845. PPL-R. 45-59

Adams, Joseph Thornton, 1796-1878. Lecture on the subject of re-annexing Texas to the United States. Delivered in New Bedford, February 10, 1845. [New Bedford] Published in the New Bedford Register, 1845. 24 p. CU-B; DLC; LNH; PHi; TxU. 45-60

Adams, Thomas F. Typographia, or the printer's instructor, a brief sketch of the origin, rise, and progress of the typographic art, with practical directions for conducting every department of an office. Third edition. Philadelphia, 1845. 282 p. CtW; ICN; MHi; NcD; NNS. 45-61

Adams, W. The fall of Croesus. By the Rev. W. Adams. New York: General Protestant Episcopal Sunday School Union, 1845. 207 p. GMilvC; NR. 45-62

Addison, Joseph, 1672-1719. The works of Joseph Addison complete in three volumes. Embracing the whole of the "Spectator," etc. New York: Harper and brothers, 1845. 3 v. ICMe; KyBgW; PWW; ScCF; OSW. 45-63

The address and reply on the presentation of a testimonial to S.P. Chase, by the colored people of Cincinnati. Cincinnati: H.W. Derby and company, 1845. 35 p. DLC; MH; NbHi; OClWHi; WaU. 45-64

Address delivered at various temperance meetings, held in the city of Boston, with an account of the grand simultaneous anniversary, February, 1845. Reported by J.R. Fitzgerald. Second thousand. Boston: Press of T.R.

Marvin, 1845. 48 p. CtY; MiD-B; MHi; MWA. 45-65

Address of claimants for indemnity for spoliations committed by the French prior to the year 1800. [New York, 1845] 8 p. CSmH. 45-66

Address of the American Republicans of Boston, to the people of Massachusetts. Boston, 1845. MBAt. 45-67

Address of the carriers of the Cincinnati Daily American Republican to its patrons, Jan. 1, 1845. Cincinnati, 1845. 4 p. OCHP. 45-68

Address of the claimants for indemnity for spoliations committed by the French, prior to the 31st of July, 1801, at a convention of claimants held at the city of New York, on October 29, 1845. [New York, 1845] 8 p. CtY; NN. 45-69

An address to Methodists on the importance of building and furnishing parsonages, read before the New London district preacher's meeting, April 8, 1845. By an itinerant. Norwich, Connecticut: Cooley, printer, 1845. 15 p. IEG; MB; MBNMHi; NcD. 45-70

Address to the clergy of all denominations of colonization [in Africa] [Washington? 1845] 15 p. MH; RPB; WHi. 45-71

Address to the Vermont and Massachusetts Railroad Company, 1845. Greenfield: Steam Press of Mirriam and Merick, 1845. 16 p. DLC; MeHi. 45-72

Addresses delivered at a temperance meeting. Boston, 1845. MB. 45-73

Adler, George J., 1821-1868. A progressive German reader, adapted to the American edition of Ollendorff's German grammar with copious notes and vocabulary, by G.J. Adler. New York: D. Appleton and company, 1845. 308 p. WHi. 45-74

Adsit, S. An address delivered before the youth's Missionary Society, of the Baptist Church, Penn Yan, July, 1845. Penn-Yan, 1845. 12 p. NHC-S. 45-75

Advent tracts. Boston: Published by J.V. Himes, [1845] 2 v. ICBB; RPE. 45-76

Aesopus. Fables of Aesop and others, translated into English: with instructive applications, and one hundred and ninety-eight illustrations by Samuel Croxall. Philadelphia: T. Cowperthwait and company, 1845. 358 p. DLC; MF; MnU; NNF; ViR. 45-77

Aetna Insurance Company. Report of the Aetna Fire Insurance Company in the city of New York, in answer to a resolution of the Assembly, transmitting statement of premiums received and taxes paid during the years 1842, 1843, and 1844. [Albany] 1845. 3 p. WHi. 45-78

Affecting history of the Dutchess of C-, who was confined nine years in a horrid dungeon under ground. Boston, 1845. CtHWatk. 45-79

Agnew, John Holmes. A manual on the christian sabbath, embracing a consideration of its perpetual obligation, change of day, utility and duties. With an introductory essay by D. Miller of Princeton, New Jersey. Philadelphia: W.S. Young, 1845. 198 p. PPM. 45-80

Agricultural almanac for the year 1846. Lancaster: Printed and sold by John Bear, [1845] 34 p. NcU; NjR. 45-81

Aikin, John, 1747-1822. Select works of the British poets, in a chronological series from Ben Johnson to Beattie. Philadelphia: Thomas Wardle, 1845. CtY; MeBa; OCX; WGr. 45-82

Ainsworth, William Harrison, 1805-1882. St. James's or the court of Queen Anne, a historical romance. New York: Burgess, 1845. 138 p. KSalW; PBm. 45-83

Akerly, J. Voltaire and Rousseau against the atheists; or essays and detached passages from those writers, in relation to the being and attributes of God. Selected and translated from the French. New York: Wiley and Putnam, 1845. 131 p. InCW; LN; NjMD; PPAN; RPA. 45-84

Alabama. Acts passed at the annual session of the general assembly of the state of Alabama; begun and held in the city of Tuscaloosa, on the first Monday in December, 1844. Tuscaloosa: John McCormick, 1845. 247 p. A-SC; In-SC; L; Mi-L; NNLI. 45-85

Alabama. Classification of the indebtedness of each county to the state bank and branches. Tuscaloosa: John M'Cormick, 1845. 14 p. TxU. 45-86

Alabama. Journal of the House of Representatives of the state of Alabama at a session begun and held at Tuscaloosa, December 2, 1844. Tuscaloosa, 1845. 403 p. A-SC. 45-87

Alabama. Journal of the Senate of the

General Assembly of the state of Alabama. Begun and held in the city of Tuscaloosa on the first Monday in December, 1844. Tuscaloosa: John M'Cormick, 1845. 291 p. A-SC. 45-88

Alabama. Message of His Excellency, Gov. Benjamin Fitzpatrick. December 2, 1845. Tuscaloosa: John M'Cormick, 1845. 12 p. NN. 45-89

Alabama. Message of His Excellency, Gov. J.F. Martin, December 16, 1845. Tuscaloosa: John McCormick, 1845. 8 p. NN. 45-90

Alabama. Report of joint examining committee on the condition of debts due the state bank and branches. Tuscaloosa, 1845. 16 p. GEU. 45-91

Alabama. Report of the commissioners appointed to examine the bank of the state of Alabama. Tuscaloosa: John Mc-Cormick, 1845. 16 p. GEU. 45-92

Albany, New York. Adventists Conference. Proceedings of the Mutual Conference of Adventists, held in Albany, April 29, 30, May 1, 1845. New York [1845?] 32 p. MWA. 45-93

Albany, New York. Laws and ordinances of the common council of the city of Albany... with the charter and the several state laws relating to the said city. Albany: Weed, 1845. 218 p. ICU; MB; NN; PU; WHi. 45-94

Albany, New York. First Baptist Church. A compendious view of the doctrine, sentiments, discipline, covenants, etc. of the First Baptist Church. Albany, 1845. 15 p. CtY; MHi. 45-95

Albany, New York. Gallery of Fine Arts. Catalogue of the first exhibition. Albany, 1846. CtY; MB; N; NN; PPL. 45-96

Albany, New York. St. Peter's Church. Report to the vestry... of the lay delegates appointed by them who attended the diocesan convention of the Protestant Episcopal Church, held in the city of New York on September 23, 1845 and continued to the 30th of the same month. Albany: Erastus H. Pease, 1845. 42 p. CtHT; DLC; MB; MiD-B; NNG. 45-97

Albion Life Insurance Company. Prospectus... New York: William Osborn, 1845. MH-BA. 45-98

Albion Mining Company. Articles of association of the Albion Mining Company, of Eagle River, Lake Superior, established July, 1845. New York: Van Norden and King, 1845. 11 p. NNE; WHi. 45-99

Albion School, Philadelphia. Catalogue of the students in the Albion School; under the direction of William H. Beach, as principal. Philadelphia, 1845. 12 p. PHi. 45-100

Albro, John Adams, 1799-1866. The father of New England. Boston: C.C. Little and J. Brown, 1845. 40 p. CtY; MBC; MiD-B; PPL; RPB. 45-101

Albro, John Adams, 1799-1866. Scripture questions. On the parables of New Testament. part I for the younger scholars. Revised edition. Boston: Massachusetts Sabbath School Society, 1845. 90 p. CtY-D; IEG; LNB; MH; NNUT. 45-102

Alcott, William Andrus, 1798-1859. Beloved physician; or life and travels of Luke the Evangelist. New York; G. Lane and C.B. Tippett, 1845. 179 p. CSt; DLC; MBC; MNBedfHi; NjMD. 45-103

Alcott, William Andrus, 1798-1859. The boy's guide to usefulness; designed to prepare the way for the young man's guide. Boston: Waite, Peirce and company, 1845. 180 p. DLC. 45-104

Alcott, William Andrus, 1798-1859. Sketches of William Penn. Boston: Waite, Peirce and company, 1845. 137 p. InCW; NCH; OO. 45-105

Alcott, William Andrus, 1798-1859. The young husband; a manual of the duties, moral, religious, and domestic, imposed by the relations of married life. Philadelphia: Lindsay, 1845. 288 p. OO. 45-106

Alcott, William Andrus, 1798-1859. The young man's guide. Worcester: S.A. Howland, 1845. 392 p. LPL. 45-107

Alcott, William Andrus, 1798-1859. Young man's guide. Fifteenth edition. Boston, 1845. PU. 45-108

Alcott, William Andrus, 1798-1859. The young man's guide. Revised and enlarged. Sixteenth edition. Boston: T.R. Marvin, 1845. 392 p. CtY. 45-109

Alcott, William Andrus, 1798-1859. The young woman's guide to excellence. Ninth edition. Boston: Waite, Peirce, 1845. 356 p. KWiU; MH; MNotn; ViU. 45-110

Alden, Albert. Pictorial map of the United States of North America. Barre, Massachusetts, 1845. 2 sheets. MB. 45-111

Alden, Joseph, 1807-1885. The cardinal flower, and other tales. Boston: Benjamin Perkins and company, 1845. 108 p. CtY; DLC; MB. 45-112

Alden, Joseph, 1807-1885. The great secret discovered; a tale for children. New York: M.W. Dodd, 1845. 65 p. OU; PEaL. 45-113

Alden, Joseph, 1807-1885. Jesus and the woman of Sychar. Boston: Massachusetts Sabbath School Society, 1845. 54 p. DLC. 45-114

Alden, Joseph, 1807-1885. The light hearted girl; a tale for children. Boston, 1845. DLC. 45-115

Alexander, Archibald, 1772-1851. Biographical sketches of the founder, and principal alumni of the Log College. Together with an account of the revivals of religion, under their ministry. Collected and edited by Rev. A. Alexander. Princeton, New Jersey: Printed by J.T. Robinson, 1845. 369 p. CU; DLC; GU; IaGG; ICN. 45-116

Alexander, Archibald, 1772-1851. The duty of Christians in relation to the conversion of the world. New York: Mission House, 1845. 21 p. ICP; NjPT; NN; NNMr; PPPrHi. 45-117

Alexander, Archibald, 1772-1851. Practical truths. New York: American Tract Society, 1845. 396 p. IaPeC. 45-118

Alexander, Archibald, 1772-1851. Suggestions in vindication of Sunday schools but more especially for the improvement of Sunday school books, and the enlargement of the plan of instruction. Revised and enlarged by the author. Philadelphia: American Sunday School Union, 1845. 42 p. InU; MB; MWA; PHi; PPPrHi. 45-119

Alexander, Archibald, 1772-1851. Thoughts on religious experience. Philadelphia: Presbyterian Board of Publication, 1845. 397 p. ICarC. 45-120

Alexander, James Waddel, 1804-1859. An address before the synod of New York by order of that body on the 22nd of October, 1845. [n.p., 1845?] 7 p. MiU; NjP; NjR; PPL; PPPrHi. 45-121

Alexander, John Henry, 1812-1867. Report on the standards of weight and measure for the state of Maryland... [Baltimore: Printed by J.D. Toy, 1845?] 213 p. CtMW; DSG; MdBE; PPAmP; Vi. 45-122

Alexander, Stephen, 1806-1883. Syllabus of ... lectures on astronomy for the use of students in the senior class in the College of New Jersey. Part 1. Princeton: John T. Robinson, 1845. 167 p. LNHT; MH; NjP; PU. 45-123

Alfieri, Vittorio, 1749-1803. The autobiography of Vittorio Alfieri, the tragic poet. Born at Asti, 1749, died at Florence, 1803. Translated with an original essay on the genius and times of Alfieri. By C. Edwards Lester. New York: Paine and Burgess, 1845. 269 p. AMob; CtB; LNH; ScCC; ViU. 45-124

Alfieri, Vittorio, 1749-1803. The autobiography of Vittorio Alfieri, the tragic poet. Translated with an original essay on the genius and times of Alfieri by C. Edwards Lester. Second edition. New York: Paine and Burgess, 1845. 269 p. IaU; MeB; NjP; PU; RNR. 45-125

Alfred University. Annual catalogues of Alfred University and Teachers Seminary. Alfred: E.S. Palmer, 1845. 16 p. NE. 45-126

Alger, Francis, 1807-1863. On the zinc mines of Franklin, New Jersey. New Haven: Printed by B.L. Hamlen, 1845. 15 p. DLC. 45-127

Alison, Archibald, 1792-1867. History of Europe, from the commencement of the French Revolution in 1789 to the restoration of the Bourbons in 1815. New York: A.S. Barnes and company, 1845. 532 p. NoLoc. 45-128

Alison, Archibald, 1792-1867. History of Europe from the commencement of the French Revolution in 1789 to the restoration of the Bourbons in 1815. New York: Harper and brothers, 1845. 4 v. IU; KyLoS; MNBedf; MoK; TSewU. 45-129

Alison, Archibald, 1792-1867. The history of Europe, from the commencement of the French Revolution in 1789 to the restoration of the Bourbons in 1815. Third edition. New York: A.S. Barnes and company, 1845. 532 p. MAnP; MMh; MShM; NWars. 45-130

Alison, Archibald, 1792-1867. History of Europe, from the commencement of the French Revolution in 1789 to the restoration of the Bourbons in 1815. Fourth edition. New York: A.S. Barnes, 1845. 532 p. CtMW; OBerB; PP; PJa; TWcW. 45-131

Alison, Archibald, 1792-1867. Miscel-

laneous essays. Reported from the
English originals with the author's cor-
rections for this edition. Philadelphia:
Carey and Hart, 1845. 390 p. KyLx; MH;
NNUT; OU; PPL. 45-132

Alleghanian. New York, 1845. v. 1-. NN.
45-133

Allegheny City. Western Theological
Seminary. Triennial catalogue of the
Western Theological Seminary at Allegheny City, Pennsylvania, February,
1845. Pittsburgh: Franklin office, 1845.
23 p. GDecCT. 45-134

Alleine, Joseph, 1634-1668. Gospel
promises; being a short view of the great
and precious promises of the Gospel.
New York and Pittsburg: Robert Carter,
1845. 167 p. OWoC. 45-135

Allen, Ann H. The housekeeper's assistant, composed upon temperance principles, with instructions in the art of
making plain and fancy cakes, puddings
with a variety of useful information and
receipts never before published, by an
old housekeeper. Boston: J. Munroe,
1845. 142 p. MWA; OCl; ViW. 45-136

Allen, Ann H. The orphan's friend and
housekeeper's assistant by an old
housekeeper. Boston: Dutton and
Wentworth's, 1845. 142 p. MH;
NNNAM. 45-137

Allen, Ethan, 1738-1789. Allen's captivity, being a narrative of Colonel Ethan
Allen, containing his voyages, travels,
etc., interspersed with political observations. Written by himself. Boston: O.L.
Perkins, 1845. 6-126 p. ICN; MB; MeBa;
NN; TxHuT. 45-138

Allen, Ethan, 1738-1789. Narrative of
captivity, from the time of his being taken
by the British near Montreal, September
24, 1775 to time of exchange May 6, 1778.
Containing his voyages and travels. Boston, 1845. 126 p. CtSoP. 45-139

Allen, Ethan, 1738-1789. Narrative of
Colonel Ethan Allen's captivity. Fourth
edition with notes. Burlington: C.
Goodrich, 1845. 120 p. DLC; MiU-C;
NjN; OU; PHi. 45-140

Allen, Joseph. Protest against
American slavery by one hundred and
seventy three Unitarian ministers. Boston: B.H. Greene, 1845. 20 p. MB; MnHi;
PHi. 45-141

Allen, Joseph, 1790-1873. Questions on
the acts of the Apostles for the higher
classes in Sunday Schools. Fourth edition. Boston, 1845. MH; MH-AH. 45-142

Allen, Joseph, 1790-1873. Questions on
the select portions of the four evangelists. Boston, 1845. 118 p. ICHi. 45-143

Allen, Joseph, 1790-1873. Questions on
the select portions of the four evangelists. Thirtieth edition. Boston: Benjamin H. Greene, 1845. MCNC. 45-144

Allen, Joseph Henry, 1820-1898. The
boys death. [Boston, 1845?] 16 p. MB;
MH. 45-145

Allen, Otis, 1804-1865. The duties and
liabilities of sheriffs, in their various relations to the public and to individuals, as
governed by the principles of common
law, and regulated by the statutes of New
York. Revised, corrected, and enlarged.
Albany: W. and A. Gould and company;
New York: Gould, Banks and company,

1845. 487 p. CU-Law; IN-SC; LU; MH-L; WaU. 45-146

Allen, Thaddeus. An inquiry into the views, principles, services, and influences of the leading men in the origination of our union. Boston: S.N. Dickinson and company, 1845. 86 p. MDeeP; MH; MiD-B; NCH; TxU. 45-147

Alley, Jerome. An address delivered before the Saint Croix Lodge of Freemasons at Calais, Maine, on Tuesday, September 30, 1845. Boston: Samuel N. Dickinson and company, 1845. 23 p. MeB; PPFM. 45-148

Allgemeine deutsche real encyklopadie fur die gebildeten stande. Conversationa lexikon. 9. originalaaflage. New York: W. Radde, 1845-1847. 14 v. OU. 45-149

The almanac and Baptist register... 1846... Philadelphia: American Baptist Publication Society, [1845] 36 p. MeHi; MHi. 45-150

Almanac, directory and business advertiser. Springfield, 1845. MBC. 45-151

Almanac for the 1846... By John Ward... [Philadelphia: Thomas Davis, 1845] 34 p. NjR. 45-152

Almanac of the American Temperance Union, for the year of our Lord and Saviour Jesus Christ, 1846... New York: American Temperance Union, [1845] 36 p. FNp. 45-153

Almanack for 1846. Anson Allen. Hartford, Connecticut: Henry Benton, [1845] MWA. 45-154

Almy, John. State of Michigan, 1845. To

emigrants. New York: I.J. Oliver, printer, 1845. 6 p. MH; MiU; MH-BA. 45-155

Alpha Delta Phi Society. Chapters, members, etc. 1845. New Haven: Hitchcock and Stafford, 1845. 21 p. MeB; NCH; OO; WHi. 45-156

Alston, Phillip William Whitmel. Christian soberness, conversion, and the witness of the spirit. Three parochial sermons, preached in Calvary Church, Memphis. Memphis: Published by the congregation, 1845. 46 p. MdBD; NjPT; NNG; TxU. 45-157

American agricultural almanac, 1846. New York: Saxton and Miles, [1845] MB; MBC; MWA. 45-158

American Agricultural Association. Constitution, by-laws and officers. New York: J.W. Oliver, 1845. 11 p. DLC; MBHO; WUA. 45-159

American agriculturist almanac. By A.B. Allen. New York, 1845. MH. 45-160

The American agriculturist almanac for 1846. New York: Saxton and Miles, [1845] 30 p. NjR. 45-161

American and Foreign Bible Society. An appeal to the friends of the Bible, and of equal rights, with reference to the rejection of an application made to the legislature of the state of New York. New York: J.R. Bigelow, 1845. 31 p. ICU; MNtCA; NHC-S; NjR; PCA. 45-162

American Anti-slavery Society. Disunion. Address of the American Anti-slavery Society and F. Jackson's letter on the pro-slavery character of the Constitution. New York: American Anti-slavery

Society, 1845. 32 p. DLC; MH; NN; TNF.
45-163

American Anti-slavery Society. Letter
to friends of the American Anti-slavery
Society, requesting their support of the
standard. Boston, 1845. 2 p. CSmH. 45-
164

American Benevolent Education and
Manual Labor Society. Constitution,
with explanatory remarks and regulations in the organization of the Institute.
New York, 1845. 8 p. MH. 45-165

American Board of Commissioners for
Foreign Missions. Manual for missionary
candidates. Boston, 1845. 40 p. MB; MH-
AH; RPB. 45-166

American Board of Commissioners for
Foreign Missions. Manual for missionary
candidates. Boston: Crocker, 1845. 39 p.
MB; MCC; NCH; NjbS. 45-167

American Board of Commissioners for
Foreign Missions. Report of the committee on anti-slavery memorials. September, 1845. With a historical statement of
previous proceedings. Boston: T.R. Marvin, 1845. 32 p. CtY; IHi; MeBat;
NcMHi; PHi. 45-168

The American book of beauty. With illustrations on steel, by eminent artists.
Edited by a lady. New York: Wilson and
company, 1845. 127 p. CtHWatk; MH;
NBuG; NjR; PU. 45-169

American boy's book comprising the
most striking and illustrative scenes and
passages in the history of our country.
Philadelphia. R.S.H. George, 1845. 196
p. MH; NBuG; NN. 45-170

The American Chesterfield or way to
wealth, honour and distinction; being
selections from the letters of Lord
Chesterfield to his son; and extracts from
other eminent authors, on the subject of
politeness with alterations and additions,
suited to the youth of the United States.
Philadelphia: Griggs and Elliot, 1845.
286 p. LNL. 45-171

American Citizen. Philadelphia, 1845-.
NIC; PHi. 45-172

American Ethnological Society. Transactions of the American Ethnological
Society. New York: Bartlet and Wilford,
1845-. GU; MNe; PPAmP; RNR; VtU.
45-173

The American farmer, and spirit of the
agricultural journals of the day; devoted
to the interest of the farmers, planters
and horticulturists of the United States.
Baltimore: Samuel Sands, 1845-. MoU;
Nc-Fay; NjR; WU-A. 45-174

American farmer's almanac. Philadelphia: Turner and Fisher, [1845] MWA.
45-175

American farmer's almanac, 1846. Calculated by David Young. New York:
Gleeley and M'Elrath, [1845] MWA. 45-
176

American fashionable letter writer,
original and selected, containing a
variety of letters... with forms of com-
plimentary cards... and rules for composition. Troy, New York: W. and H.
Merriam, 1845. 224 p. CtY; MoInRC;
MSuHi; WLacT. 45-177

The American Institute of Instruction.
Lectures delivered before the American

Institute of Instruction, at New Bedford, August, 30 and 31, 1844. Including the journal of proceedings, and a list of the officers. Boston: William D. Ticknor and company, 1845. 309 p. MLaw; MNBedf; MSa; TNB. 45-178

American Institute of the City of New York. Catalogue containing a correct list of all the articles exhibiting at the eighteenth annual fair, 1845. New York, [1845] 28 p. NjP; PWW. 45-179

American Institute of the City of New York. Charter and bylaws of the American Institute of the City of New York. New York: James Van Norden and company, 1845. 12 p. MH; NNMuCN. 45-180

American Institute of the City of New York. Report of the committee on horticulture, in conjunction with the agricultural board of the American institute, at their eighteenth annual fair, held at Niblo's garden, October, 1845. New York, 1845. 16 p. DLC; MB; NWA. 45-181

American Jewish Publication Society. Circular of the American Jewish Publication Society, to the friends of Jewish literature informing the various congregations, auxillary societies and individuals of the formation of the society and inviting their cooperation. Philadelphia, 1845. 11 p. PPDrop. 45-182

American journal of agriculture and science; devoted to the promotion of agriculture, horticulture, science, arts and industry. Albany, 1845-1848. 7 v. in 6. CtU; ICRL; LNHT; NcD; PPULC. 45-183

The American keepsake, or book for every American; and containing the Declaration of Independence, and signers names, Constitution of the United States and all the amendments. Boston: E.L. Pratt, 1845. 76 p. DLC; MH; NbHi; TxU; ViU. 45-184

The American liberty almanac, for 1846. Calculated for the horizon and meridian of Boston, New York, Baltimore, and Charleston: and for use in every part of the country. Hartford: W.H. Burleigh, [1845] 32 p. MBC; MWA; OO; TNF; WHi. 45-185

The American mechanics almanac. New York, 1845. PPL. 45-186

American mechanic's and manufactuers almanac... New York: F. Kearny, 1845. MWA. 45-187

American Musical Convention, New York, 1845. Proceedings of the American Musical Convention; held in the Broadway Tabernacle on the 8th, 9th and 10th of October, 1845. With the addresses. New York: Saxton and Miles, 1845. 80 p. DLC; ICU; MBC; NN. 45-188

American oratory; or selections from the speeches of eminent Americans [1775-1862] Compiled by a member of the Philadelphia bar. Philadelphia: E.C. and J. Biddle, 1845. 531 p. CO; DLC; GEU; KMK; NSyU. 45-189

American Party. Address of the delegates of the Native American National convention, assembled at Philadelphia, July 4, 1845. To the citizens of the United States. [Philadelphia, 1845] 16 p. DLC; PPULC. 45-190

American Party. Address of the executive committee of the American Republicans of Boston, to the people of Massachusetts. Boston: Printed by J.E. Farwell company, 1845. 17 p. MB; MH. 45-191

American Party. Address of the general executive committee of the American Republican Party of the city of New York, to the people of the United States. New York; Printed by J.F. Trow, 1845. 15 p. CtY; DLC; N; OClWHi; PPL. 45-192

American Party. Declaration of principles, comprised in the address and resolutions of the Native American convention, assembled at Philadelphia, July 4, 1845, to the citizens of the United States; revised and corrected by one of the committee. New York: T.R. Whitney, 1845. 14 p. NN; NNC. 45-193

American Party. Important testimony connected with Native American principles. The principles of the Native American Party as adopted by the National convention held at Philadelphia, July 4, 1845. [Philadelphia? 1845] 16 p. NN; PBL; PPULC. 45-194

American Party. Pennsylvania. Proceedings of the Native American state convention, held at Harrisburg, February 22, 1845: printed by order of the convention. Philadelphia: Printed by W.F. Geddes, 1845. 24 p. CtY; DLC; InU; MiD-B; MnU. 45-195

American Phonographic Corresponding Society. Constitution and list of members. Boston, [1845] 3 p. MB. 45-196

The American polite letter writer. Containing upwards of seventy letters, on various subjects written in a concise and familiar style. New York: J.O. Kane [1845?] 128 p. CoU. 45-197

The American polite letter writer. Containing upwards of seventy letters, on various subjects written in a concise and familiar style. Philadelphia: Perry, 1845. 64 p. CtHT; NN; PPL. 45-198

American practical navigator, being an epitome of navigation; containing all the tables necessary to be used with the nautical almanac... all the rules of navigation; with an appendix. By Nathaniel Bowditch. Fourteenth new stereotype edition. New York: E. and G.W. Blunt, 1845. 317, 449 p. NcAS. 45-199

The American practical navigator, being an epitome of navigation; containing all the tables necessary to be used with the nautical almanac... all the rules of navigation; with an appendix. By Nathaniel Bowditch. Fifteenth new stereotype edition. New York: E. and G.W. Blunt, 1845. 318, 451 p. MB; MSaP; WaPS; WHi. 45-200

American Protestant almanac, for 1846. New York: E. Walker, [1845] MWA. 45-201

The American Protestant magazine. June 1845-December 1849. New York: Published by the American Protestant Society, 1845-1849. DLC; IEG; OO; PPPrHi; TxU. 45-202

American Protestant Society. Annual report. 1845-. New York: Depository of the society, 1845-. DLC; IU; MH; PHi; PPPrHi. 45-203

American Protestant Society. A

chronological table of the papacy, and the persecution of Christians, from the Christian era to the present century. New York: American Protestant Society, 1845. 124 p. NNUT. 45-204

American pulpit. Worcester, 1845-1848. 4 v. MBAt; MBC; MHi; MNtCA; PCA. 45-205

American Republican Association, Hamilton County. Address published by order of the committee. No other title subject principally political parties. Cincinnati, 1845. OCHP. 45-206

The American review: a Whig journal of politics, literature, art and science. New York: Wiley and Putnam, and others, 1845- [1852] 16 v. CoGrS; MBC; NjR; PHC; ScU. 45-207

American slavery. A protest against American slavery, by one hundred and seventy three Unitarian ministers. Boston: R.H. Greene, 1845. 20 p. CBPac; DLC; MB; MH. 45-208

The American songster, containing a choice selection of eighty three songs including Tyrone Power's favourite songs. Philadelphia: W.A. Deary, 1845. 189 p. DLC; OClWHi; OU; PPULC; PSt. 45-209

American Statistical Association. Collections of the American Statistical Association, containing statistics of population in Massachusetts. Prepared by Joseph B. Felt. Boston: Charles C. Little and James Brown, 1845. v. 1-. MdHi; MsJS. 45-210

American Sunday School Union. Considerations touching the principles and objects of the American Sunday School Union. Addressed to Evangelical Christians and other citizens of the United States by the board of officers and managers of the Society. Philadelphia: American Sunday School Union, 1845. 16 p. CBPSR; NjR; NNG; PHi; PPL. 45-211

American Sunday School Union. Considerations touching the principles and objects of the American Sunday School Union. Addressed to Evangelical Christians and other citizens of the United States by the board of officers and managers of the Society. Philadelphia: American Sunday School Union, 1845. 20 p. NjR; NNUT; PPPrHi; PPULC; WHi. 45-212

American Sunday School Union. Curiosities of Egypt. Revised by the Committee of Publication of the American Sunday School Union. Philadelphia: American Sunday School Union, 1845. 180 p. ICRL; InPerM; MH; OrU. 45-213

American Sunday School Union. Important considerations touching the principles and objects of the American Sunday School Union; addressed particularly to Evangelical Christians and other citizens of England. Philadelphia: American Sunday School Union, 1845. 16 p. CtY; DLC; ICN; MB; MH-AH. 45-214

American Sunday School Union. Private devotion. By the Committee of Publication of the American Sunday School Union. Philadelphia? American Sunday School Union, 1845. 268 p. ArBaA. 45-215

American Sunday School Union. Select poetry for children compiled for the American Sunday School Union and revised by the committee of publications. Philadelphia: American Sunday School Union, [1845] 72 p. DLC; MB; PSt; ScCliTO; TxU. 45-216

The American Sunday School Union. The suppliant; or thoughts designed to encourage and aid private devotion. Revised by the committee of publication. Philadelphia: American Sunday School Union, 1845. 268 p. CBPSR; ICBB; LN; MoS; VtU. 45-217

American system of education a hand book of Anglo Saxon root words. In three parts. First part. Instructions about Anglo-Saxon root words. Second part. Studies in Anglo Saxon root words. Third part. The beginnings of the root words. By a literary association. New York: D. Appleton and company, 1845. 159 p. KTW. 45-218

American Temperance Union. Report of the executve committee of the American Temperance Union, 1845. New York: American Temperance Union, 1845. 56 p. IAlS; MoSpD; OClWHi. 45-219

American temperance union almanac for 1846. New York: American Temperance Union, [1845] MWA. 45-220

American Tract Society. Address of the executive committee. Boston, 1845. 16 p. CBPSR; MBC; MHi; NcWeM; WHi. 45-221

American turf register and racing and trotting calendar for 1845. New York: Spirit of the Times, 1846? CtY; OU. 45-222

The American Whig review: a whig journal of politics, literature, art and science. "To stand by the constitution." New York: Wiley and Putnam, 1845-1852. 16 v. CtB; IaDaP; MdBP; Nj; RP. 45-223

Americanischer stadt und land calender auf das 1846ste Jahr Christi... Philadelphia: Gedruckt und zu haben bey Conrad Zentler... [1845] 28 p. MWA; PReaHi. 45-224

American's guide: comprising the Declaration of Independence; the Articles of Confederation; the Constitution of the United States, and the constitutions of the several states composing the Union... Philadelphia: Hogan and Thompson, 1845. 419 p. CtY; KEmC; MH-L; PPL; WU. 45-225

Amherst College. Catalogue, 1845-1846. Northampton: Metcalf, 1845. 21 p. MeHi; MiD-B; MWHi. 45-226

Amicus Veritatis [pseud.] Appeal and review. An appeal from the sentence of the Bishop of New York, and a review of the trial. New York: James A. Sparks, 1845. 32 p. MiD-B. 45-227

Analysis of the cotton plant and seed. Columbia, 1845. PPL. 45-228

The anatomical remembrancer; or complete pocket anatomist. From the second London edition revised. New York: S.S. and W. Wood, 1845. 245 p. CU-M; DLC; MdBJ;W; NBMS; PPAN. 45-229

Andersen, Hans Christian, 1805-1875.
The improvisatore. Translated by Mary
Howitt. New York: Harper and brothers,
1845. 124 p. IU; MH; MnU; NN; PU. 45-
230

Andersen, Hans Christian, 1805-1875.
Life in Italy. The improvisatore... translated by M. Howitt. New York: Harper
and brothers, 1845. 124 p. NN. 45-231

Andersen, Hans Christian, 1805-1875.
Only a fiddler! and O.T.... Translated by
Mary Howitt. New York: Harper, 1845.
CtY; MBAt; MiGr. 45-232

Anderson, Robert M. The student's
review; or examinations on therapeutics,
materia medica, and pharmacy. Adapted
especially to the course of lectures
delivered in the University of Pennsylvania. Richmond: H.K. Ellyson, 1845.
[5]-296 p. DLC; IEN-M; MiDW-M;
NNN; ViU. 45-233

Anderson, Rufus, 1796-1880. A sermon
at the ordination of Mr. Edward Webb;
as a missionary to the heathen, Ware,
Massachusetts, October 23, 1845. Boston: Crocker and Brewester, 1845. 22 p.
MeBat; NcWfC. 45-234

Anderson, Rufus, 1796-1880. The
theory of missions to the heathen. A sermon at the ordination of Mr. Edward
Webb, as a missionary to the heathen,
Ware, Massachusetts, October 23, 1845.
Boston: Crocker and Brewster, 1845. 24
p. CU; ICT; NjR; OClWHi; PHi. 45-235

Anderson, S.J.P. The influence of the
Bible on liberty; an address delivered
before the Union Society of Hampden
Sidney College, September 18, 1845.
Richmond, Virginia: Printed by H.K. El-

lyson, 1845. 32 p. NcD; NjPT; PPPrHi;
ViR; WHi. 45-236

Anderson, William E. Address
delivered before the citizens of Wilmington, N.C. on the occasion of the
third anniversary of Cape Fear Lodge,
no. 2, I.O.O.F. on the 13th day of May,
1845. Richmond: Independent Odd Fellows, 8145. 16 p. NcAS; NcU. 45-237

Andrews, Ethan Allen, 1787-1858. First
lessons in Latin; or an introduction to
Andrews and Stoddards Latin grammar.
Seventh edition. Boston: Crocker and
Brewster, 1845. 216 p. MH; MnSM;
RPB. 45-238

Andrews, Ethan Allen, 1787-1858. The
first part of Jacob's and Doring's Latin
reader. Adopted to Andrews and
Stoddard's Latin grammar. Tenth edition. Boston: Crocker and Brewster,
1845. 266 p. InHu; MWHi; NmStM; OO;
ViL. 45-239

Andrews, Ethan Allen, 1787-1858. A
grammar of the Latin language; for the
use of schools and colleges. Eleventh edition. Boston: Crocker and Brewster,
1845. 323 p. CU; ICP; LNB; MoSpD;
OO. 45-240

Andrews, Stephen Pearl, 1812-1886.
The complete phonographic class book;
containing a strictly inductive exposition
of Pitman's phonography, adopted as a
system of phonetic shorthand to the
English language; especially intended as
a school book... By S.P. Andrews and
Augustus F. Boyle. Boston: Phonographic Institution, 1845. [5]-132 p.
CSmH; MB; MH; Mi; MSa. 45-241

Andrews, Stephen Pearl, 1812-1886.

The phonographic reader; a complete course of inductive reading lessons in phonography. Boston: Phonographic Institute, 1845. 36 p. DLC; M; NN. 45-242

Angell, Oliver, 1787-1858. The Union, number three, or child's third book, being the second of a series of spelling and reading books, in six numbers. Philadelphia: E. H. Butler and company, 1845. 206 p. TxH. 45-243

Angler's almanac... New York, 1845. PPL. 45-244

Annals of murder, or daring outrages, trials, confessions, etc. Philadelphia: J.B. Perry, 1845. 66 p. MH; MH-L. 45-245

Anniversary hymns and music. New York, 1845. 66 p. CtHWatk. 45-246

Annuaire de chimie comprenant les applications de cette science a la medecine et a la pharmacie... 1845-1851. New York: H. Bailliere, 1845-1851. 7 v. CtY; DLC; ICRL; OCU; PU. 45-247

The annualette: a Christmas and New Year's gift; edited by a lady. Boston: T.H. Carter and company, 1845-[1847] 98 p. LNH; MBAt; NjR; RPB. 45-248

An answer to "Questions addressed to Rev. T. Parker and his friends." By a friend indeed. Boston: Andrews, Prentiss and Studley, 1845. 24 p. CBPac; INC; MB; MH; RPB. 45-249

Answers to questions contained in Mr. Parker's letter to the Boston Association of Congregational Ministers. By one not of the Association. Boston: William Crosby and H.P. Nichols, 1845. 39 p.

CBPac; MBC; NcD; MHi; NNUT. 45-250

Anthon, Charles, 1797-1867. Anthon's Greek lessons. Part 1 and 2. New York: Harper and brothers, 1845. 2 v. NN; NNC. 45-251

Anthon, Charles, 1797-1867. Classical dictionary; containing an account of the principal proper names mentioned in ancient authors... Together with an account of coins, weights and measures... New York: Harper and brothers, 1845. 1451 p. CtY; ILM; MoS; Nh-Hi; OOxM. 45-252

Anthon, Charles, 1797-1867. First Greek lessons, containing all the inflexions of the Greek language, together with appropriate exercises in the translating and writing of Greek, for the use of beginners. New York: Harper and brothers, 1845. 238 p. GOgU; InGr; LN; NjR; ScU. 45-253

Anthon, Charles, 1797-1867. First Latin lessons containing the most important parts of the grammar of the Latin language, together with exercises in translating and writings of Latin for the use of beginners by Charles Anthon. New York: Harper and brothers, 1845. 367 p. NCoth. 45-254

Anthon, Charles, 1797-1867. A grammar of the Greek language. Principally from the German of Kuhner, with selections from Mattiae, Buttmann, Thiersch and Rost. For the use of schools and colleges. New York: Harper and brothers, 1845. 536 p. LNL; MoSMa; OWoC; TJaU; ViRU. 45-255

Anthon, Charles, 1797-1867. An introduction to Greek prose composition, with copious explanatory notes. Elucidated. New York: Harper and brothers, 1845. 270 p. CtMW; GMilvC; LNL; PLor; ScCC. 45-256

Anthon, Charles, 1797-1867. Introduction to Latin prose composition, with a complete course of exercises. New York: Harper, 1845. 327 p. CtMW; MH; MoS; PPAN; WBeloC. 45-257

Anthon, Charles, 1797-1867. Key to Anthon's Latin versification. New York: Harper, 1845. 135 p. DLC; MoFloSS; NjMD; ODW; VIRU. 45-258

Anthon, Charles, 1797-1867. Latin grammar. Part II. An introduction to Latin prose composition. New York: Harper and brothers, 1845. 327 p. TJaU; TxBradM; WPlatT; WU. 45-259

Anthon, Charles, 1797-1867. A system of Latin versification, in a series of progressive exercises, including specimens of translations from English and German poetry into Latin verse for the use of schools and colleges. New York: Harper and brothers, 1845. 327 p. GDecCT; InNd; OMC; PU; TNN. 45-260

Anthon, Charles Edward, 1822-1883. A pilgrimage to Treves, through the valley of the Meuse and the forest of Ardennes in the year 1844. New York: Harper and brothers, 1845. 128 p. In; MNBedf; NNA; PPL-R; TxU. 45-261

Anthon, Henry, 1795-1861. Parish annals. A sermon giving historical notices of St. Mark's Church in the Bowery, New York... New York: Stanford and Swords, 1845. 58 p. ICN; LU; MWA; PHi; WHi. 45-262

Anti-Sabbath Convention. Proceedings of the Anti-sabbath convention, held in the Melodeon, March 23 and 24, 1845. Boston: Published by order of the convention, Andrews and Prentiss, printers, 1845. 168 p. MLy. 45-263

Anti-slavery almanac for 1846. New York: Frich and Weed, [1845] MWA. 45-264

Anti-slavery memorials committee. Boston. Report of the committee on anti-slavery memorials. Boston: T.R. Marvin, 1845. 32 p. MLow. 45-265

The anti-Texas Legion. Protest of some free men, states and presses against the Texas rebellion, against the laws of nature and of nations. Albany: Sold at the Patriot office, 1845. 72 p. CSmH; KWiU; MBAt; PPL; Tx. 45-266

The antiquarian, and general review; comprising whatever is useful and instructive in ecclesiastical or historical antiquities. Edited by William Arthur. v.1-. March 1845-. Schenectady, New York [1845-] 2 v. CSmH; ICN; MoS; OClWHi; PHi. 45-267

The apostasy of Mr. Newman and some traces of Newmania on New Jersey soil. By a Presbyterian. Burlington, New Jersey, 1845. 24 p. CU; MCET; OCHP; PHi; WHi. 45-268

An appeal from the sentence of the bishop of New York; in behalf of his diocese. Founded on the improbabilities appearing on both sides in the late trial. New York: James A. Sparks, 1845. 32 p. MdBD; MH; NNG; OCLaw. 45-269

Appleton, Emily. Alice Mannering: or,

the nobleman's son. A tale of London, By Emily Appleton. Boston: Gleason's Publishing Hall, 1845. [5]-54 p. DLC. 45-270

Arago, Dominique Francois Jean, 1786-1853. Lectures on astronomy, translated by Dr. Lardner. New York, 1845. PPL; PPULC. 45-271

Arago, Doninique Francois Jean, 1786-1853. Popular lectures on astronomy; delivered at the royal observatory of Paris. New York: Greeley and McElrath, 1845. 96 p. CtY; MWA; NjR; NNE; PHi. 45-272

Archbold, John Frederick, 1785-1870. The law of Nisi prius; comprising the declarations and other pleadings in personal actions, and the evidence necessary to support them; with an introduction, stating the whole of the practice at nisi prius. Philadelphia: T. and J.W. Johnson, 1845. 447 p. DLC; In-SC; MoU; NcD; RPB. 45-273

Archbold, John Frederick, 1785-1870. The law of Nisi prius; comprising the declarations and other pleadings in personal actions, and the evidence necessary to support them; with an introduction, stating the whole of the practice at nisi prius. Second edition. Philadelphia: T. and J.W. Johnson, 1845. 2 v. Ct; PP; PPB; M; MH-L. 45-274

Archdeacon, Peter. A sketch of the Passaic Falls, of Peterson, New Jersey embracing a history of all the remarkable events that have occurred since the immortal Father of his country was encamped there. New York: Printed by M. O'Connor, 1845. 96 p. CtY; MdBJ; Nj. 45-275

Archenholz, Johann Wilhelm Von, 1743-1812. The history of the pirates, freebooters, or buccaneers of America. New York: Published by Charles Hobbs, 1845. 141 p. DLC; MiD-B. 45-276

Archer, William Segar, 1789-1855. Speech of Mr. Archer, of Virginia, on the joint resolution for the annexation of Texas. Delivered in the Senate, February 28, 1845. Washington: Gales and Seaton, 1845. 18 p. DLC; Tx; Vi. 45-277

Arguments and statements addressed to the legislature in relation to the petition of the city of Boston for power to bring into the city the water of Long Pond. By a remonstrant. Boston: Printed by Freeman and Bolles, 1845. 25 p. DLC; NN. 45-278

Aristotle. [pseud.] The midwife's guide, being the complete work of Aristotle. New York, 1845. CtHWatk; MBM. 45-279

Arkansas. Acts, memorials and resolutions, passed at the fifth session of the General Assembly of the state of Arkansas: Which was begun and held at the capitol, in the city of Little Rock, on November 4, 1845. Little Rock: Printed by Borland and Farley, printers to the state, 1845. 176 p. ArCH; DLC; F-SC. 45-280

Armstrong, John, 1758-1843. A treatise on agriculture, comprising a concise history of its origin and progress: the present condition of the art abroad and at home, and the theory and practice of husbandry. To which is added a dissertation on the kitchen and fruit garden. With notes by J. Buel. New York: Harper and brothers, 1845. 282 p. CtY; IGK; MH; UU. 45-281

Armstrong, Lebbeus. The temperance reformation of this 19th century. The fulfillment of divine prophecy... New York: Printed by Pudney, Hooker and Russell, 1845. 16 p. DLC; NbCrD; NN. 45-282

Armstrong, Lebbeus. Who hath woe? A sermon on the woes of intemperance in Christenden [sic], during the period of three hundred years, from the Protestant reformation in Europe to the commencement of the present century. New York: Pudney, Hooker and Russell, 1845. 16 p. IaDuU-Sem; MH; NN; NCH. 45-283

Arnold, Lemuel H. Letter in reply to the letter of John Whipple. n.p., [1845] Broadside. MH. 45-284

Arnold, Samuel George, 1806-1891. Biographical sketches of distinguished Jerseymen. Trenton, New Jersey: Press of the Emporium, 1845. 80 p. DLC; Nj; PHi; PPL; T. 45-285

Arnold, Thomas, 1795-1842. Introductory lectures on modern history, delivered in Lent term, MDCCCXLI. Edited from the second London edition, with a preface and notes by Henry Reed. New York: D. Appleton and company; Philadelphia: G.S. Appleton, 1845. 428 p. CtHT; GU; IaB; MBBC; PPA. 45-286

Arnold, Thomas, 1795-1842. Lectures on modern history. New York: D. Appleton and company, 1845. 428 p. CEu; KyDC; MBL; NPV; ScSoh. 45-287

Arnold, Thomas, 1795-1842. The miscellaneous works of Thomas Arnold... First American edition, with nine additional essays, not included in the English collection. New York: D. Appleton and company, 1845. [9]-519 p. GU; KyBDC; PPA; RPB; ScCC. 45-288

Arnold, Thomas Kerchever, 1800-1853. A practical introduction to Greek prose composition. Revised edition, with references to Kuhner's Greek grammar. Boston: J. Munroe and company, 1845. 196 p. CSto; GEU-T; MeB; TxU-T; VtU. 45-289

Arthur, Robert, 1819-1880. A popular treatise on the teeth: embracing a description of their structure, the diseases to which they are subject, and their treatment, both for the prevention and cure of those diseases... New York, Philadelphia: E. Ferrett and company, 1845. [13]-187 p. DLC; MBM; MWA; NNNAM; PPi. 45-290

Arthur, Timothy Shay, 1809-1885. Anna Milnor: the young lady who was not punctual, and other tales. New York and Philadelphia: E. Ferrett and company, 1845. 92 p. CtY; NNC; VtU. 45-291

Arthur, Timothy Shay, 1809-1885. The club room, and other temperance tales. Philadelphia: E. Ferrett and company, 1845. 160 p. CtY; DLC; TxU; PU; ViU. 45-292

Arthur, Timothy Shay, 1809-1885. The heiress. New York and Philadelphia: E. Ferrett and company, 1845. 141 p. CtY; ICN; NNC; PU; RPB. 45-293

Arthur, Timothy Shay, 1809-1885. The heiress. New York and Philadelphia: E. Ferrett and company, 1845. 160 p. MnW. 45-294

Arthur, Timothy Shay, 1809-1885. The heiress; a novel. New York and Philadelphia: E. Ferrett and company, 1845. 96 p. RPB. 45-295

Arthur, Timothy Shay, 1809-1885. Lovers and husbands: a story of married life... New York: Harper and brothers, 1845. 155 p. DLC; ICU; MnU; OO; PPL. 45-296

Arthur, Timothy Shay, 1809-1885. Madeline; or a daughter's love, and other tales. Philadelphia: H.F. Anners, [1845] 158 p. CtY; IU; NN; OM; PPULC. 45-297

Arthur, Timothy Shay, 1809-1885. The maiden: a story for my young countrywomen. Philadelphia: E. Ferrett and company, 1845. 162 p. CtY; ICN; MnU; PLFM; ViU. 45-298

Arthur, Timothy Shay, 1809-1885. Married and single; or marriage and celibacy contrasted, in a series of domestic pictures. New York: Harper and brothers, 1845. 157 p. MCli; MH; NN; OO; PU. 45-299

Arthur, Timothy Shay, 1809-1885. Tales from real life. [New York and Philadelphia?] E. Ferrett and company, 1845. 162, 71, 90 71 p. NcU. 45-300

Arthur, Timothy Shay, 1809-1885. The three eras in a woman's life. The maiden, wife and mother. Philadelphia: Henry F. Anners, 1845. 141 p. PAtM. 45-301

Arthur, Timothy Shay, 1809-1885. The two husbands and other tales. Philadelphia: Ferrett, 1845. 160 p. PBm; ViU. 45-302

Arthur, Timothy Shay, 1809-1885. The wife: a story for my young country-women. Philadelphia: E. Ferrett and company, 1845. 161 p. ICN; IU; NNC; PU; ViU. 45-303

Artists' Fund Society of Philadelphia. Catalogue of first to tenth annual exhibitions, 1835-1838; 1840-1845. Philadelphia, 1845. PHi. 45-304

Ashby, Professor. Helen Howard; or the bankrupt and broker. A mysterious tale of Boston. Boston: F. Gleason, 1845. 64 p. CtHWatk; MB; MNS. 45-305

Ashby, Professor. Viola; the redeemed. A domestic tale. Boston: Gleason's Publishing Hall, 1845. 66 p. MWA. 45-306

Ashley, Chester, 1790-1848. Speech of Mr. Ashley, of Arkansas, on the annexation of Texas: Delivered in the Senate, February 22, 1845. Washington: Printed at the Globe office, 1845. CSmH; CtY; TxU. 45-307

Ashwell, Samuel, 1798-1857. A practical treatise on the diseases peculiar to women, illustrated by cases, derived from hospital and private practice. First American from the last London edition. With notes by Paul B. Goddard. Philadelphia: Lea and Blanchard, 1845. 520 p. DLC; KyU; OU; PPC; ViU. 45-308

Ashwell, Samuel, 1798-1857. A practical treatise on the diseases peculiar to women, illustrated by cases, derived from hospital and private practice. Second complete American from the last London edition. With notes by Paul B. Goddard. Philadelphia: Lea and Blanchard, 1845. 520 p. AMoC; DLC; IaU; MH-M; NN. 45-309

Asmar, Maria Theresa, 1804-1856. Memoirs of a Babylonian princess written by herself and translated into English. Philadelphia: G.B. Zieber and company, 1845. 2 pts. MBBC; MLow; PPL-R; PPM; TN. 45-310

Asmodeus in America. [pseud.] Millertie humbug; or the raising of the wind. A comedy in five acts as performed with unbounded applause in Boston and other parts of the union. Boston: Printed for the Publishers, 1845. 18 p. MWA. 45-311

Associated Synod of North America. Minutes of the [synod] at their annual meeting, held in North Argyle, Washington County, New York, June 11th and 12th, 1845. Albany: Printed by C. Van Benthuysen and company, 1845. 10 p. MH. 45-312

Association of Masters of the Boston Public Schools. Rejoinder to the "Reply of the Hon. Horace Mann, secretary of the Massachusetts Board of Education, to the remarks of the Association of Boston Masters." Boston: C.C. Little and J. Brown, 1845. vp. ICU; MiU; NIC; OO; PPAmP. 45-313

Association of Masters of the Boston Public Schools. Report of a committee of the [association] on a letter from Dr. John Odin, Jr. and in relation to a report of the special committee of the primary school board. Boston, 1845. 18 p. MHi; RPB. 45-314

At a meeting of citizens to resist the admission of Texas as a slave state. [Boston, 1845] MB. 45-315

Atkins, Sarah. Memoirs of John Frederic Oberlin, pastor of Waldbach, in the Ban de la Roche. With an introduction by Henry Ware, Jr. Second American edition, with additions. Boston: J. Munroe and company, 1845. 320 p. CBPac; KyDC; LNH; MiD; OO. 45-316

Atkinson, Thomas, 1807-1881. National and ecclesiastical blessings. A sermon, on December 12, being the Thanksgiving day recommended to be observed by the governor of Maryland... Baltimore: D. Brunner, 1845. 14 p. MdBD; MdHi; NGH; NNG; PPL. 45-317

Atkinson, William. Remarks on a article from the Christian Examiner, entitled "Mr. Parker and his views." Boston: William Crosby and H.P. Nichols, 1845. 15 p. CBPac; MBC; MCM; MH-AH; MiD- B. 45-318

Atlantic and St. Lawrence Railroad Company. The charter and bylaws of the Atlantic and St. Lawrence Railroad Company, incorporated February 10, 1845. Portland: Thurston, Fenley and company, 1845. 23 p. DLC; Me; MeB; MeHi; MH-BA. 45-319

Atlantic and St. Lawrence Railroad Company. Report of a survey and reconnaissance of a route for [the railroad]. [Portland, Maine, 1845] 8 p. WU. 45-320

Atlee, Washington Lemuel, 1808-1878. The chemical relations of the human body with surrounding agents; a lecture introductory to a course on medical chemistry in the medical department of Pennsylvania College, for the session of 1845-1846. Philadelphia: Published by the class by Barrett and Jones, printers, 1845. 16 p. KyDC; MH-M; NNNAM; PHi; PPL. 45-321

Atlee, Washington Lemuel, 1808-1878. Memorials of W.R. Grant, M.D. n.p., 1845. PPHa; PPULC. 45-322

An atomical [sic] remembrancer. New York, 1845. NBuG. 45-323

Atwater, Lyman Hotchkiss, 1813-1883. Death disarmed of its sting. A tribute to the memory of the Hon. Roger Minott Sherman. New Haven: Printed by B.L. Hamlen, 1845. 20 p. CSmH; ICJ; MHi; NjP; WHi. 45-324

Auburn Theological Seminary. Triennial catalogue of the Theological Seminary, at Auburn, New York, January, 1845. Auburn, New York: Merrell and Hollet, 1845. 32 p. CtY; MBC; N; NAulti; NjPT. 45-325

Auburn, New York. First Presbyterian Church. A brief historical sketch of the First Presbyterian Church in Auburn. From the period of its organization to the present time. Auburn: Oliphant's Book, 1845. 32 p. NAuHi; NAuT; NNUT. 45-326

Audin, Jean Marie Vincent. History of the life, works and doctrines of John Calvin, from the French of J.M.V. Audin... Translated by Rev. John McGill... Louisville: B.J. Webb and brother, [1845] 562 p. GAM-R; GDecCT; IaDuC; InNd; MoSU. 45-327

Audubon, John James, 1780-1851. Viviparous quadrupeds of North America, by John James Audubon and John Backman. New York: J.J. Audubon, 1845-1851. 3 v. CSmH; MWiW; OCl; PP; TxU. 45-328

Audubon, John James, 1780-1851. Viviparous quadrupeds of North America, by John James Audubon and John Backman. New York: J.J. Audubon, 1845-1851. 6 v. NB; ScU. 45-329

Auferstehung und Himmel fahrt Jesu Christi. Eine Festagabe fur Kinder. Chambersburg, Pennsylvania: Druckerei der Reformirten Kirche, 1845. PPG; PPULC. 45-330

Autobiography of a reformed drunkard; or letters and recollections by an inmate of the Alms House, with illustrations. Philadelphia: Griffith and Simon, 1845. 159 p. DLC; MLow; NN; VtWinds. 45-331

Ayer, Joseph, 1793-1875. Memoir of Frances Amelia Ayer, of Lisbon, Connecticut. Died June 3, 1843, aged 14 years. Written for the Massachusetts Sabbath School Society, and revised by the committee of publication. Boston: Massachusetts Sabbath School Society, 1845. [5]-72 p. DLC; MBC; RPB. 45-332

Azais, Pierre Hyacinthe. Explanation and history of the artesian well of Grenelle. With the geological views of the author. Boston: J.N. Bang, 1845. 31 p. ICJ; MB; MBAt; MWA. 45-333

Azeglio, Massimo Tapparelli, 1798-1866. Ettore Fieramosca, or the challenge of Barletta, an historical romance of the times of the Medici. Translated from the Italian by C. Edwards Lester... New York: Paine and Burgess, 1845. 5-274 p. CtY; MeB; OC; OClW; VtU. 45-334

B

B---. A moral picture of Philadelphia. The virtues and frauds and follies of the city delineated. By Lord B---. Philadelphia: The author, 1845. 24 p. DLC; PHi. 45-335

Babcock, William Robinson, 1814-1899. Sacred melodies: a collection of hymns and spiritual songs, for the use of families, prayer meetings, class meetings, and private circles. First edition. Dansville: A.R. Knox, 1845. DLC. 45-336

Babcock's New Haven almanac for 1846. By Charles Prindle. New Haven, Connecticut: S. Babcock, [1845] MWA. 45-337

Bacheler, Origen. Episcopacy. [Pawtucket, Rhode Island, 1845] DLC. 45-338

Backwoods Girls Social Band for Improvement. Address from the Backwoods Girls Social Band for Improvement. Convened near Mountpleasant, Jefferson County, Ohio, 1845. To all tobacco eaters, smokers, and snuffers, to whom this may come, greeting. Cincinnati: Chronicle print, 1845? 11 p. DLC. 45-339

Backwoods Girls Social Band for Improvement. Address from the Backwoods Girls Social Band for Improvement. Convened near Mountpleasant, Jefferson County, Ohio, 1845. To all tobacco eaters, smokers, and snuffers, to whom this may come, greet-ing. Cincinnati: Chronicle Print, 1845? 12 p. MH; MoKU; OClWHi. 45-340

Bacon, Ezekiel, 1776-1870. Aegri Somnia. Recreations of a sick room. Utica: R.W. Roberts, printer, 1845. 107 p. ICU; MH; MPiB; NRU. 45-341

Bacon, Ezekiel, 1776-1870. Vacant hours. A sequel to "Recreations of a sick room." Utica: R.W. Roberts, 1845. 57 p. CSf; MPiB; MWA; NjR; RPB. 45-342

Bacon, Francis, 1561-1626. Essays; moral, economical and political. The conduct of the understanding, by John Locke, esq., with an introductory essay by A. Potter. New York: Harper and brothers, 1845. 299 p. GEU; InRch; MsU; OCX; PMA. 45-343

Bacon, Henry, 1813-1856. The sacred flora: or flowers from the grave of a child. Boston: A. Tompkins and B.B. Mussey, 1845. [9]-160 p. MFiHi; MH; MMeT-Hi. 45-344

Bacon, Leonard, 1802-1881. The christian alliance. Addresses of Rev. L. Bacon and Rev. E.N. Kirk, at the annual meeting of the christian alliance held in New York, May 8, 1845, with the address of the society and the bull of the Pope against it. New York: Benedict, 1845. 48, 23, 24 p. MBAt; MBrZ; NjP; NNG; PHi. 45-345

Bacon, Leonard, 1802-1881. Christian

unity; a sermon, preached before the Foreign Evangelical Society in the Bleeker Street Church, New York, May 4, 1845. New Haven, [Connecticut] Printed for the Society, 1845. 43 p. CtSoP; IaB; MWiW; NNUT; OO. 45-346

Bacon, Leonard, 1802-1881. Oration, before the Phi Beta Kappa Society of Dartmouth College, delivered July 30, 1845. Hanover: Printed at the Dartmouth Press, 1845. 23 p. DHEW; MHi; NN; PPL; TxLT. 45-347

Bacon, Nathaniel Almoran, b. 1798. A table showing the date and place of birth; to whom and when married; number of sons and daughters, date of decease; age and place of burial, of Jabez Bacon, late of Woodbury, deceased; and of his descendants bearing the name of Bacon. New Haven: Printed by Hitchcock and Stafford, 1845. 4 l. CtY; DLC; Mi; NBLIHI; MWA. 45-348

Bacon, William, 1789-1863. Salvation made sure... all christians do not obtain full assurance of hope; all... can obtain it;... way to obtain it, and importance of obtaining it. Philadelphia: Perkins and Purves, 1845. 11-156 p. ICP; MBC; MWiW; PPPrHi. 45-349

Badcock, John, fl. 1816-1830. The veterinary surgeon: or farriery taught on a new and easy plan: being a treatise on all the diseases and accidents to which the horse is liable... Philadelphia: Grigg and Elliot, 1845. 224 p. MWA; ViU. 45-350

Baddeley, Thomas, fl. 1822. A sure way to find out the true religion: in a conversation between a father and son. New

York: D. Murphy, 1845. 107 p. IRA; MoSU; NN. 45-351

Badger, L.V. Therapeutic and bathing circular. Boston: Badger, 1845. 36 p. MB. 45-352

Badger, L.V. Therapeutic and bathing circular. Second edition. Boston, 1845. MBM. 45-353

Badgley, Jonathan. An introduction to an easy practical system of philosophical grammar, unfolding the principles of our language in the inductive method, and reducing them immediately to practice. Utica: Bennett, Backus and Hawley, 1845. [5], 14-199 p. DLC; NCH; NNC; NNUt; NUt. 45-354

La Bagatelle; intended to introduce very young children to some knowledge of the French language. Boston: William Crosby and H.P. Nichols, 1845. 152 p. CtHWatk; MH; NHem; NNC. 45-355

Bagby, Arthur Pendleton, 1794-1858. Letter of Arthur Bagby, Senator in congress, to the people of Alabama. Washington: J. and G.S. Gideon, 1845. 16 p. A-Ar; DLC. 45-356

Bailey, Appleton R. The life, adventures, imprisonments and sufferings of Appleton R. Bailey. By himself. Utica: H.H. Curtiss, 1845. 16 p. NCH; NUt. 45-357

Bailey, Charles. The drop of blood; or the maiden's rescue. Springfield, 1845. 40 p. CtY; RPB; ViU. 45-358

Bailey, Ebenezer, 1795-1839. First lessons in algebra, being an easy introduction to that science; designed for the use of academies and common schools. Twenty-third improved stereotype edition. Boston: Jenks and Palmer, 1845. 252 p. DAU; MHi; RPB; TMeT. 45-359

Bailey, H.W. What I saw on the west coast of South and North America. New York, 1845. MB. 45-360

Bailey, Jacob Whitman, 1811-1857. Notes on the algae of the United States... From the American journal of science and arts, Second series. New Haven: Printed by B.L. Hamlen, 1846. 8 p. DLC; MSaP; RHi; RPB. 45-361

Bailey, Jacob Whitman, 1811-1857. Notice of some new localities of fossil and recent infusioria. New Haven, 1845. 25 p. MCM; RPB. 45-362

Bailey, Jacob Whitman, 1811-1857. On the crystals which occur spontaneously formed in the tissues of plants. New Haven: Printed by B.L. Hamlen, 1845. 18 p. DLC; MHi; NBMS; PPL; RHi. 45-363

Bailey, Keyes A. The reporter's guide; containing a complete system of short-hand writing, in ten easy lessons, with numerous illustrations; governed by the analogy of sounds, and applicable to every language. New York: The author, 1845. DLC; NCH; NN. 45-364

Bailey, Philip James, 1816-1902. Festus. A poem. New York: T.R. Knox, [1845?] 391 p. TU. 45-365

Bailey, Philip James, 1816-1902. Festus. A poem... First American edition. Boston: Benjamin B. Mussey, 1845. 416 p. CBE; DLC; MMel; PU; RPaw. 45-366

Baird, Robert, 1798-1863. Religion, in America; or an account of the origin, progress, relation to the state, and present condition of the Evangelical Churches in the United States. With notices of the Unevangelical Denominations. New York: Harper and brothers, 1845. 343 p. CBPac; GEU; LNB; MeAu; PWW. 45-367

Baird, Robert, 1798-1863. Sketches of protestantism in Italy, past and present. Including a notice of the origin, history and present state of the Waldensess. Boston: Benjamin Perkins and company, 1845. 418 p. CtSoP; KWiW; LNH; RNR; ViRut. 45-368

Baird, Thomas. Description of a tract of coal land, the property of Messrs. Richards, Baird and O'Brien, situated in Pinegrove Township, Schuylkill County... Reading, Pennsylvania: Boyer and Getz, printers, 1845. 13 p. DLC. 45-369

Baker, Archibald. An address delivered before the two literary societies of Davidson College, North Carolina, July 31, 1845. Raleigh: Printed by Weston R. Gales, 1845. 15 p. NcDaD; NcU. 45-370

Baker, Benjamin Franklin, 1811-1889. American school music book, containing a thorough elementary system, with songs, chants and hymns adapted to the use of common schools. Boston: Otis, Broaders and company, 1845. 72 p. DLC; MH; RPB. 45-371

Baker, Benjamin Franklin, 1811-1889. The Boston Musical Education Society's collection of church music; consisting of original psalm and hymn tunes, select pieces... Eighth edition. Boston: Saxton, Peirce and company, 1845. 304 p. ICRL; MWinchrHi. 45-372

Baker, Benjamin Franklin, 1811-1889. The choral, a collection of church music adapted to the worship of all denominations. Boston: Otis, Broaders and company, [1845] 320 p. ICN; MB; NNUT; RPB; TKL-Mc. 45-373

Balch, William S. A sermon preached on thanksgiving day, December 14, 1844, in the Bleeker Street Church. New York: E. Winchester, New World Press, 1845. 22 p. MMeT; MMeT-Hi; MoS. 45-374

Baldwin, Charles N. A universal biographical dictionary, containing the lives of the most celebrated characters of every age and nation... to which is added, a dictionary of the principal divinities and heroes of Grecian and Roman mythology; and a biographical dictionary of eminent living characters. New edition. Hartford: S. Andrus and son, 1845. 444 p. Ct; InNd; KHi; MdHi; MH-AH. 45-375

Baldwin, Moses. Wonderful stories. Boston: Farwell and company, 1845. 12 p. MWatP. 45-376

Baldwin, Roger Sherman. Speech of his excellency Roger Baldwin, Governor of Connecticut, to the legislature of the state, May, 1845. 20 p. Ct; MBAt. 45-377

Baldwin, Thomas, 1753-1826. A catechism; or compendium of christian doctrine and practice. Boston: New England Sabbath School Union, 1845. 36 p. DLC; NHC-S; NjPT; NN; RPB. 45-378

Baldwin, Thomas, 1753-1826. A universal pronouncing gazetteer; containing topographical, statistical and other information, of all the more important places in the known world, from the most recent and authentic sources. Philadelphia: Lindsay and Blakiston, 1845. [19]-550 p. CU; ICU; MB; PPL-R; VtBrt. 45-379

Balfe, Michael William, 1808-1870. Gypsy's dream waltz. The subject selected from Balfe's celebrated opera, the Bohemian girl. New York: Atwill, 1845. 2 p. ViU. 45-380

Balfe, Michael William, 1808-1870. The music of the Bohemian girl, consisting of six songs and three pieces. Philadelphia and New York, 1845. 11 p. MB; MH; ViU. 45-381

Ballou, Hosea, 1796-1861. Collection of psalms and hymns for Universalist societies. Sixteenth edition. Boston: B.B. Mussey, 1845. MBUPH; MnU. 45-382

Ballou, Maturin Murray, 1820-1895. Albert Simmons; or the midshipman's revenge. A tale of land and sea... Boston: F. Gleason, 1845. 47 p. DLC; MWA; RPB. 45-383

Ballou, Maturin Murray, 1820-1895. Albert Simmons; or the midshipman's revenge. A tale of land and sea... Second edition. Boston: F. Gleason, 1845. 48 p. CtY; MB. 45-384

Ballou, Maturin Murray, 1820-1895. Fanny Campbell, the female pirate captain. A tale of the revolution, by Lieutenant Murray (pseud.) Boston: F. Gleason, 1845. 100 p. CtY; DLC; MAbD; MSbra; PP. 45-385

Ballou, Maturin Murray, 1820-1895. The naval officer; or the pirate's cave. A tale of the last war. By Lieutenant Murray [pseud.] Boston: F. Gleason, 1845. 100 p. DLC; LNHT; ViU. 45-386

Ballou, Maturin Murray, 1820-1895. Red Rupert, the American buccaneer. A tale of the Spanish Indies. Boston: Gleason's Publishing Hall, 1845. CSmH; CU-B; DLC; MWA; NjP. 45-387

Baltimore, Maryland. Fifth Presbyterian Church. Church manual for the communicants, comprising their names, with the church officers; also, a brief sketch of the history of the church and the form of profession and covenant... Baltimore: Woods, 1845. MdHi; PPPr-Hi. 45-388

Baltimore, Maryland. Journal of the proceedings of the first branch of the city council of Baltimore. January session, 1845. Baltimore: Printed by James Lucas, 1845. 563 p. MdHi. 45-389

Baltimore, Maryland. Ordinances of the mayor and city council passed at the January session, 1845... December session, 1844. Baltimore: James Lucas, 1845. 130, 217 p. MdHi; MH-L; MdBB. 45-390

Baltimore, Maryland. Report of Dr. Stephen Collins, on public education; presented by him to the city council of Baltimore, as chairman of the joint committee on education. Baltimore: Printed by J. Lucas, 1845. 7 p. DHEW; DLC; NjP. 45-391

Baltimore, Maryland. Report of the trustees for the poor of Baltimore city and county. Baltimore: Printed by James Lucas, 1845. 18 p. MdHi. 45-392

Baltimore, Maryland. Report on pauper insanity; presented to the city council of Baltimore, on March 28, 1845. By Stephen Collins, Chairman of the committee. Baltimore: Printed by James Lucas, 1845. 8 p. MdHi; MH. 45-393

Baltimore, Maryland. Light Street Institute. Annual register of Light Street Institute. A classical school for boys. Baltimore, 1844-45. Baltimore: John D. Toy, 1845. 16 p. NdHi. 45-394

Baltimore and Cuba Smelting and Mining Company. Exposition, with an exhibit of the objects of the company. Baltimore: Printed by Robert Neilson, 1845. DNA; MdHi; PHi. 45-395

Baltimore and Ohio Railroad Company. Abstract of the report of the chief engineer to the president... upon the route to the city of Wheeling through Virginia, and avoiding Pennsylvania; and the other routes with which it may be compared. [Baltimore, 1845] 4 p. DBRE; DLC. 45-396

Baltimore and Ohio Railroad Company. Concluding reply of the president... to the rejoinder on the part of the city of Wheeling, delivered before the committee of roads and internal navigation, of the House of Delegates of Virginia, on January 18, 1845. [n.p., 1845] DBRE; DLC. 45-397

Baltimore and Ohio Railroad Company. Laws, ordinances and documents, relating to the Baltimore and Ohio Railroad Company, down to July 1, 1845. [Baltimore? 1845?] 236 p. DBRE; MdHi; MH; NjP; TxU. 45-398

Baltimore and Ohio Railroad Company. Proceedings of a meeting of the stockholders in Baltimore, July 12, 1845, to consider the act of the Virginia Assembly, February 19, 1845. [Baltimore, 1845] 23 p. DLC; PHi; WU. 45-399

Baltimore and Ohio Railroad Company. Report of the chief engineer upon the expediency of resuming the reconstruction of the Baltimore and Ohio Railroad between Baltimore and Harper's Ferry, November 12, 1845. [Baltimore? 1845] CSmH; DLC; MdBP; MdHi. 45-400

Baltimore and Ohio Railroad Company. Report showing the amount of salaries paid the officers of said company during the years 1842, 1843 and 1844, in conformity with orders of the House. [Annapolis?] 1845. DeGE; PPULC. 45-401

Baltimore and Susquehanna Railroad Company. Report relative to officers and agents of said company, and also in relation to the rates of charges for tolls. [Annapolis?] 1845. 10 p. DeGE; PPULC. 45-402

Baltimore directory for 1845. To which is appended a business directory... Baltimore: J. Murphy, 1845. 174, 160 p. DLC; LNT; MB; MdBS; MdBP. 45-403

Baltimore Sabbath Association. First anniversary meeting of the Baltimore Sabbath Association held on January 13, 1845. Baltimore: Evangelical Lutheran Church, 1845. 17 p. MdHi; PPPrHi. 45-404

Balzac, Honore de, 1799-1850. Harlot's progress; Colonel Chabert; the unconscious mummers. New York: Harper and brothers, [1845?] 669 p. MDanv. 45-405

Bampfield, Robert William. An essay on curvatures and diseases of the spine, including all the forms of spinal distortion. Philadelphia: Ed. Barrington and George D. Haswell, 1845. 223 p. DNLM; ICRL; NcD; PU; WU. 45-406

Bancroft, George, 1800-1891. Funeral oration on the death of General Andrew Jackson, on June 27, 1845. Charleston, South Carolina: J.B. Nixon, printer, 1845. 16 p. DLC; MB. 45-407

Bancroft, George, 1800-1891. History of the United States from the discovery of the American continent. Twelfth edition. Boston: Charles C. Little and James Brown, 1845-1893. 12 v. CSmH; MoK; OClW; PLor; WJan. 45-408

Bancroft, George, 1800-1891. Oration... death of Andrew Jackson. [Washington, 1845] 8 p. DLC. 45-409

Bancroft, Silas A. The troubadour quick step... arranged as a quick step for the piano forte. Boston: G.P. Reed, 1845. 2 p. WHi. 45-410

Bancroft, T.W. Statement of facts, concerning the source of business of the intended railroad from Worcester, Massachusetts to Nashua, New Hampshire, and an estimate of its probable cost. Worcester: Printed by H.J. Howland, [1845] 28 p. CSt; MBAt. 45-411

Bang, Theodore, pseud. The mysteries of Papermill Village. Papermill Village, New Hampshire: Walter Tufts, 1845. 31 p. CtY; MFiHi; ViU. 45-412

Bangor, Maine. Address of the mayor to the city council, March 17, 1845. Together with the annual reports. Bangor: Smith and Sayward, printers, 1845. 30 p. MeBa; MeB. 45-413

Bangor, Maine. Annual report of the receipts and expenditures of the city of Bangor, with a statement of the city debt and a schedule of the city property, for the municipal year begining March, 1844, and ending 1845. Bangor: Smith and Sayward, printers, 1845. 24 p. MeBa-Hi; MeB. 45-414

Bangs, Nathan, 1778-1862. History of the Methodist Episcopal Church. From the year 1766 to the year 1792. Third edition, revised and corrected. New York: G. Lane and C.B. Tippett, 1845. 4 v. KyBC; NNS; OBerB; OClWHi; PMA. 45-415

Banim, John, 1798-1842. Damon and Pythias, or the test of friendship. A play in five acts... Philadelphia: Turner and Fisher, 1845. CtY; MH; RPB. 45-416

Bank of Baltimore. The act of the General Assembly of Maryland granting a charter... Baltimore: Jos. Robinson, printer, 1845. 138 p. DLC; MH-BA. 45-417

Bank of the United States. The bank of the United States vs. the Philadelphia, Wilmington and Baltimore Railroad Company, [1845?] 71 p. MdHi. 45-418

The bankers weekly circular and statistical record. October 14, 1845 to May 19, 1846, No. 1-31. New York, 1845-1846. 472 p. DLC; MH-BA; PPL. 45-419

The banner of the covenant and missionary advocate. Philadelphia: Published for the board, 1845-1859. 18 v.

CSansS; MBC; NcD; PPPrHi; PPULC. 45-420

Banning, Edmund Prior, b. 1810. Common sense on chronic diseases; or a rational treatise on the mechanical cause and cure of most chronic affections of the truncal organs, of both male and female systems... Second edition. New York: Paine and Burgess, 1845. 9-199 p. NBMS; NNN; OClM. 45-421

Banning, Edmund Prior, b. 1810. On weakness of the Body, [New York, 1845] 12 p. DLC; DSG. 45-422

Bannister, Henry, 1812-1883. The prevalence of error, an earnest reason for spreading the truth: a sermon preached before the Madison County Bible Society, at their semi-annual meeting, held in Cazenovia, January 28, 1845. Published by request of the society. New York: Printed by G. Trehern, 1845. 12 p. CtMW; ICN; IEG; NcD. 45-423

Bannister, Nathaniel Harington, 1813-1847. Putnam, the iron son of '76. A national military drama, in three acts. New York: Samuel French and son, [1845] 30 p. C; OCl. 45-424

Banvard, Joseph, 1810-1887. A practical question book on the various duties which we owe to God and each other, designed as a sequel to the topical question book. Boston: New England Sabbath School Union, 1845. 131 p. ICU; NWinchrHi; MoSpD; NHC-S. 45-425

Banvard, Joseph, 1810-1887. Practical question book on the various duties which we owe to God and each other. Designed as a sequel to the topical ques-

tion book. Philadelphia, 1845. 132 p.
NHC-S. 45-426

Baptist almanac for 1846. Philadelphia:
American Baptist Publication and Sunday School Society, [1845] MWA. 45-427

The Baptist library: a republication of standard Baptist works. Edited by Charles G. Sommers, pastor of the South Baptist Church, New York. Lexington, New York: Levi L. Hill, 1845. 496 p. LNH. 45-428

The Baptist scrap book, compiled and published by Levi L. Hill. Lexington, New York, 1845. 96 p. NHC-S; NjPT. 45-429

Baptists. Alabama. Bethel Association. Minutes of the twenty-fifth anniversary of the Bethel Baptist Association, held with the Union Church, Marengo County, Alabama on October 4, 5 and 6, 1845. Macon: Printed at the Banner office, 1845. 12 p. PCA. 45-430

Baptists. Alabama. Tuskaloosa [sic] Association. Minutes. [Tuskaloosa [sic], 1845] GEU; PCA. 45-431

Baptists. Connecticut. Ashford Association. Minutes of the Ashford Baptist Association, held with the Baptist Church in Thompson, May 28 and 29, 1845. Including the proceedings, of the sabbath school convention, held at the same place, May 29. Norwich: H. Barden, printer, 1845. 14 p. Ct; NHC-S. 45-432

Baptists. Connecticut. Fairfield County Association. Minutes of the eighth session of the Fairfield County Baptist Association, held in the meeting house of the Baptist church, Stratfield, Connecticut, October 8 and 9, 1845. New York: Printed by John Gray, 1845. 15 p. PCA. 45-433

Baptists. Connecticut. Hartford Association. Minutes of the fifty-sixth anniversary of the Hartford Baptist Association, held with the Baptist Church in Bloomfield, September 10 and 11, 1845. Hartford: Burr and Smith, printers, 1845. 15 p. Ct; NHC-S; PCA. 45-434

Baptists. Connecticut. New London Association. Minutes of the twenty-eighth anniversary of the New London Baptist Association, held with the first Baptist Church, East Lyme, September 24 and 25, 1845. Norwich: John W. Stedman, printer, 1845. 20 p. Ct; NHC-S; PCA. 45-435

Baptists. Connecticut. State Convention. Twenty-second annual meeting of the Connecticut Baptist convention, held at New London, June 10, 11 and 12, 1845. Hartford: Burr and Smith, printers, 1845. 36 p. PCA. 45-436

Baptists. Connecticut. Stonington Union Association. Minutes of the Stonington Union Association, from 1772 to 1786, together with a history of the several churches composing this body. Norwich: H. Barden, printer, 1845. 82 p. M; NHC-S; PCA. 45-437

Baptists. Connecticut. Stonington Union Association. Minutes of the Stonington Union Association, held with the First Baptist Church, Groton, June 18 and 19, 1845. Norwich: H. Barden, printer, 1845. 9 p. NHC-S; PPL; RWe. 45-438

Baptists. Delaware. Delaware Association. Delaware Baptist Association, held with the Salem Church, Philadelphia, May 24, 25, and 26, 1845. New Vernon, New York: Printed at the office of the Signs of the Times, 1845. 8 p. PCA. 45-439

Baptists. Georgia, Convention. Minutes of the twenty-fourth anniversary of the Georgia Baptist convention, held at Forsyth, Monroe County, Georgia, May 16, 17 and 19, 1845. Penfield, Georgia: Printed by Benjamin Brantly, 1845. 24 p. PCA. 45-440

Baptists. Georgia. Ebenezer Association. Minutes of the thirty-first anniversary of the Ebenezer Association, convened at Richland Church, Twiggs County, on September 27, 28, 29 and 30, 1845. Macon, Georgia: Printed by S. Rose and company, 1845. 12 p. PCA. 45-441

Baptists. Georgia. Georgia Association. Minutes of the Georgia Baptist Association, held at Fishing Creek Church, Wilkes County, Georgia, on October 11 and 13, 1845. Penfield, Georgia: Printed by Benjamin Brantly, 1845. 16 p. NHC-S. 45-442

Baptists. Georgia. Hightower Association. Minutes of the Hightower Baptist Association. Minutes of the Hightower Baptist Association, held at Shady Grove Church, Forsyth County, Georgia on October 17, 18, 19 and 20, 1845. Marietta: N.M. Calder, printer, 1845. 7 p. PCA. 45-443

Baptists. Georgia. Primitive Western Association. Minutes of the Primitive Western Baptist Association, held with the Emmaus Church, Troup County, Georgia, on October 18, 19, 20 and 21, 1845. Griffin, Georgia: Printed at the Georgia Jeffersonian office, [1845?] 5 p. PCA. 45-444

Baptists. Illinois. Clear Creek Association. Minutes of the fourteenth annual meeting, held with the Shiloh Church, Pulaski County, Illinois, August 9, 10 and 11, 1845. Sparta, Illinois: Printed by O.F. M'Millan, for the association, 1845. IaB; NHC-S. 45-445

Baptists. Illinois. Colored Association. Minutes of the Wood River, Madison County, August 21-24, 1845. Alton: Telegraph office, 1845. 8 p. IaB. 45-446

Baptists. Illinois. General Association. Annual meeting of the Baptist General Association of Illinois, held at Tremont, Tazewell County, Illinois, October 18, 19 and 20, 1845. Jacksonville, Illinois: William Swett, 1845. 32 p. NHC-S; PCA. 45-447

Baptists. Illinois. Illinois River Association. The ninth anniversary of the Illinois River Baptist Association, held at La Moille, Bureau County, on June 12, 13, and 14, 1845. Ottawa: Constitutionist, printer, 1845. 16 p. NHC-S; PCA. 45-448

Baptists. Illinois. Northern Association. Minutes of the tenth anniversary of the Northern Illinois Baptist Association held with the Baptist church in Elgin, June 4 and 5, 1845. Elgin: Western Christian office, printer, 1845. 10 p. NHC-S. 45-449

Baptists. Illinois. Quincy Association. Minutes of the third annual meeting of the Quincy Baptist Association, held with the Baptist Church in Mount Sterling, Brown County, Illinois, August 8, 9, 10 and 11, 1845. Jacksonville, Illinois: William C. Swett, 1845. 15p. NHC-S. 45-450

Baptists. Illinois. Rock River Association. Minutes of the sixth session of the Rock River Baptist Association, held June 18 and 19, 1845. Rockford: A. Colton, printer, [1845] 8 p. NHC-S. 45-451

Baptists. Illinois. Vandalia Association. Minutes of the Bethel Church, Marion County, September 19, 1845. Vandalia: Office of the Baptist Helmet, 1845. IaB. 45-452

Baptists. Indiana. Flat Rock Association. Minutes of the twenty-third anniversary of the Flat Rock Baptist Association, held with the Shelbyville Church, Shelby County, Indiana, Commencing on the August 4, 1845. Greensburg, Iowa: Printed by Mills and Thomson, 1845. NHC; PCA. 45-453

Baptists. Indiana. Madison Association. Minutes of the thirteenth annual meeting of the Madison Association of Baptists, held with the Brushy Fork Church, in Jefferson County, Indiana on September 13, 14 and 15, 1845. Madison: Printed at the Christian Messenger office, 1845. PCA. 45-454

Baptists. Indiana. Tippecanoe Association. Minutes of the thirteenth annual session of the Tippecanoe Regular Baptist Church at Covington. Held with the Baptist Church at Covington, Indiana, August 22, 23, 24, and 25, 1845. Lafayette: Printed by John B. Semans, 1845. NHC-S; PCA. 45-455

Baptists. Iowa. Des Moines Association. Minutes of the seventh anniversary of the Des Moines Baptist Association, held with the Ebenezer Church, in Lee County, Iowa, on September 5 and 6, 1845. Keosaugua: Printed by J. and J.M. Shepherd, 1845. 3 p. PCA. 45-456

Baptists. Iowa. Des Moines Association. Minutes of the seventh anniversary of the Des Moines Baptist Association, held with the Ebenezer Church, in Lee County, Iowa, on September, 1845. Keosauqua: Printed by J. and J.M. Shepherd, 1845. 8 p. PCA. 45-457

Baptists. Iowa. State Convention. Minutes of the fourth annual meeting of the Baptist convention of Iowa, held at Bloomington, Muscatine County, May 30-31, 1845. [n.p., 1845] 8 p. IaHA. 45-458

Baptists. Kentucky. Bracken Association. Minutes of the forty-sixth session of th Bracken Association of United Baptists, held at Maysville, Mason County, Kentucky on September 6, 1845. Continuing until the Monday following inclusive. Maysville, Kentucky: Printed at the Eagle office, 1845. 16 p. PCA. 45-459

Baptists. Kentucky. Long Run Association. Minutes of the forty-second annual meeting of the Long Run Baptist Association, held at Harrod's Creek meeting house, Oldham County, Kentucky, on September 5, 6 and 7, 1845. Louisville: George H. Monsarrat's Power Press, 1845. 12 p. TxDaHi. 45-460

Baptists. Kentucky. Middle District Association. Ninth annual meeting of the Middle District Association of Baptists; held on July 4, 1845, at the Beech Creek meeting. Shelby County, Kentucky. Shelbyville, Kentucky: Henri F. Middleton, printer, 1845. 8 p. PCA. 45-461

Baptists. Kentucky. State annual. Minutes of the Kentucky Baptist anniversaries, held in Georgetown, October, 1845. Also an abstract of the anniversaries held in Henderson, October, 1844. Louisville: George H. Montsarrat's Steam Power Press, 1845. 44 p. PCA. 45-462

Baptists. Maine. Bowdoinham Association. Minutes of the fifty-ninth anniversary of the Bowdoinham Baptist Association, held with the church in Fayette, September 24 and 25, 1845. Portland: Charles Day and company, 1845. 12 p. MHAH; NRAB; PCA. 45-463

Baptists. Maine. Cumberland Association. Minutes of the thirty-fourth anniversary of the Cumberland Baptist Association, held with the church in Durham, S.W.B. August 26, 27 and 28, 1845. Portland: Charles Day and company, 1845. 16 p. MeB; MeHi; NRAB. 45-464

Baptists. Maine. General Conference. Minutes of the General Conference of Maine. Fryeburg, June 25, 1845. Portland: Thurston: Ilsley and company, printers, 1845. 23 p. IEN. 45-465

Baptists. Maine. Hancock Association. Minutes of the eleventh anniversary of the Hancock Baptist Association, held in the meeting house of the First Baptist Church in Bluehill, September 2, 3 and 4, 1845. Portland: Charles Day and company, printers, 1845. 16 p. NRAB; PCA. 45-466

Baptists. Maine. Kennebec Association. Minutes of the sixteenth anniversary of the Kennebec Baptist Association, held with the First Baptist Church in Bloomfield, September 16, 17 and 18, 1845. With an exhibit of the state of the churches. Farmington, Maine, J.S. Swift, printer, 1845. 24 p. MiD-B; PCA. 45-467

Baptists. Maine. Lincoln Association. Minutes of the forty-first anniversary of the Lincoln Baptist Association, held with the Baptist Church in Warren, September 17 and 18, 1845. 14 p. PCA. 45-468

Baptists. Maine. Oxford Association. Minutes of the seventeenth anniversary of the Oxford Baptist Association, held in the Baptist meeting house in Turner, September 16, 17 and 18, 1845. Portland: Charles Day and company, 1845. 16 p. PCA. 45-469

Baptists. Maine. Piscataquis Association. Minutes of the seventh anniversary of the Piscataquis Baptist Association, held with the church in Monson, September 23, 24 and 25, 1845. Portland: Charles Day and company, 1845. 16 p. MeBA; NRAB; PCA. 45-470

Baptists. Maine. Saco River Association. Minutes of the fourth anniversary of the Saco River Baptist Association, held in the Baptist Meeting house at Cornish, September 3 and 4, 1845. Saco, Maine: Printed by Noyes and Cowan, 1845. 16 p. MeBa; PCA. 45-471

Baptists. Maine. State annual. Minutes of the twenty-first anniversary of the Maine Baptist convention, held at East Winthrop, June 17, 1845. Portland: Charles Day and company, 1845. 32 p. MeBa; MHi; NRAB. 45-472

Baptists. Maine. Waldo Association. Minutes of the seventeenth anniversary of the Waldo Baptist Association, held in the Baptist Meeting house in Knox, September 9, 10 and 11, 1845. Portland: Charles Day and company, 1845. 12 p. NRAB; PCA. 45-473

Baptists. Maine. Washington Association. Minutes of the eleventh anniversary of the Washington Baptist Association. Portland: Charles Day and company, 1845. MNtcA; PCA. 45-474

Baptists. Maryland. Maryland Union Association. Minutes of the ninth meeting of the Maryland Baptist Association, held in the meeting house of the E Street, or Third Baptist Church, Washington, D.C., November 9, 10, 11 and 12, 1844. Washington: T. Barnard, printer, 1845. 20 p. PCA. 45-475

Baptists. Maryland. Maryland Union Association. Minutes of the tenth meeting of the Maryland Baptist Union Association, held in the meeting house of the First Baptist Church, Baltimore, November 5 and 6, 1845. Washington: William Q. Force, printer, 1845. 20 p. MiD-B; PCA; ViRU. 45-476

Baptists. Massachusetts. Berkshire Association. Minutes of the eighteenth anniversary of the Berkshire Baptist Association held with the Baptist church in Williamstown, October 8 and 9, 1845. Pittsfield: Charles Montague, printer, 1845. 16 p. MPiB; PCA. 45-477

Baptists. Massachusetts. Boston Association. Thirty-fourth anniversary of the Boston Baptist Association, held with the Baptist Church in Randolph, September 17 and 18, 1845. Boston: John

Putnam, printer, 1845. 19 p. CBB; PCA. 45-478

Baptists. Massachusetts. Boston Baptist Association. The thirty-fourth anniversary of the Boston Baptist Association, held with the Baptist church in Randolph, September 17 and 18, 1845. Special session. Boston: John Putnam, printer, 1845. 19 p. PCA. 45-479

Baptists. Massachusetts. Old Colony Association. Minutes of the twenty-third anniversary of the Old Colony Baptist Association, held with the Baptist Church in Kingston, October 1 and 2, 1845. Boston: John Putnam, printer, 1845. 16 p. PCA. 45-480

Baptists. Massachusetts. Salem Association. Minutes of the eighteenth anniversary of the Salem Baptist Association, held in the meeting house of the Baptist church in Methuen, September 24 and 25, 1845. Boston: John Putnam, printer, 1845. 24 p. PCA; TxFwSBS. 45-481

Baptists. Massachusetts. Sturbridge Association. Minutes of the forty-fourth anniversary of the Sturbridge Association, held with the Baptist Church in Brookfield, Massachusetts, August 28 and 29, 1845, together with the constitution. Worcester: Printed by Henry J. Howland, 1845. 17 p. MNtCA. 45-482

Baptists. Massachusetts. Westfield Association. Minutes of the thirty-fifth anniversary. Springfield: Taylor, 1845. 14 p. CtHC; PCA. 45-483

Baptists. Massachusetts. Worcester Association. Minutes of the twenty-sixth anniversary of the Worcester Baptist

Association, held with the Central Baptist Church in Southbridge, on August 21 and 22, 1845. Worcester, Henry J. Howland, 1845. 36 p. MiD-B; PCA. 45-484

Baptists. Mississippi. Aberdeen Association. Baptist association minutes. Aberdeen, Mississippi, 1845. OCHP. 45-485

Baptists. Mississippi. Choctaw Association. Minutes of the seventh anniversary of the Choctaw Baptist Association held with the church at Wahalak, Kemper County, Mississippi. Macon, Mississippi: A. and A.E. Marschalk, 1845. 10 p. MsCliBHi. 45-486

Baptists. Mississippi. Mississippi River Association. Minutes of the third annual meeting of the Mississippi River Baptist Association, held with the Jerusalem Baptist Church, Amite County, Mississippi, October 23, 24 and 25, 1845. Clinton, Louisiana: Printed by Henry Skipwith, 1845. 8 p. TxFS. 45-487

Baptists. Mississippi. Union Association. Minutes of the twenty-fifth anniversary of the Union Baptist Association, held with Bethlehem Church, Franklin County, Mississippi. Together with a synopsis of the proceedings of a convention to form a new association. n.p., 1845. 8 p. MsCliBHi. 45-488

Baptists. New Hampshire. Dublin Association. Minutes of the thirty-sixth anniversary of the Dublin Baptist Association, and the Sabbath School Convention, held with the Baptist Church, in East Washington, New Hampshire, September 2, 3 and 4, 1845.

Keene: Printed by J.J.W. Prentise, 1845. 16 p. NRAB; PCA. 45-489

Baptists. New Hampshire. Portsmouth Association. Minutes of the seventeenth anniversary of the Portsmouth Baptist Association, held at Newtown on October 1 and 2, 1845. Portsmouth: Charles W. Brewster, printer, 1845. 12 p. TxFwSB. 45-490

Baptists. New Hampshire. State Convention. Proceedings of the New Hampshire Baptist state convention, together with the New Hampshire Baptist Education Society, and the Baptist Anti-slavery Society, at their annual meetings, held at Exeter, New Hampshire, June 24, 25 and 26, 1845. Concord: Printed by Charles Young, 1845. 48 p. PCA. 45-491

Baptists. New Jersey. Central Association. Minutes of the Central New Jersey Baptist Association, held at Kingwood, October 14, 15 and 16, 1845. Lamberville: Printed by John R. Swallow, 1845. 16 p. PCA. 45-492

Baptists. New Jersey. Delaware River Association. Minutes of the Delaware River Baptist Association, held with the church at Washington, Middlesex County, New Jersey, on May 30, and 31, 1845. New Vernon, New Jersey: Printed at the sign of the times, 1845. 8 p. PCA. 45-493

Baptists. New Jersey. East New Jersey Association. Minutes of the fourth anniversary of the East New Jersey Baptist Association, held in the meeting house of the Samptown Baptist Church, on June 3, 4 and 5, 1845. New York: George B. Maigne, printer, 1845. 16 p. PCA. 45-494

Baptists. New Jersey. State Convention. Minutes of the sixteenth anniversary of the New Jersey Baptist state convention and the eighth annual meeting of the New Jersey Baptist Education Society, held in the meeting house of the Baptist Church at Piscataway, November 11, 12 and 13, 1845. New York: Printed by John Gray, 1845. 24 p. PCA. 45-495

Baptists. New Jersey. West New Jersey Association. Minutes of the thirty-fourth anniversary of the New Jersey Baptist Association, held with the Church at Allowaystown, September 9, 10, and 11, 1845. Burlington: Printed by Edmund Morris, 1845. 18 p. MiD-B; PCA. 45-496

Baptists. New York. Buffalo Association. Minutes of the thirteenth annual session of the Buffalo Baptist Association, held with the Baptist Church in Sardinia, on the September 9, 10, and 11, 1845. Buffalo: Clapp and M'Credie, printers, 1845. 16 p. MNC-H; PCA. 45-497

Baptists. New York. Canisteo River Association. Minutes of the tenth annual meeting of the Canisteo River Baptist Association, held with the Church in Almond, Septembser 10 and 11, 1845. Angelica: Erastus S. Palmer, 1845. 12 p. PCA. 45-498

Baptists. New York. Cattaraugus Association. Minutes of the tenth anniversary of the Cattaraugus Baptist Association, held with the Church in Friendship, Allegany County, July 9 and 10, 1845. Angelica: Eratus S. Palmer, 1845. 11 p. PCA. 45-499

Baptists. New York. Cayuga Association. Minutes of the forty-fifth annual meeting of the Cayuga Baptist Association, held with the Baptist church in Montezuma, Cayuga County, New York, September 18 and 19, 1845. [Auburn: U.F. Doubleday, 1845] 16 p. NHC-S; NRCR; PCA. 45-500

Baptists. New York. Chautauqua Association. Minutes of the twenty-first anniversary of the Chautauqua Baptist Association, held with the Baptist church in Sheridan, on September 3 and 4, 1845. Fredonia: Printed by W. McKinstry and company, 1845. 15 p. PCA. 45-501

Baptists. New York. Dutchess Association. Minutes of the eleventh anniversary of the Dutchess Baptist Association held in the meeting house of the First Baptist Church at Stanford, New York, October 1 and 2, 1845. New York: Printed by John Gray, 1845. 14 p. PCA. 45-502

Baptists. New York. Fairfield County Association. Minutes of the eighth session of the Fairfield County Baptist Association held in the meeting house of the Baptist Church, Stratfield, Connecticut, October 8 and 9, 1845. New York: Printed by John Gray, 1845. 16 p. NHC-S. 45-503

Baptists. New York. Genesee Association. Minutes of the twenty-seventh anniversary of the Genesee Baptist Association, held with the Oakfield and Alabama Church, June 17 and 18, 1845. Perry, New York: Curtiss, printer, 1845. 15 p. PCA. 45-504

Baptists. New York. Genesee River Association. Minutes of the seventeenth anniversary of the Genesee River Baptist Association, held with the church at West Almond, Allegheny County, June 19 and

20, 1845. Angelica: Erastus S. Palmer, 1845. 11 p. PCA. 45-505

Baptists. New York. Harmony Association. The seventh session of the Harmony Baptist Association, held in the Baptist meeting house in Busti, August 26, 27 and 28, 1845. Buffalo: Steele's Press, 1845. 21 p. NHC-S; NRCR; PCA. 45-506

Baptists. New York. Hudson River Association. The thirtieth anniversary of the Hudson River Baptist Association, held in the meeting house of the Pierrepont Street Baptist Church in the city of Brooklyn, June 17, 18 and 19, 1845. New York: Printed by John Gray, 1845. 32 p. PCA. 45-507

Baptists. New York. Livingston Association. Minutes of the fourteenth annual meeting of the Livingston Baptist Association, held with the church in Livonia, New York, June 25 and 26, 1845. Rochester: Canfield and Warren, printer, 1845. 13 p. DLC; NHC-S. 45-508

Baptists. New York. Madison Association. Minutes of the thirty-seventh annual meeting of the Madison Baptist Association, held at Morrisville, Madison County, New York, on September 9 and 10, 1845. Cazenovia: W.H. Phillips, printers, 1845. 17 p. PCA. 45-509

Baptists. New York. Missionary Convention of the State of New York. Proceedings of the twenty-fourth anniversary in Trumansburgh, October 15 and 16, 1845. Utica: Press of Bennett, Backus and Hawley, 1845. 52 p. N; NN; PCA. 45-510

Baptists. New York. Missionary Convention. Proceedings of the twenty-fourth anniversary of the Baptist missionary convention of the state of New York, held with the Baptist church in Trumansburgh, October 15 and 16, 1845. With the report of the board and treasurer... Utica: Press of Bennett, Backus and Hawley, 1845. 53 p. N; NN. 45-511

Baptists. New York. Mohawk River Association. Minutes of the sixth anniversary of the Mohawk River Baptist Association, held with Frankfort Church, June 4 and 5, 1845. Lyon's Press, [1845?] 12 p. PCA. 45-512

Baptists. New York. Monroe Association. Minutes of the eighteenth anniversary of the Monroe Baptist Association, held in the meeting house of the Baptist Church in Brockport, September 30 to October 2, 1845. Rochester: Printed by Canfield and Warren, 1845. 24 p. NRCR; PCA. 45-513

Baptists. New York. New York Association. Minutes of the fifty-fifth anniversary of the New York Baptist Association, held at the meeting house of the First Piermont Baptist Church, Rockland County, New York, on May 27 and 28, 1845. New York: Printed by John Gray, 1845. 20 p. PCA. 45-514

Baptists. New York. Oswego Association. The thirteenth anniversary... held at Hannibal, New York, September 10 and 11, 1845. Oswego: Printed by D. Ayer, 1845. 15 p. CSmH; NRCR. 45-515

Baptists. New York. Rensselaerville Association. The forty-seventh anniversary of the Rensselaerville Baptist Association, held in the meeting house of the Baptist Church of Duanesburg and Florida, September 17 and 18, 1845. Albany: Printed by J. Munsell, 1845. 12 p. PCA. 45-516

Baptists. New York. Stephentown Association. The fourteenth anniversary of the Stephentown Baptist Association, held in the meeting house of the second Baptist Church, in Nassau, Rensselaer County, New York, September 10, 11, 1845. Stephentown: Printed by Weed and Parsons, 1845. 8 p. PCA. 45-517

Baptists. New York. Union Association. Minutes of the thirty-fifth anniversary at Red Mills, Putnam County, New York, September 3 and 4, 1845. Peekskill: Printed by G.K. Lyman, 1845. 16 p. PCA. 45-518

Baptists. New York. Warwick Association. Minutes of the Warwick Baptist Association, held with the church at Brookfield, Orange County, New York, June 4 and 5, 1845. New Vernon, New York: Printed at the office of the Signs of the Times, 1845. 8 p. PCA. 45-519

Baptists. New York. Wayne Association. Minutes of the eleventh annual session of Wayne Baptist Association, held at Lyons, Wayne County, New York, on September 23 and 24, 1845. Lyons: Printed by W.N. and J. Cole, 1845. 16 p. PCA. 45-520

Baptists. New York. Worcester Association. Minutes of the fifteenth anniversary of the Worcester Baptist Association, held in the Baptist meeting house, at Westford, Otsego County, New York, July 2 and 3, 1845. Cooperstown: Printed by John H. Prentiss, 1845. 12 p. PCA. 45-521

Baptists. Ohio. Anglaise Association. Minutes of its organization and of the first annual session. Lima, Ohio, 1845. OClWHi. 45-522

Baptists. Ohio. Cleremont Association. Minutes of the twenty-ninth anniversary of the East Fork Little Miami Association of Regular Baptists. Cincinnati: L. Hommedieum and company, printers, 1845. 8 p. PCA. 45-523

Baptists. Ohio. Cleveland Association. Minutes of the fourteenth anniversary of the Rocky River Baptist Association, held at Strongsville, Cuyahoga County, Ohio. Akron, Ohio: Printed by Lane and Coggshall, 1845. 16 p. PCA. 45-524

Baptists. Ohio. Mad River Association. Minutes of the Mad River Baptist Association, at its thirty-third anniversary, September, 1845. Held with the Lost Creek Church. Springfield: Gallagher and Crain, 1845. 14 p. CSmH. 45-525

Baptists. Ohio. Marietta Association. Minutes of the twentieth anniversary of the Meig's Creek Baptist Association, held with the Little Muskingum Church, August 13 and 14. Marietta, Ohio: Printed at the Intelligencer office, 1845. 12 p. PCA. 45-526

Baptists. Ohio. Miami Association. Minutes of the Miami Association of Regular Baptists, held with the First Baptist Church of Dayton, Ohio, September 12 and 13, 1845. Dayton: Printed at the Journal office, 1845. 16 p. PCA. 45-527

Baptists. Ohio. Mohecan Association. Minutes of the 26th, 27th anniversary of the Mohecan Baptist Association.

Mansfield, Ohio: Shield and Banner, 1845-1848. 2 v. CSmH. 45-528

Baptists. Ohio. Ohio Baptist Book and Tract Society. Claims of the Ohio Baptist Book and Tract Society presented in an address to the denomination; with its consititution, a list of its officers, stockholders, etc. Zanesville, Ohio: Edwin C. Church, 1845. 16 p. OClWHi. 45-529

Baptists. Ohio. Ohio Convention. Minutes of the nineteenth anniversary of the Ohio Baptist Convention, and proceedings of other societies of the Baptist denomination in Ohio, held at Zanesville, May, 1845. Columbus: Stewart and Cole, printers, 1845. 72 p. PCA. 45-530

Baptists. Ohio. Scioto Association. Minutes of the fortieth annual meeting of the Scioto Baptist Association, held with Licking Church, Licking County, Ohio, August 16 and 18, 1845. Columbus: Stewart and Cole, printer, 1845. 15 p. PCA. 45-531

Baptists. Ohio. Wills Creek Association. Minutes of the sixth annual meeting of the Wills Creek Baptist Association, held at Tomaka Church, Coshocton County, Ohio. Zanesville, Ohio: Edwin C. Church, 1845. 10 p. MoSM. 45-532

Baptists. Pennsylvania. Abington Association. Minutes of the thirty-eighth anniversary of the Abington Baptist Association, held by appointment in the meeting house of the First Baptist Church in Honesdale, Wayne County, Pennsylvania on September 3 and 4, 1845. Greenville, Pennsylvania: Moses P. Berry, printer, 1845. 16 p. PCA. 45-533

Baptists. Pennsylvania. Central Union Association. Minutes of the fourteenth annual session of the Central Union Association of Independent Baptist Church, held in the meeting house of the Phoenixville Baptist Church, May 26 and 27, 1846. Philadelphia: King and Baird, printers, 1845. 16 p. NRAB; PCA. 45-534

Baptists. Pennsylvania. Central Union Association. Minutes of the special session of the Central Union Association of Independent Baptist Churches held in the meeting house of the Norristown Baptist Church, November 26 and 27, 1844. Philadelphia: King and Baird, printers, 1845. 28 p. NRAB; PCA. 45-535

Baptists. Pennsylvania. Clarion Association. Minutes of the eighth anniversary of the Clarion Association of Regular Baptist Churches held with the Union Church, Armstrong County, Pennsylvania, October 16, 17 and 18, 1845. Clearfield, Pennsylvania: Moore and Thompson, printer, 1845. 8 p. PCA. 45-536

Baptists. Pennsylvania. Pennsylvania Baptist Bible Society. Thirty-seventh annual report of the Society. Philadelphia, 1845. PCA. 45-537

Baptists. Pennsylvania. Pennsylvania Baptist Education Society. Minutes of anniversaries, 1844. Philadelphia, 1845. PHi; PPAmP; PCC; PP. 45-538

Baptists. Pennsylvania. Pennsylvania Baptist Education Society. Minutes of the sixth anniversary of the Pennsylvania Baptist Education Society, held with the First Baptist Church, Philadelphia. Philadelphia: King and Baird, 1845. 14 p. NRAB; PScrHi. 45-539

Baptists. Pennsylvania. Philadelphia Association. Minutes of the anniversary of the Philadelphia Baptist Association, held with the New Market Street Church in Philadelphia, October 7, 8, 9 and 10, 1845. Philadelphia: King and Baird, printers, 1845. 36 p. NRAB; PCA. 45-540

Baptists. Pennsylvania. State Convention. Minutes of the ninth anniversary of the Pennsylvania Baptist Convention, for Missionary purposes, held at Philadelphia, with the First Baptist Church, November 7-10, 1845. Philadelphia: King and Baird, printers, 1845. 48 p. NRAB; PScrHi. 45-541

Baptists. Seventh Day. Appeal for restoration of the Lord's sabbath. Fourth edition. New York: American Sabbath Tract Society, 1845. 24 p. RPB. 45-542

Baptists. South Carolina. State Convention. Minutes of the state convention of the Baptist denomination in South Carolina. Charleston: Printed by W. Riley, 1845. 36 p. GDecCT; KyLoS. 45-543

Baptists. South Carolina. Welsh Neck Association. Minutes of the fourteenth anniversary of the Welsh Neck Baptist Association, held at Cheraw, South Carolina, November 8-11, 1845. 16 p. PCA. 45-544

Baptists. Southern Convention. Proceedings of the Southern Baptist convention, held in Augusta, Georgia, May 8, 9, 10, 11 and 12, 1845. Richmond: H.K. Ellyson, printer, 1845. 20 p. MHi; MoSM; TxFwSB; ViRU. 45-545

Baptists. Tennessee. Central Association of United Baptists. Minutes of the tenth annual meeting of the Central Association of United Baptists, held with the church at Cotton Grove, Madison County, Tennessee, commencing on July 4, 1845. Jackson, Tennessee: George W. Talbot, printer, 1845. 8 p. MoSM. 45-546

Baptists. Tennessee. General Association. Proceedings of the second annual meeting of the General Association of the Baptists of East Tennessee, held at Cedar Ford, Blout County, August, 1845. Knoxville: Jas. C. Moses, printer, 1845. 12 p. PCA. 45-547

Baptists. Tennessee. Tennessee Association United Baptists, convened at the Rocky Valley meeting house, Jefferson County, Tennessee, on October, 1845. Knoxville: Jas. C. Moses, 1845. 7 p. PCA. 45-548

Baptists. Tennessee. West Tennessee Convention. Proceedings of the West Tennessee Baptist convention, held with the Spring Hill Church, Gobson County, September 12-15, 1845. Sommerville, Tennessee: Printed by Reeves and Yancey, 1845. 16 p. PCA; T. 45-549

Baptists. Texas. Union Association. Minutes of the sixth annual meeting of the Union Baptist Association, held with Mount Gillead Church, Washington County, Western Texas, on October 9, 10, and 11, 1845. La Grange, Texas: Printed at the Intelligencer office, 1845. 8 p. TxFwSB; TxU. 45-550

Baptists. Vermont. Shaftsbury Association. Minutes of the sixty-sixth anniversary of the Shaftsbury Baptist Association; held in the new meeting house in North Bennington, Vermont, June 3 and 4, 1846. East Poultney, Vermont: J.K. Seaver, printer, 1846. 11 p. MiD-B. 45-551

Baptists. Vermont. State Convention. Minutes of the twentieth anniversary held with the church in Rutland, October 9 and 10, 1845; also the Vermont Bible Society, and Vermont Anti-slavery Society, Auxiliary to the American and Foreign Society. Middlebury: J.K. Seaver, printer, 1845. PCA. 45-552

Baptists. Vermont. Woodstock Association. Sixty-first anniversary of the Woodstock Baptist Association held in the north meeting house of the Baptist Church in Mount Holly. Bellows Falls, Vermont: S.M. Blake, 1845. 12 p. PCA. 45-553

Baptists. Virginia. Albemarle Association. Minutes of the fifty-fourth anniversary of the Albemarle Baptist Association, held in the meeting house of the Free Union Church, Albemarle, August 16, 17 and 18, 1845. Charlottesville, Virginia: James Alexander, printer, 1845. 19 p. PCA; ViRu. 45-554

Baptists. Virginia. Appamattox Association. Minutes of the Appamattox Baptist Association, held at the Nottoway Church, on August 9 and 11, 1845. Lynchburg: Printed by Toler, Townley and Statham, 1845. 12 p. PCA. 45-555

Baptists. Virginia. Bible Society. Thirty-second anniversary of the Bible Society of Virginia, with the proceedings of the annual meeting, held on April 1, 1845, at the Centenary Methodist Church. Richmond: William MacFarlane, 1845. MdBD. 45-556

Baptists. Virginia. Dan River Associa-

tion. Minutes of the Dan River Baptist Association, held at Hyco meeting house, Halifax County, Virginia, August, 1845. Milton, North Carolina: Printed by C.N.B. Evans, 1845. 6 p. ViRu. 45-557

Baptists. Virginia. Dover Association. Minutes of the sixty-second annual session of the Dover Baptist Association, held with the Sharon Church, King William County, Virginia, October 10 and 11, 1845. Richmond: Printed by H.K. Ellyson, 1845. 18 p. CSmH; ViRU. 45-558

Baptists. Virginia. Dover Association. Minutes of the sixty-second annual session of the Dover Baptist Association. New edition. Richmond: Printed by H.K. Ellyson, 1845. CSmH. 45-559

Baptists. Virginia. Goshen Association. Minutes of the Goshen Baptist Association, held at Lyle's Church, Fluvanna County, Virginia, September 10-12, 1845. Richmond: Printed at the office of the Religious Herald, 1845. 16 p. ViRU. 45-560

Baptists. Virginia. Portsmouth Association. Minutes of the 55th session. Philadelphia, 1845. PCA; PPL. 45-561

Baptists. Virginia. Strawberry Association, Fall session, Cove meeting house, Bedford County, Virginia, August 31, 1844. Spring session, Mount Herman Meeting house, Bedford County, Virginia, August 31, 1844, May 10, 1845. Lynchburg: Printed by Toler, Towney and Stratham, 1845. 7 p. ViRu. 45-562

Baptists. West Virginia. Ebenezer Association. Minutes of the eighteenth anniversary of the Ebenezer Baptist Association, held with Mount Carmel

Church, Luray, Page County, Virginia, August 29 and 30, 1845. Harrisonburg, Virginia: Register office, 1845. 81 p. PCA. 45-563

Baptists. Wisconsin. Wisconsin Association. Minutes of the seventh anniversary of the Baptist Association of Wisconsin, held with the Baptist Church in Delavan, June 25 and 26, 1845. Elgin: Western Christian printer, 1845. ICU; NHC-S; WHi. 45-564

Bar, John. Bar's complete index and concise dictionary of the Holy Bible; in which the various persons, places, and subjects mentioned in it are accurately referred to; and difficult words briefly explained. Designed to facilitate the study of the sacred scriptures. Revised from the third Glasgow edition. New York: G. Lane and C.B. Tippett for the Methodist Episcopal Church, 1845. 210 p. ODecJ; OHi. 45-565

Baraga, Friedrich, 1797-1868. Abinodjiiag omasinaiganiwan. Detroit: Bagg and Harmon, printers, 1845. MBAt. 45-566

Barbauld, Anna Letitia Aikin, 1743-1825. Lessons for children translated into French, with a vocabulary. New York: Roe, Lockwood and sons, 1845. CaBVa-U; DLC; LU; MB; PPULC. 45-567

Barber, John Warner, 1798-1885. Historical collections of the state of New Jersey; containing a general collection of the most interesting facts, traditions, biographical sketches, anecdotes, etc. relating to its history and antiquities... New York: S. Tuttle, 1845. 512 p. CtB; MH; MWA; NcAS; NjT. 45-568

Barber, John Warner, 1798-1885. Historical collections of the state of New York; containing a general collection of the most interesting facts, traditions, biographical sketches, anecdotes, etc., relating to its history and antiquities. New York: Published for the authors by S. Tuttle, 1845. 616 p. CSmH; NjN; MH; NbU; RNR. 45-569

Barclay, Anthony. Proceedings of the meeting held May 26th, 1845. In furtherance of the establishment of a free church for British emigrants at the Port of New York. New York, 1845. MH. 45-570

Barker, Benjamin. Cecilia: or the white nun of the wilderness. A romance of love and intrigue. Boston: F. Gleason, 1845. 56 p. ICU; MB; MiD-B; MnU; RPB. 45-571

Barker, Benjamin. Ellen Grafton, the Lily of Lexington; or the bride of liberty. A romance of the revolution. Boston: F. Gleason, 1845. [5]-100 p. CtY; ICN; MWA; NSmB; RPB. 45-572

Barker, Benjamin. Emily Elwood; or the hermit of the crags. A romance of the last war. Boston: Gleason, 1845. 58 p. IaU; ICU; MB; OClWHi; PU. 45-573

Barker, Benjamin. Francisco; or the pirates of the Pacific. A tale of the land and sea. Boston: Gleason's Publishing Hall, 1845. DLC; ICU; KU; MB; NhD. 45-574

Barker, Benjamin. Mary Moreland; or the fortunes and misfortunes of an orphan... Boston: Gleason's Publishing Hall, 1845. 46 p. DLC; MB; MH; NSmb; RPB. 45-575

Barker, Benjamin. Zoraida; or the witch of Naumkeag. A tale of the olden times. By Egbert Augustus Cowslip [pseud.] Boston: Gleason's Publishing Hall, 1845. 48 p. ICU; MiD-B; OU. 45-576

Barker, George Arthur, 1812-1876. The white squall. [sic] A sea song. New York: Riley and company, [1845?] 7 p. MB. 45-577

Barker, Matthew Henry, 1790-1846. Fortunes of Frank Fairfield. Philadelphia, 1845. MBAt. 45-578

Barlow, John, 1798 or 9-1869. On man's power over himself... Philadelphia: Lea and Blanchard, 1845. 54 p. CtY; DNLM; ICU; MBM; WU. 45-579

Barlow, William. A letter to a committee of New York clergymen, in reply to a circular addressed by them to certain clergymen of the Diocese of New York. [New York: J.R. Winser, printer, 1845] 8 p. CtY; MdBD; MH; NNG; WHi. 45-580

Barnard, Daniel Dewey, 1797-1861. A plea for social prose, being an address delivered before the Philomathean and Eucleian Societies of the University of the City of New York, July 1, 1845. New York: Tribune Job Printing Establishment, 1845. 22 p. DLC; KyLx; MB; NjR; RPB. 45-581

Barnard, Daniel Dewey, 1797-1861. Speech of Mr. Barnard, of New York, on the annexation of Texas. Delivered in the House of Representatives, January 24, 1845. Washington: Printed by J. and G.S. Gideon, 1845. 16 p. CtY; MBAt; MWA; NBu; TxU. 45-582

Barnard, J.G. Harbor defense, by fortifications and steam vessels, considered particularly in reference to the defense of New Orleans. New York: Henry Spear, 1845. NoLoc. 45-583

Barnes, Albert, 1798-1870. The death of a mother. New York, 1845. 23 p. MH-AH. 45-584

Barnes, Albert, 1798-1870. The duties which members of the church owe to each other. New York, 1845. 23 p. MH-AH. 45-585

Barnes, Albert, 1798-1870. Practical sermons: designed for vacant congregations and families. Philadelphia: Perkins and Pruves, 1845. 3-356 p. DLC; MnSH. 45-586

Barnes, Albert, 1798-1870. The presence of God in the valley of the shadow of death: a sermon, preached in the First Presbyterian Church, Philadelphia, October 19, 1845 on the occasion of the death of Henry Neill, a ruling elder in the church, who died October 7, 1845. Philadelphia: Ashmead, 1845. 28 p. MdBP; MH-AH; NCH; PHi; PPM. 45-587

Barnes, Albert, 1798-1870. Thanksgiving sermon. The virtues and public services of William Penn. A discourse November 27, 1845. Philadelphia: W. Sloanaker; New York: W.H. Graham, 1845. 24 p. CtY; DLC; OClWHi; PPC; RPB. 45-588

Barnes, Orson. Key to Barnes's pictorial moral instructor. Syracuse: Printed at the Onon Standard office, 1845. 29 p. CtHT- W; NjR. 45-589

Barnett, Charles Zachary. Midnight; the thirteenth chime; old Saint Paul's; a melodrama, in three acts. New York: Samuel French and son, [1845] 32 p. OCl. 45-590

Barney, William Chase. Dedicated to the genius of war of Delaware. [Proceedings of the court martial of W.C. Barney] Inscribed to the officers and privates of the first troop Delaware Light Dragoons, by the author. Philadelphia, 1845. 8 p. MdHi; WHi. 45-591

Barre, Massachusetts. Evangelical Congregational Church. The articles of faith and covenant of the Evangelical Congregational Church in Barre, with a catalogue of members. Barre: Patriot Office Press, 1845. 24 p. MBC; MPiB; MWA; NBLiHi. 45-592

Barrett, Benjamin Fiske, 1808-1892. Corner stone of the New Jerusalem. New York: Bartlett and Welford, 1845. 57 p. MCNC; MsJPED; MWA; OUrC; PU. 45-593

Barrett, Samuel. Reflection in a Sunday school. Boston: Tuttle and Dennett, printers, 1845. 17 p. MB. 45-594

Barrett, Solomon. The principles of English grammar; or the self instructor: being a treatise on the constructive principles of the language. Tenth edition, revised. Utica: R.W. Roberts, printer, 1845. 96 p. CtY; NBuG; NCH; NNC; NUt. 45-595

Barrett, Thomas. Trial and execution of Thomas Barrett, who first committed a rape on the person of Mrs. Houghton and then foully murdered her to conceal his crime. Boston: Skinner and Blanchard, 1845. 24 p. MH-L; Nh; NIC-L. 45-596

Barrington, Jonah, 1760-1834. Rise and fall of the Irish nation. New York: D. and J. Sadlier, 1845. [23]-472 p. IaK; NNF; PEaL; RPAt; TJoV. 45-597

Barrow, Alexander, 1802-1846. Speech of Mr. Barrow, of Louisiana, on the resolutions from the House for the admission of Texas into the Union. Delivered in the Senate, February 19, 1845. 16 p. DLC; MBAt; MHi; WaSp. 45-598

Barrow, Isaac, 1630-1677. The pope's supremacy. To which are added a synopsis of the treatise and two complete indexes. New York: John C. Riker, 1845. 268 p. CSansS; DLC; MH; OO; PPP. 45-599

Barrow, Isaac, 1630-1677. The works of Isaac Barrow, to which are prefixed, a life of the author, by Abraham Hill, and a memoir, by James Hamilton with notes and references carefully revised; and indexes compiled expressly for this edition. New York: J.C. Riker, 1845. 3 v. CU; ICU; LNB; NcAS; ScAb. 45-600

Barrow, John, 1764-1848. A description of Pitcairn's Island and its inhabitants. With an authentic account of the mutiny of the ship Bounty, and of the subsequent fortunes of the mutineers. New York: Harper and brothers, 1845. 303 p. GAuY; IaBo; IGK; MH; RPE. 45-601

Barrow, John, 1764-1848. A memoir of the life of Peter the Great. New York: Harper and brothers, 1845. 5-320 p. LNL; OSW; RWe; ScDuE; WNaE. 45-602

Barrows, Willard, 1806-1868. A new map of Iowa. Cincinnati: Engraved and published by Doolittle and Munson; Rockingham, Iowa: Barrows, 1845. IaDa. 45-603

Barrows, Willard, 1806-1868. Notes on Iowa Territory, with a map. Map has been removed and mounted. Cincinnati, Ohio: Doolittle and Munson, 1845. 47 p. DLC; IaHA; IaU; PPFrakI; WHi. 45-604

Barstow, George, 1812-1883. Eulogy on the life and character of Andrew Jackson, at Manchester, New Hampshire, on July 12, 1845. [Manchester, 1845] 7 p. CLU; CU; MH; RPB. 45-605

Barth, M. A manual of auscultation and percussion, Agrege to the faculty of medicine of Paris and M. Henry Roger, physician to the Bureau Central of the Parisian Hospitals. Translated with additions... Philadelphia: Lindsay and Blakiston, 1845. 160 p. CtY; MeB; PPCP; OCo; RPM. 45-606

Bartlett, Edwin, 1796-1867. Guano, its origin and properties, with a practical treatise on its value and use with results. Proving it to be the most potent, portable, and the cheapest manure in the world. New Bedford: Printed by William Young, 1845. 14 p. MNBedf. 45-607

Bartlett, Edwin, 1796-1867. Guano, its origin, properties and uses; showing its importance to the farmers of the United States as a cheap and valuable manure with directions for using it. New York: Wiley, 1845. 92 p. DNAL; IaU; MH; PPULC; PU-V. 45-608

Bartlett, Edwin, 1796-1867. Guano, its origin, properties and uses; showing its

importance to the farmers of the United States as a cheap and valuable manure with directions for using it. Second edition. New York: Wiley, 1845. 92 p. DPC; IaU; MH; PPL-R; PU-V. 45-609

Bartlett, John Sherren. Maize on Indian corn; its advantages as a cheap and nutritious article of food for the poor and labouring classes of Great Britian and Ireland with directions for its use. New York, 1845. 16 p. DSG; MBHo NN. 45-610

Bartlett, William Holms Chambers, 1804-1893. Longitude by lunar culminations. [Washington: Government Printing office, 1845] 12 p. DLC; DNLM; ViFbE. 45-611

Barton, John. Perils of poetry, especially considered with references to the United States of America. Cincinnati: H.W. Derby and company, 1845. 236 p. DLC; IEG; OClWHi; OO; ViRut. 45-612

Bascom, Henry Bidleman, 1796-1850. Committee on organization, a report presented to the convention of delegates from the annual conference of the Methodist Episcopal Church. Louisville: Prentice and Weissinger, 1845. ICU; IEG; KyDC; MoSHi; OAIM. 45-613

Bascom, Henry Bidleman, 1796-1850. Methodism and slavery: with other matters in controversy between the North and the South; being a review of the manifesto of the majority, in reply to the protest of the minority, of the late general conference of the Methodist Episcopal Church, in the case of Bishop Andrew. Frankfort, Kentucky: Hodges,

Todd and Pruett, printers, 1845. 165 p. ICU; KyRE; PHi; ScU; WvU. 45-614

Batchelder, John Putnam, 1784-1868. Thoughts on the connection of life, mind, and matter; in respect to education. Utica: Bennett, Backus and Hawley, 1845. 84 p. CSmH; DLC; MWA; NNUT; WHi. 45-615

Baterlandsfreund und cantoner calender. Canton, Ohio: Peter Kaufmann, 1845. 24 p. IaHA. 45-616

Bates, Merritt. How shall a young man cleanse his way? A sermon on the death of Thomas Patterson, Albany, September 21, 1845. Albany, 1845. 12 p. CtY; MBC; MWA. 45-617

Bawr, Alexandrine Sophie, Goury de Champgrand. The maid of honour; or the massacre of St. Bartholomew. A tale of the sixteenth century. New York: Harper and brothers, 1845. 105 p. CtY; IU; KSalW. 45-618

Baxter, Richard, 1615-1691. A call to the unconverted. To which are added several valuable essays. Boston: American Tract Society, 1846. 240 p. IU; KKcBt. 45-619

Baxter, Richard, 1615-1691. The saint's everlasting rest, abridged by Benjamin Faucett. Boston: Gould, Kendall and Lincoln, 1845. 320 p. IaPeC; MBC; MeBaHi; OAsht; TxAbH. 45-620

Bayard, James. A brief exposition of the constitution of the United States with an appendix containing the Declaration of Independence... and a copious index. Philadelphia: Hogan and Thompson,

1845. 178 p. MH; OWoC; PP; PWW; RHi. 45-621

Bayle-Mouillard, Elizabeth Felicie Canard, 1796-1865. The gentleman and lady's book of politeness and propriety of deportment, dedicated to the youth of both sexes; translated from the sixth Paris edition, enlarged and improved; Fifth American edition. Philadelphia: Grigg, 1845. PPi. 45-622

Bayley, Frederic William Naylor, 1808-1853. Blue Beard. New York: Burgess, Stringer and company, 1845. 64 p. DLC; IU; NN. 45-623

Bayley, Frederic William Naylor, 1808-1853. Comic nursery tales. New York [1845] DLC. 45-624

Bayley, Frederic William Naylor, 1808-1853. Drolleries for little folks: a series of funny tales in rhyme. New York: C. Shepard, [1845?] 32 p. DLC. 45-625

Bayley, Frederic William Naylor, 1808-1853. Jack the giant killer. With illustrations by Leech. New York: Burgess, Stringer and company, 1845. 96 p. DLC; NN. 45-626

Bayley, Frederic William Naylor, 1808-1853. Little red riding hood. New York: Burgess, Stringer and company, [1845?] 64 p. DLC; NN. 45-627

Baylies, Francis, 1783-1852. Eulogy on the Honorable Benjamin Russell before the Grand Lodge of Free and Accepted Masons of the state of Massachusetts, March 10, 1845. Boston: Printed at the office of the Freemason magazine, 1845. 66 p. CtY; MBC; MWA; NUtHi; PHi. 45-628

Bayly, Thomas Haynes. David Dumps: or the budget of blunders. A tale. New York: E. Ferrett and company; Boston: S. Colman, 1845. 112 p. MdBP; MWA; NjR. 45-629

Bayly, Thomas Henry, 1810-1856. Speech of Mr. Bayly of Virginia, on the annexation of Texas. Washington: Printed at the Globe office, 1845. CSmH; CU; DLC; MMal; NBu. 45-630

The bazaar journal; devoted to all good things and good people. Philadelphia, 1845. v. 1. PHi. 45-631

Beach, Moses Yale, 1800-1868. Wealth and biography of the wealthy citizens of New York City; comprising an alphabetical arrangement of persons estimated to be worth $100,000, and upwards; with the sums appended to each name. Fifth edition, enlarged. New York: Sun office, 1845. 32 p. OO; WHi. 45-632

Beach, Moses Yale, 1800-1868. Wealth and biography of the wealthy citizens of New York City, comprising an alphabetical arrangement of persons estimated to be worth $100,000, and upwards. Sixth edition. New York: Published at the Sun office, 1845. 32 p. MdHi; MH; MWo; NUtHi; PHi. 45-633

Beach, Moses Yale, 1800-1868. Wealth and biography of the wealthy citizens of Philadelphia. Containing an alphabetical arrangement of persons estimated to be worth $50,000 and upwards, with the sums appended to each name; being useful to bankers, merchants, and others. By a member of the Philadelphia bar. Philadelphia: G.B. Zieber and company, 1845. 23 p. NcU; OClWHi; PPL; PU; WHi. 45-634

Beaconsfield, Benjamin Disraeli, 1804-1881. Alroy, Ixion in heaven, the infernal marriage and popanilla. Illustrated with explanatory notes. New York: Collier, 1845. CA; KyLo; MdBG; ScUn. 45-635

Beaconsfield, Benjamin Disraeli, 1804-1881. Coningsby; or the new generation. New York and Baltimore; W. Taylor, 1845. 136 p. DLC. 45-636

Beaconsfield, Benjamin Disraeli, 1804-1881. The novels of Benjamin Disraeli, Earl of Beaconsfield. New York: P.F. Collier and son, [1845-1870] 11 v. CSto; MdBG; MsOK; TNF. 45-637

Beaconsfield, Benjamin Disraeli, 1804-1881. Sybil; or the two nations. New York: George Routledge and sons, [1845] 489 p. ArU; LStBA; MtBiP; NGcA; ViPet. 45-638

Beaconsfield, Benjamin Disraeli, 1804-1881. Sybil; or the two nations. New York: P.F. Collier and son, [1845] 432 p. MdBG; TxElpF. 45-639

Beaconsfield, Benjamin Disraeli, 1804-1881. Sybil; or the two nations. Philadelphia, 1846. InCW. 45-640

Beaconsfield, Benjamin Disraeli, 1804-1881. Works. Philadelphia: Carey and Hart, 1845. 2 v. FTU; MBAt; NjR. 45-641

Bear Mountain Railroad Company. Reports on the Bear Mountain railroad by Edwin F. Johnson and William R. Casey, civil engineers, and on the coal and iron ores of the Bear Valley Coal Basin, by James Hall, New York state geological engineer.... New York: Jared W. Bell, 1845. 88 p. CtY; DLC; MHi; MiH; NN; PPULC. 45-642

Beattie, Robert H. An address, delivered at Ballston Spa, New York, July 4, 1845. Ballston Spa: Printed by Newell Hine, 1845. 16 p. CSmH. 45-643

Beattie, William D. Treatise on arithmetic, for common schools and academies. Fifth improved edition, with a supplement containing a large collection of additional examples. Cleveland: Younglove, 1845. 260 p. NjP; OClWHi. 45-644

The beauties of Caledonia; or gems of Scottish song, being a collection of more than fifty of the most beautiful Scotish ballads, set to music. Boston: Oliver Ditson, 1845. 99 p. CtHWatk; IaDmU; MH; NNQ; WU. 45-645

The beauties of Rechabism. By a Rechabite. Boston: James M. Usher, 1845. 104 p. DLC; MPeHi; MPiB. 45-646

The beauty of Baltimore; or the fate of the coquette. Boston: Henry L. Williams, 1845. 48 p. MB; NjR. 45-647

Beauvoir, Eugene Auguste Roger de Bully, 1806-1866. Safia; or the magic of Count Cagliostro. A Venetian Tale. Translated from the French of Roger De Beauvoir, by P.F. Christin and Eugene Lies. New York: Harper and brothers, 1845. 83 p. DLC; KyLx; IU; MeB; PPULC. 45-648

Beaver Meadow Railroad and Level Company. Reports. Philadelphia, 1845-. PPL; PPULC. 45-649

Beck, Paul. Catalogue of furniture. Philadelphia, 1845. PPL-R; PPULC. 45-650

Beckford, William, 1759-1844. Italy, Spain and Portugal, with an excursion to the monasteries of Alcobaca and Batalka. New York: Wiley and Putnam, 1845. 2 v. in 1. MeB; MH; OUrC; PU; Wv. 45-651

Beckford, William, 1759-1844. Vathek. An oriental romance. With a biographical sketch of the author. New York: Morris, Willis and Fuller, 1845. 50 p. DLC; IaDm; MNS; OO; ScSpC. 45-652

Bedford, Gunning S., 1806-1870. Introductory lecture, delivered by G.S. Bedford. New York: The medical class of the university, 1845-1846. 18 p. CtY-D; DLC; NDLM; NN. 45-653

Bedford, Gunning S., 1806-1870. Valedictory address... February 28, 1845. New York: Printed for the medical class of the university, by Joseph H. Jennings, 1845. 20 p. DLC; NBMS; NcAS; NN. 45-654

Bedford Street budget; published every Wednesday, for the students of the Latin schools and high schools, in Bedford Street, January 1-May 7, 1845; June 25-July 2, 1845. Boston, 1845-1846. 7v. in 1. DLC; MB; MBAt; PPULC. 45-655

Beecher, Catherine Esther, 1800-1878. The duty of American women to their country. New York: Harper and brothers, 1845. 164 p. CU; DLC; MWA; NBuG; WHi. 45-656

Beecher, Catherine Esther, 1800-1878. A treatise on domestic economy, for the use of young ladies at home, and at school. Revised edition. New York: Harper and brothers, 1845. 396 p. CtMW; DLC; KyLx; MWA; Vi. 45-657

Beecher, Edward. Faith essential to a complete education: an address... Charleston Female Seminary... Boston: Haskell and Moore, printers, 1845. 22 p. DLC; MH; MWelC; NjR. 45-658

Beecher, Henry Ward, 1813-1887. A discourse from moral intolerance, delivered at Bloomington, Indiana, before the Philomathean Society of the Indiana University. Indianapolis: S.V.B. Noel, 1845. 31 p. CtY; DLC; InThE; InU; NN. 45-659

Beecher, Henry Ward, 1813-1887. Lectures to young men, on various important subjects. Second edition. Salem: John P. Jewett and company; Cincinnati: William H. Moore and company, 1845. 249 p. MH-AH; MoSpD; NbCrD; NNUT; RPAt. 45-660

Beecher, Lyman, 1775-1863. Six sermons on the nature, occasions, signs, evils and remedy of intemperance. Tenth edition. New York: American Tract Society, 1845. 107 p. IaHoL; TNDL. 45-661

Beer's Carolina and Georgia almanac. Columbia: Samuel Weir, 1845. MWA. 45-662

Beethoven, Ludwig van, 1770-1827. Le desir: waltz with flute accompaniment by A. Kyle. New York, [1845] CtY. 45-663

Beethoven, Ludwig van, 1770-1827. The dream. A grand waltz with flute accompaniment by A. Kyle. New York: Homans and Ellis, 1845. CtY; PPL. 45-664

Bell, George Joseph. Inquires into the contract of sale of goods and merchan-

dise. As recognised in the judicial decisions and mercantile practice of modern nations... Philadelphia: T. and J.W. Johnson, 1845. 67, [3] p. CoU; MdBB; MsU; Nb; PP. 45-665

Bell, Luther Vose, 1809-1862. Letter on the heating and ventilation of the proposed city prison. Boston, 1845. DNLM; DSG. 45-666

Bellows, Henry Whitney, 1814-1882. Testimony of four witnesses to the divine goodness. Printed for the American Unitarian Association. Boston: J. Munroe and company, 1845. 19 p. CBPac; DLC; KyDC; MeBat; RP. 45-667

Bellows Falls, Vermont. Black River Academy. Catalogue... Bellows Falls, 1845. OCHP. 45-668

Belser, James Edwin, 1805-1859. Speech of Mr. Belser, of Alabama, on the annexation of Texas: delivered in the House of Representatives, January 3, 1845. Washington: Printed at the Globe office, 1845. 8 p. MiD-B; TxU. 45-669

Belser, James Edwin, 1805-1859. Speech of Mr. Belser, of Alabama, on the bill to admit Iowa and Florida into the Union as states. Delivered in the House of Representatives, February 11, 1845. Washington: Printed at the Globe office, 1845. 8 p. A-Ar; DLC; MiD-B. 45-670

Beman, Nathan Sidney Smith, 1785-1871. A plea for the Swiss mission in Canada: a discourse delivered in the First Presbyterian Church, Troy, October 15, 1843. Second edition. Troy, New York: Young and Hart, 1845. 36 p. CtY; MnH; NCH; PCA; RPB. 45-671

Bement, Caleb N., 1791?-1868. The American poulterer's companion: a practical treatise on the breeding rearing, fattening and general management of the various species of domestic poultry. New York: Saxton and Miles, 1845. 379 p. CoG; DNAL; MWA; NN; PPL. 45-672

Bement, Caleb N., 1791?-1868. The American poulterer's companion: a practical treatise on the breeding rearing, fattening and general management of the various species of domestic poultry. Second edition. New York: Saxton and Miles, 1845. 379 p. CtY; MB; NIC; WaPS. 45-673

Bement, Caleb N. 1791?-1868. The American poulterer's companion: a practical treatise on the breeding rearing, fattening and general management of the various species of domestic poultry. Third edition. New York: Saxton and Miles, 1845. 379 p. Ct. 45-674

Benjamin, Asher, 1773-1845. The architect, or complete builder's guide... illustrated by sixty-six engravings which exhibit the orders of architecture. Boston: B.B. Mussey and company, 1845. 83 p. CtY; MoS; NNC; TU; WHi. 45-675

Benjamin, Asher, 1773-1845. The architect, or practical house carpenter, illustrated by sixty-four engravings, which exhibit the orders of architecture, and other elements of the art; designed for the use of carpenters and builders. Fourth edition. Boston: Benjamin B. Mussey, 1845. MH; NcD; NNC; TxU; ViW. 45-676

Benjamin, Judah Philip, 1811-1884. Address delivered before the public schools of Municipality Number Two, of the city of New Orleans on the 22nd of February, 1845. New Orleans, 1845. 14 p. MH; NcD; RP. 45-677

Benner, Enos. Abhandlung uber die rechenkunst, oder practische arithmetik... Sumnytaun, [Pennsylvania] Gedruckt bei dem herausgeber, 1845. 6, 178 p. DLC; PPULC. 45-678

Bennett, Emerson, 1822-1905. League of the Miami. New edition revised and enlarged. Cincinnati: James, 1845. 116 p. In. 45-679

Bentley, Rensselaer. An introduction to the pictorial reader. Seventh thousand. New York: Saxton and Miles, etc., etc., 1845. MH. 45-680

Bentley, Rensselaer. The pictorial primer, being an introductin to the pictorial spelling book for children in families and schools. New York: Saxton and Miles; Boston: Saxton and Kelt; Philadelphia: J.M. Campbell, 1845. 48 p. MNF; NjR. 45-681

Bentley, Rensselaer. The pictorial spelling book; to which are added, examples from spelling and defining words, by placing them synonymously... New York: Sheldon and company, [1845?] 168 p. CtHWatk; NNC. 45-682

Berg, Joseph Frederick, 1812-1871. The old paths; or a sketch of the order and discipline of the Reformed Church, before the reformation, as maintained by the Waldenses prior to that epoch, and by the church of the Palatinate, in the sixteenth century. Philadelphia: J.B. Lippincott and company, 1845. NIC; NjR; NjNbS; PPPrHi; PPULC. 45-683

Beriot, Charles Auguste de, 1802-1870. Constancy: song... adapted to de Beriot's sixth air. New York, 1845. CtY. 45-684

Berk, Matthew, A. history of the Jews from the Babylonian captivity to the present time, comprising their conquests, dispersions, wanderings... Compiled from the most authentic sources. With a preface by William Jenks. Boston: M.A. Berk, 1845. NjPT. 45-685

Berks County Beneficial Society. Constitution and bylaws of the Berks County Beneficial Society, of the borough of Reading, Pennsylvania. Instituted October 15, 1840, incorporated May 25, 1841. Reading: Printed for the society, 1845. 26 p. PRea. 45-686

The Berkshire jubilee, celebrated at Pittsfield, Massachusetts, August 22 and 23, 1844. Albany: W.C. Little; Pittsfield: E.P. Little, 1845. 244 p. CtSoP; MPiB; OCHP; PHi; RPAt. 45-687

Berlin, Massachusetts. Catalogue for the year 1844/1845, 1845/1846 of the Berlin Boarding School. Worcester, 1845-1846. M; MH. 45-688

Bernard, Charles de, 1804-1850. Un beau pere. New York: F. Gaillardet, 1845. 170 p. PPM. 45-689

Berquin, Arnaud, 1740-1791. Children's companion. Translated from the French of M. Berquin. Philadelphia: J. Crissey, 1845. 143 p. CtY; RPB. 45-690

Berrian, William, 1787-1862. Enter into thy closet. New York: James A. Sparks, 1845. 233 p. DLC; NNG; RNR; VtMidSM; WNaE. 45-691

Berrien, John Macpherson. Speech of John Macpherson Berrien, of Georgia, on the joint resolution to annex Texas to the United States; delivered in the Senate of the United States, February, 1845. Washington: Printed by Gales and Seaton, 1845. 24 p. MB; MBAt; MHi; NBu. 45-692

Berteau, Felix G. New practical and theoretical method for teaching and learning the French language. New York: F.G. Berteau's Foreign Bookstore, 1845-1846. 2 v. CtHWatk; MAnP; MPiB; NNC; OO. 45-693

Berzelius, Jons Jacob, 1779-1848. The use of the blowpipe in chemistry and mineralogy. Translated from the fourth enlarged and corrected edition by J.D. Whitney. Boston: W.D. Tichnor and company, 1845. 237 p. CU-M; ICU; MeB; MSaP; PPi. 45-694

Best, William Mawdesley, 1809-1869. A treatise on the presumptions of law and fact, with the theory and rules of presumptive or circumstantial proof in criminal cases. Philadelphia: T. and J.W. Johnson, 1845. 25, 222 p. CoU; DLC; NcD; ViU-L; WaU-L. 45-695

Bethune, George Washington, 1805-1862. The fruit of the spirit. Third edition. Philadelphia: Mentz and Rovoudt, New York: Saxton and Miles, 1845. 304 p. CtY; MLow; LNHT; NGH; PLT. 45-696

Bethune, George Washington, 1805-1862. A plea for study. An oration before the literary societies of Yale College, August 19, 1845. By G.W. Bethune, minister of the Third Reformed Dutch Church of Philadelphia. Printed for the societies. Philadelphia: John C. Clark, printer, 1845. 45 p. MdHi. 45-697

Bethune, George Washington, 1805-1862. Truth the strength of freedom. A discourse on the duty of a patriot, with some allusions to the life and death of Andrew Jackson. Pronounced July 6, 1845. By G.W. Bethune, minister of the Third Reformed Dutch Church, Philadelphia. Philadelphia: Mentz and Rovoudt, 1845. 36 p. LNHT; MiD-B; NjR; OO; PPPrHi. 45-698

Bevans, James H. Address delivered the Tulli Pheboian Society of St. John's Literary Institution in Frederick, Maryland, at the annual commencement, August 5, 1845. Frederick, Maryland: John W. Baughman, 1845. 22 p. OCX. 45-699

Beveridge, William. The great necessity and advantage of public prayer and frequent communion designed to revive primitive piety. New York: James A. Sparks, 1845. 331 p. CtHT; MeBat; NGH; NjPT; ScCoT. 45-700

Beveridge, William. Sermons on the ministry and ordinances of the Church of England by the Right Reverand Father in God... New York: James Sparks, 1845. 293 p. GAGTh; InID; PPP; TChU; WNaE. 45-701

Bible. Acts of the Apostles; with notes, chiefly explanatory; designed for teaching in sabbath schools and Bible classes, and as an aid to family instruction. By Henry J. Ripley, Professor of Sacred Rhetoric and pastoral duties in the Newton Theological Institution. Boston: Gould, Kendall and Lincoln, 1845. 334 p. ScCliP. 45-702

Bible. Apocryphal books of the Old Testament proved to be corrupt additions to the word of God. The arguments of Romanists from the infallibility of the church and the testimony of the fathers in behalf of the apocrypha, discussed and refuted. By James H. Thornwell. New York: Leavitt, Trow and company, 1845. 418 p. ICN; KyLoP; MH; ScDuE; TWcW. 45-703

Bible. Apocryphal books of the Old Testament proved to be corrupt additions to the word of God. The arguments of Romanists from the infallibility of the church and the testimony of the fathers in behalf of the apocrypha, discussed and refuted. New York: Leavitt, Trow and company, 1845. 417 p. CSansS; NNUT; ScCliJ. 45-704

Bible. The apocryphal New Testament, being all the gospels, epistles, and other pieces now extant; attributed in the first four centuries to Jesus Christ. His apostles, and their companions, and not included in the New Testament by its compilers... New York: H.G. Daggers, [1845?] 184 p. DLC; NcD; NN; OkentU; TxHU. 45-705

Bible. Die Bibel; oder, Die ganze Heilige Schrift des Alten und Neuen Testaments, nach Dr. Martin Luthers Uebersetzurg. Mit einer beygefugten kurzgefassten Uebersicht des inhalts... Philadelphia: Mentz und Rovoudt, 1845-1846. 2 v. in 1. TU. 45-706

Bible. Die Bibel; oder, Die ganze Heilige Schrift des Alten und Neuen Testaments. Ubers und neu resv. von d. Leander van ess. Hildburghausen, Amsterdam and Philadelphia:

Bibliographisches Institut, 1845. 2 v. in 1. ICU. 45-707

Bible. The book of Psalms. Translated out of the original Hebrew. New York: American Tract Society [1845?] 318 p. NN. 45-708

Bible. A commentary on the Apocalypse. Andover: Allen, Merrill and Wardwell, 1845. 2 v. CU; IaU. PPL; RPB; ViLxW. 45-709

Bible. Commentary on the New Testament. By Lucius R. Paige. Boston: Benjamin B. Mussey, 1845. 414 p. CtHC; ICBB; MBC; MMeT- Hi. 45-710

Bible. The complete evangelist... Edited by William Bolles. New London, 1845. 226 p. MWA; OO. 45-711

Bible. The cottage polyglott Testament: according to the authorized version, with notes, original and selected; likewise introductory and concluding remarks to each book, polyglot references and marginal readings, chronological table, geographical index and maps... By W. Patton. Hartford: Sumner and Goodman, 1845. 718p. NjMD; NNAB. 45-712

Bible. A critical commentary and paraphrase on the Old and New Testament and the Aprocrypha, by Patrick, Lowth, Arnald, Whitby, and Lowman. A new edition with the text printed at large in four volumes. Philadelphia: Carey and Hart, 1845. 4 v. NcD. 45-713

Bible. English version of the Polyglott Bible containing the Old and New Testaments with marginal readings. Philadelphia: Biddle, 1845. ScGF. 45-714

Bible. English version of the Polyglott Bible containing the Old and New Testaments with marginal readings. Philadelphia: Sorin and Ball, 1845. MHi; MiU. 45-715

Bible. The English version of the Polyglott Bible containing the Old and New Testaments with marginal readings; together with a copious and original selection of references to parallel and illustrative passages, exhibited in a manner hitherto unattempted. Philadelphia: E.C. and J. Biddle, [1845]-1846. 23- 824, 256 p. NN. 45-716

Bible. The four gospels, translated into the Choctaw language. Boston: Printed for the American Board of Commissioners For Foreign Missions by Crocker and Brewster, 1845. 95 p. ICartC; NCaS; NNPrM; TxH. 45-717

Bible. The gospel according to John, translated into the Choctaw language... Boston: Printed from the American Board of Commissioners for Foreign Missions, by Crocker and Brewster, 1845. 95 p. NN; T. 45-718

Bible. A harmony of the four Gospels in Greek. According to the text of John. Newly arranged, with explanatory notes, by Edward Robinson... Boston: Crocker and Brewster; London: Wiley and Putnam, 1845. 235 p. DLC; KyU; MB; MiU; RPB. 45-719

Bible. A harmony of the four gospels in Greek. Newly arranged, with explanatory notes by Edward Robinson. Boston: Crocker and Brewster, 1845. 235 p. ICP; KyLoS; OU; PAtM; RPB. 45-720

Bible. A harmony of the New Testament in Greek by Ed. Robinson. Boston, 1845. MB. 45-721

Bible. The Holy Bible, containing the old and New Testaments. By Adam Clark. New York: G. Lane and C.B. Tippett, for the Methodist Church, 1845. 6 v. CoDI; GMM. 45-722

Bible. The Holy Bible, containing the Old and New Testaments. Sixteenth edition. New York: American Bible Society, 1845. NT. 45-723

Bible. The Holy Bible, containing the Old and New Testaments. The text carefully printed from the most correct copies of the present authorized translation, including the marginal readings and parallel texts; with a commentary and critical notes; designed as a help to a better understanding of the sacred writings of Adam Clarke. A new edition with the authors final corrections. New York: G. Lane, 1845. 6 v. WaU. 45-724

Bible. The Holy Bible, containing the Old and New Testaments, the text carefully printed from the most correct copies of the present. By Adam Clarke. New York: G. Lane and A.B. Tippett, for the Methodist Episcopal Church, 1845. 863 p. NoLoc. 45-725

Bible. The Holy Bible, containing the Old and New Testaments. The text of the common translation is arranged in paragraphs, such as the sense requires; the divisions of chapters and verses being noted in the margin, for reference. By James Nourse. Hartford: S. Andrus and son, 1845. 9-942, 324 p. NN. 45-726

Bible. The Holy Bible, containing the Old and New Testaments, translated out

of the original Hebrew; and with the former translations diligently compared and revised: and the Greek New Testament; printed from the text and with the various readings of Knapp: together with the commonly received English translations. Designed for the use of students. New York: J.C. Riker, 1845. 775, xix, 234, 235-248 p. CSmH; NN; NRU. 45-727

Bible. The Holy Bible, containing the Old and New Testaments, translated out of the original tongues and with the former translations diligently compared and revised. Hartford: S. Andrus and son, 1845. 811 p. NoLoc. 45-728

Bible. The Holy Bible, containing the Old and New Testaments, translated out of the original tongues and with the former translations diligently compared and revised. New York: American Bible Society, 1845. 669 p. MGrot. 45-729

Bible. The Holy Bible, containing the Old and New Testaments, translated out of the original tongues, and with the former translations diligently compared and revised with Canne's marginal notes and references; together with the apocrypha; to which is added an index... Cooperstown: Phinney, 1845. DLC; NN; WM. 45-730

Bible. The Holy Bible, containing the Old and New Testaments, translated out of the original tongues, and with the former translations diligently compared and revised, with Canne's marginal notes and references. Hartford: S. Andrus and son, 1845. 837, 656-681 p. CtY. 45-731

Bible. The Holy Bible, containing the Old and New Testaments, translated out of the original tongues, and with the former translations diligently compared and revised, with Canne's marginal notes and references. Together with the Apocrypha and Concordance. To which are added, an index, a table of text, and ... an account of the martydom of the apostles and evangelists... The text corrected according to the standard of the American Bible Society. Hartford: S. Andrus and son, 1845. 527, 78, 168, 34 p. NN. 45-732

Bible. The Holy Bible, containing the Old and New Testaments, translated out of the original tongues, and with the former translations diligently compared and revised, with Canne's marginal notes and references. Together with the Apocrypha to which are added an index; and an alphabetical table of all the names in the Old and New Testaments, with their significations. Also, tables of Scripture weights, measures and coins. Boston: B.B. Mussey, 1845. 1010 p. NcDaD; OCl. 45-733

Bible. The Holy Bible, containing the Old and New Testaments, translated out of the original tongues, and with the former translations diligently compared and revised, with references and various readings. Together with the Apocrypha. Philadelphia: Butler and Williams, 1845. 2 v. NcFayS. 45-734

Bible. The Holy Bible, containing the Old and New Testaments, translated out of the original tongues, and with the former translations diligently compared and revised. Concord, New Hampshire: Portland, Sanborn and Carter, 1845. 2 v. in 1. DLC; MeB. 45-735

Bible. The Holy Bible, containing the Old and New Testaments, translated out

of the original tongues, and with the former translations diligently compared and revised. Cooperstown: H. and E. Phinney, 1845. DLC. 45-736

Bible. The Holy Bible, containing the Old and New Testaments, translated out of the original tongues, and with the former translations diligently compared and revised. Fourth edition. New York: American Bible Society, 1845-1846. 978 p. 981-1284 p. NN. 45-737

Bible. The Holy Bible, containing the Old and New testaments, translated out of the original tongues, and with the former translations diligently compared and revised. From the authorized Oxford edition. Philadelphia: Hogan and Thompson, 1845. 1098 p. NNG. 45-738

Bible. The Holy Bible, containing the Old and New Testaments, translated out of the original tongues, and with the former translations diligently compared and revised. Hartford: S. Andrus and son, 1845. 1180 p. ViRVal. 45-739

Bible. The Holy Bible, containing the Old and New Testaments, translated out of the original tongues, and with the former translations diligently compared and revised. Hartford: S. Andrus and son, 1845. 852 p. MsJMC. 45-740

Bible. The Holy Bible, containing the Old and New Testaments, translated out of the original tongues, and with the former translations diligently compared and revised. New York: American Bible Society, 1845. 1213 p. MH-AH. 45-741

Bible. The Holy Bible, containing the Old and New Testaments, translated out of the original tongues, and with the former translations diligently compared and revised. New York: American Bible Society, 1845. 1214 p. CoCsC; IaDaM; KWiU; PPM. 45-742

Bible. The Holy Bible, containing the Old and New Testaments, translated out of the original tongues, and with the former translations diligently compared and revised. New York: American Bible Society, 1845. 1284 p. NN. 45-743

Bible. The Holy Bible, containing the Old and New Testaments, translated out of the original tongues, and with the former translations diligently compared and revised. New York: American Bible Society, 1845. 669 p. N; NNAB. 45-744

Bible. The Holy Bible, containing the Old and New Testaments, translated out of the original tongues, and with the former translations diligently compared and revised. New York: American Bible Society, 1845. 691 p. ICN. 45-745

Bible. The Holy Bible, containing the Old and New Testaments, translated out of the original tongues, and with the former translations diligently compared and revised. New York: American Bible Society, 1845. 691 p. ICN; MH-AH. 45-746

Bible. The Holy Bible, containing the Old and New Testaments, translated out of the original tongues, and with the former translations diligently compared and revised. New York: American Bible Society, 1845. 728 p. IaDaM. 45-747

Bible. The Holy Bible, containing the Old and New Testaments, translated out of the original tongues, and with the former translations diligently compared

and revised. New York: American Bible Society, 1845. 805 p. KWiU. 45-748

Bible. The Holy Bible, containing the Old and New Testaments, translated out of the original tongues, and with the former translations diligently compared and revised. New York: American Bible Society, 1845. 939, 232 p. TxU. 45-749

Bible. The Holy Bible, containing the Old and New Testaments, translated out of the original tongues, and with the former translations diligently compared and revised. New York: American Bible Society, 1845. 984 p. NcD. 45-750

Bible. The Holy Bible, containing the Old and New Testaments; translated out of the original tongues, and with the former translations diligently compared and revised. Sixth edition. New York: American Bible Society, 1845. 2 v. in 1. CBPSR; CU. 45-751

Bible. The Holy Bible, containing the Old and New Testaments, translated out of the original tongues, and with the former translations diligently compared and revised. Portland [Maine] Sanborn and Carter, 1845. 852, 259 p. ICU; MH-AH; NNUT. 45-752

Bible. The Holy Bible, containing the Old and New Testaments, translated out of the original tongues, and with the former translations diligently compared and revised. Troy, New York: W. and H. Merriam, 1845. N. 45-753

Bible. The Holy Bible, containing the Old and New testaments, translated out of the original tongues, and with the former translations diligently compared and revised; with Canne's marginal notes and references to which are added an index. Philadelphia: Jesper Harding, 1845. 768 p. MeWebr; WHi. 45-754

Bible. The Holy Bible, containing the Old and New Testaments, translated out of the original tongues... with Canne's marginal notes and references. Philadelphia: Thomas, Cowperthwait and company, 1845. CSmH. 45-755

Bible. The Holy Bible, containing the Old Testament and the New; translated out of the original tongues. Portland, 1845. 851 p. MWA. 45-756

Bible. The Holy Bible, designed for use by students. New York: J.C. Riker, 1845. 699 p. CSansS. 45-757

Bible. The Holy Bible, translated from the Latin Vulgate. The Old Testament first published at Douay, A.D. 1609 and the New Testament, first published at Rheims. New York: Edward Dunigan, 1845. 968 p. NjR; WU. 45-758

Bible. The Holy Bible, translated from the Latin vulgate; diligently compared with the Hebrew, Greek and other editions, in various languages. New York: D. and J. Sadlier, [1845] 793 p. DLC; MB; NN; ViU. 45-759

Bible. The Holy Bible, translated from the Latin Vulgate: diligently compared with the Hebrew, Greek and other editions, in various languages. With annotations by the Rev. Dr. Challoner; together with references, and an historical and chronological index. New York: 1845. 968 p. WU. 45-760

Bible. The Holy Bible, translated from the Latin Vulgate: diligently compared with the Hebrew, Greek and other editions, in various languages. With annotations by the Rev. Dr. Challoner; together with references, and an historical and chronological index. New York: D. and J. Sadlier, [1845] 793, 228 p. DLC; IEG; MB; OrCS; ViU. 45-761

Bible. The Holy Bible, translated from the Latin Vulgate: diligently compared with the Hebrew, Greek and other editions, in various languages. With annotations by the Rev. Dr. Challoner; together with references, and an historical and chronological index. Philadelphia: John Kelly, [1845?] N. 45-762

Bible. The Holy Bible, translated from the Latin Vulgate; diligently compared with the Hebrew, Greek and other editions, in various languages. New York: D. and J. Sadlier, [1845] 793 p. DLC; MB; NN; ViU. 45-763

Bible. The law of God... and with former translations diligently compared and revised. Philadelphia: C. Sherman, 5605 [1845] 5 v. MnSH; TMeSC. 45-764

Bible. Liber psalmorum. Andover: Allen, Morrell and Wardwell, 1845. 184 p. NoLoc. 45-765

Bible. The life, doctrine, and sufferings of our blessed Lord and Saviour Jesus Christ: as recorded by the four Evangelists: with moral reflections, critical illustrations, and explanatory notes by the Reverend Henry Rutter... New edition, revised and corrected. New York: Johnson, Fry and company, [1845?] 535 p. RPB. 45-766

Bible. The ministry of Jesus Christ: compiled and arranged from the four

Gospels, for families and Sunday schools; with notes and questions... By T.B. Fox. Third edition. Boston: W. Crosby and H.P. Nichols, 1845. [13]-261 p. CtHWatk; DLC; MH. 45-767

Bible. The New Testament of Our Lord and Saviour Jesus Christ. New York: American Bible Society, 1845. 344 p. MWbri; NHC-S; NNUT; NPotN. 45-768

Bible. The New Testament of Our Lord and Saviour Jesus Christ, according to the authorized version. New York: Pratt, Woodford and company, 1845. 773 p. NLock; TxShA. 45-769

Bible. The New Testament of Our Lord and Saviour Jesus Christ, according to the authorized version; with explanatory notes, practical observations, and copious marginal references. By Thomas Scott. Hartford: S. Andrus and son, 1845. 828 p. MoMM; MsCLiM; MsJMC; OrSaW-L. 45-770

Bible. The New Testament of our Lord and Saviour Jesus Christ, according to the authorized version; with explanatory notes, practical observations, and copious marginal references. By Thomas Scott. Hartford: S. Andrus and son, 1845-1855. 2 v. CtMW; CtW. 45-771

Bible. The New Testament of Our Lord and Saviour Jesus Christ, according to the commonly received version. New York: T.B. Smith, for the American and Foreign Bible Society, 1845. 346 p. MWA; NBuG. 45-772

Bible. The New Testament of Our Lord and Saviour Jesus Christ, translated from the Greek. New York: American Bible Society, 1845. 550 p. IaHA. 45-773

Bible. The New Testament of our Lord and Saviour Jesus Christ, translated out of the Latin Vulgate; diligently compared with the original Greek; and first published by the English college of Rhemes, anno, 1582. Newly revised and corrected according to the Clemintine edition of the Scriptures, with annotations... New York: D. and J. Sadlier, 1845. 14-344 p. LN; MBtS; NcA-S; NN. 45-774

Bible. The New Testament of Our Lord and Saviour Jesus Christ, translated out of the Latin Vulgate; diligently compared with the original Greek. Newly revised and corrected according to the Clementine edition of the Scriptures with annotations as approved by the Right Rev. John Hughes. New York: D. and J. Sadlier, 1845. 344 p. NcAS. 45-775

Bible. The New Testament of our Lord and Saviour Jesus Christ, translated out of the original Greek: Concord, New Hampshire: L. Roby, 1845. 254 p. NN. 45-776

Bible. The New Testament of our Lord and Saviour Jesus Christ, translated out of the original Greek: and with the former translations diligently compared and revised. Hartford: S. Andrus, 1845. 454 p. CSmH; CtY. 45-777

Bible. The New Testament of Our Lord and Saviour Jesus Christ, translated out of the original Greek: and with the former translations diligently compared and revised. New York: American Bible Society, 1845. 429 p. IAlS; OU; TxSaWi. 45-778

Bible. The New Testament of our Lord and Saviour Jesus Christ, translated out of the original Greek: and with the former translations diligently compared and revised. New York: American Bible Society, 1845. 2 v. Ia. 45-779

Bible. The New Testament of Our Lord and Saviour Jesus Christ, translated out of the original Greek: and with the former translations diligently compared and revised. New York: New York Bible and Common Prayer Book Society, 1845. 324 p. NHudH. 45-780

Bible. The New Testament of our Lord and Saviour Jesus Christ, translated out of the original Greek: and with the former translations diligently compared and revised. With a commentary and critical notes, by Adam Clarke. New edition, improved. Philadelphia: Thomas, Cowperthwait and company, 1845. 546 p. ICRL. 45-781

Bible. The New Testament of our Lord and Saviour Jesus Christ, translated out of the original Greek: and with the former translations diligently compared and revised. [Seventy-seventh edition] New York: American Bible Society, 1845. 344 p. MB; NNAB. 45-782

Bible. The New Testament of our Lord and Saviour Jesus Christ, with a commentary and critical notes, designed as a help to a better understanding of the sacred writings. New edition improved. Philadelphia: Thomas, Cowperthwait and company, 1845. 546 p. WHi. 45-783

Bible. The New Testament of Our Lord and Saviour Jesus Christ, with the marginal readings; and illustrated by original references both parallel and explanatory, and a copious selection, carefully chosen and newly arranged. Philadelphia; E.C. and J. Biddle, 1845. 256 p. TNS. 45-784

Bible. The New Testament translated from the original Greek; the four gospels by George Campbell: the Epistles by James MacKnight. Hartford: J. Gaylord Wells, 1845. 419 p. MoSU. 45-785

Bible. The New Testament translated from the original Greek; the four Gospels by George Campbell: the Epistles by James MacKnight, and the Acts and Revelations of the common version. Hartford: Isaac A. Stowe, 1845. 419 p. ICRL. 45-786

Bible. The New Testament translated from the original Greek; the four Gospels by George Campbell: the Epistles by James MacKnight, and the Acts and Revelations of the common version. Hartford: J.G. Wells, 1845. 417 p. ICU; NN. 45-787

Bible. The New Testament. Epistles of Paul. Notes, explanatory etc. on Epistles of Paul by Albert Barnes. New York: Harper and brothers, 1845. 331 p. IaDmD. 45-788

Bible. Notes, critical and practical; on the book of Joshua. By George Bush. Second edition. New York: Saxton and Miles; Boston: Saxton, Peirce and company, 1845. 221 p. InGrD; NNG. 45-789

Bible. Notes, critical and practical; on the book of Leviticus. New York: Ivison, Phinney and company, 1845. 282 p. ODaB. 45-790

Bible. Notes, critical, illustrative and practical on the book of Job, with a new translation. New York: Leavitt, Trow and company, 1845. 2 v. IaScM; ILM; KyLoP; PPLT; PPP. 45-791

Bible. Notes, critical, illustrative and practical on the book of Job, with a new translation. Third edition. New York: Leavitt, Trow and company, 1845. 2 v. DLC; LNB; NbOP; OGall. 45-792

Bible. Notes, explanatory and practical, on the acts of the apostles. Designed for Bible classes and sunday schools. Tenth edition. New York: Harper and brothers, 1845. 356 p. TChFPr. 45-793

Bible. Notes, explanatory and practical, on the Epistles of Paul to the Ephesians, Philippians, and Colossians. By Albert Barnes. New York: Harper and brothers, 1845. 331 p. DLC; IEG; MB; PPL; ViU. 45-794

Bible. Notes, explanatory and practical, on the Epistles of Paul to the Thessalonians, to Timothy, to Titus, and to Philemon. By Albert Barnes. New York: Harper and brothers, 1845. 355 p. DLC; 45-795

Bible. The phonotypic Bible; containing the Old and New Testaments; according to the authorized version. Bath: I. Pitman; Boston: Andrews and Boyle; etc., etc., 1845-. DLC. 45-796

Bible. Proverbs and other remarkable sayings of Solomon, King of Israel. Arranged under appropriate heads with indexes of Texts and subjects. Revised by the Committee of Publication of the American Sunday School Union. Philadelphia: American Sunday School Union, 1845. 171 p. ScCliP; ScCliTO. 45-797

Bible. Psalms in metre, selected from the Psalms of David; with hymns, suited to the feasts and facts of the church, and

other occasions of public worship. Buffalo: W. B. and C.E. Peck, 1845. 105 p. DLC; MB. 45-798

Bible. Psalms in metre, selected from the Psalms of David; with hymns, suited to the feasts and fasts of the church, and other occasions of public worship. Hartford: S. Andrus and son, 1845. 208 p. NBuDD. 45-799

Bible. Psalms of David, imitated in the language of the New Testament, and applied to the Christian state and worship. Claremont, New Hampshire: Manufacturing company, 1845. 573 p. PLatS. 45-800

Bible. Psalms of David, in metre: allowed by the authority of the Kirk of Scotland, and of several branches of the Presbyterian Church in the United States. With notes... by John Brown... Newburgh, New York: D.L. Proudfit; New York: [etc.] R. Carter, 1845. 424 p. MiU; N. 45-801

Bible. Psalter, or Psalms of David. Second edition. New York: James A. Sparks, 1845. 324, 29 p. NhD. 45-802

Bible. Scripture manual. New York: N.W. Dodd, 1845. 551 p. DLC; NN. 45-803

Bible. Selections from the Psalms in metre; with hymns, suited to the feasts and facts of the church. New York: D. Appleton and company, 1845. 275 p. NN; OrP; WaWW. 45-804

Bible. Selections from the Psalms in metre; with hymns, suited to the feasts and facts of the church, and other occasions of public worship. New York: Appleton, 1845. 237 p. MB. 45-805

Bible. Selections from the Psalms in metre; with hymns, suited to the feasts and facts of the church, and other occasions of public worship. New York: Harper and brothers, 1845. 124 p. NN. 45-806

Bible. Selections from the Psalms in metre; with hymns, suited to the feasts and facts of the church, and other occasions of public worship. New York: Harper and brothers, 1845. 95 p. DLC. 45-807

The Bible boy [Joseph Reed] taken captive by the Indians. Written for the American Sunday School Union. Philadelphia, [1845] 35 p. WHi. 45-808

Bible stories: with fine engraving. Worcester: J. Grout, Jr., 1845. 24 p. MWA. 45-809

Biblische beschichten des alten und neuen bundes fur dieliebe tungend. Cin Uuszug. Ausdemgrosern werte von Christoph Schmid... Cincinnati, 1845. 144 p. InGrD. 45-810

Bicentenary of the Assembly of Divines at Westminster, held at Edinburgh, July 12 and 13, 1843. Containing a full and authentic report of the addresses and conversations... with introductory sermon by Rev. Dr. Symington. Cincinnati: J.A. James, 1845. ICP; KyDC; LNB; PWW; TxAuPT. 45-811

Bickerstaff, Isaac. The Rhode Island almanac for 1845. Providence: H.H. Brown, [1845] 24 p. RPE. 45-812

Bickersteth, Edward, 1786-1850. Questions illustrating the thirty-nine articles of the Church of England; with proofs from scripture and the primitive church. Philadelphia: Herman Hooker, 1845. 9-182 p. CtHT; InID; MnHi; OrPD; WNaE. 45-813

Bickersteth, Edward, 1786-1850. A treatise on the Lord's supper, designed as a guide and companion to the holy communion. Second New York, from the ninth London edition, enlarged. New York: Stanford and Swords, 1845. CoDR; MH; TxShA. 45-814

The big guns! a few facts, comprising the naval actions of the United States Navy. Addressed to the Senate and House. By a friend of peace. [New York? 1845?] 6 p. PPULC. 45-815

Bigelow, Henry Jacob, 1818-1890. Manual of orthopedic surgery being a dissertation which obtained the Boylston prize for 1844... Boston: William D. Ticknor, 1845. 211 p. CoCsC; MdBM; MH; NBMS; WU-M. 45-816

Bilbo, William N. A dissertation on the abuse of the right of instructions, as they effect the Senate, as a political organization; Senators, as national representatives, and the representative system, the most beautiful flower of modern civilization... Nashville, [Tennessee]: Cameron and Fall, printers, 1845. 40 p. CSmH; CSt; MBAt; PPL; T. 45-817

Bindley, Charles, 1798-1850. Stable talk and table talk; or spectacles for young sportsmen, by Harry Hieover. Philadelphia: Lea and Blanchard, 1845. [13]-357 p. MeB; OU; PPM; RPAt; WaSp. 45-818

Binney, Amos, 1803-1847. Remarks made at the annual meeting of the Boston Society of Natural History, June 2, 1845; showing the origin of Natural History of the society, its influence on the cultivation of the natural sciences in New England. Boston: Freeman and Bolles, 1845. 16 p. MBAt; MH; MiD-B; MWA; PPAN. 45-819

Binney, Horace, 1780-1875. Remarks upon an ordinance now pending in the common council, to prohibit obstructions on the wharves, to the eastward of Delaware Avenue. Philadelphia, 1845. 11 p. PHi; PPULC. 45-820

Binns, John, 1772-1860. Binns magistrate's daily companion. A treatise on the office and duties of aldermen and justices of the peace, in the commonwealth of Pennsylvania. This work includes all the required forms of process and docket entries. Philadelphia: L. Johnson and company, 1845. 582 p. CU; PPL; PPM; PP; PU-L. 45-821

Binns, John, 1772-1860. Digest of the laws and judicial decisions of Pennsylvania touching the authority and duties of justices of the peace. Philadelphia: Johnson, 1845. 582 p. PPULC; PU. 45-822

Biographical memoirs of the late Henry A. Muhlenberg. New York, 1845. ICN. 45-823

Bird, Golding, 1815-1854. Urinary deposits; their diagnosis, pathology and therapeutical indications. Edited by E.L. Birkett. From the fifth London edition. Philadelphia: Lea, 1845. 227 p. DNLM; ICJ; NcD; OrU; PPF. 45-824

Bird, Joseph. The singer's first book; consisting of simple rules and easy music for common schools. Second edition. Cambridge, Massachusetts: J. Owen, 1845. 38 p. MH; NRU. 45-825

Bird, Joseph. The singer's second book; consisting of easy rules and tunes to illustrate them; also many of the most useful and popular melodies. Designed to follow the singers first book. Boston, [1845?] 64 p. MH. 45-826

Bishop Griswold Association. Constitution and bylaws, and third annual report. Philadelphia, 1845-1847. PHi; PPULC. 45-827

Bishop Griswold Association. First annual report of the Bishop Griswold Association with a list of the members affixed. Philadelphia, 1845. PPL. 45-828

Bishop Onderdonk's trial. The verdict sustained at the bar of public opinion; with remarks on Laicus and Bishop Doane. By a spectator. New York: John F. Trow, 1845. 28, 8 p. MdBD; MH; NjP; NN; PHi. 45-829

Bishop, Robert Hamilton, 1777-1855. Addresses: No. 1. To the alumni of Miami University [showing methods by which they may secure the interests of the University for generations] No. 2. To the farmers of Hamilton County [urging them to support and enlarge Mr. Cary's Academy at Pleasant Hill, Hamilton County, Ohio] Cincinnati, 1845. 12, 12 p. ICU; MH; PPPrHi. 45-830

Bishop, Robert Hamilton, 1777-1855. Circular. To the alumni of Miami University. Oxford, 1845. PPPrHi; PPULC. 45-831

Bishop, Robert Hamilton, 1777-1855. Circular. To the farmers of Hamilton County, state of Ohio. Oxford, Ohio, 1845. 12 p. PPPrHi; PPULC. 45-832

Black, Jeremiah Sullivan, 1810-1883. Eulogy on the life and character of General Andrew Jackson, delivered at Bedford, Pennsylvania, July 28, 1845. Chambersburg: Printed at the office of the Weekly Messenger, 1845. 23 p. DLC; NjR; OClWHi; PHi; TxU. 45-833

Black Hawk, 1767-1838. Life of Ma-Ka-tai-me-she-kia-kiak or Black Hawk, embracing the tradition of his nation... description of Rock River Village, manners and customs... removal of his village in 1831... his surrender and confinement at Jefferson Barraks, etc. Dictated by himself... Boston: T. Abbot, 1845. 155 p. CtHWatk; DLC; MBLiHi; MnHi; NN. 45-834

Blackley, John. Love not. Written by Mrs. Norton. Composed for the piano forte by Blackley. Philadelphia: E. Ferrett and company, 1845. 3 p. MB; MH; ViU. 45-835

Blackmore, Richard White. Doctrine of the Russian church, being the primer or spelling book, the shorter and longer catechisms and a treatise on the duty of parish priests. Translated from the Savono-Russian originals. New York: Appleton, 1845. 288 p. MiU; MnM; NRSB; WNaE. 45-836

Blackstone, William, 1723-1780. Commentaries on the laws of England: in four books; with an analysis of the work. New York: W.E. Dean, 1845. 4 v. CoCsC; MdBJ; PEaL; PU-L; WaU. 45-837

Blackstone, William, 1723-1780. Commentaries on the laws of England: in four books; with an analysis of the work. Philadelphia: J.B. Lippincott and company, 1845? 2 v. ViU-L. 45-838

Blair, Hugh, 1718-1800. Abridgement of lectures on rhetoric. New edition with appropriate questions to each chapter, by a teacher of Philadelphia. Philadelphia: Charles Bell, 1845. 230 p. IaPeC; KWiU; MiU; TxU; ViU. 45-839

Blair, Hugh, 1718-1800. Dr. Blair's lectures on rhetoric; abridged with questions. New York: W.E. Dean, 1845. 269 p. GColu; MdBS; MoSU; NjR; PWaybu. 45-840

Blair, Hugh, 1718-1800. Sermons... To which is prefixed a life and character of the author, by James Finlayson. From the last London edition. Printed verbatim from the original edition. New York: Harper and brothers, 1845. [25]-622 p. ArT; CSansS; NbOP; NCH; PWW. 45-841

Blake, Francis. Catalogue of choice wines, teas, and groceries, etc. Boston: Eastburn's Press, 1845. MH. 45-842

Blake, John Lauris, 1788-1857. Anecdotes of the American revolution; selected from Gordon's anecdotes, Gordon's letters... New York: A.V. Blake, 1845. 252 p. PP; WHi. 45-843

Blake, John Lauris, 1788-1857. First book in astronomy, adapted to the use of common schools. Boston, 1845. 120 p. PPL; PPULC. 45-844

Blake, John Lauris, 1788-1857. General biographical dictionary, comprising a

summary account of the most distin-
quished persons of all ages, nations and
professions, including more than one
thousand articles of American biography. New York: Blake, 1845. 1096 p.
IAiS; IC; InThE; MShM. 45-845

Blake, John Lauris, 1788-1857. General
biographical dictionary, comprising a
summary account of the most distinguished persons of all ages, nations and
professions, including more than one
thousand articles of American biography. Fourth edition. Philadelphia:
James J. Kay, brothers, 1846. 1096, 12 p.
ILM. 45-846

Blake, John Lauris, 1788-1857. The
juvenile companion and fireside reader,
consisting of historical and biographical
anecdotes, and selections of poetry. New
York: Alexander V. Blake and Collins,
Keese and company, 1845. 252 p.
MWinchrHi. 45-847

Blake, John Lauris, 1788-1857. The
wonders of art: containing an account of
celebrated ancient ruins; fortifications;
public edifices; monuments; and some of
the most curious and useful inventions in
modern times. Designed for the instruction of young persons. Troy, New York:
Young and Hart, 1845. 252 p. CtY-D;
DLC; NBath; NT; OC. 45-848

Blake, John Lauris, 1788-1857.
Wonders of the ocean; containing an account of the color, saltiness and probable
depth of the ocean; of its mountains of
ice, gulfs, whirlpools, currents and tides.
Cazenovia, New York: Henry and Swet-
lands, 1845. 252 p. CSmH; MH; NICLA;
NNT-C; WaPS. 45-849

Blake, John Lauris, 1788-1857. The

young orator and New York class book.
Thirteenth edition. New York: Alexander Blake, 1845. 283 p. NBuG. 45-850

Blake, John Lauris, 1788-1857. The
young orator and New York class book.
Fifteenth edition. Philadelphia: Hunt,
1846. 288 p. OC; PPULC; PU; RPB. 45-
851

Blanchard, Abijah, 1779-1852. Extract
from a sermon at the funeral of Mr. John
M'Clashan. St. Catharines, 1845. 5 p.
RPB. 45-852

Blanchard, Jonathan, 1811-1892. Secret
societies, a discourse, delivered in the
Sixth Presbyterian Church, Cincinnati,
September 7, 1845. Cincinnati: C. Clark,
1845. 14 p. CSmH; MeBat; NNUT; OC;
PPM. 45-853

Blanche de Ranzi, or the beautiful
Turkish slave. Translated from the
French for the publisher. Boston:
Gleason's Publishing Hall, 1845. 66 p.
MH; NcD. 45-854

Blandin, Philippe Frederic, 1798-1849.
Anatomy of the dental system, human
and comparative. Translated from the
French by Robert Arthur. Baltimore:
The American Society of Dental Sur-
geons, 1845. [5]-140 p. DLC; ICJ; LNT-
M; MoS; TNN. 45-855

Blanqui, Jerome Adolphe, 1798-1854.
Voyage en bulgarie pendant l'annee
1841. Philadelphia, 1845. PPL. 45-856

Bledsoe, Albert Taylor, 1809-1877. An
examination of President Edward's inquiry into the freedom of the will.
Philadelphia: H. Hooker, 1845. 234 p.
CtY; DLC; MB; PPA; ViU. 45-857

Bliss Lansingburgh almanac for 1846. Luther Bliss. Lansingburgh, New York: Pelatiah Bliss, [1845] MWA. 45-858

Bloomfield, Connecticut. Congregational Church. Confession of faith and covenant of the Congregational Church in Bloomfield, Connecticut, with a catalogue of the members, January 1, 1845. Hartford: D.B. Moseley, 1845. 8 p. Ct; MBNEH. 45-859

Bloss, Charles A. Ancient history, illustrated by colored maps and arranged to accompany a chronological chart, for the use of families and schools. Rochester: William Alling, 1845. 427 p. CtY; MH; NN; NRHi; OTifH. 45-860

Blunt, E. Great Bahama bank. New York: Blunt, 1845. PPL; PPULC. 45-861

Blunt, E. and G.W. Chart of the Gulf of Mexico, the West Indies and the Spanish Maine. New York, 1845. PPL; PPULC. 45-862

Blunt, George William, 1802-1872. Memoir of the dangers and ice of the North Atlantic Ocean. New York: E. and G.W. Blunt, 1845. 3-36 p. CtY; DLC; NN. 45-863

Blunt, Henry, 1794-1843. Lectures upon the history of our Lord and Saviour Jesus Christ. Second American edition. Philadelphia, 1845. 462 p. NcD; PPP. 45-864

Boardman, Henry Augustus. Hints on cultivating the Christian temper, by the Rev. H.A. Boardman. Philadelphia: William S. Martien, 1845. 55 p. GDecCT; PPPrHi; PPULC. 45-865

Boenninghausen, Clemens, Maria Franz Von, 1785-1864. Essay on the homoeopathic treatment of intermittent fevers; translated and edited by Charles Julius Hempel. New York: W. Radde, 1845. 56 p. DSG; MH; NN; NNNAM; PPHa. 45-866

Bogue, Thomas. A treatise on the structure, color and preservation of the human hair, Second edition. Philadelphia: J.W. Moore, 1845. 107 p. MH; MHoly; PPL. 45-867

Bolles, Isaac Newton, b. 1812. Directory and guide book for the city of Hartford, 1845. Hartford? Compiled and published by Isaac N. Bolles, 1845. 132 p. MBNEH. 45-868

Bolles, William, 1800-1883. An explanatory and phonographic pronouncing dictionary of the English language, to which is added, a vocabulary of Greek, Latin, Scripture, Christian and geographical names. New London: Bolles and Williams, 1845. 944 p. Ct; MW; OrSaW; RPAt. 45-869

Bolmar, Antoine. Book of the French verbs. Wherein the model words and several of the most difficult are conjugated affirmatively. New edition. Philadelphia: Lea and Blanchard, 1845. 173 p. NjP; NN; PPWa. 45-870

Bolmar, Antoine. Collection of colloquial phrases on every topic necessary to maintain conversation, arranged under different heads, with numerous remarks on the peculiar pronunciation and use of various words. A new edition. Revised and corrected. Philadelphia: Lea and Blanchard, 1845. 208 p. IEG; MH; NjP; NjR. 45-871

Bommer, George. New method which teaches how to make vegetable manure by a course of high fermentation to appropriate it to the nature of soils and families of plants, etc. Second edition. Revised and corrected. New York: Redfield and Savage, 1845. 90 p. DLC; MH-BA; MWA; NcU. 45-872

Bonar, Andrew Alexander, 1810-1892. Narrative of a mission of inquiry to the Jews from the Church of Scotland, 1839. Philadelphia: Presbyterian Board of Publication, 1845. 555 p. IaGG; NCH; NjPT; OO; P. 45-873

Bond, Henry. Biographical notice of the late John Ruan, M.D. Read September 2, 1845. Philadelphia: William F. Geddes, printer, 1845. 8 p. DNLM; MH; PHi; PPCP; OC. 45-874

Bonnefoux, L. Expose des eventualities et des consequences d'une guerre entre les Etats Unis et l'Angleterre, traitant les questions de l'annexaion du Texas, de l'occupation de l'Oregon, 1845. CU. 45-875

Bonnycastle, John, 1750?-1821. Bonnycastle's introduction to algebra; containing the interminate and diophantine analysis, and the application of algebra to geometry. Revised, corrected and enlarged by James Ryan. To which is added a large collection of problems by John F. Jenkins. New York: W.E. Dean, 1845. 288 p. MFiHi; MH; MoK. 45-876

The book of commerce by sea and land, exhibiting its connections with agriculture, the arts, and manufactures. To which are added a history of commerce, and a chronological table. Philadelphia:

U. Hunt, 1845. [9]-185 p. CtY; MH; NNA; PPWI; RPB. 45-877

The book of discourses. Author not given. Pittsburg: Luke Loomis, 1845. 172 p. ArPb. 45-878

The book of good examples; drawn from authentic history and biography, designed to illustrate the beneficial effects of virtuous conduct. Hartford: William J. Hamersly, 1845. 288 p. ScCoT. 45-879

Book of letters and pictures. Greenfield, 1845. 8 p. PHi; PPULC. 45-880

The book of peace. Boston: American Peace Society, 1845. 569 p. RP. 45-881

The book of peace; a collection of essays on war and peace. Boston: George C. Beckwith, 1845. 300 p. IaDmD. 45-882

The book of peace; a collection of essays on war and peace. Boston: George C. Beckwith, 1845. 412 p. IaPeC. 45-883

The book of peace; a collection of essays on war and peace. Boston: George C. Beckwith, 1845. 468 p. IGK. 45-884

The book of peace; a collection of essays on war and peace. Boston: George C. Beckwith, 1845. 500 p. CtY-D; MB; NN; OrU; PU. 45-885

The book of peace; a collection of essays on war and peace. Boston: George C. Beckwith; Philadelphia: Perkins and Purves, 1845. 548 p. CBPSR; NjR; OClWHi; PHC; PU; WHi. 45-886

The book of peace; a collection of essays on war and peace. Boston: George

C. Beckwith; Philadelphia: Perkins and Purves, 1845. 606 p. CU; ICP KWiU; MiU; OMC. 45-887

Book of pictures and verses. Greenfield, 1845. 8 p. PHi; PPULC. 45-888

Booth, F.G. The used up man. Boston: Keith's Music Publishing House, [1845] MHi. 45-889

Booth, Walter Sherman, 1827-1901. The constable's manual... by a member of the bar. Ithaca, 1845. DLC. 45-890

Booth, William A. The writings of William A. Booth, M.D. during the controversy upon slavery, which ended in the division of the Methodist Episcopal Church. Sommerville: Reeves and Yancy, 1845. 50 p. PPL; PPULC; T; TxU. 45-891

Boott, Francis, 1792-1863. Descriptions of six new North American carices. [Boston, 1845] 7 p. NNBG; RPB. 45-892

Borrow, George Henry, 1803-1881. Bible in Spain; or the journeys, adventures and imprisonments of an Englishman, in an attempt to circulate the scriptures in the Peninsula. Twelfth edition. Philadelphia: James M. Campbell; New York: L. Johnson and company, 1845. 232 p. KyDC; MH; PWW; RLa. 45-893

Bossuet, James Benign. History of the variations of the Protestant Churches... Translated from the last French edition. New York: D. and J. Sadlier and company, 1845. 2 v. ArLSJ; InCW; NjPT; PPLT; ViRu. 45-894

Boston, Thomas, 1677-1732. The crook in the lot; or a display of the sovereignty and wisdom of God. New York: Robert Carter; Pittsburg: Robert Carter, 1845. 176 p. MLow. 45-895

Boston, Massachusetts. Address of the Faneuil Hall committee on the project of a supply of pure water for the city of Boston, May 5, 1845. Boston: W.W. Clapp and Son, [1845] 32 p. DLC; MH; MiD-B; MnHi; NN. 45-896

Boston, Massachusetts. Bulfinch Street Church. Annual report of the Bulfinch Street Church. Boston, June, 1845. 16 p. MHi. 45-897

Boston, Massachusetts. Convention of delegates on the proposed annexation of Texas. Proceedings of a convention of delegates chosen by the people of Massachusetts. To take into consideration the proposed annexation of Texas to the United States. Boston, 1845. 18 p. IaU; MC; Nh-Hi; TxH. 45-898

Boston, Massachusetts. Criminal cases tried in the municipal court of Boston before Thacker. Edited by Horatec Woodman. Boston: Charles C. Little and James Brown, 1845. 733 p. Ia; MB; MWCL; U. 45-899

Boston, Massachusetts. Fellow citizens, the question is to be taken and decided in a few days, by yeas and nays whether you will accept the act for supplying the city of Boston with pure water from Long Pond or Charles River. [Boston, 1845?] 10 p. WHi. 45-900

Boston, Massachusetts. Hollis Street Church. Correspondence between the committee of the proprietors of the meeting house in Hollis Street, and the

Rev. John Pierpont which terminated in his resignation, May 10, 1845. Boston: Clapp and son, 1845. 16 p. CBPac; MBAt; MiD-B; NjR. 45-901

Boston, Massachusetts. Leyden Chapel. Plan of pews in Leyden Chapel, Green Street. [Boston, 1845] 2 v. in 1. MB. 45-902

Boston, Massachusetts. List of persons, co-partnerships, and corporations, who were taxed twenty-five dollars and upwards in the city of Boston in 1844, specifying the amount of tax on real and personal estate, severally, etc. Boston, 1845. NoLoc. 45-903

Boston, Massachusetts. Mechanics Apprentices' Library Association. Catalogue of books. Boston, 1845. MB. 45-904

Boston, Massachusetts. Messiah Church. Articles of faith and covenant and by laws of Messiah Church, Boston, with a list of the resident members, and an appendix of the members of the former Green Street and Garden Street Churches. Boston: Press of Crocker and Brewster, 1845. 33 p. MBB. 45-905

Boston, Massachusetts. Mount Vernon Congregation. Plan and valuation of the pews. Boston: Sharp, 1845. MB. 45-906

Boston, Massachusetts. Municipal register, containing rules and orders of the city council and a list of the officers of the city of Boston, for 1845. With a list of the city government, from its organization to the present time. Boston: John H. Eastburn, 1845. 85 p. MBB. 45-907

Boston, Massachusetts. Proceedings

before a joint special committee of the Massachusetts legislature, upon the petition of the city of Boston, for leave to introduce a supply of pure water into the city, from Long Pond, February and March, 1845. Boston: J.H. Eastburn, 1845. 144 p. DLC; LNH; MCM; NNC; PPAmP. 45-908

Boston, Massachusetts. Proceedings of a convention of delegates, chosen by the people of Massachusetts, and assembled at Faneuil Hall in the city of Boston, on Wednesday, the 29th day of January, 1845. Boston: Eastburn's Press, 1845. 18 p. CU; LNH; MdBJ; NNUT; TxGr. 45-909

Boston, Massachusetts. Report of the commissioners appointed by authority of the city council, to examine the sources from which a supply of pure water may be obtained for the city of Boston. Boston: J.H. Eastburn, 1845. 128 p. CtHWatk; MHi; MiD-B; TxU; WHi. 45-910

Boston, Massachusetts. Report, act of incorporation, by-laws, and general rules and regulations of the Asylum and Farm School for Indigent Boys. Boston, 1845. MH. 45-911

Boston, Massachusetts. Second Church. Order of services dedicating a new house of worship. Boston, 1845. MB. 45-912

Boston, Massachusetts. Trinity Church. Statement of the course of proceedings under the endowment known as "the Greene Foundation" for the support of an assistant minister of Trinity Church, Boston. Boston: Published by order of the Trustees, 1845. 23 p. MBD; MHi; NNG. 45-913

Boston Academy of Music. The Boston academy's collection of choruses; being a selection from the works of the most eminent composers, as Handel, Haydn, Mozart, Beethover, and together with several new and beautiful pieces by German authors, adapted to English words expressly for this work. Boston: J.H. Wilkins and R.B. Carter, 1845. 263 p. CO; MH; MiU. 45-914

Boston almanac for 1846. Boston: Thomas Groom and company, [1845] MBBG; MeHi; MPeaHi; MWA; RP. 45-915

Boston almanac for the year 1845. By S.N. Dickinson. Boston: Thomas Groom and company, [1845] 166 p. CoCsC; MAnHi; NBi; RNHi; WM. 45-916

Boston almanac for the year 1846. Boston: Printed by S.N. Dickinson and company, [1845] RPaw. 45-917

Boston almanac for the year 1846. By S.N. Dickinson. Boston: Thomas Groom and company, [1845] MNBedf; MPeHi; WHi. 45-918

Boston and Lowell Railroad Corporation. Remonstrance of the Boston and Lowell Railroad Corporation, in the matter of petitions for leave to construct railroads between Lowell and Andover. January 11, 1845. [Boston? 1845] 6 p. CSt; DBRE; ICU; M; MB; Nh. 45-919

Boston Benefit Society. Constitution. Boston: Dickinson, 1845. 16 p. MB. 45-920

Boston Concord and Montreal Railroad Company. Report of the survey from Concord to the valley of the Connecticut River at Haverhill, N.H. Meredith Bridge. Haverhill, New Hampshire: Belknap Gazette Press, 1845? 11 p. CtY; IU; MB; Nh-Hi. 45-921

Boston flute instruction book; a complete school for the flute. Boston: D. Ditson, [1845] 63 p. DLC; MH; NBuG. 45-922

The Boston friend, a novel. New York: Harper and brothers, 1845. 134 p. NBuG. 45-923

Boston guide to health and journal of arts and sciences. Edited by Dr. J.S. Sprear. Boston: Published by the editor, 1845. 376 p. CoDMS; CtY-M; DLC; MB. 45-924

Boston Mining Company. Trustees notes, and Dr. Charles T. Jackson's report. Boston, 1845. 11 p. MdBP; MHi. 45-925

Boston Missionary Society. Annual report presented January, 1846. Boston: Press of T.R. Marvin, 1845. 32 p. ICU. 45-926

The Boston Tyro. v. 1. Boston, 1845-. MB. 45-927

Botta, Carlo Giuseppe Guglielmo, 1766-1837. History of the war of the independence of the United States of America. Translated from the Italian, by George Alexander Otis... Ninth edition, revised and corrected... Cooperstown, New York: H. and E. Phinney, 1845. 2 v. CSmH; KHi; OClWHi; PMa; RJa. 45-928

Botts, Anne Charlotte Lynch, 1815-1891. Rhode Island book; selections in prose and verse, from the writings of Rhode Island citizens. Second edition. Boston: Weeks, Jordan, and company, 1845. 352 p. MdBE. 45-929

Boucharlat, Jean Louis, 1775-1848. An elementary treatise on mechanics, translated from the French of M. Boucharlat, with additions and emendations, designed to adapt it to the use of the cadets of the United States Military Academy, by Edward H. Courtenay... New York: Harper and brothers, 1845. 432 p. MoS; NCH; NjP; ViAl; WaS. 45-930

Boucicault, Dion, 1820?-1890. The old guard; a drama in one act. New York: Samuel French, [1845?] 20 p. OCl. 45-931

Boucicault, Dion, 1820?-1890. Willow copse. New York: French, [1845?] 64 p. NjP. 45-932

Boudinot, Elias, 1740-1821. Life of the Rev. William Tennent. Hartford: S. Andrus and son, 1845. 128 p. DLC; NcMHi; MWA. 45-933

Boughton, Joseph. The conspiracy, or triumph of innocence. Rochester: William H. Beach, 1845. 23 p. NRHi. 45-934

Boughton, Joseph. Solon Grind: or the thunderstruck hypocrite. New York: Burgess, Stringer and company, 1845. 120 p. MH; MWA; RPB. 45-935

Bouilly, Jean Nicolas, 1763-1842. Genevieve and Narcelin and other tales. Translated from the French by J.N. Bouilly. Boston: William Crosby and company, 1845. 168 p. MHolliHi. 45-936

The bouquet: containing the poetry and language of flowers. By a lady. Boston: B.B. Mussey, 1845. 128 p. CtY; DLC; NcD; NN; OCl. 45-937

Bourne, George, 1780-1845. A condensed anti-slavery Bible argument; by a citizen of Virginia. New York: Printed by S.W. Benedict, 1845. 91 p. DLC; MiU; NcD; TxU; ViU. 45-938

Bourne, William Oland. The sale of a distillery: a pencilling of the present age. New York: Saxton and Miles, 1845. 15 p. DLC; IU; NN; TxU; ViU. 45-939

Boutain, Louis Eugene Marie, 1796-1867. An epitome of the history of philosophy. Being the work adopted by the University of France for instruction in the colleges and high schools. Translated from the French with additions, and a continuation of the history from the time of Reid to the present day. New York: Harper and brothers, 1845. 2 v. InCW; MDeeP; OWoC; RPE; ScU. 45-940

Bowden, John William, 1798-1844. The life and pontificate of Gregory the Seventh. New York: J.R. Dunham, 1845. 304 p. CBB; NBuDD; PRosC; TSewU; WNaE. 45-941

Bowdler, John, 1783-1815. Practical Christianity, in a series of essays. First American from the Edinburgh edition. Boston: Benjamin Perkins and company, 1845. 285 p. MH; InCW; NjP; OU; WNaE. 45-942

Bowdoin College. Catalogue of the officers and students of Bowdoin College and the medical school of Maine. Boston: Samuel N. Dickenson and company,

1845. 24 p. CBPSR; Me; MeBaT; MeHi; NbHi. 45-943

Bowen, Eli, b. 1824. The coal regions of Pennsylvania, being a general geological, historical and statistical review of the anthraxite coal districts. Pottsville, Pennsylvania: B.W. Carvalic and company, 1845. MiU; PPM; PPULC. 45-944

Bowen, Elias. A sermon on ministerial education, delivered before the Oneida annual conference at Wilkes Barre, Pennsylvania, August 16, 1843. Utica, New York: R.W. Roberts, 1845. 26 p. IEG; NNMHi. 45-945

Bowen, Francis, 1811-1890. A theory of creation. A review of "Vestiges of the natural history of creation." Boston: Otis Broaders, and company, 1845. 54 p. ICMe; MB; MBC; MHi; RPB. 45-946

Bowen, Francis, 1811-1890. Critical essays on a few subjects connected with the history and present condition of speculative philosophy. Second edition. Boston: James Munroe and company, 1845. CtY; CLSU; MC; MH; NNUT. 45-947

Bower, Archibald, 1686-1766. The history of the popes. From the foundation of the See of Rome to A.D. 1758... With an introduction, and a continuation to the present time. Philadelphia: Griffith and Simon, 1845. 3 v. ICU; NNebg; PAnL; RPB; TxShA. 45-948

Bowers, Benjamin. The bachelor's escape from the snare of the fowler. Swanton: Published for the author, 1845. 35 p. VtU. 45-949

Bowlin, James Butler, 1804-1874. Speech of Mr. Bowlin, of Missouri, on the occupation of Oregon: delivered in the House of Representatives, January 29, 1845. Washington: Printed at the Globe office, 1845. 13 p. CU-B; WHi. 45-950

Boyce, James, b. 1808. Causes impeding the progress of christianity. An address delivered... September 16, 1845. Columbia, South Carolina: I.C. Morgan's Letter Press, printers, 1845. 13 p. CSmH. 45-951

Boyd, J. Family medical adviser... Philadelphia: J.B. Lippincott and company, 1845. 232 p. DLC; KBB. 45-952

Boyd, Jabez. Account of the arrest, trial, conviction and confession, for murder; by a gentleman of the neighborhood. Philadelphia, 1845. 15 p. MH-L; PHi; PPULC. 45-953

Boyd, James Robert, 1804-1890. Elements of rhetoric and literary criticism, with copious practical exercises and examples, for the use of common schools and academies; Fourth edition. New York: Harper and brothers, 1845. [17]-306 p. MeBa; NjP; NPV; ODaU; PRosC. 45-954

Boyer, Abel, 1667-1729. Boyer's French dictionary; comprising all the improvements of the latest Paris and London editions, with a large number of useful words and phrases. Boston: Benjamin B. Mussey, 1845. 530, 250 p. KyBgW; LNH; MH; OCX. 45-955

Brackenridge, Henry Marie, 1786-1871. History of the late war between the United States and Great Britain; comprising a minute account of the various military and naval operations. Philadelphia: C.H. Kay, 1845. 298 p. C; ICN; NcD; MdBE; MiD-B. 45-956

Brackett, Edward Augustus, 1818-1908. Twilight hours: or leisure moments of an artist. Boston: Printed by Freeman and Bolles, 1845. 95 p. CU; ICU; NcD; OO; TxU. 45-957

Bradbury, Osgood. Alice Marvin; or the fisherman's daughter. Boston: H.L. Williams, 1845. 50 p. CtY; MB. 45-958

Bradbury, Osgood. Emily Mansfield; or the gambler's fate. Lost but not won. Boston: Yankee office, 1845. 64 p. DLC; MB. 45-959

Bradbury, Osgood. Henriette; or the maiden and priest. Boston: H.L. Williams, 1845. 48 p. DLC; MH. 45-960

Bradbury, Osgood. Julia Bicknell; or love and murder. Founded on a recent terrible domestic tragedy. Boston: Henry L. Williams, 1845. 72 p. MB; NN; RPB; ViU. 45-961

Bradbury, Osgood. Little Emma. [Boston: H.L. Williams, 1845] RPB; ViU. 45-962

Bradbury, Osgood. Lucelle; or the young Iroquois! A tale of the Indian wars. Boston: Henry L. Williams, 1845. 75 p. MB. 45-963

Bradbury, Osgood. Mettallak; the lone Indian of the Magalloway. Boston: United States Publishing company, 1845. 66 p. CtY; NN; PPULC; ViU. 45-964

Bradbury, Osgood. Monira; or the wandering heiress. Boston: H.L. Williams, 1845. 48 p. MB. 45-965

Bradbury, Osgood. The Spanish pirate; or the terror of the ocean. Boston: H.L. Williams, 1845. 74 p. CtY; MB. 45-966

Bradbury, Osgood. Walton; or the banditt's [sic] daughter. Boston: H.L. Williams, 1845. 47 p. MB. 45-967

Bradbury, William Balchelder, 1816-1868. The school singer, or young choir's companion; a choice collection of music for singing schools, Sabbath schools... Fifth edition. New York: Newman, 1845. 204 p. IU; MH; OOxM; PPPrHi. 45-968

Bradbury, William Balchelder, 1816-1868. The school singer, or young choir's companion; a choice collection of music, original and selected. German melodies. Fifth edition. Cincinnati: William H. Moore and company, 1845. 204 p. OCoC. 45-969

Bradbury, William Balchelder, 1816-1868. The young choir or school singing book. Twenty-fifth edition. New York: Mark H. Newman, 1845. CtY; NjMD. 45-970

Bradbury, William Batchelder, 1816-1868. The young melodist; a collection of social, moral, and patriotic songs. New York: M.H. Newman, 1845. 144 p. CtY; NNU-W; RPB. 45-971

Bradford, Duncan. The wonders of the heavens, being a popular view of astronomy, including a full illustration of the mechanism of the heavens, embracing the sun, moon, and stars... Boston: Otis, Broaders and company, 1845. 371 p. CU; MdBN; NSprivi; OSW; PBa. 45-972

Bradford Junior College, Bradford, Massachusetts. Catalogue of the officers and members of Bradford Academy, Bradford, Massachusetts, for the year ending July 15, 1845. Boston: Press of T.R. Marvin, 1845. 16 p. ICU; MBradJ. 45-973

Bradley, J.D. An address to the Windham County Agricultural Society, delivered at their annual meeting, October 2, 1845. Brattleboro, Vermont: W.E. Ryther, 1845. 12 p. MH. 45-974

Braman, Milton P. Massachusetts election sermon; July 1, 1845. Boston, 1845. 85 p. PHi. 45-975

Braman, Milton Palmer, b. 1799. A discourse delivered before his excellency George N. Briggs, governor... January 1, 1845. By Milton P. Braman, pastor of the First Church in Danvers. Boston: Dutton and Wentworth, printers to the state, 1845. 85 p. CBPac; ICT; MeBat; MMeT; OClWHi. 45-976

Branch, Stephen H. A brief history of Francis Fauvel Gouraud, who is about to bamboozle the verdant? Bostonians with an exploded system of artificial memory. Boston, 1845. 12 p. MB; MH. 45-977

Brande, William Thomas, 1788-1866. A dictionary of science, literature, and art edited by W.T. Brande. Assisted by Joseph Cauvin. Illustrated by numerous engravings on wood. New York: Harper and brothers, 1845. 1352 p. NBuG; NjP; PScrM. 45-978

Brandreth, Benjamin, 1807-1880. Vegetable purgation; a natural law of the human body for its purification. New York: Peircy and Reed, printers, 1845. 16 p. DLC; MBAt; NjR; PPL; PPULC. 45-979

Brannon, P. Geology simplified and illustrated. Boston, 1845. MB. 45-980

Brazer, John, 1787-1846. A discourse on the life and character of the late Hon. Leverett Saltonstall, delivered in the North Church, Salem, Mass. Sunday, May 18, 1845. Salem: Printed at the Gazette office, 1845. 52 p. DLC; MWA; NN; OClWHi; PHi. 45-981

Breck, Joseph, 1794-1873. Catalogue of a choice collection of flower seeds, for 1845. Boston, 1845. 10 p. MH. 45-982

Breck, Joseph, 1794-1873. Catalogue of horticultural and agricultural implements and tools. Boston, 1845. 32 p. MH. 45-983

Breck, Joseph, 1794-1873. Catalogue of superb double dahlias for 1845. Also a catalogue of Phloxes, and other herbaceous plants, pinks, carnations, etc. Boston, 1845. 16 p. MH. 45-984

Breck, Joseph, 1794-1873. Catalogue of vegetable seeds, for sale at the New England Agricultural Warehouse and Seed Store. Tenth edition. Boston, 1845. 23 p. MH. 45-985

Breck, Samuel, 1771-1862. Address at the laying of the corner stone of the new hall. Philadelphia, 1845. 12 p. DeWi; PHi; PPPrHi. 45-986

Breck, Samuel, 1771-1862. Discourse before the Society of the Sons of New England of the City and County of Philadelphia, on the history of the early settlement of their country; being their first anniversary. Delivered December 21, 1844, by their president, Samuel Breck. Philadelphia: J.C. Clark, printer,

1845. 44 p. DLC; KHi; MB; PPA; WHi. 45-987

Breckenridge, William L. The confessional being the substance of a lecture. Philadelphia: Prebyterian Board of Publication, 1845. 28 p. LNH; PPPrHi. 45-988

Breckinridge, Robert Jefferson, 1800-1871. Christian pastor, one of the ascension gifts of Christ. A discourse, to vindicate the divine calling of the pastors of the Christian Church: to illustrate the devinely appointed evidence thereof; and to lift up a warning voice against prevailing errors. Baltimore: D. Owen and son, 1845. 49, 29 p. GDecCT; KyDC; MBC; PWW; NjPT. 45-989

Breckinridge, Robert Jefferson, 1800-1871. Memoranda of foreign travel: containing notices of a pilgrimage through some of the principal states of Western Europe. Baltimore: D. Owen and sons, 1845. 2 v. CSansS; DeWi; IaGG; NcU; OWoC. 45-990

Bremer, Fredrika, 1801-1856. Nina, translated by Mary Howitt. New York, 1845. 137 p. CtHWatk. 45-991

Bremer, Fredrika, 1801-1865. Life of Dalecarhia: the parsonage of Mora. Translated by William Howitt. New York: Harper and brothers, 1845. 72 p. IP; MDeeP; MH; MWA; OO; PU. 45-992

Bremer, Fredrika, 1801-1865. The midnight sun. New York, 1845. PPL. 45-993

Bremer, Fredrika, 1801-1865. The neighbors, a story of every day life; translated from the Swedish by Mary Howitt.

New York: Harper, 1845. 127 p. IP. 45-994

Brennglas, Ud. Berlin wie es ift ujdtrinft. Bon Ud. Brennglas. "Gckeffteher." New York: Wilhdlm Nadde, 1845. 36 p. LNH. 45-995

Brent, George. Address before the Philodemic Society of Georgetown College. Washington, 1845. PPL; PPM; PPULC. 45-996

Brett, Robert, 1808-1874. The doctrine of the cross, illustrated in a memorial of a humble follower of Christ. First American from the second London edition. New York: Henry M. Onderdonk and company, 1845. 164 p. CBPSR; MdBD; NNUT; WFonBG. 45-997

Brewster, David, 1781-1868. Letters on natural magic. Addressed to Sir Walter Scott, Bart. New York: Harper and brothers, 1845. [9]-314 p. GAuY; InCW; MS; NNE; WNaE. 45-998

Brewster, David, 1781-1868. The life of Sir Isaac Newton... New York: Harper and brothers, 1845. [9]-323 p. MLaw; MoRM; NcHil; OSW; WNaE. 45-999

Brewster, David, 1781-1868. A treatise on optics. A new edition, with an appendix, containing an elementary view of the application of analysis to reflexion and refraction, by A.D. Bache. Philadelphia: Lea and Blanchard, 1845. 323, [9]-95 p. CU; DLC; LNT-M; MH-M; ScCC. 45-1000

Bricher, T. Today I'm sixty-two; or the old maid's lament. The music arranged by T. Bricher. Boston: H. Prentiss, 1845. 3 p. MB; MNF. 45-1001

A bridal gift. From the fourth London edition. Hartford, 1845. MB. 45-1002

The bridal wreath, a wedding souvenir. Edited by Percy Bryant. Boston: John Wilson and son, 1845. 128 p. CtHWatk; FWpR; MBAt; NjR. 45-1003

Bridge, Horatio, 1806-1893. Journal of an African cruiser; comprising sketches of the Canaries, the Cape de Verde, Liberia, Madeira, Sierra Leone, and other places of interest on the west coast of Africa. By an officer of the United States Navy. Edited by Nathaniel Hawthorne. New York: Wiley and Putnam, 1845. 179 p. CU; MeAu; NCH; PP; RJa. 45-1004

Bridgeman, Thomas, d. 1850. The florist's guide with a monthly calendar, containing instructions for the management of greenhouse plants throughout the year. New and improved edition. New York: The author, 1845. 175 p. NNNBG; PU. 45-1005

Bridgeman, Thomas, d. 1850. The fruit cultivator's manual, containing ample directions for the cultivation of the most important fruits including the cranberry, the fig and grape. With descriptive lists of the most admired varieties. And a calendar showing the work necessary. The whole adapted to the climate of the United States. New York: The author, 1845. 175 p. MAA. 45-1006

Bridgeman, Thomas, d. 1850. The young gardener's assistant, in three parts. Containing catalogues of garden and flower seed. New York, 1845. 521 p. LNH; MdBLC; NNC; OCl. 45-1007

Bridgeport, Connecticut. First Univer-salist Church. Constitutions, confession and covenant of the First Universalist Church and Society... New York: Union and Messenger Press, 1845. 11 p. Ct. 45-1008

Bridgewater, Massachusetts. State Normal School. Proceedings of the fourth annual convention. Boston, 1845. 12 p. MBC. 45-1009

A brief account of the Lake Superior Copper Company by an original stockholder. Boston: Dickinson and company, 1845. 30 p. MBAU; MHi; NNE; NNM; PMA. 45-1010

Brief of title to large lot of ground, on the east side of Pratt Street, and five lots on west side of Pratt Street, the property of Maurice d'Hauterive. Philadelphia, 1845. 12 p. PHi. 45-1011

Brief of title to several lots in Penn Township, belonging to William D. Lewis. Philadelphia, 1845. 29 p. PHi. 45-1012

Brief of title to the real estate, situate in the County of Philadelphia, and belonging to the estate of William Masters Camac. Philadelphia, 1845. 52 p. PHi. 45-1013

Briggs, George Nixon, 1796-1861. Address to the two branches of the Legislature of Massachusetts, January 4, 1845. Boston: State printers, 1845. 18 p. ICMe; MBC; MiU; NCH; WHi. 45-1014

Briggs, George Ware. Hymns for public worship. Boston: Andrews, Prentiss and Studley, 1845. 601 p. CBPac, IEG; MH-AH; MWHi; NBLIHI. 45-1015

Brigham, Amariah, 1798-1849. Remarks on the influence of mental cultivation and mental excitement upon health. Third edition. Philadelphia: Lea and Blanchard, 1845. 204 p. DLC; ICJ; MWA; NN; ViU. 45-1016

Brighton, Massachusetts. Annual report. Cambridge, 1845. ICU; MBC. 45-1017

Brinckerhoff, Henrietta. Circulars and catalogues of Mrs. Brinckerhoff's Boarding and Day School for Young Ladies, for 1845, 1846, and 1848. Albany, 1845-1848. MHi. 45-1018

Brinckerhoff's almanac for 1846. New York: C. Brinckerhoff, [1845] MWA. 45-1019

Brinkerhoff, Jacob, 1810-1880. Speech, on the annexation of Texas: delivered in the House, January 13, 1845. [Corrected from the report of the National Intelligence of January 22, 1845] Washington, 1845. 8 p. MH; MiD-B; MMal; OClWHi; PHi. 45-1020

Brinkerhoff's Boarding and Day School for Young Ladies. Albany, New York. Circular and catalogue... [Mrs. Henrietta] Albany, 1845-. 24 p. MHi. 45-1021

Brisbane, William Henry, 1803-1878. An eulogium on the life and character of the late Honorable Thomas Morris. Delivered by request of the family of the deceased, and of the Liberty Party of Hamilton County. Cincinnati: Printed by L'Hommedieu and company, 1845. 38 p. CSmH; In; MdBJ; OCHP; TxH. 45-1022

Bristol's free almanac for 1845. Astronomical calculations made expressly for this almanac, by George R. Perkins, of Utica, which are guaranteed to be as perfect and complete as any published in the United States. Buffalo: Thomas, [1845] 32 p. DLC. 45-1023

Bristol's free almanac for 1845-1846. Astronomical calculations made expressly for this almanac by George R. Perkins. Buffalo: Thomas General Job Printer, [1845] 32 p. DLC; MoHi; MWA; NN. 45-1024

Bristol's free almanac for 1846. Batavia, New York, [1845] MB; WHi. 45-1025

Bristol's free almanac for 1846. [Buffalo, New York] William M. Cunningham, [1845] 32 p. DLC; NBuHi; NSchHi; OCHP; WHi. 45-1026

Britain Charitable Society, Boston. Annual reports. Boston, 1845-1868. 1 v. MB. 45-1027

British Charitable Society. Report of the British Charitable Society, and the constitution and regulations of the society. Boston: Printed by Tuttle and Dennett, 1845. 22 p. MWA. 45-1028

The British quarterly review. v 1. February 1845-. New York: Jackson, Walford, and Hodder, 1845-. AU; CoU; KU; MB; ViU. 45-1029

The British West Indies; a review of "A narrative of a visit to the West Indies," by a Virginian. Republished from the "Baltimore Saturday Visitor." Baltimore: Printed for the author by Sherwood and company, 1845. 14 p. CSmH; MoSM; NcD; OClWHi; PU. 45-1030

Brittan, Samuel Byron, d. 1883. The

lying wonders of Elder Jacob Knapp, exposed and refuted, by Rev. S.B. Brittan. The substance of three lectures delivered in the Universalist Church, Bridgeport, Connecticut. New York: Union and Messenger Press, 1845. 48 p. MMeT-Hi; NjR. 45-1031

The Broadway journal. Edited by C.F. Briggs, Edgar A. Poe, Henry C. Watson. v. 1- January 4, 1845- New York: Published by John Bisco, 1845-1846. 2 v. in 1. CSmH; CtY; MBAt; TxU. 45-1032

Brobst, Samuel Kistler. Die absicht und der nutzen von Sonntag-schulen, in der kurz dargestellt. Philadelphia: Thomas, 1845. 16 p. PPG; PPLT; PPULC. 45-1033

Brockenbrough, William Henry. William H. Brockenbrough's vindication. [Washington] J. and G.S. Gideon, printers, [1845?] CSmH. 45-1034

Brockport Collegiate Institute. Annual catalogue of the officers, teachers, and students of the Brockport Collegiate Institute, Brockport for the year ending January 31st, 1845. Rochester: Printed by Canfield and Warren, under the Museum, 1845. 24 p. NN; OCHP. 45-1035

Brodhead, John Romeyn, 1814-1873. Calendar to the Holland documents in the office of the Secretary of State at Albany. Transcribed from the original in the Royal Archives at the Hague and in the archives of the city of Amsterdam. Albany, 1845. 374 p. NSy. 45-1036

Brodhead, John Romeyn, 1814-1873. The final report of John Romeyn Brodhead, agent of the state of New York, to procure and transcribe documents in Europe, relative to the colonial history of said state. Made to the governor, 12th February, 1845. Albany: E. Mack, 1845. 374 p. CoMW; ICN; NjR; PHi; WHi. 45-1037

Bronson, C.P. Elocution; or mental and vocal philosophy illustrated by anecdotes, readings and engraving. New York: A.S. Barnes and company, [1845] 318 p. FWpR. 45-1038

Bronson, C.P. Elocution; or mental and vocal philosophy; involving the principles of reading and speaking. Lousiville: John P. Morton and company, 1845. 382 p. KyBgB; LAI; NcGC. 45-1039

Bronson, C.P. Elocution; or mental and vocal philosophy, involving the principles or reading and speaking. New York: A.S. Barnes and Co.; Philadelphia: Thomas, Copperwait and company: Boston: Otis Broaders and company; Louisville: Morton and Griswold, 1845. 320 p. LNH; MB; OO. 45-1040

Bronson, C.P. Elocution; or mental and vocal philosophy; involving the principles or reading and speaking. Fifth edition. Louisville: Morton and Griswold, 1845. 384 p. IaPeC; KyPr; TxU. 45-1041

Bronson, C.P. Elocution; or mental and vocal philosophy, involving the principles of reading and speaking. Fifth edition. New York: A.S. Barnes and company, 1845. 320 p. LNH; MnS; OMC; ScNC. 45-1042

Bronson, C.P. Elocution; or mental and vocal philosophy, involving the principles of reading and speaking. Fifth edition. Revised and corrected with large additions original and selected dialogues and speeches, which are copy-righted. Forty thousand. Lousiville: Morton and Griswold, [1845] 272 p. MH. 45-1043

Bronson, C.P. Elocution; or mental and vocal philosophy, involving the principles of reading and speaking. Fifth edition. Fourty-second [sic] thousand. Louisville: Morton and Griswold; Boston: O. Clapp, [1845] 384 p. CO; TxHR. 45-1044

Bronson, C.P. Elocution; or mental and vocal philosophy. involving the principles of reading and speaking. Sixth edition. Seventeenth thousand. Louisville: Morton and Griswold, 1845. 320 p. NNNAM. 45-1045

Bronson, C.P. Elocution; or mental and vocal philosophy; involving the principles or reading and speaking. Eighth edition. Louisville: Morton and Griswold, 1845. NN; OCl. 45-1046

Bronson, C.P. Elocution; or mental and vocal philosophy; involving the principles of reading and speaking. Thirty thousand. Louisville: Morton and Griswold, 1845. 284 p. IU. 45-1047

Bronson, C.P. Elocution; or mental and vocal philosophy; involving the principles of reading and speaking. Twenty-fourth edition. Lousiville: Morton and Griswold, [1845] 320 p. CSto; KyLoF; MdBS; ViU. 45-1048

Bronson, C.P. Elocution; or mental and vocal philosophy; involving the principles of reading and speaking; and designed for the development and cultivation of both body and mind, in accordance with the nature, uses, and destiny of man. Louisville: Morton and Griswold; Boston: Otis Clapp, Crosby and Nichols, Phillips, Sampson and company, [1845] 384 p. LNL. 45-1049

Bronson, C.P. Elocution; or mental and vocal philosophy; involving the principles or reading and speaking; and designed for the development and cultivation of both body and mind, in accordance with the nature, uses, and destiny of man. Fifth edition. New York: A.S. Barnes and company, 1845. 320 p. OOxM. 45-1050

Bronson, C.P. Elocution; or mental and vocal philosophy; involving the principles of reading and speaking; and designed for the development and cultivation of both body and mind, in accordance with the nature, uses, and destiny of man. Seventh edition. Lousiville: Morton and Griswold, 1845. 320 p. NoLoc. 45-1051

Bronson, Francis S. [Bronson's] traveler's directory, from New York to New Orleans. Embracing all the most important routes, with a condensed outline of the country, through which they pass. New York: J.F. Trow and company, 1845. 32 p. DLC; MsU; NNC; OOxM; ViU. 45-1052

Brook Farm Phalanx, West Roxbury, Massachusetts. Constitution of the Brook Farm Phalanx, adopted May 1, 1845. [Boston? 1845] 14 p. IU; MB; MH; MHi. 45-1053

Brooke, Henry K. Book of pirates containing narratives of the most remarkable piracies and murders, committed on the high seas; together with an account of the capture of the Amistad; and a full and authentic narrative of the burning of the Caroline. Carefully compiled for the publisher by Henry K. Brooke. Philadelphia: J.B. Perry; New York: W.W. Walker, 1845. 216 p. NSmb. 45-1054

Brooke, Henry K. Highwaymen and pirates' own book: containing historical narratives of the most celebrated robbers, pirates, etc., together with an account of the loss of the ship William Brown; and a full description of the mutiny on board the United States' brig Somers, with the execution of Spencer, Cromwell and Small. Carefully compiled for the publisher... Philadelphia: J.B. Perry; New York: Nafis and Cornish, 1845. 5-72, 5-82, 3-70 p. DLC; MdBE. 45-1055

Brookes, Richard, fl. 1750. Darby's universal gazetter. A dictionary, geo-graphical, historical, and statistical, of the various kingdoms, states, provinces, cities, towns, etc, in the world. Articles relating to the United States have been very largely extended, embracing every county, with the elements of their population arranged in tables from the census of 1840. Fourth edition. Philadelphia: Grigg and Elliot, 1845. 988 p. IaHi; IG; LNHT; MiGr; ViU. 45-1056

Brookes, Richard, fl. 1750. A new universal gazetter of the known world. Boston: Phillips and Sampson, 1845. 56 p. KyLoS; MeHi; MWA; TxShA; ViU. 45-1057

Brookfield Academy, Clarkville, New York. Annual catalogue year ending December 24, 1845. Hamilton: Waldron and Baker, 1845. 16 p. NN. 45-1058

Brookfield Association. Doings and report of the Auxiliary Foreign Mission Society of the Brookfield Association, at their twenty-second annual meeting in Charlton, October 21, 1845. West Brookfield: Merriam and Cooke, 1845. 23 p. MWA. 45-1059

Brooklyn, New York. Church of the Saviour. By-laws of the First Unitarian Congregational Society, worshiping in the Church of the Saviour, Brooklyn. With the by-laws of the Board of Trustees and blank form of deed of pews, and such extracts from the laws of the state as relate to similar religious societies. Brooklyn, 1845. 18 p. CtY. 45-1060

Brooklyn, New York. Pierrepont St. Baptist Church. Articles of faith, with the covenant, of the Pierrepont St. Baptist Church, Brooklyn Long Island, adopted at the constitution of the church, April, 1840. New York: George B. Maigne, 1845. 12 p. PCA. 45-1061

Brooklyn alphabetical and street directory, and yearly advertiser, for 1844-5. Compiled and published by Henry R. and William J. Hearne and Edwin Van Nostrand. Brooklyn: Stationers' Hall works, [1845] 268 p. NNA; NSmb. 45-1062

Brooklyn city directory for 1845 and 1846. To which is added, a list of the charter officers, law courts, public officers, state officers, sheriffs, and county clerks, and map of the city of New York. Also an almanac for 1845. Brooklyn: Silas H. Crowell, 1845. CSmH; NBLiHi. 45-1063

Brooklyn Clerical Union. Constitution, laws and names of members. Brooklyn, 1845. NBLiHi. 45-1064

Brooklyn, New York and Long Island ferry bill; brief argument on behalf of the applicants. Brooklyn, 1845. NBLiHi. 45-1065

Brooks, Charles, 1795-1872. The Christian in his closet; or prayers for individuals, adapted to the various ages, conditions and circumstances of life. Boston: Munroe and company, 1845. 316 p. CBPac; KWiU; MBAU; MNtCA; NjMD. 45-1066

Brooks, Charles, 1795-1872. The Christian in his closet; or prayers for individuals, adapted to the various ages, conditions and circumstances of life. Second edition. Boston: Munroe and company, 1845. MBAt; MB-FA; MH. 45-1067

Brooks, Charles Timothy, 1813-1883. A poem pronounced before the Phi Beta Kappa Society, at Cambridge, August 28, 1845. Boston: Charles C. Little and James Brown, 1845. 36 p. CSmH; MeB; MWA; RNR; TxU. 45-1068

Brooks, Nathan Covington, 1809-1898. First lessons in Latin; a series of exercises, analytical and synthetical, in Latin syntax. First edition. Philadelphia: Thomas, Cowperthwait, and company, 1845. 234 p. MdBD; MdHi; PPA; PPULC; RNR. 45-1069

Brooks, Nathan Covington, 1809-1898. First lessons in Latin; a series of exercises, analytical and synthetical, in Latin syntax; designed as an introduction to Ross' Latin grammar, but suited to any other grammar of the language. Second edition. Philadelphia: Thomas, Cowperthwait, and company, 1845. 234 p. MdBS; PU. 45-1070

Brooks, Samuel. The slave holder's religion. Cincinnati: Sparhawk and Lytle, printers, 1845. 47 p. DLC; MiU; NN; OClWHi; OO. 45-1071

Broom, Herbert, 1815-1882. A selection of legal maxims, classified and illustrated. Philadelphia: T. and J.W. Johnson, 1845. [31]-286 p. CoU; Ct; MdBB; MsU; PP. 45-1072

Brother and sister, or grace illustrated in the conversion and happy death of Isaac M. and Almira Rowe. By their pastor. Philadelphia: Presbyterian Board of Publication, 1845. 47 p. DLC. 45-1073

Brother and sister, or grace illustrated in the conversion and happy death of Isaac M. and Almira Rowe. By their pastor. Philadelphia: Presbyterian Board of Publication, 1845. 64 p. DLC;NjPT; ViRut. 45-1074

Brother angel. An Italian romance. Founded on the most thrilling incidents of Italian history in the sixteenth century. New York: H.G. Daggers, 1845. 68 p. DLC; ICU. 45-1075

Brother Jonathan: or the American boy's songster. A collection of the most popular naval, patriotic, comic and sentimental American songs... New York: [1845?] [95]-152 p. CU. 45-1076

Brough, John, 1811-1865. Address of, delivered before the Olive Branch Lodge, no. 34, of the Independent Order of Odd Fellows, at Newark, Ohio. October 2, 1845. Newark, Ohio, 1845. 20 p. OClWHi; OHi. 45-1077

Brougham and Vaux, Henry Peter Brougham, 1778-1868. Dialogues on instinct; with analytical view of the researches on fossil osteology. Philadelphia: E. Ferrett and company, 1845. 203 p. KyLx; ICP; MH; OClW; PAtM. 45-1078

Brougham and Vaux, Henry Peter Brougham, 1778-1868. Lives of men of letters and science, who flourished in the time of George III. Philadelphia: Carey and Hart, 1845. CtY; IEG; MH-AH; PP; PU. 45-1079

Brougham and Vaux, Henry Peter Brougham, 1778-1868. Lives of men of letters and science, who flourished in the time of George III. Philadelphia: Carey, 1845-1846. 2 v. CU; ICJ; MNt; NWM; OMC. 45-1080

Brougham and Vaux, Henry Peter Brougham, 1778-1868. Lives of men of letters and science, who flourished in the time of George III. Philadelphia: Carey, 1845-1847. 2 v. CSmH; PPULC; PP-W. 45-1081

Brougham, John, 1810-1880. The fine ould [sic] Irish gentleman. Boston: Reed, 1845. 5 p. MB; NN. 45-1082

Brougham, John, 1810-1880. The incendiary; a tale of love and revenge. Boston: Williams, 1845. 40 p. CtY; IaU; MB; NNC. 45-1083

Brown, Aaron Venable, 1795-1859. Texas and Oregon. Letter and speeches of the Hon. A.V. Brown, of Tennessee, in reply to the Hon. John Quincy Adams on the annexation of Texas, and on the bill for the organization of a territorial government over Oregon. Washington: Blair, 1845. 31 p. CtY; DLC; NN; Tx. 45-1084

Brown, Edward. Echoes of nature. Philadelphia: E.C. and J. Biddle, 1845. 140 p. CtY; MB; MWA; PHi; RPB. 45-1085

Brown, Francis H. Pavonia polka waltz... New York, 1845. CtY. 45-1086

Brown, Francis H. The sultans band march, for the pianoforte, respectfully dedicated to his pupil, Master Charles Legay. Boston: G.P. Reed, [1846] 3 p. MWar. 45-1087

Brown, Francis H. Will you come to my mountain home? New York, 1845. CtY; ViU. 45-1088

Brown, Goold, 1791-1857. Brown's grammar improved... New York: S.S. Wood, 1845. 335 p. IaU; RPB. 45-1089

Brown, Goold, 1791-1857. The first lines of English grammar; being a brief abstract of the author's larger work designed for young learners. New York: Samuel S. and William Wood, 1845. 108 p. MB; MH; NNC; RPB. 45-1090

Brown, Goold, 1791-1857. The institutes of English grammar... and a key to the oral exercises: to which are added four appendixes... New York: S. and William Wood, 1845. 312 p. KHi; MB; MBuG; NNC; NRSB. 45-1091

Brown, James. An English syntithology, developing the constructive principles of the English language, in appropriate technical terms. Third edition. Philadelphia: H. Grubb, 1845. 3 v. NNC; OClW; OO. 45-1092

Brown, John Ball, 1784-1862. Reports of cases in Boston Orthopedic Institution, for cure of deformities of human frame, with observations on spinal curvature. Boston: D. Clapp, 1845. 35 p. CtY; MHi; MWA; Nh; RPB. 45-1093

Brown, John J. American angler's guide; being a compilation from the works of popular English authors, from Walton to the present time. Together with the opinion and practices of the best American anglers. By an American angler. New York: Burgess, Stringer and company, 1846. 224 p. MAnP; MH; NCasti; OC; RPAt. 45-1094

Brown, John M. Christmas home; or the household festival and other poems. New York: C. Shepard, 1845. 142 p. IEG; MeB. 45-1095

Brown, Richard. Sacred architecture; its rise, progress and present state... London and New York: Fisher and son, 1845. 304 p. CtY; DLC; NcRS; T. 45-1096

Brown, Simeon. Four lectures on the divine conduct in predestination, the unbelief of the Jews, etc. Zanesville, Ohio: Lutheran Standard office, 1845. 30 p. PPPrHi; PPULC. 45-1097

Brown, William Henry, 1808-1883. Portrait gallery of distinguished American citizens, with his biographical sketches and facsimiles of original letters. Hartford, Connecticut: E.B. and E.C. Kellogg, 1845. 111 p. CtB; InG; NcD; PP; WLac. 45-1098

Brown, William John, 1805-1857. Speech of Mr. Brown, of Indiana, on the annexation of Texas: delivered in the House, January 14, 1845. Washington: Printed at the Globe office, 1845. 8 p. CSmH; CtY. 45-1099

Browne, Peter Arrell, 1782-1860. Lecture upon the naturalization law of the United States. Philadelphia: J. Richards, printer, 1845. 24 p. DLC; OCHP; WHi. 45-1100

Browning, Elizabeth Barrett, 1806-1861. A drama of exile: And other poems. New York: Henry G. Langley, 1845. 2 v. InCW; KU; MB; OAU; RPAt. 45-1101

Browning, William Shergold, d. 1874. A history of the Huguenots. A new edition, continued to the present time. Philadelphia: Lea and Blanchard, 1845. GEU-T; ICT; O; PPiPPr; VtStjA. 45-1102

Browns almanac, No. 9, for 1846. Claremont: Claremont Manufacturing Company, 1845. [15], 18-69 p. MAm. 45-1103

Brown's almanac, pocket memorandum and account book for 1846. Concord, New Hampshire: John F. Brown, [1845] 68 p. MHi; NhHi. 45-1104

Brown's almanack. Portland: Sanborn and Carter, 1845. MWA. 45-1105

Brown's almanack for 1846. Second edition. Concord, New Hampshire: John F. Brown, [1845] MWA. 45-1106

Brown's business man's almanac for 1846. Springfield, Massachusetts: Ben F. Brown, [1845] MWA. 45-1107

Brumby, R.T. Letters of Professor R.T. Brumby, on the importance of a geological survey of Alabama. Published in the State Journal and Flag, in November and December, 1844. Tuscaloosa, Alabama:

Printed by William H. Fowler, 1845. 25 p. A-Ar; DLC; MoS; NN; TxU. 45-1108

Bruno, C. Muscogee waltz. Boston: Ditson, 1845. MB. 45-1109

Bruton, James, 1815-1867. Cut for partners! A laughable farce. New York: Samuel French, [1845] 50 p. OCl. 45-1110

Bryan, James, 1810-1881. Report on the state of the lying in hospitals of Europe to the managers of the Preton Retreat, and to the obstetrical committee of the College of Physicians. Philadelphia: King and Baird, printers, 1845. 23 p. DLC; PHi; PPL-R; PPPG. 45-1111

Bryan, John A. Union of the Atlantic and Pacific Oceans, at or near the Isthmus of Panama, examined and discussed by John A. Bryan. In a series of letters addressed to the National Institute, at Washington. [Washington?] Published under the direction of Francis Markoe, Jr., secretary of the institute, [1845] 27 p. ICN; MHBA; MiD-B. 45-1112

Bryant, William Cullen, 1794-1878. Poems collected and arranged by the author. New York: D. Appleton and company, 1845. MH; NcDaD; PPCCH; PPULC. 45-1113

Bryant, William Cullen, 1794-1878. Selections from the American poets. New York: Harper and brothers, 1845. [13]-316 p. InCW; MB; MoSM; OClW; RWe. 45-1114

Bryce, Campbell R. Address delivered before Palmetto Lodge, No. 5, I.O.O.F.... May 17, 1844. Columbia, South Carolina:

Printed by A.S. Johnston, 1845. 32 p. GDecCT. 45-1115

Buchanan, James. Last letter of Mr. Buchanan to Mr. Pakenham on the American title to Oregon. Baltimore: Constitution office, 1845. CSmH; MBAt; MiD-B; NjR; TxU. 45-1116

Buck, Charles, 1771-1815. Anecdotes, religious, moral and entertaining, alphabetically arranged and interspersed with a variety of useful observations. From the ninth London edition. Boston: Otis, Broaders and company, 1845. 154 p. ICRL; IEG; OClW; WHi. 45-1117

Buck, Charles, 1771-1815. Theological dictionary containing definitions of religious terms; a comprehensive view of every article in the system of divinity... Woodward's new edition published from the last London edition, corrected to 1844. Philadelphia: Uriah Hunt and son, 1845. 478 p. MWC; PEdg; ViRu. 45-1118

Buck, Charles, 1771-1815. Theological dictionary containing definitions of religious terms; a comprehensive view of every article in the system of divinity... Woodward's new edition published from the last London edition, corrected to 1844. Philadelphia: Uriah Hunt and son, 1845. 631 p. MBAt; MWA; NjMD; NPalK; TChU. 45-1119

Bucke, Charles, 1781-1846. Ruins of ancient cities; with general and particular accounts of the rise, fall and present condition. New York: Harper, 1845. 2 v. IGK; MsU; PP; RPE; WM. 45-1120

Buckstone, John Baldwin, 1802-1879. The green bushes; or, a hundred years ago. An original drama in three acts. New

York: Samuel French, [1845] 50 p. OCl; PPL; PPULC. 45-1121

Buckstone, John Baldwin, 1802-1879. The snapping turtles; or, matrimonial masquerading; a duologue, in one act. New York: R.M. DeWitt, [1845] 18 p. IaU; MdBP. 45-1122

Budington, William Ives, 1815-1879. The history of the First Church, Charlestown, in nine lectures with notes. Boston: Charles Tappan, 1845. 258 p. CoD; DLC; MWA; NBu; WHi. 45-1123

Buffalo, New York. Board of Trade. Constitution, by-laws and organization of the Board of Trade of the city of Buffalo: constituted January 16, 1844. Published by order of the Board. Buffalo: Clapp and M'Credie, 1845. 16 p. NBuHi. 45-1124

Buffalo, New York. City Bank of Buffalo. Inventory of assets of the City Bank of Buffalo to be sold at auction at the merchants' exchange in the city of Buffalo, December 12, 1845. Buffalo, 1845. 32 p. C; IU; NBuHi. 45-1125

Buffalo, New York. Pollard Total Abstinance Society. Songs and odes. Buffalo: Faxon and company, 1845. 56 p. NBuG. 45-1126

Buffalo Nursery and Horticultural Garden, Buffalo, New York. Descriptive catalogue of fruit and ornamental trees, shrubbery and plants, cultivated and for sale at the Buffalo Nursery and Horticultural Garden, by Benjamin Hodge. Buffalo: Press of C.F.S. Thomas, [1845] CSmH; NN. 45-1127

Buffon, Georges Louis Leclerc, 1707-

1785. Buffon's natural history of man. Cooperstown: H. and E. Phinney, 1845. 2 v. MiU-C. 45-1128

Buist, Robert, 1805-1880. American flower garden directory; containing practical directions for the culture of plants in the flower garden for every month in the year. Third edition. Philadelphia: Carey and Hart, 1845. 341 p. ICU; MSaP; NICAr; RJa; WGr. 45-1129

Bulfinch, Stephen Greenleaf, 1809-1870. Lays of the gospel... Boston: J. Munroe and company, 1845. 194 p. CBPac; LNH; MoS; TxU; WHi. 45-1130

Bullard, Asa, 1804-1888. The pretty alphabet. Boston: Sabbath School Society 1845. 16 p. NNC. 45-1131

Bullard, Ebenezer W. Joy in the dedication of the sanctuary; a sermon, delivered January 22, 1845, at the dedication of the house of worship, erected by the Calvinistic Congregational Church and Society. Fitchburg, [Massachusetts] S. and C. Shepley, 1845. 24 p. IaGG; MiD-B; MWA; NN; RPB. 45-1132

Bullard, Henry Adams, 1788-1851. Lecture upon the comparative condition of man in ancient and modern times, pronounced in New Orleans, March 24, 1845. [New Orleans?] 1845. 26 p. MB; MH. 45-1133

Bullions, Peter, 1791-1864. Practical lessons in English grammar and composition; for young beginners: being an introduction to the principles of English grammar, with copious exercises, and directions for their use. Fifth edition, revised. New York: Pratt, Woodford and company, 1845. 144 p. IaHi. 45-1134

Bullions, Peter, 1791-1864. Practical lessons in English grammar and composition; for young beginners: being an introduction to the principles of English grammar, with copious exercises, and directions for their use. Sixth edition, revised. New York: Pratt, Woodford and company, 1845. 132, 12 p. CtHWatk; MH; MLow. 45-1135

Bullions, Peter, 1791-1864. Principles of English grammar; comprising the substance of the most approved English grammars extant. Eleventh edition. New York: Pratt, Woodford and company, 1845. 216 p. CtHWatk; DLC; WGr. 45-1136

Bullions, Peter, 1791-1864. Principles of English grammar; comprising the substance of the most approved English grammars extant. Twelfth edition. New York: Pratt, Woodford and company, 1845. 216 p. ICMcHi; MoS; OOxM; ViU. 45-1137

Bullions, Peter, 1791-1864. Principles of English grammar; comprising the substance of the most approved English grammars extant. Thirteenth edition. New York: Pratt, Woodford and company, 1845. 216 p. InI; ODW. 45-1138

Bullions, Peter, 1791-1864. The principles of Greek grammar; comprising the substance of the most approved grammars extant, for the use of colleges and academies. Eighth edition. New York: Pratt, Woodford and company, 1845. 312 p. IaHi; OO; PP; PPULC; TMeL. 45-1139

Bullions, Peter, 1791-1864. The principles of Greek grammar; comprising the substance of the most approved grammars extant, for the use of colleges and academies. Ninth edition. New York: Pratt, Woodford and company, 1845. 312 p. ICP; NIC. 45-1140

Bullions, Peter, 1791-1864. The principles of Latin grammar; comprising the substance of the most approved grammars extant, for the use of colleges and academies. Second edition. New York: Pratt, Woodford and company, 1845. 312 p. CSt. 45-1141

Bullions, Peter, 1791-1864. The principles of Latin grammar; comprising the substance of the most approved grammars extant, for the use of colleges and academies. Ninth edition. New York: Pratt, Woodford and company, 1845. 312 p. ICP. 45-1142

Bullions, Peter, 1791-1864. The principles of Latin grammar; comprising the substance of the most approved grammars extant, for the use of colleges and academies. Tenth edition. New York: Pratt, Woodford and company, 1845. 312 p. CtHWatk; MH; OO. 45-1143

Bumstead, Josiah Freeman, b. 1797. Mr. Bumstead's defence of his school books in reply to S.S. Greene. [Boston, 1845] CtHWatk; MB; MH; MHi; RPB. 45-1144

Bumstead, Josiah Freeman, b. 1797. My first school book to teach me, with the help of my instructor, to read and spell words, and understand them. By a friend of mine. Boston: T.R. Marvin, 1845. 108 p. MB; MBC; MH; RPB. 45-1145

Bumstead, Josiah Freeman, b. 1797. Spelling and thinking combined; or the spelling book made a medium of

thought. Boston: T.R. Marvin, 1845. MH.
45-1146

Bumstead, Josiah Freeman, b. 1797.
Third reading book in the primary
school. Boston: William D. Ticknor and
company, 1845. 160 p. MH; NNT-C. 45-
1147

Bunbury, Selina, b. 1802. The abbey of
Innismoyle: a story of another century.
First American edition. Philadelphia:
J.M. Campbell, 1845. 173 p. PPULC; PU.
45-1148

Bunyan, John. The water of life, or a discourse, showing the richness and glory of
the grace and spirit of the Gospel, as set
forth in scripture by this term. The water
of life. Baltimore: R. Douglass, 1846. 35
p. MdHi. 45-1149

Bunyan, John, 1628-1688. The holy war
made by King Shaddai upon Diabolus, to
regain the metropolis of the world, or the
losing and taking again of the town of
Mansoul... A new edition, with notes by...
Reverend George Burder... Hartford,
1845. [15] 255 p. CtY; IaDmU; MWA;
MWar. 45-1150

Bunyan, John, 1628-1688. The little
pilgrim's progress. Philadelphia: Smith
and Peck, 1845. 192 p. MB; PP; PPULC.
45-1151

Bunyan, John, 1628-1688. The pilgrim's
progress. Most carefully collated with the
edition containing the author's last additions and corrections. With explanatory
notes by T. Scott, and a life of the author
by Josiah Condor. Fifth American edition. Philadelphia: Presbyterian Board of
Publication, 1845. 554 p. FU; NN; PBa;
PPULC. 45-1152

Bunyan, John, 1628-1688. The pilgrim's
progress from this world to that which is
to come. Delivered under the similitude
of a dream. In two parts. With original
notes by T. Scott. Hartford: S. Andrus
and son, 1845. 360 p. IU; NN; OO; PPPr-
Hi; PPULC. 45-1153

Bunyan, John, 1628-1688. The pilgrim's
progress from this world to that which is
to come. Delivered under the similitude
of a dream. With a sketch of the author's
life by Stephen B. Wickens. New York:
Carlton and Porter, [1845?] 478 p. CoCs;
NN; OClW; ViU. 45-1154

Bunyan, John, 1628-1688. The pilgrim's
progress from this world to that which is
to come. Delivered under the similitude
of a dream. With a sketch of the author's
life by Stephen B. Wickens. New York:
Lane and Tippett, 1845. 478 p. MB; ViU.
45-1155

Burder, George, 1752-1832. Village
sermons; or one hundred and one plain
and short discourses, on the principal
doctrines of the Gospel; intended for the
use of families, Sunday schools, or companies assembled for religious instructions in country villages. Philadelphia:
Gregg and Elliot, 1845. 476 p. ILM. 45-
1156

Burdett, Charles, b. 1815. The Elliot
family; or the trials of New York
seamstresses... Second Thousand. New
York: E. Winchester, 1845. [9]-162 p.
CSmH; CtY; IaMP. 45-1157

Burdett, Charles, b. 1815. Never too
late. New York: D. Appleton and company, 1845. 180 p. CtY; FU; NN; PPULC.
45-1158

Burgess, George, 1809-1866. Missionary heart; annual sermon to the Board of Missions. June 18, 1845. New York: Daniel Dana, Jr., 1845. 19 p. PHi; RPB. 45-1159

Burgess, Robert. Dreams of the morning. Pittsburgh: Printed by Johnston, 1845. 119 p. InU; NBuG; PWW. 45-1160

Burghalder, Christian. The spirit of languages, in English and German exercises. Cincinnati, Ohio: Jacob Ernst, 1845. 302 p. CoHi; IaDuU; IU; OCU; ODaU. 45-1161

Burhaus, Hezekiah. The scientific spelling book, containing the principles of English orthography and pronunciation, in which the sounds of letters, syllables, and words are critically investigated and systematically arranged ... compiled for the use of schools. New York: Baker and Crane, 1845. 252 p. WOshT. 45-1162

Burke, Andrew. Address delivered before the Henry Baldwin Institute, on January 16, 1845. Pittsburg: Johnston and Stockton, 1845. 18 p. MeB; PHi; PPL; PPULC. 45-1163

Burleigh, Charles Calistus, 1810-1878. Thoughts on the death penalty. Philadelphia: Printed by Merrihew and Thompson, 1845. 144 p. DLC; ICMe; OCLaw; PPM; WU. 45-1164

Burleigh, William Henry. Tyranny of intemperance: an oration delivered in the Methodist Episcopal Church, New Haven, before the I.O. of R., the S. of T., and the Washingtonians, July 4, 1845. Published by request. New Haven: W. Storer, 1845. 18 p. Ct; CtY; IC; ICJ; MoS. 45-1165

Burnap, George Washington, 1802-1859. Expository lectures on the principal passages of the Scriptures which relate to the doctrine of the Trinity. Boston: James Munroe and company, 1845. 336 p. IEG; KyLoP; PPWe, RNR; VtU. 45-1166

Burnap, George Washington, 1802-1859. Memoir of Henry Augustus Ingalls, with selections from his writings. New York: The Metropolitan Association, 1845. IEG; MH; MiD. 45-1167

Burnap, George Washington, 1802-1859. Miscellaneous writings of George W. Burnap. Collected and revised by the author. Baltimore: John Murphy, 1845. [13]-343 p. CBPac; GMM; MB; NN; WHi. 45-1168

Burnap, U.C. The manifestations of God; a discourse by U.C. Burnap, pastor of Appleton Street Church, Lowell, Massachusetts. Boston: T.R. Marvin; New York: Mark H. Newman, 1845. MBC; MeLewB; MLow; NjPT. 45-1169

Burnet, Gilbert, 1643-1715. Exposition of the thirty-nine articles of the Church of England, with an appendix containing the Augsburg Confession, Creed of Pope Pius IV. New York: Appleton, 1845. 585 p. InID; MdW; NNG; PPLT; ViRut. 45-1170

Burns, Jabez, 1805-1876. Pulpit cyclopaedia, and Christian ministers companion; containing three hundred and sixty skeletons and sketches of sermons and eighty two essays on Biblical learning, theological studies and the composition and delivery of sermons. New York: D. Appleton, 1845. 616 p.

CtHT; MNF; OMC; PCC; ScCoT. 45-1171

Burns, Robert, 1759-1796. The works of Robert Burns; with an account of his life... to which are prefixed... by James Currie, M.D. including additional poems, extracted from the last edition edited by Allan Cunningham. Philadelphia: J. Crissy, 1845. FA; KU; MoRH. 45-1172

Burr, C.C. Substance of an extemporaneous oration on the Irish repeal; delivered in Troy, October 23... New York: Printed at the Irish Volunteer office, 1845. 28 p. CtHWatk; NNAIHI. 45-1173

Burr, Charles Chauncey. Review of Rev. Dr. Berg's three discourses in favor of capital punishment. Philadelphia, 1845. 47 p. MB; NIC; PHi; PPL; WHi. 45-1174

Burritt, Elihu, 1810-1879. Letter to the liberty convention. Cincinnati, 1845. PPL; PPULC. 45-1175

Burritt, Elijah Hinsdale, 1794-1879. The geography of the heavens, and class book of astronomy: accompanied by a celestial atlas. Fifth edition. New York: Huntington and Savage, 1845. 332 p. CtSoP; MnM; NNC; ViRU; WBeloC. 45-1176

Burroughs, Charles, 1787-1868. Sermon on death of Lieut. B.S.B. Darlington, in St. John's Church, Portsmouth, New Hampshire, March 9, 1845, by Rev. Chas. Burroughs. n.p.: n.p., 1845. 11 p. PHi; PPULC. 45-1177

Burrow, Reuben, 1798-1868. A discourse on Christian baptism, embracing discourses, on the baptism of the Holy Ghost and christian communion; to which is added an essay entitled "The kingdom of Christ not of this world." Lebanon, Tennessee: Banner of Peace, 1845. 265 p. IEG; LNB; NcMHi; T; TKL-Mc. 45-1178

Burruss, J.C. One hundred and ten reasons for being a Universalist. Richmond, 1845. 8 p. MMeT. 45-1179

Burton, Robert, 1577-1640. The anatomy of melancholy, what it is. A new edition. By Democritus minor [pseud.] Philadelphia: E. Claxton and company, 1845. MnU. 45-1180

Burton, William Evans, 1802-1860. The baronet's daughter, and the secret cell. Boston: H.L. Williams, 1845. MnU; NN. 45-1181

Bury, John William. The family of Leck of Bedlington in the county of Durham, and the charity of John George Leake in New York, United States. [Compiled from the printed reports of the legislature of the state of New York and other sources. Communicated by John William Bury, esq. Newcastle: Printed by M.A. Richardson, 1845] 14 p. DLC. 45-1182

Bush, George, 1796-1859. Anastasis; or the doctrine of the resurrection of the body, rationally and scripturally considered. New York: Wiley and Putnam, 1845. 396 p. CBPac; KyU; MeBaT; MH; TNP. 45-1183

Bush, George, 1796-1859. Anastasis; or the doctrine of the resurrection of the body, rationally and scripturally considered. Second edition. New York:

Wiley and Putnam, 1845. 396 p. CtY; Ia-FayU; MWa; NbCrD; OO. 45-1184

Bush, George, 1796-1859. New church miscellanies. New York, 1845. NB. 45-1185

Bush, George, 1796-1859. The resurrection of Christ; in answer to the question, whether he rose in a spiritual and celestial, or in a material and earthly body. New York: J.S. Redfield, 1845. 92 p. CBPSR; DLC; NjMD; PBa; RP. 45-1186

Bush, George, 1796-1859. The resurrection of Christ; in answer to the question, whether he rose in a spiritual and celestial, or in a material and earthly body. New York: Wiley and Putnam, 1845. 92 p. DLC; MBAt; NN; NNUT. 45-1187

Bush, George, 1796-1859. The soul; or an inquiry into Scriptural psychology, as developed by the use of the terms, soul, spirit, life, etc., viewed in its bearings on the doctrine of the resurection. New York: J.S. Redfield, 1845. 141 p. ArCH; DLC; InGrD; OUrC; PU. 45-1188

Bushnell, Horace, 1802-1876. A discourse on the moral uses of the sea. Delivered on board the packet ship Victoria, Captain Morgan, at sea, July, 1845. Published by request of the captain and passengers. New York: M.W. Dodd, 1845. 20 p. Ct; DLC; MiD-B; MWA; PCA. 45-1189

The business guide and legal companion, containing a selection of forms, for mercantile and money transactions... interest and money tables, and tables of weights and measures, compiled by a member of the Massachusetts Bar. Boston: Redding and company, 1845. 60 p. DLC; IaDaP; MB. 45-1190

The bustle; a philosophical and moral poem. By the most extraordinary man of the age... Boston: B. Marsh, 1845. 82 p. DLC; MH. 45-1191

Butler, Alban, 1711-1773. The lives of the fathers, martyrs, and other principal saints. Compiled from original monuments and other authentic records. Illustrated with the remarks of judicious modern critics and historians. Baltimore: Metropolitan Press, 1845. CSansS; KyOw; MiDSH; NbOC; PV. 45-1192

Butler, Alban, 1711-1773. The lives of the fathers, martyrs, and other principal saints: compiled from original monuments and other authentic records. Second American edition. Philadelphia: Eugene Cummisky, 1845. 12 v. CStclU. 45-1193

Butler, Charles, 1750-1832. Horae biblicae; being a connected series of notes on the text and literary history of the Bibles, or sacred books of the Jews and Christians; and on the bibles or books accounted sacred by the Mahometans, Hindus, Parsees, Chineese... Boston: J. Munroe and company, 1845-1918. DLC; IEG; MBC; NCaS; RPAt. 45-1194

Butler, Charles, 1802-1897. Communication of the agent of the foreign holders of Indiana state bonds, to His Excellency James Whitcomb, governor of Indiana, December, 1845. Indianapolis: J.P. Chapman, 1845. 24 p. CSmH. 45-1195

Butler, Charles, 1802-1897. Letter of Charles Butler, esq. to the legislature of Indiana, in relation to the public debt. Indianapolis: Morrison and Spause, 1845. 107 p. CU; In; MiU; NN. 45-1196

Butler, Charles. American lady. Philadelphia, 1845. NN. 45-1197

Butler, E.K. The Berkshire jubilee. Ode. Written for the Berkshire jubilee by Mrs. E.K. Butler. Albany: Wear C.; Little; Pittsfield: E.P. Little; Albany: C. Van Benthuysen, 1845. 6 p. MPiB. 45-1198

Butler, Joseph, 1692-1752. Analogy of religion, natural and revelaed to the constitution and course of nature. A dissertation: On personal identity. On the nature of virtue. With an account of the author by Samuel Halifax. New York: Robert Carter, 1845. 312 p. CBB; KyWA; NCox; NHudH; ODa. 45-1199

Butler, Joseph, 1692-1752. The works of the Right Reverend Father in God, Joseph Butler. Late Bishop of Durham... To which is prefixed an account of the character and writings of the author, By Samuel Halifax, late Lord Bishop of Gloucester. New York: Robert Carter, 1845. 303 p. FDeS; GMM; OClW; ViAl-Th. 45-1200

Butler, Noble, 1819-1882. A practical grammar of the English language. Louisville, Kentucky: Morton and Griswold, [1845] [5]- 216 p. CtHWatk; DLC; NNC. 45-1201

Butler, Samuel, 1612-1680. Hudibras, in three parts; written in the time of the late wars. With a life of the author, annotations, and an index. Hartford, 1845. CtY; MPiB; NIC; NhT; PPL. 45-1202

Buying experience or how to spend a dollar by Thomas Teller. New Haven, 1845? 64 p. CtY. 45-1203

Byron, George Gordon Noel Byron, 1788-1824. Childe Harold's pilgrimage, a romaunt. Philadelphia: George S. Appleton; New York: D. Appleton and company, 8145. 298 p. WBur. 45-1204

Byron, George Gordon Noel Byron, 1788-1824. The poetical works of Lord Byron. Philadelphia: J.B. Lippincott and company, 1845. 608 p. NHon; OrU. 45-1205

Byron, George Gordon Noel Byron, 1788-1824. The works of Lord Byron, in verse and prose, including his letters, journals, etc. with a sketch of his life. New York: Alexander V. Blake, 1845. 627 p. MPalY; NcGa; PPA; PPULC. 45-1206

Byron, George Gordon Noel Byron, 1788-1824. The works of Lord Byron, including the suppressed poems, also a sketch of his life. by J.W. Lake. Complete in one volume. Philadelphia: Grigg and Elliott, 1845. 764 p. IaDu; MeBa; NBuU; NcU; OTifH. 45-1207

C

Cabell, Edward Carrington, 1816-1896. Florida contested elections; statement of E.C. Cabell, submitted to the committee on contested elections of the House. [Washington] J. and G.S. Gideon, [1845?] 13 p. DLC; NN; Vi. 45-1208

Caesar, C. Julius. C. Julii Caesaris, que extant, interpretatione et notis illustravit Johannes Godivinus... The notes and interpretations translated and improved by Thomas Clark. New edition... Philadelphia: Thomas, Cowperthwait and company, 1845. 304 p. ViU. 45-1209

Caesar, C. Julius. Caesar. Translated by William Duncan. New York: Harper and brothers, 1845. 2 v. ODW; OO. 45-1210

Caesar, C. Julius. Commentaries on the Gallic war; and the first book of the Greek paraphrase; with English notes, plans of battles, and historical, geographical, archaeological indexes by Charles Anthon. New York: Harper and brothers, 1845. 493 p. InGrD; LNP; MH; NBuU; NCaS. 45-1211

Caesar, C. Julius. Commentaries on the Gallic war; with a dictionary and notes by Professor W.A. Andrews. Boston: Crocker and Brewster, 1845. 378 p. CtY; IaDuU; MB; MH; NNC; OO. 45-1212

Caesar, C. Julius. The first six books of Caesar's commentaries on the Gallic war, adapted to Bullions' Latin grammar by Rev. Peter Bullions. New York: Pratt, Woodford and company, 1845. 312 p. CtY; DLC; MtHi; NN; PPULC. 45-1213

Caesar, C. Julius. The first six Books of Caesar's commentaries on the Gallic war; with an introduction. Third edition. New York, 1845. CtY. 45-1214

Caesar Borgia; or the times of Pope Alexander VI. An Italian romance. Translated from the French. New York: H.G. Daggers, 1845. 48 p. NN. 45-1215

Cairns, John T., 1805-1854. The recruit: a compilation of exercises and movements of infantry, light infantry, and riflemen, according to the latest improvements. Respectfully dedicated to the recruits of the United States. New York: E. Walker, 1845.[9]-160 p. DLC; MWA; NWM; NcRA. 45-1216

Caldwell, George A. Speech of Mr. Caldwell on the annexation of Texas, delivered in the House, January 21, 1845. Washington, 1845. 12 p. DLC; ICN; MHi; NcD; PHi. 45-1217

Caldwell, Merritt, 1806-1848. A practical manual of elocution: embracing voice and gesture... Philadelphia: Sorin and Ball; [etc., etc.] 1845. [15]-331 p. DLC; IaDuU; MH; NN; PPL. 45-1218

Calendar to the European documents, copies of which are in the office of the Secretary of State of New York. Albany, 1845. PPL; PPL-R. 45-1219

Calhoon, William, 1772-1851. A treatise on the ordinances and officers of the Church of God. By the Rev. William Calhoon, a member of the presbytery of Lexington, Virginia. Philadelphia: W.S. Martien, 1845. 51 p. MH-AH; NcMHi; NjPT; Vi. 45-1220

Callcott, John Wall, 1766-1821. A musical grammar in four parts. Fifth edition. Boston: James Loring, 1845. 216 p. CtHWatk; DLC; MeB; MH. 45-1221

Calles, Abraham, 1773-1845. Lectures on the theory and practice of surgery. By the late Abraham Calles, M.D. Edited by Simon M'Coy. Philadelphia: Barrington and George D. Haswell, 1845. 420 p. CSt-L; KyU; PPiAH; PU; Vi. 45-1222

Cambridge, Massachusetts. How to settle the Texas question; address to the friends of free institutions in Massachusetts and other free states. [Boston? 1845] 11 p. MnU; NNC. 45-1223

Cambridge, Massachusetts. First Parish Sunday School Library. Catalogue of the First Parish Sunday School Library, Cambridge: Metcalf and company, printers to the University, 1845. 4-36 p. M; MiD-B. 45-1224

Cambridge Washington Academy, Cambridge, New York. Catalogue of the officers and students of Cambridge Washington Academy, in Cambridge, Washington County, New York, for the year 1845. Troy, New York: Printed at the Daily Wig office, 1845. 15 p. InID. 45-1225

Cameron, Lucy Lyttleton Butt, 1781-1858. The farmer's daughter. New York:

Robert Carter; Pittsburgh: Thomas Carter, 1845. OMC. 45-1226

Camp, George Sidney. Democracy... New York: Harper and brothers, 1845. 249 p. DLC; GAuY; InCW; MnU; NBuCC. 45-1227

Campbell, George, 1719-1796. The philosophy of rhetoric. A new edition. New York: Harper and brothers, 1845. 435 p. GDecCT; IaCrC; KHi; MdAN; MiToC. 45-1228

Campbell, Thomas, 1777-1844. The poetical works of Thomas Campbell. Philadelphia: John Locken, 1845. 288 p. CSmH; CtY; IU; NBuG; PU. 45-1229

Campbell, Thomas, 1777-1844. The poetical works of Thomas Campbell. Philadelphia: Lea and Blanchard, 1845. WGr. 45-1230

Campbell, Thomas, 1777-1844. The poetical works of Thomas Campbell, complete with a memoir of the author by Washington Irving, and remarks upon his writings by Lord Jeffery. Philadelphia: Lea and Blanchard, 1845. 434 p. AMob; CoD; ICU; LN; MoSpD. 45-1231

Campbell, William W., 1806-1881. Address and poem, delivered at the dedication of the hall of Alpha chapter of the order of United Americans, April 1, 1845. New York, 1845. 24 p. WHi. 45-1232

Can abolitionists vote or take office under the United States Constitution? New York: American Anti-slavery Society, 1845. 39 p. MsJS; TxU. 45-1233

Canal Convention, Terre Haute, Indiana. Address to the citizens of Indiana by the Committee of the Canal Convention... Which convention assembled at Terre Haute, May 22, 1845, to consider the best mode of applying the land granted by the General government, for extending the Wabash and Erie Canal, to the Ohio, at Evansville. Terre Haute, 1845. CtHt. 45-1234

Canal Convention, Terre Haute, Indiana. Proceedings of the canal convention; assembled at Terre Haute, May 22, 1845, for the purpose of considering the best mode of applying the proceeds of the liberal grant of land by the genral government, towards extending the Wabash and Erie Canal to the Ohio River, at Evansville. Terre Haute, Indiana, 1845. 15 p. In. 45-1235

Canandaigua Academy. Catalogue of the trustees, teachers and students of Canandaigua Academy. Canandaigua: Printed by George L. Whitney, 1845. 11 p. NCanHi; NGH. 45-1236

A candid appeal to candid Protestants, in refutation of the mistakes and misrepresentations of the Rev. Dr. Booth, of the Cincinnati Protestant; made in several discourses delivered in Columbus, Ohio, against the Catholic Church and Catholic morality, on the 20th and 21st of July, 1845. By a Catholic layman and citizen of Columbus. Columbus: C. Scottland Company, 1845. 36 p. ICLoy; MB; PHi; PPL-R. 45-1237

Canfield and Warren's directory of the city of Rochester, for 1845-1846. With a map. Rochester: Canfield and Warren, 1845. NRHi. 45-1238

Cannon, Charles James, 1800-1860.

Father Felix; a tale. New York: Edward Dunigan, 1845. CtY; ViU. 45-1239

Canton, Massachusetts. Annual report of the School Committee of Canton. April 7, 1845. [Dedham, 1845] 6 p. MH. 45-1240

Captain Simon Suggs, late of Talapoosa Volunteers, together with taking the census and other Alabama sketches. Philadelphia: Carey and Hart, 1845. ICN. 45-1241

The captured slave, in there acts. Buffalo: Printed for the author, 1845. 40 p. PPG; PPULC. 45-1242

Cardell, William Samuel, 1780-1828. The story of Jack Halyard. The sailor boy, or the virtuous family designed for American children in families and schools. Philadelphia: Uriah Hunt and son, 1845. PPeSchw; PPULC; RPB. 45-1243

Carey, John L. Slavery in Maryland briefly considered. Baltimore: J. Murphy, 1845. 51 p. CU; ICN; KyLx; NjMD; PHi. 45-1244

Carleton, William, 1794-1869. Farm legends. New York: Harper and brothers, 1845. 131 p. OkPer. 45-1245

Carleton, William, 1794-1869. Phelim O'Tooles courtship and the poor scholars. Philadelphia: Carey and Hart, 1845. 98 p. WU. 45-1246

Carleton, William, 1794-1869. Phil Purcel and other tales of Ireland. Philadelphia: Carey and Hart, 1845. MB; MdBP. 45-1247

Carll, M.M. Mother's manual, and infant instructor. Fourth edition, improved and enlarged. New York. Paine and Burgess, 1845. 175 p. DLC; ICarbT; MB; RPB. 45-1248

Carlyle, Thomas, 1795-1881. Critical and miscellaneous essays. A new edition, complete in one volume. Philadelphia: Carey and Hart, 1845. 568 p. CoU; CtY; LU; NN; PPL. 45-1249

Carlyle, Thomas, 1795-1881. The life of Friedrich Schiller. From the second London edition. New York: D. Appleton and company, 1845. 280 p. MB; NB; NCan; OO; PPULC. 45-1250

Carlyle, Thomas, 1795-1881. Past and present. Third edition. New York: William H. Colyer, 1845. 205 p. ICU; KMar; MeB; NjP; PP. 45-1251

Carmoly, Eliakim, 1802?-1875. History of the Jewish physicians, from the French of E. Carmoly, with notes. By John R.W. Dunbar. Baltimore: Printed by J. Murphy, [1845?] 94, 34 p. DLC; MdBJ; NNN; PPCP; WU. 45-1252

Caroline Hargrave, the merchant's daughter; being the first series of the mysteries of Salem or modern witchcraft. Salem: Varney, Parsons, and company, 1845. 36 p. DLC; MWA; NjP; PU; ViU. 45-1253

Carp River Mining Company. Articles of association. Boston: Eastburn's Press, 1845. 12 p. M. 45-1254

Carpenter, John M., b. 1804. The duty of the churches to recognize and appreciate their pastors. A sermon on behalf of the widows' fund; delivered before the New Jersey Association, at their annual meeting, held in the meeting house of the Baptist Church in Allowaystown, New Jersey.... Philadelphia: King and Baird, printers, 1845. 16 p. MH-AH; NjR; OClWHi; PCA; RPB. 45-1255

Carpenter, William Benjamin, 1813-1885. Principles of human physiology, with their chief applications to pathology, hygiene, and forensic medicine. Especially designed for the use of students. Second American, from the last London edition. With notes and additions, by Meredith Clymer... Philadelphia: Lea and Blanchard, 1845. [25]-643 p. DLC; Ia; MBuU-M; Nh; PMA. 45-1256

Carpenter, William Benjamin, 1813-1885. Principles of human physiology. Fourth American edition. Philadelphia: Lea and Blanchard, 1845. PPHa; PPULC. 45-1257

Carpenter, William Henry, 1813-1899. Claiborne the Rebel; A romance of Maryland, under the proprietary... New York: E. Ferrett and company, 1845. 104 p. DLC; MdBE; MdHi; PPL. 45-1258

Carrier's address, Cincinnati. New year's address to the patrons of the Daily Enquirer and message by the Carrier, January 1, 1845. n.p., 1845. Broadside. OCHP. 45-1259

Carroll, Charles, 1737-1832. Journal of Charles Carroll of Carrollton, during his visit to Canada in 1776, as one of the commissioners from Congress... Baltimore: Maryland Historical Society, 1845. 84 p. CSmH; ICN; KyLoF; MH; PHi. 45-1260

Carrollton, Louisiana. An act to incorporate the town of Carrollton passed by the legislature of Louisiana. Carrollton, 1845. 6 p. MH-L. 45-1261

Carruthers, William Alexander, 1800-1846. The knights of the horse-shoe: a traditionary tale of the cocked hat gentry in the Old Dominion... Wetumpka, Alabama: Charles Yancey, 1845. 248 p. CSmH; IaCrM; NcU; NN. 45-1262

Carson, Alexander, 1776-1844. Baptism in its mode and subjects. With a sketch of his life by John Young. First American edition, revised by the committee of publication. Philadelphia: American Baptist Publication Society, 1845. 502 p. IU; NRAB; PCC; PPULC. 45-1263

Carson, Joseph, 1808-1876. Introductory lecture on therapeutics. Philadelphia, 1845. PPC; PPCP; PPULC. 45-1264

Carson, Joseph, 1808-1876. Lectures on pharmacy delivered in the Philadelphia College of Pharmacy. Philadelphia, 1845. PPC; PPCP; PPULC. 45-1265

Cartee, Henry S. Grand trumpet gallopade. Boston, 1845. 3 p. MB; RHi. 45-1266

Carter, T.J. Map of Portsmouth and Concord Railroad shewing its connection with other railroads. November, 1845. Boston, 1845. Nh; Nh-Hi. 45-1267

Carter, T.J. Report of the engineer on the routes surveyed for the Portsmouth and Concord Railroad. Portsmouth, 1845. 16 p. DBRE; Nh-Hi. 45-1268

Carter, T.J. Report of the engineer on the routes surveyed for the Vermont Central Railroad from Connecticut River at Hartford, Vt., to Lake Champlain, at Burlington. Boston: S.N. Dickinson, printer 1845. 12 p. DBRE; ICU. 45-1269

Carvosso, William, 1750-1834. The great efficacy of simple faith in the atonement of Christ, exemplified in a memoir of Mr. William Carvosso, sixty years a class leader in the Wesleyan Methodist Connection. Written by himself and edited by his son. New York: Published by G. Lane and C.B. Tippett for the Methodist Episcopal Church, 1845. 348 p. IaMpI; LNB; PwmpDS-Hi; TNS. 45-1270

Cary, Thomas Greaves, 1791-1859. The dependence of the fine arts for encouragement, in a republic, on the security of property... an address, delivered before the Boston Mercantile Library Association, November 18, 1844. Boston: C.C. Little and J. Brown, 1845. 39 p. CtHWatk; MB; MWA; NCH; PHi. 45-1271

Cary, Thomas Greaves, 1791-1859. A practical view of the business of banking. Boston: Published in Hunt's Merchant Magazine, 1845. 16 p. CtHT; IU; MWA; MH-BA. 45-1272

Cary, Thomas Greaves, 1791-1859. Profits on manufactures at Lowell. A letter from the treasurer of the corporation to John S. Pendleton, esq., Virginia. Boston: C.C. Little and J. Brown, 1845. 23 p. CU; ICN; MPiB; PHi; RP. 45-1273

Cary, Thomas Greaves, 1791-1859. Result of manufactures at Lowell. A letter from the treasurer of a corporation to John S. Pendleton, Esq., Virginia. Boston: Charles C. Little and James Brown, 1845. 23 p. LNH. 45-1274

The case of William Livingston and fifteen hundred other citizens of Lowell. Boston, 1845. 28 p. DBRE; DLC; MH; Nh. 45-1275

The casket: a souvenir for 1845. New York: Edward Kearney, printed by G.B. Maigne, [1845] 395 p. FStP; MnU; NjR; WU. 45-1276

A casket of four jewels for young Christians. Boston, 1845. IEG. 45-1277

Cass, Lewis, 1782-1866. Speech of the Hon. Lewis Cass, of Michigan, on the defence of the country, delivered in the Senate. Washington: Union office, 1845. 7 p. MH; Mi; Nh-Hi; NjR; NWM. 45-1278

Cass, Lewis, 1782-1866. Speech of the Hon. Lewis Cass, of Michigan, on the European interference in American affairs. Delivered in the Senate, January 26, 1845. Washington: Printed at the Union office, 1845. 8 p. CSmH; MH; MiD-B; NBu; PHi. 45-1279

Casselberry, Isaac, 1821-1873. A description of certain fossil bones found near Evansville, [Iowa?] with speculations concerning the animal, of which they are remains. Evansville: Printed at the Courier office, 1845. 8 p. CtY; IaHi; MoS; PHi; OC. 45-1280

Casserly, Patrick S. A complete system of Latin prosody, for the use of schools, colleges, and private learners. New York: Casserly and sons, 1845. 143 p. CtHWatk; MB; MH; PScrM; RPB. 45-1281

Casserly, Patrick S. Latin prosody, for the use of schools, colleges, and private learners; on a plan entirely new. New York: Casserly and sons, 1845. 143 p. DLC; WOccR. 45-1282

Castania, Christophorus Plato, b. 1814. The Greek captive; a narrative of the captivity and escape of Christophorus Plato Castania, during the massacre on the Island of Scio by the Turks. Written by himself. Worcester: Henry J. Howland, 1845. 100 p. MH; MWA. 45-1283

The castle on the rock from the London edition. New York: General Protestant Sunday School Union, 1845. 63 p. MiD-B. 45-1284

Castleton Medical College. Thirty-third circular of Castleton Medical College. Albany: Printed by C. Van Benthuysen and company, 1845. 15 p. Nh. 45-1285

Castleton Medical College. Thirty-fourth circular of Castleton Medical College. Albany: Printed by the Knickerbocker office, 1845. 15 p. OO. 45-1286

Catalogue of valuable books principally in the French language to be sold at public sale, 1845 at the residence of the late Joseph Bonapart at Bordentown, New Jersey. [Philadelphia: United States Job Printing office, 1845] 8 p. Nj. 45-1287

A catechism in three parts. Twelfth edition. Boston: S.G. Simpkins, 1845. MWHi. 45-1288

Catechism of the Christian doctrine, published with the approbation of the most Rev. Archbishop Eccleston. Baltimore: Metropolitan Press, 1845. MdW. 45-1289

Catechism of the distinctive doctrines of the Evangelical Protestants and the Roman Catholic Church. Completed by several ministers of the District Synod of Duisburg, in Germany. First American edition, translated from the German. New York: Henry Ludwig, 1845. 71 p. CSansS; MBAt. 45-1290

Catholic Apostolic Church. The christian liturgy and book of common prayer; containing the rites of the Apostolic Catholic, or Universal Church of Christ. Boston: Ticknor, 1845. 464 p. KWiU; MB; MCET; NNP; PPL. 45-1291

Catholic Church. Christian liturgy and book of common prayer; containing the administration of the sacraments and other rites and ceremonies of the Apostolic Catholic or Universal Church of Christ. Boston, 1845. ICU; MBAt; MH; PPL-R. 45-1292

The Catholic keepsake. Edited by Prof. Walter. Baltimore: Murphy and company, [1845?] 252 p. DLC. 45-1293

The Catholic keepsake. Edited by Prof. Walter. Philadelphia: M. Fithian, [1845] 252 p. DLC; LNL. 45-1294

Catlin, George, 1796-1872. Catlin's North American Indian portfolio. Hunting scenes and amusements of the Rocky Mountains and prairies of America. From drawings and notes of the author, made during eight years' travel amongst forty-eight of the wildest and most remote tribes of savages in North America. New York: J. Ackerman, 1845.

16 p. CU-B; ICN; M; MBAt; NR. 45-1295

Catlin, George, 1796-1872. Letters and notes on the manners, custom and condition of the North American Indians. Written during eight years' travel, from 1832 to 1839, amongst the wildest tribes of Indians in North America. Fifth edition. n.p., 1845. NoLoc. 45-1296

Cattanio, P.A. Der geographische bildersaal. Philadelphia: George W. Gorton, 1845. PPG; PPeSchw. 45-1297

Cattermole, Richard, 1795?-1858. The great civil war of Charles I and the Parliament. By the Rev. Richard Cattermole. With engravings from drawings by George Cattermole under the superintendence of Mr. Charles Heath. New York: Appleton and company, 1845. 2 v. KyCov; MdBJ. 45-1298

Cattermole, Richard, 1795?-1858. The great civil war of Charles I and the Parliament. By the Rev. Richard Cattermole. Second edition. New York: Appleton and company, 1845. 2 v. CtHT; MoK; Vi. 45-1299

Caulkins, Frances Manwaring, 1795-1869. History of Norwich, Connecticut, from its settlement in 1660, to January 1845. Norwich: T. Robinson, 1845. 9-359 p. MH; NhD; OClWHi; PHi; RPAt. 45-1300

Causes of the Kensington riots explained in a series of letters to the Hon. Daniel O'Connell. By a Pennsylvanian; a Dutchman. Number 1. Philadelphia: A.H. Rowand, 1845. 1 p. MiD-B; PHi. 45-1301

Cayuga County, New York. Rules of the court of common pleas of the County of Cayuga. Adopted May 30, 1845. Prepared by Benjamin F. Hall. Auburn: J.C. Derby and company, 1845. 44 p. NN. 45-1302

Cazenave, Pierre Louis Alphee, 1802-1877. Manual of diseases of the skin, revised and corrected. New York: Langley, 1845. OCGHM. 45-1303

Cazneau, Jane Maria McManus, 1807-1878. Texas and her presidents. With a glance at her climate and agricultural capabilities. By Corinne Montgomery. New York: Winchester, 1845. 122 p. CtY; MWA; NcD; NHi; NN. 45-1304

Ceba, Ansaldo, 1565-1623. The citizen of a republic, what are his rights, his duties, and privileges, and what should be his education. New York: Paine and Burgess, 1845. 190 p. CU; IaU; KyLx; MoS; PPG. 45-1305

Cecil, Richard, 1748-1810. The works of the Rev. Richard Cecil late minister of St. John's Chapel, Redford-row, London, New York: Carter, 1845-7. 3 v. ABBS; CU; DLC; KyLoS; NCH. 45-1306

Cellini, Benvenuto, 1500-1571. Memoirs of Benvenuto Cellini, a Florentine artist; written by himself... Translated by Thomas Roscoe. New York: Wiley and Putnam, 1845. 2 v. OCX; RNR; TBriK; ViU; WvC. 45-1307

Central convention of the New Jerusalem. The memorist; or catechetic lessons drawn from the spiritual exposition of the word of God, which is now revealed for the use of the New Jerusalem. Baltimore: Published by the acting committee of the central convention, 1845. 48 p. MCNC; PBa. 45-1308

Chadwick, Edwin, 1800-1890. A report on the results of a special inquiry into the practice of interment in towns. Made at the request of Her Majesty's principal secretary of state for the home department. Philadelphia: Printed by C. Sherman, 1845. 7-48 p. CSt-L; ICJ; MH; OSW; PPM. 45-1309

Chadwick, L.T. The willow bank waltz, composed for the piano forte and respectfully dedicated to his friend Edwin Scranton, esq. New York: Firth, Pond and company, etc., etc., etc., 1845. 6 p. CoU; IG. 45-1310

Chafrone, Hester Mulso, 1727-1801. Letters on the improvements of the mind; addressed to a lady. With a biographical sketch of the author. Hartford: S. Andrus and son, 1845. 176 p. KCou. 45-1311

Challoner, Richard, 1691-1781. The garden of the soul; a manual of fervent prayers, pious reflections and solid instructions. New York: D. and J. Sadlier, 1845. 450 p. GDecCT. 45-1312

Challoner, Richard, 1691-1781. A short history of the first beginning and progress of the Protestant religion gathered out of the best Protestant writers by way of question and answer. New York: D. and J. Sadlier, 1845. 72 p. ArLSJ; ICU; MdBLC; WMMU. 45-1313

Chalmers, George, 1742-1825. An introduction to the history of the revolt of the American colonies; being a comprehensive view of its origin, derived from the state papers contained in the public offices of Great Britain. Boston: J. Munroe and company, 1845. 2 v. FSa; IaU; NcD; PPA; WaS. 45-1314

Chalmers, Thomas, 1780-1847. Discourses on the application of Christianity to the commercial and ordinary affairs of life. New York: Robert Carter, 1845. 377 p. KKcBT; MoSpD; NcHil; NjP; OBerB. 45-1315

Chalmers, Thomas, 1780-1847. Discourses on the Christian revelation. View in connection with the modern astronomy, to which are added discourses illustrative of the connection between theology and general science. New York: Robert Carter, 1845. 358 p. KyDC; MdBJ; NBuG; OCo; TJaL. 45-1316

Chalmers, Thomas, 1780-1847. Natural theology. New York and Pittsburgh: Robert Carter, 1845. 2 v. IEG; MTop; NP; OMans; TxU. 45-1317

Chalmers, Thomas, 1780-1847. On natural theology. New York and Pittsburgh: Robert Carter, 1845. 2 v. InThE; LU; NjPT; ScDuE; TBriK. 45-1318

Chalmers, Thomas, 1780-1847. On the miraculous and internal evidences of the Christian revelation, and the authority of its records. New York and Pittsburgh: Robert Carter, 1845. 2 v. LNB; NbOM; NjPT; TxBrdD; ViAl. 45-1319

Chalmers, Thomas, 1780-1847. Sketches of moral and mental philosophy; their connection with each other; their bearings on doctrinal and practical Christianity. New York and Pittsburg: R. Carter, 1845. [13]-420 p. MiU; NbOM; PPWe; ScDuE; TxBrdD. 45-1320

Chamberlayne, Israel, 1795-1875. The past and the future... a sermon occasioned by the death of Rev. Seth Mattison, late of the Genesee Annual Conference, delivered... Vienna, September, 1844. Rochester: Printed by David Hoyt, 1845. 23 p. CSmH; IEG; MoKU; NCH; NN. 45-1321

Chambers, Robert, 1802-1871. Explanations; a sequel to vestiges of the natural history of creation. Philadelphia: Carey and Hart, 1845. 142 p. CtY. 45-1322

Chambers, Robert, 1802-1871. Historical sketches of English and American literature. Embracing an account of the principal productions of the most distinguished authors in Great Britain and the United States, from the earliest to the present period. Hartford: Edward Hopkins, 1845. [9]-328 p. ICBB; MHi; NNUT; OMC. 45-1323

Chandler, Elizabeth Margaret, 1807-1834. Essays, philanthropic and moral, by Elizabeth Margaret Chandler; principally relating to the abolition of slavery in America. Philadelphia: T.E. Chapman, 1845. 120 p. MdBJ; MWH; PHC; ViU. 45-1324

Chandler, Elizabeth Margaret, 1807-1834. The poetical works of Elizabeth Margaret Chandler; with a memoir of her life and character by Benjamin Lundy. Philadelphia: T.E. Chapman; New York: Baker, Crane and Day, 1845. 180 p. InRchE; MdBJ; MWH; PSC- Hi; RPB. 45-1325

Chandler, Joseph Ripley, 1792-1880. An oration delivered at the laying of the cornerstone of a monument on Mount

Zion in Ephrata, Lancaster County, Pennsylvania, September 11, 1845. Philadelphia, 1845. 32 p. DeWI; MH; NjR; PHi; PPFM. 45-1326

Channing, Walter, 1786-1876. My own times, or 'tis fifty years since. [Boston? 1845] 34 p. CtY; MB; MBCo; NIC; RPB. 45-1327

Channing, Walter, 1786-1876. Of the medical profession, and of its preparation. An introductory lecture, read before the medical class of Harvard University, November 5, 1845... Boston: D. Clapp, Jr., 1845. 32 p. ICMe; MBM; MH; RPB. 45-1328

Channing, Walter, 1786-1876. Parliamentary sketches and water statistics. Being another word addressed to the citizens of Boston, in support of supplying the city with the pure water of Long Pond... Boston: Benjamin H. Greene, 1845. 28 p. CtY; MB-FA; MBM; MH; MWA. 45-1329

Channing, William Ellery, 1780-1842. Self culture, with a biographical sketch of the author. Boston: James Munroe, 1845. MAbD; MH; MWA; NjMD; RHi. 45-1330

Channing, William Ellery, 1780-1842. The works of William E. Channing. Fourth complete edition. Boston: James Munroe and company, 1845. 6 v. ICBB; MB-W; NjP; RLa; ScU. 45-1331

Chapard, Francis G. Dreams on the ocean. New York, 1845. 60 p. DLC. 45-1332

The chapel hymn book. Fifth edition.

Boston: S.C. Simpkins, 1845. 288 p. DLC; NNUT. 45-1333

Chapin, Alonzo Bowen, 1808-1858. A classical spelling book, containing rules and reasons for English orthography and pronunciation... New York: Alexander V. Blake, 1845. 180 p. CtHWatk; IAIS; MWHi; NSyU; RPB. 45-1334

Chapin, Alonzo Bowen, 1808-1858. A primitive church. New Haven: S. Babcock, 1845. 432 p. CBCDS. 45-1335

Chapin, Alonzo Bowen, 1808-1858. A view of the organization and order of the primitive church as presented in scripture and history, to the end of the second century; with the apostolic succession to the present day. New Haven: Babcock, 1845. 432 p. InUpT; PP; TChU; ViAl. 45-1336

Chapin, Edwin Hubbell, 1814-1880. Address delivered before Montezuma Lodge, January 27, 1845. Also an original poem delivered on the same occasion. [n.p.] 1845. CSmH; RPB. 45-1337

Chapin, Edwin Hubbell, 1814-1880. Discourses on various subjects. Boston: Abel Tompkins, 1845. 213 p. FStP; IaMp; MB; MMeT. 45-1338

Chapin, Edwin Hubbell, 1814-1880. Discourses on various subjects. Second edition. Boston, 1845. RPE. 45-1339

Chapin, Edwin Hubbell, 1814-1880. Hours of communion. Boston: A. Tompkins and B.B. Mussey, 1845. 160 p. MB; MMeT; MWat; NCaS. 45-1340

Chapin, Edwin Hubbell, 1814-1880. Hours of communion. Boston: A.

Tompkins and B.B. Mussey, 1845. 6 p. MB. 45-1341

Chapin, Edwin Hubbell, 1814-1880. The mission of little children. A discourse. Boston: Abel Tompkins, 1845. 16 p. ICMe; MBAt; MBC: MH; MWA. 45-1342

Chapin, Edwin Hubbell, 1814-1880. Occasional sermon, delivered before the United States' General Convention of Universalists, held in Boston, September 17, 1845. Boston: A. Thompkins, 1845. 20 p. MHi; MiD-B; MMeT-Hi; NNUT; OO. 45-1343

Chapin, William, 1802-1888. Chapin's ornamental map of the United States with plans of the world, British possessions, West Indies and Columbia. New York: W. Chapin, E.J.B. Taylor, 1845. NIC. 45-1344

Chapin, William, 1802-1888. Complete gazetter of the United States of North America, containing a general view of the United States and of each state and territory. New York: T. and E.H. Ensign, 1845. 371 p. CLU; MWA; NIC; PPM. 45-1345

Chapin, William, 1802-1888. A complete reference gazetteer of the United States of North America. The whole forming a complete manual of reference on the geography and statistics of the United States. New York: Published by T. and E.H. Ensign, 8145. 371. CLU; IaHi; MWA; NUt; TxU. 45-1346

Chaplain and Connecticut Railroad. Proceedings of a meeting. Boston: Eastburn's Press, 1845. 18 p. MH-BA. 45-1347

Chapman, Ezekiel Jones. Critical and explanatory notes on many select passages in the New Testament, being such as are hard to be understood, being attended with more or less difficulty to common readers.... [Utica: R.W. Roberts] 1845. NUt; OO; USlC. 45-1348

Chapman, Ezekiel Jones. Critical and explanatory notes of many select passages in the New Testament. Third edition with corrections and improvements. Utica: R.W. Roberts, 1845. 360 p. IEG; MoU; NUt; OO. 45-1349

Chapman, Nathaniel, 1780-1853. Notes on lectures, in the University of Pennsylvania, with an appendix, containing a few remarks on Asiatic cholera and yellow fever, by a physician. Philadelphia: William S. Young, 1845. 131 p. NBMS; NNNAM; PPCP; PPL. 45-1350

Chappell, Absolom Harris, 1801-1878. Speech on the annexation of Texas to the United States, in the House of Representatives, January 26, 1845. Washington, 1845. MBAt; NBu. 45-1351

Chapsal, Charles Pierre, 1788-1858. Lecons et modeles de litterature francaise. New York: R. Lockwood and son, 1845. 360 p. CtHT; IaGG; MB; MH; MNat. 45-1352

Chaptal de Chanteloup, Jean Antoine Claude, 1756-1832. Chymistry [sic] applied to agriculture, with a preliminary chapter on the organization, structure, etc., of plants; by Sir Henry Davy. New York: Harper and brothers, 1845. 359 p. IJ; MH; OClW; SCGrw. 45-1353

Charleston, South Carolina. Chamber of Commerce. Answers by the Charleston Chamber of Commerce to questions proposed by the secretary of the treasury, respecting the operation of the tariff. Charleston, 1845. 24 p. DLC; MBAt. 45-1354

Charleston, South Carolina. French Protestant Church. Preamble and rules for the French Protestant Church of Charleston adopted at a meeting of the corporation held on the 12th and the 19th November, 1842. Charleston, 1845. 26 p. NoLoc. 45-1355

Charleston, South Carolina. Meeting on religious instruction of negroes. Proceedings of the meeting in Charleston, South Carolina, May 13-15, 1845, on the religious instruction of the negroes, together with the report of the committee, and the address to the public. Published by order of the meeting. Charleston, South Carolina: Printed by B. Jenkins, 1845. 72 p. CSmH; DLC; ICU; NN; ScCC. 45-1356

Charleston, South Carolina. Second Presbyterian Church. Manual for communicants. Charleston, South Carolina: B. Jenkins, printer, 1847. 34 p. NjPT. 45-1357

Charleston Female Tract Society for Evangelizing the West. Annual Report. n.p., 1845-1846. ICU; MBC. 45-1358

Charleston Library Society, Charleston, South Carolina. A catalogue of the books of the Charleston Library Society, purchased since 1826, with a list of present officers and members. Published by order of the society. Charleston: Miller and Browne, 1845. 2 v. DLC; KyLoS; NN; ScU. 45-1359

Charlestown, Massachusetts. List of persons assessed a state, town and county tax, in the town of Charlestown, for the year 1844. Published by order of the town. Charlestown: Aurora Power Press, 1845. 56 p. DLC; MB; MH; MiD-B. 45-1360

Charlton, Robert Milledge, 1807-1854. The romance of life, a historical lecture, delivered before the Georgia Historical Society, on January 14, 1845. Savannah: Printed by E.C. Councell, 1845. 19 p. IEG; MH; NN; PHi; ViU. 45-1361

A chart exhibiting the phrenological character of --- as given by ---. Pittsburgh: Whitney, Dumars and Wright, 1845. 12 p. MH. 45-1362

Chase, Horace, 1788-1875. New Hampshire probate directory; containing all the statue laws relating to courts of probate and proceedings therein. Concord, G.P. Lyon, 1845. 318 p. DLC; MB; MH; Nh-Hi. 45-1363

Chase, Pliny Earle, 1820-1886. The good scholar's easy lessons in arithmetic. Philadelphia: U. Hunt and son, 1845. DLC; PHC; MWHi. 45-1364

Chase, Pliny Earle, 1820-1886. A key to the first and second parts of the elements of arithmetic. Philadelphia: Uriah Hunt and son, 1845. 50 p. MH; NNC; MWHi. 45-1365

Chateaubriand, Francois Auguste Rene, 1768-1848. Beauties of Christianity. Translated from the French, by Frederic Shoberl. With a preface and notes by the Rev. Henry Kett. Philadelphia: M. Carey, 1845. 524 p. CStclU. 45-1366

Cheek, Henry. Cheek's farriery; a complete treatise on the causes and symptoms of the diseases of the horse, and their remedies. Memphis, 1845. 100 p. MsCliM; T; TU. 45-1367

Cheever, George Barrell, 1807-1890. The American common place book of prose, a collection of eloquent and interesting extracts from the writings of American authors. Cooperstown: H and E. Phinney, 1845. 468 p. NBuG. 45-1368

Cheever, George Barrell, 1807-1890. Lectures on the Pilgrim's progress, and on the life and times of John Bunyan. Third edition. New York: Wiley and Putnam, 1845. 514 p. CSansS; GDecCT; KEmC; MeBat, NjP. 45-1369

Cheever, George Barrell, 1807-1890. Lectures on the Pilgrim's progress, and on the life and times of John Bunyan. Fourth edition. New York: E. Walker, 514 p. MB; NjPT; PSC; ViRut; WBeloC. 45-1370

Cheever, George Barrell, 1807-1890. Wanderings of a pilgrim in the shadow of Mont Blanc... New York: Wiley and Putnam, 1845. 166 p. CtY; MB; RPAt; ScCC; WEau. 45-1371

Cheever, Henry P. The rival brothers; or the corsair and privateer. A tale of the last war... Boston: Gleason's Publishing Hall, 1845. 66 p. InU; MB; MH; MWA. 45-1372

Cherokee almanac for the year of our Lord 1846... [1845] GHi; NcWsM. 45-1373

Cherokee Nation. Memorial of the Cherokee Indians who have become citizens of the state of North Carolina, for the value of their property unlawfully sold by agents in the employment of the United States, February 10, 1845. [Washington, 1845] 3 p. NcU; NN. 45-1374

Cherokee primer. Third edition. Park Hill: Mission Press, John Candy, 1845. 28 p. NN. 45-1375

Cherokee primer. Fourth edition. Park Hill: Mission Press, John Candy, 1845. 28 p. MBAt. 45-1376

Chesapeake and Delaware Canal Company. Address of the board of president and directors... to the stock and loan-holders of that company. Philadelphia: J.C. Clark, printer, 1845. 48 p. DLC; ICU; MdHi; MH; PPAmP. 45-1377

Chesapeake and Ohio Canal Company. Communication from the president and directors of the Chesapeake and Ohio Canal Company, in relation to the bonds issued by the state for the subscription to the capital stock. [Annapolis? 1845] 16 p. ViU. 45-1378

Chesapeake and Ohio Canal Company. Communication from the president and directors of the Chesapeake and Ohio Canal Company, to the governor of Maryland, January 15, 1845. [Annapolis? 1845] 35 p. DLC; ViU. 45-1379

Chesapeake and Ohio Canal Company. Communication from the president and directors of the Chesapeake and Ohio Canal Company, to the governor of Maryland. [Annapolis? 1845] 39 p. DLC; ViU. 45-1380

Chesapeake and Ohio Canal Company.

Proceedings of the stockholders of the company, in general meetings during the year 1844. [Frederick?] 1845. 31 p. DLC; OClWHi; ViU. 45-1381

Chesapeake and Ohio Canal Company. Special report of the president and directors of the Chesapeake and Ohio Canal Company, submitting certain acts for the acceptance of the stockholders, in general meeting assembled, April 29, 1845; together with the proceedings of the stockholders thereon. Washington: Printed by Gales and Seaton, 1845. 26 p. DLC; ViU. 45-1382

Cheshire Pastoral Association. Christian hymns for public and private worship. A collection compiled by a committee of the association. Boston, 1845. 454 p. DLC; IEG; MH-AH. 45-1383

Cheshire Pastoral Association. Christian hymns for public and private worship. A collection compiled by a committee of the Cheshire Pastoral Association. Second edition. Boston: W. Crosby and H.P. Nichols, 1845. 454 p. MB; MeB. 45-1384

Cheshire Pastoral Association. Christian hymns for public and private worship. A collection compiled by a committee of the Cheshire Pastoral Association. Third edition. Boston: Crosby, 1845. 454 p. ICN; MH; MH-AH. 45-1385

Cheshire Railroad Company. Bylaws and act of incorporation and general railroad laws. Keene, 1845. 27 p. ICJ; MiHi. 45-1386

Chesterfield, Philip Dormer Stanhope, 1694-1773. Letters, sentences, and Max-

ims. New York: Burt, [1845?] 343 p. CSjoSC; MdCatS. 45-1387

Chesterfield, Philip Dormer Stanhope, 1694-1773. The works of Lord Chesterfield, including his letters to his son, etc. First complete American edition. New York: Harper and brothers, 1845. 647 p. IaScM; KyDC; MH; NbOC; NjMD. 45-1388

Chicago city directory and business advertiser. A business advertiser and general directory of the city of Chicago for the year 1845-1846, together with a historical and statistical account. Second year of publication. By J. Wellington Norris. Chicago: J. Campbell and company, 1845. [13]-156 p. DLC; ICHi; MH. 45-1389

Chicago medical and surgical journal. Chicago, 1846-1848. MdBM. 45-1390

Child, David Lee. The taking of Naboth's Vineyard, or history of the Texas conspiracy, and an examination of the reasons given by the Hon. J.C. Calhoun, Hon. R.J. Walker and others, for the dismemberment and robbery of the Republic of Mexico. New York: S.W. Benedict and company, 1845. 32 p. MH; MHi; MNF; PHi. 45-1391

Child, Lydia Maria Francis, 1802-1880. The American frugal housewife, dedicated to those who are not ashamed of economy. Thirty-first edition enlarged and corrected by the author. New York: S.S. and W. Wood, 1845. 130 p. CtHWatk; MH; NcU; OO. 45-1392

Child, Lydia Maria Francis, 1802-1880. Brief history of the condition of women in various ages and nations. Revised and corrected by the author. Fifth edition. New York and Boston: C.S. Francis and company, 1845. 2 v. in 1. CtY; Ia; MWA; PPM; RWe. 45-1393

Child, Lydia Maria Francis, 1802-1880. Flowers for children. For children from four to six years. New York, 1845. 178 p. DLC; RPB; ViU. 45-1394

Child, Lydia Maria Francis, 1802-1880. The girl's own book. New York: Clark Austin and compnay, [1845?] [13]-288 p. CtY. 45-1395

Child, Lydia Maria Francis, 1802-1880. History of the condition of women in various ages and nations. Fifth edition revised. New York, 1845. 2 v. MW; OCel. 45-1396

Child, Lydia Maria Francis, 1802-1880. Letters from New York. New York: C.S. Francis and company, 1845. 287 p. DeWi; NjMD; NGH; OrU; VtB. 45-1397

Child, Lydia Maria Francis, 1802-1880. Letters from New York. Third edition. New York: C.S. Francis and company, 1845. 288 p. DLC; ICU; NBu; RP; TxU. 45-1398

Child, Lydia Maria Francis, 1802-1880. Philothea: a Grecian romance... New and corrected edition. New York: C.S. Francis and company; Boston: J.H. Francis, 1845. [9]-290 p. LNT; MiGr; OO; PBa; WU. 45-1399

Childbirth: its pains greatly lessened, its perils entirely obviated. Being an account of an experiment recently made in London. With allusions to several cases in this country... New York: H.G. Dog-gers, 1845. 58 p. DLC; ICJ; MdBJ; NNN; PPCP. 45-1400

Children of Mary. Manual of the children of Mary. Baltimore: Hedian and O'Brien, 1845. 321 p. DLC. 45-1401

Childs, George. Drawing book of objects: studies from still life. Second edition. Philadelphia: J.W. Moore, 1845. NRMA. 45-1402

Child's book of poetry. Worcester: Jonathan Grant, Jr., [1845?] 24 p. MWA; NN. 45-1403

The child's delight: a present for young people. Edited by a Lady. Philadelphia: George S. Appleton and company, 1845. 152 p. DLC; RPB. 45-1404

The child's gem for 1845. Edited by Mrs. S. Colman. Boston: T.H. Carter and company, 1845. 96 p. MHoilliHi. 45-1405

The child's own book. Boston: Munroe and Francis, 1845. 620 p. MBev. 45-1406

The child's pictorial mentor for the year; containing amusing instruction characteristic of each month. Second edition. Worcester, 1845. 58 p. MnU; MWA. 45-1407

Chimes, rhymes, and jingles: entered according to act of Congress in the year 1845, by Munroe and Francis. Boston: Munroe and Francis, 1845. 160 p. NNC. 45-1408

Chipman, Daniel, 1765-1850. The life of Hon. Nathaniel Chipman, formerly member of the U.S. Senate and chief justice of the state of Vermont. Boston: Little and Brown, 1845. 402 p. DLC; MWA; MiD; NN; PHi. 45-1409

Chipman, Samuel. The temperance lecturer; being facts gathered from a personal examination of all the jails in the state of New York. Albany, 1845. 72 p. MBC; NN. 45-1410

Chippewa Copper Mining Company. Constitution of the Chippewa Copper Mining Company, report of Col. C.W. Cutter's exploration of the mineral regions of Lake Superior. Boston: Eastburn's Press, 1845. 32 p. M; MiHCH. 45-1411

Chittenden, H.A. A reply to the charge of heresy. Addressed to the members of the North Congregational Church, Hartford, Connecticut, 1845. Boston: Christian Publishing Society, 1845. 28 p. Ct; ICN; OClWHi. 45-1412

Chivers, Thomas Holley. The lost pleiad; and other poems. New York: Edward O. Jenkins, 1845. 32 p. CSmH; CtHT; MH; NcAS; NN. 45-1413

Chouquet, Gustave. First lessons in learning French. New York: Roe Lockwood and son, 1845. 106 p. MH; MWHi. 45-1414

Christian doctrinal advocate and spiritual monitor. v. 1-. 1845. Matt's carners, 1845-. PCG; PPULC. 45-1415

Christian family magazine; devoted to religion, literature, science, and general intelligence. Edited and published by D.S. Burnet. Cincinnati: Printed for the editor by R.P. Brooks, 1845. v. 1-. CBPac; NcD; TKimJ; TNDC. 45-1416

The christian sabbath of divine authority, and obligatory on men to be observed on the first day of the week. Northampton, 1845. 24 p. MBC. 45-1417

Christian Sentinel. East Windsor Hill, Connecticut. Conducted by an association of gentlemen. Hartford, 1845-1847. 2 v. CBPSR; CtY; MBC; NbCrD; NhD. 45-1418

Christina: the little pilgrim's progress. Part II. Philadelphia: Loomis and Peck, 1845. 95 p. MeBaHi. 45-1419

Christison, Robert, 1797-1882. A treatise on poisons in relation to medical jurisprudence physiology and the practice of physics. First American from the fourth Edinburg edition. Philadelphia: Ed Barrington and George D. Haswell, 1845. 792 p. CU-M; ICJ; KyU; MBP; ViU. 45-1420

A Christmas and New Year's present. New York: J. Riker, 1845. 208 p. MBC; NPLaK. 45-1421

The Christmas tree. A Christmas and New Year's gift from the children of the Warren Street Chapel: January 1st, 1845. Boston: Office of the Christian world, 1845. 17 p. MB; MPeHi; NNC; RPB. 45-1422

Christmasia; neu rai o nodweddiadan neilldnol, y diweddar barchedig christmas evans. Utica: Choeddedig gan R. Edwards, 1845. 64 p. CtY; NIC; WM. 45-1423

Christy, Edward P. Christy's far famed and original band of Ethiopian minstrels. Buffalo: Clapp and M'Oredio, [1845] 16 p. NBuHi. 45-1424

Chumasero, John Chamberlain, 1816-1903. The landlord and tenant, a tale of the present day, founded on facts. By the author of "Mysteries of Rochester." Rochester: William H. Beach, 1845. 39 p. NRHi. 45-1425

Chumasero, John Chamberlain, 1816-1903. Laura, the Sicilian girl; a tale of Sicily. By the author of "Scenes in Italy." Rochester: William H. Beach, 1845. 40 p. NRHi. 45-1426

Chumasero, John Chamberlain, 1816-1903. The mysteries of Rochester. Rochester: W.H. Beach, 1845. 96 p. NR; NRHi; NRU. 45-1427

Chumasero, John Chamberlain, 1816-1903. The mysteries of Rochester. Second edition. Rochester: William H. Beach, 1845. CtY; NR; NRHi. 45-1428

Church, Alonzo, 1793-1862. A discourse delivered before the Georgia Historical Society, on the occasion of its sixth anniversary, on Wednesday, 12th February, 1845. [Athens, Georgia: "Southern Whig,"] 1845. 34 p. CSmH; MHi; NIC; PHi; TxU. 45-1429

Church, Benjamin, 1639-1718. The history of the great Indian war of 1675 and 1676 with notes and appendix by S.G. Drake. Revised edition. New York: H. Dayton, [1845] 360 p. MdU; NIC; NjP; OClWHi. 45-1430

Church, Benjamin, 1639-1718. The history of the great Indian war of 1675 and 1676, commonly called Philip's war. Also, the old French and Indian wars, from 1689 to 1704. With numerous notes and an appendix. Revised edition.

Hartford: S. Andrus and son, [1845] 360 p. CtY; GEU; MH; MHa; NCH. 45-1431

Church, Benjamin, 1639-1718. The history of the great Indian war of 1675 and 1676, commonly called Philip's war; also the old French and Indian wars from 1689 to 1704, by Thomas Church with numerous notes and an appendix by Samuel G. Drake. Second edition. New York: H. Dayton, 1845. 360 p. InI; NN. 45-1432

Church, Edward. French spoken. A new system of teaching French. Boston: B.B. Mussey, 1845. MB; MBAt; MH; NBuG. 45-1433

Church, Edward. French spoken. A new system of teaching French. Second edition. Boston: Benjamin B. Mussey, 1845. 30 p. CtMW; MH; NNC; PHC. 45-1434

Church, Edward. French spoken. A new system of teaching French. Third edition. Boston: S.N. Dickinson, 1845. 301 p. MH; NNC; PHi; PPULC; RPB. 45-1435

Church, Pharcellus. Permanency of the pastoral relation. A sermon... before the ministerial conference of the Monroe Baptist Association, at Ogden, July 2, 1845. Rochester: Sage and brother, 1845. 24 p. CSmH; MB; MWelC; NN; RPB. 45-1436

Church, W.A. Patterns of inlaid tiles from churches in the diocese of Oxford. Wallingford: Payne, 1845. 3 p. CtY; NN; NNC; PPF; PPULC. 45-1437

Church almanac for 1846. New York: Protestant Episcopal Tract Society, [1845] MWA; NBLIHI; NNA; OrPD. 45-1438

The church almanac for 1846... Second edition. New York: The Protestant Episcopal Tract Society, [1845] 48 p. IEG; MWA; WHi. 45-1439

Church of Jesus Christ of Latter Day Saints. A collection of sacred hymns for the Church of Jesus Christ of Latter Day Saints. Pittsburgh, 1845. DLC. 45-1440

Church psalmist; or psalms and hymns, for the public, social, and private use of Evangelical Christians. Fifth edition. New York: Mark H. Newman, 1845. 653 p. IaCrM; IU; NSyHi; TWcW. 45-1441

The churchman: an illustrated weekly news magazine. 1845-. New York, 1845-. v. 1-. OCl; PCC. 45-1442

The churchman's companion in the closet; or a complete manual of private devotions. Edited by Francis E. Paget. New York: D. Appleton and company; Philadelphia: George S. Appleton, [1845] 327 p. MDB; MoBolS; NbOM. 45-1443

Cicero, Marcus Tullius. M.T. Ciceronis. Orationes qualdam selectae, in useum delphini, cum interpretative et historia succincta M.T. Ciceronis. Stereotyped from the second edition corrected and improved with a life of Cicero in English. Philadelphia: Thomas, Cowperthwait and company, 1845. 367 p. GOgU; OAlM; ScCC; TxU. 45-1444

Cicero, Marcus Tullius. Offices; translated by Thomas Cockman. New York: Harper and brothers, 1845. 343 p. LNP. 45-1445

Cicero, Marcus Tullius. Orationes quaedam selectae... Bostoniae, sumptibus R.S. Davis, 1845. MBC; MH; MoS; NcGC. 45-1446

Cicero, Marcus Tullius. The orations, translated by Duncan, the officers by Cockman and the Cato and Daelius by Melworth. New York: Harper and brothers, 1845. 3 v. ODaGSG; OSW. 45-1447

Cicero, Marcus Tullius. Select orations. With English notes, critical and explanatory and historical geographical and legal indexes. New edition with improvements. New York: Harper and brothers, 1845. 518 p. CU; LStBA; MH; PReaA; WAxN. 45-1448

Cincinnati, Ohio. Catalogue of paintings and sculpture exhibiting at the fireman's fair given by the ladies for the benefit of Fire Engine and Hose Company, no. 5, at Washington Hall, commencing June 16, 1845. [Cincinnati, 1845?] 4 p. OCHP. 45-1449

Cincinnati, Ohio. Celebration of the forty-fifth anniversary of the first settlement of Cincinnati and the Miami County on the 26th day of December, 1844 by natives of Ohio. Cincinnati: Shreve and Gallagher, 1845. OMC. 45-1450

Cincinnati Astronomical Society. The annual address delivered before the Cincinnati Astronomical Society. Cincinnati: R.P. Brooks, 1845. 56 p. CSmH; CtY; MBC; MH; OClWHi. 45-1451

Cincinnati Historical Society. Annals of the Cincinnati Historical Society. Published by order of the Society. Cincinnati: R.P. Donogh and company, 1845. 20 p. DLC; MH; MiU; OMC; PPPrHi. 45-1452

Cincinnati Historical Society. Annual of the Cincinnati Historical Society. Published by order of the society. Cincinnati: R.P. Donogh and company, 1845. 12 p. M; MWA; OClWHi. 45-1453

Ciocci, Raffaele. Iniquities and barbarities practiced at Rome in the nineteenth century. Philadelphia: T.B. Peterson, [1845] MnU. 45-1454

Ciocci, Raffaele. A narrative of iniquities and barbarities practiced at Rome in the nineteenth century. Third American from the second London edition. Philadelphia: J.M Campbell; New York: Saxton and Miles, 1845. 140 p. CSansS; OC; OO; P. 45-1455

Circumnavigation of the globe. An historical account of the circumnavigation of the globe, and of the progress of discovery in the Pacific Ocean, from the voyage of Magellan to the death of Cook. New York: Harper and brothers, 1845. 366 p. OSW. 45-1456

Cist, Charles, 1793-1868. The Cincinnati miscellany; or antiquities of the West and pioneer history and general and local statistics. Compiled from the Western general advertiser, from October 1st, 1844 to April 1st [1846] Cincinnati: C. Clark, 1845-1846. 2 v. CtMW; ICU; MBAt; MH; OCX. 45-1457

Cist, Lewis Jacob, 1818-1885. Trifles in verse; a collection of fugitive poems. Cincinnati: Robinson and Jones, 1845. [13]-184 p. CSt; InThE; MoSM; OCY; TxU. 45-1458

Citizen and farmer's almanac. Desilver and Mier, 1845. MWA. 45-1459

Citizen's and farmer's almanac for 1846. Original calculations by Edward Hagerty. Baltimore: John T. Hanzsche, [1845] MdHi; MWA; NCH. 45-1460

City Fire Insurance Company. Report of the City Fire Insurance Company in the City of New York in answer to a resolution of the Assembly. [Albany] 1845. 3 p. WHi. 45-1461

City sights for little folks. Philadelphia: Smith and Peck, 1845. 191 p. OClWHi; MH; NPV. 45-1462

Civis, Pseud. Romanism incompatible with republican institutions. By Civis. New York: Published by the American Protestant Society, 1845. 107 p. CtHC; GEU-T; MiU; MMeT; NN. 45-1463

Clack, Franklin Hulse. An address delivered on the anniversary of the birthday of Washington, before the Philomathian Society of Mount St. Mary's College, Maryland, February 22, 1845. Washington, 1845. 8 p. DLC; MBAt. 45-1464

Claggett, Rufus. The American expositor, or intellectual definer. Designed for the use of schools. New York: Paine and Burgess, 1845. 190 p. MFiT; NN; OClWHi; RHi; WaPS. 45-1465

Claggett, Rufus. Elocution made easy: containing rules and selections for declamation and reading. New York: Paine and Burgess, 1845. 144 p. KyBC; MH; NjP; OkHi; ViU. 45-1466

Claimants on Mexico. New York, 1845. 12 p. CtY; CU; PPL. 45-1467

Claims of the Baptist Book and Tract

Society. Lanesville, 1845. 16 p. MBC. 45-1468

Clapp, Caleb. A sermon on occasion of the decease of Dr. Daniel Dayton delivered at the Chruch of the Nativity, New York. New York: Henry M. Onderdonk and company, 1845. 26 p. MBD. 45-1469

Clapp, Eliza Thayer. Studies in religion. By the author of "Words in a Sunday School." New York: C. Shepard, 1845. 230 p. CBPac; DLC; MeB; MH; MH-AH. 45-1470

Clark, A. Address at the celebration of the anniversary of St. John the Baptist, before the members of the Masonic Fraternity, June 24, 1845 at Logansport, Indiana. Logansport: Printed at the "Logan Chief office," 1845. 10 p. NNFM. 45-1471

Clark, Abraham. Sketch of Abraham Clark. Trenton, 1845. PPL. 45-1472

Clark, George W. The liberty minstrel, Fourth edition. New York: Benedict, 1845. 184 p. LU; MBC; NcD; NIC; OO. 45-1473

Clark, George W. The liberty minstrel. Fourth edition. New York: Leavitt and Alden, 1845. 184 p. CoD; IU; MeBa; MH; PHC. 45-1474

Clark, John Alonzo, 1801-1843. Awake, thou sleeper! by the late Rev. J.A. Clark. Second edition. New York and Pittsburgh: Robert Carter, 1845. 244 p. CtMW; MdW; MeBat; NjMD; OClW. 45-1475

Clark, John Alonzo, 1801-1843. The

pastor's testimony. Fifth edition revised and corrected by the author. New York and Pittsburgh; R. Carter, 1845. 240 p. IaCrM; IU; NjMD. 45-1476

Clark, John Alonzo, 1801-1843. Walk about Zion, Seventh edition. New York and Pittsburgh: Carter, 1845. LN; MCET; OLiS. 45-1477

Clark, Lewis Garrard, 1812-1897. Narrative of the sufferings of Lewis Clarke, during a captivity of more than twenty five years among the Algerines of Kentucky, one of the so called Christian States of North America. Dictated by himself. Boston: David H. Ela, 1845. 108 p. DLC; MBAt; MWA; PPAmP; WaS. 45-1478

Clark, Lewis Gaylord, 1808-1873. The knickerbocker sketch book. A library of select literature. New York: Burgess, Stringer and company, 1845. 243 p. ArU; CtY; ICU; MB; MWA; NN. 45-1479

Clark, Lincoln, 1800-1886. Eulogy upon the life, character and death of General Andrew Jackson, delivered on July 19, 1845, before the societies and citizens of Tuscaloosa, and published at their request. Tuscaloosa: Printed by M.D.J. Slade, 1845. 40 p. Ct; DLC; GEU; TCh; TxU. 45-1480

Clark, Rufus W. War with Mexico. A sermon preached in the North Church, Portsmouth, New Hampshire, September 7, 1845. [Portsmouth] C.W. Brewster, printer, 1845. 16 p. MC; MH; MWA; NjR. 45-1481

Clark, Thomas March, 1812-1903. An efficient ministry. A sermon preached before the sixty-first annual convention of the Protestant Episcopal Church in the state of Pennsylvania. Philadelphia: King and Baird, 1845. 16 p. MiD-B; OO; PHi. 45-1482

Clark, Uriah. An exposure of assults made upon universalism by Rev. messrs. Wisner, Curry, Hatfield, Smith, Dr. Cox, etc. by Rev. Uriah Clark. Delivered by request in the First Universalist Church at Lockport, on Sunday afternoon, April 13th, 1845. Rochester: Western Luminary office, 1845. 17 p. MMeT. 45-1483

Clarke, Adam, 1760?-1832. Christian theology. Selected from his published and unpublished writings and systematically arranged. With a life of the author by Samuel Dunn. New York: G. Lane and C.B. Tippett for the Methodist Episcopal Church, 1845. 438 p. ArSpr; DLC; ILM. 45-1484

Clarke, Adam, 1760?-1832. A dissertation on the use and abuse of tobacco. Baltimore: Sherwood and company, 1845. 36 p. MdBMP; MdBP. 45-1485

Clarke, Edward, d. 1891. A sermon delivered at Middlefield, Massachusetts, March 26, 1845, at the funeral of Deacon David Mack... With an appendix... Amherst: J.S. and C. Adams, printers, 1845. 16 p. CtSoP; DLC; MNF; NNG; RPB. 45-1486

Clarke, Irwin. Sufferings of ... during captivity in Kentucky.... Boston: Ela, 1845. 108 p. MB; MBAt; MWA; NNNR. 45-1487

Clarke, James Freeman, 1810-1888. The peculiar doctrine of Christianity, or reconciliation by Jesus Christ. Boston:

Office of the Christian World, 1845. 27 p. ICMe. 45-1488

Clarke, James Freeman, 1810-1888. A sketch of the history of the doctrine of atonement. Boston: James Munroe and company, 1845. 34 p. MBC; MeB; MH; OO; RPB. 45-1489

Clarke, William, 1800-1838. The boy's own book; a complete encyclopedia of all the diversions, athletic, scientific and recreative, of boyhood youth. Sixth American edition. Boston: Munroe and Francis, 1845. 316 p. ICU; MH; NcAS. 45-1490

Clarkson, William K. The constitution. New York: Printed for the author, 1845. 147 p. DLC; MH; NN; NNS; OOC. 45-1491

The class book of nature, comprising lessons on the universe, the three kingdoms of nature, and the form and structure of the human body. With questions and numerous engravings. Edited by J. Frost, Ninth edition. Hartford: Belknop and Hamersley, 1845. 283 p. NIC-A. 45-1492

Clater, Francis, 1756-1823. Every man his own cattle doctor; containing the causes, symptoms, and treatment of all the diseases incident to oxen, sheep and swine and a sketch of the anatomy and physiology of neat cattle. Philadelphia: Lea and Blanchard, 1845. 251 p. ICMc-Hi. 45-1493

Clater, Francis, 1756-1823. Every man his own farrier; containing the causes, symptoms, and most approved methods of cure, of the diseases of horses. First American from the twenty-eighth London edition. With notes and additions by J.S. Skinner. Philadelphia: Lea and Blanchard, 1845. KyDC; NB; NSyU; P. 45-1494

Claxton, Christopher. History and description of the steamship Great Britain, built at Bristol for the Great Western Steamship Company; to which are added, remarks on the comparative merits of iron and wood as materials for ship building. New York: J.S. Homans, 1845. 28 p. CU; DLC; LNH; MWA; NNE. 45-1495

Clay and Fielinghuysen [sic] almanac for 1845. New York: Turner and Fisher, 1845. MWA; PPL. 45-1496

Clay, Cassius Marcellus, 1801-1903. Appeal of Cassius M. Clay, to Kentucky and the world. Boston: J.M. Macomber and E.L. Pratt, 1845. 35 p. CtSoP; ICU; OClWHi; PPL; RP. 45-1497

Clay, Cassius Marcellus, 1810-1903. To the people of Kentucky. [Lexington? 1845?] 8 p. KyLx; MBAt; MH. 45-1498

Claybaugh, Joseph. The comparative dignity and importance of the office of the gospel ministry and an address to the students of the theological seminary at Oxford, Ohio, under the care of the Second Associate Synod of the West, delivered at the opening of its seventh session, November 9, 1845. Rossville: J.M. Christy, 1845. 24 p. CSmH; OClWHi; PPPrHi. 45-1499

Cleaveland, Elisha Lord, 1800-1866. A sermon occasioned by the death of Charles W. Hinman, delivered on April 27, 1845. New Haven: Hitchcock and Staf-

ford, 1845. 18 p. CtSoP; CtY; OCl; RPB. 45-1500

Cleaveland, John Payne, 1799-1873. The people's claim on the scholar. An address before the "Society of inquiry," in Wabash College, Iowa, July 22, 1845. Published by request. Cincinnati: Printed by E. Shepard, 1845. 24 p. CSmH; ICP; NCH; OUrC; PPPrHi. 45-1501

Clerical Society of Brooklyn. Constitution and laws of the Clerical Society of Brooklyn, New York; with the names of the members and the inaugural address of the late president... Maurice William Dwight. Instituted January 3, 1844. Embracing members of several denominations of Evangelical Christians. Brooklyn: Printed by order of the Society, 1845. 16 p. MB; MBC; NN; NjR. 45-1502

Cleveland, Charles Dexter, 1802-1869. First Latin book. Being the author's original "First lessons in Latin," thoroughly revised and remodeled, with numerous improvements. Philadelphia: Thomas, Cowperthwait and company, 1845. [9]-219 p. DLC; GHi; ILM; MB; MNBedf. 45-1503

Cleveland, Charles Dexter, 1802-1869. Second Latin book, being the first part of Jacobs' and Doring's "Elementarbuch," adapted to the author's Latin grammar. Philadelphia: Thomas, Cowperthwait, and company, 1845. 299 p. GHi; IaHi; MB; NjPT; OTifH. 45-1504

Cleveland and Pittsburgh Railroad Company. Report of the survey and estimates of the Cleveland and Pittsburgh Railroad. By Col. S. Dodge, engineer.

Akron: Dewey and Elkins, 1845. 7 p. OClWHi. 45-1505

Clifton Coal Company. Extracts from reports made by a commiteee of the Maryland Legislature. Charter of the Clifton Coal Company, by the legislature of Maryland. New York, 1845. MdBP; OClWHi. 45-1506

Clingman, Thomas Lanier, 1812-1897. Memoranda of the late affair of honor between Hon. T.L. Clingman, of North Carolina and Hon. William L. Yancey of Alabama. [Washington? 1845] 8 p. ArU; ICN; LU; MH; NjP; OClWHi. 45-1507

Clingman, Thomas Lanier, 1812-1897. Speech of Mr. Clingman... on the late presidential election, January 6, 1845. Washington: Gideon, 1845. 16 p. CtY; MBAt; MWA; NcD; PHi. 45-1508

Clinton, George William, 1807-1885. Address delivered at the dedication of Erie tent, No. 30, I.O. of R. in the city of Buffalo, October 24, 1845. Buffalo: C.E. Young, 1845. 16 p. DLC; NBu. 45-1509

Coale, William Edward, 1816?-1865. An essay to describe the best mode of treating... fractures of the thigh. Boston: Thomas H. Webb and company, 1845. 48 p. CtY; MBM; NNN; RHi; RPM. 45-1510

Coates, Reynell, 1802-1886. Physiology for schools. Fourth edition, revised. Philadelphia: Butler and Williams, 1845. [25]- 333 p. ICJ; LNB; PHi; PPULC. 45-1511

Cobb, Howell, 1815-1868. Speech of Mr. Cobb, of Georgia, on the annexation of Texas: delivered in the House, January

22, 1845. Washington: Printed at the Globe office, 1845. 8 p. CtY; DLC. 45-1512

Cobb, Lyman, 1800-1864. Cobb's arithmetical rules and tables. Designed for the use of small children in families and schools. Trenton: Davenport, 1845. 35p. MB. 45-1513

Cobb, Lyman, 1800-1864. Cobb's new juvenile reader, No. 1, or first reading book, containing interesting, moral, and instructive reading lessons, composed of easy words of one and two syllables. Designed for the use of small children in schools and families. New York: Caleb Bartlett, 1845. 108 p. MoU; NRivHi. 45-1514

Cobb, Lyman, 1800-1864. Cobb's new juvenile reader; or second reading book containing interesting moral and instructive reading lessons composed of easy words of one, two and three syllables in which all the words in the first reading lesson not contained in any reading lesson in No. 1.... New York: Caleb Bartlett, 1845. 144 p. NFred. 45-1515

Cobb, Lyman, 1800-1864. Cobb's new juvenile reader no. III or third reading book. New York: Calab Bartlett, 1845. 216 p. NFred. 45-1516

Cobb, Lyman, 1800-1864. Cobb's new sequel to the juvenile readers; or fourth reading book. New York: Caleb Bartlett, 1845. 240 p. MH; NHem; PReaAT. 45-1517

Cobb, Lyman, 1800-1864. Cobb's new spelling book, in six parts. Ithaca, New York: Andres, Woodruff, and Gauntlett,

1845. 168 p. MH; NIDHi; OCHP; PPe-Schw; PScrHi. 45-1518

Cobb, Lyman, 1800-1864. New North American reader; or fifth reading book. New York: Caleb Bartlett, 1845. 384 p. CtHWatk; InPerM; MiU; OClWHi; PWW. 45-1519

Cobb, Lyman, 1800-1864. New North American reader; or fifth reading book: containing a great variety of interesting, historical, moral and instructive reading lessons in prose and poetry... designed for the use of the highest classes in schools and academies. Cincinnati: B. Davenport, 1845. 384 p. NjR; WvW. 45-1520

Cobb, Lyman, 1800-1864. The reticule and pocket companion, or miniature lexicon of the English language. Stereotype edition. New York: Harper and brothers, 1845. 832 p. MH; NjP; WGrNM. 45-1521

Cobbett, William, 1763-1835. Cobbett's legacy to labourer's; or what is the right which the lords, baronets and squires have to the lands of England? In six letters addressed to the working people of England. With a dedication to Sir Robert Peel, Bart. New York: D. and J. Sadlier, 1845. 104 p. ODaMSJ. 45-1522

Cobbett, William, 1763-1835. Cobbett's legacy to parsons in six letters, addressed to the church parsons in general. New York: D. and J. Sadlier, 1845. 104 p. IRivf; MdBS; OClJC; WOccR. 45-1523

Coe, Benjamin Hutchins, 1799-1883. Drawing book of trees. New York, 1845. CtHwatk. 45-1524

Coe, Benjamin Hutchins, 1799-1883.

Easy lessons in landscape drawing, etc. New York, 1845. CtHWatk. 45-1525

Coe, Benjamin Hutchins, 1799-1883. A new drawing book of American scenery. New York: Saxton and Miles, 1845. 24 p. MWinchrHi. 45-1526

Coffin, Charles, 1779-1851. The lives and services of Major General John Thomas, Colonel Thomas Knowlton, Colonel Alexander Scammell, Major General Henry Dearborn. New York: Egbert, Hovey and King, printers, 1845. 222 p. ICN; MeHi; MNF; Nh-Hi; OCHP. 45-1527

Coffin, James Henry, 1806-1873. Solar and lunar eclipses. Familiarly illustrated and explained with the method of calculating them. According to the theory of astronomy as taught in New England colleges. New York: Collins brothers and company, 1845. 83 p. IaMp; LU; MeB; NBuG; PU. 45-1528

Coffin, Joshua, 1792-1864. A sketch of the history of Newbury, Newburyport, and West Newbury, from 1635 to 1845. Boston: S.G. Drake, 1845. [9]-416 p. CtMW; FSa; MnHi; OO; PPA. 45-1529

Coffin, Robert A. An essay on the uses and advantages of town organization. Boston: Fowle and Capen, 1845. 65 p. CtY; MB; MConw; MWA; TxU. 45-1530

Cogswell, Jonathan, 1782-1864. Discourses on practical and experimental subjects. New Brunswick, New Jersey: Terhune's, 1845. 228 p. ICP; NN; PPPr-Hi; PPULC. 45-1531

Coit, Thomas Winthrop, 1803-1885. Forms of prayer, or sameness of words no hindrance to devotion. A sermon, by Rev. T.W. Coit, Rector of Trinity Church, New Rochelle, New York. New York: Churchman's Bookstore, 1845. 23 p. CtHT; IEG; MdBD; Nh; PHi. 45-1532

Coit, Thomas Winthrop, 1803-1885. Puritanism; or a churchman's defense against its aspersions, by an appeal to its own history. New York: D. Appleton and company; Philadelphia: G.S. Appleton, 1845. [13], 527 p. IaDa; KyLos; NcU; RNR; ViAl. 45-1533

Colburn, Warren, 1793-1833. Arithmetic upon the inductive method of instruction. Being a sequel to intellectual arithmetic. Boston: Jordan, Swift and Wiley, 1845. 245 p. MB; MiU; NjR; NNC. 45-1534

Colburn, Warren, 1793-1833. Colburn's first lessons. Intellectual arithmetic upon the inductive method of instruction. Boston, [1845?] MB. 45-1535

Colburn, Warren, 1793-1833. Intellectual arithmentic, upon the inductive method of instruction. Boston: William J. Reynolds and company, 1845. 172 p. MH. 45-1536

Colburn, Warren, 1793-1833. An introduction to algebra, upon the inductive method of instruction. Boston: Swift and Wiley, 1845. 274 p. OCL. 45-1537

Colburn, Warren, 1793-1833. Key containinng answers to the examples in the sequel to intellectual arithmetic. Boston: Edward J. Peet, 1845. 70 p. ICU; MB; MBU-E; MHi; MiU. 45-1538

Colby, Benjamin. A guide to health, being an exposition of the principles of the Thomsonian system of practice, and their mode of application in the cure of every form of disease; embracing a concise view of the various theories of ancient and modern times. Third edition, enlarged and revised... Milford, New Hampshire: J. Burns, 1845. [13]-181 p. MBM; NCH; PPCP; PPHa. 45-1539

Colby College, Waterville, Maine. Catalogue of the library of Waterville College, in Waterville, Maine. Waterville: J.S. Carter, 1845. 47 p. CSmH; ICN; MB; MeBa; MH. 45-1540

Colcord, Munroe. Trial of Munroe Colcord, Elihu Colcord, John A. Webster, etc., for the murder of Dolly Sever. By an attorney at law. Exeter, New Hampshire: Charles C. Dearborn, 1845. 46 p. DLC; MH-L; Nh-Hi; NIC-L. 45-1541

Cole, Albert, 1809?-1845. A tribute of affection to the memory of the late Rev. George W. Cole. Portland, [Maine] W. Hyde, 1845. [13]-300 p. CSmH; ICT; MeB; NN; OClWHi. 45-1542

Cole, Frederick Wing, 1815-1845. Poems... with a sketch of his life and character, by Rev. S.W. Fisher. Albany: C. Van Benthuysen and company, 1845. 128 p. DLC; IEG; MWA; OMC; PPM. 45-1543

Cole, Timothy. The sacred songster: a collection of hymns for prayer and conference meetings. Partly original. Lowell, 1845. 96 p. RPB. 45-1544

Coleridge, Samuel Taylor, 1772-1834. Aids to reflection. With the author's last corrections. To which is prefixed a preliminary essay by J. M'Vickar. Sixth edition, revised and corrected. New

York: Swords, Stanford, and company, 1845. 324 p. NbCrD; NNoe; OO. 45-1545

Coleridge, Samuel Taylor, 1772-1834. The works of Samuel Taylor Coleridge, prose and verse... Philadelphia: Thomas. Cowperthwait and company, 1845. 546 p. IaCW; KIn; MShM; PWWJS; WaU. 45-1546

Colhoun, John B. The world's unbelief in religious mysteries; a sermon by the Rev. John B. Colhoun. Philadelphia: B.E. Smith, 1845. 12 p. DLC; MdBD; NNG; PPL; PPULC. 45-1547

Collamer, Jacob. Speech of Mr. J. Collamer, of Vermont, on the annexation of Texas. Delivered in the House... January 23, 1845. [Washington: Printed at Gideon's, 1845] 16 p. CSmH; KHi; MH; MiD-B; MWA. 45-1548

A collection of interesting tracts, explaining several important points of Scripture of Doctrines. Published by order of the general conference. New York: G. Lane and C.B. Tippett, for the Methodist Episcopal Church, 1845. 378 p. InUpT; NcMHi; TxAbM. 45-1549

Collection of songs and pianoforte music. Boston? 1845. 64 p. MB. 45-1550

Colles, Abraham, 1773-1843. Lectures on the theory and practice of surgery. Edited by Simon M'Coy. Philadelphia: E. Barrington and G.D. Haswell, 1845. 420 p. DLC; ICJ; MiU; NcD; PU. 45-1551

Collet, Pierre, 1693-1770. Life of St. Vincent of Paul, founder of the Congregation of the Mission and of the Sisters of Charity... Baltimore: Metropolitan Press, 1845. 347 p. CtHT; InNd; MdW; MH; ViL. 45-1552

Collier, David. David Collier's einleitung zum richtigen verstande und nutzlicher lesung der heiligen schrift; aus dem Englischer ubersetzt von F.E. Rambach. Neu Berlin, Pennsylvania: Reissner, 1845. 525 p. CLCo; CtMW; IaDuW; OBerB; PreaAT. 45-1553

Collier, Robert Ruffin, 1805-1870. To the citizens of Petersburg. January, [n.p.] 1845. 24 p. PPPrHi; PPULC. 45-1554

Collins, Stephen. Miscellanies. Second edition. Philadelphia: Carey and Hart, 1845. [3]-308 p. CtY; MdBP; NjP; Vi; WaS. 45-1555

Collins, William, 1721-1759. The poetical works of Collins, Gray and Beattie. With a memoir of each. New York: Turner and Hayden, 1845. 308 p. IaMp; KyU; MiDD; NNUT; OO. 45-1556

Collot, Alexander G., b. 1796. Progressive French anecdotes and questions: intended as a reading, reciting, and question book and forming a guide preceded by "Collot's French dialogues and phrases," to conversational French narration. Philadelphia: James Kay, 1845. 233 p. MFmR; PHar; ScCMu. 45-1557

Collot, Alexander G., b. 1796. Progressive French dialogues and phrases: consisting of a systematic collection of conversations on familiar subjects and also of select idioms and proverbs... Philadelphia: J. Kay, jun. and brother, 1845. 226 p. IU; MH; NNU-W. 45-1558

Collot, Alexander G., b. 1796. Progressive French grammar and exercises, on the basis of Levizac's French grammar. Philadelphia: J. Kay, jun. and brother, 1845. ICU; MeB; MH; OCY; TNJU. 45-1559

Collot, Alexander G., b. 1796. Progressive pronouncing French reader; on a plan new, simple and effective: Being a course of interesting and instructive lessons. Selected from the works of the best prose writers and poets. Preceded by a collection of easy fables. Philadelphia: James Kay, Junior and brother, 1845. 288 p. CtY; KyLoS; MeBa; NSyHi. 45-1560

Collyer, William Bengo, 1732-1854. A treasure of truth upon seventy subjects, from the writings of Rev. W.B. Collyer. Selected and arranged by Rev. John O. Choules. New York: L. Colby, 1845. IaDuU; ICU; OClW. 45-1561

Colman, George, 1762-1836. The poor gentleman. A comedy in five acts. With the stage business, cast of characters, costumes, relative positions, etc. as performed at the Park Theatre. New York: Samuel French, [1845?] 72 p. CSt; ICU. 45-1562

Colman, Pamela Chandler. New stories for little boys; original and selected. Boston: S. Colman, 1845. 96 p. NWebyC. 45-1563

Colman, Pamela Chandler. New stories for little girls; original and selected. Boston: S. Coleman, 1845. 95 p. CtY. 45-1564

Colombat, Marc, 1797-1851. A treatise on the diseases and special hygiene of females. Translated from the French, with additions, by Charles D. Meigs. A new edition, revised. Philadelphia: Lea and Blanchard, 1845. 719 p. DLC; NcD; OClM; PPC; PPULC. 45-1565

Colombat, Marc, 1797-1851. A treatise upon the diseases and hygiene of the organs of the voice. By Colombat de L'Isere. Translated by J.F.W. Lane. Boston: Otis, Broaders and company, 1845. 220 p. CU-M; MB; NNUT; PPAN; RNR. 45-1566

Colonel David Mack, the faithful steward who died in Middlesfield, Massachusetts. New York, [1845] 24 p. MWA. 45-1567

Colquhoun, Janet Sinclair, 1781-1846. The world's religion, as contrasted with genuine Christianity. New York: Carter, 1845. 207 p. CtHWatk; ICBB; PP. 45-1568

Colton, Joseph Hutchins, 1800-1893. The western tourist, or emigrant's guide through the states of Ohio, Michigan, Indiana, Illinois, and Missouri and the territories of Wisconsin and Iowa. New York: J.H. Colton, 1845. InU; NNUT. 45-1569

The columbian almanac, for the year 1846. Wilmington, [Delaware] John B. Porter, [1845] [36] p. MWA; WHi. 45-1570

Combe, Andrew, 1797-1847. The physiology of digestion considered with relation to the principles of dietetics. From the third Edinburgh, revised and enlarged. New York: W.H. Colyer; Boston: Lewis and Sampson, 1845. 287 p. DNLM; MsU; NBMS; OClW; ScOrC. 45-1571

Combe, Andrew, 1797-1847. The principles of physiology applied to the preservation of health, and to the improvement of physical and mental education. From the seventh Edinburgh edition. New York: Harper and brothers, 1845. CtY; MeAu; MiThr; OCX; ScCMu. 45-1572

Combe, Andrew, 1797-1847. A treatise on the physiological and moral management of infancy. For the use of parents. From the fourth Edinburgh edition. New York: W.H Colyer, 1845. 296 p. NN. 45-1573

Combe, George, 1788-1858. The constitution of man considered in relation to external objects. Hartford: S. Andrus and son, 1845. 60 p. CSansS; IaHoL; OWoC; PP; TxU. 45-1574

Combe, George, 1788-1858. The constitution of man considered in relation to external objects. New York, 1845. MH; OClStM. 45-1575

Combe, George, 1788-1858. The constitution of man considered in relation to external objects. From the third enlarged Edinburgh edition. Erie, Pennsylvania: O.D. Spafford, 1845. 389 p. CSmH; OO. 45-1576

Combe, George, 1788-1858. The constitution of man considered in relation to external objects. Seventeenth American edition, materially revised and enlarged. Boston: T.H. Webb and company, 1845. 436 p. MB; NbCrD; PPHa; PPULC. 45-1577

Combe, George, 1788-1858. Moral philosophy; or the duties of man considered in his individual, social and domestic capacities. New York: W.H.

Colyer, 1845. 372 p. CtHWatk; LNB; MB. 45-1578

Combe, George, 1788-1858. Moral philosophy, or the duties of man considered in his individual, social and domestic capacities. From the revised and enlarged Edinburgh edition. Cooperstown, New York: W. H. Colyer, 1845. 25-372 p. MB. 45-1579

Comfort, John W. The practice of medicine on Thomasonian principles, adapted as well to the use of families as to that of the practitioner. Philadelphia: A. Comfort, 1845. 522 p. NbU-M; P; PPHa; ViU. 45-1580

Comfort, John W. Thomsonian practice of midwifery, and treatment of complaints peculiar to women and children. Philadelphia: A. Comfort, 1845. 215 p. DLC; MBM; OClWHi; PPCP; PPHi. 45-1581

The comic forget me not songster, being the latest, and best collection of the most popular comic songs, as sung by choice spirits of the age. Philadelphia, 1845. 154 p. IU; RPB. 45-1582

Comings, A.G. Mirror of Christian evidences. Conducted by A.G. Comings. Boston: Published by A.G. Comings, 1845. 42 p. DLC; MBAt; MBNMHi. 45-1583

Comings, A.G. The reign of peace. A series of discourses. Boston, 1845. 124 p. MB; PPULC; PSC. 45-1584

Comlie, George, 1788-1858. A system of phrenology complete American edition from the fourth and last revised and enlarged Edinburgh. New York: William

H. Colyer; Boston: Phillips and Sampson, 1845. 516 p. InLW; WU. 45-1585

Comly, John, 1773-1850. Comly's reader, and book of knowledge; with exercises of spelling and defining, intended for the use of schools, and for private instruction. Philadelphia: Thomas L. Bonsal, 1845. 212 p. NjR; PHi; PPM; PSC-Hi. 45-1586

Comly, John, 1773-1850. A new spelling book, compiled with a view to render the arts of spelling and reading easy and pleasant to children... to which is added a variety of useful exercises. Philadelphia: Kimber and Sharless, 1845. 180 p. CtY. 45-1587

Commercial Bank of Pennsylvania. Act to extend the charter of the Commercial Bank of Pennsylvania. Philadelphia, 1845. 15 p. PHi. 45-1588

Commuck, Thomas, d. 1856. Indian melodies; harmonized by Thomas Hastings. New York: G. Lane and C.B. Tippet, 1845. 144 p. CSmH; ICN; MH; NjMD; PPi. 45-1589

The communion of saints the communion of the Bible. Dover, New Hampshire: Published by the trustees of the Freewill Baptist Printing Establishment, 1845. 45 p. NjPT; OO; RPB; WHi. 45-1590

The community at West Roxbury, Massachusetts. [Boston, 1845?] 8 p. MH. 45-1591

A compend of Bible truth. Philadelphia, 1845. 186 p. DLC; NjPT. 45-1592

The complete history of Ireland, from the earliest times; being compiled from a connected continuation by approved standard writers. New York: R. Martin and company, [1845?] 2 v. in 1. CtHT; IU; MiU; NNAIHi. 45-1593

A complete history of the Marquis De Lafayette, Major General in the Army of the United States of America, in the war of the Revolution; embracing an account of his late tour through the United States, to the time of his departure September 1825. Hartford: S. Andrus and son, 1845. 504 p. IC; LNB; OO; Vi; WBeloC. 45-1594

A comprehensive summary of English and American Tory and biography, from the earliest period to the present day: with a sketch of natural philosophy and general astronomy, adapted to the use of American schools and the general reader, by Augustus J.H. Duganne. Philadelphia: Grubb and Reazor, 1845. 11-314 p. KyLoSX. 45-1595

Comstock, John Lee, 1789-1858. Elements of chemistry, in which the recent discoveries in the science are included and its doctrines familiarly explained. Fiftieth edition. New York: Pratt, Woodford and company, 1845. 420 p. CtHWatk; WvB. 45-1596

Comstock, John Lee, 1789-1858. Elements of chemistry, in which the recent discoveries in the science are included and its doctrines familiarly explained. Fifty-first edition. New York: Pratt, Woodford and company, 1845. 420 p. OrUM. 45-1597

Comstock, John Lee, 1789-1858. Elements of chemistry, in which the recent discoveries in the science are included and its doctrines familiarly explained. Fifty-second edition. New York: Pratt, Woodford and company, 1845. 420 p. CLSU; NbLU; OkentC. 45-1598

Comstock, John Lee, 1789-1858. Elements of chemistry, in which the recent discoveries in the science are included and its doctrines familiarly explained. Fifty-third edition. New York: Pratt, Woodford and company, 1845. 420 p. MH; NPV; OO; TxU-T. 45-1599

Comstock, John Lee, 1789-1858. Elements of chemistry, in which the recent discoveries in the science are included and its doctrines familiarly explained. Fifty-fourth edition. New York: Pratt, Woodford and company, 1845. 420 p. CtMW; TxNbE. 45-1600

Comstock, John Lee, 1789-1858. Elements of chemistry, in which the recent discoveries in the science are included and its doctrines familiarly explained. Fifty-fifth edition. New York: Pratt, Woodford and company, 1845. 420 p. ScU. 45-1601

Comstock, John Lee, 1789-1858. An introduction to mineralogy; adapted to the use of schools and private students... Twelfth edition. New York: Pratt, Woodford and company, 1845. 369 p. DLC; LU; MiThr; MoS; ViRut. 45-1602

Comstock, John Lee, 1789-1858. An introduction to the study of botany, including a treatise on vegetable physiology and descriptions of the most common plants in the middle and northern states. Eleventh edition. New York: Pratt, Woodford and company, 1845. MoS; NSYU; OO; PWCHi. 45-1603

Comstock, John Lee, 1789-1858. Outlines of geology, intended as a popular treatise on the most interesting parts of the science, together with an examination of the question whether the days of creation were indefinite periods. Fifteenth edition. New York: Pratt, Woodford and company, 1845. 396 p. CtHWatk; ODW; PPi; PMA; WvED. 45-1604

Comstock, John Lee, 1789-1858. Outlines of physiology, both comparative and human, in which are described the mechanical, animal, vital and sensorial organs and functions. Eighth edition. New York, Pratt, Woodford and company, 1845. NBCP; OClC; OClM; OO. 45-1605

Comstock, John Lee, 1789-1858. A system of natural philosophy: in which the principles of mechanics, hydrostatics... are familiarly explained. To which are added questions for the examination of pupils. New York: Pratt, Woodford and company, 1845. CoU; MH; Nh. 45-1606

Comstock, John Lee, 1789-1858. A system of natural philosophy: in which the principles of mechanics, hydrostatics... are familiarly explained. To which are added questions for the examination of pupils. Sixtieth edition. New York: Pratt, Woodford and company, 1845. 360 p. CLO; MoS. 45-1607

Comstock, John Lee, 1789-1858. A system of natural philosophy: in which the principles of mechanics, hydrostatics... are familiarly explained. To which are added questions for the examination of pupils. Sixty-first edition. New York: Pratt, Woodford and company, 1845. 360 p. MWHi. 45-1608

Comstock, John Lee, 1789-1858. A system of natural philosophy: in which the principles of mechanics, hydrostatics... are familiarly explained. To which are added questions for the examination of pupils. Sixty-second edition. New York: Pratt, Woodford and company, 1845. MH; OAU. 45-1609

Comstock, John Lee, 1789-1858. A system of natural philosophy: in which the principles of mechanics, hydrostatics... are familiarly explained. To which are added questions for the examination of pupils. Sixty-third edition. New York: Pratt, Woodford and company, 1845. 360 p. IU. 45-1610

Comstock, John Lee, 1789-1858. A system of natural philosophy: in which the principles of mechanics, hydrostatics... are familiarly explained. To which are added questions for the examination of pupils. Sixty-fourth edition. New York: Pratt, Woodford and company, 1845. WvH. 45-1611

Comstock, John Lee, 1789-1858. A system of natural philosophy: in which the principles of mechanics, hydrostatics... are familiarly explained. To which are added questions for the examination of pupils. Sixty-fifth edition. New York: Pratt, Woodford and company, 1845. TxU-T. 45-1612

Comstock, John Lee, 1789-1858. A system of natural philosophy: in which the principles of mechanics, hydrostatics... are familiarly explained. To which are added questions for the examination of pupils. Sixty-sixth edition. New York: Pratt, Woodford and company, 1845. 360 p. MSwan; NPtv. 45-1613

Comstock, John Lee, 1789-1858. A system of natural philosophy: in which the principles of mechanics, hydrostatics... are familiarly explained. To which are added questions for the examination of pupils. Sixty-seventh edition. New York: Pratt, Woodford and company, 1845. 360 p. OrSaW. 45-1614

Comstock, John Lee, 1789-1858. A system of natural philosophy: in which the principles of mechanics, hydrostatics... are familiarly explained. To which are added questions for the examination of pupils. Sixty-eighth edition. New York: Pratt, Woodford and company, 1845. MH. 45-1615

Comstock, John Lee, 1789-1858. A system of natural philosophy: in which the principles of mechanics, hydrostatics... are familiarly explained. To which are added questions for the examination of pupils. Sixty-ninth edition. New York: Pratt, Woodford and company, 1845. MH; OCU; RPB. 45-1616

Condie, David Francis, 1796-1875. Annual oration. The Philadelphia Medical Society, by appointment, at the opening of its session of 1844-5. Philadelphia: King and Baird, 1845. 24 p. MB; NNNAM; PU; WU. 45-1617

Condie, David Francis, 1796-1875. A practical treatise of disease of children. Philadelphia: Lea and Blanchard, 1845. 696 p. NPla. 45-1618

Condit, Joseph D. A sermon occasioned by the death of Mrs. Irene M. Tuck, and delivered at Ludlow, Massachusetts, August 29, 1844. Springfield, Massachusetts: Smith and Taylor, 1845. 12 p.

CtSoP; MBC; MNF; NjPT; RPB. 45-1619

The condition, influence, rights of women. Albany, 1845. IU. 45-1620

The condition, influence, rights and appeal of women from J.A. Segur, Mary Wollstonecraft, Thomas Carey, Matthew Herttell, etc. Third edition. Albany, 1845. DLC; IU; MH. 45-1621

The confession of a rum seller. Boston, 1845. 214 p. MB; MH; MH- AH. 45-1622

The confessions of a magnetizer being an expose of animal magnethism. Boston: Gelason, 1845. 50 p. CtY; DNLM; ICN; MnU; RPB. 45-1623

Confessions of Saint Augustin, Bishop of Hippo, and Doctor of the church: to which is prefixed a sketch of his life. A new edition. New York, 1845. 55 p. IaDaSA; MoSU. 45-1624

The congregational almanac for the year of our Lord and Saviour Jesus Christ, 1846... Calculated for New England, New York and the Western states. By a congregationalist. Boston: C.C. Dean, 1845. 60 p. MeHi; MdBJ; MnHi; MWA. 45-1625

Congregational almanac. By a congregationalist. Boston, 1845. MHi. 45-1626

Congregational Churches in New Hampshire. Minutes of the general association of New Hampshire, at their annual meeting held in Portsmouth, August 26, 1845. Portsmouth: Charles W. Brewster, 1845. 32 p. ICP. 45-1627

Congregational Churches in Connecticut. Minutes of the General Association of Connecticut, at their meeting in Plainfield: June, 1845. With an appendix, containing the report on the state of religion. New Haven: Printed by J.H. Benham, 1845. 50 p. NcMHi. 45-1628

Congregational Churches in Connecticut. Psalms and hymns for Christian use and worship. Prepared and set forth by the General Association of Connecticut. New Haven: Durie, 1845. 712 p. IEG; MeBat; PPPrHi; RPB. 45-1629

Congregational Churches in Iowa. Constitution, articles of faith, rules of business and general principles of church polity. Burlington: Hawkeye office, 1845. 12 p. IaCrM; MBC; MH; NN; NNUT. 45-1630

Congregational Churches in Massachusetts. Minutes of the general Association of Massachusetts, at their session in Westminister, June, 1845. With the narrative of the state of religion, and the pastoral letter. Boston: Press of Crocker and Brewster, 1845. 58 p. MA; MiD-B. 45-1631

Congregational Churches in Massachusetts. Unfinished report of the Committee on Congregationalism. Boston, 1845. 52 p. MBC. 45-1632

Congregational Churches in Vermont. Extracts from the minutes of the general convention at their session at Danville, June, 1845. Windsor: Chronicle Press, 1845. 28 p. ICP; MiD-B. 45-1633

Connecticut. Journal of the House, of the state of Connecticut, May session,

1845. Hartford: John L. Boswell, 1845. 248 p. Mi; MoU. 45-1634

Connecticut. Journal of the Senate of the state of Connecticut, May session, 1845. Hartford: John L. Boswell, 1845. 270 p. MoU. 45-1635

Connecticut. Legislative roll: rules of the House, Joint Rules of proceedings and joint standing committee. Hartford: John L. Boswell, 1845. Ct. 45-1636

Connecticut. List of insane poor persons who have received aid from the state during the past year. Hartford: John L. Boswell, 1845. 8 p. Ct. 45-1637

Connecticut. Proceedings at the annual convention of the Connecticut Medical Society. Norwich: J.G. Cooley, 1845. 24 p. Ct. 45-1638

Connecticut. Public acts passed by the General Assembly of the state of Connecticut, in the years 1839, 1840, 1841, 1842, and 1843. Hartford: John L. Boswell, 1845. 240 p. IaU-L; In-SC; W. 45-1639

Connecticut. Public acts passed by the General Assembly of the state of Connecticut, May session, 1845. Hartford: John L. Boswell, 1845. 69 p. CSfLaw; IaU-L; NNLI; Wa-L. 45-1640

Connecticut. Report of the Committee on education. Hartford: J.L. Boswell, 1845. 63 p. Ct; CtSoP; CtY; DE; MB. 45-1641

Connecticut. Report of the directors of the Connecticut state prison to the General Assembly. Hartford: John L. Boswell, 1845. 31 p. Ct. 45-1642

Connecticut. Report of the joint select committee to whom was referred that part of the Governor's message relating to the insane poor. Hartford: John L. Boswell, 1845. 13 p. Ct. 45-1643

Connecticut. Report of the joint standing committee on banks to whom was referred the bank commissioners' report. Hartford, 1845. 8 p. Ct; CtSoP; CtY. 45-1644

Connecticut. Resolutions and private acts passed by the General Assembly of the state of Connecticut, May session, 1845. Hartford: John L. Boswell, 1845. 173 p. MdBB. 45-1645

Connecticut. Resolutions and private acts passed by the General Assembly of the state of Connecticut. Hartford: John L. Boswell, 1845. 184 p. Ar-Hi; In-SC; Nv; T; W. 45-1646

Connecticut. Speech of His Excellency, Roger S. Baldwin to the Legislature of the state. Hartford: John L. Boswell, 1845. 20 p. CtSoP; CtY; MB; NNUT. 45-1647

Connecticut. Tabular statement of the number of representatives from the several counties and towns in Connecticut and of the tax paid by each, with the numerical ratio of the representations to the population and to the taxation. Hartford: John L. Boswell, 1845. 8 p. Ct; CtSoP; MB. 45-1648

Connecticut annual register, and United States calendar for the 1845. Hartford: Samuel Green, [1845] 176 p. Ct. 45-1649

Connecticut Washington Total

Abstinence Society. First annual report. New Haven: Peck, White and Peck, 1845. 40 p. CtY; NN. 45-1650

Connecticut Washington Total Abstinence Society. First annual report. New Haven: Storer, 1845. 28 p. CtY; NN. 45-1651

Constitution a pro-slavery compact; or selections from the Madison Papers and etc. Second edition, enlarged. New York: American Anti-slavery Society, 1845. 131 p. KyLx. 45-1652

The constitution and history of the English Church; a catechism for the use of parachial schools. Philadelphia: George and Wayne, 1845. 16 p. NcU. 45-1653

Constitutionality of a bridge at Albany, as shown in the remarks of D. Bull, Jr. and B.F. Butler, and the opinion of Chief Justice Savage in the Troy Bridge Case. Albany, 1845. 20 p. MHi; MH-L. 45-1654

The controversy between Massachusetts and South Carolina. Boston, 1845. NcD. 45-1655

Convention of Friends of Freedom in the Southern and Middle States. Proceedings of the great convention of the friends of freedom in the eastern and middle states, held in Boston, October 1, 2 and 3, 1845. Lowell: Pillsbury and Knap, 1845. 34 p. MB; MLow; NSyU; RPB. 45-1656

Convention of the Friends of Freedom in the Eastern and Middle States, Boston, 1845. Proceedings of the great convention. Lowell: Pillsbury and Knapp,

New edition. 1845. 34 p. CtY; MH; NBuG; OClWHi; RPB. 45-1657

Conversations on common things, or guide to knowledge. For the use of schools and families by a teacher. Boston: Munroe and Francis, 1845. 288 p. MChiA. 45-1658

Conversion of the Earl of Rochester. Philadelphia: Presbyterian Board of Publication, 1845. 28 p. IaDuU-Sem. 45-1659

Cook, Eliza, 1818-1889. The poems of Eliza Cook: Comprising Melaia; together with her miscellaneous pieces... Philadelphia: U. Hunt and son, 1845. 288 p. CtHT-W; MH; MWA; NbU; PU. 45-1660

Cooke, Parsons, 1800-1864. The good minister of Jesus Christ: a sermon preached at the installation of Rev. Willard Child, as pastor of the First Congregational Church in Lowell, October 1, 1845. Lowell, [Massachusetts] Milton Bonney, 1845. 39 p. CSmH; ICN; MBC; NN; RPB. 45-1661

Cooke, Parsons, 1800-1864. A history of German anabaptism, gathered mostly from German writers living in the age of the Lutheran Reformation, and embracing a full view of the peasants' wars, the celestial prophets, and other fanatics of that day, and of the historical connection between the present Baptists and the Anabaptists... Boston: C. Tappan, 1845. 412 p. IGK; KMK; MBC; MsU; NHC-S. 45-1662

Cooke, Parsons, 1800-1864. A parallel between German anabaptism and modern fanticisms, with an antidote to the latter. Boston, 1845. 54 p. MBC; MH-AH. 45-1663

Cookman, George Grimston, 1800-1841. Speeches delivered on various occasions by George C. Cookman, of the Baltimore annual conference, and chaplain to the Senate of the United States. New York: G. Lane and C.B. Tippett, for the Methodist Episcopal Church, 1845. 139 p. NcD; TJaLam. 45-1664

Cooley, Arnold James. A cyclopaedia of several thousand practical receipts and collateral information in the arts, manufactures and trades, including medicine, pharmacy and domestic economy. New York: D. Appleton and company, 1845. 576 p. NRAM; PPL-R. 45-1665

Coolidge, James Ivers Trecothick, 1817-1913. A three years ministry. A sermon preached February 9, 1845, at the Purchase Street Congregational Church, being the third anniversary of his ordination. Boston: Samuel N. Dickinson, 1845. 20 p. CtY; DLC; MH-AH; MiD-B; RPB. 45-1666

Coombe, Pennell. Address at the temperance celebration in Easton, July 4, 1845. Easton, 1845. 18 p. PHi. 45-1667

Coons, George W. The conqueror conquered; or the Christian's triumph over death, a funeral discourse in reference to the death of Mrs. Ann C. Brinkley, wife of Robert C. Brinkley of the city of Memphis. Delivered at Nashville, Tenn., October 26, 1845. Memphis: Eagle Press, 1845. 16 p. T; TxU. 45-1668

Cooper, Astley Paston, 1768-1841. The anatomy and diseases of the breast. To which are added his various surgical papers, now first published in a collected form. Philadelphia: Lea and Blanchard, 1845. 188 p. IaU; NcU; PPi; RNR; Vi. 45-1669

Cooper, Astley Paston, 1768-1841. The anatomy of the thymus gland, by Sir Astley Cooper. From the last London edition. Philadelphia: Lea and Blanchard, 1845. 37 p. ViU. 45-1670

Cooper, Collin Campbell. Identities of light and heat of caloric and electricity... Philadelphia: Grigg, 1845. 96 p. PHi; PPAN; PPL; PU. 45-1671

Cooper, James Fenimore, 1789-1851. The chainbearer; or the littlepage manuscripts. Boston: Houghton, Mifflin and company, 1845. 467 p. MF. 45-1672

Cooper, James Fenimore, 1789-1851. The chainbearer; or the littlepage manuscripts. New York: Burgess, Stringer and Company, 1845. 2 v. CSmH. 45-1673

Cooper, James Fenimore, 1789-1851. The chainbearer; or the littlepage manuscripts. First edition. New York: Burgess, Stringer and company, 1845. 2 v. CtHWatk; MHa; MWA; PPL-R; WM. 45-1674

Cooper, James Fenimore, 1789-1851. The deerslayer; or the first warpath. A tale. Philadelphia: Lea and Blanchard, 1845. 2 v. in 1. NCosh; NN; PJA; PPL. 45-1675

Cooper, James Fenimore, 1789-1851. The history of the navy of the United States of America; abridged in one volume. Philadelphia: Thomas, Cowperthwait and company, 1845. 447 p. IG; MSa; NjR; ViU. 45-1676

Cooper, James Fenimore, 1789-1851. Homeward bound; or the chase. A tale of the sea. New York: Burgess, Stringer, and company, 1845. 2 v. in 1. CtY; RPB. 45-1677

Cooper, James Fenimore, 1789-1851. Mercedes of Castile; or the voyage to Cathay. New York: Bugess, Stringer and company, 1845. 2 v. in 1. MB; MeB. 45-1678

Cooper, James Fenimore, 1789-1851. Ned Myers; or a life before the mast; edited by J. Fenimore Cooper, in one volume. New York: Stringer and Townsend, 1845. 232 p. WM. 45-1679

Cooper, James Fenimore, 1789-1851. Notions of the Americans; picked up by a traveling bachelor. New edition. Philadelphia: Lea and Blanchard, 1845. 2 v. in 1. KyLo; OCY; ViU. 45-1680

Cooper, James Fenimore, 1789-1851. The pioneers; or the sources of the Susquehanna. Philadelphia: Lea and Blanchard, 1845. 2 v. in 1. MWinchrHi; NcDaD; NCosh; PPL. 45-1681

Cooper, James Fenimore, 1789-1851. The prairie. New York: Printed by Hurst, 1845. 483 p. PAlt-K. 45-1682

Cooper, James Fenimore, 1789-1851. The red rover, a tale. New edition. New York: Burgess, Stringer, and company, 1845. 2 v. RPB. 45-1683

Cooper, James Fenimore, 1789-1851. Satanstoe; or the littlepage manuscripts.

A tale of the colony. New York: Burgess, Stringer and company, 1845. 2 v. CtY; MnU; MWA; OClWHi; RPAt. 45-1684

Cooper, James Fenimore, 1789-1851. The spy. A tale of the neutral ground. New York: Burgess, Stringer and company, 1845. 2 v. DLC; MdBE. 45-1685

Cooper, James Fenimore, 1789-1851. The spy; a tale of the neutral ground. A new edition. New York: Burgess, Stringer and company, 1845. 2 v. DLC. 45-1686

Cooper, James Fenimore, 1789-1851. The two admirals. A tale. New York: Burgess, Stringer and company, 1845. 2 v. CtY. 45-1687

Cooper, James Fenimore, 1789-1851. The two admirals. A tale. New York: Burgess, Stringer, and company, 1845. 2 v. in 1. CtY; GEU. 45-1688

Cooper, James Fenimore, 1789-1851. Wing and wing; or Le Feu Follet; a tale. In two volumes. New York: Burgess, Stringer and company, 1845. 2 v. in 1. GEU. 45-1689

Cooper, James Fenimore, 1789-1851. Wyandotte, or the hutted knoll, a tale. Philadelphia: Lea and Blanchard, 1845. 2 v. MeB. 45-1690

Cooper, Joseph T. True issue, or the confession of faith and the associate testimony, in reference to the civil magistrate's power in matters of religion, compared; with an inquiry as to the propriety of altering the former. Philadelphia: Young, 1845. PHi; PPPr-Hi. 45-1691

Cooper, Samuel, 1780-1848. A dictionary of practical surgery from the seventh London edition, revised, corrected, and enlarged. With numerous notes and additions... together with a supplementary index, in which the science is brought down to the present period by D.M. Reese. New York: Harper and brothers, 1845. LNB; MB; MoS; NClsM; NNN. 45-1692

Cooper, Samuel, 1789-1876. A concise system of instructions and regulations for the militia and volunteers of the United States. New edition, with additions and improvements. Philadelphia: Frank Desilver, 1845. 303 p. MBMHiM; MH; MWHi; WU. 45-1693

Cooper, Thomas, 1759-1839. On the connection between geology and the Pentakuch, in a letter of Prof. Tilliman, from Thomas Cooper... To which is added an appendix. Boston: Abner Kneeland, 1845. 72 p. IEN-M; OO; TxDaM. 45-1694

Copeland, B.F. Report of a committee of citizens of Roxbury against the adoption of the city form of government. n.p., [1845] MBAt. 45-1695

Copeland, John. A discourse, preached on the funeral occasion of the Rev. Charles Sherman, Troy, New York, March 12, 1844. Published by special request of the offical board of North Second Street Church; viz. where Mr. Sherman had held his pastoral charge. Canandaigua: Printed by George L. Whitney, 1845. 32 p. CtMW; N; PPPrHi. 45-1696

Copley, Esther Hewlett. Kind words for the kitchen; or illustrations of humble life. New York: M.W. Dodd, 1845. 263 p. MPiB; NN. 45-1697

Copper Falls Mining Company. Articles of association and agreement. Boston: S.N. Dickinson and company, 1845. 10 p. MH-BA; Mi. 45-1698

The coral maker. Revised by D.P. Kidder. New York: G. Lane and C.B. Tippett, 1845. 2 parts. NNC. 45-1699

Cormenin, Louis Marie de Lahaye, 1788-1868. The history of the popes, their crime, murders, poisonings, parricides, adulteries and incests, from St. Peter to Gregory the sixteenth, including the history of the Saints, martyrs, fathers of the church... Philadelphia: Campbell, 1845. MWA; PPiW; PPPrHi. 45-1700

Cornaro, Louis, 1467-1566. The discourses and letters of Louis Cornaro, on a sober and a temperate life. With a biography of the author by Piero Maroncelli, and notes and an appendix by John Burdell. New York: Fowlers, 1845. PPPrHi. 45-1701

Cornell, Silas. A description of Silas Cornell's improved terrestrial globe, with the manner of using it. Intended for the use of schools, academies, and families. Second edition. Rochester: Published by the author, 1845. 36 p. CSt; CtY; MNBedf; N. 45-1702

Correctional Association of New York. First report of the Prision Association of New York including the Constitution and bylaws and a list of officers and members. New York: Published by the association, 1845. 138 p. NBuG; RPB. 45-1703

Correspondence on the subject of life and death. Boston: J.P. Mendum, 1845. 81 p. ICMe. 45-1704

Cotter, John Rogerson. The mass and rubrics of the Roman Catholic Church. Translated into English with notes and remarks. New York: D. Appleton and company, 1845. 177 p. ICU; LN; MH; NN; TxU. 45-1705

Cottom's Virginia and North Carolina almanack for 1846. Calculations by David Richardson. Richmond, Virginia: Peter Cottom, [1845] MWA; Vi. 45-1706

Cotton, Henry G. A treatise on the powers and duties of justices of the peace in the state of Illinois. Ottawa, [Illinois] published by the author, 1845. 548 p. CSmH; ICL; IP. 45-1707

Cotton from the pod to the factory; a popular view of the natural and domestic history of the plant, the adaption and improvement of the cotton factory to its present state of perfection. New York: Homans and Ellis, 1845. 77 p. MBC; NBuG; NcD; NN. 45-1708

Cotton lord... New York: Dagger, 1845. 120 p. CtHT. 45-1709

Couch, Paul. The duty of sinners to make themselves a new heart. A sermon. Boston: Jordon and Wiley, 1845. 12 p. MBC; NjPT. 45-1710

Count Ludwig, and other romances. With stories by Douglas Jerrold, Thomas Moore, the poet, W.H. Ainsworth, and Allen Cunningham. Now first collected into a single volume. New York: Published by H.G. Daggers, 1845. 120 p. DSG; NjP; RPB. 45-1711

Country walks for little folks. Philadelphia: Smith and Peck, 1845. 191 p. CtY; MB; NUt. 45-1712

The covenanter; devoted to the principles of the Reformed Presbyterian Church. Philadelphia, 1845. ICP; MH; NIC; PHi; PPPrHi. 45-1713

Covington, Kentucky. Licking Valley Register. Address of the carrier of the Licking Valley Register to its patrons Covington, January 1, 1846, [1845? Broadside. NbHi. 45-1714

Cowell, Joseph, 1792-1863. Thirty years passed among the players in England and America: interspersed with anecdotes and reminiscences of a variety of persons directly or indirectly connected with the drama during the theatrical life of Joe Cowell, comedian. Written by himself New York: Harper and brothers, 1845 103 p. CtY; MH; PU. 45-1715

Cowper, Thomas, 1731-1800. The works of Cowper and Thomson; including many letters and poems. Philadelphia: Grigg and Elliot, 1845. 573 p. CSmH; MdW; NBuCC; ODaM. 45-1716

Cowper, William, 1731-1800. The task; a poem, for the use of schools and academies. Boston: Phillips and Sampson, 1845. MH; NjP; PPF. 45-1717

Cowper, William, 1731-1800. The task, and other poems; by William Cowper, with numerous illustrations, engraved by Chenney, Cushman, etc. from the drawing by John Gilbert. Philadelphia: Carey and Hart, 1845. 324 p. MBBC; MH; MLy; NCaS; PPF. 45-1718

Cox, Abraham L. The rejected article,

in reply to Dr. S.P. White's "Case of tumor of the shoulder," in the May number of the New York Journal of Medicine and Science. New York: Printed for the author, 1845. [3]-35 p. CtY; NBMS; Nh; NNN; PPCP. 45-1719

Cox, Edward Jenner. Practical treatise on medical inhalation, with numerous cases demonstrating the curative powers of the local application of various remedies in bronchitis, consumption, and other diseases of the respiratory organs. Second edition. Philadelphia: Penington, 1845. 117 p. NNNAM; PPCP; PPHPI. 45-1720

Cox, Francis Augustus, 1783-1853. History of the English Baptist Missionary Society, from A.D. 1792 to A.D. 1842. Boston: W.S. Damrell, 1845. 2 v. in 1. Ct; ICU; MB; MNtCA; Nh. 45-1721

Coxe, Arthur Cleveland, 1818-1896. Hallowe'en, a romount with lays meditative and devotional. Hartford: H.S. Parsons, 1845. 189 p. CtY; MiD; NNC; OO; ViU. 45-1722

Coxe, Arthur Cleveland, 1818-1896. Saul, a mystery. New York: D. Appleton and company; Hartford: H.S. Parsons, 1845. 297 p. ICU; MH; NNG; PP; TxU. 45-1723

Coxe, John Redman. Considerations respecting the recognition of friends in another world; on the affirmed descent of Jesus Christ into hell; on phrenology in connexion with the soul, end on the existence of a soul in brutes. Philadelphia: George S. Appleton, 1845. 89 p. ICU; MBC; NjPT; OrPD; TNV. 45-1724

Coxe, Margaret, b. 1800. Floral emblems; or moral sketches from flowers... Cincinnati: H.N. Derby and company; New York: D. Appleton and company, 1845. 144 p. CtY; MBAt; OO; PU; RPB. 45-1725

Coxe, Margaret, b. 1800. Young lady's companion, and token of affection, in a series of letters. Second edition. Columbus: I.N. Whiting. 348 p. MH. 45-1726

Coxe, Margaret, b. 1800. Young lady's companion, and token of affection, in a series of letters. Third edition. Columbus: I.N. Whiting, 1845. 348 p. FWpR; MsNF; MWA; OClWHi. 45-1727

Coxe, Richard Smith, 1792-1865. Review of the relations between the United States and Mexico, and of the claims of citizens of the United States against Mexico. Washington: Ritchie and Heiss, 1845. 71 p. CSmH; DLC; MdBP; MH; NN. 45-1728

Coyle, Fitzhugh. Letter to the President of the United States, respecting certain debts due by the Post Office Department, and the conduct of P.G. Washington, auditor in relation thereto. [Washington? 1845?] DLC; PHi. 45-1729

Coyle, R. Map of Liberia; compiled from data on file in the office of the American Colonization Society under the direction of W. McLain. Baltimore: Weber, 1845. MB; MdBJ; PPAmP; PPL. 45-1730

Crabb, George, 1778-1851. English synonymes explained in alphabetical order, with copious illustrations and examples drawn from the best writers... New York and London: Harper and brothers, 1845. 535 p. CBPSR; DLC; IEG; MnHi; NNG. 45-1731

Crabbe, George, 1754-1832. The poetical works of Crabbe, Heber, and Pollok, completed in one volume. Philadelphia: Grigg and Elliot, 1845. 396 p. CtW; CtY; GA; LNT; O. 45-1732

Cranch, Christopher Pearse, 1813-1892. Address delivered before the Harvard Musical Association, in the chapel of the University at Cambridge, August 28, 1845. Printed at the request of the society. Boston: Printed by S.N. Dickinson and company, 1845. 21 p. CtY; MB; MBAt. 45-1733

Cranfield, Richard. The useful Christian: a memoir of Thomas Cranfield, for about fifty years a devoted Sunday school teacher. Revised by the Committee of publication of the American Sunday School Union. Philadelphia: American Sunday School Union, 1845. 5-227 p. NN. 45-1734

Cravath, Oren, 1806-1874. A case of withdrawal from the Presbyterian Church with the reasons for so doing. Cortland Village, 1845. 16 p. DLC; MBC. 45-1735

Craven, Henry Thornton, 1818-1905. Done brown; a farce in one act. New York: Samuel French, [1845?] 20 p. OCl. 45-1736

Crawford, Gilbert. A humble enquiry into the subject of regeneration by motives: being an essay delivered before the Presbytery of Genesee, by order, at Perry, Wyoming County, New York, on September 9, 1845. Rochester: Printed

by McConnell and Curtis, 1845. 31 p CSmH; MBC; NN. 45-1737

Crawford, Lucy. The history of the White Mountains from the first settlement of Upper Coos and Pequaket. By Lucy, wife of Ethan Allen Crawford Portland: F.A. and A.F. Garrish, 1845 228 p. MHi. 45-1738

Crazy Jane; or the melancholy fate of Jane Henry, who, ruined and abandoned by a faithless lover, is tempted to a most heinous [sic] crime, and banished from her father's house under her ill treatment and the influence of shame and remorse becomes a maniac... New York, 1845. 14 p. NoLoc. 45-1739

Creighton, Andrew, 1790-1855. The history of Arabia, ancient and modern; containing a description of the country, an account of its inhabitants... and a comprehensive view of its natural history... New York: Harper and brothers, 1845. 2 v. InCW; OO; OSW; RWe; ScNC. 45-1740

Crihfield, Arthur. Orations on the origin and destiny of man, on the evidences of the Christian religion and on the reformation of society. Second edition. Cincinnati, 1845. 303 p. OCHP. 45-1741

Crittenden, A.F. Inductive and practical system of double entry bookkeeping on an entirely new plan containing twelve sets of books. Philadelphia: E.C. and J. Biddle, 1845. 208 p. CtY; DLC; MB; MH; PU. 45-1742

Crittenden, A.F. An inductive and practical system of double entry bookkeeping on an entirely new plan. Having a general rule, deduced from the definition of debtor and creditor, applied to the journalizing of all transactions: containing twelve sets of books for imparting a general knowledge of the science. School edition. Philadelphia: E. and S. Biddle, 1845. 131 p. NSyHi. 45-1743

Crocker, William P. Map of the Boston, Concord and Montreal Railroad from Concord to Haverhill, N.H., July, 1845. Boston, 1845. 97 p. MB; Nh-Hi. 45-1744

Crockett, David, 1786-1836. An account of Col. Crockett's tour to the north and down east in the year of our Lord 1834. New York: Nafis and Cornish, 1845. 234 p. OO; RP; TxU; WaU 45-1745

Crockett, David, 1786-1836. The life of Martin Van Buren, heir-apparent to the government and the appointed successor of General Andrew Jackson... New York: Nafis and Cornish, 1845. 209 p. DeWi; LU; MiGr; OU; RP. 45-1746

Crockett, David, 1786-1836. A narrative of the life of David Crockett, of the state of Tennessee... Written by himself. New York: Nafis and Cornish; Philadelphia: John B. Perry, 1845. 211 p. DLC; MsOk; MMilt; NjR; RP. 45-1747

Crockett's almanac for 1846. Boston: James Fisher, [1845] MWA. 45-1748

Crockett's almanac for 1846. Philadelphia: Turner and Fisher, [1845] MWA. 45-1749

Croes, Robert Brown. The anniversary lecture, pronounced before the historical society of the county of Vigo, Indiana, on March 14, 1844... rector of St. Stephen's Church, Terre Haute. Cincinnati: Printed by R.P. Donogh and company, 1845. 23 p. CSmH; In; MBAt; NNC; PPPrHi. 45-1750

Croghan, John. Rambles in the Mommoth cave during the year 1844. By a visitor. Louisville, Kentucky: Morton and Griswold, 1845. IaDaM; KyRe; MdBE; NN; ViU. 45-1751

Croly, George, 1780-1860. Life and times of his late majesty George the Fourth. With anecdotes of distinguished persons of the last fifty years. New and improved. New York: Harper and brothers, 1845. 414 p. CtB; InCW; LN; OCX; PU. 45-1752

Croly, George, 1780-1860. Marston; or the memoirs of a statesman. Complete in one volume. Philadelphia: Lea and Blanchard, 1845. 255 p. CtY; LNHT; MB; MH; OFH. 45-1753

Crompton, Susan Fanny. Stories for Sunday afternoons. From the creation to the advent of the Messiah. Boston, [1845?] MH. 45-1754

Cromwell, Oliver, 1599-1658. Letters and speeches; edited by Thomas Carlyle. New York: Wiley and Putnam, 1845. 2 v. DLC; MnM; MWA; OrPR; PPA. 45-1755

Cromwell, Oliver, 1599-1658. Oliver Cromwell's letters and speeches with elucidations. By Thomas Carlyle. New York: Wiley and Putnam, 1845. 2 v. CtB; LNH; MWal; PPL-R; WU. 45-1756

Cross, Jeremy L., 1783-1861. The templar's chart or hieroglyphic monitor; containing all the emblems and hieroglyphics explained in the valiant and magnanimour order of Knights of the Red Cross, Knights Templars and Knights of Malta to which are added lessons, exhortations, prayers, charges, songs. Second edition with improvements. New York: Jeremy L. Cross, 1845. 223 p. IEG; MBevHi; OClJC; PPFM; Tx-BrdD. 45-1757

Cross, Robert B. An anniversary lecture, pronounced before the Historical Society of the county of Vigo, Indiana, 14th of March, 1844. Cincinnati: R.P. Donogh and company, 1845. 23 p. NNUT. 45-1758

Croswell, Harry, 1778-1858. A manual of family prayer; adapted to the various seasons of the ecclesiastical year; with prayers and thanksgiving, for special occasions. Second edition, revised and corrected. New Haven: S. Babcock, 1845. 248 p. CtMW; DLC; InID; NBu; PPM. 45-1759

Croswell, William, 1804-1851. Church of the Advent. A letter to the Bishop of Massachusetts, occasioned by his late letter to the clergy. Together with the resolutions of the wardens and vestry. Boston: Printed by Tuttle and Dennett, 1845. 28 p. DLC; MWA; NjR; PPL; RPB. 45-1760

Crouch, Frederick William Nicholls, 1808-1896. Kathleen Mavourneen. New York, [1845] CtY. 45-1761

Crowe, John Finley, 1787-1850. A review of Mr. MacMaster's speech before the synod of Indiana, October 4, 1844. Madison, [Wisconsin] Jones and Lodge, 1845. 28 p. In; IU; NjPT; NNUT; PPPrHi. 45-1762

Crowen, T.J. Every lady's book; an in-

structor in the art of making every variety of plain and fancy cakes, pastry, confectionary, blanc mange, jellies, ice creams, also, for the cooking of meats, vegetables, etc. By a lady of New York. New York: J.K. Wellman, 1845. 144 p. IHi; MH; NPV. 45-1763

Crowen, T.J. The management of the sick room. Compiled from the latest medical authorities, by a lady of New York under approval of Charles A. Lee. Third edition. New York, 1845. 107 p. DSG; IEN-M; MH; MWA; NbU. 45-1764

Crown Point, New York. First Congregational Church. Confession of faith and covenant of the First Congregational Church. Organized September 10, 1804. Troy, 1845. NoLoc. 45-1765

Cruden, Alexander, 1701-1770. A complete concordance to the Holy Scriptures with an introduction by the Rev. David King. New edition. Boston: Gould, 1845. 568 p. IEG; LN; OC. 45-1766

Cruden, Alexander, 1701-1770. A complete concordance to the Holy Scriptures with an introduction by the Rev. David King. Third edition. Boston: Gould, Kendall and Lincoln, 1845. 563 p. FE NHunt; OO. 45-1767

Cruden, Alexander, 1701-1770. A complete concordance to the Holy scriptures, by Alexander Cruden. A new and condensed edition with an introduction by the Rev. David King. New York: Lewis Colby, 1845. 568 p. WStfSF. 45-1768

Cruel boy, and other pieces. Worcester: J. Grant, Jr. [1845- 1847?] 16 p. MWA. 45-1769

Cruikshank, George, 1792-1878. The bachelor's own book, being twenty-four passages in the life of Mr. Lambkin. Boston: Redding and company, 1845. 24 p. CtY; MBevHi; MdBP; MH. 45-1770

Cruikshank, George, 1792-1878. George Cruikshank's omnibus a vehicle for frolic and fun. Philadelphia: E. Ferret and company, 1845. 72 p. CtY; ICU. 45-1771

Cruikshank, George, 1792-1878. More good wings from Cruikshank's Omnibus; a vehicle for fun and frolic. Philadelphia: E. Ferrett and company, 1845. 72 p. MH; PHi. 45-1772

Crump, William Hanby. The world in a pocket book; or universal popular statistics. Third edition, enlarged and improved, with appendix, of changes and events, down to the present time. Philadelphia: Appleton, 1845. 195 p. LNHT; MBC; NGlc; NPV; ViR. 45-1773

Crump, William Hanby. The world in a pocket book; or universal popular statistics. Fourth edition, enlarged and improved, with appendix, of changes and events, down to the present time. Philadelphia: Appleton, 1845. 195 p. MB; MH; PPL-R; RPB; TWcW. 45-1774

Cruttenden, David Henry, 1816-1874. The systematic arithmetic, or arithmetic arranged in its natural order. Schenectady: L. Riggs, 1845. 280 p. DLC. 45-1775

Cultivator almanac. by Luther Tucker. New York: W.H. Carey and company, 1845. MWA. 45-1776

Cultivator almanac. By Luther Tucker.

Richead [sic] Long Island: G.O. Wells, 1845. MWA. 45-1777

Cultivator almanac for 1846. By Luther Tucker. Albany, New York: Andrew Leighton, [1845] MWA. 45-1778

Cultivator almanac for 1846. By Luther Tucker. Albany, New York: Luther Tucker, [1845] MWA; PHi; WHi. 45-1779

Cultivator almanac for 1846. By Luther Tucker. East Rutland, Vermont: W.E.C. Stoddard, [1845] MWA. 45-1780

Cultivator almanac for 1846. By Luther Tucker. New York: Mark H. Newman, [1845] MWA. 45-1781

Cultivator almanac for 1846. By Luther Tucker. New York: Payne and Burgess, [1845] MWA. 45-1782

Cultivator almanac for 1846. By Luther Tucker. New York: William K. Cornwell, [1845] MiU; MWA. 45-1783

Cultivator almanac for 1846. By Luther Tucker. Rochester: Samuel Hamilton... [1845?] NBuHi. 45-1784

Cultivator almanac for 1846. By Luther Tucker. Rochester: William Alling, [1845?] NRU. 45-1785

Cumberland University. Lebanon, Tennessee. Catalogue of the officers and students of Cumberland University. Lebanon, Tennessee, 1845. 8 p. MHi; T. 45-1786

Cuming, Francis H. Christian resignation: a sermon delivered at the Presbyterian Church, Ann Arbor, Michigan, at the funeral of Col. William A. Abel, September 19, 1843. Troy, New York: From the press of J.C. Kneeland and company, 1845. 19 p. MiD-B; NN. 45-1787

Cumings, Samuel. The western pilot; containing charts of the Ohio River and of the Mississippi, from the mouth of the Missouri to the Gulf of Mexico; accompanied with directions for navigating the same, and a gazetter. Revised and corrected every year by Capts. Charles Ross and John Klinefelter. Cincinnati: C. Conclin, 1845. 144 p. KU; MnM; NN; OClWHi. 45-1788

Cumming, Hiram. Secret history of the perfidies, intrigues and corruptions of the Tyler Dynasty, with the Mysteries of Washington City, connected with that vile administration, in a series of letters... Washington and New York: Published by the author, 1845. 64 p. DLC; MB; MBAt; NCH; Vi. 45-1789

Cundall, Joseph, 1818-1895. Tales of the Kings of England: Richard II to Elizabeth. New York: Wiley and Putnam, 1845. 224 p. MGrovLA. 45-1790

Cunningham, A.C. The mystery of disease revealed; or guide to the inexperienced; the origin and progression of diseases, and their effectual remedies, or the confidential doctor at home. New York, 1845. 101 p. DNLM; DSG. 45-1791

Cunningham, John William, 1780-1861. World without souls. Second edition. New York and Pittsburg: Robert Carter, 1845. 177 p. NN; NN-As. 45-1792

Cunynghame, Arthur Augustus Thur-low. The opium war; being recollections of service in China. Philadelphia: G.B. Zieber and company, 1845. 25-271 p. CU; MBAt; NNS; OUrC; RNR. 45-1793

Curr, Joseph, d. 1847. Familiar instructions in the faith and morality of the Catholic Church compiled from the works of the most approved Catholic writers. From the fourth Dublin edition revised and corrected. Boston: Patrick Donahoe, 1845. 152 p. ICLay; MdBS; MoFloSS. 45-1794

Currier, Edward. The political text book; containing the Declaration of Independence with the lives of the signers; the farewell addresses of George Washington and Andrew Jackson.... Cooperstown: E. Phinney, 1845. 512 p. NJost; NN. 45-1795

Curwen, Samuel, 1715-1802. Journal and letters of the late Samuel Curwen, judge of admiralty, etc., a loyalist refugee in England... Third edition. By George Atkinson Ward. New York: Leavitt, Trow and company, 1845. 672 p. InFtw; MdHi; MiD-B; NcD; ScCF. 45-1796

Cushing, Luther Stearns, 1803-1856. Charge to the jury in causpriocy case. Commonwealth vs. W.P. Eastman, et al. Boston, 1845. MH. 45-1797

Cushing, Luther Stearns, 1803-1856. Manual of parliamentary practice. Rules of proceedings and debate in deliberative assemblies. Boston: W.J. Reynolds, 1845. 173 p. CSmH; MB; MH; MH- AH; RPAt. 45-1798

Cushing, Luther Stearns, 1803-1856. Manual of parliamentary practice. Rules of proceedings and debate in deliberative assemblies. Second edition. Boston: Reynolds, 1845. 173 p. Ct; MB; MBAt; MSSC; MWA. 45-1799

Cushing, Luther Stearns, 1803-1856. Manual of parliamentary parctice. Rules of proceedings and debate in deliberative assemblies. Fourth edition. Boston: Reynolds, 1845. 173 p. IaU; ICU; MH; OO; TxU. 45-1800

Cushman, Robert Woodward, 1800-1868. A pure Christianity the world's only hope. New York: Lewis Colby, 1845. 115 p. IaDmU; NjHo; PCA; RPB; ViRU. 45-1801

Cushman, Robert Woodward, 1800-1868. A pure christianity the world's only hope. Third edition. New York: Published by Lewis Colby, 1845. 115 p. TxHuT. 45-1802

Cutter, Calvin, 1807-1872. Anatomy and physiology designed for schools and families. With 150 engravings. Boston: Printed by S.N. Dickinson and company,

1845. 262 p. CtHWatk; DLC; MH-M; MLy; WU-M. 45-1803

Cutter, Calvin, 1807-1872. Physiological family physician. West Brookfield: Merriam and Cook, printers, 1845. 218 p. MH-M; MWA; RPB. 45-1804

Cutting, James A. A short treatise on the care and management of bees and the construction of the changeable bee-hive. Bradford, Vermont: A.B.F. Hildreth, 1845. VtMidbC. 45-1805

The cyclopaedia of practical medicine: comprising a treatise on the nature and treatment of diseases, materia medica and therapeutics, medical jurisprudence, etc. Edited by John Forbes. Philadelphia: Lea and Blanchard, 1845. 4 v. MdUM; ScCoB; ViRA. 45-1806

Czerny, Carl. Piano-forte instructor. Boston: Howe, [1845] MQ. 45-1807

D

Daboll, Nathan, 1750-1818. Daboll's complete schoolmaster's assistant: being a plain comprehensive system of practical arithmetic, adapted to the use of schools in the United States. New London, Connecticut: Bolles and Williams, 1845. 249 p. DAU. 45-1808

Dagg, John Leadley, 1794-1884. An essay in defence of strict communion. Penfield, [Georgia] Printed by B. Brantley, 1845. 74 p. GU; NCH-S; NjPT. 45-1809

Dahlmann, Fredrich Christoph. The history of the English revolution. Translated from the German by H.E. Lloyd. Frankfort, Ohio: M.C. Jungel, 1845. InU. 45-1810

Daily, William Mitchell, 1812-1877. Discourses from the pulpit. Cincinnati: R.W. Carroll and company, 1845. 306 p. LU; MsJPED. 45-1811

Daily bread. Philadelphia: Presbyterian board, 1845. MWiW. 45-1812

Daily times. May 1, 1845-March 24, 1846. Washington City, [1845-1846] DLC; ICU. 45-1813

The daily union. Washington, 1845-1859. DLC; ICU; NR; PHi; TxU. 45-1814

Daily's universal gazetteer. A dictionary, geographical, historical and statistical. Fourth edition. Philadelphia and New York, 1845. 988 p. DLC. 45-1815

Dakin, Samuel D. Brief sketch of the plan of a sectional floating dry dock combined with a permanent stone basin and platform... New York: Printed by P. Miller, 1845. 93 p. DLC; IaB; LNH; NNE; PReaHi. 45-1816

Dallam, James Wilmer, 1818-1847. A digest of the laws of Texas: containing a full and complete compilation of the land laws; together with the opinions of the Supreme Court. [1840-1844] Baltimore: Printed by J.D. Toy, 1845. [9]-632 p. DLC; OCLaw; PPB; RPL; WaU. 45-1817

Dallam, James Wilmer, 1818-1847. The lone star: a tale of Texas; founded upon incidents in the history of Texas... New York, Philadelphia: E. Ferrett and company, 1845. 95 p. DLC; RPAt; Tx; TxGr. 45-1818

Dallas, George Mifflin, 1792-1864. Obsequies in honor of Andrew Jackson. Eulogium, on the occasion of the Jackson obsequies at Washington Square, in the city of Philadelphia, June 26, 1845, with a notice of the civic and military procession on that day. Philadelphia: Mifflin and Parry, printers, 1845. 16 p. MiD-B; OCHP; PHi; PPL; PPM. 45-1819

Dalzel, Andrew, 1742-1806. Analekta hellenika or collectanea graeca minora;

with notes, partly compiled and partly written by Andrew Dalzel. Sixth American edition. New York: Dean, 1845. 299 p. IaDmD; LNL; MNS; OClW; PU. 45-1820

Dalzel, Andrew, 1742-1806. Collectanea Graeca majora, ad usum academicae juventutis accommadoata... Fourth edition. Philadelphia: Thomas, 1845. 2 v. MH; MiU; NcU; NPV; PMA. 45-1821

Dana, Daniel, 1771-1859. A discourse delivered in the First Presbyterian Church in Newburyport, on November 19, 1844, it being the fiftieth anniversary of the author's ordination. Newburyport, [Massachusetts] John G. Tilton, 1845. 32 p. CSmH; IU; MNe; OClWHi; TxU. 45-1822

Dana, Edmund L. Address delivered before the Mathetean Society, Wyoming Seminary, Kingston... Pennsylvania. Wilkes Barre, 1845. 14 p. NjPT. 45-1823

Dana, James Dwight, 1813-1895. Notice of Dr. Blum's treatise on pseudomorphous minerals and observations on pseudomorphism. New Haven, 1845. 28 p. MH-Z; NNC; PPAN. 45-1824

Dana, James Dwight, 1813-1895. Origin of the constituent and adventitial minerals of trap and the allied rocks, by James D. Dana; extracted from the American journal of science. New Haven: B.L. Hamlen, 1845. 18 p. ICJ; ICU; NNN; PPAN. 45-1825

Dana, Joseph, 1769-1849. Liber primus, or first book of Latin exercises. To which have been added, colloquies from Erasmus; with a vocabulary. Fifteenth edi-

tion, revised and corrected. Boston, 1845. 252 p. TxBrdD. 45-1826

Dana, Richard Henry, 1815-1882. Seaman's friend; containing a treatise on practical seamanship... a dictionary of sea terms. Fourth edition. Boston: Charles C. Little and James Brown; New York: Mark H. Newman and E. and G.W. Blunt; Philadelphia: Carey and Hart, 1845. MNan; MSaP. 45-1827

Dana, William Coombs, 1810-1880. A transatlantic tour; comprising travels in Great Britain, France, Holland, Belgium, German, Switzerland and Italy. Philadelphia: Perkins and Purves, 1845. 391 p. MBC; MWH; Nh; PPL-R; ScSoh. 45-1828

Daniel, Henry, 1786-1873. Trial of H. Daniel, for the murder of Clifton R. Thomson. Compend of the testimony, with the concluding argument on the part of the commonwealth by M.V. Thomson. Cincinnati, 1845. NIC-L; PP; PPB. 45-1829

Daniell, Edmund Robert, d. 1854. A treatise on the practice of the High court of the chancery, with some practical observations on the pleading in that court. From the London edition. Harrisburg: M'Kinley and Lescure, 1845-46. 3 v. CtY; DLC; MiU-L; NjR; WaU-L. 45-1830

Daniels, William M. A correct account of the murder of Generals Joseph and Hyrum Smith at Carthage on June 27, 1844. Mauvoo, Illinois: J. Taylor, 1845. 24 p. CoD; CSmH; IHi; NHCS; UU. 45-1831

Dante, Alighieri, 1265-1321. The vision: or hell, purgatory, and paradise, of Dante Alighieri. Translated by the Rev. Henry Francis Cary. New York: D. Appleton and company, 1845. 587 p. LNB; MeAu; NCH; PHC; RPAt. 45-1832

Danvers, Massachusetts. South Church. The articles of faith and covenant of the South Church, Danvers; with a list of the members. Salem: Salem Observer Press, 1845. 11 p. MBNEH; MPeHi; WHi. 45-1833

Danvers, Massachusetts. Unitarian Church. Order of exercises at the Unitarian Church in Danvers... November 1, in the 97th year of his age. Danvers: Danvers Courier Press, [1845] Broadside. MPeHi. 45-1834

Danville, Kentucky. Centre College. Annual catalogue. Danville, Kentucky: J.F. Zimmermann and J.J. Barbee, printers, 1845. 15 p. NjPT. 45-1835

Daring exploits and perilous adventures; being a record of thrilling narratives, heroic achievements, hazardous enterprises, etc. Hartford: Ezra Strong, 1845. 504 p. MWHi. 45-1836

De darkie's comic all-me-nig for 1846. Calculated by David Young. Pennsylvania: Colon and Adriance, [1845] DLC; MWA; WHi. 45-1837

De darkie's comic all-me-nig for 1846. Calculated by David Young. Philadelphia: Turner and Fisher, [1845] MB; MWA; RPB. 45-1838

De darkie's comic all-me-nig for 1846. Calendar by David Young, Philomath. Boston: James Fisher, [1845] MWA. 45-1839

Darley, William Henry Westray, 1801-1872. Cantus ecclesiae; or the sacred chorister, being a collection of... the best standard compositions... many original composition, by American authors. Second edition. Philadelphia: Thomas, Cowperthwait and company, 1845. 300 p. MB; MH; NBuDD; NNG; PP. 45-1840

Darley, William Henry Westray, 1801-1872. Cantus ecclesiae, or the sacred chorister; being a collection of psalm and hymn tunes, chants, sentences, and anthems. With a system of instruction in vocal music by L. Meignen. Third edition. Philadelphia: Thomas, Cowperthwait and company, 1845. 300 p. MHi. 45-1841

Darling, Noyes. An address upon injurious insects; delivered before the New Haven Horticultural Society, October 1, 1845. New Haven: J.H. Benham, 1845. 51 p. CtY; MBHo; MH; MiD-B; NUtHi. 45-1842

Darrach, William, 1796-1865. Lectures on medical obedience, introductory to the course of theory and practice of medicine in the medical department of Pennsylvania College, Philadelphia, for the session of 1845-1846. Philadelphia: Barrett and Jones, 1845. 15 p. CSt-L; DLC; NNC-M; NNNAM; PHi. 45-1843

Dartmouth College. Catalogue of the officers and students for 1845-6. Hanover: Printed at the Dartmouth Press, 1845. 24 p. MWHi. 45-1844

D'Arusmont, Frances Wright, 1795-1852. Biography, notes and political letters of Frances Wright D'Arusmont. From the first British Edition. New

York: John Windt, 1845. 2 v. MH. 45-1845

Darwin, Charles Robert. 1809-1882. Journal of researches into the natural history and geology of the countries visited during the voyage of H.M.S. Beagle round the world under the command of Fitz Roy. New York: D. Appleton and company, 1845. 512 p. KyU; NcU; NN; OCan; ScGrwL. 45-1846

Daughters of temperance. New York City. Good Samaritan Union, No. 3. Constitution and bylaws of Good Samaritan Union... of the city of New York. New York: Piercy and Reed, 1845. DLC. 45-1847

Daughter's own book; or practical hints from a father to his daughter. Sixth edition. Philadelphia: Grigg and Elliot, 1845. 240 p. DLC; NcD; NEas; OCl; PU. 45-1848

Daunt, William Joseph O'Neill, 1807-1894. A catechism of the history of Ireland, ancient and modern. Boston: P. Donahoe, 1845. ICU; MBBC; MH; MWH. 45-1849

Davenport, Bishop. History of the United States, containing all the events necessary to be committed to memory; with the Declaration of Independence, the Constitution of the United States, and a table of chronology, for the use of schools. A new edition, corrected and improved. Philadelphia: Uriah Hunt and son, 1845. 144 p. DLC; NcHiC; PSC-Hi. 45-1850

Davenport, Richard Alfred, 1777?-1852. Sketches of imposture, deception and credulity. Philadelphia: G.B. Zieber and company, 1845. 283 p. ICBB; LNT; NCH; PU; RPA. 45-1851

David, Urbain. Les Anglais a la Louisiane, en 1814 et 1815; poeme en 10 chants. Nouvelle Orleans: R.G. Jewell, 1845. [6]-60 p. AU; CtY; IU; LNHT; MiU. 45-1852

David Turner's select classical and English school, Richmond, Virginia. Catalogue... 1844-1845. Richmond, Ritchie and Dunnavant, [1845] Vi. 45-1853

Davidson, David. Connexion or sacred and profane history, being a review of the principal events in the world. New York: Robert Carter, 1845. 3 v. NSchU; OU; TKC; TxShA; ViRut. 45-1854

Davidson, Lucretia Maria, 1808-1825. Poetical remains of the late Lucretia Maria Davidson, collected and arranged by her mother; with a biography, by Miss Sedgwick. New edition, revised. Philadelphia: Lea and Blanchard, 1845. 25-248 p. LNT; MH; PU; OCl; WBB. 45-1855

Davidson, Margaret Miller, 1823-1838. Biography and poetical remains of the late Margaret Miller Davidson. A new edition revised. Philadelphia: Lea and Blanchard, 1845. 248 p. CtY; DCU; NcD; TNP; ViU. 45-1856

Davidson, Robert, 1808-1876. A plea for Presbyterianism. Philadelphia: Presbyterian Board of Publication, 1845. 35 p. MAnP; NcD. 45-1857

Davies, Charles, 1798-1876. Arithmetic designed for acedemies and schools [with answers]. Philadelphia: A.S. Barnes and company, 1845. 340 p. CtHT-W; InEvW; MH; MNS; OO. 45-1858

Davies, Charles, 1798-1876. Elementary algebra; embracing the first principles of the science. New York: A.S. Barnes and company, 1845. 279 p. KyLxT; MH; NbCrD; OO; TxD-T. 45-1859

Davies, Charles, 1798-1876. Elementary geometry, with applications in mensuration. New York: A.S. Barnes and company, 1845. 216 p. MB; PLFM. 45-1860

Davies, Charles, 1798-1876. Elements of algebra, including Sturm's theorem. Translated from the French of M. Bourdon. Adapted to the course of mathematical instructions in the United States. New York: A.S. Barnes and company, 1845. 368 p. CSt; KTW; MH; ODaY; OO. 45-1861

Davies, Charles, 1798-1876. Elements of analytical geometry; embracing the equations of the point, the straight line, the comic sections, and surfaces of the first and second order. Revised edition. New York: A.S. Barnes and company, 1845. 352 p. CLO; NPV; OOxM; TxU; ViU. 45-1862

Davies, Charles, 1798-1876. Elements of surveying and navigation; with a description of the instruments and the necessary tables... Eighth edition. New York: A.S. Barnes and company, 1845. 188, 71, 100 p. ABBS; CtY; IaFayU; NFred. 45-1863

Davies, Charles, 1798-1876. First lessons in arithmetic. Designed for beginners. New York: A.S. Barnes and

company, 1845. 168 p. CtHWatk; IU. 45-1864

Davies, Charles, 1798-1876. First lessons in geometry, with practical applications in mensuration and artificers, work and mechanics. Hartford: A.S. Barnes and company, 1845. 252 p. MHolliHi. 45-1865

Davies, Charles, 1798-1876. Key to Davies arithmetic; for the use of teachers only. New York: A.S. Barnes and company, 1847. MH; OrU. 45-1866

Davies, Charles, 1798-1876. Key to Davies arithmetic; with additional examples; for the use of teachers only. New York: Barnes, 1845. 278 p. CtHWatk; InLogCM; ViRU. 45-1867

Davies, Charles, 1798-1876. New elementary algebra embracing the first principles of the science. Edited by J.H. Van Amringe. New York, Chicago, [etc.] 1845. InGrD. 45-1868

Davies, Samuel, 1724-1761. Sermons on important subjects, with the life and times of the author, by Albert Barnes. Fourth edition. New York: Robert Carter, 1845. 3 v. MoSpD; OO; PCC; ScCoB; TKC. 45-1869

Davis, Asahel, b. 1791. Antiquities of Central American and the discovery of New England by the Northmen, etc. Thirteenth edition from the twelfth Boston edition. Troy, New York: N. Tuttle, 1845. 22 p. DLC; NIC. 45-1870

Davis, Asahel, b. 1791. Discovery of New England by the Northmen, five hundred years before Columbus; with an introduction on the antiquities of

America and on the first inhabitants of Central America. Thriteenth edition for the twelfth Boston edition. Troy: N. Tuttle, 1845. 22 p. DLC; NH; NjR; NN; WHi. 45-1871

Davis, Garrett, 1801-1872. Speech of Mr. Davis, of Kentucky, on the annexation of Texas. Delivered in the House, January 14, 1845. [Washington, 1845] 16 p. DLC; ICU; MBAt; MHi. 45-1872

Davis, John Francis, 1795-1890. The Chinese, a description of the empire of China. New York: Harper and brothers, 1845. 2 v. GAuY; InCW; MnU; OSW; PWW. 45-1873

Davis, Joseph B. Sermon at the dedication of the Freewill Baptist chapel, Roxbury, Massachusetts, November, 1845. Dover, New Hampshire, 1845. 12 p. MeLewB; MH-AH; RPB. 45-1874

Davis, Pardon. Davis' modern practical English grammar. Adapted to the American system of teaching. Philadelphia: Uriah Hunt and son, 1845. 7-175 p. CtHT-W; NNC. 45-1875

Davis, Samson. Human physiognomy or the art of discerning the mental and moral character of man. Compiled from English and French philosophers. New York: Wilson and company, 1845. 80 p. MB. 45-1876

Davis, Thomas K. Our national literature: valedictory oration before the senior class in Yale College. New Haven, 1845. 16 p. MBC. 45-1877

Day, George Edward, 1815-1905. Report on the institutions for the deaf and dumb in Central and Western

Europe in 1844. To the directors of the New York institution. Albany: Carroll and Cook, printers, 1845. MH; MWA; PPL-R; PPM. 45-1878

Day, Guy Bigelow. A poem and the valedictory oration by Thomas Kirby Davis. Pronounced before the senior class in Yale College, July 2, 1845. Published by request of the class. New Haven: Printed by B.L. Hamlen, 1845. 40 p. M; NBuG; NjPT; PPM; RPB. 45-1879

Day, Hartley W. The Boston numeral harmony; or Day and Beal's phonography of music, believed to be the most comprehensive and simple musical notation ever published in the world. The elements embrace a newly invented musical notation and sight singing method. Boston, [1845] 79 p. CSmH; CtMW; NN; PPPrHi; WHi. 45-1880

Day, Jeremiah, 1773-1867. An introduction to algebra, being the first part of a course of mathematics, adapted to the method of instruction in the American colleges. Fifty-second edition. New Haven: Durrie and Peck; Philadelphia: Smith and Peck, 1845. 332 p. MShM; NJam. 45-1881

Day, Jeremiah, 1773-1867. An introduction to algebra, being the first part of a course of mathematics, adapted to the method of instruction in the American colleges. Fifty-third edition. New Haven: Durrie and Peck; Philadelphia: Smith and Peck, 1845. 332 p. KWiU; MWHi; Nh; NRivHi; TWeW. 45-1882

Day, Jeremiah, 1773-1867. A key to Day's algebra and mathematics; with questions for examination, general principles, explanations and solutions with tables of logarithms. New York: Clark and Austin, 1845. 472 p. DAU; GMilvC. 45-1883

Day, Parsons E. District school grammar. The elementary principles of English grammar, accompanied by appropriate exercises in parsing, with an appendix. Fourth edition. Ithaca: Published by D.D. and A. and S. Spencer, 1845. 142 p. NNC. 45-1884

Day, Parsons E. District school speaker. A collection of pieces for public declamation. In three parts: containing a choice variety of exercises in prose, poetry, and dialogue; original and selected. Ithaca: D.D. and A. and S. Spencer, 1845. 156 p. CtY; MiGr; N; NRHi; RPB. 45-1885

Day, Thomas, 1748-1789. History of Sandford and Merton. A new edition. Revised and abridged. By Thomas Teller [pseud.] New Haven: S. Babcock, [1845] 64 p. CtY; DLC; MWHi; OCl; NB. 45-1886

Dayton, William Lewis. Speech of Mr. Dayton, of New Jersey, against the annexation of Texas. Delivered in the Senate, February 24, 1845. Washington: J. and G.S. Gideon, printers, 1845. 25 p. DLC; NjP; NNC; PHi. 45-1887

Dean, Christopher C. The gospel kite. Written for the Massachusetts Sabbath School Society and revised by the committee of publication. Boston: Sabbath School Society, 1845. 32 p. MChiA. 45-1888

Dean, Christopher C. The teachings of nature, or the songs of the earth. Boston, 1845. 84 p. RPB. 45-1889

Dean, Ezra. Speech of Mr. Dean, of Ohio, on the annexation of Texas: delivered in the House, January 10, 1845. [Washington, 1845?] DLC; MBAt; NBu; PHi. 45-1890

Dean, Joseph Joy. Devotions to the sacred heart of Jesus... Philadelphia: H. and C. McGrath, 1845. 358 p. LN; OCX. 45-1891

Deane, James, 1801-1858. Illustrations of fossil footmarks. Boston, 1845. 8 p. DLC; MB. 45-1892

Deane, James, 1801-1858. Illustrations of fossil footmarks. Boston, 1845-1847. DLC. 45-1893

Deane, James, 1801-1858. Notice of a new species of batrachian footmarks. New Haven, 1845. MB. 45-1894

Dearborn, William L. Report of surveys of railroad routes. Boston: Eastburn's Press, 1845. 57 p. MH-BA. 45-1895

Defoe, Daniel, 1661?-1731. The history of the devil: containing his original; a state of his circumstances; his conduct, public and private... interspersed with many of the devils adventures. Sixth edition. Boston: Dow and Jackson, 1845. 296 p. CU; ICN; IGK; MNe. 45-1896

Defoe, Daniel, 1661?-1731. The little Robinson Crusoe. Philadelphia: Loomis and Peck, 1845. 95 p. CtY; PPeSchW. 45-1897

Defoe, Daniel, 1661?-1731. The life and adventures of Robinson Crusoe; revised with special references to moral tendency and adapted to the capacity of the young. Philadelphia: E.C. Biddle, 1845. MH. 45-1898

Defoe, Daniel, 1661?-1731. The life and adventures of Robinson Crusoe, who lived twenty-eight years in an uninhabited island... Philadelphia: T. Wardle, 1845. 251 p. CtY. 45-1899

Defoe, Daniel, 1661?-1731. The life and adventures of Robinson Crusoe. With a life of the author. Portland: S.H. Colesworthy, 1845. 134 p. CtY; MeB; MH; MWA; WHi. 45-1900

Defoe, Daniel, 1661?-1731. Novels and miscellaneous works of Daniel Defoe. New York, 1845. MB. 45-1901

DeGraff, Simon. The modern geometrical stair builder's guide, being a plain practical system of hand railing, embracing all its necessary details, and geometrically illustrated by twenty-two steel engravings. Together with the use of the most important principles of practical geometry. Syracuse, New York: Published by the author, 1845. 68 p. DLC; NNC; OCX; WaPS. 45-1902

Delabarre, Christophe Francois, 1787-1862. A treatise on second dentition, and the natural method of directing it: followed by a summary of stomatic semeology. Translated from the French, for the American Library of Dental Science. Baltimore: American Society of Dental Surgeons, 1845. 5-171 p. ICJ; MdBM; NBMS; OC; TNN. 45-1903

DeLancey, William Heathcote, 1797-1865. Episcopal address to the annual convention of the diocese of western New York, August 20, 1845. Utica: H.H.

Curtiss, printer, 1845. 40 p. CSmH; MH; NBuDD; NN; NUt. 45-1904

Delaware. Address of Thomas Stockton, esq., the governor of Delaware, at his inauguration, January 21, 1845. Dover, Delaware: S. Kimmey, printer, [1845] 13 p. CSmH. 45-1905

Delaware. Laws of the state of Delaware; passed at a session of the General Assembly, commenced and held at Dover, on Tuesday the seventh day of January, in the year of our Lord 1845, and of the Independence of the United States. Dover: S. Kimmey, 1845. 99 p. In-SC; MdBB; Nj; Wa. 45-1906

Delaware. Laws of the state of Delaware; passed at a session of the General Assembly, commenced and held at Dover, on Tuesday the seventh day of January, in the year of Our Lord, one thousand eight hundred and forty-five. The sixty-ninth. Dover: S. Kimmey, 1845. 707, 104 p. IaU; In-SC; NNLI; Mi-L. 45-1907

Delaware. University. Catalogue of the officers and students, of Delaware College, Newark, Delaware, 1844-1845. Wilmington, Delaware: Porter and Naff, printers, 1845. 23 p. PPM. 45-1908

Delaware and Maryland farmer's almanac for 1846. Philadelphia: J. M'Dowell, [1845] MWA. 45-1909

Delaware and Maryland farmer's almanac for 1846. New edition. Philadelphia: J. McDowell, 1845. MWA. 45-1910

Delaware Mutual Safety Insurance Company, Philadelphia. The company... authorized to make marine, inland navigation and fire insurance. [Philadelphia] H. Evans, 1845. 15 p. PPM. 45-1911

DeLeon, Edwin, 1818-1891. Position and duties of young America. An address delivered before the two literary societies of the South Carolina College, December, 1845. 26 p. CU; MH; MHi; MnHi; ScU. 45-1912

Delta Phi. New Jersey Epsilon, Rutgers College. Catalogus fratrum. A.N.C. Collegio Rutgersensi. [New York, 1845] MB; NN. 45-1913

Delta Phi. New York Alpha, Union University. Catalogus octo decennis fratrum. A.N.E. Collegio Concordiae dedicato. [New York, 1845] NN. 45-1914

Delta Phi. New York Delta. Columbia University. Catalogus fratrum. G.N.E. Collegio Columbiae. [New York, 1845] NN. 45-1915

Delta Phi. New York Gamma. New York University. Catalogus quadriennis fratrum. B.N.E. Universitate. [New York, 1845] NN. 45-1916

Democratic Association, Washington, D.C. Oregon. Published by the Democratic Association of Washington, D.C. Washington City: J. Heart, printer, [1845] 4 p. CSmH. 45-1917

Democratic expositor and United States journal for the country. Washington, 1845-1846. V. 1-. A-Ar; DLC; OClWHi; TxU. 45-1918

Democratic Party. Ohio. Letter to the secretary of the treasury, on the effect of the tariff of 1842; on the agricultural and other interests of the west. By a committee of the democratic convention of Hamilton County, Ohio. Cincinnati: 1845. 24 p. ICU. 45-1919

The Democritus of Boston. School committee scrap book. Boston, 1845. MB. 45-1920

Dempster, J. Benefit and danger of society: an address to the Ladies Mutual Improvement Association of Newbury Seminary, November 14, 1845. Newbury, Vermont: L.J. McIndoe, 1845. 8 p. MBNMHi. 45-1921

Dempster, William Richardson, 1809-1871. A home in the heart... By E. Cook. Boston, 1845. CtY. 45-1922

Dempster, William Richardson, 1809-1871. The May queen. Poetry by Alfred Tennyson. Boston: Ditson, 1845. 29 p. KU; MB; MNF; NBuG; NN. 45-1923

Dempster, William Richardson, 1809-1871. When the night wind bewaileth; or never more, never more. Boston: Oliver Ditson, 1845. 7 p. MB; NN; ViU. 45-1924

Dendy, Walter Cooper, 1794-1871. The philosophy of mystery. New York: Harper and brothers, 1845. 442 p. CSt; GEU; KyLoP; OU; PPi. 45-1925

Denison, Charles Wheeler, 1809-1881. The American village, and other poems. Boston: Henry B. Skinner and company, 1845. [5] 143 p. CtY; ICU; MB; MsSC; ScCoB. 45-1926

Dennery, Adolphe Phillippe, 1811-1899. Noemie. A drama in two acts. From the French of Dennery and Clement, translated and adapted by T.W.

Robertson... New York: R.M. DeWitt, [1845] 25 p. MdBE; MdBP; NIC. 45-1927

Dens, Peter. Extracts from the theological works of the Rev. Peter Dens, on the nature of confession, and the obligation of the seal. New edition. New York, 1845. PPL; PPM; PPPrHi. 45-1928

Denton, Daniel. A brief description of New York, formerly called New Netherlands with the places thereunto adjoining... New York: William Gowans, 1845. 16 p. DLC; MB; MiU; NNF; PPL. 45-1929

Denton, Daniel. A brief description of New York, formerly called New Netherlands with the places thereunto adjoining... New York: William Gowans, 1845. 79 p. DFH; NNC; PHi; VtU. 45-1930

Denton, Daniel. A brief description of New York, formerly called New Netherlands with the places thereunto adjoining... New York: William Gowans, 1845. 23, 57, 16 p. Nh. 45-1931

Denton, Daniel, 1656-1696. A brief description of New York, formerly called New Netherlands, with the places thereunto adjoining... New edition, with introduction and copious historical notes. New York: William Gowens, 1845. 57 p. DLC; MdBP; OrU; PBL; ViU. 45-1932

Denton, Daniel, 1656-1696. A brief description of New York, formerly called New Netherlands, with the places thereunto adjoining... New edition, with introduction and copious historical notes. New York: William Gowens, 1845. 79 p. MHi; NjNbS; OFH; PPL. 45-1933

Denton, Daniel, 1656-1696. A brief description of New York, formerly called New Netherlands, with the places thereunto adjoining... New edition, with introduction and copious historical notes. Philadelphia: Press of the Historical Soceity of Pennsylvania, 1845. 16 p. DLC; MB-B; MnH; NjP; PPL. 45-1934

Denton, Daniel. A brief description of New York, formerly called New Netherlands with the places thereunto adjoining... A new edition, with an introduction and copious historical notes, by Gabriel Furman... New York: William Gowans, 1845. 17,57 p. CtMW; MBC; NjR; OCHP; PPL. 45-1935

Derby, Elias Hasket, 1803-1880. The case of William Livingston and fifteen hundred other citizens of Lowell, petitioners for a cross railroad from Lowell to Andover... Boston: Dutton and Wentworth's, printer, 1845. 28 p. DBRE; MHi; MNBedf; NH; P. 45-1936

Description of the dial of the seasons. A chart, illustrating the sun's declination at all seasons. Philadelphia, 1845. NjR. 45-1937

Description of the improved truss bridge, invented by Nathaniel Rider. Patented, October, 1845. New York, 1845. DLC. 45-1938

Description of the monument on Groton Heights with the inscription and names. New London, 1845. 12 p. CtHWatk. 45-1939

Description of Washington's monument, and of the public buildings in Baltimore. Baltimore: Printed by James Young, 1845. 12 p. CSmH; PHi. 45-1940

Deslandes, Leopold. Manhood; the causes of its premature decline, with directions for its perfect restoration; addressed to those suffering from the destructive effects of excessive indulgence, solitary habits... Translated from the French, with many additions, by an American physician. Boston, 1845. MBM; MdToH; NN; PPM. 45-1941

Deslix, P.J.A. Digest of the reported decisions of the supreme court of Louisiana, from December, 1838, to February, 1843. New Orleans: J.L. Sollee, 1845. 533 p. DLC; LNH; NNLI; TxHuT; WaU. 45-1942

Deutsches lefebuch jur aufanger... Boston: Phillips and Sampson, and S.G. Simpkins, 1845. 222 p. MFiHi. 45-1943

DeVeaux, Samuel, 1789-1852. The traveller's own book, to Saratoga Springs, Niagara Falls and Canada... Fifth edition. Buffalo: Faxon and company, 1845. 251 p. Ia; MiD-B; MWA; NBu; RPB. 45-1944

Dewey, Orville, 1794-1882. The character and claims of sea faring men. A sermon. New York: C.S. Francis and company, 1845. 19 p. CBPac; MiD-B; NIC; PPM; RPB. 45-1945

Dewey, Orville, 1794-1882. Rights, claims and duties of opinion. An address delivered before the Berry Street ministerial conference, May 28, 1845. Boston: Crosby and Nichols, 1845. 23 p. CtHWatk; DLC; MB; MiU; MWiW. 45-1946

DeWindt, Carolina Amelia Smith. Melzinga: a souvenir. By C.A.D. New York,

1845. 175 p. CSmH; DLC; IU; MWA; Nh-Hi. 45-1947

DeWolf, Lyman E. The constable's guide, being a treatise on the duties of constables in the State of Pennsylvania. Ithaca: Mack, Andrus and company, 1845. 176 p. P. 45-1948

DeWolf, Orrin. Warning to the young. Trial of Orrin DeWolf for the murder of William Stiles, at Worcester, January 14, 1845, including his confession. Third edition. Worcester: Thomas Drew, 1845. Ct; MW; PP; WaU-L. 45-1949

The diadem for 1845-[1847] A present for all seasons, with splendid engravings after pictures by Sally, Leutz, Huntington, etc. Philadelphia: Carey and Hart, 1845-[1847] 3 v. MB; NjR; MnU; OMC; PP. 45-1950

Dick, John, 1764-1833. Lectures on the Acts of the Apostles. Second edition. New York and Pittsburg: Robert Carter, 1845. 407 p. CSansS; IaGG; KyLoP; ScCliJ; TJaU. 45-1951

Dick, Thomas, 1774-1857. Celestial scenery; or the wonders of the planetary system displayed. Illustrating the perfections of deity and a plurality of worlds. Philadelphia: Biddle, 1845. ICN; KyLoS; MH; NNUT; TJaL. 45-1952

Dick, Thomas, 1774-1857. The christian philosopher or the connection of science and philosophy with religion. Uniform edition, from the eighth London edition, revised, corrected and enlarged. Philadelphia: E.C. Biddle, 1845. ICN; MH; PU; TxShA; ViU. 45-1953

Dick, Thomas, 1774-1857. An essay on

the sin and the evils of covetousness, and the happy effects which would flow from a spirit of christian beneficence. Uniform edition. Philadelphia: E.C. and J. Biddle, 1845. 304 p. ICN; MH; MHoly; NNUT; PPIU. 45-1954

Dick, Thomas, 1774-1857. On the improvement of society by the diffusion of knowledge, or an illustration of the advantages which would result from a more general dissemination of rational and scientific information among all ranks. Hartford: Sumner and Goodman, 1845. MBC. 45-1955

Dick, Thomas, 1774-1857. On the improvement of society by the diffusion of knowledge, or an illustration of the advantages which would result from a more general dissemination of rational and scientific information among all ranks. Philadelphia: Biddle, 1845. 386 p. ICN; MH. 45-1956

Dick, Thomas, 1774-1857. On the mental illumination and moral improvement of mankind; or an inquiry into the means by which a general diffusion of knowledge and moral principle may be promoted. Philadelphia: Biddle, 1845. 425 p. DLC; ICN; MH; PPPrHi. 45-1957

Dick, Thomas, 1774-1857. The philosophy of a future state. Philadelphia: E.C. and J. Biddle, 1845. 4 v. in 2. ICN; KOl; PAtM; PU; TJaL. 45-1958

Dick, Thomas, 1774-1857. The philosophy of religion or an illustration of the moral laws of the universe. Philadelphia: Biddle, 1845. 391 p. ICN; KyLoP; MH. 45-1959

Dick, Thomas, 1774-1857. The philosophy of religion or an illustration of the moral laws of the universe. Philadelphia: E.C. Biddle, 1845. 386 p. IaFd; KyLoS; MdBMC; PAtM; TNP. 45-1960

Dick, Thomas, 1774-1857. The sideral heavens, and other subjects connected with astronomy, as illustrative of the character of the Deity and of an infinity of worlds. Philadelphia: E.C. Biddle, 1845. 394 p. IaHoL; ICN; MH; PAtM; TJaL. 45-1961

Dick, Thomas, 1774-1857. The works of Thomas Dick. Hartford: Sumner and Goodman, 1845. 4 v. in 1. InPerM; IU; OMC; TU. 45-1962

Dickens, Charles, 1812-1870. The chimes! A goblin story of some bells that rang an old year out, and a new year in. New York: E. Winchester, New World Press, 1845. 32 p. CtY; NN. 45-1963

Dickens, Charles, 1812-1870. The chimes! A goblin story of some bells that rang an old year out, and a new year in. New York: Harper and brothers, 1845. 31 p. MBAt; MWA; NN; RPB; WaU. 45-1964

Dickens, Charles, 1812-1870. The chimes! A goblin story of some bells that rang an old year out, and a new year in. Philadelphia: Lea, 1845. 96 p. MB; MeLeB; MH; MW; PPL-R. 45-1965

Dickens, Charles, 1812-1870. Christmas carol in prose, being a ghost story of Christmas. New York: Harper and brothers, 1845. 31 p. MWA; ViU. 45-1966

Dickens, Charles, 1812-1870. The cricket on the hearth. A fairy tale of home. Philadelphia: Henry Altemus company, 1845. 192 p. OkDun. 45-1967

Dickens, Charles, 1812-1870. The haunted man and the ghost's bargain, a fancy for Christmas time. Philadelphia: T.B. Peterson, 1845. 27 p. NSyHi. 45-1968

Dickens, Charles, 1812-1870. Joseph Grimaldi, the clown. New York: H.C. Doggers, 1845. 114 p. MH; ViU. 45-1969

Dickens, Charles, 1812-1870. Life and adventures of Martin Chuzzlewit. [New York: Harper and borthers, 1845?] 312, 31, 32, 31 p. WaPS. 45-1970

Dickens, Charles, 1812-1870. The life and adventures of Nicholas Nickleby. Philadelphia: Lea and Blanchard, 1845. 403 p. CtY; MB; MeU; OCl; PU. 45-1971

Dickens, Charles, 1812-1870. Sketches by Boz, illustrative of everyday life and everyday people. New edition, complete. Philadelphia: Lea and Blanchard, 1845. 268 p. MMh; OFH. 45-1972

Dickinson, Andrew, 1801-1883. The city of the dead: and other poems. New York: Saxton and Miles, 1845. [7]-108 p. DLC; MeB; NNC; OWoC; TxU. 45-1973

Dickinson, Daniel Stevens, 1800-1866. Opinions and decisions on the question whether the bill for conditionally releasing the New York and Erie Railroad Company from the state loan, is a majority bill. Albany, 1845. 19 p. CSt; NNE. 45-1974

Dickinson, Daniel Stevens, 1800-1866. Speech of Mr. Dickinson, of New York,

on the annexation of Texas: delivered in the Senate of the United States, February 22, 1845. Washington: Printed at the Globe office, 1845. 13 p. CSmH; MH; NBu; NN. 45-1975

Dickinson College. Register for the academical year 1845-1846. Carlisle, Pennsylvania: John D. Toy, printer, 1845. 23 p. KyLx; MBNMHi. 45-1976

Dickson, David, 1583?-1663. Sum of saving knowledge; or a brief sum of Christian doctrine. Philadelphia: Presbyterian Board of Publication, 1845. 36 p. IaDuU. 45-1977

Dickson, Samuel, 1802-1869. The principles of the chrono-thermal system of medicine; with fallacies of the faculty. In a series of lectures originally delivered in 1840, at the Egyptian Hall, Piccadilly, London. New, enlarged and improved. First American from the third London [people's] edition. New York: J.S. Redfield; Boston: Redding and company; [etc., etc.,] 1845. [9]- 228 p. CSt-L; DLC; IEN-M; OCLW; WMAM. 45-1978

Dickson, Samuel Henry, 1798-1872. Essays on pathology and therapeutics, being the substance of the course of lectures delivered by Samuel Dickson... in the medical college of the state of South Carolina... Charleston: McCarter and Allen, 1845. 2 v. DLC; MBM; NcD; RPM; ViU. 45-1979

Dickson, Samuel Henry, 1798-1872. Remarks on certain topics connected with the general subject of slavery... Charleston: Observer Office Press, 1845. 35 p. CtY; MH; MoS; NcAS; PPL. 45-1980

A dictionary of select and popular quotations, which are in daily use: taken from the Latin, French, Greek, Spanish, and Italian languages; together with a copious collection of law maxims and law terms; translated into English with illustrations, historical and idiomatic. Sixth American edition, corrected with additions. Philadelphia: Grigg and Elliot, 1845. 312 p. ICU; LNH-T; MiDU-L; TU; WPew. 45-1981

Didimus, Henry. New Orleans as I found it. New York: Harper and brothers, 1845. 125 p. DLC; LNH; MWA; PHi; TxU. 45-1982

Dillahunty, Edmund, 1765-1852. Address delivered by the Hon. Edmund Dillahunty to the students of Franklin College, October 15th, 1845. Franklin College, Tennessee, 1845. 28 p. CSmH; T; TKL-Mc; TxU. 45-1983

Dillahunty, Edmund, 1765-1852. Address to the Grand Lodge of the state of Tennessee. Nashville: Charles A. Fuller, 1845. 12 p. IaCrM. 45-1984

Dillahunty, Edmund, 1765-1852. Masonic address, delivered by Hon. Ed. Dillahunty before the Lebanon Lodge No. 98 on the 31st of December, 1844. Lebanon, Tennessee: Printed by McClain and Dunnington, 1845. 19 p. IaCrM; LNMas. 45-1985

Dillaway, Charles Knapp, d. 1889. Roman antiquities, and ancient mythology. Seventh edition. Boston: Gould, 1845. 144 p. CtY; IaWas; NcWfC; PReaAT. 45-1986

Dimick, Leverett. The wood dealer's companion: containing a wood measure

giving the amount of cords and feet, of any load or pile of four feet wood from one to fifty feet in length, and from one to nine feet high... Also... a table showing the value of any number of feet of wood from one to one hundred and twenty-eight, at various prices. Glen's Falls, New York: M. and T.J. Strong, 1845. 49, 49, [9] p. DLC; MBAt; NBuG. 45-1987

Dimmick, Luther Fraseur, 1790-1860. A sermon preached at the funeral of Woodbury Dimmick, son of Aaron Quimby of Danville, New Hampshire, who died October 2, 1843, aged eight and one-half years. Concord: A. McFarland, 1845. 11 p. MH; NhDO; Nh-Hi; OO. 45-1988

Directory and guide book, for the city of Hartford, 1845. Compiled and published by Isaac N. Bolles. [Hartford: Printed at the office of the Republican Courier, 1845.] 132 p. Ct; DLC; MH. 45-1989

Directory of the city of Detroit, and register of Michigan for the year 1845. By James H. Wellings. Detroit: Harsha and Willcox, 1845. 121, 46 p. MWA. 45-1990

Directory of the city of Newark for 1845-1846. By B.F. Pierson. Newark, New Jersey: Aaron Guest, printer, 1845. 244 p. NjMo. 45-1991

A discourse on the life and character of Joseph. September 14, 1845. Boston, 1845. 13 p. NIC. 45-1992

Discussion of the merits of Noah Webster's orthography, and Lyman Cobb's school books, in "Soc. Teachers and Friends of Education" in New Jersey. New York, 1845. 27 p. CtHWatk. 45-1993

The dispensatory [sic] of the United States of America. Sixth edition carefully revised. Philadelphia: Grigg and Elliot, 1845. 1322 p. CU; MH-M; OMC; WaPS. 45-1994

Disraeli, Isaac, 1766-1848. Amenities of literature, consisting of sketches and characters of English literature. New York: J. and W.G. Langley, 1845. 2 v. ArLP; GMM; KyU; MBBC; OCM. 45-1995

Disraeli, Isaac, 1766-1848. Amenities of literature, consisting of sketches and characters of English literature. Second edition. New York: J. and W.G. Langley, 1845. 2 v. NNUT; OUr; TJoV; WNaE. 45-1996

Dix, Dorothea Lynde, 1802-1887. Memorial soliciting a state hospital for the insane, submitted to the Legislature of Pennsylvania, February 3, 1845. Harrisburg: J.M.G. Lesure, 1845. DLC; DNLM; MB; PP; PPL. 45-1997

Dix, Dorothea Lynde, 1802-1887. Memorial soliciting a state hospital for the insane, submitted to the Lesgislature of Pennsylvania, February 3, 1845. Philadelphia: I. Ashmeade, printer, 1845. 52 p. Ct; MH; KyLx; Nj; PHi. 45-1998

Dix, Dorothea Lynde, 1802-1887. Memorial soliciting a state hospital for the insane, submitted to the Legislature of New Jersey; January 23, 2845. Printed by order of the legislature of New Jersey. Second editon. Trenton, 1845. 46 p. CtY; DLC; OSW; NHi; Phi. 45-1999

Dix, Dorothea Lynde, 1802-1887. Memorial soliciting attention to the condition of necessities of idiots, epileptics, and the insane, poor, in the state of New Jersey. Trenton, 1845. 30 p. MdBJ. 45-2000

Dix, Dorothea Lynde, 1802-1887. Memorial. To the honourable the Senate and General assembly of the state of New Jersey. [Trenton, 1845] 39 p. DLC; PPL. 45-2001

Dix, Dorothea Lynde, 1802-1887. Remarks on prisons and prison discipline in the United States. Boston: Printed by Munroe and Francis, 1845. 104 p. CU; DLC; NjR; PPAmP; RPB. 45-2002

Dix, Dorothea Lynde, 1802-1887. Remarks on prisons and prison discipline in the United States. First edition. Philadelphia, 1845. 104 p. PHi. 45-2003

Dix, Dorothea Lynde, 1802-1887. Remarks on prisons and prison discipline in the United States. Second edition, from the first Boston edition. Philadelphia: Joseph Kite and company, 1845. 108 p. IaB; IEU; MWA; NcD; PU. 45-2004

Dix, Dorothea Lynde, 1802-1887. A review of the present condition of the state penitentiary [sic] of Kentucky, with brief notices and remarks upon the jails and poor houses in some of the most populous counties. Written by request. Printed by order of the legislature. Frankfort, [Kentucky] A.G. Hodges, state printer, 1845. 40 p. CtY; DLC; MH; MoSHi; WHi. 45-2005

Dix, John, 1800?-1865? Local loiterings, and visits in the vicinity of Boston. By a looker-on. Boston: Redding and company, 1845. 147 p. DLC; ICN; MHi; MWA; NjR. 45-2006

Dix, John, 1800?-1865? Pen and ink sketches: by a cosmopolitan. To which is added Chatterton: a romance of literary life. Boston: W. Hayden and T.M. Brewer, 1845. 198 p. DLC; LNH; MBBC; MeU; WHi. 45-2007

Dixon, Edward Henry, 1808-1880. A treatise on diseases of the sexual organs; adapted to popular and professional reading, and the exposition of quackery, professional and otherwise. New York: Burgess, Stringer and company, 1845. 260 p. MdBM; NBMS; PPCP; RPM; WMAM. 45-2008

Dixon, Edward Henry, 1808-1880. A treatise on diseases of the sexual organs; adapted to popular and professional reading, and the exposition of quackery, professional and otherwise. New York: Taylor, 1845. 260 p. CtY-M; DLNM. 45-2009

Dixon, John, b. 1795. The twin brothers: being the lives of John and James Dixon, born at Naworth Park, Cumberland, England. Thirty-first edition. Albany: Printed by Munsell and Tanner, 1845. 72 p. DLC; MiGr. 45-2010

Dixon, Joshua. Scriptural examination of the church catechism, revised and adapted to the liturgy of the Protestant Episcopal Church, with notes, by G.A. Smith. Fourth edition. Philadelphia: Hooker, 1845. 231 p. MBD; PPLt. 45-2011

Doak, Samuel, 1749-1830. Lectures on human nature. Adapted to the use of students at college, academies, or in other schools, or in private. To which is added an essay on life. Jonesborough, Tennessee: F. Gifford and company, 1845. 104 p. CtY; TKL; T; TU. 45-2012

Doane, George Washington, 1799-1859. The bishops address to the members of the senior class at St. Mary's Hall, at the closing exercises of the summer term, September 24, 1845. Burlington: Printed by Edmond Morris, 1845. 44 p. MdBD; MH. 45-2013

Doane, George Washington, 1799-1859. The church, a debtor to all the world: the rector's Christmas offering to the parishioners of St. Mary's Church, Burlington; for 1845. Burlington, New Jersey: E. Morris, 1845. 16 p. Ct; DLC; MWA; NGH; PPPrHi. 45-2014

Doane, George Washington, 1799-1859. Civil government a sacred trust from God; the anniversary oration before the New Jersey Society of Cincinnati, at Trenton, July 4, 1845. Burlington, [New Jersey] E. Morris, printer, 1845. 36 p. CSmH; DLC; MWA; NNUT; PPM. 45-2015

Doane, George Washington, 1799-1859. Episcopal address to the sixty-second annual convention in St. Mary's Church, Burlington, May 28, 1845. Burlington: Missionary Press, 1845. 40 p. CtHT; DLC; MiDMCh; NBuDD; PHi. 45-2016

Doane, George Washington, 1799-1859. In corporation with Christ, the source and channel of the spiritual life: the fifth charge to the clergy of the Diocese of New Jersey... Burlington: Missionary Press, 1845. 31 p. CSmH; MdBD; MiD-B; MWA; NNG. 45-2017

Doane, George Washington, 1799-1859. Jesus of Nazareth, who went about doing good, the model for the church and for the ministry: the sermon at the annual commencement of the General Theological Seminary... Burlington: E. Morris, 1845. 18 p. DLC; InID; MWA; NBuDD; PPM. 45-2018

Doctor Wistar's free almanac for 1846. Boston: Seth W. Fowle, [1845] MeLewB; MHi; MWA. 45-2019

Doddridge, Philip, 1702-1751. An address to the head of a family, on the subject of family religion. By P. Doddridge. Philadelphia: Presbyterian Board of Publication, 1845. 24 p. CU; IaDuU-Sem; NcD; NN; PPL. 45-2020

Doddridge, Philip, 1702-1751. The family expositor, or a paraphrase and version of the New Testament, with critical notes and a practical improvement to each section, with a memoir of the author, by N.W. Fiske. Fifteenth edition. Amherst, Mass.: John S. and Charles Adams, 1846. 1006 p. IaFairP; LRuL; MShM. 45-2021

Doddridge, Philip, 1702-1751. The rise and progress of religion in the soul in a course of serious and practical addresses, suited to persons of every character and circumstances with a devout meditation and prayer, subjoined to each chapter. New York: Leavitt and Allen, 1845. 288 p. OCl. 45-2022

Doddridge, Philip, 1702-1751. The rise and progress of religion in the soul in a course of serious and practical addresses, suited to persons of every character and circumstances with a devout meditation and prayer, subjoined to each chapter. Philadelphia, 1845. 323 p. OCl. 45-2023

Dodge, D.L. Battle of that great day of God Almighty. New York, 1845. MB. 45-2024

Dods, John Bovee. Thirty short sermons on various important subjects both doctrinal and practical. Boston: Thomas Whittemore, 1845. 348 p. LNT; MH; NCaS. 45-2025

Dodsley, Robert, 1703-1764. The economy of human life: translated from an Indian manuscript, to which is prefixed an account of the manner in which the said manuscript was discovered; in a letter from an English gentleman residing in China. New Haven: S. Babcock, 1845. 160 p. IEG; LNH; MB; WWea. 45-2026

Dodworth, Allen. Devilshoof [sic] quick step, as performed with universal applause, by Dodworth's New York cornet band; arranged from Balf's opera of the Bohemian girl, by Allen Dodworth. New York: Firth, Hall and Pond, 1845. 5 p. NN; WHi. 45-2027

Doerinckel, Frederick. Havemeyer's grand march. New York, 1845. CtY. 45-2028

Doggett's New York City supplement directory; containing the removals, so far as ascertained, occasioned by the great fire, July 19th, 1845. To which is added a street key showing the occupants of the building destroyed. New York: John Doggett, Jr., 1845. 440 p. MH; NNS. 45-2029

Dolby, Thomas, 1782-1856. Golden apples in silver pictures; being the Christian economy of human life. Third American edition. New York: Axford, [1845] 112 p. NjP. 45-2030

Doll, Henry. Jesus' witnesses; or the "Great salvation" exemplified in the experience of those who profess to have obtained this inestimable blessing. To which are added, aphorisms and reflections, relating to that important doctrine. Baltimore: Parsons and Preston, 1845. 347 p. DLC; IEG; NNG; NNMHi; PAtM. 45-2031

The dollar farmer, a monthly publication. By Prentice and Weissinger. Louisville, Kentucky: Printed and published at the office of the Louisville Journal, 1845. 192 p. DLC; KyLxT; KyU. 45-2032

Donaldson, Joseph, 1793-1830. Recollections of the eventful life of a soldier. By the late Joseph Donaldson, sergeant in the Ninety-fourth Scots Brigade. Philadelphia: G.B. Zieber and company, 1845. [9]-231 p. KyHop; MH; MoSU; NNS; RNR. 45-2033

Donizetti, Gaetano, 1797-1848. Belisarius. Words by Cammarano. New Orleans, 1845. 30 p. CtY. 45-2034

Donizetti, Gaetano, 1797-1848. Oh! Summer night; serenade Don Pasquale, arranged for viola and guitar by L.J. Bill. New York, 1845. CtY; ViU. 45-2035

Donovan, Edward, 1768-1837. The natural history of British quadrupeds; consisting of coloured figures, accompanied with scientific and general descriptions. New edition. New York: Bohn, 1845. PPM. 45-2036

Dore, James. Youth invited to the celestial Canaan. Boston: Massachusetts Sabbath School Society, 1845. 72 p. MSwan. 45-2037

Douglas, James Smith. Homoeopathy. A lecture before the Hygeian Society, of the Hamilton Literary and Theological Institution, April, 1845. Hamilton, New York: Printed by Walron and Baker, 1845. 29 p. A-Ar; DSG; NCH-S; NN; PPHa. 45-2038

Douglas, James Smith. A lecture before literatry and theological institution, April, 1845. Hamilton, New York: Waldron and Baker, 1845. 29 p. WU-M. 45-2039

Douglas, Stephen Arnold, 1813-1861. Atlantic and Pacific Railroad. A letter from the Hon. S.A. Douglass [!] to A. Whitney, esq. [Quincy, Illinois: Woods and Flagg, printers, 1845] 8 p. CSmH. 45-2040

Douglas, Stephen Arnold, 1813-1861. Speech of Mr. Douglas, of Illinois, on the annexation of Texas: delivered in the House, January 6, 1845. [Washington? 1845] 7 p. MBAt; MH; NBu; NcU; PHi. 45-2041

Douglass, David Bates, 1790-1849. Further statement of facts and circumstances connected with the removal of the author from the Presidency of Kenyon College, in answer to "The reply of trustees," etc. Albany: Erastus H. Pease, 1845. 71 p. CtHT; MWA; NNG; OHi; RPB. 45-2042

Douglass, Frederick, 1817-1895. Narrative of the life of Frederick Douglass, an American slave. Written by himself. Boston: Published at the Anti-slavery office,

1845. 125 p. DLC; GAU; ICHi; MeB; NcD. 45-2043

Dover, George. Lives of the most eminent sovereigns of modern Europe. New York, 1845. MBC. 45-2044

Dow, Ann Eliza. The life and adventures of, being a true narrative. Burlington, Vermont: Published for the author, 1845. 24 p. MWA; VtHi. 45-2045

Dow, E. Dean. Remarks on forms of prayer in sameness of words no hindrence to devotion. New York, 1845. Nh. 45-2046

Dow, Joseph. Plan of Exeter village, New Hampshire, 1845. Boston, 1845. Nh-Hi. 45-2047

Dowling, John, 1807-1878. The history of Romanism; from the earliest corruptions of christianity to the present time. New York: Edward Walker, 1845. 671 p. KyU; NbUHi; NcD; NjR; PU. 45-2048

Dowling, John, 1807-1878. The history of Romanism; from the earliest corruptions of christianity to the present time. Third edition. New York: Edward Walker, 1845. 671 p. MB; NbCrD; NjR; ViU. 45-2049

Dowling, John, 1807-1878. The history of Romanism; from the earliest corruptions of christianity to the present time. Fourth edition. New York: Edward Walker, 1845. 671 p. CSansS; DLC; ICU; MoSW; NNUT. 45-2050

Dowling, John, 1807-1878. The history of Romanism; from the earliest corruptions of christianity to the present time. Fifth edition. New York: Edward

Walker, 1845. 671 p. IaGG; MH; MsU. 45-2051

Dowling, John, 1807-1878. The history of Romanism; from the earliest corruptions of christianity to the present time. Sixth edition. New York: Edward Walker, 1845. 671 p. CSansS; DLC; ICU; MoSW; NNUT. 45-2052

Dowling, John, 1807-1878. The history of Romanism; from the earliest corruptions of christianity to the present time. Seventh edition. New York: Edward Walker, 1847. 671 p. KKcBT; MBr; Sc-CliP. 45-2053

Dowling, John, 1807-1878. The history of Romanism; from the earliest corruptions of christianity to the present time. Eighth edition. New York: Edward Walker, 1845. 671 p. IaB; DAU; MH-AH; RPB; WvU. 45-2054

Downing, Andrew Jackson, 1815-1852. The fruits and fruit trees of America; or the culture propagation and management in the garden and orchard of fruit trees generally with descriptions of all the finest varieties of fruit, native and foreign cultivated in this country. New York: Wiley and Putnam, 1845. 594 p. DLC; NBuG; PPL- R; RPAt; Wv. 45-2055

Doyle, Robert Emmet. Address delivered before the Philodemic Society of Georgetown College, District of Columbia on February 24, 1845. To which are prefixed the remarks of Richard H. Clarke, of the District of Columbia, previous to his reading Washington's farewell address... Washington: Printed by Gales and

Seaton, 1845. 19 p. CSmH; MdHi; MH. 45-2056

Drake, Benjamin Michael, 1800-1860. An address on education, delivered before the students of the female collegiate academy, at Port Gibson, Mississippi, 25th July, 1845 by Rev. B.M. Drake. Jackson, Mississippi: Printed at the Southron [sic] office, 1845. 16 p. CSmH; DLC. 45-2057

Drake, Samuel Gardner, 1798-1875. The book of the Indians; or biography and history of the Indians of North America from its first discovery to the year 1841. Ninth edition with large additions. Boston: Mussey, 1845. CtMW; IHi; MH; NRU; ScDuE. 45-2058

Drake, Samuel Gardner, 1798-1875. Catalogue of the private library of Samuel Gardner Drake, of Boston, chiefly relating to the antiquities, history and biography of America. Boston, 1845. 80 p. CtSoP; MH; MHi; PPL; WHi. 45-2059

Drake, Samuel Gardner, 1798-1875. Genealogical and biographical account of the family of Drake in America. With some notices of the antiquities connected with the early times of persons of the name in England... Boston: Printed at the private press of G. Coolidge, for S.G. Drake, 1845. 9-51 p. CtY; ICN; MiD-B; MnHi; RHi. 45-2060

Draper, Bourne Hall. The juvenile naturalist; or walks in the country. New York, 1845. MDeeP. 45-2061

Draper, Bourne Hall. The youth's book of nature, or the four seasons illustrated. Being familiar descriptions of natural history, made during walks in the country. New York: D. Appleton and company, 1845. 2 v. in 1. NN. 45-2062

Draper, Bourne Hall. The youths' book of nature or the four seasons by Rev. B.H. Draper. New York: D. Appleton and company; Philadelphia: George S. Appleton, 1845. 237 p. NcNb. 45-2063

Draper, John William, 1811-1882. An introductory lecture to the course of chemistry: on the relations and nature of water. New York: Medical class of the University, 1845-1846. 15 p. DLC; DNLM; NN. 45-2064

Draper, John William, 1811-1882. On the allotropism of chlorine as connected with the theory of substitution. New Haven: B.L. Hamlen, 1845. 24 p. DLC; NN. 45-2065

Draper, John William, 1811-1882. A treatise on the forces which produce the organization of plants; with an appendix containing several memoirs on capillary attraction, electricity and the chemical action of light. Second edition. New York: Harper, 1845. 216 p. CtY; OCl; PPAmP; ScU; WM. 45-2066

Drayton, Boston Jenkins. Address before the First Baptist Chruch Temperance Society, on their anniversary in August 1845. Charleston: Published by the Society, 1845. 20 p. MdBJ. 45-2067

Dromgoole, George Coke, 1797-1847. Speech of Mr. Dromgoole, of Virginia, on the annexation of Texas: delivered in the House, January 24, 1845. Washington: Printed at the Globe office, 1845. 16 p. DLC; MBAt; MdBJ; PU; Vi. 45-2068

Druitt, Robert, 1814-1883. Principles and practice of modern surgery. Philadelphia: Lea and Blanchard, 1845. PPJ. 45-2069

Dublin, New Hampshire. Report of the superintending school committee. Keene, 1845. 23 p. M. 45-2070

DuBois, Robert Patterson, 1805-1887. A discourse on the origin and history of the Presbyterian Church and congregation of New London, in Chester County, Pennsylvania, delivered by the pastor Robert P. DuBois, August 6th, 1845. Philadelphia: King and Baird, 1845. 24 p. MBAt; MNBedf; NjPT; PHi; PPPrHi. 45-2071

Dudley, John, 1805-1898. Shall we save our country, or the duty of prayer from Rulrrs, [sic] as a means of self preservation. A sermon, delivered at Quechee Village, Thanksgiving Day, November 27, 1845. 12 p. ICN; MBAt; MiD-B; MWA; NcD. 45-2072

Dudley, Massachusetts. Congregational Church. Historical notice of the Congregational Church in Dudley, with the articles of faith, covenant, etc. Worcester: Printed by Henry J. Howland, 1845. 16 p. MBC; MBNEH; MWA; OMC. 45-2073

Duer, John, 1782-1858. The law and practice of marine insurance, deduced from a critical examination of the adjudged cases; the nature and analogies of the subject, and the general usage of commercial nations. New York: John S. Voorhies, 1845-[1846] 2 v. CU; ICJ; TMeB; WaU. 45-2074

Duer, William Alexander, 1780-1858. A course of lectures on the constitutional jurisprudence of the United States... New York: Harper and brothers, 1845. 419 p. CU; GAuY; InCW; LNP; WM. 45-2075

Duff, Alexander. The Jesuits; their origin and order, morality and practices, supression and restoration. Philadelphia: Presbyterian Board of Publication, 1845. 107 p. IU; LNHT; MdW; NjPT; PPiW. 45-2076

Duff, Joseph. Traveller's guide. A map of the Ohio and Mississippi Rivers. Extending from Pittsburgh to the Gulf of Mexico... Cincinnati: George Conclin, 1845. IGK; MB; OClWHi; PHi. 45-2077

Duff-Gordon, Lucie Austin, 1821-1869. The French in Algiers. The soldier of the foreign legion. The prisoners of Abd-el-Kader. New York: Wiley and Putnam, 1845. FOA; GEU; LNP; PPL-R; RWe. 45-2078

Duganne, Augustine Joseph Hickey, 1823-1884. Harp of religion. Philadelphia: Henry Logstretch, 1845. 128 p. CU; InRchE; NSyU. 45-2079

Duganne, Augustine Joseph Hickey, 1823-1884. The knights of the seal; or the mysteries of the three cities; a romance of men's hearts and habits. Philadelphia: Colon and Adriance, 1845. 204 p. DLC; KEmT; MB. 45-2080

Duggan, Joseph Francis, b. 1817. My own wild Irish girl. Boston: Reed, 1845. 3 p. MB. 45-2081

Dumas, Alexandre, 1802-1870. Amaury. Translated from the French of Alexandre Dumas. By E.P. New York:

Harper and brothers, 1845. 106 p. DLC; IC; LNH; MnM; OClStM. 45-2082

Dumas, Alexandre, 1802-1870. The Corsican brothers. Corsica-Paris. Translated from the French by a pupil of Mons. G.J. Hubert Sanders. Philadelphia: G.B. Zieber and company, 1845. 63 p. MHi; NCatS; PPL. 45-2083

Dumas, Alexandre, 1802-1870. The memoirs of a physician by Alexandre Dumas. New York: Stringer and Townsend, late Burgess, Stringer and company, 1845. 347 p. NoLoc. 45-2084

Dumas, Alexandre, 1802-1870. The regent's daughter. Translated from the French of Alexandre Dumas. By Charles H. Town. New York: Harper and brothers, 1845. 124 p. DLC; IU; MWA; NjR; RPB. 45-2085

Dumas, Alexandre, 1802-1870. La Reine Margot. New York: Bureau du Courrier des Etats-Unis, 1845. PPL-R. 45-2086

Dumas, Alexandre, 1802-1870. Vingt ans apres, ou les trois Mousquetaires sous mazarin. New York: Bureau du Courrier des Etats-Unis, 1845. PPL-R. 45-2087

Duncan, Alexander, d. 1852. Speech of Mr. Duncan, of Ohio, delivered in the House, January 29, 1845. [Washington? 1845] DLC; N; OrP; WHi. 45-2088

Duncan, Alexander, d. 1852. Speech of Mr. Duncan, of Ohio, in the House, February 19, in committee on the army aprorpriation bill. [Washington, 1845] 16 p. DLC; MH; NNC. 45-2089

Duncan, Mary Grey Lundie. Memoir of Mrs. Mary Lundie Duncan. Being recollections of a daughter, by her mother. Second edition. New York: Robert Carter 1845. 310 p. IaB; NSyHi; PPPrHi. 45-2090

Duncan, Mary Grey Lundie. Memoir of Mrs. Mary Lundie Duncan by her mother. Third edition. New York: Robert Carter, 1845. 310 p. ScCoT. 45-2091

Dunglison, Robley, 1798-1869. An introductory lecture, delivered before the class of institutes of medicine, in Jefferson Medical College, November 3, 1845. Philadelphia: The class, 1845. 24 p. DNLM; IEN; MH-AH; MeB; NjR. 45-2092

Dunglison, Robley, 1798-1869. Medical lexicon. A dictionary of medical science, containing a concise account of the various subjects and terms; with the French and other synonyms; notices of climate... Fifth edition. Philadelphia: Lea and Blanchard, 1845. 771 p. ArU-M; CU-M; MnHi; OTU; PPCP. 45-2093

Dunlap, James D. A book of forms: containing six hundred of the most approved precedents for conveyancing and for practice in the courts of the commonwealth; also, for use in public offices and for men in business generally, adapted to the present acts of assembly... Philadelphia: E.C. and J. Biddle, 1845. 362 p. IaLyYMA; MdU; Nc-SC; PAtM; PPB. 45-2094

Dunn, John. The Oregon Territory, and the British North American fur trade. With an account of the habits and customs of the principal native tribes on the northern continent. Philadelphia: G.B. Zieber and company, 1845. 13-236 p. CSmH; MB; MBAt; NN; WaSp. 45-2095

Dunn, Samuel. Christian theology. Second edition. New York: G. Lane and C.B. Tippett, 1845. 438 p. NcHPC. 45-2096

Dunton, Joseph. A guide to a practical knowledge of sacred geography, classified and arranged systematically for the use of families and Sabbath schools. Third edition. Ithaca: Mack, Andrus and company, 1845. [9]-48 p. CSmH; DLC; MH; NRMA. 45-2097

Durbin, John Price, 1800-1876. Observations in the East, chiefly in Egypt, Palestine, Syria, and Asia Minor. New York: Harper and brothers, 1845. 2 v. CU; FMU; MB; OOxM; PPA. 45-2098

Durbin, John Price, 1800-1876. Observations in the East, chiefly in Egypt, Palestine, Syria, and Asia minor. New York: Harper and brothers, 1845-1847. 2 v. PMA. 45-2099

Durivage, Francis Alexander, 1814-1881. Edith Vernon: or crime and retribution. A tragic story of New England, founded upon fact. Boston: F. Gleason, 1845. [9]-52 p. CSmH; DLC; NjR; NN; RPB. 45-2100

Durivage, Francis Alexander, 1814-1881. Mike Martin; or the last of the highwaymen. A romance of reality... Boston: Charles H. Brainard, 1845. 48 p. MB; MH; MHi; MWA. 45-2101

Durivage, Francis Alexander, 1814-1881. Popular cyclopaedia of history; ancient and modern, forming a copious historical dictionary of celebrated institutions, persons, places, and things; with notices of the present state of the principal cities, countries, and kingdoms of the known world. Hartford: Case, Tiffany and Burnham, 1845. 717 p. MeBa; MnHi; OO; TxDaM; WaPS. 45-2102

Durivage, Oliver Everett. The stage struck Yankee; a farce, in one act. New York: S. French, [1845?] 16 p. MH; OCl. 45-2103

Durlacher, Lewis. A treatise on corns, bunions, the diseases of nails and the general management of the feet. Philadelphia: Lea and Blanchard, 1845. [19]-134 p. MeB; NIC; OC; PPM; WMAM. 45-2104

Dutchess and Ulster farmer's almanac for 1846. By David Young. Poughkeepsie, New York: William Wilson, [1845] MWA. 45-2105

Duty, Mark. The blind man's production; or mathematical instructor; a short and comprehensive work, designed for the use of farmers, mechanics, merchants, steam boat clerks, market people. Cleveland: T.H. Smead, 1845. 56 p. CSmH. 45-2106

Dwight, Nathaniel, 1770-1831. The lives of the signers of the declaration of Independence. New York: Harper and brothers, 1845. 373 p. LNH; OO; ScU; TNF; WJan. 45-2107

Dwight, Theodore, 1796-1866. The history of Connecticut, from the first settlement to the present time. New York: Harper and brothers, 1845. 450 p. CtY; LN; OCY; PWW; TSewU. 45-2108

Dwight's American magazine and family newspaper; for the diffusion of useful knowledge and moral and religious principles. Edited by T. Dwight. New York, 1845-. v. 1-. AzU; DLC; MB: NcD; TxU. 45-2109

Dwyer, John Hanbury. An essay on elocution: with elucidatory passages from various authors, to which are added remarks on reading prose and verse, with suggestions to instructors of the art. Fifth edition, with additions. Albany: W.C. Little, 1845. [7]-300 p. CtHWatk; DLC; MdBS; NjP; PU. 45-2110

Dymond, Jonathan, 1796-1828. Essays on the principles of morality, and on the private and political rights and obligations of mankind. New York: Collins, brothers and company, 1845. [15]-576 p. CoD; CtMW; GEU; NbU; MNS. 45-2111

E

Eagle Fire Insurance Company. Report... in the city of New York, in answer to a resolution of the Assembly, [transmitting statements of premiums received and taxes paid for the years, 1842, 1843 and 1844] [Albany, 1845] 3 p. WHi. 45-2112

Earle, Pliny. A visit to thirteen asylums for the insane in Europe. By Pliny Earle, physician to Bloomingdale Asylum for the insane, New York. New York: Egbert, Hovey and King, printers, 1845. 82 p. KWiU; OO. 45-2113

East, John. My Saviour: or devotional meditations, in prose and verse, on the names and titles of the Lord Jesus Christ. Tenth edition. Boston, 1845, CtY. 45-2114

East River Mutual Fire Insurance Company. Report in answer to a resolution of the assembly. [Transmitting statement of premiums received and taxes paid during the years 1842-1844] [Albany, 1845] 2 p. WHi. 45-2115

Eastburn, Manton, 1801-1872. Short treatise on the rite of confirmation. Boston: Gould, Kendall and Lincoln, 1845. 21 p. RPB. 45-2116

Eastburn, Manton, 1801-1872. Short treatise on the rite of confirmation. Boston: Tract Committee of the diocese of Massachusetts, 1845. 21 p. MBAt; MBD; MPiB; MWA; RPB. 45-2117

Eastern Railroad Company. Remonstrance of the Eastern Railroad Company, [1845] 3 p. DLC; M. 45-2118

Eastman, Buell. A practical treatise on diseases peculiar to women and girls; to which is added an eclectic system of midwifery. Also the treatment of diseases of children, and the remedies used in the cure of diseases; particularly adapted to the use of heads of families and midwives. Connersville, 1845. 182 p. DLC; In; OCLloyd. 45-2119

Easy lessons for young readers. Worcester: S.A. Howland, [1845?] MWA. 45-2120

Eaton, Horace, 1810-1883. The field and the work of the medical profession; an address delivered before the associated alumni of Castleton Medical College. Albany: Printed by C. Van Benthuysen and company, 1845. 31 p. DLC; ICU; MBM; NN; VtMidbC. 45-2121

Eaton, John Henry, 1790-1856. Memoirs of Andrew Jackson, late major-general and commander in chief of the southern division of the army of the United States. Compiled by a citizen of Massachusetts. Philadelphia: [T.K. and P.G. Collins] 1845. 334 p. CoU; MnHi 45-2122

Eaton, John Henry, 1790-1856 Memoirs of Andrew Jackson, late major general and commander in chief of the southern division of the army of the United States. Compiled by a citizen of Massachusetts. Philadelphia: [T.K. and P.G. Collins] 1845. 334 p. ICN. 45-2123

Eaton, John Henry, 1790-1856. Memoirs of Andrew Jackson, seventh president of the United States; containing a full account of his Indian campaigns, and defense of New Orleans... Compiled by a citizen of New York. Auburn, New York: James C. Derby; Geneva, New York: George H. Derby and company, etc., 1845. 270 p. CSfA. 45-2124

Eaton, M. Five years on the Erie Canal: an account of some of the most striking scenes and incidents, during five years' labor on the Erie Canal, and other inland waters, by Dea. M. Eaton, missionary of the American Bethel Society. Utica: Bennett, Backus and Hawley, 1845. [19]-156 p. CSmH; DLC; MWA; NhD; WyU. 45-2125

Eberle, John, 1787-1838. A treatise on the diseases and physical education of children. Third edition. Philadelphia: Grigg and Elliot, 1845. 555 p. DNLM; IaU; MoU; OMC. 45-2126

Eberle, John, 1787-1838. A treatise on the practice of medicine. With notes and additions by George M'Clellan. Sixth edition. Philadelphia: Grigg and Elliot, 1845. 2 v. in 1. CSt-L; InU-M; MoSMed; NcGA; TNP. 45-2127

Eddy, Ansel Doane, 1798-1875. A review of the prelatical principles, as anti-republican and unevangelical. New York: Leavitt, Trow and company, 1845. 44 p. MiD-B; NCH; NjR; PHi; PPPrHi. 45-2128

Edes, Richard Sullivan, 1810-1877. Discourse delivered at Bolton, December 26, 1844, at the re-dedication of the church belonging to the First Parish... minister of said parish. Worcester: Printed by Henry J. Howland, 1845. 15 p. MBAt; MHi; MiD-B; MWA; RPB. 45-2129

Edgar, Mary C. A Catholic story; or four month's residence in the house of a convert from Protestantism... Philadelphia: M. Fithian, 1845. 108 p. MH-AH. 45-2130

Edgeworth, Maria, 1767-1849. Castle Rachrent: essay on Irish bulls; Essay on the noble science of self justification... New York: Harper, 1845. MCon. 45-2131

Edgeworth, Maria, 1767-1849. Frank. New York: Harper, 1845. 477 p. NNCo-Ci. 45-2132

Edgeworth, Maria, 1767-1849. The little dog Trusty, the cherry orchard, and the orange man. Selected by Mrs. Colman. Boston: B.B. Mussey, [1845] 64 p. MH. 45-2133

Edgeworth, Maria, 1767-1849. Tales and novels. New York: Harper, 1845-1846. 18 v. in 9. MsNF; TNJ. 45-2134

Edmond, Amanda M. Carey, 1824-1862. The broken vow and other poems. Boston: Gould, Kendall and Lincoln, 1845. 324 p. AzPrHi; ICU; MH; NhD; TxU. 45-2135

Edson, Ambrose. Letters to the conscience: or the grounds of solicitude and hope. Fourth edition. New York:

Shepard, Oliver and company, 1845. 145 p. GDecCT. 45-2136

Edson, William J. The vocal guide, a first book for schools and classes in vocal music: containing a systematic arrangement of the elements of art, adapted to the modern mode of teaching by the aid of the black board... New York: Saxton and Miles, 1845. 152 p. OO. 45-2137

Education in Romish seminaries, a letter in answer to certain inquiries respecting the propriety of selecting as places of education, seminaries professedly under the control of religious societies of the church of Rome, by a presbyter of the Protestant Episcopal Church. New York: C. Shepard, 1845. 14 p. CtHT; MdBD; NN; PHi; PPPrHi. 45-2138

Edwards, Jonathan, 1703-1758. Hatak yoshuba uhleha hut chihowa anukhobela ya ibbak toyuka. Sinners in the hands of an angry God. A sermon... Park Hill: John Candy and John F. Wheeler, 1845. 28 p. MBAt. 45-2139

Edwards, Jonathan, 1703-1758. History of the work of redemption; a reprint from the Worcester edition, without alteration, mutilation or omission. New York: Leavitt, 1845. 516 p. IaU; MNP; TxU. 45-2140

Edwards, Jonathan, 1703-1758. Sinners in the hands of an angry God. Philadelphia: Presbyterian Board of Publication, 1845. 16 p. IaDuU-S; OClWHi. 45-2141

Edwards, Jonathan, 1703-1758. Thoughts on the revival of religion in New England, 1740. To which is prefixed a narrative of the surprising work of God in Northampton, Massachusetts, 1735.

New York: American Tract Society 1845. 446 p. ICU; IU; NPV; OCl. 45-2142

Edwards, Jonathan, 1703-1758. A treatise concerning religious affections A reprint from the Worcester edition without alteration, mutilation or omission. New York: Leavitt, Trow and company, 1845. 228 p. IU; MeWC; MNoanNP; McSalL. 45-2143

Eggleston, Nathaniel Hillyer. God among the nations; a discourse delivered on the occasion of the late state fast.. Hartford: Edwin Hunt, 1845. 24 p CtSoP; CU; MBC; MiD-B; WHi. 45 2144

The Egyptian. New York; G. Lane and C.B. Tippett, 1845. 180 p. NNMHi; PPF 45-2145

Eley, James Norman. The American florist; or a guide to the management and cultivation of plants in conservatories greenhouses, rooms and gardens. Hartford: Printed by E. Geer, 1845. [13] 183 p. Ct; IU; MB; MSaP; TxU. 45-2146

The elfin queen, ballad adopted to a beautiful Italian melody and arranged for the piano forte. Baltimore: F.D. Benteen, 1845. 2 p. CSt. 45-2147

Elias, John, 1774-1841.Traethawd ar y sabboth yn hwn yr ystyrir, I. Moesoldeb y gorchynyn II. Newi diad y diwrnod dan yr Oruchwyliaeth newydd III. Sancteiddiad y sabboth; ynghyd ag anaryu an nogaethau a chyfarwydd iadau i'w sanctsiddiaw of. Utica: Evan E. Roberts 1845. 64 p. NUt. 45-2148

Eliot, Samuel Atkins, 1798-1862. An article on public and private charities in

Boston. From the North America Review for July, 1845. Cambridge, Massachusetts: Metcalf and company, 1845. 27 p. CtHWatk; IaHi; MB; MH-AH; RPB. 45-2149

Eliot, Thomas D. Anniversary address, delivered before the American Institute of the city of New York, October 17, 1845. New York: James Van Norden and company, printers, 1845. MBNMHi; MNBedf; PPL-R. 45-2150

Eliot, Thomas Dawes, 1808-1870. Anniversary address delivered before the American Institute of the City of New York, at the Broadway Tabernacle, October 17, 1845, during the eighteenth annual fair. New edition. New York: James Van Norden and company, 1845. 19 p. DLC; MWA. 45-2151

Eliot, William Greenleaf, 1811-1887. A manual of prayer, for public and private worship; with a collection of hymns. Second edition. Boston: Munroe, 1845. 304 p. CBPac; CtY; ICP; MH-AH; MMal. 45-2152

Ella Herbert, or self denial. By a lady. Boston, 1845. 71 p. DLC; MH. 45-2153

Ellet, Charles, 1810-1862. The position and prospects of the Schuylhill Navigation Company. Philadelphia, 1845. 36 p. ICU; MBAt; MH; NNE; PPF. 45-2154

Ellet, Charles, 1810-1862. The Reading Railroad. By Charles Ellet, Jr. New York: J.F. Trow and company, printers, 1845. 28 p. CtY; MH-BA; MnHi; NNE; PPL. 45-2155

Elliot, Jonathan, 1784-1846. The debates in the several state conventions on the adoption of the federal constitution, as recommended by the general convention at Philadelphia, in 1787. Together with the journal of the federal convention... Second edition with considerable additions. Philadelphia: J.B. Lippincott and company, 1845. 5 v. TU. 45-2156

Elliot, Jonathan, 1784-1846. The debates in the several state conventions on the adoption of the federal constitution, as recommended by the general convention at Philadelphia, in 1787. Together with the journal of the federal convention... Second edition with considerable additions. Washington: Taylor and Maury, 1845-1854. 5 v. ICU; ICJ; OO; PPB; PU-L. 45-2157

Elliot, Jonathan, 1781-1846. Debates on the adoption of the federal constitution, in the cnvention held at Philadelphia in 1787; with a diary of the debates of the congress of the confederation... Washington: Printed for the editor, 1845. 641 p. Az; MeB; NR; PPL-R; WHi. 45-2158

Elliot, Jonathan, 1784-1864. The funding system of the United States and of Great Britain, with some tabular facts of other nations touching the same subject. Prepared under a resolution of the House. Washington: Blair and Rives, printers, 1845. 1299 p. CSf; MdBE; MiD; RPB; TxU. 45-2159

Elliot, Samuel Hays, 1809-1869. Emily Maria. A true narrative. New York: The American Tract Society, [1846] 72 p. ICP; ViU. 45-2160

Elliott, Charles, 1792-1869. Indian missionary reminiscences. Principally of the

Wyandot Nation. In which is exhibited the efficacy of the gospel in elevating ignorant and savage men. New York: G. Lane and C.B. Tippett, 1845. 216 p. KU; MBC; NNC. 45-2161

Elliott, Thomas Odingsell. An oration delivered at the New Theatre at Charleston, before the Cincinnati Society and '76 Association of the July 4, 1845. Charleston: Miller and Browne, 1845. 26 p. NcU. 45-2162

Ellis, Chesselden. Speech of Mr. Ellis, of New York, on the annexation of Texas: Delivered in the House, January 25, 1845. Washington: Printed at the Globe office, 1845. 13 p. CtY; LNH; NBu; TxU. 45-2163

Ellis, George Edward, 1814-1894. The christian ministry and its fruits. A sermon, preached at the installation of Rev. Horatio Alger, as pastor of the West Church, in Marlborough, Massachusetts, January 22, 1845.... Boston: James Munroe and company, 1845. 38 p. CtY; ICMe; MBC; MHi; RPB. 45-2164

Ellis, George Edward, 1814-1894. A collection of Psalms and hymns for the sanctuary. Boston: James Munroe and company, 1845. 658 p. CBPac; IEG; MBAU; MMeT; RPB. 45-2165

Ellis, George Edward, 1814-1894. A discourse delivered at the dedication of the first meeting house of the First Church and Society, in Somerville, Massachusetts, September 3, 1845. Boston: James Munroe and company, 1845. 24 p. CCBPac; MH-AH; NN; PL; RPB. 45-2166

Ellis, George Edward, 1814-1894. Let-

ters upon the annexation of Texas, addressed to Hon. J. Quincy Adams, as originally published in the Boston Atlas under the signature of Lisle. Boston: White, Lewis and Potter, 1845. 47 p. CU; ICN; MHi; MWA; TxU. 45-2167

Ellis, Rufus, 1819-1885. The claims of New England Society upon the young student. An address, delivered before the social union of Williston Seminary, Easthampton, Massachusetts. Northampton, [Massachusetts] Printed by John Metcalf, 1845. 16 p. CBPSR; CSmH; CU; MHi. 45-2168

Ellis, Samuel. Address delivered at the opening of the Grand Division of the Sons of Temperance of Maine at Augusta. Boston: White, Lewis and Potter, printers, 1845. 21 p. MB; MWA. 45-2169

Ellis, Sarah Stickney, 1812-1872. The daughters of England, their position in society, character and responsibility. New York: Henry G. Langley, 1845. 125 p. KBB; MH; PLT. 45-2170

Ellis, Sarah Stickney, 1812-1872. Family monitor and domestic guide. New York, 1845. InBra. 45-2171

Ellis, Sarah Stickney, 1812-1872. Home; or the iron rule. A domestic story. New York: Harper and brothers, 1845. 164 p. 45-2172

Ellis, Sarah Stickney, 1812-1872. Irish girl and other poems. New York: James Langley, 1845. 263 p. NjR. 45-2173

Ellis, Sarah Stickney, 1812-1872. Look to the end; or the Bennet's abroad. New York: Harper and brothers, 1845. 142, 16 p. IU; MeB; MWA; NjR; ViAl. 45-2174

Ellis, Sarah Stickney, 1812-1872. Mothers of England, their influences and responsibility. New York, 1845. IP; KBB; MH. 45-2175

Ellis, Sarah Stickney, 1812-1872. Pictures of private life... Author's edition, complete in one volume. [First and second series] New York: J. and H.G. Langley, 1845. [7]-125, [7]-140 p. InNd; KBB; MB; NR. 45-2176

Ellis, Sarah Stickney, 1812-1872. The poetry of life. Author's edition complete in one volume. New York: J. and H.G. Langley, 1845. 184 p. CU; InNd; KyLx; MB; MH; MiD. 45-2177

Ellis, Sarah Stickney, 1812-1872. The prose works of Mrs. Ellis... New York: J.G. Langley, 1845. 2 v. CtB; LNB; MWA; NjN; Vi. 45-2178

Ellis, Sarah Stickney, 1812-1872. The select works of Mrs. Ellis... New York: J. and H.G. Langley, 1845. CtMW; Ia; InNd; MShM; MWA; NcU. 45-2179

Ellis, Sarah Stickney, 1812-1872. A voice from the vintage on the force of example: addressed to those who think and feel. New York: J. and H.G. Langley, 1845. 54 p. InNd; MB; MH; MoS. 45-2180

Ellis, Sarah Stickney, 1812-1872. The wives of England, their relative duties, domestic influence and social obligations. Author's edition. New York: J. and H.G. Langley, 1845. 122 p. KBB; MH; MoKCM. 45-2181

Ellis, Sarah Stickney, 1812-1872. The women of England, their social duties and domestic habits. Uniform edition. New York: J. and H.G. Langley, 1845. 125 p. KBB; MoKCM. 45-2182

Ellison, William J. An oration delivered on July 4, 1845, in Williamston, North Carolina. New York: Shipman, 1845. 19 p. NcWfc. 45-2183

Ellmer castle: A Roman Catholic story of Ireland in the nineteenth century. Revised American edition. Philadelphia: Wilson and Stokes, 1845. 201 p. MdBP; MdBLC; NjR. 45-2184

Ellwanger and Barry, Rochester, New York. Descriptive catalogue of fruits, ornamental trees, flowering shrubs and plants, cultivated and for sale... at the Mount Hope Botanic Garden and Nurseries. Rochester, New York: 1845. 42 p. N. 45-2185

Ellyson's Richmond directory, and business reference book. Carefully arranged for 1845-1846. Richmond: H.K. Ellyson, [1845] CSmH; PPL-R; ViW. 45-2186

Elmer, Lucius Quintius Cincinnatus. Speech of Mr. Elmer, of New Jersey, on the Rhode Island controversy. Delivered in the House, February 28, 1845. Washington: Printed at the Globe office, 1845. 8 p. MH; MiD-B; MWA; NjR; RHi. 45-2187

Elmira Academy. Public exhibition phamplet. Elmira, 1845. 2 p. NE. 45-2188

Elssler, Fanny, 1810-1884. The letters and journal of Fanny Ellsler. Written before and after her operatic campaign in the United States. New York: H.G. Daggers, 1845. 65 p. CtHWatk; IEN; MH; MiD; PPL. 45-2189

Elton's comic all-my-nack, 1846. New York: Elton, [1845] MWA. 45-2190

Elton's comic almanack. New York: [1845] CU. 45-2191

Elton's funny almanack, 1846. New York, New York: Elton, [1845] MWA; NNMuCN. 45-2192

Elwood, Anna Katharine Curteis. Memoirs of the Literary Ladies of England from the commencement of the last century. Philadelphia: G.B. Zieber and company, 1845. 336 p. CtY; IU; MB; NN; PPL. 45-2193

Elyria, Ohio. A comparison of the different routes of the Cleveland, Columbus and Cincinnati Railroad. Cleveland: Younglove's steam Power Press, 1845. 20 p. OClWHi. 45-2194

Embury, Emma Catherine Manley, 1806-1863. American wild flowers in their native haunts. With plates and landscape views, by E. Whitefield. New York: D. Appleton and company, 1845. 256 p. CtY; IC; LNT; MB. 45-2195

Embury, Emma Catherine Manley, 1806-1863. American wild flowers in their native haunts. With plates and landscape views, by E. Whitefield. Second edition. New York: D. Appleton and company, 1845. MH; MoSB. 45-2196

Embury, Emma Catherine Manley, 1806-1863. The blind girl, with other tales. New York: Harper and brothers, 1845. 222 p. CtY; IU; NGos; ODW; ViU. 45-2197

Emerson, Benjamin Dudley, 1781-1872. Introduction to the national spell-

ing books, with easy and progressive reading lessons, for the use of primary schools. New edition, revised and enlarged. Claremont, New Hampshire: Claremont Manufacturing Company, 1845. MH. 45-2198

Emerson, Benjamin Dudley, 1781-1872. The second class reader; designed for the use of the middle class of schools in the United States. Claremont, New Hampshire: Claremont Manufacturing Company, 1845. 168 p. MH; NhU; PReaAT. 45-2199

Emerson, Benjamin Dudley, 1781-1872. The second class reader; designed for the use of the middle class of schools in the United States. Philadelphia: Hogan and Thompson, 1845. 168 p. WvMc. 45-2200

Emerson, Benjamin Dudley, 1781-1872. The third class reader designed for the use of the younger classes in the schools of the United States. Bradford, Vermont: Asa Low, 1845. 160 p. NoLoc. 45-2201

Emerson, Benjamin Dudley, 1781-1872. The third class reader designed for the use of the younger classes in the schools of the United States. Claremont, New Hampshire: Claremont Manufacturing Company, 1845. MH. 45-2202

Emerson, Benjamin Dudley, 1781-1872. The third class reader designed for the use of the younger classes in the schools of the United States. Philadelphia: Hogan and Thompson, 1845. 160 p. PHi; VtMorr. 45-2203

Emerson, Frederick, 1788-1857. The case of Frederick Emerson vs. Charles

Davis and Alfred S. Barnes... Boston: S.N. Dickinson and company, 1845. DLC. 45-2204

Emerson, Frederick, 1788-1857. Key to the North American arithmetic. Part second and part third. Boston: Jenks and Palmer, etc., etc., 1845. 72 p. DLC; MB; MH; Nh-Hi; WaS. 45-2205

Emerson, Frederick, 1788-1857. North American arithmetic. Part first, for young learners. Boston, 1845. CtHWatk. 45-2206

Emerson, Frederick, 1788-1857. North American arithmetic. Part first, for young learners. Claremont, 1845. CtHWatk. 45-2207

Emerson, Frederick, 1788-1857. North American arithmetic. Part second, uniting oral and written exercises. Boston: Jenks and Palmer, 1845. 216 p. MH; RPB. 45-2208

Emerson, Frederick, 1788-1857. North American arithmetic. Part second, uniting oral and written exercises. Boston: Russell, [1845?] 190 p. IaU. 45-2209

Emerson, Frederick, 1788-1857. North American arithmetic. Part second, uniting oral and written exercises. Philadelphia: Hogan and Thompson, 1845. 216 p. DLC; MB; NIC; PHi; RPB. 45-2210

Emerson, Frederick, 1788-1857. North American arithmetic. Part third, for advanced scholars. Boston: Jenks and Palmer and company, 1845. 288 p. DLC; ICBB; MB; MBarn; OClWHi. 45-2211

Emerson, Frederick, 1788-1857. Outlines of geography and history, present-ing a concise view of the world. Philadelphia: Hogan and Thompson, 1845. 144 p. MoS; MLow. 45-2212

Emerson, Joseph, 1777-1833. Emerson's lessons on the old testament; being a part of a biblical outline. Boston: Crocker and Brewster, 1845. 122 p. MLow. 45-2213

Emerson, Joseph, 1777-1833. Emerson's lessons on the old testament; being a part of a biblical outline. Fifth edition. Boston: Crocker and Brewster, 1845. MH-AH. 45-2214

Emerson, Joseph, 1777-1833. Questions adopted to Whelpleys compend of history. Twelfth edition. New York: Collins, brothers and company, 1845. 69 p. KWiF; OWoC. 45-2215

Emerson, Joseph, 1777-1833. Questions and supplement to Goodrich's history of the United States. A new edition, revised and adapted to the enlarged edition of the history. Boston: Jenks and Palmer, 1845. 192 p. CU; KyDC; MH; MHa. 45-2216

Emerson, Ralph Waldo, 1803-1882. Essays: second series. Boston: J. Munroe and company, 1845. 313 p. CSt; ICN; FTU; MBAt; NPV. 45-2217

Emerson, Ralph Waldo, 1803-1882. Nature: addresses, and lectures. Philadelphia: David McKay, 1845. 346 p. IaCorn. 45-2218

Emma Somerville; or the violated sanctuary; an interesting tale, by an American lady. Lowell: N. Dayton; Boston: Lewis and Sampson, 1845. 127 p. CtY; MWA; RPB. 45-2219

Emma Willard School, Troy, New York. Catalogue of the officers and pupils of the Troy Female Seminary, for the academic year, commending September 18, 1844 and ending August 6, 1845, together with the conditions of admittance, etc. Troy: N. Tuttle, 1845. NGlf. 45-2220

Emmons, Ebenezer, 1799-1863. Introductory address, delivered before the class of the Albany Medical College, at the commencement of the session of 1845-1846. Albany: Printed by Carroll and Cook, 1845. 24 p. MWiW; NjR; NN; NNNAM; PPHa. 45-2221

Emmons' Charlestown directory... Charlestown: Charles P. Emmons, 1845-1872. 13 v. MBAt; MBNEH. 45-2222

Emory, John, 1789-1835. A defence of "our fathers," and of the original organization of the Methodist Episcopal Church against the Rev. Alexander M'Claine, and others. Fifth edition. New York: G. Lane and C.B. Tippett, 1845. 154 p. ArSsJ; GAGTh; IaHoL; MsMer-N; TChU. 45-2223

Emory, John, 1789-1835. The episcopal controversy reviewed, by John Emory. Late one of bishops of the Methodist Episcopal Church. Edited by his son, from an unfinished manuscript. New York: G. Lane and C.B. Tippett for the Methodist Episcopal Church, 1845. 380 p. GAGTh; GEU-T; IaOskJF; KBB; MnSH. 45-2224

Emory, Robert, 1814-1848. History of the discipline of the Methodist Episcopal Church. New York: G. Lane and C.B. Tippett, 1845. 364 p. CtMW; IaU; ODaB; NcD; PPP. 45-2225

The encourager; a monthly magazine for children. Edited by Daniel P. Kidder. New York: Lane and Tippett, for the Sunday School Union of the Methodist Episcopal Church, 1845. 288 p. DLC; NcU; NHt. 45-2226

Encylopaedia Americana. A popular dictionary of arts, sciences, literature, history, politics and biography. A new edition. Philadelphia: Lea and Blanchard, 1845-1855. 14 v. NcCJ; NPalK; Nj; PPCC; PU. 45-2227

Enfield, Connecticut. First Congregational Church. Historical notice of the Congregational Church, in Enfield, Connecticut, with the confession of faith, the covenant, and a chronological catalogue of the members since 1783. Hartford, Connecticut: J. Gaylord Wells, 1845. 28 p. Ct; MWA; MBLIHI. 45-2228

Engelmann, George, 1809-1884. Plantae lindheimerianae; an ememeration of F. Lindheimer's collection of Texan plants, with remarks, and descriptions of new species, etc. Boston: Freeman and Bolles, 1845-1850. 2 pts. LNH; MH; MnU; PPAN; RPB; TxD-T. 45-2229

Engles, William Morrison, 1797-1867. Rills from the fountain of wisdom, or the book of proverbs arranged and illustrated. Philadelphia: Presbyterian Board of Publication, 1845. 188 p. LNL; NjPT; OWoC; PPL; ViRut. 45-2230

English, Williams B. Rosina Meadows, the village maid; or temptations unveiled. A local domestic drama in three acts. New York: S. French, [1845] 52 p. C; CtY. 45-2231

English German and German English

dictionary containing all the words in general use, designating the various parts of speech in both languages compiled from the dictionaries of Lloyd, Nohden, Flugel and Sporschil. Philadelphia: Mentz and Rouvoudt, 1845. 498 p. CtHWatk; MtBil. 45-2232

An English woman in Egypt, letters from Cairo written during a residence there in 1842-1844 with E.W. Lane. Philadelphia, 1845. PPL-R. 45-2233

English woman in Russia; impressions of society and manners of the Russian at home, by a lady. New York: Charles Scribner, 1845. 316 p. RNR. 45-2234

Enlargement of the Schuylkill navigation. No. 2. Philadelphia, 1845. 2 v. DLC; ICJ; MB; MBAt; PPF. 45-2235

Enquiry into the propriety of granting charters of incorporation for manufacturing and other purposes in South Carolina. By one of the people. Charleston: Walker and Burke, 1845. 14 p. GU; ScU; WHi. 45-2236

Ensign and Thayer, publishers, New York. Map of the world on Mercator's projection. New York, 1845. Nh. 45-2237

Entick, John, 1703?-1773. Tyronis thesarus; or Entick's Latin-English dictionary, with a classical index of the preterperfects and supines of verbs, designed for the use of schools. Carefully revised and augumented throughout by the Rev. M.G. Sarjant. Baltimore: Joseph Neal, 1845. 620 p. NoLoc. 45-2238

Episcopal City Mission, Boston. Act of incorporation and by-laws of the Episcopal City Mission, 1844. Boston: Joseph G. Torrey, 1845. 12 p. NNUT. 45-2239

An episcopal mission to seamen in New York. [New York?] 1845. CtHT. 45-2240

Episcopal observer. Boston, 1845. v. 1-. CtHT; MB; MBC; PPL; TxU. 45-2241

Epitome of the art of spiritual navigation; or a voyage to heaven recommended: By a christian mariner. With explanatory notes by Edward Hare. Philadelphia: James Harmstead, 1845. 144 p. ICBB; PPiRPr. 45-2242

Epps, John, 1804-1869. Domestic homoeopathy; or rules for the domestic treatment of the maladies of infants, children, and adults, and for the conduct and the treatment during pregnancy, confinement, and suckline. Second American from the Fourth London edition. Boston: O. Clapp, 1845. 239 p. MBM; NBMS; NN; PPHa. 45-2243

Erie Canal Company of Pennsylvania. Second annual report of the Erie Canal Company, to the legislature of Pennsylvania, for the year 1844. Harrisburg: J.M.G. Lescure, 1845. 5 p. OSW; PHi. 45-2244

Erskine College. Due West, South Carolina. The annual catalogue of the officers and students of Erskine College. Sessions of 1845. Greenville: O.H. Wells, 1845. 11 p. GDecCT. 45-2245

Ertheiler, Moritz. A phrase book in English and German. New York: Greeley and McElrath, etc., etc., 1845. 172 p. MH; MWHi. 45-2246

Eschenburg, Johann Joachim, 1743-

1820. Classical antiquities being part of the "Manual of classical literature," from the German of J.J. Eschenburg, by N.W. Fiske. Philadelphia: Biddle, 1845. 331 p. IaMpl; LNP; MdBJ; PPWe; RNPL. 45-2247

Eschenburg, Johann Joachim, 1743-1820. Manual of classical literature. From the German with additions by N.W. Fiske. Fourth edition. [Seven thousand] Philadelphia: C.C. and J. Biddle, etc., etc., 1845. 690 p. MH; NcAS. 45-2248

Esquirol, Jean Etienne Dominique, 1772-1840. Mental maladies. A treatise on insanity. Translated from the French, with additions, by E.K. Hunt. Philadelphia: Lea and Blanchard, 1845. 496 p. ICU- R; IJI; NNU-M; PPCP; TxSaO. 45-2249

Essay on the evils of the banking system as conducted in the United States. Philadelphia, 1845. MBAt. 45-2250

Essex County, Massachusetts. Society for the promotion of Agriculture, Horticulture and Manufactures. Constitution, revised and amended, October 2, 1845. Newark, 1845. 11 p. WU-A. 45-2251

Essex South Conference on Foreign missions. Report of the committee presented at Marblehead, July 9, 1845. Salem: Henry Whipple, 1845. 12 p. MWA. 45-2252

Essling, Fred. The true test; or the way to distinguish envy from criticism. Louisville: Noble and Dean, 1845. ICU; KyLo; PPL-R. 45-2253

Etiquette for gentlemen; or short rule and reflections for conduct in society. By a gentleman. Philadelphia: Lindsay and Blakiston, 1845. 224 p. ICN. 45-2254

Etiquette for ladies; with hints on the presentation, improvement, and display of female beauty. Philadelphia: Lindsay and Blakiston, 1845. 224 p. MWA; NIC PHi; WKenHi. 45-2255

Ettwein, John. Remarks on the traditions of the Indians of North America Philadelphia, 1845. PPL. 45-2256

Eva Labree: or the rescued chief. A tale of the city and forest. By Tom Shortfellow, [pseud.] Boston: Gleason's Publishing Hall, 1845. 66 p. ICU; MB; NSmb 45-2257

Evangelical Lutheran Church in the United States. Collection of hymns and prayers, for public and private worship Published by order of the Evangelical Lutheran Joint Synod of Ohio. Zanesville: Lutheran Standard office, 1845. 368 p. OCoC. 45-2258

Evangelical Lutheran Church in the United States. Proceedings of the thirteenth convention of the general synod Baltimore: Printed at the publication Rooms, 1845. 96 p. ICartC; OSW. 45-2259

Evangelical Lutheran Joint Synod of Ohio and Other States. A collection of hymns and prayers, for public and private worship. Zanesville: Printed at the Lutheran Standard office, 1845. 368 p NNUT. 45-2260

Evangelical Lutheran Joint Synod of Ohio. Minutes of the fifth session con vened in Lancaster, Ohio, May 17, 1845. Zanesville: Printed at the Lutheran Standard office, 1845. 26 p. OCoC. 45-2261

Evangelical Lutheran Synod and Ministerium of North Carolina. Minutes of the Evangelical Lutheran Synod and Ministerium of North Carolina. Salisbury: Printed at the Carolina Watchman office, 1845. 29 p. ICartC. 45-2262

Evangelical Lutheran Synod and Ministerium of Pennsylvania. Verhandlunged der 98sten jahrlichen versammlung des Deutschen Ministeriums. Sumnytaun, 1845. 44 p. PHi. 45-2263

Evangelical Lutheran Synod and Ministerium of Virginia. Bericht der Verrichtungen der Synode Salem, North Carolina: Gedruct bey Blum und Sohn, 1845. 44 p. NcWsM. 45-2264

Evangelical Lutheran Synod of Maryland. Proceedings of the twenty-seventh annual session. Baltimore: Printed at the publication rooms, 1845. 43 p. ICartC; OSW. 45-2265

Evangelical Lutheran Synod of Miami. Proceedings of a convention and of the first and second sessions. Baltimore: Printed at the publication rooms, 1845. 39 p. ICartC; ICN; OSW. 45-2266

Evangelical Lutheran Synod of Ohio. Proceedings of the tenth session of the English Synod. Baltimore: Printed at the publication rooms, 1845. 32 p. OSW. 45-2267

Evangelical Lutheran Synod of the West. Proceedings of the tenth annual convention of the Synod. Baltimore: Printed at the publication rooms, 1845. 35 p. OSW. 45-2268

Evangelical Lutheran Synod of Virginia. Minutes of the fifteenth annual session held in Shepherdstown, May 8-12, 1845. Baltimore: Printed at the publication rooms, 1845. 38 p. NcU. 45-2269

Evangelical Lutheran Tennessee Synod. Twenty-fifth session. Ecclesiastical annals. Report of the translations of the Evangelical Lutheran Tennessee Synod, during the twenty fifth session, convened at Zion's church, Shenandoah County, Virginia. From the 6th to the 9th of October, 1845. Also a treatise on infant baptism by Dr. Martin Luther. Salem; Printed by Blum and son, 1845. 16 p. ScCoT. 45-2270

Evangelical repository. Devoted to the principles of the reformation, as set forth in the formularies of the Westminster Divines, and witnessed for by the Associate Synod of North America. Edited by Joseph T. Cooper. Philadelphia: William S. Young, 1845. InU; NcWfC; MBC. 45-2271

Evans, J. National ingratitude lamented: a sermon preached in Charlestown, South Carolina, September 14, 1744, a day of public fast. Charlestown, 1845. 31 p. MH. 45-2272

Eveline Newville; or a spirit, yet a woman too. By a lady of the South... New York: Burgess, Stringer and company, 1845. 108 p. CtY; DLC; NN; ViU. 45-2273

Evelyn of Alleyne Cliff; or the two lovers. A romance of the Highlands. By Tom Shortfellow [pseud] Boston:

Gleason's Publishing Hall, 1845. 42 p. CtY; RPB; ViU. 45-2274

Everest, Charles William, 1814-1877. The poets of Connecticut; with biographical sketches. Hartford: Case, Tiffany and Burnham, 1845. 468 p. NIC; MnSM. 45-2275

Everest, Charles William, 1814-1877. The snow drop; a gift for a friend. Edited by C.W. Everest... New York: J.S. Redfield, 1845. 128 p. CtHWatk; CtSoP; RPB; TxU. 45-2276

Everest, Charles William, 1814-1877. Vision of death and other poems. Hartford: Robins and Smith, 1845. [11]-127 p. CtHT; CtHWatk; CtY; MB; Mi. 45-2277

Everett, Alexander Hill, 1790-1847. Critical and miscellaneous essays. To which are added a few poems. Boston: J. Munroe and company, 1845. 563 p. AzU; CtMW; KyLoP; MeB; PPA. 45-2278

Everett, Alexander Hill, 1790-1847. Critical and miscellaneous essays. To which are added a few poems. Boston: James Munroe and company, 1845-1846. 2 v. ICU; MoSM; NRU-W; NhPet; OCY; TMeC. 45-2279

Everett, Alexander Hill, 1790-1847. Poems. Boston: James Munroe and company, 1845. 105 p. ICU; KyBC; MH; MLy. 45-2280

Every man his own gardener; an account of every vegetable production cultivated for the table, by the plough and the spade. New York: Homans and Ellis, [1845] 92 p. MB; NIC; NN. 45-2281

Every man's doctor: or family guide to health, containing a condensed description of the various causes and symptoms of diseases. To which is added one hundred and fifty recipes. New York: J.K. Wellman, 1845. 72 p. MiD-B; OU. 45-2282

Every Philadelphian's book, and stranger's guide. Philadelphia: Thomas, Cowperthwait and company, 1845. 56 p. DLC; PHi. 45-2283

Ewbank, Thomas, 1792-1870. Specimens of ancient oracular and fighting colipiles: with remarks on dragons and other fire breathing monsters of mythology and the middle ages, being a supplement to his treatise on hydraulics and mechanics. New York: The author, 1845. [5]-31 p. ICN; LNH; MBAt; MS; NIC. 45-2284

Ewing, M.C. Description of the water power at the great falls of the Potomac. n.p., 1845. Map. NHi. 45-2285

Ewing, M.C. The water power at the Great Falls of the Potomac. Washington: Printed by J. and G.S. Gidion, [1845] 7 p. DLC; MH- AH. 45-2286

Executor's and administrator's guide; containing the revised statutes relating to wills and testaments; the distribution of the estates of intestates; and the rights, powers and duties of executors and administrators with the lastest amendments. New York, 1845. 132 p. MH-L. 45-2287

Exercises on phonography; or writing by sound, natural and rational method of writing all languages by one alphabet.

New York: J. Donlevy, 1845. 24 p. MdBP. 45-2288

Emmet, Robert. The life, trial and conversations of Robert Emmet, leader of the Irish insurrection of 1803. New York: R. Coddington, 1845. 132 p. DLC; MBC; MdBS; MH; NjP. 45-2289

F

Fables showing the number of emigrants and recaptured Africans sent to the colony of Liberia by the government of the United States. Washington, 1845. 128 p. CU; DLC; MWA; NN; PU. 45-2290

Fact to correct fancies; or short narratives compiled from the biography of remarkable women. Written for children. By a mother. New York: C.D. Frances and company, 1845. 186 p. MBedf; NN; PP; TxU. 45-2291

Factory life as it is. By an operative. [Lowell, 1845] 8 p. MB; RPB. 45-2292

Facts for the people of Barre touching the hostile attack of Rev. A. Royce of this town, upon the Methodist Episcopal Church, in a tract entitled "Considerations for the people of Barre." Montpelier: Poland and Briggs, printers, 1845. 51 p. MB; MiD-B. 45-2293

Fairbanks, Joseph. The experience of Joseph Fairbanks, of Farmington, Maine. Farmington: J.S. Swift, printer, 1845. 62 p. MeLewB. 45-2294

Fairchild, Ashbel Green. The Great Supper; or an illustration and defense of some of the doctrines of grace. In three discourses. Second edition, revised and enlarged, with an introduction by Rev. Alexander T. McGill, D.D. Pittsburg: Luke Loomis, 1845. [9]-172 p. ICP; IEG; OSW; TBriK. 45-2295

Fairchild, Joy Hamlet, 1790-1859. A full and accurate report of the trial of Rev Joy H. Fairchild, before the municipal court of the city of Boston, for adultry with Miss Rhoda Davidson. Boston Purdy and Bradley, 1845. 24 p. M, MBNEH; MH; PP. 45-2296

Fairchild, Joy Hamlet, 1790-1859 Statement and review of the whole case of the Reverend Jay H. Fairchild from it's commencement to it's termination, compiled from original documents, by a member of the Suffolk bar. Boston. Wright's Steam Press, 1845. 104 p. MBC MoU; NBLiHi; Nh. 45-2297

Fairchild, Joy Hamlet, 1790-1859 Times report. Trial of Rev. Joy Hamlet Fairchild. On a charge of adultery with Miss Rhoda Davidson. Boston, 1845. 44 p. Nh; N-L. 45-2298

Fairchild, Joy Hamlet, 1790-1859. Trial of Rev. Joy Hamlet Fairchild. On a charge of adultery with Miss Rhoda Davidson. Reported for the Boston Daily Times. By J.E.P. Weeks, 1845. Boston, 1845. 32 p. DLC; NN. 45-2299

Fairchild, Joy Hamlet, 1790-1859. Trial of Rev. Joy Hamlet Fairchild. On a charge of adultery with Miss Rhoda Davidson. Reported for the Boston Daily Times. By J.E.P. Weeks, 1845. [Third edition] Boston, 1845. 46 p. MH; NIC-L. 45-2300

Fairchild, Joy Hamlet, 1790-1859. The truth revealed. Statements and review of the whole case of the Reverend Joy Fairchild... Compiled from original documents, by a member of the Suffolk Bar. With an appendix. Boston: Wright's Steam Press, 1845. 104 p. CBPSR; DLC; NjR; OMC; WaU-L. 45-2301

The fairy cabinet; fairy tales translated from the French and German. Boston, 1845. MBAt. 45-2302

Falconer, Thomas, 1805-1882. The Oregon question; or a statement of the British claims to the Oregon Territory, in opposition to the pretensions of the government of the United States. With a chronological table, and a map of the territory. New York: W. Taylor, 1845. 40 p. MH; PHi; RPB; ScC; WHi. 45-2303

Falconer, Thomas, 1805-1882. Reply to Mr. Greenhow's answer: with Mr. Greenhow's rejoinder. [Washington? 1845?] 4 p. CU-B; NHi. 45-2304

Family almanac and Franklin Calendar for 1846. Troy, New York: W. and H. Merriam, [1845] MWA. 45-2305

The family almanac for the year 1845, containing calculations for five different latitudes and intended for general use in the United States. New York: Collins, Brother and company, 1845. 15 p. MWA. 45-2306

Family christian almanac for 1846. By David Young. New York, New York: American Tract Society, [1845] IAlS; MPeHi; MWA; MWHi; NjR. 45-2307

Family doctor and medical almanac for

1846. Boston: Comstock and Ross, [1845] MWA. 45-2308

The family manual, containing things worth knowing. Edited by Timothy Trainer, formerly an officer in the British Army. New York, 1845. 32 p. InU; MBC; MH; MoSM. 45-2309

Faneuil Hall committee on the project of a supply of pure water. Address of the committee... for the city of Boston, May 5, 1845. Boston: From the press of W.W. Clapp and son, [1845] 32 p. CtY; MH. 45-2310

Farley, Frederick A. Grounds for rejecting the text of the three heavenly witnesses... with concession of trinitarians upon the same. Boston: J. Munroe, 1845. 24 p. IEG; MeBat; MMeT-Hi; PPM; RP. 45-2311

Farmer, George O. The beloved one. Boston: Bradlee and company, 1845. CtY; MB. 45-2312

Farmer, George O. A world of love at home. Boston: Bradley and company, 1845. 2 p. MB. 45-2313

Farmer, John, 1789-1838. Map of the surveyed part of Michigan. New York, 1845. ICU. 45-2314

Farmer's almanac. Baltimore: Armstrong and Berry, [1845] IaHA. 45-2315

The farmer's almanac for 1846. Astronomical calculations by Zadock Thompson. Newbury, Vermont: F. and H. Keys, [1845] MWA. 45-2316

Farmer's almanac for 1846. By David

Young. New York, New York: C. Small, [1845] MWA. 45-2317

Farmer's almanac for 1846. By David Young. New York, New York: Collins brothers and company, [1845] MWA. 45-2318

Farmer's almanac for 1846. By David Young. New York, New York: T.W. Strong, [1845] MWA. 45-2319

Farmer's almanac for 1846. By David Young. Newark, New Jersey: Benjamin Olds, [1845] MWA. 45-2320

Farmer's almanac for 1846. By David Young. Rahway, New Jersey: John Pearson, [1845] NjR. 45-2321

Farmer's almanac for 1846. By David Young. Trenton, New Jersey: Charles Scott, [1845] MWA. 45-2322

Farmer's almanac for 1846. Calculations by John Ward. Philadelphia: Thomas Davies, [1845] MWA. 45-2323

Farmer's almanac for the year 1846. By David Young, New Brunswick, New Jersey: John Terhune, [1845] 35 p. MWA; NjR. 45-2324

Farmer's almanac for the year 1846. By David Young. Newark, New Jersey: Benjamin Olds, [1845] MWA; NjR. 45-2325

Farmer's almanac for the year of our Lord 1846. By David Young. New York: H. and S. Raynor, [1845] MWA; NjR; WHi. 45-2326

The farmer's almanack, calculated on a new and improved plan for 1846. Boston,

Carter, Hendee and company, 1845. CU. 45-2327

The farmer's almanack, calculated on a new and improved plan, for the year of our Lord, 1845. Boston: Carter, Hendee and company; [etc., 1845] CU. 45-2328

Farmer's almanack for 1846. By David Young. Ithaca, New York: Mack, Andrus and company, [1845] MWA. 45-2329

Farmer's almanack for 1846. By Robert B. Thomas. Portland, Maine: H.H. Little and company, [1846] MWA. 45-2330

Farmer's almanack for 1846. Calculations by Zadock Thompson. Montpelier, Vermont: E.P. Walton and sons, [1845] MWA. 45-2331

Farmer's almanack for 1846. Calculations by Zadock Thompson. Newbury, Vermont: F. and H. Keyes, [1845] MWA. 45-2332

The farmer's almanack for the year of our Lord 1845; by Robert B. Thomas. Boston: Jenks and Palmer, 1845. MBev-Hi; MHa; MPeHi; MWa; RNHi. 45-2333

Farmer's almanack for the year of our Lord 1846. Boston: Samuel N. Dickinson and company, printers, [1845] RPE. 45-2334

Farmers' almanac, for the year of our Lord 1846. By David Young. New York: H. and S. Raynor, [1845] 34 p. WHi. 45-2335

The farmer's and farrier's almanac for 1846. Philadelphia: John B. Perry, [1845] MWA; NjR. 45-2336

Farmer's and mechanic's almanac for 1846. Philadelphia: Mentz and Rovandt, [1845] MWA. 45-2337

Farmer's and planter's almanac for 1846... Salem, North Carolina: Blum and son, [1845] NcAS. 45-2338

Farmer's calendar for 1846. By Edward Hagerty. Baltimore, Maryland: Cushing and brother, [1845] MWA. 45-2339

The farmer's library. New York: Greeley and McElrath, 1845-1848. 3 v. IC; ICMcHi; NjR. 45-2340

Farnham, Thomas Jefferson, 1804-1848. History of Oregon Territory, it being a demonstration of the title of these United States of North America to the same. Second edition. New York: W. Taylor; Boston: Saxton and Kelt, etc., etc., 1845. [7]-83 p. MH; MWA; OCl; ViU. 45-2341

Farnham, Thomas Jefferson, 1804-1848. Mexico: its geography, its people, and its institutions: with a map, containing the result of the latest explorations of Fremont, Wilkes, and others. New York: H. Long and brother, 1845. IG; PHi. 45-2342

Farr, Edward. Select poetry, chiefly devotional of the reign of Queen Elizabeth. Collected and edited for the Parker Society. Cambridge [U.S.?] Printed at the university press, 1845. 2 v. IaU; IP; LNT; MH; TBriK. 45-2343

Farrar, Eliza Ware Rotch, 1791-1870. The young lady's friend. New York: S. and William Wood, 1845. 432 p. ViU. 45-2344

Farren, George. The common forms and rules for drawing and answering an original bill in Chancery, as directed and suggested by the new orders of court and report cases... Boston: Webb and company, 1845. 132 p. MH; Nj; OCLaw; PPB; WaU. 45-2345

Fashionable American letter writer: containing a variety of plain and elegant letters, on business, love, courtship, marriage, relationship, friendship, etc. With forms... Troy, New York: W. and H. Merriam, 1845. 224 p. Ct; N. 45-2346

Fate of the Steamship President, which sailed from New York, March 11, 1841, bound for Liverpool. Boston, 1845. 34 p. MB; MH; MWA; RWe. 45-2347

Fauvel-Gouraud, Francois. Phreno-mnemotechny; or the art of memory: the series of lectures, explanatory of the principles of the system, delivered in New York and Philadelphia, in the beginning of 1844. New York: H.G. Langley, 1845. DCL; ICJ. 45-2348

Fauvel-Gouraud, Francois. Phreno-mnemotechny; or the art of memory: the series of lectures, explanatory of the principles of the system, delivered in New York and Philadelphia, in the beginning of 1844. New York and London: Wiley and Putnam, 1845. 566 p. GHi; MeB; NbOM; RP; WaPS. 45-2349

Fauvel-Gouraud, Francois. Programme of Prof. Fauvel-Gouraud's public experimental lectures: being a selection of the principal scientific, historical, statistical, geographical and literary facts or questions, which are answered from memory. New York:

Phreno-Mnemotechnic Depot, 1845. 96 p. DLC; MH; MHi; NIC; NNS. 45-2350

Fays' boarding school for boys. Elizabethtown, New Jersey: Baltimore, 1845. NjP. 45-2351

Fearne, Charles, 1742-1794. An essay on the learning of contingent remainders and executory devises. Fourth American, from the tenth London edition; containing the notes, cases, and other matter added to the former editions, by Charles Butler... Philadelphia, Robert H. Small, 1845. 2 v. DLC; NcU; NNU; PV-L; WaU-L. 45-2352

The Federalist, on the new constitution, written in the year 1788, by Alexander Hamilton, James Madison, and John Jay... Sixth edition. Washington: J. and G.S. Gideon, 1845. 391 p. GDecCT; MeAug; MiU-C; PP; RJa. 45-2353

Fehr, J.H.A. Essay on homeopathia, with a glance at allopathia. Lexington: Inguirer office printer, 1845. 48 p. DLC; DNLM; KyDC; OC. 45-2354

Felt, J.P. System of astronomy on the copernican of true principles, with tables... Salem, Massachusetts: Ives and Pease, 1845. 32 p. CSt; DLC; MH; MSaP; PU. 45-2355

Felt, Joseph Barlow, 1789-1869. Annals of Salem. Second edition. Salem: W. and S.B. Ives; Boston: James Munroe and company, 1845- 1849. 2 v. CoPu; IHi; Me; NhM; OClWHi. 45-2356

Female Institute of the Tennessee Annual Conference, Athens, Alabama. Catalogue of the officers and students of the Tennessee conference of the Female Institue for the year 1844-1845. Athens, Alabama, 1845. 15 p. GEU. 45-2357

Fenelon, pseud. Letters to the Rt. Rev. John Hughes, Catholic Bishop of New York, upon the present system of public education; with suggestions for a plan more effectual and less expensive; recommending itself to the approbation of christians of all denominations. Philadelphia: M. Fithian, 1845. 31 p. WStfSF. 45-2358

Fenelon, Francois de Salignac de la Mothe, 1651-1715. Les adventures de Telamaqui, fils d'Ulysse, par M. Fenelon. Nouv. ed. avec la signification des mots les plus difficiles en anglais au bas do chaque page. a laquelle on a ajonte, un petit dictionaire, mythologique et geographique, pour faciliter l'intelligence de cet ouvrage. Boston: Phillips, Sampson and company; Philadelphia: E. Barrington and G.D. Haswell, [1845?] 420 p. CSt; ICU; MtU; ViU. 45-2359

Ferguson, Adam. The history of the progress and termination of the Roman government. Philadelphia: Thomas Wardle, 1845. 493 p. CtY; IJI; NcGv; OCX; ScDuE. 45-2360

Fergusson, William, 1808-1877. A system of practical surgery... Second edition, with notes and added illustrations. Philadelphia: Lea and Blanchard, 1845. 639 p. A-Ar; CSt-L; MBM; PPCP; ViRMC. 45-2361

Fessenden, Guy Mannering, 1804-1871. The history of Warren, Rhode Island, from the earliest times; with particular notices of Mossasoit and his family. Providence: H.H. Brown, 1845. 125 p.

DLC; MHi; NIC; PPL; OClWHi. 45-2362

Fessenden, Thomas Green, 1771-1837. The complete farmer and rural economist; containing a compendious epitome of the most important branches of agriculture and rural economy. Seventh edition, revised, improved and enlarged. Boston: Otis, Broaders and company; Philadelphia: Thomas, Cowperthwait and company, 1845. 345 p. ScCleA. 45-2363

Fessenden, Thomas Green, 1771-1837. The new American gardener, containing practical directions on the culture of fruits and vegetables; including landscape and ornamental gardening, grapevines, silk, strawberries, etc., etc.... Seventeenth edition. Boston: Otis, Broaders and company, 1845. 306 p. InWefU; NNNBG; OCHP; PMA. 45-2364

Fessenden, Thomas Green, 1771-1837. The new American gardener, containing practical directions on the culture of fruits and vegetables; including landscape and ornamental gardening, grapevines, silk, strawberries, etc., etc.... Eighteenth edition. Boston. 1845. 306 p. MoSB; WU-A. 45-2365

A few hasty reasons, why the mission of the United States at Vienna should be restored. Washington, [1845] DLC; MBAt. 45-2366

A few incidents of travel in England connected with the immutable principles of truth, called the Gospel of Jesus Christ. Boston: J. Gooch, 1845. 24 p. MB. 45-2367

Ficklin, Olando Bell, 1808-1886.

Speech of Mr. Ficklin on the annexation of Texas: delivered in the House, January 23, 1845. Washington, 1845. 14 p. MBAt; MHi; NBu; PHi. 45-2368

Fido, or the faithful friend. New York: E. Kearny, 1845. MH. 45-2369

Finney, Charles Grandison, 1792-1875. Letters on revivals. Puluski, New York: W.E. Wright, 1845. 169 p. CSmH; MiD; MnSH; OO; WaPS. 45-2370

The fireman's call, as sung by George Washington Dixon... Boston: [Oliver, Ditson] 1845. CtY; MHi. 45-2371

Firemen's Insurance Company of the City of New York. Report... in answer to a resolution of the assembly, transmitting statements of premiums received and taxes paid for the years 1842, 1843 and 1844. [Albany, 1845] 3 p. WHi. 45-2372

First book for sunday schools. Printed for the use of the South Parish School, Portsmouth, New Hampshire. Fifth edition. Boston: Crosby, 1845. 36 p. NNC. 45-2373

Fish, Francis G. St. Ann's Church [Brooklyn, New York] from the year 1784 to the year 1845... By a Sunday school teacher. Brooklyn: F.G. Fish, 1845. 220 p. Ct; ICN; MiD; MnHi; NBuG. 45-2374

Fisher, George Thomas. Photogenic manipulation: containing the theory and plain instructions in the art of photography. Philadelphia: Carey and Hart, 1845. 60, 48 p. MdBP; MLow; NhM; PPF. 45-2375

Fisher, Redwood S., 1762-1856. Circular and prospectus of the national magazine. New York, 1845. PPL. 45-2376

Fisher, Samuel Ware, 1814-1874. The purpose of God, in the early death of the Christian illustrated; a sermon occasioned by the death of Miss Mary S. Dwight. Albany: Erastus H. Pease, 1845. 32 p. CtY; MBAt; MPiB; MWA; NjR. 45-2377

Fisher, Samuel Ware, 1814-1874. The supremacy of mind: a lecture, introductory to the eleventh annual course of lectures before the Young Men's Association of the city of Albany. Albany: Munsell and Tanner, printers, 1845. 49 p. ICMe; MnHi; MWA; OCHP; PHi. 45-2378

Fisher, Thomas, 1801-1856. Dial of the seasons, or a portraiture of nature. Philadelphia: Carey and Hart, 1845. 217 p. DLC; ICBB; MH; NN; PPA. 45-2379

Fisher, Thomas T. Eulogy on the life and character of Gen. Andrew Jackson. Louisville, Kentucky: G.H. Monsarrat and company, 1845. 9 p. T. 45-2380

Fisher, Thomas T. Eulogy on the life and character of Gen. Andrew Jackson. Louisville, Kentucky: G.H. Monsarrat and company, 1845? 16 p. NcU. 45-2381

Fisher, William Logan. History of the institution of the sabbath day, being a plea for liberty of conscience in opposition to sabbath conventions. Philadelphia: Merrihew and Thompson, printers, 1846. 194 p. CtY; DeWI; ICN; MBAt; PHi. 45-2382

Fisher's comic almanac. New York, 1845. CtY. 45-2383

Fisher's comic almanac for 1846. Boston: James Fisher, [1845] [36] p. MHi; MWA. 45-2384

Fisher's magazine and industrial record. New York: Reduval Cushing, 1845-1846. 3 v. DLC; MBAt. 45-2385

Fisher's national magazine and industrial record. v. 1-. June, 1845-. New York: Fisher, Redwood, 1845-. MiMarq-Hi. 45-2386

Fisk, Benjamin Franklin, d. 1832. A grammar of the Greek language. Twenty-sixth edition. Boston: Robert S. Davis, etc., etc., 1845. 263 p. LStBA; MBC; MH. 45-2387

Fisk, Theophilus. Our country; its dangers and destiny. An address delivered before the cadets of the Norwich University, at the annual commencement, August 20, 1840. Washington: Printed at the office of the United States Journal, 1845. 16 p. Ct; MBAt; MH; NcU; OClWHi. 45-2388

Fitch, Asa, 1809-1879. An essay upon the wheat-fly, and some species allied to it. From the American Quarterly Journal of Agriculture and Science. Albany: Printed by Carroll and Cook, 1845. 32 p. CtHWatk; MSaP; NjR; MBHo. 45-2389

Fitch, Asa, 1809-1879. Memorial of A. Fitch being a rejoinder to a monument placed before the Senate by Charles Gould. [Washington, 1845] 20 p. MH. 45-2390

Fitch, W. Mosely. An inaugural dissertation on the sympathies of the system. Submitted to the dean and faculty of the medical college of the state of South Carolina, for the degree of M.D. Charleston, South Carolina: J.B. Nixon, printer, 1845. 18 p. GDecCT; NBMS; PPCP. 45-2391

Fitz, Asa, b. 1810. The American school song book, enlarged and improved. Boston: William J. Reynolds and company, and W.B. Fowle, 1845. 5-160 p. MBevHi; MDOVC; MNF; MPiB; OCl. 45-2392

Fitzgerald, J.R. Addresses delivered at various temperance meetings held in the city of Boston, with an account of the grand simultaneous anniversary, February, 1845. Reported by J.R. Fitzgerald, esq. Boston: Press of T.R. Marvin, 1845. 48 p. MB; MBNMHi; MWA; WHi. 45-2393

Flavel, John, 1630?-1691. The method of Grace, in the Holy Spirits applying to the souls of men, the eternal redemption contrived by the Father and accomplished by the Son. First American edition, revised and somewhat abridged. New York: American Tract Society, [1845] 560 p. IaU; MH; MH-AH; ViU. 45-2394

Fleetwood, John. The life of our Lord and Saviour Jesus Christ: containing a full and accurate history from his taking upon himself our nature, to his crucifixion, resurrection and ascension. Hartford: Case, Tiffany and Burnham, 1845. 660 p. MeLewB. 45-2395

Fleming, Charles, 1806-1875. A new and complete French and English and French dictionary, on the basis of the royal dictionary English and French, and French and English... with complete tables of the verbs. Second edition, revised and enlarged. Philadelphia: Carey and Hart, 1845. 1376 p. DLC; IU; MiU; NcD; PPL. 45-2396

Fletcher, Abel. History, objects and principles of the order of the Sons of Temperance; an address delivered in Richmond, Virginia, December 2, 1844. Philadelphia: Gibson and Porter, printers, 1845. 28 p. DLC; MB; PPC; PPL; RP. 45-2397

Fletcher, James, 1811-1832. History of Poland from the earliest period to the present time. New York: Harper and brothers, 1845. 339 p. InCW; MeAu; OCX; ScDuE. 45-2398

Fletcher, John William, 1729-1785. Appeal to matter of fact and common sense; or a rational demonstration of man's corrupt and lost state. New York: Lane, 1845. 214 p. CoD; PPLT. 45-2399

Fletcher, John William, 1729-1785. Checks to antinomianism in a service of letters to Rev. Mr. Shirley and Mr. Hill. New York: G. Lane and C.B. Tippett, 1845-1846. 2 v. KMcpC; MH-AH; OkU; PP. 45-2400

Fletcher, Thomas. Eulogy on life and character of Andrew Jackson, at the Methodist Episcopal Church, Jackson, Mississippi, July 22, 1845. Jackson, 1845. 8 p. PHi. 45-2401

Flint, Timothy, 1780-1840. Biographical memoir of Daniel Boone, the first settler of Kentucky; interspersed with incidents in the early annals of the country. Cincinnati: G. Conclin, 1845.

252 p. DLC; In; KyBgW; OCHP; ViU. 45-2402

Florence de Lacey; or the coquette. A novel. New York: E. Winchester, 1845. 106 p. DLC; MH; NN; ViU. 45-2403

Flow gently sweet Ofton. Philadelphia: G. Willig, 1845. 3 p. MB; ViU. 45-2404

Flowers of melody; eight popular songs and ballads. New York: E. Ferrett and company, [1845?] 12 p. MH. 45-2405

Flugel, Johann Gottfried, 1788-1885. Flugels' complete dictionary of the German and English languages. Adapted to the English student, with great additions and improvements. Third edition. Boston: Charles C. Little and James Brown, 1845. 2 pts. MH; MH-L. 45-2406

Flugel, Johann Gottfried, 1788-1885. Flugel's dictionary of the German and English languages, abridged: in two parts. Carefully compiled from the London edition of Flugel's larger dictionary. Second edition. Boston: C.C. Little and J. Brown, 1845. 2 v. in 1. OO. 45-2407

Flygare-Carlen, Emilie Smith, 1807-1892. The Foster brothers; a romance. Translated from the Swedish. New York: William H. Colyer, 1845. 155 p. NjR; OMC. 45-2408

Flygare-Carlen, Emilie Smith, 1807-1892. The magic goblet; or the consecration of the church of Hammarby. Translated from the original Swedish. New York: William H. Colyer, 1845. 152 p. DLC; IEN; MB; NjR. 45-2409

Folger, Alfred M. The family physician being a domestic medical work, written

in plain style. Cottrell: G.H. Joyce, 1845. 320 p. DNLM; NcAS; NcD; Sc; WaPS. 45-2410

Follen, Charles, Theodore Christian, 1796-1840. Deutsches Lesebuch fur aufanger. 9 ausgabe. [German reader for beginners. Ninth edition] Boston: S.G. Simpkins, 1845. 222 p. CU; ICU; MFiHi; MH; PPL. 45-2411

Follen, Charles, Theodore Christian, 1796-1840. A practical grammar of the German language. Tenth edition, stereotyped. Boston: Samuel G. Simpkins, 1845. KyBC; MH; NNC. 45-2412

Follen, Charles, Theodore Christian, 1796-1840. Practical grammar of the German language. Eleventh edition. Boston, 1845. IaFair; DLC; IaWas; MBAt; MW; OO. 45-2413

Follen, Eliza Lee Cabot, 1787-1860. The birthday; a sequel to the well spent hour. Boston: Follen, 1845. IEG. 45-2414

Folsom, George, 1802-1869. A French and English pronouncing dictionary, on the basis of Nagent's with many new words in general use. New York: Alexander V. Blake, 1845. 376 p. Vt-Morr. 45-2415

Fontaine, A. b. 1798. The book of prudential revelations or the golden Bible of nature and reason and the confidential doctor at home. Boston: The author, 1845. 507 p. FDef; IEN-M; MdBM; NNNAM; PLFM. 45-2416

Fontaine, A. b. 1798. A manual full of comforts, revelations and instructions. Boston, 1846. 107 p. DLC. 45-2417

Fontaine, A. b. 1798. Practical key to the confidential doctor at home, in accordance with the book of prudential revelations and the golden bible of nature. Boston, 1845. 53 p. DLC; DNLM; IENM; PPC; PPCP. 45-2418

Foot, Andrew Hull, 1806-1863. Farewell temperance address; delivered before the crew of the United States frigate Cumberland, November 1, 1845. Boston: Samuel N. Dickinson and company, printers, 1845. 8 p. CtY; WHi. 45-2419

Forbes, Darius. The christian's duty to society. A sermon: preached October 20, 1844. Boston: Printed by B.B. Mussey, 1845. 16 p. CtY; MBAt; MMeT; PPL-R. 45-2420

Forbes, Darius. An exposition and defence of oddfellowship... Boston: B.B. Mussey, 1845. 96 p. MWHi; MWA; WHi. 45-2421

Force, William Quereau, 1820-1880. Picture of Washington and its vicinity for 1845, to which is added: the Washington guide, containing a congressional directory, residences of public officers, and other useful information. Washington: W.Q. Force, 1845. 146 p. MBAt; MdHi; NBu; PPL; RPAt. 45-2422

Force, William Quereau, 1820-1880. The Washington guide; containing a congressional directory and residences of public officers, with other useful information. Washington: W.Q. Force, 1845. DLC. 45-2423

Forget me not, a gift for 1846. Edited by A.A. Phillips. New York: Nafis and Cornish, 1845. ICN; MWA; NBuG; NPV; ViU. 45-2424

Formby, Henry. A visit to the East; comprising Germany and the Danube, Constantinople, Asia Minor, Egypt and Idumea. New York: James R. Dunham, 1845. 134 p. ICU; MB; NBuDD; PP; TSewU. 45-2425

Forstall, Edmund J. Agricultural productions of Louisiana, embracing valuable information relative to the cotton, sugar and molasses interests, and the effects upon the same of the tariff of 1842. [New Orleans] 1845. 43 p. AU; CtY; ICU; PPL; WHi. 45-2426

Foster, Benjamin Franklin. A concise treatise on commercial book keeping elucidating the principles and practice of double entry and the modern methods of arranging merchants' accounts. Fifth edition. Boston: T.R. Marvin, 1845. 184 p. ICRL; MeB; MH. 45-2427

Foster, Benjamin Franklin. Theory and practice of book keeping. Boston: T.R. Marvin, 1845. MH. 45-2428

Foster, Benjamin Wood, 1810-1881. Practical system of bookkeeping by double and single entry. Fifth edition. Boston: Saxton and Huntington, 1845. MH. 45-2429

Foster, Benjamin Wood, 1810-1881. A practical system of bookkeeping by single entry, exemplified in two sets of books; containing various forms of bills, mercantile calculations, etc. Fourth edition. Boston: J. French, 1845. 35 p. CtY; MB. 45-2430

Foster, J. Heron. A full account of the

great fire at Pittsburgh, on April 10, 1845; with the individual losses, and contribution for relief. Compiled by J. Heron Foster. Pittsburgh: J.W. Cook, 1845. 52 p. CSansS; KyDC; NjR; OFH; PHi. 45-2431

Foster, James, 1697-1753. The married state; its obligations and duties. With hints on the education of a family. Third edition. Hartford, [1845?] CtY. 45-2432

Foster, James, 1697-1753. The married state; its obligations and duties. With hints on the education of a family. Third edition. New York, 1845. CtY. 45-2433

Foster, John, 1770-1843. Foster's essays. Essays in a series of letters... Hartford: S. Andrus and son, 1845. 133 p. CSansS; IaHoL; MBrockKC; OWoC. 45-2434

Foster, Stephen S. The brotherhood of thieves. A true picture of the American church and clergy. Cincinnati, 1845. PPL. 45-2435

Foster and Dickinson's oneida almanac. By G.R. Perkins. Utica: R.W. Roberts, 1845. MWA. 45-2436

Foucaud, U. Edward. Book of illustrious mechanics of Europe and America with a supplementary chapter on American mechanics and their inventions. Edited by John Frost. Hartford: Hammersley, 1845. IaDaM; MB; MChi; MH. 45-2437

Fougue, Friederich de la Motte. The hermit of Markworth. The two captains. Boston: Jordan and Wiley, 1845. MBBCHS. 45-2438

Fowle, William Bentley, 1795-1865. The common school speller; in which about 14,000 words of the English language are carefully arranged by classification and association. Thirtieth edition. Boston: William B. Fowle and N. Capen, 1845. 204 p. ICU; MBev-F; MH; MHaHi. 45-2439

Fowle, William Bentley, 1795-1865. The companion to spelling books... Boston: William B. Fowle and N. Capen, 1845. 144 p. CtHWatk; MB; MH; NNC; PU. 45-2440

Fowle, William Bentley, 1795-1865. An elementary geography for Massachusetts children. By William B. Fowle and Asa Fitz. Boston: Fowle and Capen, [1845] 224 p. CSt; MHi; NNC; OClWHi; RPB. 45-2441

Fowle, William Bentley, 1795-1865. Familiar dialogues and popular discussions. Fourth edition. Boston: Charles Tappan; New York: M.H. Newman, 1845. 286 p. FLlS; MB; MH. 45-2442

Fowler, Lorenzo Niles, 1811-1896. Synopsis of phrenology and physiology, comprising a condensed description of the functions of the body and mind. Boston: Samuel Harris, 1845. 24 p. NN. 45-2443

Fowler, Orson Squire, 1809-1887. Fowler on matrimony, or phrenology applied to the selection of congenial companions for life. New York: Fowler, 1845. 108 p. CtY-M; MBM; OO. 45-2444

Fowler, Orson Squire, 1809-1887. Fowler on temperance, founded on phrenology and physiology; or the laws of life and the principles of the human constitution, as developed by the science of phrenology and physiology, applied to total abstinence from all alcoholic and intoxicating drinks. Fourth edition, enlarged and improved. New York: O.S. and L.N. Fowler, 1845. 32 p. CtY-M; MoS; WHi. 45-2445

Fowler, Orson Squire, 1809-1887. Fowler's practical phrenology; giving a concise elementary view of phrenology. With references... Twenty-second edition, enlarged and improved. New York: O.S. and L.N. Fowler; Boston: Saxton and Peirce's phrenological depot, 1845. 71 p. CoD; DLC; IaBo; MnS; NjR. 45-2446

Fowler, Orson Squire, 1809-1887. Phrenology proved, illustrated, and applied, accompanied by a chart... together with a view of the moral and theological bearing of the science. Thirtieth edition, enlarged and improved. New York: L.N. Fowler, etc., etc., 1845. 430 p. CSb; DLC; ICU; Oak; RPB. 45-2447

Fox, Mary L. The ruined deacon. A true story. Boston: D.H. Ela and company, 1845. 36 p. CtY; InU; MWH; NjP; PU. 45-2448

Fox, Thomas Bayley, 1808-1876. Allegories and christian lessons for children. Boston: William Crosby and H.P. Nichols, 1845. 144 p. MH; NNC; MNotn; WHi. 45-2449

Foxe, John, 1516-1587. Book of martyrs; or a history of the lives, sufferings and triumphant deaths of the primitive as well as protestant martyrs. Now improved by important alterations and additions by Charles A. Goodrich.

Hartford: E. Hunt, 1845. 597 p. CBPSR; MeBat; NN; ODaM; RAu. 45-2450

Foxe, John, 1516-1587. A history of the lives, sufferings, and triumphant deaths of the primitive as well as the Protestant martyrs from the commencement of Christianity to the latest periods of pagan and popish persecution. New edition. Philadelphia: J.M. Campbell, 1845. 638 p. MH; MnSM; PPPrHi; ScNC; ViAl. 45-2451

France. Code of instruction on the organization and superintendence of light houses and beacons on the coast of France. Translated from the French. Washington, 1845. 55 p. CtMW; NNE. 45-2452

Franklin, Augustus. The widow's pirate son; or Pauline Coustry, the corsair's mate. A tale of the province of Massachusetts. Boston: H.L. Williams, 1845. 48 p. DLC; MB. 45-2453

Franklin, Benjamin, 1706-1790. The life of Benjamin Franklin; containing the autobiography, with notes and a continuation. By Jared Sparks. Boston: C. Tappan, 1845. 612 p. CtY; IaGG; NB; MMh; OrU. 45-2454

Franklin, Benjamin, 1706-1790. Memoirs, written by himself with his most interesting essays, letters and miscellaneous writing. New York: Harper and brothers, 1845. 2 v. IaHi; InCW; MChi; NjR; OCX. 45-2455

Franklin, Benjamin, 1706-1790. The works of Dr. Benjamin Franklin, consisting of essays, humorous, moral and literary, with his life written by himself.

Hartford: S. Andrus and son, 1845. 304 p. ICartC; MHi; PLF; ScP; WHi. 45-2456

Franklin, Massachusetts. Church. The confession of faith and covenant of the church in Franklin, Massachusetts. From the manuscript of Nathaniel Emmons, late pastor. Boston: S.N. Dickinson and company, printers, 1845. 8 p. MWA. 45-2457

Franklin almanac. Calculated by John Armstrong. Pittsburgh, Pennsylvania: Johnston and Stockton, 1845. MWA. 45-2458

Franklin almanac for 1846. Calculations by George Perkins. New York, New York: Edward Kearny, [1845] MWA. 45-2459

The franklin almanac for 1846. Calculations by George Perkins. Rochester: E. Shepard and company; New York: E. Walker and company, [1845] MWA; NCH; WHi. 45-2460

The franklin almanac for 1846. Calculations by George Perkins. Utica: Benjamin F. Brooks, [1845?] NUt. 45-2461

Franklin almanac for 1846. Calculations by John Armstrong. Pittsburgh, Pennsylvania: Johnston and Stockton, [1845] MWA. 45-2462

Franklin almanac for 1846. Calculations by John Ward. Philadelphia: Thomas Davis, [1845] MWA; NjR. 45-2463

Fraser, Charles. Address on the birthday of General Washington, delivered at the request of the Washington Light Infantry, on the 22d of February, 1845. Charleston: Printed by Walker and Burke, 1845. MB; NN; ScC; WHi. 45-2464

Fraser, James Baillie, 1783-1856. Historical and descriptive account of Persia, from the earliest ages to the present time. Illustrated by a map and several engravings. New York: Harper and brothers, 1845. 345 p. InCW; LN; OSW; RPE; WM. 45-2465

Fraser, James Baillie, 1783-1856. Mesopotamia and Assyria, from the earliest ages to the present time; with illustrations of their natural history. New York: Harper, 1845. [17]-336 p. MB; PWW; RPE; TxU; WNaE. 45-2466

Frazee, Bradford. An improved grammar of the English language on the inductive system; with which elementary and progressive lessons in composition are combined for the use of schools and academies. Philadelphia: Sorin and Ball, 1845. 192 p. CoU; CtW; GDecCT; NjP; PLFM. 45-2467

Frazee, Bradford. An improved grammar of the English language on the inductive system; with which elementary and progressive lessons in composition are combined for the use of schools and academies. Second edition. Philadelphia: Sorin, 1845. 192 p. CtW; CtMW. 45-2468

Frazer, Richard. Statement relative to diseases on board of emigrant vessels. [n.p.] 1845. PPL. 45-2469

Free Produce Association of Friends of Philadelphia Yearly Meeting. Circular to our fellow members of the religious

Society of Friends. Philadelphia, 1845. 2 p. PHC. 45-2470

Free state rally and Texan chainbreaker, November 15-January 12, 1845, [1846] Boston, 1845-1846. v. 1-. MBAt; NIC; TxU. 45-2471

The free will Baptist register, for the year of our Lord 1845. Dover: William Burr, 1845. 84 p. MHa; MWA; NhHi. 45-2472

Freemasons. Alabama. Proceedings of the Grand Lodge of the state of Alabama, convened in the city of Tuscaloosa, December 1, 1845. Tuscaloosa: John McCormick, 1845. 60 p. NNFM. 45-2473

Freemasons. Georgia. Constitution of the Grand Lodge of Georgia, as amended at its sessions of 5843 and 5844 and submitted to and approved by the subordinate Lodges and received and acknowledged at the Grand Communication, 7th of November, 5845. Macon: S. Rose, 1845. 8 p. NNFM; PPFM. 45-2474

Freemasons. Illinois. Proceedings of the Grand Lodge of ancient free and accepted Masons of the state of Illinois, at its sixth annual communication held in the town of Jacksonville, October, 5845. Chicago: Ellis and Fergus, 1845. 138 p. NNFM. 45-2475

Freemasons. Indiana. Proceedings of a grand communication of the grand lodge of Indiana for 1845. Indianapolis: S.V.B. Noll, 1845. 56 p. MBFM. 45-2476

Freemasons. Indiana. Proceedings of a grand communication of the grand lodge of Indiana, begun and held in the Masonic hall in the city of Indianapolis on Monday the 26th day of May, 1845. Indianapolis: S.V.B. Noel, 1845. 59 p. IaCrM; MBFM; NNFM; OCM. 45-2477

Freemasons. Indiana. Proceedings of the grand royal arch chapter of Indiana at the first communication in the city of Indianapolis. Richmond: Halloway and Davis, 1845. TxWFM. 45-2478

Freemasons. Iowa. By-laws of Iowa City Royal Arch Chapter. Iowa City: Jessie Williams, 1845. 11 p. IaCrM. 45-2479

Freemasons. Iowa. Proceedings of the Grand Lodge of Iowa, at the second grand annual communication in Iowa City, on Tuesday, January 6th, 1845. Bloomington: Jno B. Russell, printer, 1845. 58 p. NNFM. 45-2480

Freemasons. Iowa. Proceedings of the Grand Lodge of Iowa, held in Iowa City, on Tuesday, January 6, A.L. 5845. Bloomington: J.B. Russell, 1845. 47 p. IaDaM. 45-2481

Freemasons. Kentucky. Proceedings of the Grand Lodge of Kentucky, at a grand annual communication in the city of Lexington, commencing August 25, 1845. Frankfort: Hodges, Todd and Pruett, 1845. 86 p. NNFM. 45-2482

Freemasons. Louisiana. Grand lodge of free and accepted Masons of the ancient York rite of the state of Louisiana. New Orleans: J.L. Sollee, 1845. 16 p. IaCrM; NNFM; OCM. 45-2483

Freemasons. Louisiana. Proceedings of grand lodge of Masonic Lodge in Louisiana; meeting in 1845. New Orleans: J.L. Sollee, 1845. 14 p. IaCrM. 45-2484

Freemasons. Maine. Act of incorporation and by-laws adopted by the grand royal Arch Chapter of Maine. Incorporated January 19, 1822. Portland: A.S. Shirley and son, 1845. 36 p. NNFM; PPFM. 45-2485

Freemasons. Maine. Grand lodge of the most ancient and honorable fraternity of free and accepted Masons, of the state of Maine. Portland: A. Shirley and son, 1845. 24 p. NNFM. 45-2486

Freemasons. Maryland. Constitution of the Grand Lodge of Free and Accepted Masons of Maryland, as amended and adopted at the May Communication together with the by-laws adopted at the November Communication. Baltimore: Joseph Robinson, 1845. 27 p. IaCrM; PPPrM. 45-2487

Freemasons. Maryland. Proceedings of the Grand Lodge of free and accepted Masons of Maryland and of the Grand Stewards' Lodge, from June to December, 1845. Baltimore: Joseph Robinson, 1845. TxWFM. 45-2488

Freemasons. Maryland. Proceedings of the Grand Lodge of Maryland, at its annual communication, held at the Masonic Hall, in the city of Baltimore, on Monday, 19th day of May, 1845. Baltimore: Joseph Robinson, 1845. 56 p. PPL; TxWFM. 45-2489

Freemasons. Maryland. Proceedings of the grand royal arch chapter, of the state of Maryland in the city of Baltimore on the 18th November, 1844. Baltimore:

Joseph Robinson, 1845. 18 p. NNFM. 45-2490

Freemasons. Massachusetts. Regulations of the Grand Royal arch chapters of Massachusetts, revised and adopted March 11, 5845. Boston: Tuttle and Dennett, 1845. 48 p. IaCrM. 45-2491

Freemasons. Mississippi. The constitution of the M.W. Grand Lodge of Mississippi, together with resolutions in force. Natchez, Mississippi: Printed at Courier office, 1845. 15 p. IaCrM. 45-2492

Freemasons. Mississippi. Extract from the proceedings of the grand lodge of the state of Mississippi, at the grand annual communication; held at the Masonic Hall in the city of Natchez, January, 1845. Natchez: Printed at the Courier office, 1845. 116 p. MsFM. 45-2493

Freemasons. New Hampshire. A journal of the proceedings of the Grand Lodge of New Hampshire, at their annual communication, holden at Concord, June 10th and 11th, 1845. Exeter: Charles E. Folson, 1845. 41 p. LNMas. 45-2494

Freemasons. New York. Constitution of the ancient and honourable fraternity of free and accepted masons, in the state of New York. Collected and digested by order of the Grand Lodge of the said state. New York: Joseph M. Marsh, 1845. 56 p. IaCrM; PPFM. 45-2495

Freemasons. New York. Constitution of the most ancient and honorable fraternity of free and accepted Masons of the state of New York. New York: Joseph M. Marsh, 1845. 61 p. NNFM; NUt; PPFM. 45-2496

Freemasons. New York. Proceedings of Grand Chapter of Masonic Lodge in New York state; meeting held in 1844. Albany: American Masonic Register office, 1845. 9 p. IaCrM. 45-2497

Freemasons. New York. Proceedings of Grand Lodge of Masonic Lodge in the New York state; meeting held in 1845. New York: Joseph M. Marsh, 1845. 64 p. IaCrM. 45-2498

Freemasons. New York. Transactions of the grand lodge of the most ancient and honorable fraternity of free and accepted Masons of the state of New York, from the 4th of September, 1844 to the 6th of June, 1845. New York: Joseph M. Marsh, 1845. 64 p. NNFM; OCM. 45-2499

Freemasons. North Carolina. Proceedings of the Grand Lodge of Ancient York Masons, of North Carolina. Raleigh: Thomas Loring, 1845. 62 p. IaCrM; LNMas; NNFM; OCM; TxWFM. 45-2500

Freemasons. Ohio. Journals of proceedings of the grand council of royal and Select Masters, for the state of Ohio at the annual grand communication, held at Columbus, October 23, 1845. n.p., 1845. LNMas. 45-2501

Freemasons. Ohio. Proceedings of the grand chapter of royal arch Masons of the state of Ohio, at the annual grand communication held at Columbus, Ohio. Columbus: C. Scott and company, 1845. 18 p. ODaM. 45-2502

Freemasons. Ohio. Proceedings of the grand convention of free Masons, in the state of Ohio, held at Chillicothe,

January 4, 1808. Columbus: C. Scott, and company, 1845. 32 p. NNFM. 45-2503

Freemasons. Ohio. Proceedings of the Grand encampment of Knights Templar of the state of Ohio, at its third session held at the city of Columbus, October 21, 1845. Columbus: C. Scott and company, 1845. 37 p. NNFM. 45-2504

Freemasons. Ohio. Proceedings of the Grand Encampment of Knights Templars, of the state of Ohio, at their third session, held at the city of Columbus, October 21, 1845. Columbus: C. Scott and company, 1845. 18 p. NNFM. 45-2505

Freemasons. Ohio. Proceedings of the Grand Encampment of Knights Templars, of the state of Ohio. At its third session, held at Columbus, 1845. Columbus: C. Scott and company, 1845. 12 p. ODaM. 45-2506

Freemasons. South Carolina. Rules and regulations for the government of the grand royal arch chapter of South Carolina, February 23, 1843, with constitution of the United States Royal arch chapter, September, 1844. Charleston: Burgess and James, printer, 1845. 24 p. PHi. 45-2507

Freemasons. Texas. Transactions of the right worshipful grand lodge of free and accepted Masons of the Republic of Texas at its eight grand annual communication. W 45-2508

Freemasons. United States. Constitution of the general grand chapter of royal arch Mason, for the United States of America, as revised and adopted September, 1844. Baltimore: Joseph Robinson, 1845. 19 p. PPFM. 45-2509

Freemasons. Virginia. Proceedings of the grand royal arch chapter of Virginia. Richmond: John Warrock, 1845. 20 p. NNFM. 45-2510

Freemasons. Virginia. Proceedings of a grand annual communication of the Grand Lodge of Virginia. Richmond: John Warrock, 1845. 65 p. NNFM; OCM. 45-2511

Freemasons. Wisconsin. Constitutions of the most worshipful Grand Lodge of Wisconsin and general regulations for the government of the craft under its jurisdiction. Platteville: Jerome L. Marsh, 1845. 38 p. MBFM. 45-2512

Freemasons. Wisconsin. Proceedings of the Grand Lodge of Wisconsin at a Grand Annual Communication. Platteville, Wisconsin: Jerome L. Marsh, 1845. 86 p. IaCrM; MBFM; NNFM; WHi. 45-2513

Freewill Baptist founded in New Hampshire. Sacred melodies for conference and prayer meetings and for social and private devotion. Seventh edition. Dover: Trustees of the Freewill Baptist Printing Establishment, 1845. 224 p. NcU. 45-2514

Fremont, John Charles, 1813-1890. Exploring expedition to the Rocky Mountains, in 1842 and to Oregon and North Carolina, in the years 1843-1844. Washington, 1845. 693 p. MtHi. 45-2515

Fremont, John Charles, 1813-1890. Narrative of the exploring expedition to the Rocky Mountains in the year 1842,

and to Oregon and North California i the years 1843-44. Reprinted from the o ficial copy. Second edition. Washingto H. Polkinhorn, 1845. 278 p. CS; KyL NNNBG; PHi. 45-2516

Fremont, John Charles, 1813-189(Narrative of the exploring expedition t the Rocky Mountains in the year 184: and to Oregon and North California i the years 1843-44. Reprinted from the o ficial copy. Second edition. Washingtor Taylor, Wilde and company, 1845. 278 NjR; NNBG; OMC; ViU; WaSp. 45 2517

Fremont, John Charles, 1813-1890 Report of the exploring expedition to th Rocky Mountains in the year 1842, an to Oregon and North California in th years, 1843 and 1844. Printed by order o the House of Representatives Washington: Blair and Rives, 1845. 58 p. CU-B; KyLxT; MeBa; PCC; WaU. 45 2518

Fremont, John Charles, 1813-1890 Report of the exploring expedition to th Rocky Mountains in the year 1842, an to Oregon and North California in the years, 1843 and 1844. Printed by order o the House of Representatives Washington: Gales and Seaton, 1845 693 p. OrP; PEaL; RNR; ViU; Wa. 45-2519

French, Benjamin Brown, 1800-1870 The changes of the earth, a poem. Delivered before the Capitol Hill Institute, in the city of Washington. [Washington, 1845?] 15 p. DLC. 45-2520

French, Richard. Letter of Hon. Richard French to fellow citizens of the inth congressional district of Kentucky. Washington? 1845? 8 p. NNC. 45-2521

Friends, Society of. A declaration of New England yearly meeting of Friends, upon various Christian doctrines. Providence: Knowles and Vose, 1845. 23 . MNtcA; NBuG. 45-2522

Friends, Society of. Declaration of the Seneca Nation of Indians in general council assembled, with the accompanying documents, also an address to the chiefs and people of that nation. Baltimore: W. Woody, 1845. 53 p. MBu; NRMA; PHC; WHi. 45-2523

Friends, Society of. Green Street Monthly Meeting. An epistle from the Monthly Meeting of Friends, of Philadelphia, held at Green Street, to its members. Philadelphia: John Richards, 1845. 5 p. PHC; PSC-Hi. 45-2524

Friends, Society of. Joint committee on Indian affairs. Report of the proceedings of an Indian council held at Cattaraugus, in the state of New York. Baltimore: Printed by William Woody, 1845. 34 p. DLC; MBAt; MdHi; MH; PHi. 45-2525

Friends, Society of. Narrative of facts and circumstances that have tended to produce a secession from the society in New England. Providence: Knowles and Vose, 1845. 43 p. MBC; MNtcA; NBuG. 45-2526

Friends, Society of. New York Yearly Meeting. An account of the times and places of holding the quarterly, monthly, and preparative meetings, and meetings for worship, constituting the New York Yearly Meeting of Friends. New York, 1845. 32 p. PHC. 45-2527

Friends, Society of. Philadelphia Monthly meeting. Address of... to its members. Philadelphia: Chapman and Jones, 1845. MH. 45-2528

Friends, Society of. Philadelphia Yearly Meeting. Circular to out fellow members of the religious society of friends. [Philadelphia, 1845] MH. 45-2529

Friends, Society of. Report of the committee on education. At a yearly meeting held in Philadelphia, by adjournment from the 21st of the fourth month to the 25th of the same, inclusive, 1845. n.p.: Joseph Kite and company, [1845] 12 p. NjR. 45-2530

Friends, Society of. Report of the proceedings of an Indian council held at Cattaraugus, in the state of New York, 7th month, 1845. Baltimore: William Wooddy, 1845. 34 p. DLC; MBAt; MdHi; MH; PHi. 45-2531

Friends, Society of. Rhode Island Quarterly Meeting. An address from the Rhode Island Quarterly Meeting of Friends, to the members of that religious society within the limits of New England Yearly meeting and elsewhere. New York: Piercy and Reed, 1845. 48 p. DeWi; MiD-B; PHC; RNR; WHi. 45-2532

Friends, Society of. To the members of the Society of Friends in Pennsylvania and elsewhere. Philadelphia: Merrihew and Thompson, 1845. 8 p. PHC. 45-2533

Friends, Society of. Western Quarterly meeting. To the members of the Society of Friends in Pennsylvania and elsewhere. Philadelphia: Printed by Merrihew and Thompson, 1845. 8 p. MB; NIC. 45-2534

Friends almanac for the year 1846. By Jos. Foulke. Philadelphia: Elijah Weaver, [1845] 47 p. MWA; Nj. 45-2535

Friend's Boarding School. Annual catalogue of the officers and pupils of the Friend's Boarding School, Washington, Dutchess County, New York for 1845. Poughkeepsie: Platt and Schram, 1845. 12 p. NP. 45-2536

Friends of Freedom. Proceedings of the great convention of the Friends of Freedom in the eastern and middle states held in Boston October 1, 2, 3, 1845. Lowell, 1845. 34 p. MBM; PHi. 45-2537

Friendship's offering; A Christmas, New Years and birthday present for 1845. Boston: Lewis and Sampson, 1845. 340 p. KU; LNH; MeBaT; TJaL; ViL. 45-2538

Frost, John, 1800-1859. The American speaker, containing numerous rules, observations, and exercises on pronounciation, pauses, inflections, accents and emphasis... Philadelphia: Thomas, Cowperthwait and company, 1845. 448 p. KU; NjP. 45-2539

Frost, John, 1800-1859. The battle grounds of America, illustrated by stories of the revolution. With fourteen engravings. Auburn: J.C. Derby, 1846. 252 p. NIC. 45-2540

Frost, John, 1800-1859. The beauties of French history. New York: Alexander V. Blake, 1845. 252 p. DLC; IaDmU; IU; MSbo; ViU. 45-2541

Frost, John, 1800-1859. The birds of the air. By Robert Ramble. Philadelphia, Crissy, 1845. 144 p. DLC. 45-2542

Frost, John, 1800-1859. The book of the army: comprising a general military history of the United States, from the period of the revolution to the present time. Compiled from the best authorities. New York: D. Appleton and company; Philadelphia: G.S. Appleton, 1845. [12] 446 p. InThE; LNH; MdBLC; PPL-R; Vi. 45-2543

Frost, John, 1800-1859. Elements of English grammar; with progressive exercises in parsing. Boston: Jenks and Palmer, 1845. 108 p. MB. 45-2544

Frost, John, 1800-1859. The heroes and battles of the American revolution; or thrilling stories and anecdotes of that eventful period. By a veteran soldier. Philadelphia: W.P. Hazard, 1845. 252 p. DLC; ICN; MB; OU; ViU. 45-2545

Frost, John, 1800-1859. The heroes and battles of the American revolution; or thrilling stories and anecdotes of that eventful period. By a veteran soldier. Fifth edition. New York: Saxton and Miles, 1845. 240 p. MHi; NTi; RWe; WAsN. 45-2546

Frost, John, 1800-1859. History of the United States; for the use of common schools. Philadelphia: Thomas, Cowperthwait, 1845. 324 p. MBevHi; MdW; PAtM; TN. 45-2547

Frost, John, 1800-1859. History of the United States; for the use of common schools. Second edition. Philadelphia: E.C. Biddle, 1845. 324 p. NBLiHi; O. 45-2548

Frost, John, 1800-1859. The pictorial book of commodores comprising lives of distinguished commanders in the navy of the United States. Compiled from the best authorities. New York: Nafin and Cornish, etc., etc., 1845. 9, 440 p. CtY; POA; IaDa; OClW; PP. 45-2549

Frost, John, 1800-1859. Pictorial life of Andrew Jackson; embracing anecdotes, illustrative of his character. For young people. Philadelphia: Lindsay and Blakiston, 1845. 183 p. DLC; FMU; MH; MWA; NcD. 45-2550

Frost, John, 1800-1859. Robert Ramble's visit to the grand menagerie; with full descriptions and anecdotes of the animals. Philadelphia: J. Crissy, 1845. 144 p. NN. 45-2551

Frost, John, 1800-1859. Stories of the American revolution; comprising a complete anecdotic history of that great national event. Philadelphia: E. Ferritt and company, 1845. 252 p. DLC; IaMpI; MNS; OO. 45-2552

Frost, John, 1800-1859. The wonders of history comprising remarkable battles, sieges, feats of arms, and instances of courage, ability and magnanimity occurring in the annals of the world from the earliest ages to the present time. New York: Nafis and Cornish, 1845. 567 p. NNebg. 45-2553

Frothingham, Nathaniel Langdon, 1793-1870. Deism or Christianity: Four discourses, by N.L. Frothingham. Boston: William Crosby and H.P. Nichols, 1845. 77 p. ICU; MH; NjR; OO; RNR. 45-2554

Frothingham, Nathaniel Langdon,

1793-1870. Recollections of Rev. F.W.P. Greenwood. A sermon preached after his death and selections from his writings. Boston: James Munroe and company, 1845. 46 p. ICMe; M; MWA; OCHP; PPM; RP. 45-2555

Frothingham, Richard, 1812-1880. The history of Charlestown, Massachusetts. Charlestown: Charles P. Emmons; Boston: Charles C. Little and James Brown, 1845-1849. 368 p. DLC; MBevHi; MdBP; Nh; PHi. 45-2556

Fry, Elizabeth. A brief memoir of the late Elizabeth Fry. Philadelphia: Henry Longstreth, 1845. 33 p. MNBedf; PHC. 45-2557

Fry, Joseph Reese. Leonora; a lyrical drama in three acts. Words by J.R. Fry; music by W.H. Fry. First performed at the Chestnut Street Theatre. Philadelphia: King and Baird, 1845. 34 p. NRU; PPM; RPB. 45-2558

Fry, William Henry, 1815-1864. Affection waltz and love not quick step. Philadelphia: Willig, 1845. 2 p. MB. 45-2559

Fuller, Andrew, 1754-1815. The atonement of Christ and the justification of the sinner arranged from the writings of the Rev. Andrew Fuller by the editor of his complete works. New York: American Tract Society, 1845. 396 p. KyLoP; ViRu. 45-2560

Fuller, Andrew, 1754-1815. The atonement of Christ and the justification of the sinner arranged from the writings of Rev. Andrew Fuller. By the editor of his complete works. Philadelphia: American

Tract Society by Baptist Publication Society, 1845. 396 p. ViRut. 45-2561

Fuller, Andrew, 1754-1815. The Calvinistic and Socinian system. New York: Colby, 1845. 405 p. PPM. 45-2562

Fuller, Andrew, 1754-1815. The complete works of the Rev. Andrew Fuller; with a memoir of his life by Andrew Gunton Fuller. Reprinted from the third London edition; revised with additions, by Joseph Belcher. Philadelphia: American Baptist Publication Society, 1845. 3 v. AMaJ; IaK; KKcBT; ViRU. 45-2563

Fuller, Andrew, 1754-1815. Dialogues, letters and essays. New York: Colby, 1845. 478 p. PPM. 45-2564

Fuller, Andrew, 1754-1815. Expository discourses on Genesis: with practical reflections. New York: L. Colby, 1845. CtY; PPM. 45-2565

Fuller, Andrew, 1754-1815. The gospel, its own witness. New York: Colby, 1845. 501 p. NRAB; PPM. 45-2566

Fuller, Andrew, 1754-1815. The gospel worthy of all acceptation. New York: Colby, 1845. 424 p. PPM. 45-2567

Fuller, Andrew, 1754-1815. Miscellanies. New York: Colby, 1845. 514 p. PPM. 45-2568

Fuller, Andrew, 1754-1815. Sermons on various subjects. New York: Colby, 1845. 447 p. PPM. 45-2569

Fuller, Richard, 1804-1876. Domestic slavery considered as a scriptural institution in a correspondence between the Rev. Richard Fuller... and the Rev. Francis Wayland... Revised and corrected by the authors. New York: L. Colby; Boston: Gould, Kendall and Lincoln, 1845. 254 p. IaPeC; LNH; MBC; TxH; WBelo C. 45-2570

Fuller, Richard, 1804-1876. Intrepid faith: a sermon on the death of the Rev. William Tomlinson Brantly, with a sketch of his life and character; delivered at the request of the First Baptist Church of Charleston, South Carolina, May 18 1845. Charleston: Published by the church, 1845. 40 p. GU; KyLoS; MdHi NjPT; RPB. 45-2571

Fuller, Samuel, 1802-1895. Characteristic exellences of the liturgy. Boston: Tract committee of the Diocese of Massachusetts, 1845. 28 p. AMob; IEG MBD; MHi; NNC. 45-2572

Furman, Gabriel, 1800-1854. Address delivered before the Queens County Agricultural Society, at its third anniversary, at Jamica, October 10, 1844 Jamaica, [Long Island] Printed by C.S Watrous, 1845. 24 p. MB; NB; PPL NBLIHI. 45-2573

Furness, William Henry, 1802-1896. A brief statement of the Christian view of the atonement. Printed for the American Unitarian Association. Boston: J. Munroe and company, 1845. 14 p. CBPac ICMe; MeB; MH; PHi. 45-2574

Furness, William Henry, 1802-1896 The exclusive principle considered. Two sermons on Christian Unity and the truth of the gospels. By William Furness, pastor of the First Unitarian Congregational Church in Philadelphia. Boston

Benjamin H. Greene, 1845. 28 p. CBPac; CMe; MH-AH; OO; RPB. 45-2575

Furness, William Henry, 1802-1896. A funeral discourse. May 4th, 1845. Philadelphia, 1845. 14 p. ICU; MHi; PPL. 45-2576

Furness, William Henry, 1802-1896. A thanksgiving discourse by William H. Furness. November 27th, 1845. [Philadelphia, 1845?] 20 p. DHEW; CMe; KyLx; MHi. 45-2577

Furness, William Henry, 1802-1896. Two discourses, delivered in the First Congregational Unitarian Church on January 26, and February 2, 1845. Philadelphia: Printed by J. Crissy, 1845.

28 p. ICMe; MBAU; OCHP; PHi; WHi. 45-2578

Furness, William Henry, 1802-1896. A word for peace. A christmas discourse, December 25, 1845. Printed by request. Philadelphia: J. Crissy, 1845. 14 p. IaGG; ICN; MBAt; MBAU; MHi. 45-2579

Fysh, Frederic, d. 1867. The divine history of the church; or a catechism of the apocalypse, with a plan of the apocalyptic drama; and a chronological table of the principal events prefigured, arranged according to apocalyptic time. With an introduction by Richard Newton. Philadelphia: George and Wayne, 1845. 347 p. NjPT; NN; PPL; PPL-R. 45-2580

G

Gaines, Edmund Pendleton, 1777-1849. The case of General Gaines and wife versus Richard Relf and Beverly Chew, in the Circuit court of the United States for the state of Louisiana. New Orleans: Printed by J. Cohn, 1845. 60 p. DLC; MdBP; PPL. 45-2581

Galbraith, John, 1794-1860. A letter to Rev. Henry Tullidge, containing some comments upon a work entitled "The refuge of lies and the covert from the storm," written by Rev. B.J. Lane, designed to refute Universalism. Erie, 1845. 40 p. MBAt; NCaS; NIC; OU. 45-2582

Gale, George Washington, 1789-1861. A brief history of Knox College, situated in Galesburg, Knox County, Illinois. With sketches of the first settlement of the town... Cincinnati, [Ohio] Printed by C. Clark, 1845. 32 p. IaB; ICU; MBC; MLow; OClWHi. 45-2583

Gale, Leonard Dunnell, 1800-1883. Elements of natural philosophy: embracing the general principles of mechanics, hydrostatics, hydraulics, pneumatics, acustics, optics, electricity, galvanism, magnetism and astronomy. Eleventh edition. New York: Mark H. Newman, 1845. 276 p. InGrD; NN; OOxM. 45-2584

Galena, Illinois. First Presbyterian Church. A brief history of the First Presbyterian Church, Galena, Illinois, for the use of its members. Also the confession of faith, covenant, and rules of sai church... Galena: Printed by W.C.E Thomas, 1845. 16 p. MnHi; PPPrHi. 45 2585

Gallatin, Albert, 1761-1849. Notes o the semi-civilized nations of Mexico Yucatan and Central America. [Nev York: Bartlett and Welford; Londoni Wiley and Putnam, 1845] 352 p. CSi ICN; MdBP; MiU-C; NN. 45-2586

Gallaudet, Thomas Hopkins, 1787 1851. Bible stories with practical illustra tions and remarks on the fall. [In th Cherokee language] Second edition Park Hill: Cherokee Nation; John Cand and John F. Wheeler, 1845. 24 p. ICN MBAt. 45-2587

Gallaudet, Thomas Hopkins, 1787 1851. The child's book on the soul; tw parts in one. Hartford, Connecticut Belknap and Hamersley, 1845. 80 p PWaybu. 45-2588

Gallup, Joseph Adams, 1769-1849 Outlines of the institutes of medicine founded on the philosophy of humai economy, in health, and in disease. Nev York: Collins, brothers and company 1845. 2 v. DNLM; MBCo; RNR. 45-258

Gallup, Joseph Adams, 1769-1849 Outlines of the institutes of medicine founded on the philosophy of humai economy, in health, and in disease Second edition, revised. New York: Col lins, brothers and company, 1845. 2 v. MH-M; NBMS; NNNAM; VtU. 45-2590

Galt, John, 1779-1839. Lawrie Todd, or the settlers in the woods. Revised and corrected, with a new introduction, notes, etc., by the author. With an original preface, by Grant Thornburn. New York: Farmer and Daggers, 1845. 174 p. MB; MH; NNG; OClStM. 45-2591

Galt, John, 1779-1839. The life of Lord Byron. New York: Harper and brothers, 1845. 334 p. GAuY; InCW; MeAu; OWoC; WHi. 45-2592

Gammell, William, 1812-1889. Lives of Roger Williams, Timothy Dwight, and Count Pulaski. Boston: Charles C. Little and James Brown, 1845. 446 p. IP; NNC; NNS; OClWHi; WNaE. 45-2593

Gannett, Ezra Stiles, 1801-1871. A discourse delivered at the dedication of the Unitarian Church, Montreal, May 11, 1845. Boston: William Crosby and H.P. Nichols, 1845. 40 p. MBAt; MBAU; MiD-B; RPB. 45-2594

Gannett, Ezra Stiles, 1801-1871. The faith of the Unitarian Christian explained, justified and distinguished. Printed for the American Unitarian Association. Boston: J. Munroe and company, 1845. 36 p. ICMe; MH; MMeT-Hi; MWA; NjR. 45-2595

Gannett, Ezra Stiles, 1801-1871. The faith of the Unitarian Christian explained, justified and distinguished. Printed for the American Unitarian Association. Boston: J. Munroe and company, 1845. 40 p. CBPac; ICMe; MWA; NCH; OO. 45-2596

Gannett, Ezra Stiles, 1801-1871. Mr. Parker and his views. An article from the Christian examiner and religious miscellany. Boston: Crosby and Nichols, 1845. 30 p. CBPac; IEG; MBC; NcD; OC. 45-2597

Gannett, Ezra Stiles, 1801-1871. Peace not war. A sermon preached in the Federal Street Meeting House. December 14, 1845. Boston: Joseph Dowe, 1845. 24 p. IaGG; MeB; NNG; OClWHi; RPB. 45-2598

Gannett, Ezra Stiles, 1801-1871. Questions addressed to Rev. T. Parker and his friends. Boston: Halliburton and Dudley, 1845. 16 p. CBPac; MBAt; MH; RPB. 45-2599

Garber, C.H. The seeker; or the exiled spirit, and other poems. Philadelphia: United States Job Printing office, 1845. 154 p. NNC; NNUT; PHi. 45-2600

Gardner, Catharine E. A memoir of the late Joseph Peabody from Hunt's merchant's magazine, for August, 1845. New York: G.W. Wood, 1845. 19 p. ICN; MH-AH; MHi; MSaP; PPL-R. 45-2601

Garland, Hugh A., 1805-1854. Oration, in commemoration of Andrew Jackson. Richmond: P.D. Bernard, printer, 1845. 23 p. DLC; MH; MW; NcD; NjR. 45-2602

The garland, or a token of friendship. A christmas and new year's gift. Boston: Phillip Sampson and company, 1845. 288 p. MWA. 45-2603

Garlington, A.C. Address delivered before the literary societies of Erskine College, Abbeville district, South

Carolina, on the sixth anniversary, September 17, 1845. Greenville, South Carolina: Printed by O.H. Wells, 1845. 14 p. CSmH; GDecCT; MH; TBriK. 45-2604

Gatchell, Joseph. The disenthralled; being reminiscences in the life of the author. Third edition. Troy, 1845. 78 p. CtHWatk; IEGG; PHi. 45-2605

Gaume, Jean Joseph, 1802-1879. The catechism of perserverance from the beginning of the world down to our own days. Translated from the tenth French edition. New edition. New York: Benziger brothers, [1845] 4 v. MoK. 45-2606

Gaussen, Louis, 1790-1863. Theopneusty or the plenary inspiration of the Holy Scriptures. Translated by Edward Norris Kirk. Third American from the second French edition. New York: John S. Taylor and company, 1845. 410 p. CSt; GMM; MH; NjPT; ODaB. 45-2607

The gavel: a monthly periodical devoted to odd fellowship and general literature. By C.C. Burr and John Tanner. Albany: J. Munsell, 1845. 324 p. DLC; MH; MnU; NAl; NSmB. 45-2608

Geauga County Teacher Institute. Catalogue. Geauga County Teachers' Institute held October, 1845. Chardon, Ohio: Whites office, 1845. 16 p. MiD. 45-2609

Gems of devotion: a selection of prayers for the use of Catholics. Baltimore: Metropolitan printers, [1845] 336 p. MdBS. 45-2610

Gems of sacred poetry. Third edition.

Boston: Saxton and Kelt, 1845. 128 p. Ct; MB; MH. 45-2611

General Association of Massachusetts. Minutes of the General Association of Massachusetts at their session in Westminister with the narrative of the state of religion, and the pastoral letter. Boston: Crocker and Brewster, 1845. 58 p. NjR. 45-2612

General family directory. New York: Comstock and company, 1845. MWA. 45-2613

General Synod of the Evangelical Lutheran Church in the United States. Hymns, selected and original, for public and private worship. Thirty-seventh edition. Baltimore, General Synod, 1845. CtY; OCoC. 45-2614

General view of Colportage as conducted by the American Tract Society in the United States. New York: American Tract Society, 1845. 48 p. MH; MBC; NNG. 45-2615

General view of Colportage as conducted by the American Tract Society in the United States, May, 1845. New York: Printed at the Society's house by Daniel Fanshaw, 1845. 48 p. NNMr. 45-2616

Genesee Wesleyan Seminary, Lima, New York. Catalogue of the officers, faculty, and students of the Genesee Wesleyan Seminary. Rochester: S. Hamilton, printer, 1845. 31 p. CSmH; MWA. 45-2617

Geneva, New York. Laws and ordinances of the trustees of the village of Geneva. To which are prefixed the village charter, passed May 6, 1837, and the ιcts amendatory thereof. Geneva: Ira Merrell, printer, 1845. 34 p. NRU. 45-2618

Geneva College. Register of Geneva College for the academical year, 1844-1845. Geneva: Ira Merrell, printer, 1845. 32 p. CtY; MH. 45-2619

Geneva College. Register of Geneva College for the academical year, 1845-1846. Geneva: Ira Merrell, printer, 1845. 32 p. CSmH; MBC; MH; NGH; NSyU. 45-2620

Geneva Medical College. Geneva, New York. Catalogue of the college, session of 1844-1845. Geneva: Ira Merrell, printer, 1845. 19 p. CtY; MBC; MH; NNNAM. 45-2621

Geneva Medical College. Geneva, New York. Circular for 1845. Buffalo: Thomas, General Job printer, 1845. 10 p. OSG; NGH. 45-2622

Geological Society of America. Abstract of the proceedings of the sixth annual meeting of the association of American geologists and naturalists, held in New Haven, Connecticut, April, 1845. New Haven: B.L. Hamlen, printer, 1845. 87 p. MB; MoS; NjR. 45-2623

George Cruikshank's table book, edited by Gilbert Abbott and Beckett. With twenty two illustrations. Philadelphia: Carey and Hart, 1845. ICU; MH; MWA; TxHi. 45-2624

George Washington University. Circular. Washington, 1845. 1 v. Ct. 45-2625

Georgetown, Massachusetts. Harmony Cemetery. Bylaws of the Harmony Cemetery, with the names of officers for 1844-1845. Haverhill, Essex Banner, 1845. 10 p. MHa. 45-2626

Georgia. Acts of the state of Georgia, 1845. Columbus, Georgia: S.W. Flourney, 1845. 231 p. GU; Ia; MdBB; Mi-L; R. 45-2627

Georgia. A codification of the statute laws of Georgia, including the English statutes of force; in four parts. To which is prefixed a collection of state papers of English, American and state origin. Savannah: John M. Cooper, 1845. 990 p. GMBC; IU; TJaL; ViU-L; WaU-L. 45-2628

Georgia. Governor's message. November 4, 1845. Fellow citizens of the Senate and House. [Milledgeville?] 1845. 22 p. GU-De. 45-2629

Gesenius, Friedrich Heinrich Wilhelm, 1786-1842. Hebrew grammar. Translated from the eleventh German edition. Translated By T.J. Conant, with a course of exercises. Fourth edition. Boston: Gould, Kendall and Lincoln, 1845. 325 p. CoCsC; IEG; MH; OrPD; ScDuE. 45-2630

Gesta Romanorum. Evenings with the old story tellers; select tales from the Gesta Romanorum, etc. New York: G.P. Putnam's sons, 1845. IdU. 45-2631

Gesta Romanorum. Evenings with the old story tellers; select tales from the Gesta Romanorum, etc. New York: Wiley and Putnam, 1845. 155 p. CtY; MH; NNC; OClW; RWe. 45-2632

Gesta Romanorum. Select tales from Gesta Romanorum, etc. New York:

Wiley, 1845. 155 p. CSfU; IaBo; LNL; NcWfC; TBrik. 45-2633

Gettysburg. Theological Seminary of the United Lutheran Church in America. General catalogue and constitution, 1845. Theological seminary of the general synod of the Evangelical Lutheran Church in the United States. Gettysburg: H.C. Neinstedt, 1845. 20 p. MeHi; NNUT; OSW; PPLT. 45-2634

Gettysburg College, Gettysburg, Pennsylvania. Annual catalogue of the officers and students in Pennsylvania College. Gettysburg: H.C. Neinstedt, 1845. 20 p. MBC; PPM. 45-2635

Getz, George. Getz's forms. A general collection of precedents in conveyancing, in which examples are given, in sufficient variety, to enable the schrivener, conveyancer, and man of business to draw instruments of writing legally and correctly... Third edition, revised, enlarged and improved. Philadelphia: Thomas, Cowperthwait and company, 1845. 270 p. IaDmD-L; In-SC; MH-L; PP. 45-2636

Gibbes, Robert Wilson, 1809-1866. Description of the teeth of a new fossil animal found in the green sand of South Carolina. [Philadelphia, 1845] 3 p. MH-Z; NIC. 45-2637

Gibbes, Robert Wilson, 1809-1866. National Institute. Review of first, second and third bulletins of the National Institute and the address of J.R. Poinsett, January 4, 1841, and of Levi Woodbury, January 15, 1845. [Columbia, South Carolina, 1845] DLC. 45-2638

Gibbon, Edward, 1737-1794. The his-

tory of the decline and fall of the Roman empire. A new edition, to which is added a complete index of the whole work. Chicago, Illinois: Belfield, Clark and company, [1845] 5 v. NjHo; PPins; ViU. L. 45-2639

Gibbon, Edward, 1737-1794. The history of the decline and fall of the Roman empire. A new edition, to which is added a complete index of the whole work. Philadelphia: Henry T. Coates and company, 1845. 668 p. IaDuN; MA; WvWe 45-2640

Gibbon, Edward, 1737-1794. The history of the decline and fall of the Roman empire. New York: A.L. Burt, [1845] AzPh; KSalW; MdU: NNC; RP. 45-264

Gibbon, Edward, 1737-1794. The history of the decline and fall of the Roman empire. New York: Harper, 1845. 6 v. FEv; IaA; MSan; OCU; WNei. 45-2642

Gibbon, Edward, 1737-1794. The history of the decline and fall of the Roman empire. New York: Harper and brother 1845. 5 v. FEv; NbOP; NNC. 45-2643

Gibbon, Edward, 1737-1794. The history of the decline and fall of the Roman empire. New York: W. Lovell company 1845. 6 v. IdB; MeAu; NcLoC; WU. 45-2644

Gibbon, Edward, 1737-1794. The history of the decline and fall of the Roman empire. With notes by the Rev. H.H. Milman. A new edition to which is added complete index of the whole work. Chicago and New York: Belford, Clark and company, 1845. 5 v. NjHo; ViU-L 45-2645

Gibbs, William, b. 1785. Family notices collected by William Gibbs, of Lexington, Massachusetts. [Lexington, Massachusetts, 1845] 8 p. MH; MWA; MnHi; WHi. 45-2646

Gibbs, Wolcott, 1822-1908. An inaugural dissertation on a natural system of chemical classification... Princeton, New Jersey: Printed by J.T. Robinson, 1845. 59 p. CSt-L; MdBJ; NBM; PU-S; RPB. 45-2647

Gibson, William, 1788-1868. Institutes and practice of surgery: being the outline of a course of lectures. Seventh edition, improved and altered. Philadelphia: James Kay, Jr. and brothers: Pittsburgh: C.H. Kay, 1845. 2 v. CU; ICJ; LNB; MdBM; PPWa. 45-2648

Giddings, Joshua Reed, 1795-1864. Speech of Mr. Giddings, of Ohio, on the annexation of Texas. Delivered in the House, January 22, 1845. [Washington: J. and G.S. Gideon, printers, 1845. 16 p. MBAt; MHi; NIC; PHi; TxU. 45-2649

Giesebrecht, Ludwig. The seven sleepers, as performed by the Philadelphia Sacred Music Society. Music by C. Loewe. Words translated from the German. Philadelphia, 1845. 16 p. MH; PHi. 45-2650

A gift: a Christmas, New Year and birthday present, 1845. Philadelphia: Carey and Hart, 1845. 300 p. ArU; MAm; MWA; TxU; WGr. 45-2651

A gift for Julia. Third edition. Boston: J.M. Usher, 1845. 100 p. NNU-W. 45-2652

Gilbert, Ann Taylor, 1782-1866. Hymns for infant minds, by the author of original poems and nursery rhymns. New edition, edited by Thomas Teller. New Haven: S. Babcock, [1845] 64 p. CtY. 45-2653

Gillespie, William Mitchell, 1816-1868. Rome; as seen by a New Yorker in 1843-1844... New York: Wiley and Putnam, 1845. 216 p. CtMW; KWiU; MB; OCY; PPA. 45-2654

Gillies, John, 1712-1796. Historical collections relating to remarkable periods of the success of the gospel. Compiled by the John Gillies. Published originally in 1754. Kelso: Rutherford, 1845. 582 p. ICN; NN; PPL; PPPrHi. 45-2655

Gillies, John, 1712-1796. Memoirs of Rev. George Whitefield... Revised and corrected with large additions and improvements to which is appended an extensive collection of his sermons and other writings. Hartford: Edwin Hunt, 1845. ICU; LNB; NbOP; OO; TMeSC. 45-2656

Gilman, Caroline Howard, 1794-1888. Oracles from the poets; a fanciful diversion for the drawing room. New York and London: Wiley and Putnam, 1845. 242 p. CtHT; InU; MWA; PU; ScC. 45-2657

Gilman, Caroline Howard, 1794-1888. Stories and poems for children. New York: C.S. Francis and company; Boston: J.H. Frances, 1845. [9]-179 p. MB; NcD. 45-2658

Gilman, Samuel, 1791-1856. Unitarian Christianity no novel device. A discourse delivered on May 25, 1845, being the 24th anniversary of the Charleston Unitarian Book and Tract Society... to which is added the report of the managers on that occasion. Charleston, South Carolina: Printed by Walker and Burke, 1845. 22 p. ICU; WHi. 45-2659

Gilmanton Academy, Gilmanton, New Hampshire. Order of exercises for the annual exhibition of students, 1845, 1847. Gilmanton, 1845-1847 Nh-Hi. 45-2660

Gilpin, Henry Dilworth, 1801-1860. Address delivered at the University of Pennsylvania, before the Philomathean Society, on the occasion of their biennial celebration, May 23, 1845. Philadelphia: King and Baird, printers, 1845. 30 p. MiD-B; NCH; PHi; PPAmP; Vi. 45-2661

Gilpin, Thomas, 1776-1853. Genealogy of the Gilpin family in England, A.D. 1200-1800, taken from the papers of Joshua Gilpin, esq. By his brother, Thomas Gilpin. Philadelphia, 1845. PPPrHi. 45-2662

Gilroy, Clinton G. The art of weaving; with account of its rise and progress. New York, 1845. 537 p. MW. 45-2663

Gilroy, Clinton G. History of silk, cotton, linen, wool and other fibrous substances; including observations on spinning, dyeing and weaving. New York: Harper and brothers, 1845. 464 p. MnU; NBu; OrP; RPB; WU. 45-2664

Gilroy, Clinton G. The history of silk, cotton, linen, wool and other fibrous substances; including observations on spinning, dyeing and weaving. also an account of the pastoral life of the ancients, their social state and attainments in the domestic arts. New York: Harper and brothers, 1845. 464 p. DLC; ICJ; MB; OrPS; RPB. 45-2665

Gipsey's dream waltz, the subjec selected from Balfe's celebrated opera the "Bohemian girl." New York: Atwill 1845. 2 p. MB. 45-2666

The Girard almanac for 1846. Philadel phia: Thomas L. Bonsal, [1845] 34 p MWA; NjR. 45-2667

Girard Trust Corn Exchange Bank Philadelphia. Prospectus. Philadelphia 1845. PHi. 45-2668

Gish, J. Wealthy citizens of Lancaster County, Pennsylvania. Lancaster, D.S Keiffer, [1845] 17 p. CSmH; PPL. 45 2669

Giustiniani, L. Papal Rome as it is; By a Roman. With an introduction... Philadel phia: James M. Campbell, 1845. 224 p ICP; KyLoP; MWA; NNUT; PLT. 45 2670

Gleig, George Robert, 1796-1888. The hussar, by the author of the Subaltern Gleig. Philadelphia: G.B. Zieber and company, 1845. DLC; NN; PPL-R RPAt. 45-2671

Glenn, James. The city and country con trasted: a poem... New York: Privately printed, 1845. DCL; MH; NBuG. 45 2672

Gliddon, George Robbins, 1809-1857 Ancient Egypt, her monuments hieroglyphics, history and archaeology New edition, revised. Baltimore, 1845 CMC; CtY; MdBP; NIC; NWM. 45-267.

Glimpses on the wonderful. New York Wiley and Putnam, 1845. 155 p. DLC MWA; NUt; OO. 45-2674

Glover, Charles William, 1806-1863. The melodies of many lands... by C. Jefferys. New York, 1845. CtY. 45-2675

Glover, Stephen, 1812-1870. A home that I love. Song arranged for the Spanish guitar by Francis Weiland. Philadelphia: Lee and Walker, 1845. 3 p. MB. 45-2676

Godfrey's almanac for 1846. Brattleboro, Vermont: Joseph Steen, [1845] MWA. 45-2677

Godfrey's almanack for the year 1846. By Albert Godfrey. Keene, New Hampshire: J. and J.W. Prentiss, [1845] 44 p. MB; MWA; NhHi; NjR. 45-2678

Godwin, Mary Wollstonecraft, 1759-1797. A vindication of the rights of woman, with strictures on political and moral subjects. With a biographical sketch of the author. New York: G. Vale, 1845. 214 p. IaCr; LNH; MiD; OClWHi; PBa. 45-2679

Goethe, Johann Wolfgang von, 1749-1832. Essays on art. Translated by Samuel Gray Ward. Boston: J. Munroe and company, 1845. 263 p. CtY; InRch; MeAug; ScU; WU. 45-2680

Goethe, Johann Wolfgang von, 1749-1832. Faust; a dramatic poem, by Goethe. Translated into English prose with notes, etc. by A. Hayward. Second American from the Thrid London edition. Lowell: Bixby and Whiting, 1845. 320 p. CtY; CU; DLC; MWA; NjP; ViU. 45-2681

Goethe, Johann Wolfgang von, 1749-1832. Herman and Dorothea... New York, 1845. MH. 45-2682

The golden rule: a dialogue between little Grace and her mother. Boston: Massachusetts Sabbath School Society, 1845. 72 p. RPE. 45-2683

The golden rule: a weekly gazette, devoted to odd fellowship, popular literature and general intelligence. New York: E. Winchester, 1845-1848. V. 1-8. NUtHi; PPL. 45-2684

Goldsborough, Louis Malesherbes, 1805-1877. A reply to an attack made upon the navy of the United States, by Samuel E. Coues, president of the Peace Society, in which a brief notice is taken of the recent July 4th oration, delivered at Boston by Charles Sumner. Portsmouth: C.W. Brewster, 1845. 23 p. MBAt; MdAN; Nh; Nh-Hi; WHi. 45-2685

Goldsbury, John, 1795-1890. The common school grammar. A concise and comprehensive manual of the English grammar... Sixth edition. Boston: J. Munroe, 1845. 94 p. MB; PU-Penn; RPB; TxGR; WU. 45-2686

Goldsbury, John, 1795-1890. A concise and comprehensive manual of English grammar... Sixth edition. Boston: J. Munroe and company, 1845. CtHWatk; MH. 45-2687

Goldsmith, Henry. Catechism for Hebrew children. New York, 1845. 20 p. PPDrop. 45-2688

Goldsmith, Oliver, 1728-1774. Abridgement of the history of England from the invasion of Julius Caesar to the death of George Second and a continuation to the War of 1845. Greenfield: Massachusetts: A. Phelps, 1845. 444 p. NSyU. 45-2689

Goldsmith, Oliver, 1728-1774. Goldsmith's history of Greece, from the earliest state to the death of Alexander the Great. New York: G. Lane and C.B. Tippett for the Sunday School Union of the Methodist Episcopal Church, 1845. 175 p. GEU; NcD. 45-2690

Goldsmith, Oliver, 1728-1774. The Grecian history, from the earliest state to the death of Alexander the Great. Revised and corrected, and a vocabulary of proper names appended; with prosodial marks, to assist in their pronunciation. Philadelphia: Grigg and Elliot, 1845. 322 p. NcC; P; OCX. 45-2691

Goldsmith, Oliver, 1728-1774. History of England. Greenfield, Massachusetts: A. Phelps, 1845. 444 p. IaPeC. 45-2692

Goldsmith, Oliver, 1728-1774. History of Greece from the earliest state to the death of Alexander the Great. New York: G. Lane and C.B. Tippett, 1845. 175 p. NjMD. 45-2693

Goldsmith, Oliver, 1728-1774. A history of the earth, and animated nature. A new edition with corrections and alterations. Philadelphia: Grigg and Elliott, 1845. 4 v. in 2. AzT; DNLM; MH. 45-2694

Goldsmith, Oliver, 1728-1774. The miscellaneous works of Oliver Goldsmith, with an account of his life and writings. Stereotyped from the Paris edition, edited by Washington Irving. Philadelphia: J. Crissy, 1845. 527 p. CSf; MoS; NcAS; PFal; ViU. 45-2695

Goldsmith, Oliver, 1728-1774. Pinnock's improved edition of Dr.

Goldsmith's abridgment of the history o Rome. First American, corrected anc revised from the twelfth English edition. Philadelphia: Thomas, Cowperthwai and company, 1845. 395 p. DLC; ICU MH; NGH; TNT. 45-2696

Goldsmith, Oliver, 1728-1774 Pinnock's improved edition of Dr Goldsmith's history of England from the invasion of Julius Caesar to the death o George II. Forty-fifth edition from the thirty-fifth English edition. Philadelphia Thomas, Cowperthwait and company 1847. CtY; MH. 45-2697

Goldsmith, Oliver, 1728-1774 Pinnock's improved edition of Dr Goldsmith's history of England, from the invasion of Julius Caesar to the death o George II, with a continuation to the year 1832. With questions for examination Sixteenth American corrected anc revised from the twenty-fourth Englis edition. Philadelphia: Thomas, Cow perthwait and company, 1845. 468 p MDeeP; MH; NNQ; PU; TxU-T. 45 2698

Goldsmith, Oliver, 1728-1774 Pinnock's improved edition of Dr Goldsmith's history of Greece, for the use of schools. Philadelphia: Thomas Cowperthwait and company, 1845. 372 p GEU; NcD; NSchU; ViU. 45-2699

Goldsmith, Oliver, 1728-1774. Poems plays and essays; an account of his writ ings and life; to which is added critica dissertation on his poetry. By J. Aikin New York: Turner, 1845. 384 p. CtY; LN NKeen; OClW; PPL. 45-2700

Goldsmith, Oliver, 1728-1774. Poetica works of Oliver Goldsmith. Illustrated by wood engravings from ten designs of C.W. Cope and others. With a biographical memoir. Edited by Bolton Corney. New York: Harper and brothers, 1845. 235 p. C; IEG; MB; NCH; NcRSM. 45-2701

Goldsmith, Oliver, 1728-1774. The vicar of Wakefield: a tale. New York: Wiley and Putnam, 1845. 175 p. CtY; IaMp; MeB; MH; RJa. 45-2702

Goldsmith, Oliver B. Goldsmith's gems of penmanship, containing various examples of the caligraphic art, embracing the author's system of mercantile penmanship. New York: The author, 1845. 36 p. DLC; ICN; NcAS; NhD. 45-2703

Good, John Mason, 1764-1827. The book of nature. From the last edition. Hartford: Belknap and Hamersley, 1845. 25-467 p. IaMp; MeGr; MoS; PP; WMAM. 45-2704

Good, Peter Peyto, 1789-1875. The family flora and meteria medica botanica, containing the botanical analysis, natural history, and chemical and medical properties of plants. Elizabethtown, New Jersey: The author, [1845] CtSoP; MdUC; NRU; PHC; RPM. 45-2705

Good, Peter Peyto, 1789-1875. The family flora and materia medica botanica, containing the botanical analysis, natural history, and chemical and medical properties of plants. New York: Author, 1845. 1 v. CO; DNLM; FDes; NCH; PPL. 45-2706

Goodell, William, 1792-1878. Address read at the New York state library convention, held at Port Byron, July 25 and 26, 1845. Albany: Albany Patriot, 1845. 14 p. NCanHi; NUtHi; OO; PPL; TxLT. 45-2707

Goodell, William, 1792-1878. Comeouterism. The duty of secession from a corrupt church. Boston: Cornhill, 1845. 38 p. MiD-B; MWA; NUt; PHi; PPL. 45-2708

Goodell, William, 1792-1878. Comeouterism. The duty of secession from a corrupt church. New York: American Anti-slavery Society, 1845. 38 p. CtSoP; MH; NNUT; TxU; WHi. 45-2709

Goodell, William, 1792-1878. Views on American constitutional law, in its bearing upon American slavery. Second edition, revised with additions. Utica: Lawson and Chaplin, 1845. 163 p. GEU; ICU; LNH; PHi; WHi. 45-2710

Goodman, William. The social history of Great Britain during the reigns of the Stuarts, beginning with the seventeenth century, being the period of settling the United States. Second edition. New York: W.H. Colyer, 1845. 2 v. LN; MWH; OHi; RPAt; Vi. 45-2711

Goodrich, Charles Augustus, 1790-1862. A child's book on the creation. Second edition. Park Hill: Cherokee Nation, Mission Press, 1845. 14 p. ICN; InNd; MBAt. 45-2712

Goodrich, Charles Augustus, 1790-1862. The child's history of the United States. Designed as a first book of history for schools. Illustrated by numerous anecdotes. Improved from the thirty-first edition. Philadelphia: Thomas, Cowperthwait and company, 1845. [7]-175 p.

DLC; MiU; NcAS; OClWHi; PPWI. 45-2713

Goodrich, Charles Augustus, 1790-1862. History of the Church, from the birth of Christ to the present time, life of Christ, history of several Protestant denominations, sketches of martyrs... Brattleboro, Vermont: G.H. Salisbury, 1845. 14-504 p. MBNMHi; MMET; NhFr; VtBrt; WHi. 45-2714

Goodrich, Charles Augustus, 1790-1862. A history of the United States of America, on a plan adapted to the capacity of youth... Enlarged from the one hundredth edition. Boston: Jenks, Palmer, and company, 1845. MH; MiD-B; MWHi. 45-2715

Goodrich, Charles Augustus, 1790-1862. Questions and supplement to Goodrich's history of the United States. By Joseph Emerson. New edition, revised and adapted to the enlarged edition of the history. Boston: Jenks and Palmer, 1845. 192 p. MiD-B. 45-2716

Goodrich, Charles Augustus, 1790-1862. The universal traveller; designed to introduce readers at home to an acquaintance with the arts, customs, and manners of the principal modern nations on the globe... Hartford, [Connecticut] Robins and Smith, 1845. 504 p. ICU; LU; MnHi; MWA; OU. 45-2717

Goodrich, Chauncey Allen, 1790-1860. Lessons in Latin Parsing; containing the outlines of the Latin grammar, divided into short portions, and exemplified by appropriate exercises in parsing. Twentieth edition. New Haven: Durrie and Peck; Philadelphia: Smith and Peck,

1845. 214 p. CtHWatk; CtY; MNBedf MnSS. 45-2718

Goodrich, Samuel Griswold, 1793 1860. Book of quadrupeds for youth Brattleboro, Vermont, 1845. MB. 45 2719

Goodrich, Samuel Griswold, 1793-1860. The child's botony. Eleventh edi tion. Boston: Jenks and Palmer, 1845 MH. 45-2720

Goodrich, Samuel Griswold, 1793 1860. Curiosities of nature: by the autho of Peter Parley's tales. Boston: Thompson, Brown and company, 1845 320 p. MB; MiGr; MMal; WM. 45-2721

Goodrich, Samuel Griswold, 1793-1860. Dick Boldhero; or a tale of adventures in South America. By the author of Peter Parley's tales. Philadelphia: Sorir and Ball, 1845. 167 p. CtY; NN; OClWHi; ViU. 45-2722

Goodrich, Samuel Griswold, 1793-1860. Enterprise, industry and art of man as displayed in fishing, hunting, commerce, navigation, mining, agriculture and manufactures. Boston: Bradbury, Soden and company, 1845. 335 p. CU; DLC; MB; PU; ViU. 45-2723

Goodrich, Samuel Griswold, 1793-1860. Enterprise, industry and art of man, as displayed in fishing, hunting, commerce, navigation, mining, agriculture and manufactures. New York: J. Allen, 1845. 335 p. ICN; NcU; OO; ViU; WaS. 45-2724

Goodrich, Samuel Griswold, 1793-1860. Every day book for youth. Worester: Grout, 1845. 14-293 p. OO. 45-725

Goodrich, Samuel Griswold, 1793-860. The first book of history for hildren and youth. By the author of 'eter Parley's tales. Revised edition. 3oston: C.J. Hendee, etc., 1845. MH; lcWsM; PReaHi. 45-2726

Goodrich, Samuel Griswold, 1793-860. The fourth school reader. Louis-ille: J.P. Morton and company, 1845. 40 p. OCX. 45-2727

Goodrich, Samuel Griswold, 1793-860. A glance at philosophy, mental, noral and social. By the author of Peter 'arley's tales. Boston: Bradbury, Soden nd company, 1845. [7]-320 p. DLC; 4Hi; NIC; TxU; ViU. 45-2728

Goodrich, Samuel Griswold, 1793-860. A glance at philosophy, mental, noral and social. By the author of Peter 'arley's tales. Boston: J.E. Hickman, 1845] [7]-320 p. CU; LNT; NhM; 4mAlb; TxGR. 45-2729

Goodrich, Samuel Griswold, 1793-860. A glance at philosophy, mental, noral and social. By the author of Peter 'arley's tales. New York: J. Allen, 1845. 7]-320 p. NbU; NcU; NFred; ViU. 45-.730

Goodrich, Samuel Griswold, 1793-860. A glance at philosophy, mental, noral and social. By the author of Peter 'arley's tales. Philadelphia: T.K. and '.G. Collins, 1845. 320 p. CtY; MiGr; 4nHi; RPB; ViR. 45-2731

Goodrich, Samuel Griswold, 1793-860. A glance at philosophy, mental,

moral and social. By the author of Peter Parley's tales. Philadelphia: Thomas, Cowperthwait and company, 1845. 320 p. CoDR; CtY; ICU; RJa; ViLxW. 45-2732

Goodrich, Samuel Griswold, 1793-1860. History of the Indians of North and South America. By the author of Peter Parley's tales. Boston, 1845. 320 p. MBL; MHi. 45-2733

Goodrich, Samuel Griswold, 1793-1860. A home in the sea; or the adventures of Philip Brusque. Designed to show the nature and necessity of government. By the author of Peter Parley's tales. Philadelphia: Sorin and Ball, 1845. 167 p. ICN; DLC; MH; RPB; ViU. 45-2734

Goodrich, Samuel Griswold, 1793-1860. Illustrative anecdotes of the animal kingdom: by the author of Peter Parley's tales. Boston: Bradbury, Soden and company, 1845. 336 p. CSmH; DLC; MHi; Wa. 45-2735

Goodrich, Samuel Griswold, 1793-1860. Illustrative anecdotes of the animal kingdom: by the author of Peter Parley's tales. Boston: New York: J. Allen, 1845. 336 p. KyLo; MSaP; NjR; RPB; ViU. 45-2736

Goodrich, Samuel Griswold, 1793-1860. Lights and shadows of African history. Boston, 1845. 336 p. MHi. 45-2737

Goodrich, Samuel Griswold, 1793-1860. Lights and shadows of European history. Boston, 1845. 320 p. MHi. 45-2738

Goodrich, Samuel Griswold, 1793-1860. Literature, ancient and modern. By the author of Peter Parley's tales. Boston: Bradbury, Soden and company, 1845. 336 p. DLC; MHi; NIC; RPB; ViU. 45-2739

Goodrich, Samuel Griswold, 1793-1860. Literature, ancient and modern. By the author of Peter Parley's tales. New York: J. Allen, 1845. 336 p. CSmH; NN; NNC; PU; ViU. 45-2740

Goodrich, Samuel Griswold, 1793-1860. Lives of benefactors. Boston: Thompson, Brown and company, [1845] 320 p. IaDaIC; MiGr; MLaw; Nv; WHi. 45-2741

Goodrich, Samuel Griswold, 1793-1860. Lives of celebrated women. Boston: Thompson, Brown and company, [1845] 352 p. IaScM; MBoy; MNan; OClWHi; WHi. 45-2742

Goodrich, Samuel Griswold, 1793-1860. Manners and customs of the principal nations of the globe. Boston: Bradbury, Soden and company, 1845. [5]-352 p. IaMp; KyBC; MB; RPaw; ViU. 45-2743

Goodrich, Samuel Griswold, 1793-1860. The manners, customs, and antiquities of the Indians of North and South America. By the author of Peter Parley's tales. Boston: Bradbury, Soden and company, 1845. 336 p. MnHi. 45-2744

Goodrich, Samuel Griswold, 1793-1860. A national geography for schools... New York: Huntington and Savage, 1845. 108 p. DLC; MH; NcAS; PP; TxU-T. 45-2745

Goodrich, Samuel Griswold, 1793-

1860. New second reader, Edited by Butler. Louisville, [1846] CtHWatk. 45-2746

Goodrich, Samuel Griswold, 1793-1860. Peter Parley's book of anecdotes. Illustrated by engravings. Philadelphia: Thomas, Cowperthwait and company, 1845. 144 p. CtY; ICU; MnS. 45-2747

Goodrich, Samuel Griswold, 1793-1860. Peter Parley's book of fables. Hartford: R.A. White, 1845. 128 p. TxD-T. 45-2748

Goodrich, Samuel Griswold, 1793-1860. Peter Parley's common school history... Philadelphia: Butler and Williams. 1845. 309 p. CtHwatk; MH; NN; PPWI. 45-2749

Goodrich, Samuel Griswold, 1793-1860. Peter Parley's geography for beginners. New York: Huntington and Savage. 1845. 160 p. IEG; MH; MiD; MiD-B. NcU. 45-2750

Goodrich, Samuel Griswold, 1793-1860. Peter Parley's tales about ancient and modern Greece. Philadelphia: Thomas, Cowperthwait and company. 1845. 199 p. NbM; ViU. 45-2751

Goodrich, Samuel Griswold, 1793-1860. Peter Parley's tales about ancient Rome, with some account of modern Italy. Philadelphia: Thomas, Cowperthwait, 1845. 208 p. CtY; ICU; PHC; TJaU. 45-2752

Goodrich, Samuel Griswold, 1793-1860. Peter Parley's tales about the Islands in the Pacific Ocean. Philadelphia: 1845. 144 p. PHi. 45-2753

Goodrich, Samuel Griswold, 1793-

1860. Peter Parley's tales about the sun, moon, and stars. Philadelphia: Thomas, Cowperthwait, 1845. 116 p. ICU; NN. 45-2754

Goodrich, Samuel Griswold, 1793-1860. Peter Parley's universal history, on the basis of geography. For the use of families. New York: York, Nafis and Cornish, etc., etc., 1845. 2 v. ICU; MH; TxComT. 45-2755

Goodrich, Samuel Griswold, 1793-1860. A pictorial geography of the world, comprising a system of universal geography, popular and scientific. Boston: C.D. Strong, 1845. [2 v.] 1008 p. MnSS; MWA; PPL; RNHi; RWe. 45-2756

Goodrich, Samuel Griswold, 1793-1860. A pictorial geography of the world, comprising a system of universal geography, popular and scientific. Thirteenth edition. Boston: C.D. Strong, 1845. 2 v. ICRL; MiU; PPL. 45-2757

Goodrich, Samuel Griswold, 1793-1860. A pictorial history of America; embracing both the northern and southern portions of the New World... Hartford: E. Strong, 1845. 813 p. CoHi; CtY; MHa; MiU; NjMD. 45-2758

Goodrich, Samuel Griswold, 1793-1860. A pictorial history of England. Philadelphia: E.H. Butler and company, 1845. 448 p. FNp; KyLxT; LNB; NdAS; PBm. 45-2759

Goodrich, Samuel Griswold, 1793-1860. A pictorial history of France for schools. Philadelphia: Sorin and Ball, 1845. 347 p. KyHi; MH; NN; ScCC; TxH. 45-2760

Goodrich, Samuel Griswold, 1793-1860. A pictorial history of the United States, with notices of the portions of America north and south. For the use of schools. Philadelphia: Sorin and Ball, 1845. 354 p. CtHT-W; OCHP; PJA; TNP; ViU. 45-2761

Goodrich, Samuel Griswold, 1793-1860. A pictorial natural history, embracing a view of the mineral, vegetable, and animal kingdoms. For the use of schools. Boston: James Munroe and company, 1845. 415 p. MH; MnU; NIC; TxU-T. 45-2762

Goodrich, Samuel Griswold, 1793-1860. The second book of history, including the modern history of Europe, Africa, and Asia. Illustrated by engravings and sixteen maps and designed as a sequel to the "First book of history." Revised edition. Boston: C.J. Hendee, and James and Palmer, 1845. 192 p. CSmH; DLC; NWebyC. 45-2763

Goodrich, Samuel Griswold, 1793-1860. Stories about the earth, sun, moon and stars; from the works of Peter Parley [pseud.] New York: Baker, Crane and Day [1845?] 8 p. NN. 45-2764

Goodrich, Samuel Griswold, 1793-1860. A tale of the revolution, and other sketches. By Peter Parley [pseud.] Philadelphia: Sorin and Ball, 1845. 160 p. DLC; ICN; NRU; ODW; ViU. 45-2765

Goodrich, Samuel Griswold, 1793-1860. The tales of Peter Parley about Africa. With engravings. Revised edition. Philadelphia: Thomas, Cowperthwait, 1845. 138 p. ViU. 45-2766

Goodrich, Samuel Griswold, 1793-

1860. The tales of Peter Parley about America. With engravings. Revised Edition. Philadelphia: Thomas, Cowperthwait aand company, 1845. 144 p. DLC; InFtwL; OU. 45-2767

Goodrich, Samuel Griswold, 1793-1860. The tales of Peter Parley about Asia. Revised edition. Philadelphia: Thomas, Cowperthwait and company, 1845. MH. 45-2768

Goodrich, Samuel Griswold, 1793-1860. The third reader for the use of schools. Boston: Otis, Broaders and company, 1846. 180 p. CtHWatk; PPM; OO. 45-2769

Goodrich, Samuel Griswold, 1793-1860. The truth finder; or the story of inquisitive Jack, by the author of Peter Parley's tales. New York: Harper and brothers, 1845. 162 p. DLC; RPB. 45-2770

Goodrich, Samuel Griswold, 1793-1860. The truth finder; or the story of inquisitive Jack, by the author of Peter Parley's tales. Philadelphia, 1845. 162 p. MBAt; ODW. 45-2771

Goodrich, Samuel Griswold, 1793-1860. The wonders of geology, by the author of Peter Parley's tales. Boston: Bradbury, Soden and company, 1845. 291 p. KyBgW; MB-FA; LN; NP; ViU. 45-2772

Goodrich, Samuel Griswold, 1793-1860. The world and its inhabitants. By the author of Peter Parley's tales. Boston: J.E. Hickman, 1845. 328 p. CU-I. 45-2773

Goodrich, Samuel Griswold, 1793-

1860. The world and its inhabitants. By the author of Peter Parley's tales. Boston: Soden and company, 1845. 528 p. DLC; MB; RPB; ViU; WaS. 45-2774

Goodrich, Samuel Griswold, 1793-1860. The world and its inhabitants. By the author of Peter Parley's tales. New York: J. Allen, 1845. 328 p. MWA; NcU; ViU. 45-2775

Goodrich, Samuel Griswold, 1793-1860. The world and its inhabitants. By the author of Peter Parley's tales. Philadelphia: Thomas, Cowperthwait and company, [1845] 328 p. CtY; OClWHi; PCC; PPWa; ViLxW. 45-2776

Goodrich, Samuel Griswold, 1793-1860. The young American; or book of government and law; showing their history, nature and necessity. For the use of schools. Seventh edition. New York: Turner and Hayden, 1845. 282 p. CoCra. 45-2777

Goodrich, Samuel Griswold, 1793-1860. The young American; or book of government and law; showing their history, nature and necessity. For the use of schools. Eighth edition. New York: Turner and Hayden, 1845. 282 p. DLC; ICRL; NBP. 45-2778

Goodwin, Nathaniel, 1782-1855. Descendants of Thomas Olcott, one of the first settlers of Hartford, Connecticut. Hartford: Press of Case, Tiffany and Burnham, 1845. [13]-63 p. CtMW; ICN; MH; PHi; RHi. 45-2779

Gordon, John, d. 1845. Petition of John Gordon for a reprieve to Governor James Fenner with other documents.

Compiled by S.S. Rider. Providence, 1845? RPB. 45-2780

Gordon, John, d. 1845. Synopsis of trial for murder, supreme court, Rhode Island and particulars of execution of John Gordon with appendix. Boston: Skinner and Blanchard, 1845. 64 p. MH; MH-L. 45-2781

Gordon, Thomas Francis, 1787-1860. Indices to public documents. Papers explanatory of the plan of Gordon's proposed index of public documents, laid before the House by Mr. Burke. [Washington] Blair and Rives, printers, 1845. 7 p. CSf; DLC; MiU; OO; RPB. 45-2782

Gore, Catherine Grace Frances Moody, 1799-1861. Abednego, the money lender; a novel. New York: F. Ferrett and company, 1845. 119 p. RPB. 45-2783

Gore, Catherine Grace Frances Moody, 1799-1861. Agathonia; a romance. New York, 1845. PPL. 45-2784

Gore, Catherine Grace Frances Moody, 1799-1861. Cecil; or the adventures of a coxcomb. A romance. New York: Farmer and Daggers, 1845. 398 p. CtY; MdBP; NN. 45-2785

Gore, Catherine Grace Frances Moody, 1799-1861. Self. New York: Harper and brothers, 1845. 176 p. CtY; MB; MH; RPAt; ScC. 45-2786

Gorman, John B. Philosophy of animated existence; to which is added a brief medical account of the middle regions of Georgia. Philadelphia: Sorin

and Ball, 1845. 17-570 p. CtY; GEU; NNN; PPCP; TxH. 45-2787

Gotteschalc, pseud. Letters to Messrs. A. Young and M. Bird, containing strictures on their recent publications, entitled "The great dinner," and "Error unmasked," and in defence of the principles of Calvinism, as set forth in Mr. Fairchild's work "The great supper." Pittsburgh: Loomis, 1845. 150 p. CSansS; ICP; PPins; PPPrHi; ViRut. 45-2788

Goudy's Illinois farmer's almanac and repository of useful knowledge, for the year 1846. Springfield: E.T. Goudy, [1845. 31] p. IHi. 45-2789

Goudy's Illinois farmer's almanac for 1846. Springfield, Illinois: E.T. Goudy, [1845] MWA. 45-2790

Gough, John B. Narrative of the conduct and conversation during his late absence. New York: Lewis C. Donald, 1845. 16 p. MB. 45-2791

Gough, John Bartholomew, 1817-1886. An autobiography. Boston: The author 1845. 180 p. MH; MWA; PHi; PP. 45-2792

Gough, John Bartholomew, 1817-1886. An autobiography. Three thousand. Boston: The author, 1845. 172 p. MB; MCoh; NjPT; NN; PHi. 45-2793

Gough, John Bartholomew, 1817-1886. An autobiography. Fourth thousand. Boston: The author 1845. MH; MNowdHi; OO. 45-2794

Gough, John Bartholomew, 1817-1886. An autobiography. Fifth thousand. Boston: The author 1845. CtY; MH; MnHi; NNP. 45-2795

Gough, John Bartholomew, 1817-1886. An autobiography. Sixth thousand. Boston: The author 1845. 172 p. MBNMHi; ScSpW. 45-2796

Gough, John Bartholomew, 1817-1886. An autobiography. Seventh thousand. Boston: The author 1845. 172 p. LNDil; MeB. 45-2797

Gough, John Bartholomew, 1817-1886. An autobiography. Eighth thousand. Boston: The author 1845. 172 p. DLC; OC; MPiB; OO; RPB. 45-2798

Gough, John Bartholomew, 1817-1886. An autobiography. Ninth thousand. Boston: The author 1845. 172 p. Ct; LNB; ScCliP. 45-2799

Gough, John Bartholomew, 1817-1886. An autobiography. Eleventh thousand. Boston: The author 1845. 172 p. MWA. 45-2800

Gough, John Bartholomew, 1817-1886. An autobiography. Twelfth [sic] thousand. Boston: The author 1845. 180 p. ViRut. 45-2801

Gough, John Bartholomew, 1817-1886. An autobiography. Thirteenth thousand. Boston: The author 1845. 180 p. NNC. 45-2802

Gough, John Bartholomew, 1817-1886. An autobiography. Fourteenth thousand. Boston: The author 1845. 180 p. TNP. 45-2803

Gough, John Bartholomew, 1817-1886. An autobiography. Fifteenth thousand.

Boston: The author 1845. 184 p. DLC; OrU; NHerm. 45-2804

Gould, J. The claims of the American and Foreign Bible Society, maintained and vindicated; in reply to Rev. H. Blodgett's defence of the American Bible Society, and the common English version. By J. Gould and John Winter. Warren, Ohio: W.J. Tait, 1845. 52 p. CSmH; IaU; ICU; OClWHi; PCA. 45-2805

Gould, John W. Forecastle yarns. Edited by his brother Edward S. Gould. Baltimore: W. Taylor and company; New York: W. Taylor, 1845. 64 p. CtY; RPB. 45-2806

Gould, Marcus Tullius Cicero, 1793-1860. The art of shorthand writing. Compiled from the latest European publications with sundry improvements, adapted to the present state of literature in the United States. Revised Stereotype edition. Philadelphia: U. Hunt and son, 1845. 15-1 60 p. MdW; MnU; NN; ViU. 45-2807

Govett, R. Open or strict communion? Judgement pronounced on the question by the Lord Jesus, himself. Norwich, 1845. 36 p. NjPT. 45-2808

Govett, R. Sin after baptism; or a long neglected command of the Lord Jesus; recommended to believers. Norwich, 1845. 23 p. NjPT. 45-2809

Gow, Neil. A practical treatise on the law of partnership, with an appendix of precedents and a supplement, containing all the new decisions to the present period. Third edition, with considerable alterations and additions, with notes and references to American decisions, by Edward B. Ingraham. Philadelphia: Robert H. Small, 1845. 500, 84 p. IaMp; Md; MoKU; Nj; PP. 45-2810

Gowans bibliotheca americana. New York: W. Gowans, 1845-1869. 5 v. ICN; MiU; NNC; OCl; RHi. 45-2811

Gozlan, Leon, 1806-1866. Les nuits de Pere La Chaise. New York: Bureau de Courrier des Etats Unis, 1845. NN; PPL-R. 45-2812

Graeter, Francis. German and English phrases and dialogues, for the use of students in either language, collected by Francis Graeter. Fifth edition, enlarged and improved. Philadelphia: Thomas, 1845. 252 p. CtMW; MdBS; MnOw; PPG; ViU. 45-2813

Graglia, C. Italian pocket dictionary: in two parts... Preceded by an Italian grammar. First American from the fourteenth London edition, with corrections and additions. Boston: Wilkins, Carter and company, 1845. 482 p. GDecCT; MMilt; NcAs; NCH; NRU-W. 45-2814

Graham, George Frederick. English synonyms classified and explained, with practical exercises, designed for schools and private tuition. Edited with an introduction and illustrative authorities, by Henry Reed. New York, Cincinnati, and Chicago: American Book company, [1845] 344 p. GMM; InR; LNL; OrP; TxSaO. 45-2815

Grahame, James, 1790-1842. The history of the United States of North America, from the plantation of the British colonies till their assumption of national independence. Second edition,

enlarged and amended. Boston: C.C. Little and J. Brown, 1845. 4 v. CtY; MWA; NNC; OHi; TxU. 45-2816

Grahame, James, 1790-1842. The history of the United States of North America, from the plantation of the British colonies till their assumption of national independence. Second edition, enlarged and amended. Philadelphia: Blanchard and Lea, 1845. 4 v. ArU; CtSoP; MdW; NcAS; ScCliP. 45-2817

Grant, Asahel, 1707-1844. The Nestorians; or the lost tribes. Containing evidence of their identity, an account of their manners, customs, and ceremonies, together with sketches of travel in ancient Assyria, Armenia, Media, and Mesopotamia and illustrations of Scripture prophecy. New York: Harper and brothers, 1845. 385 p. CL; LNP; Me; PWW; ScDuE. 45-2818

Grant, William Robertson, 1811-1853. An introductory lecture to the course of anatomy and physiology in the medical department of Pennsylvania College, Philadelphia, delivered, November 4, 1845. Philadelphia: Published by the class, 1845. 15 p. MdU-M; NNNAM; PHi; PPL; PPM. 45-2819

Granville, Massachusetts. First Church of Christ. The Granville jubilee, celebrated at Granville, Massachusetts, August 27 and 28, 1845. Springfield: H.S. Taylor, 1845. 139 p. CtSoP; ICN; MWA; Nh; RPB. 45-2820

Granville, Massachusetts. First Church of Christ. The Granville jubilee, celebrated at Granville, Massachusetts, August 27 and 28, 1845. New edition.

Springfield: H.S. Taylor, 1845. 139 p. CtSoP; ICN; MWA; Nh; RPB. 45-2821

A graphic account of the alarming riots at St. Mary's Church in April 1822... By a reporter. Philadelphia, 1845. PPL. 45-2822

Grattan, Thomas Cooley, 1792-1864. A chance medley of light matter. A collection of eleven sketches, tales, etc. New York: Harper and brothers, 1845. 140 p. CLU; DLC; MB; MH; NN. 45-2823

Graves, Hiram Atwill, 1813-1850. The family circle; its affections and pleasures. Boston: Gould, Kendall and Lincoln, 1845. 128 p. MB; MBAt. 45-2824

Gray, A.B. Map of that part of the mineral lands adjacent to Lake Superior ceded to the United States by the treaty of 1842 with the Chippewas comprising that district between Chocolate River and Fond Du Lac. Washington, 1845. MdBP. 45-2825

Gray, Asa, 1810-1888. The botanical text book for colleges, schools and private students. Second edition. New York: Wiley and Putnam, 1845. 509 p. CU; MH; NNNBG; OrB; VtU. 45-2826

Gray, Frederick Turell, 1804-1855. An address before the Boston Young Men's Total Abstinence Society, November 24, 1845. Boston: Christian World, 1845. 32 p. MB. 45-2827

Gray, James, 1770-1824. A dissertation of the coincidence between the priesthoods of Jesus Christ and Melchisedec, in three parts... Together with a sketch of the life of Jesus Christ. Hagerstown,

Maryland: William Stewart, 1845. NbOP; PLT; PU. 45-2828

Gray, James, 1770-1824. A dissertation of the coincidence between the priesthoods of Jesus Christ and Melchisedec, in three parts... Together with a sketch of the life of Jesus Christ. Philadelphia: James M. Campbell, etc., 1845. 158 p. GAU; NbOP; OkHi; PPLT; TChU. 45-2829

Gray and Hart's catalogue of Christmas and New Year presents. Splendidly illustrated and standard books. Philadelphia, 1845. KyDC. 45-2830

Graydon, Alexander, 1752-1818. Memoirs of his own time. With reminiscences of the men and events of the revolution. Philadelphia: Printed by Lindsay and Blakiston, 1845. 24, 13, 504 p. MHi; MShr. 45-2831

Graydon, William, 1759-1840. Forms of conveyancing and of practice with explanatory notes and references, by R.E. Wright. New edition. Philadelphia: Kay, 1845. 612 p. IaFair; PHi; PPL-R; PP; PU. 45-2832

Grayson, William John, 1788-1863. Slavery in the South; a review of Hammond's and Fuller's letters and Chancellor Harper's memoir on that subject. From the Oct. no. of the Southern Quarterly. [Charleston: Walker and Burke, 1845] 24 p. CU; GDecCT; MBAt; OClWHi; PPL. 45-2833

The Great battle. Remarks on "the battle of that great day of God almighty." Taken from a series of unpublished letters. By a father. New York: J.S.Redfield, 1845. 65 p. MBC; MdBP; WHi. 45-2834

Great Britain. A complete and accurate account of the debate in the House of Commons, on Tuesday, July 9, 1782 in which the cause of Mr. Fox's resignation and the great question of American independence came under consideration. Philadelphia: Color and Adriance, 1845. 64 p. Ct; ICN; MBC; PHi; PPL. 45-2835

Great Britain. Reports of cases argued and determined in the Court of King's Bench. By Edward Hyde East. Second American edition with notes by G.M. Wharton. Philadelphia: Lea and Blanchard, 1846. 16 v. C; Ia; MWiW; NNLI; WaU. 45-2836

Great Falls, New Hampshire. Congregational Church. Articles of faith and covenant. [n.p.] 1845. 8 p. MBC. 45-2837

Great Western Almanac for 1846. Calculations by C.F. Egelmann. Philadelphia: Jos. McDowell, [1845] MWA. 45-2838

Greater, Francis. Deutsche und Englische Redensarten und Gespraeche 5. Stereotyp-Ausgabe. Philadelphia: Thomas, Cowperthwait und co., 1845. PPG. 45-2839

Greeley, Horace, 1811-1872. Protection and free trade. The question stated and considered. [New York: Greeley and McElrath, 1845] 16 p. C; MiD-B. 45-2840

Greely, Stephen Sewall Norton. A funeral sermon preached at Newmarket, New Hampshire, April 20, 1845, on the death of Mrs. Helen St. John, wife of Gilbert A. Grant, esquire. Boston: Printed

by S.N. Dickinson and company, 1845. 16 p. ICMe; MBNEH; MiD-B; MoSpD; Nh-Hi. 45-2841

Green, Augustus R. On the episcopacy of the African Methodist Episcopal Church. Pittsburgh, 1845. PPL. 45-2842

Green, Charles C. The Nubian slave. Boston: Bela Marsh, 1845. 8 p. MB; MBC; NIC. 45-2843

Green, Henry G., 1824-1845 Confession of Henry G. Green, as written by himself in a letter to a friend... to which is added his trial and sentence and his letter to his mother... Albany, 1845. 31 p. MoU. 45-2844

Green, Henry G., 1824-1845 Confession of Henry G. Green, who was executed for the murder of his wife, at Troy, New York, on September 10, 1845, as given to the Rev. Robert B. Van Kleeck and the Rev. George C. Baldwin. Troy: R. Rose and F. Belcher, from the press of N. Tuttle, 1845. 12 p. MoU; MWA; N-L; NjR. 45-2845

Green, Henry G., 1824-1845. Trial of Henry G. Green for the murder of his wife, containing... the letter to his mother to Green, a poem suggested for the occasion. Troy: Printed for the publisher, 1845. 48 p. MB; NjR; NN; PHi; PP. 45-2846

Green, Jonas. A familiar exposition of homoeopathy, or the new system of curing diseases. Illustrating its superiority over the present system of medicine. Washington: J. and G.S. Gideon, printers, 1845. 12 p. DLC; DNLM; NNNAM. 45-2847

Green, Jonathan S. Notices of Bartimeus and Hawaii, two christian Sandwich Islanders. By Rev. J.S. Green and Rev. E.W. Clark. Boston: Massachusetts Sabbath School Society, 1845. 126 p. MBC; MH; MWA; NNC. 45-2848

Green, Thomas Jefferson, 1801-1863. Journal of the Texian expedition against Mier; subsequent imprisonment of the author... and final escape from the Castle of Pervte. First edition. New York: Harper and brothers, 1845. 487 p. AzU; CU; ICN; MWA; TxGR. 45-2849

Green mountain almanac for 1846. Calculations by George Perkins, for the East. Montpelier, Vermont: Clarke and Collins, [1845] DLC. 45-2850

Greene, Jonathan Harrington, b. 1812. An exposure of the arts and miseries of gambling; designed especially as a warning to the youthful and inexperienced against the evils of that odious and destructive vice. Second edition, improved. Boston: Redding and company, 1845. 324 p. ICJ; MB; MWA; NcD; NN. 45-2851

Greene, Jonathan Harrington, b. 1812. The gambler's mirror; designed to expose the wiles of the gambling and sporting gentry, and intended to warn the community against the evil tendency of their desperate habits. Boston: Redding, 1845. MH. 45-2852

Greenhow, Robert, 1800-1854. Answer to the strictures of Mr. Thomas Falconer of Lincoln's Inn, on the history of Oregon and California. [Washington, 1845] 7 p. CHi; DLC; OrHi; PPL; RPB. 45-2853

Greenhow, Robert, 1800-1854. The geography of Oregon and California, and the other territories on the northwest coast of North America; illustrated by a new and beautiful map of those countries. Boston: Printed for the author by Freeman and Bolles, 1845. 42 p. CtY, NcGW; NNC; OrHi. 45-2854

Greenhow, Robert, 1800-1854. The geography of Oregon and California, and the other territories on the northwest coast of North America; illustrated by a new and beautiful map of those countries. New York: M.H. Newman, 1845. 42 p. CU; MnHi; NNC; PPL; RPB 45-2855

Greenhow, Robert, 1800-1854. The history of Oregon and California, and the other territories on the northwest coast of North America... Second edition revised, corrected and enlarged. Boston Charles C. Little and James Brown, 1845 492 p. CHi; IaHi; MiU-C; MWA TxDaM. 45-2856

Greenhow, Robert, 1800-1854. The history of Oregon and California, and the other territories on the northwest coast of North America... Third edition revised, corrected and enlarged. New York: D. Appleton and company, 1845 492 p. GEU; NcGW; OrHi; PPL; WaPS 45-2857

Greenleaf, Benjamin, 1786-1864. Introduction to the national arithmetic, on the inductive system; combining the analytic and synthetic methods with the cancelling system. Boston: Robert Davis, and Gould, Kendall and Lincoln: New York Robinson and Pratt and company, etc. etc., 1845. 196 p. MH; MiU; OSW; TxU T. 45-2858

Greenleaf, Benjamin, 1786-1864. Key to the national arithmetic, exhibiting the operation of the more difficult questions in that work. Boston: R.S. Davis, 1845. CtHWatk; MB; OrU. 45-2859

Greenleaf, Benjamin, 1786-1864. Mental arithmetic. Mental arithmetic upon the inductive plan; for beginners. Boston: R.S. Davis, etc., 1845. 67 p. CtHWatk; DLC; MH; PU. 45-2860

Greenleaf, Benjamin, 1786-1864. The national arithmetic, on the inductive system; containing also... book keeping; forming a complete mercantile arithmetic. Boston: Robert S. Davis, and Gould, Kendall and Lincoln; New York: Pratt, Woodford and company... 1845. 324 p. CtY; MAnP; MBevHi; VtMidbC. 45-2861

Greenleaf, Simon, 1783-1853. A discourse commemorative of the life and character of the Hon. Joseph Story... Pronounced... 1845... Boston: C.C. Little and J. Brown, 1845. 48 p. CU; LNH; MnHi; Nh; ScCC. 45-2862

Green's Connecticut annual register and United States calendar, for 1845: to which is prefixed an almanac. Hartford: Samuel Green, 1845. 176 p. CtNb. 45-2863

Greenwald, Emanuel, 1811-1885. Address delivered before the students of the Carrollton Academy, at the close of the first session of that institution... Carrollton, Ohio: T.W. Collier, 1845. 12 p. CSmH; OClWHi. 45-2864

Greenwood Cemetery. Brooklyn, New York. Greenwood Cemetery: its rules, regulations, etc. with an appendix containing a catalogue of proprietors, etc. New York: Houel, Macoy and Van Buren, printers, 1845. 8, 37 p. DLC; TNP. 45-2865

Greg, William Rathbone, 1809-1881. Creed of christendom: its foundations and superstructure. New York, 1845. MdBP. 45-2866

Gregg, Josiah, 1806-1850. Commerce of the prairies; or the journal of a Santa Fe trader, during eight expeditions across the great western prairies, and nine years residence in Northern Mexico. Second edition. New York: J. and H.G. Langley, 1845. 2 v. in 1. CoD; IaHi; MnHi; PU; TxWB. 45-2867

Gregg, O. Ormsby. Pittsburgh, her advantageous position and great resources, as a manufacturing and commercial city, embraced in a notice of sale of real estate. Pittsburgh, 1845. 40 p. MB; NN; PHi; PPins; WHi. 45-2868

Gregg, William, 1800-1867. Essays on domestic industry; or an enquiry into the expediency of establishing cotton manufacturing in South Carolina. Charleston: Burgess and James, 1845. 63 p. A-Ar; MBAt; NcU; ScCC; TxU. 45-2869

Gregorian and other ecclesiastical chants, adapted to the Psalter and Canticles, as they are pointed to be sung in churches. Reprinted from the Second London edition. With a supplement from other sources. Fourth edition. New York: J.A. Sparks, 1845. 38 p. MdBP. 45-2870

Gregory, George, 1754-1808. A concise history of the Christian Church from its first establishment to the present time compiled from the work of Dr. G. Gregory, with numerous additions and improvements. New York: G. Lane and C.B. Tippett, 1845. 446 p. DLC; MdBJ; TChU. 45-2871

Gregory, Henry. The church not a sect; although everywhere spoken against. A sermon preached in St. Paul's Church, Syracuse, May 25, 1845. Published by request. Syracuse: L.W. Hall, 1845. 16 p. InID; MBAt; NSy; NSyHi. 45-2872

Grey, Elizabeth Caroline. The bosom friend. A novel. New York: Harper and brothers, 1845. 134 p. DLC; MdCatS; ScC; ViU. 45-2873

Grey, Elizabeth Caroline. The gambler's wife. A novel. New York: Harper and brothers, 1845. 155 p. IU; MdBP; PPL; ViU. 45-2874

Grey, Elizabeth Caroline. Hyacinthe; or the contrast. Philadelphia: T.B. Peterson and brothers, 1845? 7-100 p. CtY; NdBP; NN. 45-2875

Grey, Elizabeth Caroline. Novels and tales. New York, 1845-1850. PPL. 45-2876

Grey, Elizabeth Caroline. Novels and tales. Philadelphia, 1845- 1849. PPL. 45-2877

Gridley, Philo, 1796-1864. An address delivered before the literary societies of Hamilton College, July 22, 1845, Clinton, New York. Utica: R.W. Roberts, printer, 1845. 29 p. CSmH; MH; NN; TxU; WHi. 45-2878

Grier's Carolina and Georgia almanac for the year of our Lord, 1846... Calcula-

tions by Robert Grier, residing in Butts County, Georgia. Macon, Georgia: J.M. Boardman, 1846. GMWa. 45-2879

Griffin, George, 1778-1860. Suffering's of Christ. New York: Harper, 1845. CtHC; LNP; MeBaT; MWiW; NCH. 45-2880

Griffin, Mary M. Drops from Flora's cup, or the poetry of flowers, with a floral vocabulary. Boston: G.W. Cottrell and company; New York: T.W. Strong, 1845. 160 p. IaU; MB; NcU; NHem; NNC. 45-2881

Griffin, Robert H. Oration delivered before the members of the Grand Lodge of Georgia, Magnolia Encampment, No. 1, Oglethorpe Lodge No. 1 and Live Oak Lodge No. 3 of the Independent Order of Odd fellows on the occasion of the second celebration of the order in Savannah on Thursday, February 6th, 1845. Savannah: E.C. Councell, 1845. 16 p. ScC. 45-2882

Grigg, John, 1792-1864. Grigg's southern and western songster: being a choice collection of the most fashionable songs, many of which are original. Philadelphia: Grigg and Elliott, 1845. 324 p. TMeC. 45-2883

Griggs, Leverett, 1808-1883. Infant baptism explained and defended, with a warrant for believers and their children. Hartford: D.B. Moseley, 1845. 106 p. CSansS; CtHC; CtY; MBC; OO. 45-2884

Grimes, Green, b. 1809. A secret worth knowing. A treatise on the most important subject in the world: simply to say, insanity. Nashville, Tennessee: Nashville

Union, 1845. 94 p. GEU; MoSU; NN; TkL-Mc. 45-2885

Grimes, James Stanley, 1807-1903. Etherology; or the philosophy of mesmerism and phrenology, including a new philosophy of sleep and of consciousness. New York: Saxton and Miles; Philadelphia: James M. Campbell; Boston: Saxton, Pierce and company, 1845. 350 p. ICJ; RPM; MNF; NNNAM; PPA. 45-2886

Grimshaw, William, 1782-1852. History of England, from the first invasion by Julius Caesar, to the accession of Victoria. In 1837... Accompanied by a book of questions and a key for the use of schools. Philadelphia: Grigg and Elliot, 1845. 330 p. DLC. 45-2887

Grimshaw, William, 1782-1852. History of France; from the foundation of the monarchy to the death of Louis XVI. Philadelphia: Grigg and Elliot, 1845. 302 p. ICartC. 45-2888

Grimshaw, William, 1782-1852. History of the United States, from their first settlement as colonies, to the period of the fifth census, in 1830. Accompanied by a book of questions and a key. Philadelphia: Grigg and Elliot, 1845. 326 p. ICLoy; MH; NNC; MoU; ScU. 45-2889

Grimshaw, William, 1782-1852. Ladies lexicon and parlour companion. Containing nearly every word in the English language, and exhibiting the plurals of nouns and the participles of verbs; being also particularly adapted to the use of academies and schools. Philadelphia: Grigg and Elliot, 1845. 405 p. MBC; OCHP; OCU. 45-2890

Grimshaw, William, 1782-1852. The life of Napoleon, with the history of France, from the death of Louis XVI, to the year, 1821. Philadelphia: Grigg and Elliot, 1845. 285 p. MiD-U; OMC; NNG. 45-2891

Grimshawe, Thomas Shuttleworth. A memoir of the Rev. Leigh Richmond, of Trinity College, Cambridge, rector of Turvey, Bedfordshire, and chaplin to his royal highness the late Duke of Kent. New York: M.W. Dodd, 1845. 362 p. IaGG; GEU; NjMD; TJaL; ViPet. 45-2892

Griscom, John Hoskins, 1809-1874. The sanitary condition of the laboring population of New York. With suggestions for its improvement. A discourse delivered on December 30, 1845, at the repository of the American Institute. New York: Harper and brothers, 1845. 58 p. CSt-L; ICJ; MB; NNUT; PHi. 45-2893

Griswold, Alexander Viets, 1766-1843. The office of sponsors in baptism. By the late bishop of the Eastern Diocese. Boston: The tract committee, Massachusetts, 1845. 16 p. AMob; MBD; MHi; NjPT; RHi. 45-2894

Griswold, Rufus Wilmot, 1815-1857. The poetry of love. Boston: Isaac Tompkins, 1845. 128 p. NBuG. 45-2895

Griswold, Rufus Wilmot, 1815-1857. The poetry of the passions. Philadelphia: J. Locken, 1845. 288 p. CtHT-W; MPiB; NN; PU; RPB. 45-2896

Griswold, Rufus Wilmot, 1815-1857. The poetry of the sentiments. Philadelphia: John Locken, 1845. 320 p. CtY; KPea; NjR; RPB. 45-2897

Griswold, Rufus Wilmot, 1815-1857. The poets and poetry of America. Sixth edition. Philadelphia: Carey and Hart, 1845. 476 p. CtY; IaU; MH; NN; ViU. 45-2898

Griswold, Rufus Wilmot, 1815-1857. The poets and poetry of England, in the nineteenth century. Philadelphia: Carey and Hart, 1845. 504 p. MH; NIC; PHC; PP; PPL. 45-2899

Griswold, Rufus Wilmot, 1815-1857. The poets and poetry of England, in the nineteenth century. Second edition. Philadelphia: Carey and Hart, 1845. 504 p. DLC; IaU; KyU; PMA; ViU. 45-2900

Griswold, Stanley, 1763-1815. Overcoming evil with good: a sermon at Wallingford, Connecticut, before numerous friends of the constitution, March 11, 1801. New Haven, 1845. 24 p. CtY; MBC. 45-2901

Grobe, Charles. La liberti: variations... sur un chant national espagnol... pour le piano. Philadelphia, 1845. CtY. 45-2902

Groesbeck, Herman J. Eulogy on the life and character of General Andrew Jackson, delivered in the Methodist Church, Covington, on June 28, 1845. Covington: Printed at the Kentucky Intelligence office, 1845. 20 p. MoSHi; T. 45-2903

Grosh, Aaron Burt, 1803-1884. Washingtonian pocket companion: containing a choice collection of temperance hymns, songs, odes, glees, duets, choruses, etc., with music arranged by

W.L. Seaton. Fourth edition. Utica, New York: B.S. Merrell, 1845. 160 p. CSmH; MnU; NN; NUtHi; OClWHi. 45-2904

Gross, Samuel David, 1805-1884. Elements of pathological anatomy; illustrated by colored engravings and two hundred and fifty woodcuts. Second edition, thoroughly revised, and greatly enlarged. Philadelphia: E. Barrington and George D. Haswell, 1845. 822 p. IaU; GU-M; MdBJ; PPi; TNV. 45-2905

Grosvenor, D.A. The laws of Ohio respecting colored people, shown to be unjust. Hudson, 1845. 16 p. MBC. 45-2906

Groton, Massachusetts. Constitution of the artillery company. Boston: George H. Brown, printer, 1845. 8 p. MH; MWA. 45-2907

Guenee, Antoine, 1717-1803. Letters of certain Jews to Monsieur Voltaire, containing an apology for their own people, and for the Old Testament with critical reflections, and a short commentary extracted from a greater.... Translated by the Rev. Philip Lefanu. Second American edition with correction. Paris, Kentucky: G.C. Moore; Covington, Kentucky: J.L. Newby, 1845. 612 p. LNH; NNG; OCl; PU. 45-2908

Guide for strangers and visitors through the city of New York. Second thousand. Revised and enlarged. New York, 1845. NN. 45-2909

Guide to painting and water colors, containing directions for forming shades or tints by mixing colors: those necessary for coloring landscapes and other scenery: their names, varieties and different uses.

New York: C.P. Huestis, 1845. NN. 45-2910

Guizot, Elizabeth Charlotte Pauline, 1773-1827. The young student; or Ralph and Victor... From the French by Samuel Jackson. New York: Appleton, 1845. 3 v. CtY; PP; PU; ScDuE. 45-2911

Guizot, Francois Pierre Guillanne, 1787-1874. General history of civilization in Europe, from the fall of the Roman Empire to the French revolution. Third American, from the second English edition, with occasional notes, by C.S. Henry. New York: George Appleton and company; Philadelphia: George S. Appleton, 1845. IU; MdBP; PPDrop; RJa. 45-2912

Gummere, John, 1784-1845. A treatise on surveying; containing the theory and practice; to which is prefixed a perspicuous system of plane trigonometry. Fourteenth edition carefully revised and enlarged by the addition of articles on the theodolite, levelling and topography. Philadelphia: Kimber and Sharpless, 1845. 266 p. LNL; MH; MoK; MNF. 45-2913

Gurley and Hill. Catalogue of a choice and valuable library of rare, curious, and standard works on American history, chiefly relating to the early history of New England, New York, New Jersey by Messrs Gurley and Hill, New York Long Room, November 20th. New York, 1845. 23 p. CtMW; NN. 45-2914

Gurney, Joseph John, 1788-1847. Thoughts on habit and discipline. Philadelphia: Henry Longstreth, 1845. 309 p. CtHT; InRchE; KyLx; MWA; PuU. 45-2915

Guthrie, George James, 1785-1856. On the anatomy and diseases of the urinary and sexual organs. Containing the anatomy of the bladder and the urethra, and the treatment of the obstructions to which these passages are liable. From the third London edition. Philadelphia: Lea and Blanchard, 1845. 9-159 p. Ia; IEN-M; LNOP; NRAM; PPi. 45-2916

Guthrie, William. The christian's great interest; or the trial of a saving interest in Christ, and the way to attain it. With an introductory essay by the Rev. Thomas Chalmers. Philadelphia: Presbyterian Board of Publication, 1845. 274 p. TxBrd-D; TxHR. 45-2917

Guy, Joseph, 1784-1867. Guy's elements of astronomy, and an abridgement of Keith's new treatise on the use of globes. New American edition. Thirtieth edition. Philadelphia: Thomas, Cowperthwiat and company, 1845. 136, 173 p. ICP; MiD; NTEW; PPWa; TKL. 45-2918

Guy, William Augustus, 1810-1885. Outline of general pathology. New York: 1846. DLC; OOC. 45-2919

Guy, William Augustus, 1810-1885. Principles of forensic medicine. First American edition. With notes and additions, by Charles A. Lee. New York: Harper and borthers, 1845. 711 p. CSt- L; IaU-L; PPCP; ViU; WaU. 45-2920

Guy, William Augustus, 1810-1885. Principles of medical jurisprudence, with so much of anatomy, physiology, pathology... First American edition, edited by C.A. Lee. New York: Harper and brothers, 1845. 711 p. CtY; Ia; LNOP; MBM; PU. 45-2921

H

Habermann, Johann, 1516-1590. Das kleine gebet buch. New York: William Radde, 1845. PPeSchw. 45-2922

The habits of good society; a handbook for ladies and gentlemen; with thoughts, hints and anecdotes concerning social observations, nice points of taste and good manners; and the art of making one's self agreeable. From the last London edition. New York: Carleton, 1845. 430 p. NGlf. 45-2923

Hackley, Richard S. Lands in East Florida. Washington, 1845. PPL. 45-2924

Hackley, Richard S. Protest of R.S. Hackley's heirs respecting their lands. Washington, 1845. PPL. 45-2925

Hadley, Amos, 1825-1908. Literary hours of the laboring man, early history of Dumbarton, two addresses with additions and amendations before the Dunbarton Lyceum, October 18, 1844 and January 31, 1945. Concord: A. McFarland, 1845. 27 p. MnHi; NhD. 45-2926

Hagerstown town and country almanack. By J.F. Egelman. Hagerstown: J. Giuben [sic] 1845. MWA. 45-2927

Hague, William, 1808-1887. The relation of christianity to politics. A discourse delivered on the day of public thanksgiving, November 28, 1844. Boston: William D. Ticknor and company, and William S. Damrell, 1845. 32 p. MBAt; MiD-B; MWA; NHC-S. 45-2928

Hague's Christian almanac for 1846. By Thomas Hague. Philadelphia: Printed for the author, [1845] MWA. 45-2929

Hahn-Hahn, Ida Marie Luise Sophie Friederike Gustava Grafin von, 1805-1880. The Countess Faustina. New York: Winchester, 1845. MBBCHS; MdBP; NN; OU. 45-2930

Hahn-Hahn, Ida Marie Luise Sophie Friederike Gustava Grafin von, 1805-1880. Travels in Sweden, sketches of a journey to the north. Translated from the German. New York: E. Winchester, 1845. 55 p. NN; NNC; PPi; TxHuT. 45-2931

Hahnemann, Samuel, 1755-1843. The chronic diseases; their specific nature and homoeopathic treatment. Translated and edited by Charles J. Hempel. With a preface by Constantine Hering. New York: W. Raddle, 1845. 202 p. DLC; IGK; PPHa; RPB; TxWB. 45-2932

Haines, Isaac S. Catechism on chemistry, adapted to the course of lectures delivered in the University of Pennsylvania. Third edition. Philadelphia: J.G. Auner, 1845. [13]-160 p. IEN-M; MH; PPCP; ViRMC; WBB. 45-2933

Hale Apollos. A harmony of prophetic

hronology. Boston: Joshua V. Himes, 845. 92 p. MWA. 45-2934

Hale, C.V.R.M. Ellen Elliott. New York, 1845. MB. 45-2935

Hale, C.V.R.M. Saturday evenings; a eries of moral and religious essays. New York: John Douglas, 1845. 262 p. CSans-; DLC; MiD; NB; PPM. 45-2936

Hale, C.V.R.M. Tales of our own country. Ellen Elliott or a happy home in Alabama. New York: Burgess, Stringer, and company, 1845. 96 p. A-Ar; ICN; MB. 45-2937

Hale, Charles, 1831-1882. A description of the Washington Islands: and in particular the island of Nukahiwa, the principal of the group: with some account of the manners, customs, etc. of the inhabitants... Compiled from the work of Mr. Dalyhmple... Boston: Printed for the editor, 1845. 46 p. DLC; MB; MH; MWA; NCH. 45-2938

Hale, Edward Everett. How to conquer Texas before Texas conquers us. Boston, 1845. 16 p. DLC; ICN; MBC; MWA. 45-2939

Hale, John Parker, 1806-1873. Letter from John P. Hale, of New Hampshire, to his constituents, on the proposed annexation of Texas. Washington: Blair and Rivers, [1845] 8 p. A-Ar; MdBP; MWA; PHi; ViU. 45-2940

Hale, Nathan, 1784-1863. Inquiry into the best mode of supplying the city of Boston, with water, for domestic purposes, in reply to the pamphlets of Mr. Wilkins and Mr. Shattuck, and also to some of the representations to the committee of the legislature, on the hearing of the petition of the city. By a member of the late board of water commissioners. Boston: Eastburn's press, 1845. 70 p. CtY; ICU; MBAt; MiU; NN. 45-2941

Hale, Salma, 1787-1866. History of the United States, from their first settlement as colonies to the close of the administration of Mr. Madison in 1817. New York: Harper and brothers, 1845. 2 v. LU; MsU; OCY; ScGrw; ScU. 45-2942

Hale, Salma, 1787-1866. History of the United States, from their first settlement as colonies to the close of the war with Great Britain in 1815, to which are added questions, adapted to the use of schools. Revised edition. Cooperstown, New York: H. and E. Phinney, 1845. 298, 26 p. CtY; MH; MiHi; MiU; NCH. 45-2943

Hale, Sarah Josepha Buell, 1788-1879. Alice Ray: a romance in rhyme. Philadelphia, 1845. 37 p. CSmH; DLC; MnU; PPL. 45-2944

Hale, Sarah Josepha Buell, 1788-1879. Keeping house and housekeeping: a story of domestic life... New York: Harper and brothers, 1845. 143 p. ICBB; MWA; NjP; RPAt; VtMidSM. 45-2945

Halevy, Jacques Francois Fromental Elis, 1799-1862. Bright star of hope. Philadelphia: Lee and Walker, 1845. 5 p. MB. 45-2946

Halevy, Jacques Francois Fromental Elis, 1799-1862. La reine de Chypie, opera, paroles, de Saint Georges. Translated by B.H. Revoil. New York, 1845. MBAt. 45-2947

The half-yearly abstract of the medical

sciences. Being a practical digest of the contents of the British and continental medical works. Edited by W.H. Rankin. New York and Philadelphia: Henry C. Lea, 1845-1874. 58 v. IaDaM; KyLxT; LNB; NIC; PU. 45-2948

Haliburton, Thomas Chandler, 1796-1865. Jude Haliburton's yankee stories. Philadelphia: T.B. Peterson and brother, [1845?] 2 v. in 1. NBuG; ViRut. 45-2949

Hall, Alfred G. Womanhood: causes of its premature decline, respectfully illustrated. Being a review of the changes and derangements of the female constitution, a safe and faithful guide to mothers, during gestation, before and after confinement, with medical advice... Second edition, revised and enlarged. Rochester, Printed by E. Shepard, 1845. [17]-188 p. DLC; MB; MBM. 45-2950

Hall, Anna Maria Fielding, 1801-1881. Groves of Blarney. New York: E. Ferrett and company, 1845. 107 p. NjR; RPAt. 45-2951

Hall, Anna Maria Fielding, 1800-1881. Private purse and other tales. New York: C.S. Frances and company; Boston: J.H. Francis, 1845. DLC; MBAt. 45-2952

Hall, Anna Maria Fielding, 1800-1881. Sketches of Irish character. Illustrated edition. New York, Philadelphia: E. Ferrett and company, 1845. 5-383 p. DLC; ICU; MH; NBuG; PBa. 45-2953

Hall, Anna Maria Fielding, 1801-1881. The whiteboy, a story of Ireland in 1822. New York: Harper and brothers, 1845. 151 p. IC; MBL; MdHi; MH. 45-2954

Hall, Basil, 1788-1844. Selections from fragments of voyages and travels... Boston: Sexton and Keet, 1845. 239 p. KTW MB; OClWHi; PSC; TxShA. 45-2955

Hall, Charles Radclyffe, 1819-1879. Mesmerism: its rise, progress, and mysteries in all ages and countries, being a critical inquiry into its assumed merit and history of its mock marvels, hallucinations, and frauds. First American edition, from... the London Lancet. New York: Burgess, Stringer and company 1845. 166 p. DLC; LNL; MH; NN; RPB 45-2956

Hall, David, 1683-1756. A mite into the treasury; or some serious remarks on that solemn and indispensable duty of duly attending assemblies for divine worship Philadelphia: J. Richards, 1845. 63 p MH; PHi; PSC-Hi. 45-2957

Hall, Edward Brooks, 1800-1865. Purity and charity. A discourse in behalf of the children's friends' society, delivered in Providence, October 7, 1845. Providence: Charles Burnett, Jr., 1845. 16 p MB; NN; PCA; RPB. 45-2958

Hall, Edwin, 1802-1877. The voice of blood from the ground; a sermon preached at Norwich, Connecticut. February 16, 1845. New York: Benedict and company, 1845. 16 p. NN. 45-2959

Hall, John, 1783-1847. The primary reader, designed for the younger reading classes in common schools in the United States. Fourth edition. Hartford: Robins and Smith, 1845. 144 p. CtY. 45-2960

Hall, John, 1783-1847. The reader's guide, containing a notice of the elementary sounds in the English language; instructions for reading both prose and verse, with numerous examples for illustration, and lessons for practice. Tenth edition. Hartford: Robins and Smith; New York: Huntington and Savage, 1845. 333 p. CtY. 45-2961

Hall, John, 1783-1847. The reader's manual. Designed for the use of common schools in the United States. Hartford: Robins and Smith, [etc., etc.] 1845. 312 p. NN. 45-2962

Hall, John Vine, 1774-1860. Sinner's friend. Boston: Sabbath School Society, 1845. MdW. 45-2963

Hall, John Vine, 1774-1860. Sinner's friend, or the disease of sin, its consequences, and the remedy. Boston: Massachusetts Sabbath School Society, 1845. 360 p. MTop. 45-2964

Hall, Joseph, 1574-1656. A selection from the writings of Joseph Hall... With observations of some specialities in his life, written with his own hand. Edited by A. Hunting Clapp. Andover: Allen, Morrill and Wardwell; New York: M.H. Newman, 1845. 333 p. CtY; GDecCT; MTop; NhD; OO. 45-2965

Hall, Lyman W. Elementary outline of mental philosophy, for the use of schools... Cleveland, Ohio: M.C. Younglove; Akron: Dewey and Elkins, 1845. IaMpI; ICJ; OAkU; OCLWHi; OO. 45-2966

Hall, Nathaniel, 1805-1875. The christian ministry. A sermon preached at the ordination of Mr. Hiram Withington as pastor of the First Congregational Church in Leominster... December 25, 1844. Boston: William Crosby and H.P.

Nichols, 1845. 30 p. CBPac; ICMe; MBAU; NNUT; RPB. 45-2967

Hall, Nathaniel, 1805-1875. Consolations in the death of children. A sermon. Boston: Leonard C. Bowles, 1845. 8 p. MH; MWA. 45-2968

Hall, Nathaniel, 1805-1875. Do justly. A sermon preached at Dorchester... December 14, 1845. Boston: William Crosby and H.P. Nichols, 1845. 16 p. CBPac; ICMe; MH-AH; NcD; RPB. 45-2969

Hall, Samuel Read, 1795-1877. School history of the United States. Boston: B.B. Mussey, 1845. MH; OMC. 45-2970

Hall, Willard, 1780-1875. Address before the literary societies of Delaware College, at commencement, June 25, 1845. Newark, Delaware. Philadelphia: Isaac Ashmead, printer, 1845. 40 p. MBAt; MdHi; NcD; PHi; PWW. 45-2971

Hall, Willard. 1780-1875. A plea for the Sabbath; addressed to the legal profession in the United States. Baltimore: Baltimore Sabbath Association, 1845. 12 p. DLC; MH; NcD; PHi; WHi. 45-2972

Hallam, Henry, 1777-1859. View of the state of Europe during the Middle Ages. From the sixth London edition. New York, 1845. 568 p. GEU; InCW; MdBD; MChi; ScDuE. 45-2973

Halleck, Fitz-Greene, 1790-1867. Alnwick castle. New York: Dearborn, 1845. 98 p. NjN. 45-2974

Halleck, Fitz Greene, 1790-1867. Alnwick castle, with other poems. New

York: Harper and brothers, 1845. 104 p. LNH; MoS; MWA; OCY; TNT. 45-2975

Halleck, Fitz-Greene, 1790-1867. Alnwick castle, with other poems. New York: Harper, 1845. 64 p. DLC; OHi. 45-2976

Halleck, Fitz-Greene, 1790-1867. Selections from the British poets. New York: Harper and borthers, 1845. 360 p. LN; OClW; OCX. 45-2977

Halleck, Henry Wager, 1815-1872. Message from the president of the United States, communicating [in compliance with a resolution of the Senate] a copy of the report on national defence, made to the engineering department. [Washington] 1845. 76 p. CSf; LNH; TxU. 45-2978

Hallock, Gerard, 1806-1866. Review of the tract controversy; being substantially a reprint of an editorial article in the New York Journal of Commerce, of April 19th, 22d and 24th, 1845. New York: Leavitt, Trow and company, 1845. 62 p. ICP; MeBat; NjR; PPL-R. 45-2979

Hallworth, Thomas. Rational mnemonics; or assistance for the memory, resulting from a philosophical direction of natural principles. New York: A.V. Blake and D.D. Wickham, 1845. 2 v. in 1. CtHWatk, IEG; MB; NNS; ViU. 45-2980

Hamilton, Alexander, 1757-1804. Letters of Pacificus and Helvidius on the proclamation of neutrality of 1793, by Alexander Hamilton, [Pacificus] and James Madison, [Helvidius] to which is prefixed the proclamation. Washington:

J. and G.S. Gideon, 1845. 102 p. CSmH; DLC; KHi; NcD; PU. 45-2981

Hamilton, Edward, 1812-1870. Songs of sacred praise; or the American collection of psalm and hymn tunes, anthems, sentences and chants. Boston: Phillips and Sampson, 1845. 328 p. CtY; KyBC; MWA; PPM; RPB. 45-2982

Hamilton, Frank Hastings, 1813-1836. Monograph on Strabismus, with cases Buffalo: Jewett: Thomas and company 1845. 69 p. IaU; ICJ; MH-M; NBuU-M; OClM. 45-2983

Hamilton, William Thomas, 1796-1884. The duties of masters and slaves respectively; or domestic servitude as sanctioned by the Bible; a discourse, delivered in the Government Street Church, Mobile, Alabama, on December 15, 1844. Mobile: F.H. Brooks, 1845. 24 p. A-Ar; DLC; KyDC; LU; PPPrHi. 45-2984

Hamilton, William Thomas, 1796-1884. A plea for the liberal education of woman; an address delivered at the annual examination of the female seminary, at Marion, Alabama, July 17, 1845. New York: J.F. Trow and company, 1845. 28 p. A-Ar; MB; MHi; NcD; TxDaM. 45-2985

Hammond, Jabez Delano, 1778-1855. The history of political parties in the state of New York, from the ratification of the federal constitution to December, 1840... Third edition, corrected and revised. Cooperstown, New York: H. and E. Phinney, 1845. 2 v. GA; LU; MS; NNS; O. 45-2986

Hammond, James Henry, 1807-1864.

Governor Hammond's letters on southern slavery: addressed to Thomas Clarkson, the English abolitionist. [Charleston: Walker and Burke, printers, 1845] 32 p. AU; DLC; ICU; KyLx; ScU. 45-2987

Hammond, James Henry, 1807-1864. Two letters on slavery in the United States, addressed to Thomas Clarkson, esq. Columbia: Allen, McCarter and company, 1845. 51 p. CU; DLC; GAU; PHi; RPB. 45-2988

Hanna, John Smith. Petition of John S. Hanna, remonstrating against the annexation of Texas. [Washington, 1845] 3 p. CSf; DLC; MBAt; OO; TxU. 45-2989

Hannigan, Dennis. The orange girl of Venice; or the downfall of "The council of ten." New York: John Slater, 1845. 59 p. MH; RPB. 45-2990

The harbinger, devoted to social and political progress. New York: Burgess, Stringer and company, 1845-. v. 1-. DLC; ICN; MBAt; TxU; WvC. 45-2991

Hardin, John J. Speech of Mr. Hardin, on the annexation of Texas, delivered in the House, January 15, 1845. [Washington: J. and G.S. Gideon, printers, 1845] 15 p. CtY; DLC; IHi; MB; WHi. 45-2992

The hare-bell. Third edition. Hartford, 1845. MB; MH. 45-2993

The hare-bell; a token of friendship. Fourth edition. Hartford: Parsons, 1845. 192 p. CtHT. 45-2994

Harkey, Simeon Walcher. Address delivered at the funeral obsequies in honor of the late Andrew Jackson, Frederick City, Maryland, July 8, 1845. Frederick: Printed at the office of the Frederick Examiner, 1845. 26 p. OSW; PPLT; RPB; WHi. 45-2995

Harp and hickory tree. Address eulogistic of Andrew Jackson delivered before the democratic association. [New York? 1845?] NN. 45-2996

Harrington, Henry Francis. The responsibleness of American citizenship; A sermon preached on occasion of the "Anti-rent" disturbances, December 22, 1844. By Henry F. Harrington, minister of the First Unitarian Church in Albany. Printed by request. Albany: Weare C. Little, 1845. 23 p. CtHC; IEN-M; MBAt; NAl; NCH. 45-2997

Harrington, Isaac. A key to illustrations of arithmetic. New York: Baker, Crane and Day, 1845. 157 p. DLC. 45-2998

Harris, Chapin Aaron. The principles and practice of dental surgery. Second edition, revised, modified and greatly enlarged. Philadelphia: Lindsay and Blakiston, 1845. 600 p. DLC; MdBM; MiU; PCC; TxDaBM. 45-2999

Harris, H.A. The horse thief: or the maiden and negro. A tale of the prairies. Boston: Gleason's Publishing Hall, 1845. [5]-66 p. DLC; ICN; KEmT; MB; TNF. 45-3000

Harris, L.W. The good hope. A sermon delivered at the funeral of Mr. George Brown. Boston: Freeman and Bolles, 1845. 15 p. ICMe. 45-3001

Harris, Nicholas. A complete system of practical bookkeeping, in six sets of books. Also a series of concise rules for performing various computations in business. Hartford: Case, Tiffany and company, 1845. 230 p. CtHWatk; LRuL; MH; NNC. 45-3002

Harris, William, 1792-1861. Lectures on puerperal fevers. Philadelphia: T. and G. Town, 1845. 50 p. DLC; GMW; PPHi; PPPrHi; PU. 45-3003

Harris, William Cornwallis, 1807-1848. The highlands of Ethiopia. From the first London edition. New York: J. Winchester: New World Press, 1845. 392 p. NNA; NR; PPAN; PPP. 45-3004

Harris, William Thaddeus, 1826-1854. Epitaphs from the old burying ground in Cambridge. With notes. Cambridge: J. Owen, 1845. 192 p. DLCj; IaHa; MH; NhD; PPL. 45-3005

Harrison, John Pollard, 1796-1849. Elements of materia medica and therapeutics. Cincinnati: Desilver and Burr, 1845. 2 v. ArU-M; CSt-L; DSG; NBMS; PPiAM. 45-3006

Harrison, John Pollard, 1796-1849. Elements of materia medica and therapeutics. Philadelphia: Thomas, Cowperthwait and company, 1845. ArU-M; MoSMed; NBMS; OClM; OCGHM. 45-3007

Harrison, John Pollard, 1796-1849. Sources, evils and correctives of professional discontent; an introductory lecture, delivered November 4, 1845. Cincinnati: Ben Franklin Printing House, 1845. 16 p. CSmH; NBMS; OCGHM; OClWHi; PPPrHi. 45-3008

Harrison, Robert, 1796-1858. The

Dublin dissector, or manual of anatomy; comprising a description of the bones, muscles, vessels, nerves and viscera; also the relative anatomy of the different regions of the human body, together with the elements of pathology. Second American from the fifth enlarged Dublin edition, with additions by Robert Watts, Jr.... New York: J. and H.G. Langley, 1845. 541 p. DLC; LNOP; MnU; NNN; OrUM. 45-3009

Harrison, Samuel Alexander, 1822-1890. Individual influence. An address delivered before the Lyceum of St. Michaels, October 10, 1845. Baltimore: Armstrong and Berry, 1845. 23 p. MdHi. 45-3010

Harroway, J. The sunny hours of childhood. New York, 1845. CtY. 45-3011

Hart, John Seely, 1810-1877. A brief exposition of the constitution of the United States for the use of common schools. Philadelphia: Butler and Williams, 1845. 13-100 p. CtHT-W; IaDmU; MBC; NjR; PPeSchw. 45-3012

Hart, John Seely, 1810-1877. Class book of poetry; consisting of selections from distinguished English and American poets from Chaucer to the present day. Philadelphia: Butler and Williams, 1845. 384 p. CtY; MB; MdBJ; NjR; NNC 45-3013

Hart, John Seely, 1810-1877. A class book of prose; consisting of selections from distinguished English and American authors, from Chaucer to the present day. Philadelphia: Eldredge and brothers, 1845. 384 p. DLC; NjP; NN; PPD. 45-3014

Hart, John Seely, 1810-1877. English grammar: or an exposition of the principles and usages of the English language. Philadelphia: E.H. Butler and company, 1845. 7-192 p. CtHT-W; IaMp; MoS; NhD; WU. 45-3015

Hart, John Seely, 1810-1877. Questions to White's universal history. Philadelphia: Lea and Blanchard, 1845. 36 p. TNJU. 45-3016

Hartford, Connecticut. Atheneum Lyceum. Constitution, by-laws, rules of order and standing resolutions. Hartford, 1845. 13 p. CtY. 45-3017

Hartford, Connecticut. North Church. Catalogue together with its history articles of faith, and bylaws. Hartford: E. Gleason, 1845. 24 p. MH-AH. 45-3018

Hartford, Connecticut. Park Congregational Church. Catalogue of the North Church, Hartford. Hartford: E. Gleason, 1845. 24 p. Ct. 45-3019

Hartford County Agricultural Society. Address, October 3, 1845, by I.W. Stuart; together with the reports of the committees, and the transactions of the society. Hartford: Printe by E. Gleason, 1845. 83 p. DLC; NcD; NIC; NN. 45-3020

Hartley, Robert Milham, 1796-1881. Removal of alms house from Bellevue. New York, 1845. NN. 45-3021

Hartman, Christian B. The rudiments of arithmetic in questions and answers. Lancaster, Pennsylvania: John H. Pearsol, printer, 1845. 64 p. NN. 45-3022

Hartwell, Jesse, 1771?-1860. The wars of Michael and the dragon: on a succinct versification of the Bible: to which is prefixed a birthday poem. Painesville, Ohio: C.B. Smythe, printer, 1845. 160 p. CSmH; DLC; NNUT; OClWHi; RPB. 45-3023

Hartzel, Jonas. Sermon on regeneration. Warren, Ohio: A.W. Parker, [1845] 16 p. OClWHi. 45-3024

Harvard University. Catalogue of students attending medical lectures in Boston, 1844-45 with a circular of the faculty. Boston: D. Clapp, Jr., 1845. 12 p. MBNMHi; MdBD; NBuU-M; TNP. 45-3025

Harvard University. Catalogue of the officers and members of the Harvard Natural History Society. Cambridge: Metcalf and company, 1845. 17 p. MH. 45-3026

Harvard University. A catalogue of the officers and students of Harvard University, for the academical year 1845-46. Cambridge: Metcalf and company, 1845. 67 p. DLC; NbHi. 45-3027

Harvard University. A catalogue of the students of law at Harvard University, from the establishment of the law school to the end of the spring term in the year 1845. Cambridge, 1845. 65 p. MBC; MHi; MNBedf. 45-3028

Harvard University. Catalogus senatus academici et eorum qui numera et officia gesserunt, quique alicujus gradus lauren donati sunt, in Universitate Harvardians. Cantabrigiae: Metcalf, 1845. 102 p. KyLx; MiD-B; MiU; NCH. 45-3029

Harvard University. Laws of Harvard University, relative to undergraduates.

Cambridge: Metcalf and company, printers, 1845. 40 p. CtY; DLC; MH; MH-AH; MiD-B. 45-3030

Harvard University. Orders and regulations of the faculty of Harvard University. Cambridge: Metcalf and company, printers, 1845. 14 p. CtY; DLC; VtU. 45-3031

Harvard University. Report of a committee of the overseers of Harvard University, concerning the requirements for admission to the university. Salem: Printed at the Gazette office, 1845. 12 p. DLC; MBAt; MBC; MHi; NNC. 45-3032

Harvard University. Report of a committee of the overseers of Harvard University, on the division of time for recitations. [Boston, 1845] 10 p. DLC; MB; MH; MHi; MH. 45-3033

Harvard University. Report on diminishing the cost of instruction of Harvard University, together with a minority report on the same subject. [Boston? 1845?] 32 p. DHEW; ICJ; MHi; MiU; OO. 45-3034

Harvard University. Report on filling up vacancies in the clerical part of the permanent board of overseers of Harvard University. [Boston, 1845] 10 p. DLC; MB; MBC; MH; OO. 45-3035

Harvard University. Harvard Natural History Society. A catalogue of the officers and members, 1845. Cambridge: Printers to the University, 1845-1866. 5 v. M. 45-3036

Haskel, Daniel, 1784-1848. A chronological view of the world; exhibiting the leading events of universal his-

tory. Collected chiefly from the article "chronology" in the new Edinburgh encyclopaedia. Edited by Sir David Brewster with an enlarged view of important events and a continuation to the present time. Collected from authentic sources. New York: J.H. Colton, 1845. 267 p. IaDuU; KyLxT; MiOC; OClWHi; PP. 45-3037

Haskel, Daniel, 1784-1848. A complete descriptive and statistical gazetteer of the United States of America, containing a particular description of the states, territories, counties, districts... with an abstract of the census and statistics for 1840... By Daniel Haskel... and J. Calvin Smith... New York: Sherman and Smith, 1845. 752 p. CSt; DLC; MnHi; OCHP; ScU. 45-3038

Haskett, William Jay. An abstract of the laws of the state and ordinances of the corporation of the city of New York, in relation to vessels, wharves, slips, piers, basins, wrecks and salvage. [New York] Herald Book and Job Printing office, 1845. 86 p. CU; MiU-L; NNC; RPJCB. 45-3039

Hastings, Lansford Warren. The emigrants' guide, to Oregon and California, containing scenes and incidents of a party of Oregon emigrants; a description of Oregon; scenes and incidents of a party of California emigrants; and a description of California; with a description of the different routes to those countries... Cincinnati: George Conclin, 1845. 152 p. CU-B; InU; MnHi; NbCrD; OCY. 45-3040

Hastings, Thomas, 1784-1872. The christian psalmist; or Watts' psalms and hymns, with copious selections from other sources. The whole carefully revised and arranged, with directions for musical expression. New York: D. Fanshaw, 1845. CtHWatk; DLC; ICN; MdBD; PPPrHi. 45-3041

Hastings, Thomas, 1784-1872. The Manhattan collection of psalms and hymn tunes and anthems. New York: Fanshaw, 1845. PPPrHi. 45-3042

Hastings, Thomas, 1784-1872. The psalmodist; a choice collection of Psalm and hymn tunes, chiefly new; adapted to the very numerous metres now in use, together with chants... Cincinnati: Moore and company, 1845. 352 p. CtHWatk; IEG; NUtHi; OCHP; OO. 45-3043

Hatfield, Robert Griffith, 1815-1879. The American house carpenter... Second edition. New York and London: Wiley and Putnam, 1845. 254, 32 p. CtHC; ICAB; MChi; RNR. 45-3044

Hatfield, Robert Griffith, 1815-1879. The American house carpenter: a treatise upon architecture, cornices and mouldings, framing, doors, widows, and stairs. Together with the most important principles of practical geometry. Second edition. New York: Wiley, 1845. 272 p. CU; ICA; NIC; NNC; PP. 45-3045

Hauff, Wilhelm, 1802-1827. The Jew Suss; a tale of Stutgard, in 1737. Translated from the German of Hauff. Philadelphia: J.W. Moore, 1845. 132 p. NN. 45-3046

The haunted house: a temperance dream. Rochester: Sold at Dewey's News Room, 1845. CtY; DLC; NRU. 45-3047

Haverford College. Address of the managers of Haveford School Association to the stockholders and others interested in the institution. Philadelphia: J. Kite and company, [1845] 8 p. MH; PHC; PHi. 45-3048

Haweis, Thomas, 1734-1820. The communicant's spiritual companion, or an evangelical preparation for the Lord's supper in which are shown the nature of the ordinance, and the dispositions requisite for a profitable participation thereof. With meditations and helps for prayer suitable to the subject. Philadelphia: H. Hooker, 1845. MH; NNG. 45-3049

Hawes, Joes, 1789-1867. An address delivered at the eighth anniversary of the Mount Holyoke Female Seminary, South Hadley, Massachusetts July 31, 1845. Published by vote of the trustees. Boston: William D. Ticknor and company, 1845. 24 p. CtHWatk; NNG; PHi. 45-3050

Hawes, Joel, 1789-1867. Dignity of the teachers office. Boston, 1846. DLC; RPB. 45-3051

Hawes, Joel, 1789-1867. A father's memorial of an only daughter. Discourse, First Church, Hartford, December 9, 1844. By the pastor of the First Congregational Church. Hartford: D.B. Moseley, 1845. 30 p. Ct; CtY; ICN; MBNMHi; PPPrHi. 45-3052

Hawes, Joel, 1789-1867. Lectures to young men, on the formation of character. Fifteenth edition. Hartford: Belknap and Hammersley, 1845. 172 p. RKi; RJa. 45-3053

Hawes, Joel, 1789-1867. A looking glass

for ladies; or the formation and excellence of the female character. An address delivered at Hartford, on Sunday evening, August 24, 1845. Boston: W.D. Ticknor and company, 1845. 28 p. CtY; DLC; ICN; MB; MBC. 45-3054

Hawes, Joel, 1789-1867. Prosperous journey by the will of God. Second edition. Hartford, 1845. 24 p. Ct. 45-3055

Hawes, Joel, 1789-1867. A prosperous journey by the will of God. A discourse delivered July 7, 1844. Third edition. Hartford: Mosely, 1845. 24 p. Ct; CtHC; CtY; CtHT-W. 45-3056

Hawes, Joel, 1789-1867. Religion of the east with impressions of foreign travel. Hartford: Belknap and Hamersley, 1845. 215 p. CtSoP; IaB; MH; OMC; RPAt. 45-3057

Hawker, Robert, 1753-1827. The poor man's evening portion: being a selection of a verse of scripture, with short observations, for every day in the year; intended for the use of the poor in spirit who are rich in faith and heirs of the kingdom. New edition. Philadelphia: T. Wardle, 1845. 360 p. DLC; ICBB; KSteC; NN; PPM. 45-3058

Hawker, Robert, 1753-1827. The poor man's morning portion, being a selection of a verse of Scripture with short observations for every day in the year, intended for the use of the poor in spirit who are rich in faith and heirs of the kingdom. A new edition. Philadelphia: T. Wardle, 1845. 372 p. DLC; NhD; ViU. 45-3059

Hawker, Robert, 1753-1827. Zion's pilgrim; or the way to the heavenly Canaan. New York: Robert Carter, 1846. MLow; ODW. 45-3060

Hawks, Francis Lister, 1798-1866. The American forest, or Uncle Philip's conversations with the children about the trees of America. New York: Harper and brothers, 1845. MH; NcU; RPE; ScGrw. 45-3061

Hawley, S. The fulness of the Jews. The restoration of the Jews and subsequent probation to the Gentiles. Boston: H.B. Pratt, 1845. 72 p. NjR. 45-3062

Hawthorne, Nathaniel, 1804-1864. Twice told tales... Boston: James Munroe, 1845. 2 v. CtMW; DLC; NRHi. 45-3063

The hawthorn; a Christmas and New Year's present, 1845. New York: J.C. Riker, 1845. 208 p. ICU; MB; NjR; RPB; WU. 45-3064

Hay, George, 1729-1811. The scripture doctrine of miracles displayed: in which their nature, etc. are impartially examined and explained according to the light of revelation, and the principles of sound reason. First American edition, corrected and revised with notes. New York: Casserly and sons, 1845. 2 v. MnSS; MoSU; PV. 45-3065

Hay, George, 1729-1811. The scripture proof of miracles displayed. First American edition, corrected and revised, with notes. New York: Casserly and sons, 1845. 2 v. ArLSJ; DLC; MiD; MnSS; PV. 45-3066

Haydock, George. Incidents in the life of George Haydock, ex-professional wood sawyer of Hudson. Hudson:

Columbia Washingtonian, printer, 1845. 48 p. MH; MWA. 45-3067

Hayes, John Lord, 1812-1887. Remarks made at a Democratic meeting in Portsmouth, on the 7th January 1845. In defence [sic] of the course of P.J. Hale, Member of Congress in relation to the annexation of Texas. [Portsmouth, 1845] 12 p. CtY; MBAt; MH; NNC; TxU. 45-3068

Haynes, Dudley Cammet, 1809-1888. A practical view of Christian missions. Portland, Maine: William Hyde, 1845. 120 p. ICT; MeLe; NBuG; NcWsW; NNMa. 45-3069

Hayward, H.L. An occasional address, delivered before the Cayuga Association of Universalists, at its session in Genoa, September 24, 1845. Rochester: Printed by W. Houghes, 1845. 16 p. MMeT-Hi; NCaS; NNC. 45-3070

Hayward, John, 1781-1862. The book of religions, comprising the views, creeds, sentiments, or opinions of all the principal religious sects in the world. Fifth edition. Concord, New Hampshire: I.S. Boyd, 1845. 443 p. CO; MB; MLow; MWA; UU. 45-3071

Haywood, William Henry, 1801-1852. Speech of Mr. Haywood, on the annexation of Texas, delivered in the Senate, January 14, 1845. Washington, 1845. 13 p. DLC; NcU; PHi. 45-3072

Hazard, Rowland Gibson, 1801-1888. Address delivered before the Washington County Association for the improvement of public schools, at Wickford, January 3, 1845. Providence: B.F.

Moore, 1845. 42 p. CtY; DHEW; MBC; OO; ViU. 45-3073

Hazard, Rowland Gibson, 1801-1888. Essay on the philosophical character of Channing. Boston: James Munroe and company, 1845. 40 p. CBPac; LNH; NNC; RNR; VtU. 45-3074

Hazen, Edward. The grammatic reader. No. 1. New York, 1845. CtHWatk; MH. 45-3075

Hazen, Edward. The grammatic reader. No. 3. New York, 1845. CtHWatk. 45-3076

Hazen, Edward. The panorama of professions and trades; or every man's book. Embellished with eighty-two engravings. Philadelphia: Uriah Hunt and son, 1845. 320 p. CSf; NbU; PRHi; ScC; ViU. 45-3077

Hazen, Edward. Popular technology; or professions and trades. New York: Harper and brothers, 1845. 2 v. in 1. IGK; InCW; NNC; RPE; RWe. 45-3078

Hazen, Edward. The speller and definer; or class book no. 2. Designed to answer the purposes of a spelling book and to supersede the necessity of the use of a dictionary as a class book. Philadelphia: U. Hunt and son, 1845. 215 p. CtHT-W; IEG; MH; PHi; ViU. 45-3079

Hazlett, Thomas. Address before the literary society of Macedon academy. Rochester: J.M. Patterson and company, 1845. 16 p. CSmH. 45-3080

Hazlitt, William, 1778-1830. Characters of Shakespeare's plays. New York: Wiley and Putnam, 1845. 229 p. CtB; MNe; MjR; RAp; TxU. 45-3081

Hazlitt, William, 1778-1830. Lectures on the dramatic literature of the age of Elizabeth... New York: Wiley and Putnam, 1845. 218 p. CtY IaMp; MPiB; NOg; OCY. 45-3082

Hazlitt, William, 1778-1830. Lectures on the dramatic literature of the age of Elizabeth; delivered at the survey inst. Second editon. New York: Wiley, 1845. 218 p. PU. 45-3083

Hazlitt, William, 1778-1830. Lectures on the dramatic literature of the age of Elizabeth. Third edition. New York: Wiley and Putnam, 1845. MiD. 45-3084

Hazlitt, William, 1778-1830. Lectures on the English poets by William Hazlitt from the third London edition. Edited by his son. New York: Wiley and Putnam, 1845. 255 p. IaAS; MWA; OClW; PHi; RWe. 45-3085

Hazlitt, William, 1778-1830. Table talk: opinion on books, men and things. First American edition. New York: Wiley and Putnam, 1845. 2 v. in 1. CtMW; ICJ; KWiU; MWA; TWoW. 45-3086

Heacock, Reuben B. Claims of Reuben B. Heacock, on the government of the United States, for property destroyed by the enemy, in the late war. Buffalo: Printed by Manchester and Brayman, 1845. 20 p. CSmH; MiD-B; PHi. 45-3087

Head, Francis Bond, 1793-1875. Bubbles from the Brunnen's of Nassau, by an old man. New York: Wiley and Putnam, 1845. 228 p. CU; IaMp; MB; RNR; ViRU. 45-3088

Head, Francis Bond, 1793-1875. Life in Germany; or a visit to the springs of Germany by "an old man" in search of health New York, [1845?] Part 2. NN 45-3089

Headley, Joel Tyler, 1813-1897. The Alps and the Rhine; a series of sketches by J.T. Headley. New York: Baker and Scribner, 1845. 138 p. CU; MBC; NjP OMC; RPAt. 45-3090

Headley, Joel Tyler, 1813-1897. The Alps and the Rhine; a series of sketches by J.T. Headley. New York: Wiley and Putnam, 1845. 138 p. LNP; MiD MNBedf; MWA; OC. 45-3091

Headley, Joel Tyler, 1813-1897. Letters from Italy. New York: Wiley and Putnam, 1845. 224 p. CtHT; LNH; MPiB NNS; RJa. 45-3092

Headley, Joel Tyler, 1813-1897. Man's separate existence, a sermon preached in Stockbridge, Massachusetts, September 1845. Pittsfield: Montaque, 1845. 12 p CtHC; MCH; MWA. 45-3093

Health, a home magazine devoted to the physical culture and outdoor life New York, 1845-1875. DLC. 45-3094

Heberden, William, 1710-1801. Commentaries on the history and cure of diseases. From the last London edition Philadelphia: Ed. Barrington and George D. Haswell, 1845. 214 p. ICJ GU-M; NBMS; PP; TNV. 45-3095

Hebrew Orphan Asylum, New York Constitution and bylaws of the Hebrew Benevolent Society. April 8th, 1822. New York, 1845. 15 p. PPDrop. 45-3096

Hedding, Elijah. A discourse on the administration of discipline. Preached before the New York, Providence, New England and Maine Conferences: and published at their request. New York: Lane and Tippett, for the Methodist Episcopal Church, 1845. 91 p. IaFayU; KBB; OBerB; Or; PPM. 45-3097

Hedge, Levi, 1766-1844. Elements of logic; or a summary of the general principles and different modes of reasoning. Stereotype edition. Cooperstown: H. and E. Phinney, 1845. 178 p. MH; MiU; NjP; PPA; OSW. 45-3098

Heidelburgh Catechism. The Heidelburgh catechism or a summary of Christian doctirine as used by the German Reformed Church in the United States of America. Revised and corrected with additional proof texts. Seventh edition. Chambersburg, Pennsylvania: Printed at the office of publication, 1845. 55 p. ViRut. 45-3099

Heine, Heinrich, 1797-1856. Deutschland, ein wintermaerchen. New York: Renouard, 1845. 88 p. MH; PU. 45-3100

Hemans, Felicia Dorothea Browne, 1793-1835. The complete works of Mrs. Hemans, reprinted entirely from the last English edition. Edited by her sister. New York: D. Appleton and company: Philadelphia: George S. Appleton, 1845. 2 v. FTa; ICU; NcD; PSC- Hi; ViU. 45-3101

Hemans, Felicia Dorothea Browne, 1793-1835. The forest sanctuary; lays of many lands, and other poems. New York: Francis, 1845. DLC; MB; MChi; MHa; NcDurN. 45-3102

Hemans, Felicia Dorothea Browne, 1793-1835. Poems by Felicia Hemans, with an essay on her genius, by H.T. Tuckerman. Edited by Rufus W. Griswold. New York: Leavitt and Allen, [1845?] NBuG. 45-3103

Hemans, Felicia Dorothea Browne, 1793-1835. Poems by Felicia Hemans, with an essay on her genius, by H.T. Tuckerman. Edited by Rufus W. Griswold. Philadelphia: Sorin and Ball, 1845. 347 p. DLC; MnHi; MsN; OCoY; PPi. 45-3104

Hemans, Felicia Dorothea Browne, 1793-1835. The poetical works of Mrs. Hemans. With memoir. New York: D. Appleton and company, 1845. 654 p. CSmH; MH; NBuG; NNUT. 45-3105

Hemans, Felicia Dorothea Browne, 1793-1835. The skeptic; siege of Valencia; and other poems. By Felicia Hemans, edited by her sister. New York: S. Francis and company, 1845. [6]-386 p. LNL; MB; MChi; OCMtSM; TJo. 45-3106

Hemans, Felicia Dorothea Browne, 1793-1835. Songs of the affections; and other poems. From the last London edition. Edited by her sister. New York: C.S. Francis and company; Boston: J.H. Francis, 1845. CoU; MB; RPB. 45-3107

Hemans, Felicia Dorothea Browne, 1793-1835. Songs; scenes and hymns of life, and other poems, edited by her sister. New York: S.S. Francis, 1845. 335 p. KHayF; MB; MHa. 45-3108

Hemans, Felicia Dorothea Browne, 1793-1835. Tales and historic scenes: and other poems. From the last London edition. Edited by her sister. New York: C.S. Francis and company; Boston: J.H. Francis, 1845. 356 p. InRch; MB; MHa; TJo; WaS. 45-3109

Hemans, Felicia Dorothea Browne, 1793-1835. The vespers of Palermo; records of women and other poems. New York: Francis, 1845. MAnP; MB; MChi; MLen; PPM. 45-3110

Hemans, Felicia Dorothea Browne, 1793-1835. The works of Felicia Hemans; edited by her sister [Mrs. Owen]. Reprinted from the last London edition. With an essay on her genius, by Mrs. Sigourney. New York: C.S. Francis; Boston: J.H. Francis, 1845. 3 v. CtY; LNH; MAnP; NGle; TNV. 45-3111

Hempel, Charles Julius, 1811-1879. On eclecticism in medicine; or a critical review of the leading medical doctrines. An inaugural thesis presented at the New York University on the first of March, 1845. New York: William Radde, 1845. 45 p. DLC; NN; NNNAM; PPCP; PPHa. 45-3112

Hempel, Charles Julius, 1811-1879. A treatise on the use of arnica in cases of contusions, wounds, strains, sprains... with a number of cases illustrative of the use of that drug. New York: William Radde, 1845. 16 p. MnU; NN; NNNAM; PPHa. 45-3113

Henderson, John, 1795-1857. Speech of Mr. Henderson, on the resolution for the annexation of Texas, in the Senate, February 20, 1845. [Washington, 1845] 16 p. DLC; MH; NBu; OClWHi; WHi. 45-3114

Henderson, William Augustus. Modern

domestic cookery and useful receipt book... enlarged and improved, by D. Hughson, with specifications of approved patent receipts... consisting of all the most serviceable preparations for domestic purposes. Boston: L. Tompkins, 1845. 360, [3]-61 p. ICJ; NNNAM; NNT-C. 45-3115

Hening, William Waller, 1768-1828. Maxims in law and equity, comprising Noy's maxims, Francis's maxims, and Branch's principia legis et aequitatis, with a translation of the Latin maxims and references to modern authorities. Richmond, 1845. 168 p. MH-L. 45-3116

Hening, William Waller, 1768-1828. Maxims in law and equity, comprising Noy's maxims, Francis's maxims, and Branch's principia legis et aequitatis, with a translation of the Latin maxims, and references to modern authorities, both British and American. Philadelphia: T. and J.W. Johnson, 1845. 166 p. NNIA; Nv; OCoSc; ScU-L. 45-3117

Henn, Frederick. Exchange tables, showing the value of the United States currency in British sterling, of any sum from one cent to ten thousand dollars, at the different rates of premium, from par to twelve and three quarters per cent, by quarter per cent advances progressively. New York: P.A. Meiser, 1845. 18 p. LU; NNC. 45-3118

Henni, John Martin, 1805-1881. Facts against assertions; or a vindication of Catholic principles against misrepresentations, calumnies and falsehoods, embodied in the "Thanksgiving sermon" delivered by J.J. Miter, in the Congregational Church of Milwaukee, December 12, 1844. By Philalethes. Milwaukee:

Courier, Printer] 1845. [3]-170 p. MoSU; WHi; WSofSF. 45-3119

Henry, Joseph, 1799-1878. The coast survey. An article from the Princeton Review, for April, 1845. Princeton, New Jersey: Printed by J.T. Robinson, 1845. 4 p. MB; NjP; NN; PPAmP; PU. 45-3120

Henry, Matthew, 1662-1714. The communicant's companion. With an introductory essay by the Rev. John Brown. New York and Pittsburg: Robert Carter, 1845. 295 p. KBB; TKC. 45-3121

Henry, Philip, 1631-1696. Christ all in all to believers; or what Christ is made to believers, in forty real benefits. Philadelphia: Presbyterian Board of Publication, 1845. 391 p. IEG; MTop; NjPT; OOxW; TxBrdD. 45-3122

Henry, Thomas Charlton, 1790-1827. Letters to an anxious inquirer, designed to relieve the difficulties of a friend under serious impressions. Fourth edition. Philadelphia: Presbyterian Board of Publication, 1845. 308 p. DLC; NbOP; P; TxBrdD. 45-3123

Henshaw, John Prentiss Kewley, 1792-1852. A vindication of the Protestant Episcopal Church, in an address on the occasion of laying the corner stone of Grace Church, Providence on April 8th, 1845. Providence: Book and Tract Depository of the Diocese of Rhode Island, 1845. CtY; MWA; RPB. 45-3124

The Herald of freedom. N.P. Rogers, editor. Concord, New Hampshire, 1845-1846. 2 v. in 1. DLC; IU; MBAt; MnU; NcA-S. 45-3125

Herbert, George, 1593-1633. The country parson: his character and rule of holy life. Andover, Allen, Morrill and Wardwell, 1845. 59 p. MBC. 45-3126

Herbert, Henry William, 1807-1858. The innocent witch. A continuation of Ruth Whalley; or the fair puritan. A romance of the Bay Province... Boston: Henry L. Williams, 1845. 50 [i.e., 48] p. MB. 45-3127

Herbert, Henry William, 1807-1858. My shooting box. By Frank Forester, [pseud.] Philadelphia: Carey and Hart, 184?. 179 p. CU; DeWi; MnU; PPL; ViU. 45-3128

Herbert, Henry William, 1807-1858. A protege of the Grand Duke: a tale of Italy. Boston: F. Gleason, 1845. 50 p. ICU; MB: MnU; RPB. 45-3129

Herbert, Henry William, 1807-1858. The revolt of Boston. A continuation of Ruth Whalley; or the fair puritan. A romance of the Bay Providence. Boston: Henry L. Williams, 1845. 48 p. MB; MH; RPB. 45-3130

Herbert, Henry William, 1807-1858. Ruth Whalley; or the fair puritan. A romance of the Bay Providence. Boston: Henry L. Williams, 1845. 72 p. DLC; MB; MWA. 45-3131

Herbert, Henry William, 1807-1858. The Warwick woodlands; or things as they were there twenty years ago. By Frank Forester, [pseud.] Philadelphia: G.B. Zieber, 1845. 168 p. CtY; CU; MH; NN. 45-3132

Herbert, Thomas. The republican hymn book. Second edition. Covington, Kentucky: Published for the author, 1845. 287 p. MnU. 45-3133

Herbert, Thomas. The republican hymn. Covington, 1845. MH. 45-3134

Hering, Constantin, 1800-1880. Domestic physician. Third American edition revised with additions from the author's manuscript of the Fifth German edition together with the additions of Drs. Goullon, Gross, and Stapf to which is added a chapter on the diseases of women. Philadelphia: C.L. Radema, 1845. 412 p. DLC; ICU; MWA; PPCP. 45-3135

Herodotus. The history of Herodotus; taken by Henry Carey. New York: American Book company, 1845. 568 p. NcD. 45-3136

Herttell, Thomas, 1771-1849. Correspondence on the subject of life and death. Boston: J.P. Mendum, 1845. 81 p. ICMe; NN; OCHP. 45-3137

Herttell, Thomas, 1771-1849. The spirit of truth. Boston: Printed and published at the Boston Investigator offfice, 1845. 72 p. ICMe; OC; WLacT. 45-3138

Herttell, Thomas, 1771-1849. Thomas Herttell's epistolary correspondence with Dr. Thomas Cooper, of Columbia, South Carolina, during his last sickness, on the subject of human life, death, etc... New York: G. Vale, 1845. 50 p. NN. 45-3139

Hervey, Henry. Discourses to different ages and classes. Springfield, Ohio: Printed at the office of the Presbyterian of the West, 1845. 112 p. DLC; IaMp; ICartC; NjP; OClWHi. 45-3140

Hervey, James, 1714-1758. Meditation and contemplations. New York: Rober Carter, 1845. 2 v. in 1. GDecCT; ICU KyRe; MBedf. 45-3141

Hervey, James, 1714-1758. Meditation and contemplations. To which is prefixe the life of the author. Philadelphia: Sori and Ball, 1845. 2 v. in 1. ICU; MoLeb NbCrD; O; PHi; TxH. 45-3142

Hervey, Thomas Kibble, 1799-1859 The book of Christmas; descriptive of th customs, ceremonies, traditions, supersti tions, fun, feeling and festivities of th Christmas season. New York: Wiley an Putnam, 1845. 230 p. CtY; MB; NBuG PPM; OCY. 45-3143

Hetherington, William Maxwell, 1803 1865. History of the church of Scotland from the introduction of Christianity t the period of the disruption in 1843 Fourth American from the third Edin bourgh edition. New York: Carter, 1845 500 p. GMM; InHam; MiD; PCC OWoC. 45-3144

Heuberer, Charles F. The America girl. Our hearts are with our native land Song composed for the pianoforte. Bos ton: Henry Prentiss, 1845. 5 p. MB; MNF 45-3145

Heuberer, Charles F. The happies land, ballad. Boston: Prentis, 1845. MB MBNEC; MoS. 45-3146

Heuberer, Charles F. Jackson's Sword a national song. By A. Durivage. Boston 1845. CtY. 45-3147

Heuberer, Charles F. "Know'st thou the land where groves of citrons flower?' New York, 1845. CtY. 45-3148

Hewitt, John Hill, 1801-1890. I'm still hine own; written and adapted to a favorite melody. Baltimore, 1845. CtY. 45-3149

Hewitt, John Hill, 1801-1890. Love strong in death. Baltimore, 1845. CtY. 45-3150

Hewitt, John Hill, 1801-1890. The oratoric of Jephtha, written and composed by John H. Hewitt. Baltimore: Bull and Tuttle, 1845. 11 p. NN; RPB; WaU. 45-3151

Hey, Wilhelm, 1789-1854. The child's picture and verse book. New York: D. Appleton, 1845. MH; ViU. 45-3152

Hibbard, Freeborn Garretson, 1811-1895. The Bible: its influence upon science and civilization; an address delivered before the Gennesee Philosophical Society at its annual meeting in Lima, New York, July 16, 1845. Rochester: Printed for Samuel Hamilton, 1845. 24 p. CSmH; MoS; NSyU. 45-3153

Hibbard, Freeborn Garretson, 1811-1895. Christian baptism, in two parts. Part first, its subjects: Part second, its, mode, obligation, import, and relative order. New York: G. Lane and C.B. Tippett, for the Methodist Episcopal Church, 1845. 328, 218 p. MoSC; NBuG; PCA; TJaL; ScOrC. 45-3154

Hibbe, Gustof Clemens. Wanderings of a philihellene from the German of Schoicke. New York: H.G. Daggers, 1845. 43 p. DLC. 45-3155

Hibernian Society for the Relief of Emigrants from Ireland. Act of incorporation, bylaws, etc.... Philadelphia: Severns and Magill, printers, 1845. 28 p. MiD-B; PPL; PPPrHi. 45-3156

Hibernicus, pseud. What brings so many Irish to America. A pamphlet. New York: Published for the author, 1845. NN. 45-3157

Hickok, Laurens Persius, 1798-1888. Theology as a science. An address, on the occasion of his inauguration to the chair of Christian theology, in the theological seminary at Auburn, January 8, 1845. Auburn, New York: H. and J.C. Ivison, 1845. 39 p. CtHC; ICP; MBC; NjR; PPPrHi. 45-3158

Hicks, Edward, 1780-1849. A word of exhortation to young friends; presented to them without money and without price. By a poor illiterate minister. Philadelphia: J. Richards, 1845. 36 p. MH; PSC-Hi; PHC; PPM. 45-3159

Hidden, Ephraim Nelson. A sermon preached at Chichester, New Hampshire, October 15, 1845, at the ordination of Charles Willey. Gilmanton: A. Prescott, 1845. 20 p. MBC; MeHi; MH. 45-3160

Hiester, John P. Notes of travel: being a journal of a tour in Europe. Philadelphia: J.M. Campbell, 1845. [5]-272 p. DNLM; MB; MdBE; PAtM; PU. 45-3161

Hildreth, Richard, 1807-1865. The history of the United States of America. Revised edition. New York: Harper and brothers, 1845. 579 p. 3 v. ILM. 45-3162

Hildreth, Richard, 1807-1865. Native Americanism detected and exposed. By

a native American. Boston: for the
author, 1845. 36 p. IU; NNC. 45-3163

Hildreth, Richard, 1807-1865. The
slave; or memoirs of Archy Moore. Fifth
edition. Boston, 1845. NoLoc. 45-3164

Hildreth, Richard, 1807-1865. The
white slave; or the Russian peasant girl.
New York: Harper and brothers, 1845.
210 p. KyLx. 45-3165

Hill, Anne. Progressive lessons in painting flowers and fruit, comprising twenty-
four lessons or studies, on six sheets.
Designed for the use of schools and
private pupils. Philadelphia: E.C. Biddle,
1845. DLC; DSI; DP. 45-3166

Hill, B.L. Medical eclectism; an introductory lecture delivered before the class
of the Eclectic Medical Institute. Cincinnati: W.L. Mendenhall, 1845. 16 p.
OClWHi. 45-3167

Hill, Thomas, 1818-1891. An elementary treatise on arithmetic designed as an
introduction to Peirce's course of pure
mathematics, and as a sequel to the arith-
metics used in the high schools of New
England. Boston: J. Munroe and company, 1845. 85 p. MB; MH; NNC; OU;
ViU. 45-3168

Hill, V.C. New York sacred musicale
[sic] of sacred music. New York: Saxton
and Miles, 1845. KyDC. 45-3169

Hills, Chester. Builder's guide, a practical treatise on Grecian and Roman architecture, together with specimens of
the Gothic style. Revised and improved
with additions of villa and schoolhouse
architecture. Hartford: Case, Tiffany and
Burnham, 1845. 96 p. MdBP. 45-3170

Hill's Tennessee, Alabama and Mississippi almanac and state register, for the
year of our Lord 1846. By J.B. Hill. Fayetteville, Tennessee: E. Hill, [1845] T. 45-
3171

Hill's Tennessee, Alabama and Mississippi almanac and state register, for the
year of our Lord, 1846. Fayetteville, Tennessee: E. Hill, [1845] [100] p. T. 45-317.

Hillsborough, New Hampshire. Repor
of the selectmen of Hillsborough, fo
1844 and 1845. Nashua, 1845. 10 p. MHi
45-3173

Himes, Joshua Vaughan, 1805-1895
Hymns of the millennial harp; origina
and selected. Arranged for the use of the
adventists. Boston: Joshua V. Himes
1845. 275 p. CBB; NNUT. 45-3174

Himmlisches palmgartlein; oder
Messbuchlein. Cincinnati: L. Meyer and
company, 1845. PPG. 45-3175

Hine, James. I wander by the brookside
A ballad. Composed by James Hine. Boston: G.P. Reed, 1845. 7 p. KU. 45-3176

Hinman, J.L. Review of paper money
banking in a letter to a clergyman. Calculated financially for the latitude and longitude of Ohio, but will serve without
material variation for most parts of the
United States. Second edition. Cuyahoga
Falls, Ohio: H. Canfield, 1845. 31 p. CtY
45-3177

Hinman, Royal Ralph, 1785-1868. Firs
Puritan settlers. Catalogue of the names
of the first Puritan settlers of the colony
of Connecticut with the time of their ar-
rival in the colony and their standing in

society, etc. Hartford: Gleason, 1845. 367 p. DLC; MWA; NN; PHi; PP. 45-3178

Hirst, Henry Beck, 1813-1874. The coming of the mammoth, the funeral of time, and other poems... Boston: Phillips and Sampson, 1845. 9-168 p. IU; MH; MnU; PP; TxU. 45-3179

An historical account of the circumnavigation of the globe, and of the progress of discovery in the Pacific Ocean, from the voyage of Magellan to the death of Cook. New York: Harper and brothers, 1845. 366 p. IEG; LU; MnU; OSW; RPE. 45-3180

History and description of Woburn and its abbey. Woburn, Massachusetts, 1845. MdBP. 45-3181

The history and philosophy of courtezanism, as connected with morals and legislation. By an ex-alderman. New York: [Howard, Lowe and company] 1845. 72 p. DLC. 45-3182

History and record of the proceedings of the people of Lexington and its vicinity, in the suppression of the true American, from the commencement of the movement on August 14, 1845, to its final termination on Monday, the 18th of the same month. Lexington, [Kentucky] Virden, printer, 1845. DLC; OC. 45-3183

History of all denominations of Christians in the United States. New York, 1845. 68 p. DLC; MB. 45-3184

History of England; for families and schools. Philadelphia: Thomas, Cowperthwait and Company and Carey and Hart, 1845. 168 p. GMilvC. 45-3185

The history of Hans Egede and the Moravian missionaries. From the London edition. Boston: Sunday School Society, 1845. MH. 45-3186

The history of Ireland, from the invasion by Henry the Second to the present times. Being a compilation of the philosophical and statistical points to be found in the most approved writers on the subject. New York: R. Martin and company, 1845. 2 v. MB; MBrZ; NNF; RPM; WHi. 45-3187

History of Mary Gutzlaff. Boston: Massachusetts Sunday School Union, 1845. MBC. 45-3188

The history of our blessed Lord in easy verse for young children with illustrations from the London edition. New York: General Protestant Episcopal Sunday School Union, 1845. 40 p. MHa; MHi; RPB. 45-3189

A history of Texas; or the emigrant's guide to the new republic by a resident emigrant, late from the United States with a brief introduction by the Rev. A.B. Lawrence. New York: Nafis and Cornish, 1845. 275 p. DLC; OSW; PAtM; TxHR; Vi. 45-3190

History of the ivory crucifix, or statue of Christ carved from a solid block of ivory, by a monk in the convent of St. Nicholas, at Genoa Italy. [New York, 1845] 12 p. DLC; MB; NN. 45-3191

A history of the murder of Coloner George Davenport. July 4, 1845. Galena, Illinois, 1845. MH. 45-3192

Hitchcock, Calvin, 1787-1867. A discourse delivered before the Pastoral Association of Massachusetts, in Park Street Church, Boston, May 27, 1845. Boston: Press of T.R. Marvin, 1845. 23 p. MeBat; MTa; Nh; NjR. 45-3193

Hitchcock, Calvin, 1787-1867. Historical notices on congregationalism. A discourse, delivered before the Pastoral Association of Massachusetts... Boston: Press of T.R. Marvin, 1845. 23 p. CBB; IaB; MoSpD; MWiW; WHi. 45-3194

Hitchcock, Edward, 1793-1864. The American academic system defended. An address delivered at the dedication of the new hall of Williston Seminary, in Easthampton, January 28, 1845. Amherst: J.S. and C. Adams, 1845. 29 p. CtSoP; ICU; MDeeP; MLy; OO. 45-3195

Hitchcock, Edward, 1793-1864. The coronation of winter; a discourse delivered at Amherst College and Mount Holyoke Seminary, soon after a remarkable glacial phenomenon, in the winter of 1845. Amherst: J.S. and C. Adams, 1845. 24 p. CtY; ICN; MBC; NjR; PPPrHi. 45-3196

Hitchcock, Edward, 1793-1864. The coronation of winter; a discourse delivered at Amherst College and Mount Holyoke Seminary, soon after a remarkable glacial phenomenon in the winter of 1845. Second edition. Amherst: J.S. and C. Adams, 1845. Ct; ICU; MH; NjR; WHi. 45-3197

Hitchcock, Edward, 1793-1864. Elementary geology. Third edition revised and improved with an introductory notice by John Pye Smith. New York: Mark H. Newman, 1845. 352 p. CtY; GAuY; MB; OClW; RPB. 45-3198

Hitchcock, Edward, 1793-1864. The highest use of learning: an address delivered at his inauguration to the presidency of Amherst College... Published by the trustees. Amherst: J.S. and C. Adams, printers, 1845. 51 p. CoCsC; IaGG; MAnP; OrU; PLT. 45-3199

Hitchcock, Ethan Allen, 1798-1870. Memorial to the Congress of the United States from officers of the United States army, on the subject of Brevet and staff rank. Corpus Christi, 1845. 23 p. MdBJ; ScU; TxU. 45-3200

Hitchcock, Ethan Allen, 1798-1870. De obfuscationibus or a glimmering light on Mesmerism. New York: Charles S. Francis and company, 1845. 39 p. DLC; PPT; Vt. 45-3201

Hoare, Clement, 1789-1849. A practical treatise on the cultivation of the grape vine on open walls. Third American edition. Boston: William D. Ticknor and company, 1845. 192 p. ICU; MHing; NNNBG; OCo; VtU. 45-3202

Hobart, Nathaniel, d. 1840. Life of Emanuel Swedenborg, with some account of his writings. Second edition. Boston: T.H. Carter and company, 1845. 236 p. CtY; MB; MWA; PPM; WHi. 45-3203

Hoblyn, Richard Dennis, 1803-1886. A dictionary of terms used in medicine and the collateral sciences. First American from the second London edition. Revised with numerous additions, by Isaac Hays. Philadelphia: Lea and Blanchard, 1845. 402 p. CtY; FSa; MB; NBuG; ViRMC. 45-3204

Hock, Walter Farquhar. The cross of Christ or meditations on the death and passion of our Blessed Lord and Savior. New York: D. Appleton and company, 1845. 172 p. CSfCW; MdBD; NdCatS; Nh; OrPD. 45-3205

Hodge, Charles, 1797-1878. Abolitionism. [Princeton, 1845] 24 p. KyLx; MBAt; OClWHi; T. 45-3206

Hodge, Charles, 1797-1878. A brief account of the last hours of Albert B. Dod. November 20th, 1845. Princeton: John T. Robinson, [1845] 16 p. ICU; MB; MBAt; MH; NN; NjP. 45-3207

Hodge, Charles. Review of Beman on the atonement. First published in biblical repertory, January, 1845. Philadelphia: Presbyterian Board of Publication, 1845. 95 p. CtHC; IEG; MBC; MWiW. 45-3208

Hoerner, James. Catholic melodies; or a compilation of hymns, anthems, psalms, etc. with appropriate airs and devotional exercises for the ordinary occasions of Catholic duty and worship. Baltimore: John Murphy, 1845. 264 p. CStclU; MdBS; MdHi. 45-3209

Hoffman, Charles Fenno, 1806-1884. The vigil of faith.and other poems. Fourth edition. New York: Harper and brothers, 1845. 7-164 p. CtY; KyLo; NNUT; RPAt; TxU. 45-3210

Hoffman, David, 1784-1854. Circular to students of law in the United States. Philadelphia, 1845. MBAt. 45-3211

Hoffman, David, 1784-1854. To his excellency, James K. Polk. By David and Charles F. Mayer. [n.p.] 1845. 8 p. DLC. 45-3212

Hoffman's Albany directory and city register, for the years 1845-1846... Albany: Printed by L.G. Hoffman, 1845. ICN; KHi; NCH; NN; PP. 45-3213

Hofland, Barbara Wreaks Hoole, 1770-1844. Reflection; a tale. Boston: Gordon, Swift and Wiley, 1845. 161 p. MB; MMilt. 45-3214

Hofland, Barbara Wreaks Hoole, 1770-1844. Self-denial. A tale. Boston: Jordan, Swift and Wiley, 1845. 154 p. MB; MnHi; NNC. 45-3215

Hogan, William, 1790-1848. Auricular confession and Popish nunneries. Boston: Saxton and Kelt, 1845. 219 p. CtHC; MB; MBC; MH; TxDaM-P. 45-3216

Hogan, William, 1790-1848. Synopsis of popery as it was as it is. Boston: Redding and company, 1845. 219 p. KyLxT; MBAt; MBC; PAtM; PPM. 45-3217

Hogan, William, 1790-1848. Synopsis of popery as it was as it is. Boston: Saxton and Kelt, 1845. 219 p. DLC; MB; MH; OClW; TxDaM-P. 45-3218

Hogarth, George, 1783-1870. Musical history, biography and criticism. With an original preface by H.C. Watson. New York: H.G. Daggers, 1845. CtY; MH; MoS; NBuG; RNR. 45-3219

Hogg, James, 1770-1835. Winter evening tales, collected in among the cottages in the South of Scotland. Hartford: S. Andrus and Son, 1845. 2 v. MBAt; MH; MoK; OClStM. 45-3220

Holberg, Ludwig, 1684-1754. Neils Klim's journey under the ground, being a narrative of his wonderful descent to the subterranean lands; together with an account of the sensible animals and trees inhabiting the Planet Nazar and the firmament. Translated from the Danish by John Grierlow. Boston: Saxton, Peirce and company, 1845. 190 p. IU; MH; NeBe; PU; TxU. 45-3221

Holbrook, Edwin A. Nature and grace compared; a poetic sermon preached at Malone and Westville, New York, June 8 and 15, 1845. Burlington: Chauncey Goodrich, 1845. 22 p. MMeT; NCaS; Vt. 45-3222

Holcomb, Frederick. Mysteries of divine providence. A funeral sermon on the death of Mr. Frederick Merriam, with a passing notice of other deaths in the same family. Hartford: W. Faxon, 1845. 12 p. CtHT; CtY-D. 45-3223

Holdich, Joseph, 1804-1893. Christ, not self, the object of preaching. Boston: American Pulpit, 1845. CtHC. 45-3224

Holding, Joseph. The liberal soul shall be made fat and the honest statesman and politician shall be rewarded their labor and works will follow them through life. Tarboro: Press, 1845. NcU. 45-3225

Holiday tales. The magical watch. Mr. Bull and the giant atmodes [sic] Old Pedro. Adventures of a bee. Philadelphia: George S. Appleton; New York: D. Appleton and company, 1845. 120 p. NRHi. 45-3226

Holland, Elihu Goodwin. The natural evidence on the being of God, and the immortal life. Bath, New York: Steuben Co., 1845. 30 p. CtY; ICMe; MB; MH-AH; MWA. 45-3227

Holland, John, 1794-1872. Memoirs of the life and ministry of the Rev. John Summerfield, with an introductory letter by James Montgomery. Sixth edition New York: J.K. Wellman, 1845. 460 p. MBAt; MiD-B; OkLaw; TxSaT; WBelo-C. 45-3228

Holland, John, 1794-1872. Memoirs of the life and ministry of the Rev. John Summerfield. With an introductory letter by James Montgomery. Seventh edition. New York: J.K. Wellman, 1845. 460 p. MB; MeB; NBuG; NT; TxDaM. 45-3229

Holmes, Edward, 1797-1859. The life of Mozart including his correspondence. New York: Harper and brothers, 1845. 379, 4 p. CtMW; GEU; MeSaco; PAnL; RWoH. 45-3230

Holmes, George Frederick, 1820-1897. Address delivered before the Beaufort District Society; by G.F. Holmes. 23d April, 1845. Columbia: A.S. Johnston, 1845. 26 p. ScU. 45-3231

Holmes, Isaac Edward, 1796-1867. Speech of Mr. Holmes on the annexation of Texas to the United States. Delivered in the House, January 14, 1845. [Washington, 1845] 7 p. CSt; KHi; MH; MiD-B; PHi. 45-3232

Holt, Daniel, 1810-1883. Views of homoeopathy; with reasons for examining and admitting it as a principle in medical science. New Haven: J.H. Benham, 1845. 48 p. CtHT; DSG; MH-AH; OC; PPHa. 45-3233

Holyday tales. Philadelphia: G.S. Appleton, 1845. 120 p. MH; NN. 45-3234

Home Missionary Society of the City of Philadelphia. Annual report of the Board of Managers. Philadelphia: Merrihew, 1845-. PPPrHi. 45-3235

Homer, James Lloyd. A short inquiry into the commercial policy of the United States; or the right principles of revenue laws and international commerce, by a merchant of Boston. Boston: William D. Ticknor and company, 1845. 22 p. ICU; M; MH; NN; PHi. 45-3236

Homerus. The first three books of Homer's Iliad, according to the ordinary text, and also with the restoration of the digamma, to which are appended English notes, critical and explanatory, a metrical index and Homeric glossary by Charles Anthon. [Text in Greek] New York: Harper and brothers, 1845. 599 p. DLC; LN; NjMD; PMA; TxU. 45-3237

Homerus. The Iliad of Homer, translated by Alexander Pope. New York: Barnes, 1845. 2 v. LStBA; MdMWM; MH; NIC; TxBradM. 45-3238

Homerus. The Odyssey, according to the text of Wolf; with notes for the use of schools and colleges. By John Owen. New York: Leavitt, Trow and company, 1845. 12, 516 p. DLC; ICP; MH-AH; NjP; PLFM. 45-3239

Homerus. The Odyssey of Homer. Translated by Alexander Pope. Philadelphia: James Crissey, 1845. 2 v. LNHT; NboM: NIC; NSyHi. 45-3240

A homily for the times. The lofty and lowly; a sermon for the eleventh Sunday after Trinity. By a presbyter of New Jersey. Published by necessity. New York: Stanford and Swords, 1845. 28 p. CtMW; CtW; MH-AH; NNG. 45-3241

Homman, J.W. The nurses' and mothers' medical preceptor; designed to aid nurses and mothers in the treatment of children and the sick. Boston: Wright's Steam Power Press, 1845. 108 p. OU. 45-3242

Homoeopathic pioneer. v. 1. No. 1. Syracuse, 1845. DNLM; DSG; NNNAM; PPHa. 45-3243

Honest John's farmers almanac... West Brookfield, Massachusetts, 1845. DLC. 45-3244

Honest John's farmer's almanack for 1846. By Honest John Smith. West Brookfield, Massachusetts: George W. Minck, [1845] MH; MHi; MWA. 45-3245

Honest John's farmer's almanack for the year 1846. By Honest John Smith. Boston: Benjamin B. Mussey, [1845] 48 p. MHi; MWA. 45-3246

Hood, Charles. Gonzalvo: or the fall of Grenada. Boston: W.D. Ticknor and company, 1845. 377 p. IU; MBAt MWA; OO; RPB. 45-3247

Hood, Thomas, 1799-1845. Mrs. Peck's pudding: a humorous paper by Charles Dickens and a dramtic sketch by Sir E. Sutton Bulwer, with illustrations by Darley. Philadelphia: Carey and Hart, 1845. CSmH; MHa RPAt. 45-3248

Hood, Thomas, 1799-1845. Poems. New York: Wiley and Putnam, 1845. PRosC. 45-3249

Hood, Thomas, 1799-1845. The poetical works of Thomas Hood. Serious poems. Philadelphia: Porter and Coates, 1845. 288 p. MdBLD; MoSMa; NGlc; PPi; PRosC. 45-3250

Hood, Thomas, 1799-1845. Prose and verse. New York: Wiley and Putnam, 1845. 2 v. CtMW; GDecCT; ICU; ODa; PU. 45-3251

Hood, Thomas, 1799-1845. Whimsicalities, a periodical gathering. Philadelphia: Lea and Blanchard, 1845. 292 p. MB; MBL; MNBedf; NNS; RPAt. 45-3252

Hood, Thomas, 1799-1845. The works of Thomas Hood. Edited with notes by his son and daughter. New York: Ward, Lock, and company, 1845. 459 p. NbOC. 45-3253

Hook, Theodore Edward, 1788-1841. Gilbert Gurney; a novel, by Theodore Hook. Philadelphia: Carey and Hart, 1845. 303 p. MB; MNe; NcAS; PPL-R. 45-3254

Hook, Theodore Edward, 1788-1841. Snowdon. A novel. New York: E. Ferrett, 1845. 112 p. MdBP; NjP; PBm; ViU. 45-3255

Hook, Theodore Edward, 1788-1841. The widow. a Novel. Philadelphia: Ferrett, 1845. 112 p. PBm. 45-3256

Hooker, Edward William, 1794-1875. The cultivation of the spirit of missions in our literary and theological institutions. Boston: T.R. Marvin, 1845. 24 p. MBC; MWiW; NcMHi. 45-3257

Hooker, Edward William, 1794-1875.

Memoir of Mrs. Sarah L. Huntington Smith, late of the American mission in Syria. Third edition. New York, 1845. 396 p. ICU; KyCov; MBr; MH; OSW. 45-3258

Hooker, Richard, 1553/4-1600. The works of Mr. Richard Hooker with an account of his life and death, by Isaac Walton, arranged by the Rev. John Keble. New York: D. Appleton and company, 1845. 2 v. MsJPED. 45-3259

Hooker, Thomas, 1586-1647. The poor doubting christian drawn to Christ... with... author's life and introduction, by Edward Hooker. Hartford: Robins, 1845. 167 p. CtSoP; IEG; InCW; MiKC; OWervO. 45-3260

Hooper, John. The doctrine of the second advent, briefly stated in an address to the members of the Church of England, in the parish of Westbury, Wilts. From the Second London edition. Circleville, Ohio: Religious Telescope office, 1845. 22 p. MdBD; NNG. 45-3261

Hooper, Johnson Jones, 1815?-1863. Adventures of Captain Simon Suggs, late of the Tallapoosa volunteers; together with "Taking the Census," and other Alabama sketches. Philadelphia: T.B. Peterson and brothers, 1845. 201 p. MBAt; MsAb. 45-3262

Hooper, Johnson Jones, 1815?-1863. Some adventures of Captain Simon Suggs, late of the Tallapoosa Volunteers; together with "Taking the census," and other Alabama sketches. By a country editor... Philadelphia: Carey and Hart, 1845. 201 p. MB; MBAt; NcAS; PPiU; TxU. 45-3263

Hooper, Lucy, 1816-1841. The lady's book of flowers and poetry; to which are added, a botanical introduction, a complete floral dictioary; and a chapter on plants in rooms. Edited by Lucy Hooper. New York: J.C. Riker, 1845. 275 p. CtY: NRHi; TJon. 45-3264

Hooper, Ralph Lambton. Joy and peace in believing; or hints for obtaining the blessing. First American for the Third London edition with an introduction by Rev. H.V.D. Johns. Baltimore: Armstrong and Berry, 1845. 133 p. PPM. 45-3265

Hooper, Robert, 1773-1835. Lexicon medicum; or medical dictionary containing an explanation of the terms in anatomy, botany, etc... Thirteenth American edition. New York: Harper and brothers, 1845. 2 v. in 1. LNOP; MdBM; Nh; PPCP; OAsht. 45-3266

Hooper, William. A sermon delivered in the Union meeting house in Amherst, Sunday May 11, 1845. Concord: Balm and Gilead, 1845. 11 p. CSmH; MMeT. 45-3267

Hope, James, 1801-1841. Principles of pathological anatomy; adapted to the cyclopedia of practical medicine and it's elements. With two hundred and sixty beautifully coloured illustrations. First American edition. Edited by L.M. Lawson. Philadelphia: Lindsay and Blakiston, 1845. 359 p. DNLM; IU-M; KyU; MBM; PPCP. 45-3268

Hope, John C. Sermon, delivered before the missionary society. Baltimore: Printed at the Publication Rooms, 1845. 24 p. OSW. 45-3269

Hope, Matthew Boyd, 1812-1859. A discourse designed to show that physiological inquiries are not unfriendly to religious sentiment. Delivered in the Tenth Presbyterian Church, Philadelphia, January 18, 1845. Philadelphia: Jefferson Medical Class, 1845. CSansS; DNLM; ICN; NjPT; PPPrHi. 45-3270

Hopkins, J.G. The northern railroad in New York, with remarks on the western trade. Boston: Freeman and Bolles, 1847. 31 p. CtY; IU; MB; MnHi; OClWHi. 45-3271

Hopkins, John Henry, 1792-1868. Episcopal government. A sermon preached at the consecration of the Rev. Alonzo Potter as bishop of the diocese of Pennsylvania; by the Rt. Rev. John Henry Hopkins, bishop of the diocese of Vermont. Philadelphia: King and Baird, 1845. 24 p. Nh; NN; PPL; RPB; TSewU. 45-3272

Hopkins, Louisa Payson, 1812-1862. On the acts of the Apostles. Written for the Massachusetts Sabbath School Society, and revised by the committee of publication. Boston: Massachusetts Sabbath School Society, 1845. 155 p. MBC; MChiA; MMeT. 45-3273

Hopkins, Mark, 1802-1887. Burdens to be cast upon the Lord. A sermon before the American Board of Commissioners for Foreign Missions, at the thirty-sixth annual meeting, Brooklyn, New York, September, 1845. Boston: Press of Crocker and Brewster, 1845. 31 p. CU; ICP; MBC; NjR; PPPrHi. 45-3274

Hopkins, Mark, 1802-1887. A sermon before the American Board of Commissioners of Foreign Missions, at the thirty-sixth annual meeting, Brooklyn, New York, September, 1845. New edition. Boston: Press of Crocker and Brewster, 1845. 31 p. MeBat; MNtCA; Nh. 45-3275

Hopkins, Mark, 1802-1887. A sermon delivered at Pittsfield, August 22, 1844, on the occasion of the Berkshire Jubilee. Albany: Weare C. Little; Pittsfield: E.P. Little, 1845. 34 p. ICMe; MB; MPiB; NN; RPB. 45-3276

Hopkins, Mark, 1802-1887. A sermon preached before the annual convention of the congregational ministers of Massachusetts, in Boston, May 29, 1845. Boston: Press of T.R. Marvin, 1845. 32 p. CU; MPiB; PPL; RPB; PPPrHi. 45-3277

Hopkins, Mark, 1802-1887. A sermon preached before the annual convention of the Congregational ministers of Massachusetts, in Boston, May 29, 1845. Boston: T.R. Marvin, 1845. 32 p. CU; MBC; NcD; PPPrHi; RPB. 45-3278

Horatius Flaccus, Quintus. The works of Horace with English notes critical and explanatory. New edition with corrections and improvements. New York: Harper and brothers, 1845. 681 p. GHi; IaSc; MnU; OCX; ODaU. 45-3279

Horne, George, 1730-1792. A commentary of the book of Psalms, in which their literal and historical sense, as they relate to King David and the people of Israel, is illustrated; and their application to Messiah, to the church, and to individuals as members there of, is pointed out. New York and Pittsburg: Robert Carter, 1845. 536 p. CU; GDecCT; InID; ODaB; ScCoT. 45-3280

Horne, R.H. The new spirit of the age.

Edited by R.H. Horne. New York: Harper and brothers, 1845. 365 p. MBNEH; NFred; RKi; ScGrw. 45-3281

Horne, Leonard and Company. Catalogue of a splendid and unequaled collection of Chinese and rare books. Boston, 1845. 50 p. DLC. 45-3282

Horner, Gustavus R.B. Medical topography of Brazil and Uruguay... Philadelphia: Lindsay and Blakiston, 1845. 296 p. CSt-L; DNLM; ICJ; PPAmP; PU. 45-3283

Horton, George Moses, 1798-ca. 1880? The poetical works of George M. Horton, the colored bard of North Carolina, to which is prefixed the life of the author, written by himself. Hillsborough: D. Heartt, 1845. 96 p. MH; NcRR; NcU. 45-3284

Hosmer, William Howe Cuyler, 1814-1877. The months. Boston: W.D. Ticknor and company, 1845. 71 p. CSmH; DLC; MB. 45-3285

Housekeeper's almanac: and the young wife's oracle, containing over 200 valuable receipts in cookery, confectionary, pastry, etc., etc. New York: Nafis and Cornish, 1845. 11 p. NUtHi. 45-3286

Housekeeper's annual and ladies register for 1846. Boston: Crosby and Nichols, [1845] MWA. 45-3287

Houston, George Smith, 1811-1879. Speech of Mr. Houston, of Alabama, on the bill reducing and graduating the price of the public lands of the United States. Delivered in the House, February 5, 1845. [Washington? 1845?] 8 p. DLC; MH; PHi; TxU. 45-3288

Houston, Thomas. Manual of hymns; a collection of hymns, for social and family worship. Compiled by Thomas Houston and Alfred Bellamy. Chittenango, New York: John Dow, printer, 1845. CSmH; DLC; IC; NBuG. 45-3289

Houstoun, Matilda Charlotte Jesse Fraser, 1815?-1892. Texas and the Gulf of Mexico; or yachting in the new world. Philadelphia: G.B. Zieber and company, 1845. [13]-288 p. CU; ICU; KHi; PU; TxGR. 45-3290

How shall we vote on the water act? Boston, 1845] 24 p. DLC; MBAt; MHi; NNC; WHi. 45-3291

Howard, Charles Wallace, 1811-1876. A sermon delivered at the re-opening and dedication of the French Protestat Church of Charleston, South Carolina, on Sunday, May 11, 1845. Charleston: Burgess and James, printers, 1845. 24 p. CtHC; MH-AH; PPPrHi; RPB; ScU. 45-3292

Howard, Henry, 1792-1874. Outlines of medical jurisprudence. Intended to promote the studies of the medical and law students who attended his lectures. Third edition. Charlottesville: R.C. Noel and company, 1845. 159 p. NcD; Vi; ViU. 45-3293

Howe, Edward. The fairy bell waltz; composed and arranged for the piano forte. New York: Firth and Hall, 1845. 2 p. MNF; ViU; WHi. 45-3294

Howe, Henry, 1816-1893. Historical collections of Virginia; containing a collection of the most interesting facts, traditions, biographical sketches, anecdotes, etc., with geographical and statis-

tical descriptions... Charleston, South Carolina: Babcock and company, 1845. 544 p. CtB; GAuY; Nh-Hi; RWe; ViU. 45-3295

Howe, James Hervey. Our country: its origin, position and destination. An oration delivered in North-East, New York, July 4, 1845. [Pougkeepsie: E.B. Killey, printer, 1845] 15 p. CtY; MBAt; NNUT; WHi. 45-3296

Howe, Leonard and company. American historical, and English standard works. Catalogue of valuable books, comprising many rare historical works relating to America... Boston: Printed by Alfred Mudge, 1845. 49 p. MiU-C. 45-3297

Howe, Leonard and company. Bibliotheca americana. Catalogue of a splendid and unequaled collection of choice and rare books on America, ancient and modern... Boston, 1845. 50 p. DLC; MiU-C. 45-3298

Howe, Uriah Tracy. An address delivered to the members of the Ohio Mechanics Institute at its eight annual fair. Cincinnati: Sparhawk and Lytle, 1845. 21 p. CSmH; NN; OCHP. 45-3299

Howell, Robert Boyte Crawford, 1801-1868. The responsibilities of educated men. An oration delivered before the Society of Alumni of Georgetown College at the annual commencement, June 26, 1845. By Robert Howell of Nashville, Tennessee. Georgetown, Kentucky: Society of Alumni, 1845. 12 p. KyLoS; MBAt; MH; NN; PCA. 45-3300

Howitt, Mary Botham, 1799-1888. Alice Franklin. A tale. New York: D. Appleton and company, 1845. 174 p. CtY; ICU; MDux; MH. 45-3301

Howitt, Mary Botham, 1799-1888. The author's daughter. A tale. New York: Harper and brothers, 1845. 71 p. IU; MBL; MH; NjR. 45-3302

Howitt, Mary Botham, 1799-1888. Hope on! Hope ever! or the boyhood of Felix Law. New York: D. Appleton, 1845. 212 p. AAP; ICartC; MH. 45-3303

Howitt, Mary Botham, 1799-1888. Little coin, much care. New York: D. Appleton, 1845. 171 p. MoS; NFrf. 45-3304

Howitt, Mary Botham, 1799-1888. My own story; or the autobiography of a child. New York: D. Appleton and company, 1845. MA; MnU; NBuG; NN; NT. 45-3305

Howitt, Mary Botham, 1799-1888. My uncle the clockmaker. A tale. New York: D. Appleton and company and George S. Appleton, 1845. 130 p. ICBB; NNC; OClW; PU; ViU. 45-3306

Howitt, Mary Botham, 1799-1888. No sense, like common sense, or some passages in the life of Charles Middleton. New York, 1845. IEG. 45-3307

Howitt, Mary Botham, 1799-1888. The poetical works of Howitt, Milman, and Keats. Complete in one volume. Philadelphia: Thomas, Cowperthwait and company, 1845. 607 p. InLog; MBrad; MiKL; NPen; ViRVMI. 45-3308

Howitt, Mary Botham, 1799-1888. The poetical works of Howitt, Milman, and Keats. Philadelphia: Thomas, Cow-

perthwait and company, 1845. 447, 75 p InU. 45-3309

Howitt, Mary Botham, 1799-1888 Strive and thrive; a tale. New York: D Appleton, 1845. 175 p. OClW; OO. 45 3310

Howitt, Mary Botham, 1799-1888. The two apprentices. A tale for youth. New York: D. Appleton and company Philadelphia: George D. Appleton, 1845 175 p. DLC; MH; NHem; PPL; RNR. 45 3311

Howland, Esther Allen, 1801-1860 American economical housekeeper, and family receipt book. Second edition Worcester: W. Allen, 1845. 124 p FTaSU. 45-3312

Howland, Esther Allen, 1801-1860 American economical housekeeper, and family receipt book. Worcester: W Allen, [1845] 124 p. KMK. 45-3313

Howland, Esther Allen, 1801-1860 American economical housekeeper, and family receipt book. Stereotype edition Cincinnati: H.W. Derby and company 1845. 108 p. ICJ; MCR; MiU. 45-3314

Howland, Esther Allen, 1801-1860. The New England economical housekeeper, and family receipt book. Stereotype edition. Worcester: S.A. Howland, 1845 104 p. DLC; MWA; OO; ViW. 45-3315

Hoyle's games; containing the established rules and practice of whist, quadrille, piquet, quinze, oingt-un, cassino, put, etc. Philadelphia: Henry F. Anners, [1845] 269 p. ICN; MB; NiP; OCl; WHi. 45-3316

Hoyt, Ralph, 1806-1878. A chant of life and other poems with sketches and essays. New York: Hoyt, 1845. 32 p. ICU; NN-W; RPB. 45-3317

Hoyt, Ralph, 1806-1878. Night; a poem in two parts... New York, 1845. 60 p. RPB. 45-3318

Hubback, John, 1811-1885. A treatise on the evidence of succession to real and personal property and peerages. Philadelphia: T. and J.W. Johnson, 1845. 551 p. CoU; IU-L; MdBB; NcD; TxSC. 45-3319

Hubbard, James. M. The national blues quick step. New Haven, 1845. CtY. 45-3320

Hubbard, William Joseph; 1802-1864. Arguments on behalf of Joseph Tilden and others, remonstrants, on the hearing of the petition of the mayor of the city of Boston, on behalf of the city council for a grant of the requisite powers to construct an aqueduct from Long Pond to the city, before a joint special committee of the Massachusetts legislature, March 5, 1845. Boston: Press of T.R. Marvin, 1845. 54 p. IU; MiD-B; NN; PPL; WHi. 45-3321

Hubner, Johann, 1668-1731. Hubner's Bibliche historien asu dem alten und neuen Testamente. For the youth and public schools newly revised according to the requirements of our time. Philadelphia: Mentz and Rovoudt, 1845. 490 p. PNazMHi. 45-3322

Hudson, Charles, 1795-1881. Speech of Mr. Hudson, of Massachusetts, on the annexation of Texas. Delivered in the House, January 20, 1845. [Washington, 1845] 15 p. CtY; IEN-M; MWA; NNC; WHi. 45-3323

Hudson, Robert E. Signal book for Boston Harbor. Boston: J. Howe's Sheet Anchor Press, 1845. 86 p. MB; MH; MSaP. 45-3324

Hudson River Indians. Report on the aboriginal names and geographical terminology of New York. New York, 1845. 43 p. MWA. 45-3325

Hughes, Jeremiah, 1783-1848. A brief sketch of Maryland, its geography, boundaries, history, government, legislation, internal improvements, etc. [Baltimore?] Printed for the Publisher, 1845. 245 p. DLC; MdBP; MdHi; WHi. 45-3326

Hughes, John Taylor, 1819-1862. Doniphan's expedition; containing an account of the conquest of New Mexico; General Kearney's overland expedition to California. Cincinnati, 1845. PPL. 45-3327

Hughes, Margaret Smith. Letter... to her father, narrating the loss of the packet ship Poland, on her way from New York to Havre, May 16, 1840. An offering to the Pennsylvania Academy of the fine arts, from Christopher Hughes. Baltimore: J.D. Toy, [1845] 34 p. CtY; DLC; NIC; PHi; PPL. 45-3328

Hughes, Thomas P. Sylwedd pregeth ar y balm o gilead; hefyd cweledigaeth myngdd nebo, a pherlau galfaria; yn cynnwys caniadau a hymnau New Yddion, ar amrywiol destynau ysgrythrol... Utica: Argraffwyd gan R.W. Roberts, 1845. 48 p. NUt. 45-3329

Hugo, Victor Marie, 1802-1885. The Rhine. New York: Wiley and Putnam, 1845. 291 p. IaMp; KyLx; OCY; RPAt; WM. 45-3330

Hugo, Victor Marie, 1802-1885. Sketches and legends of the Rhine. New York: Cornish, Lamport and company, 1845. 291 p. ICU; InThE; KEmT; MoS; OCh. 45-3331

Hulett, Thomas G. Every man his own guide to the falls of Niagara, or the whole story in few words... To which is added a chronological table, containing the principal events of the late war between the United States and Great Britain. Fifth edition. Buffalo: Faxon and company, 1845. MH; NN; PHI; PPL. 45-3332

Hulett, W.E. Every stranger his own guide to Niagara Falls. The latest and most comprehensive work yet before the public. Containing a table of distances and the intermediate places on the five principal routes leading from Niagara Falls to Albany, via Montreal, Quebec and Saratoga Springs. Buffalo: Steele's Press, 1845. DLC; MB; MH; RPB. 45-3333

Hull, Joseph Darling. A plea for religious newspapers; a sermon preached to his own people on the Lord's day, December 29th, 1844 by a Connecticut pastor. Hartford: D.B. Moseley, 1845. 23 p. CtY; IEG; MBC; MMeT; NjPT. 45-3334

Hullihen, Simon P. Essay on cleft palate and its treatment. Baltimore: John W. Woods, 1845. 11 p. DLC; NNNAM. 45-3335

Humane Society of the Commonwealth of Massachusetts. History of the society with a selected list of premiums awarded by the trustees, from its commencement to the present time; including extracts from the correspondence, a statement of the funds, and a list of the officers and members. Boston: S.N. Dickinson, 1845. 954 p. DLC; IU; MBC; MH; OO. 45-3336

Humboldt, Alexander, freiherr von, 1769-1859. Cosmos: a survey of the general physical history of the universe. New York: Harper and brothers, 1845. DLC; MWA; NN; PPL; TxU. 45-3337

Hume, David, 1711-1776. Essay on miracles. New York: G. Vale, 1845. 33 p. NN. 45-3338

Humphrey, Charles, 1791-1850. A collection of practical forms in suits at law; also precedents of contracts, conveyances, wills, etc.... Albany: W. and A. Gould and company; New York: Gould, Banks and company, 1845. 2 v. CoU; DLC; InSC; OMC; TU. 45-3339

Humphrey, Heman, 1779-1861. Thirty four letters to a son in the ministry. Second edition. New York: Mark H. Newman, 1845. 352 p. CtY; MiU; NNUT; PAtM; RPB. 45-3340

Humphrey, Heman, 1779-1861. Valedictory address, delivered at Amherst College, by Rev. Heman Humphrey, on leaving the presidential chair, April 15, 1845. Published by the trustees. Amherst: J.S. and C. Adams, printers, 1845. 23 p. CtMW; IaGG; MWA; NN; TxU. 45-3341

Humphreys, David, 1782-1818. Memoirs of the life, adventures, and military exploits of Israel Putnam, Senior Major-general in the Revolutionary Army of the United States, and next in rank to General Washington. Ithaca, New York: Mack, Andrus and company, 1845. 141 p. KyLoP; MWA; NCH; NN; PHi. 45-3342

Hunt, Freeman, 1804-1858. The library of commerce; practical, theoretical and historical. New York: Hunt's Merchant Magazine, 1845. 342 p. DLC; ICU; MH; OOxM; PU. 45-3343

Hunt, John. Hours of reflection; on horror and pleasure... [Schenectady?] 1845. 324 p. CtMW; MB; MBAt; MWA; RPB. 45-3344

Hunt, Leigh, 1784-1859. Imagination and fancy; or selections from the English poets, illustrative of those first requisites of their art; with markings of the best passages, critical notices of the writers, and an essay in answer to the question, "What is poetry?" New York: Wiley and Putnam, 1845. 225 p. CtB; MoS; OCY; PPA; RLa. 45-3345

Hunt, Leigh, 1784-1859. The indicator: a miscellany for the fields and the fireside... New York: Wiley and Putnam, 1845. 2 v. in 1. CSf; IU; MNan; OZaN; PHC. 45-3346

Hunt, Leigh, 1784-1859. Rimini and other poems. Boston, 1845. 124 p. CtNwchO. 45-3347

Hunt, Leigh, 1784-1859. Selections from the English poets... New York, 1845. CU. 45-3348

Hunt, Richard S. A new guide to Texas: consisting of a brief outline of the history of its settlement, and the colonization and land laws... by Richard Hunt and Jesse F. Randel, Houston, Texas. New York: Sherman and Smith, 1845. 62 p. IaDL; NUtHi; Tx. 45-3349

Hunt, Thomas Poage, 1784-1859. The wedding days of former times. Philadelphia: Griffith and Simon; New York: Saxton and Miles, 1845. 87 p. MiD-B; MLow; MWA; PPM. 45-3350

Hunt, Thomas Poage, 1794-1876. Jesse Johnson and his times. Philadelphia: Griffith and Simon, 1845. 77 p. NN; PPPrHi. 45-3351

Hunt, Washington, 1811-1867. Speech of Mr. Hunt, of New York, on the naturalization laws, and frauds on the ballot box; in the House of Representatives, December 29, 1845. Washington, 1845. CtHC; DLC; MBAt; MH; NBu. 45-3352

Hunter, William. The case, William Hunter, in equity, versus the inhabitants of Marlboro... Worcester: Press of H.J. Howland, 1845. 5, 554 p. MB; MHi; MMarl; ViU-L. 45-3353

Hunter, William. Preparation for death. A discourse, delivered at Howard, Steuben County, New York, April 8, 1845, and occasioned by the death of Mrs. Eliza S. Rose, wife of the Rev. L. Rose. Bath, New York: Hull and Wittemore, printers, 1845. 16 p. NNUT; NRU. 45-3354

Hunter, William, 1811-1877. The minstrel of Zion: a book of religious songs accompanied with appropriate music, chiefly original. By Rev. William Hunter and Rev. Samuel Wakefield.

Philadelphia: Sorin, 1845. 216 p. DLC; ICN; NNUT; PPPrHi. 45-3355

Hunter, William, 1811-1877. Select melodies; comprising the best of those hymns and spiritual songs in common use, not to be found in the standard Episcopal Methodist hymn book: as also, a number of original pieces. Cincinnati: Printed at the Methodist Book Concern, R.P. Thompson, printer, 1845. 320 p. DLC; NNMHi; OC. 45-3356

Hunter, William, 1811-1877. Select melodies; comprising the best of those hymns and spiritual songs in common use, not to be found in the standard Episcopal Methodist hymn book: as also, a number of original pieces. Philadelphia: Sorin and Ball, 1845. 320 p. CtY-D. 45-3357

Huntington, B.W. Individuality. An address, delivered before the Philomatic Society, of the University of Alabama; at its twelfth anniversary. Tuscaloosa: Printed by M.D.J. Slade, 1845. 26 p. AU; KyLoS; NN; PPPrHi. 45-3358

Huntington, Elisha. Address on the organization of the government, April 7, 1845. Lowell, 1845. Nh. 45-3359

Huntington, Ezra Abel, 1813-1901. The house of God, and the law of the House. A sermon preached at... Albany... December 3, 1845. Albany: Erastus H. Pease, 1845. 46 p. CtY; DLC; ICT; MBC; MnHi. 45-3360

Huntington, Frederic Dan, 1819-1904. A discourse at the South Congregational Church, in Boston, on the first Sunday in the year... Boston: Leonard C. Bowles, 1845. 24 p. CtY; ICMe; MBAU; MWA NNC. 45-3361

Huntington, Frederic Dan, 1819-190 The relations and duties of the rich to th poor, and especially to this charity. A ser mon delivered in behalf of the Warre Street Chapel at the ninth anniversary the opening of the building, January 2 1845. Boston: Dutton and Wentwort 1845. 15 p. CBPac; MBAU; MiD-B NNG; OO. 45-3362

Huntington, Frederic Dan, 1819-1904 The relations and duties of the rich to th poor, and especially to this charity. A ser mon delivered in behalf of the Warre Street Chapel at the ninth anniversary o the opening of the building, January 2 1845. Second edition. Boston: Dutto and Wentworth, 1845. 15 p. NN; OCHF 45-3363

Huntington, Jabez Williams, 1788 1847. Speech of Mr. Huntington, of Con necticut, on the resolution for th annexation of Texas to the United States and its admission as a state, into th union. Delivered in the Senate, Februar 21 and 22, 1845. [Washington? 1845] 1 p. CtY; DLC; MBAt; MHi; NNC. 45 3364

Huntington, William, 1745-1813. Th Arminian skeleton, or the Arminian dis sected and anatomized. Charleston, Il linois: B. Monroe and W.W. Bishop printers, 1845. 180 p. ICN; MWA; NN 45-3365

Huntington, Zebulon, 1766-1851. The exile of Connecticut: composed by him self in the decline of life. Being a concise narrative of the life of Zebulon Hun tington, till almost four score years o

...ge. [Enfield? New Hampshire, 1845?]
8 p. DLC; DSI. 45-3366

Hurlbut, Elisha P. Essays on human
...ghts and their political guaranties. By
...P. Hurlbut, Counselor at law in the city
...f New York. New York: Greely and Mc-
...lrath, 1845. 219 p. A-Ar; CtHC; OO;
...U; ScU. 45-3367

Hurwitz, Hyman, 1770-1844. Hebrew
...ales, selected and translated from the
...ritings of the ancient Hebrew sages.
...oston: William Crosby, 1845. 100 p.
...LM; LU; NN; OC; WM. 45-3368

Hurwitz, Hyman, 1770-1844. Hebrew
...ales, selected and translated from the
...ritings of the ancient Hebrew sages.
...hiladelphia: Jewish Publication
...ociety, 1845. 14-120 p. OCH. 45-3369

Hutchins' improved almanac... for the
...ear of our Lord, 1846, being the second
...fter bissextile, or leap year, and the
...eventith year of American inde-
...endence... By David Young. New York:
...I. and S. Raynor, [1845] MWA; NjMo;
...VHi. 45-3370

Hutchins' improved for 1846. By David
Young. New York: Charles Small, [1845]
MWA. 45-3371

The hyacinth: or affection's gift. A
christmas, new years and birthday
present for 1846. Philadelphia: Henry F.
Anners, [1845-1855] 11 v. FSar; KU;
MWA; NIC. 45-3372

Hyde, Orson. Speech of Mr. Orson,
delivered before the High Priest's
quorum in Nauvoo, April 27, 1845, upon
the course and conduct of Mr. Sidney
Rigdon... Joseph, Illinois: Printed by
John Taylor, 1845. 36 p. CSmH; NN. 45-
3373

Hymns for the use of Sabbath schools;
published for the Sabbath School Missionary Board of Central New York.
Utica: Press of Bennett, Backus and
Hawley, 1845. 32 p. KHi; MWA. 45-3374

Hymns of the Holy Church. Hartford:
Henry S. Parsons, 127 p. NYStJ. 45-3375

I

I wish father was rich. Boston: Sabbath School Society, 1845. 16 p. MLex. 45-3376

Ide, George Barton, 1804-1872. The ministry demanded by the present crisis. Philadelphia: American Baptist Publication Society, [1845] 102 p. DLC; ICU; MiU; NRAB; PPT. 45-3377

Illinois. Abolition petitions: report of the minority of the committee to whom were refereed the different petitions in relation to the people of color. [Springfield, 1845] 2 p. WHi. 45-3378

Illinois. An act to establish and maintain common schools in the state of Illinois: passed the General Assembly of said state at their session. Springfield: Walters and Weber, 1845. 26 p. ICHi; MB. 45-3379

Illinois. Addressing the judges out of office... preamble and resolutions removing the chief justice and associate justices of the supreme court, with pledge of re-election at reduced salaries for the purpose of financial retrenchment. [Springfield, 1845] 1 p. WHi. 45-3380

Illinois. Communication from the Governor, of Illinois, in relation to the late mission of Messrs. Leavitt and Oakley to London, on business connected with the Illinois and Michigan Canal. [Springfield, 1845] 3 p. WHi. 45-3381

Illinois. Communication from the Governor, of Illinois, transmitting a letter to the Senate from Baring Brothers and company, and Magniac, Jardiner and company, of London, January 2, 184. [Springfield, 1845] 7 p. WHi. 45-3382

Illinois. Communication from the Governor, Thomas Ford, in relation to the Northern Cross Railroad; also submitting to the General Assembly sundry documents and letters in relation to the late system of internal improvement. Springfield, 1845. 34 p. WHi. 45-3383

Illinois. Communication from the Governor, Thomas Ford, on state indebt-edness. [Springfield, 1845] 2 p. WHi. 45-3384

Illinois. In relation to the Mormon war at Nauvoo, Hancock County. February 26, 1845. [Springfield, 1845] 2 p. WHi. 45-3385

Illinois. Indictment against Richard Eels for aiding a negro slave belonging to a person in Missouri to escape. [Springfield, 1845] 1 p. WHi. 45-3386

Illinois. Journal of the House of Representatives of the fourteenth General Assembly of the state of Illinois at thier regular session, begun and held at Springfield. December 2, 1844 Springfield: Walters and Weber, [1845] CSmH. 45-3387

Illinois. Laws of the state of Illinois, passed by the fourteenth General Assembly, at their regular session, began [sic] and held at Springfield, December 2nd, 1844. Springfield: Walters and Weber, 1845. 384 p. A-SC; IaU-L; In-SC; MdBB; RPL. 45-3388

Illinois. The memorial of a committee of the state school convention, held at Peoria in October last, upon the subject of common school education, December 7, 1844. Springfield: Walters and Weber, [1845] 16 p. DLC; IHL; MH. 45-3389

Illinois. Relinquishment of a portion of the salaries of the supreme judges. [Springfield, 1845] 8 p. WHi. 45-3390

Illinois. Report of minority and majority of Penitentiary committee. [Springfield, 1845] 3 p. WHi. 45-3391

Illinois. Report of the auditor in relation to the quantity of lands taxable, increase of state revenue by taking lands taxes from counties, statistical information relating to amount of taxes received from each county for 1843 and 1844, etc. [Springfield, 1845] WHi. 45-3392

Illinois. Report of the auditor of public accounts. Springfield. Walter and Weber, 1845. 8 p. IHi. 45-3393

Illinois. Report of the Committee on finance to which was referred so much on the message of the Governor as relates to the state debt, increased taxation, and to which has also been referred various bills and resolutions on the subject of the state debt. January 13, 1845. [Springfield, 1845] 14 p. IHi; WHi. 45-3394

Illinois. Report on the State Bank of Illinois. [Springfield, 1845] 2 p. WHi. 45-3395

Illinois. Reports made to the House of Representatives of the state of Illinois at their session begun and held at Springfield, December 2, 1844. 2 v. in 1. Springfield: Walters and Weber, 1845. Mi. 45-3396

Illinois. Reports made to the Senate and House of Representatives of the state of Illinois, at their session begun and held at Springfield, December 2, 1844. New edition. Springfield: Walters and Weber, 1845. 2 v. in 1. Mi. 45-3397

Illinois. Revised statutes of the state of Illinois, adopted by the General Assembly of said state, at its regular session held in the years, 1844-1845. Together with an appendix... Springfield: Walters and Weber, pritners, 1845. DLC; IU; NcD; PPT; WaU-L. 45-3398

Illinois. Revised statutes of the state of Illinois, adopted by the General Assembly of said state, at its regular session, held in the years, A.D., 1844-45. Revised and prepared by M. Brayman. Springfield: Williams Walters, 1845. 749 p. Az; CoU; CSt; IU; MdBB. 45-3399

Illinois. Saline lands. Report from the auditor in relation to the avails arising from the saline lands, January 28, 1845. [Springfield, 1845] 4 p. WHi. 45-3400

Illinois. School Convention, 1844. The memorial of a committee of the state school convention, held at Peoria in October last, upon the subject of common school education. Springfield, 1845. 30 p. WHi. 45-3401

Illinois. Tract books and record of town lots of the state: communication from the auditor, January 6, 1845. [Springfield, 1845] 4 p. WHi. 45-3402

Illinois College. Catalogue of the officers and students for the year ending June, 1845. Springfield: Goudy's Job office, 1845. 19 p. IHi. 45-3403

The illustrated Bible history; a compilation of the important events recorded in the Old and New Testaments. New York: Wilson and company, 1845. MH; NNC; TNV. 45-3404

The illustrated family magazine. For the diffusion of useful knowledge. Boston: Bradbury, Soden and company, 1845-1846. 4 v. in 2. DLC; MB; MSBHi; NIC; RWe. 45-3405

Imitatio Christi. The following of Christ, in four books by Thomas A. Kempis translated from the original Latin by the Rt. Rev. and Ven. Richard Challoner. Second American edition. Baltimore: J. Murphy, 1845. 551 p. MdBD. 45-3406

Imitatio Christi. Imitation of Christ rendered into English from the original Latin by Johy Payne. New edition. Boston: Gould, 1845. 228 p. PU. 45-3407

Imposure, deception, credulity. Philadelphia, 1845. PPPH-I. 45-3408

Incidents of travel. New York: Harper, 1845. 2 v. MiKL. 45-3409

Indiana. Annual report of the auditor of the state of Indiana, for the fiscal year ending October 31, 1845. Indianapolis: J.P. Chapman, 1845. InU; WHi. 45-3410

Indiana. Annual report of the commissioners and superintendent on the erection of the hospital, to the governor of the state of Indianapolis, 1845. OO; WHi 45-3411

Indiana. Annual report of the superintendent of the Indiana state prison to the General Assembly. December 8, 184! Indianapolis: J.P. Chapman, 1845. InU 45-3412

Indiana. Annual report of the treausre of the state to the General Assembly. Indianapolis: J.P. Chapman, 1845. InU WHi. 45-3413

Indiana. Catalogue of the trustees, officers and students of the University a Bloomington, 1844. Bloomington Printed by Christian Record office, 184! MH; PPPrHi. 45-3414

Indiana. Circular of the trustees of the Indiana Asylum for the Education of the Deaf and Dumb, and the rules of internal economy. Indianapolis: G.A. and J.P Chapman, 1845. 8 p. In; MB; PPL; WHi 45-3415

Indiana. Communication from the Governor and memorial of bondholder to the General Assembly. January, 1846 Indianapolis, 1845. 6 p. WHi. 45-3416

Indiana. Communication from the Governor in reply to a resolution of the Senate in relation to Charles Butler agent for foreign bondholders. December 27, 1845. Indianapolis, 1845. 5 p MiD-B; WHi. 45-3417

Indiana. Communication of the Agent of the Foreign Holders of Indiana state bonds to His Excellency James White

:omb, governor of Indiana, December, 1845. Indianapolis, 1845. 24 p. WHi. 45-3418

Indiana. Documents of the twenty-ninth session of the General Assembly of the state of Indiana, begun and held at the town of Indianapolis, December 2, 1844. Indianapolis: J.P. Chapman, 1845. InFtw. 45-3419

Indiana. An enumeration of the white male inhabitants over twenty one years of age, reported to the House by the auditor of the state. [Indianapolis, 1845] 3 p. WHi. 45-3420

Indiana. General laws of the state of Indiana, passed at the twenty-ninth session of the General Assembly begun on the first Monday in December, 1844. Indianapolis: J.P. Chapman, 1845. 112 p. A-SC Az; IaHi; L; OCLaw. 45-3421

Indiana. Governor's message delivered to the General Assembly. December 2, 1845. Indianapolis, 1845. 12 p. WHi. 45-3422

Indiana. Journal of the House of Representatives of the state of Indiana, during the thirtieth session of the General Assembly. Indianapolis: J.P. Chapman, 1845. InLB; LU; WHi. 45-3423

Indiana. Journal of the Indiana State Senate, during the thirtieth of the General Assembly, commencing December 1, 1845. Indianapolis: J.F. Chapman, 1845. 754 p. ICU; InGrD; LU. 45-3424

Indiana. Laws of a local nature, passed and published at the twenty-ninth session of the General Assembly of the state of Indiana, begun at Indianapolis on the first Monday in December, 1844. Indianapolis: J.P. Chapman, 1845. 314 p. Ar-SC; Ia; MdBB; Nj. 45-3425

Indiana. Laws of a local nature, passed and published at the twenty-ninth session of the General Assembly of the state of Indiana. Begun at Indianapolis on the first Monday in December, 1844. Indianapolis: J.P. Chapman, 1845. 314 p. Ar-SC; Ia; In-SC; Nb; W. 45-3426

Indiana. Message of the Governor and accompanying documents from bondholders on the subject of the state debt, January 3, 1845. Indianapolis, 1845. 6 p. WHi. 45-3427

Indiana. Message of the governor, delivered to the General Assembly of the state of Indiana, December 2, 1845. Indianapolis: J.P. Chapman, 1845. In; WHi. 45-3428

Indiana. Report of the Adjutant general's office. Indianapolis, 1845-. IGJ; MB; WHi. 45-3429

Indiana. Report of the auditor of the state in answer to a resolution of the Senate relating to canals and other internal improvements. Indianapolis, 1845. WHi. 45-3430

Indiana. Report of the Committee [Senate] on education in relation to the deaf and dumb. Indianapolis: G.A. and J.P. Chapman, 1845. DSG. 45-3431

Indiana. Report of the state bank showing their condition on the third Saturday in November, 1844. Indianapolis: J.P. Chapman, 1845. InU; WHi. 45-3432

Indiana. Report on the subject of hospitals for the insane, by John Evans, M.D. made to the Commissioners of the Lunatic Asylum of Indiana, June 22, 1845. Indianapolis, 1845. 10 p. WHi. 45-3433

Indiana. Report to the General Assembly by the Department of Public Instruction. Indianapolis: J.P. Chapman, 1845. InU; WHi. 45-3434

Indiana. Reports of the majority and minority of the committee on canals and internal improvements on a resolution of the Senate in relation to the Wabash and Erie Canal, January 4, 1845. Indianapolis, 1845. In; InU; WHi. 45-3435

Indiana. Reports of the majority and minority of the Committee on elections of the House on a charge of defalcation against Allen T. Rose of Clay County, January, 1845. Indianapolis, 1845. 32 p. WHi. 45-3436

Indiana. Second Report of the president of the state bank to the general assembly. December, 1845. Indianapolis: J.P. Chapman, 1845. InU. 45-3437

Indiana. University. Catalogue... Bloomington, 1845. 16 p. MH. 45-3438

Indiana Asbury University, Greencastle. First quinquennial catalogue of the Platonean Society of Asbury University. Greencastle, 1845. 14 p. NoLoc. 45-3439

Indiana Medical College, La Porte, Indiana. Annual circular and catalogue of the officers and students of the La Porte University, session, 1844-1845. Chicago: J. Campbell, 1845. DLC; PPC. 45-3440

Ingersoll, Charles Jared, 1782-1862 Historical sketch of the second war between the United States of America and Great Britain, declared by an act of congress, June 18, 1812, and concluded b peace, February 15, 1815. Philadelphia Lea and Blanchard, 1845-1849. 2 v. GU MNe; MWA; PRHi; ViRU. 45-3441

Ingersoll, Charles Jared, 1782-1862 Speech of Mr. Ingersoll, of Pennsylvania on the annexation of Texas, delivered in the House, January 3, 1845 [Washington, 1845] 4 p. CtY; TxHU. 45 3442

Ingersoll, George Goldthwait, 1796 1863. Home a thanksgiving sermon preached at King's Chapel. Boston: Wil liam Crosby and H.P. Nichols, 1845. 24 p DLC; MBAt; MnHi; VtU; WHi. 45-344

Ingersoll, George Goldthwait, 1796 1863. Unitarianism the "Way of the Lord." First series. Boston: James Mun roe and comapny, 1845. 46 p. ICMe IEG; MBC; MeB; RP. 45-3444

Ingraham, Joseph Holt, 1809-1860. The adventures of Will Wizard. Corporal o the Saccarapa Volunteers. Boston: H.L Williams, 1845. 32 p. MeU; PU. 45-344

Ingraham, Joseph Holt, 1809-1860 Alice May, and Bruising Bill. Boston Gleason's Publishing Hall, 1845. 50 p CtY; MeB; MnU; NSmb; ViU. 45-3446

Ingraham, Joseph Holt, 1809-1860 Bertrand; or the story of Marie de Heywode; being a sequal to Marie the fugitive... Boston: H.L. Williams, 1845 40 p. CtY; RPB. 45-3447

Ingraham, Joseph Holt, 1809-1860.

Black Ralph; or the helmsman of Hurlgate! A tale. Boston: H.L. Williams at the Yankee office, 1845. 47 p. CtY; InU; MB; RPB. 45-3448

Ingraham, Joseph Holt, 1809-1860. Charles Blackford; or the adventures of a student in search of a profession. Boston: Yankee office, 1845. 48 p. CtY; ICU; MAbD; MeU; MH. 45-3449

Ingraham, Joseph Holt, 1809-1860. Clipper yacht; or Moloch, the money lender! a tale of London and the Thames. Boston: H.L. Williams, 1845. 54 p. CU; KEmT; MiD-B; NjR. 45-3450

Ingraham, Joseph Holt, 1809-1860. The cruiser of the mist. New York: Burgess, Stringer and company, 1845. 52 p. CSmH; MeU; MsU. 45-3451

Ingraham, Joseph Holt, 1809-1860. The dancing feather; and its sequel Morris Graeme... New York and Boston: H.L. Williams, 1845-1847. 92 p. DHU; DLC; MsU; NjP; OClWHi. 45-3452

Ingraham, Joseph Holt, 1809-1860. The dancing feather, or the amateur free booters. Boston: H.L. Williams, 1845. 48 p. CtY; DLC; MeU; OClWHi. 45-3453

Ingraham, Joseph Holt, 1809-1860. Edward Austin; or the hunting flask. A tale of the forest and town. Boston: F. Gleason, 1845. 66 p. LNH. 45-3454

Ingraham, Joseph Holt, 1809-1860. Fleming Field; or the young artisan. A tale of the days of the stamp act. New York: Burgess, Stringer and company, 1845. 96 p. MeU; MWA; MWH; NcD. 45-3455

Ingraham, Joseph Holt, 1809-1860. Forrestal; or the light of the reef. A romance of the blue waters. Boston: H.L. Williams, 1845. 140 p. CtY; MeB; PU; TxU; ViU. 45-3456

Ingraham, Joseph Holt, 1809-1860. Frank Rivers; or the dangers of the town. Boston: Yankee office, 1845. 47 p. TxU. 45-3457

Ingraham, Joseph Holt, 1809-1860. Freemantle; or the privateersman; a nautical romance of the last war. Boston: George W. Reeding and company, 1845. 46 p. ICU; MH. 45-3458

Ingraham, Joseph Holt, 1809-1860. Grace Weldon; or Frederica, the bonnet girl. Boston: H.L. Williams, 1845. 108 p. DLC; MeU; MnU. 45-3459

Ingraham, Joseph Holt, 1809-1860. Harry Harefoot; or the three temptations. A story of city scenes. Boston: H.L. Williams, 1845. 61 p. CtY; ICU; MnU; PU; ViU. 45-3460

Ingraham, Joseph Holt, 1809-1860. Henry Howard; or the noes make one yes. Boston: Henry L. Williams, 1845. 32 p. DLC; MeU; NcD; RPB. 45-3461

Ingraham, Joseph Holt, 1809-1860. Herman de Ruyter; or the mystery unveiled. Being a sequel to the beautiful cigar vender. Boston: Yankee office, 1845. 48 p. CtY. 45-3462

Ingraham, Joseph Holt, 1809-1860. Josephene; or the maid of the gulf. New York: Dick and Fitzgerald, [1845?] 95 p. ViU. 45-3463

Ingraham, Joseph Holt, 1809-1860. The

knights of seven lands. Boston: F. Gleason, 1845. 64 p. CtY; ICU; NjP; NNC; PU. 45-3464

Ingraham, Joseph Holt, 1809-1860. Marie; or the fugitive. A romance of Mount Benedict. Boston: H.L. Williams, 1845. MeB; NcAS; RPB. 45-3465

Ingraham, Joseph Holt, 1809-1860. Mary Wilbur; or the deacon and the widow's daughter. Boston: Yankee office, 1845. CtY; NCD; RPB; ViU. 45-3466

Ingraham, Joseph Holt, 1809-1860. The mast ship; or the bombardment of Falmouth. Boston H.L. Williams, 1845. 50 p. CtY; MeU; ViU. 45-3467

Ingraham, Joseph Holt, 1809-1860. The midshipman, on the couvette and brigantine; a tale of land and sea. Boston: Gleason's Publishing Hall, 1845. 64 p. CtY; IaU; MB; MH; PU. 45-3468

Ingraham, Joseph Holt, 1809-1860. Montezuma, the serf; or the revolt of the Mexitili. A tale of the last days of the Aztec Dynasty. Boston: H.L. Williams, 1845. 2 v. CSmH; DLC; IEN; RPB; TxDaM. 45-3469

Ingraham, Joseph Holt, 1809-1860. Morris Graeme; or the cruise of the sea slipper. A sequel to the dancing feather. Boston: H.L. Williams, 1845. 50 p. ICU; RPB. 45-3470

Ingraham, Joseph Holt, 1809-1860. Neal Nelson; or the siege of Boston: A tale of the revolution. Boston: Henry L. Williams, 1845. 48 p. KEmT; MH. 45-3471

Ingraham, Joseph Holt, 1809-1860. Norman; or the privateersman's bride. A sequel to freemantle. Boston: Yankee office, 1845. 43 p. CtY; DLC; PU; ViU. 45-3472

Ingraham, Joseph Holt, 1809-1860. Paul Deverell; or two judgements for one crime. A tale of the present day. Boston: H.L. Williams, 1845. 72 p. CtY; MeU; NNC; PU; RPB. 45-3473

Ingraham, Joseph Holt, 1809-1860. The pirate chief; or the cutter of the ocean. New York: Garrett, [1845?] 99 p. NjP. 45-3474

Ingraham, Joseph Holt, 1809-1860. Rafael; or the twice condemned. A tale of Key West. [Boston: H.L. Williams, 1845] 47 p. DLC; ICU; MeU; MH; MWA. 45-3475

Ingraham, Joseph Holt, 1809-1860. A romance of the sunny south; or feathers from a traveller's wing... Boston: H.L. Williams, 1845. MeU; TxDaM. 45-3476

Ingraham, Joseph Holt, 1809-1860. Scarlet feather; or the young chief of the Abenaquies. A romance of the wilderness of Maine. Boston: F. Gleason, 1845. 66 p. CtY; MWA; NN; PU; RPB. 45-3477

Ingraham, Joseph Holt, 1809-1860. The Spanish galleon; or the pirate of the Mediterranean. A romance of the Corsair Kidd. Boston: F. Gleason, 1845. 64 p. ICU; MB; MH; NcAS; ViU. 45-3478

Ingraham, Joseph Holt, 1809-1860. Will Terril; or the adventures of a young gentleman born in a cellar... Boston: Yankee office, 1845. 48 p. MeU; MH. 45-3479

Ingraham, Joseph Holt, 1809-1860. The wing of the wind: a novelette of the sea. New York: Burgess, Stringer and company, 1845. 96 p. DLC; MeU; MnU; NNC; ViU. 45-3480

Ingram, J.K. The pirate's revenge or a tale of Don Pedro and Miss Lois Maynard. Boston: Wright's Steam Power Press, 1845. DLC. 45-3481

Innes, William. Letter addressed to an approving but undecided beaver. From London edition. Boston: Sabbath School Society, 1845. CtHC; OO. 45-3482

An inquiry into the causes and origin of slavery in the United States. No. 4. By an American citizen. To which is prefixed a letter from a member of congress, to the author. Philadelphia: W.S. Young, printer, 1845. 8 p. MH; NIC. 45-3483

An inquiry into the propriety of granting charters of incorporation for manufacturing and other puposes in South Carolina. By one of the people. Charleston: Printed by Walker and Burke, 1845. 14 p. A-Ar. 45-3484

The investigator and advocate of independence, science, religion, literature, etc. [Washington: C. Drew, 1845-1846.] 2 v. DLC; MBC; MdBP NBu. 45-3485

Iowa. Journal of the convention for the formation of a constitution for the state of Iowa, begun and held at Iowa City. Iowa City: Jesse Williams, 1845. 224 p. IaHi; MH-L. 45-3486

Iowa. Journal of the council of the seventh Legislative Assembly of the Territory of Iowa. Iowa City: Williams and Palmer, 1845. 231 p. DLC; Ia; IaU-L. 45-3487

Iowa. Journal of the House of Representatives of the Seventh Legislative Assembly of the Territory of Iowa. Fort Madison, Iowa: R. Wilson Albright, 1845. 255 p. Ia. 45-3488

Iowa. Laws of Iowa. Passed by the extra session of the Legislative Assembly which commenced on the 17th day of June 1844. Iowa City: Williams and Palmer, 1845. 159 p. IaCrM; In-SC. 45-3489

Iowa. Laws passed at extra session of Legislative Assembly, begun June, 1844, also the laws of the regular session. Iowa City: Williams and Palmer, 1845. 157 p. IaCr; MiL; Nj; NNLI. 45-3490

Iowa. University. Extracts from the laws of Iowa in regard to Iowa City University, chapter 41. Iowa City, 1845. 8 p. IaCrM. 45-3491

Ireland, John, 1761-1842. The shipwrecked orphans: a true narrative of the shipwreck and sufferings of John Ireland and William Doyley. Written by John Ireland. New Haven: S. Babcock, [1845] 64 p. CtY; MBAt; MH. 45-3492

Irish eloquence. The speeches of the celebrated Irish orators, Philips, Curran, Gratton... and Robert Emmett. Philadelphia: E.C. and J. Biddle, 1845. 178, 370 p. LU; MeBaT; MH; NcD; PNT. 45-3493

Irving, Edward, 1792-1834. Interpretations of Old Testament prophecies quoted in the new. By a celebrated English divine. First American edition. Published by Rev. Isaac P. Labogh. New York: Marks and Craft, 1845. 372 p.

CtHC; GDecCT; KyLoP; NNG; ViRut. 45-3494

Irving, Washington, 1783-1859. Astoria; or anecdotes of an enterprise beyond the Rocky Mountains. New York: Syndicate Trading Company, [1845] 952 p. PWerv. 45-3495

Irving, Washington, 1783-1859. Bracebridge Hall; or the humorists. By Geoffrey Crayon. New York, 1845. MdAN. 45-3496

Is the diocese of New York vacant. [New York, 1845] 58 p. MB; NN. 45-3497

Isaacs, Nicholas Peter, b. 1784. Twenty years before the mast; or life in the forecastle... New York: J.P. Beckwith, 1845. 199 p. DLC; FOA; ICN; MBAt; MiD-B. 45-3498

Isabel; or the trials of the heart. A tale for the young. New York: Harper and brothers, 1845. 182 p. CtY; DLC; PU; RPE; Viu. 45-3499

The Italian walt, arranged for the pianoforte, by an amateur. Boston, 1845. 2 p. MH. 45-3500

Ithaca Academy. Catalogue of the trustees, teachers, and students of the Ithaca Academy, for the year ending July 23 1845. Ithaca, New York: Mack, Andrus and company, printers, 1845. 16 p NIDHi; NIT. 45-3501

Ives, Elam, 1802-1864. Beethoven collection of sacred music; comprising themes... New edition. New York: Paine and Burgess, 1845. NN. 45-3502

Ives, Elam, 1802-1864. The musical spelling book: a new method of instruction in the rudiments of music; together with musical recreations as a relief from study. New York: Paine and Burgess 1845. CtHWatk; CtY; ICN; MH; NNUT 45-3503

Ives, Eli. New method, which teaches how to make vegetable manure, by a course of high fermentation, in fifteen days, without cattle, as good and more durable than farm manure; to appropriate it to the nature of soils and families of plants, and with great economy... Second edition revised and corrected. New York: Redfield and Savage, 1845. 90 p. MWA. 45-3504

J

Jackson, Andrew, 1767-1845. A sketch of the life of General Andrew Jackson; and of the battle of New Orleans, with an engraving of the battleground, written for the Knickerbocker Magazine. New York: I. Smith Homans, 1845. 16 p. ICN; MiD-B; MWA; NcU; WHi. 45-3505

Jackson, Charles Thomas, 1805-1880. Dr. Charles T. Jackson's report to the trustees of Lake Superior Copper Company. November, 1845. Boston: Beals and Green, 1845. 19 p. DLC; MB; MiD-B; NNE; GNNM; RPB. 45-3506

Jackson, Charles Thomas, 1805-1880. Views and map, illustrative of the scenery and geology of the state of New Hampshire. Boston: Thurston, Torry and company, 1845. 20 p. CtY; ICJ; MBAt; MH-Z; OCU. 45-3507

Jackson, Daniel, b. 1790. Alonzo and Melissa; or the unfeeling father, a tale founded on facts. New York: Leavitt and Allen brothers, 1845. 187 p. RPB. 45-3508

Jackson, Isaac Wilber, 1805-1877. Elements of conic sections. Compiled by I.W. Jackson. Second edition. Albany: O. Steele, 1845. 87 p. CtY; DLC; NCH; PU; RPB. 45-3509

Jackson, Samuel, 1787-1872. Lecture, introductory to a course on the institutes of medicine, in the University of Pennsylvania, delivered November 11, 1845. Philadelphia: Printed by John Young, 1845. 32 p. DNLM; MBAt; NBMS; PHi; PPM. 45-3510

Jackson, William, b. 1794. Christian's legacy: with an appendix, containing a compendium of the Holy Bible. Designed for making the reading and study of the Holy Scriptures more easy... Ninth edition. Philadelphia: Published by the author, 1845. KWiU. 45-3511

Jacobs, Friedrich, 1764-1847. First part of Jacob's Latin reader, adapted to Bullion's Latin grammar. New York, 1845. MiD; NBuG; NRU; OrU; OUrC. 45-3512

Jacobs, Friedrich, 1764-1847. Greek reader, selected principally from the work of Friedrich Jacobs, with English notes... New York: Harper and brothers, 1845. 614 p. MeHi; PAtM; PMA. 45-3513

Jacobs, Friedrich, 1764-1847. Greek reader, with improvements, additional notes, and corrections, by David Patterson. Tenth New York edition from the ninth German edition, corrected and improved, with numerous notes, additions and alterations not in any former edition. New York: W.E. Dean, 1845. 214, 97 p. DLC; KAStB; TxSaWi; ViL. 45-3514

Jacobs, Friedrich, 1764-1847. Greek reader, with improvements, additional notes, and corrections, by David Patterson. Tenth New York edition from the ninth German edition, corrected and improved, with numerous notes, additions and alterations not in any former edition. Philadelphia: J.B. Lippincott and company, 1845. 214, 97 p. IaDaSA; LNVrS; OSW; TxU. 45-3515

Jacobs, Friedrich, 1764-1847. Latin reader by Friedrich Jacobs and William Doring. With notes and illustrations partly translated from the German, and partly drawn from other sources, by John D. Ogilby. Eighth edition from the seventh German edition. New York: W.E. Dean, 1845. DLC; KyBC; MiD; NBuG. 45-3516

Jacobs, Friedrich, 1764-1847. Latin reader. First part with vocabulary and English notes for the use of schools, academies, and colleges. Philadelphia: Uriah Hunt and son, 1845. 259 p. IaShen; ScOrAM. 45-3517

Jahr, Gottlieb Heinrich Georg, 1800-1875. A short elementary treatise upon homoepathia. Second French edition. Translated by Edward Bayard. New York: William Radde, 1845. 90 p. ICJ; MBM; NNN. 45-3518

James, George Payne Rainsford, 1799-1860. The ancient regime. A tale. New York: Harper and brothers, 1845. 2 v. in 1. KvU; MH; NjP; ScU. 45-3519

James, George Payne Rainsford, 1799-1860. Arrah Neil; or times of old. A romance. New York: Harper, 1845. 139 p. NNC. 45-3520

James, George Payne Rainsford, 1799-1860. The brigand. A romance. New York: Farmer and Daggers, 1845. 176 p. MeB; ViU. 45-3521

James, George Payne Rainsford, 1799-1860. Charles Tyrrell; or the bitter blood New York: Harper and brothers, 1845. 2 v. in 1. LNH; PU. 45-3522

James, George Payne Rainsford, 1799-1860. The history of Charlemagne. New York: Harper and brothers, 1845. InCW MsU; OT; RWe; ScDuE. 45-3523

James, George Payne Rainsford, 1799-1860. The history of chivalry. New York Harper and brothers, 1845. 342 p. MeAu MoSM; NbOC; OCX; OWoc. 45-3524

James, George Payne Rainsford, 1799-1860. The man-at-arms; or Henry de Cerons; a romance. New York: Harper and brothers, 1845. 2 v. IaDuC; NN; PU 45-3525

James, George Payne Rainsford, 1799-1860. The smuggler, a tale. New York: Harper and brothers, 1845. DLC; MBL; MH; NRMA. 45-3526

James, John Angell, 1785-1859. Elizabeth Bales: a pattern for Sunday school teachers. New York, [1845?] 89 p ICP. 45-3527

James, John Angell, 1785-1859. The flower faded; or memoir of Clementine Cuvier, daughter of Baron Cuvier; with reflections by J.A. Angell. From the tenth London edition. New York: John S. Taylor and company, 1845. 147 p. MLow; NbCrD. 45-3528

James, John Angell, 1785-1859. Grateful recollections. An address to the church assembling in Carr's Lane, Birningham, on completing the fortieth year of his pastorate. Birminham: Hudon, 1845. 70 p. MH. 45-3529

James, John Angell, 1785-1859. The narriage ring: or how to make home happy. Ten thousand. Boston: Gould, Kendall and Lincoln, 1845. 128 p. OO. 45-3530

James, John Angell, 1785-1859. The narriage ring: or how to make home happy. Twelve thousand. Boston: Gould, Kendall and Lincoln, 1845. 128 p. CoCsC. 45-3531

James, John Angell, 1785-1859. The young man from home. New York: American Tract Society, [1845] 231 p. AU; MoU. 45-3532

James, John Angell, 1785-1859. The young man from home. New York: D. Appleton and company, 1845. 195 p. MeBa; MiGr; NB. 45-3533

James River and Kanawha Company, Richmond, Virginia. Amended regulations for the James River and Kanawha Canal, adopted by the body of stockholders at their tenth annual meeting in December, 1844, together with tables of tolls and distances. Richmond: Sheperd and Colin, 1845. 46 p. IU; MH; Vi; ViU. 45-3534

Jameson, Anna Brownell Murphy, 1794-1860. Memoirs of celebrated female sovereigns. New York: Harper and brothers, 1845. 2 v. IGK; MMen; NcWsS; ODa; WNaE. 45-3535

Jameson, Anna Brownell Murphy, 1794-1860. Memoirs of the early Italian painters. Boston: Houghton, Osgood and company, 1845. 502 p. IQ. 45-3536

Jamieson, Alexander. A grammar of rhetoric and polite literature: comprehending the principles of language and style, the elements of taste and criticism; with rules for the study of composition and eloquence. Twenty-fifth edition. New Haven: A.H. Malthy, 1845. 306 p. LNUrs; OO. 45-3537

Jarman, Thomas, 1800-1860. A treatise on wills. First American edition. With notes and references to American decisions, by J.C. Perkins, esq. Boston: C.C. Little and J. Brown, 1845. 2 v. DLC; GU-L; MWiW; PP; WU-L. 45-3538

Jarvis, Charles Wesley. Songs of fancy, eight in number, original, arranged and adapted. New York, 1845. CtY; MB. 45-3539

Jarvis, Charles Wesley. Songs of the campaign. Eight songs, comic, serious, and amusing. Part I. Philadelphia: Ferrett and company, [1845] MB. 45-3540

Jarvis, Edward, 1803-1884. Lectures on the necessity of the study of physiology, delivered before the American Institute of Instruction, at Hartford, August 22, 1845. Boston: William D. Ticknor and company, 1845. 55, 36 p. Ia; MH; MWA; NjR; NNNAM. 45-3541

Jarvis, Edward, 1803-1884. What shall we do with the insane of the Western Country? [Louisville, 1845] 45 p. DNLM; MHi. 45-3542

Jarvis, Samuel Farmar, 1786-1851. A chronological introduction to the history of the church, being a new inquiry into the true dates of the birth and death of Our Lord and Saviour Jesus Christ; and containing an original harmony of the four Gospels, now first arranged in the order of time. New York: Harper and brothers, 1845. ICU; KMK; LN; OrPD; ScCC. 45-3543

Jay, John, 1817-1894. Facts connected with the presentment of Bishop Onderdonk: a reply to parts of the Bishop's statement. By John Jay, one of the counsel originally employed by the presenting bishops. New York: Stanford and Swords; Philadelphia: G.S. Appleton, 1845. 23 p. CtHT; DLC; MBC; PPM; RNR. 45-3544

Jay, John, 1817-1894. Jay's Pamphlet reviewed, being a brief answer to a reply to parts of the Bishop's statement, by John Jay, a looker on. New York: H.M. Onderdonk, 1845. 12 p. MdToH; MB; CtY; NjR; WHi. 45-3545

Jay, William, 1769-1853. Evening exercises for the closet: for every day in the year. New York: R. Carter, 1845. 2 v. in 1. NNG. 45-3546

Jay, William, 1769-1853. Morning exercises for the closet, for every day in the year. New York: Robert Carter, 1845. 2 v. in 1. CBPSR. 45-3547

Jay, William, 1769-1858. Address delivered before the American Peace Society, at its annual meeting, May 26, 1845. Boston: American Peace Society, 1845. 31 p. IHi; MB; NN; PPPrHI; RPB. 45-3548

Jay, William, 1769-1853. The christian contemplated in a course of lectures delivered in Argyle Chapel, Bath. New York and Pittsburgh: Robert Carter 1845. 380 p. ScCliP. 45-3549

Jayne's medical almanac and guide to health, 1845. Philadelphia: Printed by Dr. D. Jayne and son, 1845. 41 p. MHi MsJS; NSchHi. 45-3550

Jefferson and Company. Memoria proposing an immense saving to government on the Congressional Printing. n.p. [1845?] 11 p. DLC; MNBedf. 45-3551

Jefferson College, Cannonsburg, Pennsylvania. Catalogue of the officers and students of Jefferson College, July, 1845 Pittsburgh: George Parkin, 1845. 16 p PWW. 45-3552

Jeffreys, Henry, 1788-1849. The religious objection to tetotalism. By Archdeacon Jeffreys. Second American edition. Charlottesville, [Virginia Printed at the Intelligencer office, 1845 16 p. MB; NNG; Vi. 45-3553

Jegli, John B. John B. Gegli's Louisville directory. Louisville, Kentucky: J.C Noble, [1845] 3 v. ICHi; ICU. 45-3554

Jenison, Silas H. An address delivered at the annual fair of the Addison County Agricultural Society, October, 1844 Middlebury: J. Cobb, Jr., printer, 1845 MBAt; VtMidSM. 45-3555

Jenkins, John Stilwell, 1818-1852. Life and public services of General Andrew Jackson. Including the most important of his state papers and the eulogy delivered at Washington, June 21, 1845; by George Bancroft. New York and Chicago Franklin Publishing Company, [1845?] MH. 45-3556

Jerram, Jane Elizabeth Holmes. The child's own story book; or tales and dialogues for the nursery. First American from the third London edition. Philadelphia: George S. Appleton; New York: D. Appleton and company, 1845. 192 p. NHem. 45-3557

Jerrold, Douglas William, 1803-1857. The history of St. Giles and St. James. New York: Burgess, Stringer and company, 1845. 202, 24 p. CtY; LNH; MdBP; MH; OFH. 45-3558

Jerrold, Douglas William, 1803-1857. Mrs. Caudle's curtain lectures, By "Punch." With illustrations. Hartford: S. Andrus and son, 1845. 156 p. CtSoP, MNF; NIC; OCX. 45-3559

Jerrold, Douglas William, 1803-1857. Mrs. Caudle's curtain lectures, By "Punch". With illustrations. Philadelphia: Carey and Hart, 1845. 5-42 p. CBPac; MH; PPi; TxDaM. 45-3560

Jerrold, Douglas William, 1803-1857. Mrs. Caudle's curtain lectures, delivered during thirty years, by Mrs. Margaret Caudle, and suffered by Job. New York: E. Winchester, 1845. 30 p. CSfCP; NjR. 45-3561

Jerrold, Douglas William, 1803-1857. Mrs. Caudle's curtain lectures, delivered during thirty years, by Mrs. Margaret Caudle, and suffered by Job, her husband. New York: E. Winchester, 1845. 26 p. MH; MWA; NjR; NN. 45-3562

Jerrold, Douglas William, 1803-1857. Mrs. Caudle's curtain lectures, delivered during thirty years, by Mrs. Margaret Caudle, and suffered by Job, her husband. New York: E. Winchester, 1845. 40 p. CtY; MH; NN. 45-3563

Jerrold, Douglas William, 1803-1857. Mrs. Caudle's curtain lectures, delivered during thirty years, by Mrs. Margaret Caudle, and suffered by Job, her husband. New York: E. Winchester, 1845. 48 p. MH; NN. 45-3564

Jerrold, Douglas William, 1803-1857. Mrs. Caudle's curtain lectures, delivered during thirty years, by Mrs. Margaret Caudle, and suffered by Job, her husband. New York: W. Taylor, 1845. 26 p. MH; NN. 45-3565

Jerrold, Douglas William, 1803-1857. Story of a feather. Philadelphia: Carey and Hart, 1845. 191 p. CtHT-W; MB; MH; NNC; RPA. 45-3566

Jerrold, Douglas William, 1803-1857. Time works wonders; a comedy in five acts... Boston: Saxton and Kelt, 1845. 66 p. CtY; MPiB; NcU; PPL; RPA. 45-3567

Jester. Boston, 1845. v. 1, No. 1. MB. 45-3568

Jester. [Weekly] Boston, 1845. v. 1-. Nu. 1. MB. 45-3569

Jesuits. Constitution of the Jesuites. New York: Sheldon and company, 1845. 522 p. IaPeC. 45-3570

The Jew, at home and abroad... Philadelphia: American Sunday School Union, [1845] 188 p. CoD; DLC; ICP; MWiW; PPLT. 45-3571

Jewett, Charles, 1807-1879. Temperance lyrics. Compiled by Charles Jewett. Boston: Isaac Thompkins, 1845.

48 p. CSmH; CtHWatk; MHi; NN. 45-3572

Jewett, Milo Parker, 1808-1892. The mode and subjects of baptism... Ninth thousand. Stereotype edition. Philadelphia: American Baptist Publication and Sunday School Society, 1845. 108 p. IEuC; KyLoS; MH-AH. 45-3573

Jewsbury, Geraldine Endsor, 1812-1880. Zoe. The history of two lives. New York: Harper and brothers, 1845. 143 p. CtY; IU; NN; TxU; VtU. 45-3574

Jimeson, M.P. An original exhibition of some of the difficulties of Westminster Calvinism. Pittsburgh: Printed by N.M. Poindexter, 1845. 133 p. IaShen; InUpT; PPi; PPins; WvU. 45-3575

Job Caudle's dinner table harangues. Revealed in self defence, by the ghost of Mrs. Caudle. New York: E. Winchester, 1845. 32 p. CtY; MB; MoKU; MWA. 45-3576

Jocelyn, Edwin. A prize essay on the duties of parents in relation to their schools. Written for the Essex County Teachers Association. By Edwin Jocelyn, principal of the Saltonstall School, Salem. Salem: Ives and Pease, 1845. 16 p. IaU; MB; NjR; OO; PHi. 45-3577

John Ronge, the holy coat of treves, and the new German Catholic Church. New York: Harper and brothers, 1845. 172 p. GDecCT; MB; NNUT; VtU; WBeloC. 45-3578

Johnson, Andrew, 1808-1875. Letter of Andrew Johnson, of Tennessee, to his constituents. Washington: J. and G.S. Gideon, printers, 1845. 29 p. DLC MdBP; TKL-Mc. 45-3579

Johnson, Artemas Nixon, b. 1817. The musical class book, for the use of female seminaries, high schools, adult and juvenile singing schools, and private classes. Boston: George P. Read, 1845. 30 p. MB; MH; NNUT. 45-3580

Johnson, Elizabeth, fl. 1834. Exercise for private devotion. Second edition Boston: Simpkins, 1845. IGK; MB MBC; MB-FA. 45-3581

Johnson, Herschel Vespasian, 1812 1880. Oration on the life and character o Andrew Jackson, delivered at the re quest of the citizens of Baldwin County in the representative chamber, at Mil ledgeville, Georgia, on July 16, 1845 Milledgeville, 1845. 16 p. DLC; NcD. 45 3582

Johnson, Lorenzo Dow, 1805-1867 Memoria technica; or the art of memory Lowell: Stearns and Taylor, 1845. 36 p. 7 p. CtY; MWA; Nh. 45-3583

Johnson, Lorenzo Dow, 1805-1867 Memoria technica; or the art of memory New edition. Lowell: Stearns and Taylor 1845. 36 p. MB; MH. 45-3584

Johnson, Samuel Roosevelt, 1802-1873 O worship the Lord in the beauty of holi ness. A sermon at the consecration of St Mary's Church, Delphi, Indiana, o Thursday, August 21, 1845. New York Stanford and Swords, 1845. In; MH-AH NNC; RPB. 45-3585

Johnson, T.W. A brief history of the rise and progress of the temperance reform with historical facts... also, a condensed history of the causes and events of the Irish rebellion of '98... Glen's Falls: Strong, 1845. 56 p. NCH; PPM; Vi. 45-3586

Johnson, Walter Rogers, 1794-1852. Abstract of Professor Johnson's report to the secretary of the Navy of the United States respecting forest improvement coal. New York: George F. Nesbitt, 1845. 8 p. M; MH; MH-BA. 45-3587

Johnson, Walter Rogers, 1794-1852. On the Nile aulluvium of Nubia. Extract of a letter from Dr. Richard Lepsius... to Dr. S.G. Morton, relative to the language of the Bishareens of Nubia, and the alluvial deposits of the Nile. With an analysis of those deposits. [Philadelphia, 1845] 8 p. DLC; IU; MB; PPAN; RPB. 45-3588

Johnson, Walter Rogers, 1794-1852. A report to the navy department of the United States on American coals, applicable to steam navigation and to other purposes. Extracted from the American Journal of Science. New Haven: Printed by B.L. Hamlen, 1845. 28 p. DLC; TxU. 45-3589

Johnson, William. An examination of a book entitled discourses on the apostolical successions. New York: Stanford and Swords, 1845. 47 p. NGH. 45-3590

Johnson, William Bullein, 1782-1862. The church's argument for Christianity for the apostolic succession. New York: Sparks, 1845. 175 p. PPM; ViU. 45-3591

Johnson, William Lupton. Primitive state of man; the rector's offering for 1845, being the 6th pastoral address to the parishioners of Grace Church,

Jamaica, Long Island. Jamaica, 1845. MWA; NBLIHI; NNC; NSmb; TSewU. 45-3592

Johnston, Alexander Keith, 1804-1871. The national atlas of historical, commercial and political geography. New York: D. Appleton and company, 1845. 41 p. MH-AH. 45-3593

Johnston, James Finlay Weir, 1796-1855. Catechism of agricultural chemistry and geology, with an introduction by J.P. Norton; from the eighth English edition with notes and additions by the author, prepared expressly for this edition. Albany: Pense, 1845. 74 p. CtHT; MB; MNowdHi; NCH; PU; TNV. 45-3594

Johnston, James R. A discourse delivered at the opening of the synod of New York in the city of Brooklyn. By the moderator. Goshen: Printed by Mead and Webb, 1845. 50 p. NjPt; NjR, PPPr-Hi. 45-3595

Johnston, James R. A discourse delivered on the occasion of the dedication of the Presbyterian Church of Hamptonburgh... Goshen: Printed by Mead and Webb, 1845. 29 p. MB; MH-AH; MWA; NjR; PPPrHi. 45-3596

Johnston, John, 1806-1879. A manual of chemistry, on the basis of Dr. Turner's elements of chemistry. A new edition. Philadelphia: Thomas, Cowperthwait and company, 1845. 480 p. CtY; NjR; NNAN. 45-3597

Johnston, William, 1804-1891. An address on female education, delivered at Columbus, December 31, 1844. Columbus: C. Scott and company, 1845. 23 p. InU; MdBJ; MH; OClWHi; OO. 45-3598

Johnstone, Christian Isobell, 1781-1857. Nights of the round table; or stories of Aunt Jane and he friends. Philadelphia: Zieber and company, 1845. 252 p. MB; MB; NIC; PPL-R; RPA. 45-3599

Johnstone, John, 1778-1855. A sermon preached in the Presbyterian Church, Jersey City, September 14, 1845, on the occasion of the death of David Henderson. Jersey City, Press of the Advertiser, 1845. CSmH; CtY; PPPrHi. 45-3600

Jones, Charles Colcock, 1804-1883. A catechism, of scripture doctrine and practice, for families and Sabbath schools, designed also for the oral instruction of colored persons. Sixth edition. Charleston: D.W. Harrison, 1845. 154 p. ScCliJ. 45-3601

Jones, F. Miss Candle's complaint. Philadelphia, 1845. CtY. 45-3602

Jones, John Beauchamp, 1810-1866. Wild western scenes; a narrative of adventures in the western wilderness, forty years ago; wherein the conduct of Daniel Boone.... By a squatter. Philadelphia: E. Ferrett and company, 1845. 247 p. CtY; DLC; PU. 45-3603

Jones, John Paul, 1747-1792. Life of Rear Admiral John Paul Jones, chevalier of the military order of merit, and of the Russian order of St. Anne... Compiled from his original journals and correspondence: including an account of his services in the American revolution, and in the war between the Russians and Turks in the Black Sea. Illustrated with numerous engravings, from original

drawings by James Hamilton. Philadelphia: Walker and Gillis, 1845. 11-399 p. CtY; KyLx; MdAN; TxDaM; ViU. 45-3604

Jones, Joseph. Religious lacon; or holy thought. New York: Y.S. Redfield, 1845. 142 p. MBC. 45-3605

Jones, Justin. The burglars; or the mysteries of the league of honor. An American tale. By Harry Hazel. [Pseud. Boston: Gleason, 1845. 64 p. CtY; NNC; PU; RPB. 45-3606

Jones, Justin. The king's cruisers; or the rebel and the rover. By Harry Hazel [Pseud.] New York: Everet D. Long [1845?] ICU; NjP; ViU. 45-3607

Jones, Justin. The nun of St. Ursula, or the burning of the convent. A romance of Mount Benedict. By Harry Hazel [pseud.] Boston: F. Gleason, 1845. [9]-64 p. DLC; MB; MiD-B; MMal; MWA. 45-3608

Jones, Justin. The rival chieftains; or the brigands of Mexico. A tale of Santa Anna and his times. By Harry Hazel [pseud. Boston: Gleason's Publishing Hall, 1845. 54 p. CU-B; ICU; MWA; RPB. 45-3609

Jones, Justin. The West Point cadet; or the young officer's bride. A romance in real life, by Harry Hazel [pseud.] Boston: F. Gleason, 1845. 100 p. CSfCW; CtY; NSmb; NWM. 45-3610

Jones, Pascal. My uncle Hobson and I; or slashes at life with a free broad axe. New York: D. Appleton and company; Philadelphia: G.S. Appleton, 1845. 268 p. DLC; ICU; MH; PPL; RPB. 45-3611

Jones, Thomas P. New conversations on chemistry, adapted to the present state of that science; where in its elements are clearly and familiarly explained. Philadelphia: Gregg and Elliot, 1845. 332 p. CtY. 45-3612

Jones, William, 1762-1846. The history of the Christian Church, from the birth of Christ to the XVIII. Century: Including the very interesting account of the Waldenses and Albigenses. Fourth American from the fifth London edition. Wetumpka, Alabama: Charles Yancey, 1845. 505 p. AMaJ; DLC; NcD; OrU; TxWB. 45-3613

Jones, Z. Elements of arithmetic. Adapted to the use of common schools and academies. Part I. Exeter: F. Grant, 1845. MH. 45-3614

Josephus, Flavius. The works of Flavius Josephus, the learned and authentic Jewish historian and celebrated warrior, containing twenty books of the Jewish war, and the life of Josephus. Philadelphia: Grigg and Elliot, 1845. 2 v. ArBaA; CtY; LNHT; MAnA; NjPT. 45-3615

Josephus, Flavius. The works of Flavius, the learned and authentic Jewish historian and celebrated warrior. Translated by William Whiston. Buffalo: N. G. Ellis, 1845. 648 p. MiAbC. 45-3616

Jouffroy, Theodore Simon, 1796-1842. Introduction to ethics, including a critical survey of moral systems. Translated from the French of Jouffroy. Boston: J. Munroe and company, 1845. 2 v. ICMe; MiOC; OO; PU; TNDL. 45-3617

Journal of agriculture, containing the best current production in promotion of agricultural improvements, including the choicest prize essays issued in Europe and America. John S. Skinner, editor. New York: Greeley, 1845-1848. 3 v. CtY; IU; LNH; NcD; P; WU-A. 45-3618

Journal of prison discipline and philanthropy... Philadelphia, 1845-1919. 74 v. in 25. CSt; InU; MB; NcD; PU. 45-3619

The journeyman mechanic's account book, on a new plan. Boston, 1845. 32 p. MH; MH-BA. 45-3620

Judd, Gideon Noble, 1789-1860. Nonconformity to the world, by the renewing of the mind. New York: M.W. Dodd, 1845. 84 p. NCats; NNUT. 45-3621

Judd, Sylvester, 1789-1860. A discourse touching the causes and remedies of intemperance. Preached February 2, 1845. Augusta: W.T. Johnson, 1845. 40 p. CtY; RPB; WHi. 45-3622

Judd, Sylvester, 1813-1853. Margaret. A tale of the real and ideal, blight and bloom; including sketches of a place not before described, called Mons Christi... Boston: Jordan and Wiley, 1845. 3-460 p. DLC; ICMe; MBBC; PU; RPB. 45-3623

Judd, Willard, 1804-1840. A compilation of miscellanies from the writings of Rev. Willard Judd; with a brief memoir of the author, by Orrin B. Judd. New York: Lewis Colby, 1845. 120 p. CSmH; NHC- S; NNNG; TxAbH. 45-3624

Judd, Willard, 1804-1840. Memoirs and remains, embracing a review of Professor Stuart, a compilation of miscellanies, and a biographical sketch of O.B. Judd, with an introductory essay by S.H. Cone. New

York: L. Colby, 1845. 452 p. CtMH; IaDmU; NjMD; PCA; RPB. 45-3625

Judkins, Jesse P., 1815-1867. Introductory lecture, to a course on descriptive and surgical anatomy; delivered in Cincinnati; November 3, 1845. Cincinnati: H.C. and J.B. M'Grew, printers, 1845. 12 p. DLC; NNNAM; OCIM; OCIWHi; WU-M. 45-3626

Judson, Emily Chubbuck, 1817-1854. Memoir of Sarah B. Judson, member of the American Mission at Burmah. By Fanny Forester, pseud. New York: L. Colby, 1845. 250 p. NCH. 45-3627

Jung-Stilling, Johann Heinrich, 1740-1817. The autobiography of Heinrich Stilling... Translated from the German of S. Jackson. New York: Harper and brothers, 1845. 187 p. CtMW; CtY; DLC; LN; PHC. 45-3628

Junius, pseud. The letters of Junius, from the latest London edition. New York: Leavitt and Allen, [1845?] 2 v. in 1. MWH. 45-3629

Junius, pseud. The letters of Junius, from the latest London edition. Philadelphia, 1845. 2 v. in 1. CU; IU; KyDC; OO; ScDa. 45-3630

Junius, pseud. The letters of Junius, from the latest London edition. Philadelphia: J. Locken, 1845. 2 v. IaDmD; IU; LStBA; MdCatS; NbOP. 45-3631

Junkin, David Xavier, 1808-1888. The oath a divine ordinance, and an element in the social constitution; its origin, nature, ends, efficacy, lawfulness, obligations, interpretation, form and abuses. New York: Wiley and Putnam, 1845. 223 p. DLC; IaK; KyDC; PU; RPA. 45-3632

Junkin, George, 1790-1868. A plea for north eastern Pennsylvania. The tenth Baccalaureate in Lafayette College. Easton, Pennsylvania: J.P. Hetrich, printer, 1845. 24 p. DLC; ICMe; MH- AH; PEaL; PPM. 45-3633

Junkin, George, 1790-1868. Truth and freedom: a sermon, delivered at the opening of the general assembly of the Presbyterian Church, at Cincinnati, May 15, 1845. Cincinnati: Printed by R.P. Donogh and company, 1845. 28 p. ICP; MH-AH; OCIWHi; PPaL; PPPrHi. 45-3634

Justitiae, Amici. The verdict unsealed; being a review of the testimony given before the court convened for the trial of the bishop of New York. New York: Henry M. Onderdonk, 1845. 36 p. CtY; MdToH; OCLaw; PPL. 45-3635

Juvenalis, Decimus Junius. Decimi Junii Jevenalis et auli persii flacci satirae expurgate, notes illustrate. Curavit F.P. Leverett. Bostaniae: Wilkins, Carter and company, 1845. 252 p. MWH; NcDaD; TMeSC; TxShA. 45-3636

The juvenile gem for 1845. Edited by Mrs. Hofland. New York: E. Kearney, 1845. 252 p. MnU; NjR; NNC; ODaV; TBriK. 45-3637

K

Kames, Henry Home, 1696-1782. Elements of criticism, with analyses and translations of ancient and foreign illustrations. Edited by Abraham Mills. New edition. New York: Huntington and Savage, 1845. 504 p. GA; IaOakJF; KyDC; NFred. 45-3638

Kane, Robert John, 1809-1890. Elements of chemistry, including the most recent discoveries and applications of the science to medicine and pharmacy, and the arts. An American edition, by John William Draper. New York: Harper and brothers, 1845. 704 p. ICU- R; MH-M; MCM; PPi; ViRA. 45-3639

Kate Kearney; ballad. New York, [1845] CtY. 45-3640

Kathleen O'Moore; ballad. New York, [1845] CtY. 45-3641

Katholischer katechismus, herausgegeben mit genehmingung des hochw. Bischofs von Pittsburg, Dr. Mich. O'Connor, von der Versammlung des allerheiligsten erlosers. Pittsburg: Gedruckt bei Victor Scriba, 1845. 160 p. DCU; NStc. 45-3642

Keep, John, 1781-1870. Congregationalism, and church action: with the principles of Christian union, etc... New York: S.W. Benedict and company, 1845. 143 p. CBPSR; IaGG; MBC; MeBat; OClWHi. 45-3643

The keepsake; a Christmas, New Years and birthday present for 1845. New York: D. Appleton and company, 1845. 288 p. ICN; NN; PSt; RPE; TxU. 45-3644

Keese, John, 1805-1856. The forest legendary, or metrical tales of the North American woods; edited by John Keese. No. 1. New York: William Van Norden and Josiah Adams, 1845. 96 p. MB; NLag; NRMA; TxU. 45-3645

Keese, John, 1805-1856. The poet's gift; illustrated by one of her painters. Boston: T.H. Carter and company, 1845. 320 p. IaDuU; MH; MWA; OO; WU. 45-3646

Keese, John, 1805-1856. The poets of America; illustrated by one of her painters. Fifth edition. New York: S. Colman, [1845] 2 v. ICN. 45-3647

Keightley, Thomas, 1789-1872. The history of England from the earliest period to 1839. From the second London edition. New York: Harper and brothers, 1845. 5 v. GAuY; InRchE; OSW; ScGrw; WM. 45-3648

Keith, Charles H. Boston flute instruction book: a complete school for the flute. Boston: Ditson, [1845] 63 p. CtHWatk; MB. 45-3649

Kelley, Robert Reid. Persecutions in Madeira in the nineteenth century; being an exposition of facts. Translated from the Portuguese by Manuel J. Gonsalves. New York: American Protestant Society, 1845. 86 p. CSfCW; LU; MB; NNMr; TChU. 45-3650

Kellogg, Edward, 1790-1858. Currency: the evil and the remedy. Third edition. New York: W.H. Graham, 1846. 48 p. CtY; MH; NjR; NN; PPM. 45-3651

Kellogg, Edward, 1790-1858. Currency: the evil and the remedy. Fourth edition. New York: W.H. Graham, [1845?] NoLoc. 45-3652

Kellogg, Ezra B. The true Christian. A sermon... Alton: The Telegraph office, 1845. 11 p. IHi; MdBD; NNG; OCHP. 45-3653

Kellogg, Lewis, 1805-1882. The cost of intemperance; a discourse... Whitehall... 1845. Troy, New York: [1845?] CSmH; NjPT. 45-3654

Kemble, Marie Theresa DeCamp, 1774-1838. The day after the wedding; a farce in one act. New York: Samuel French, [1845?] 22 p. OCl. 45-3655

Kendall, Ezra Otis, 1818-1899. Atlas of the heavens; showing the places of the principal stars, clusters and nebulae; designed to accompany the uranography... Philadelphia: Butler and Williams, 1845. 68 p. MCAVS; MLexHi; NIC; OCX; PU. 45-3656

Kendall, Ezra Otis, 1818-1899. Uranography; or a description of the heavens; designed for academies and schools; accompanied by an atlas of the heavens, showing the places of the stars, clusters, and nebalae. Philadelphia: Butler, 1845.

365 p. ICP; MH; PPF; OCX; ViU. 45-3657

Kendall, George Wilkins, 1809-1867. Narrative of the Texan Santa Fe expedition, comprising a description of a tour through Texas... and final capture of the Texans, and their march as prisoners, to the city of Mexico. New York: Harper and brothers, 1845. 2 v. CSmH; KyU; OCHP. 45-3658

Kendall's clarinet instruction book; a complete school for the clarinet. Containing progressive exercises, marches, quick-steps; waltzes, popular melodies, jigs, solos, and duets. Boston: O. Ditson, [1845] ICN; MB; MH. 45-3659

Kendrick, Asahel Clark, 1809-1895. The ancient and modern civilizations contrasted. An address delivered before the Aeonian Society of the Hamilton Literary and Theological Institution, on July 30, 1845. Hamilton: Waldron and Baker, 1845. 26 p. CSmH; MNtCA; NN; PPC; PPL. 45-3660

Kendrick, Asahel Clark, 1809-1895. Greek Ollendorff; being a progressive exhibition of the principles of the Greek grammar; designed for beginners in Greek. New York: D. Appleton and company, 1845. 371 p. PPM. 45-3661

Kennebec and Portland Railroad Company. Act incorporating the Kennebec and Portland Railroad Company, approved April 1, 1836, and additional acts, approved April 9, 1841, and March 31, 1845. Augusta, Maine: Severance and Dorr, 1845. 11 p. DBRE; M; MeB. 45-3662

Kennedy, Andrew, 1810-1847. Speech

of Mr. Kennedy, on the Oregon bill, in the House, February 1, 1845. [Washington, 1845] 4 p. DLC; WHi. 45-3663

Kennedy, Grace, 1782-1825. Profession is not principle: or the name of christian is not christianity. From the sixth Edinburgh edition. New York: Robert Carter, 1845. CtHC; MsG. 45-3664

Kennedy, John Pendleton, 1795-1870. Discourse on the life and character of George Calvert, the first Lord Baltimore: made by John P. Kennedy, before the Maryland Historical Society, December 9, 1845, being the second annual address to that association. Baltimore: J. Murphy, 1845. 50 p. A-Ar; DLC; DeWi; LNH; OMC; PPi. 45-3665

Kennedy, John Pendleton, 1795-1870. Speech on the annexation of Texas. Delivered in the House, January 11, 1845. [Washington, 1845] 16 p. IaGG; MdBP; MdHi; NBu; TxU. 45-3666

Kennedy, John Pendleton, 1795-1870. To the mechanics, manufactures, and workingmen of the city of Baltimore. Baltimore: Printed by Samuel Sands, 1845. 16 p. MBAt; MdBP; NcD; PPM; ViU. 45-3667

Kenrick, Francis Patrick, 1796-1863. The primacy of the apostolic see vindicated. Philadelphia: M. Fithiam, 1845. 488 p. ICN; MiD- B; NNF; ODaU. 45-3668

Kenrick, William, 1789-1872. The new American orchardist; or an account of the most valuable varieties of fruit of all climates adapted to cultivation in the United States. Seventh edition, enlarged and revised with a supplement. Boston: Otis, Broaders and company, 1845. 450 p. DNAL; NNBG; WU. 45-3669

Kenrick, Winslow R. A new exposition of the prophecies of Daniel. Framingham, Massachusetts: Published by the author, 1845. 90 p. NoLoc. 45-3670

Kent County, Delaware. First biennial report of the superintendent of free schools. Dover, Delaware: S. Kinney, printer, 1845. 16 p. CSmH; MH; PHi. 45-3671

Kentucky. Acts of the General Assembly of the commonwealth of Kentucky: Passed at December session, 1844. Frankfort: A.G. Hodges, state printer, 1845. 245 p. A-SC; IaU-L; In-SC; KyLoB; Mi-L. 45-3672

Kentucky. Acts of the General Assembly of the Commonwealth of Kentucky: Passed at the December session, 1844. Published by authority. Frankfort, Kentucky: A.G. Hodges, state printer, 1845. 354 p. Ky. 45-3673

Kentucky. Journal of the House of the commonwealth of Kentucky, begun and held in the town of Frankfort, December 31, 1845 and of the commonwealth, the fifty-fourth. Frankfort: A.G. Hodges, state printer, 1845. 506 p. CoU; InU; KyDC; KyLoB; NcU. 45-3674

Kentucky. Journal of the Senate of the commonwealth of Kentucky, begun and held in the town of Frankfort, on December 31, 1845, and of the commonwealth, the fifty-fourth. Frankfort: A.G. Hodges, state printer, 1845. 378 p. InU; KyHi; NcU. 45-3675

Kentucky. Message of the governor of Kentucky to the General Assembly. Frankfort, 1845-. MiU; PPL. 45-3676

Kentucky. Report of the commissioners appointed by the governors of Tennessee and Kentucky to run and remark certain portions of the boundry line between said states, November 8, 1845. [Frankfort, 1845] 4 p. WHi. 45-3677

Kentucky. Report of the commissioners appointed to settle with the president of the bank of the commonwealth and the commissioners of the sinking fund. [Frankfort, 1845] 70 p. WHi. 45-3678

Kentucky. Report of the superintendent of public instruction. Frankfort, Kentucky, 1845-. DLC; M. 45-3679

Kentucky. Reports communicated to both branches of the legislature of Kentucky, at the December session, 1845. Frankfort, Kentucky: A.G. Hodges, state printer, 1845. 733 p. Ky; Nj. 45-3680

Kentucky. Response of the Bank of Kentucky to the interrogatories propounded by the joint committee of the legislature on banks. [Frankfort, 1845] 49 p. WHi. 45-3681

Kentucky. Special report of the board of internal improvement in reference to a settlement with the Green and Barren River commissioners, January 15, 1845. [Frankfort, 1845] 9 p. WHi. 45-3682

Kenyon, William Asbury, 1817-1862. Miscellaneous poems, to which are added writings in prose. Chicago, Illinois: Printed by Jas. Campbell and company, 1845. 208 p. CSmH; ICHi; O; OkU. 45-3683

Kenyon College, Gambier, Ohio. Catalogue of the Theological Seminary of the Diocese of Ohio; Kenyon College, and Kenyon Grammar Schools, 1844-1845. Gambier, Ohio: G.W. Meyers, 1845. 23 p. WNaE. 45-3684

Kenyon College, Gambier, Ohio. Catalogue of the Theological Seminary of the Diocese of Ohio; Kenyon College, and Kenyon Grammar Schools, 1846-1847. Gambier, Ohio: G.W. Meyers, 1845. 22 p. MeHi; NN. 45-3685

Ker, Leander. History of liberty, its origin, character and progress: an address delivered before the Athenaean Society of the University of Missouri, at Columbia, July 30, 1845. Columbia: William F. Switzler, 1845. 35 p. DCU; MdBP. 45-3686

Ker, Leander. Slavery consistent with Christianity, a lecture. Second edition. Baltimore, 1845. 31 p. MHi. 45-3687

Kerfoot, John Barrett, 1816-1881. The confidence of a certain faith. A sermon in the chapel of the College of St. James, on November 23, 1845. Baltimore: Joseph Robinson, 1845. 16 p. CtHT; DLC; MdHi; NcU; PLT. 45-3688

Kerner, Justinus Andreas Christian, 1786-1862. The seeress of Prevorst, being revelations concerning the inner life of man and the interdiffusion of a world of spirits in the one we inhabit. New York: Harper and brothers, 1845. 119 p. IaK; ICN; MB; MeBa; VtU. 45-3689

Kerney, Martin Joseph, 1819-1861. A compendium of ancient and modern history; with questions adapted to the use of schools and academies; also an appendix. Baltimore: Owen, Kurtz and company, 1845. 530 p. DLC; InNd; KyCovV; MiD-U; MoSF. 45-3690

Kerr, David. The certainty of salvation through Christ: a sermon preached on Whit-sunday, May 11, 1845. New Orleans: J.E. Steele, 1845. 33 p. ICN; MdBD; NNG. 45-3691

Kidder, Daniel Parish, 1815-1891. Little Rose; or stories on the Lord's prayer and other scriptures. Edited by D.P. Kidder. New York: Lane and Tippett, 1846. 170 p. DLC; OCl. 45-3692

Kidder, Daniel Parish, 1815-1891. Mormonism and the Mormons; a historical view of the rise and progress of the sect self-styled Latter Day Saints. New York: G. Lane and C.B. Tippet, 1845. 341 p. CSansS; MB; MiD; UU; WHi. 45-3693

Kidder, Daniel Parish, 1815-1891. The sea star. Revised by the editor. New York: Lane, 1845. NB; ODW; ScOrC. 45-3694

Kidder, Daniel Parish, 1815-1891. Sketches of residence and travels in Brazil, embracing historical and geographical notices of the empire and its several provinces. Philadelphia: Sorin and Ball; London: Wiley and Putnam, 1845. 2 v. GU; ICJ; MnSH; PPA; WHi. 45-3695

Kidder, Daniel Parish, 1815-1891. The temptation; or Henry Thornton. Showing the progress and fruits of intemperance. Revised by D.P. Kidder. 90 p. CtY. 45-3696

Kilbourne, Payne Kenyon, 1815-1859.

The family memorial. A history and genealogy of the Kilbourn family, in the United States and Canada, from the year 1635 to the present time... Hartford: Brown and Parsons, 1845. 151 p. CtY; DLC; MWA; OHi; WHi. 45-3697

Kilbourne, Payne Kenyon, 1815-1859. History and genealogy of the Kilbourne family in the United States and Canada, 1635-1845. Hartford, Connecticut, 1845. 151 p. CtSoP. 45-3698

Kimball, Caleb, 1798-1879. The holy Spirit resisted. Boston: Benjamin Perkins and company, 1845. 108 p. DLC; InAndC; MA. 45-3699

Kimball, Caleb, 1798-1879. The holy Spirit resisted. Second edition. Boston: Benjamin Perkins and company, 1845. 108 p. MB. 45-3700

Kimball, Caleb. The happy choice. Boston: Massachusetts Sabbath School Society, 1845. MH; MTop. 45-3701

King, A.C. The western grammar of the English language, adapted to the modern improved system of lecturing, the use of select and common schools, and the private learner... By A.C. King and George H. Spencer. Terre Haute: T. Dowling, printer, 1845. 96 p. CtY. 45-3702

King, Charles, 1789-1867. A review of the trial of the Right Rev. Benjamin T. Onderdonk. New York: Stanford and Swords, 1845. 16, [8] p. Ct; MiD-B; NNG; NNUT; PPL. 45-3703

King, George I. Success: the criterion of ministerial authority. A sermon preached before the Oswego Presbytery, at the installation of Rev. R. Richard Kirk, Bishop of the Congregational Church in Camden, New York, October 7, 1845... Published at the request of the Congregational Church. Utica: R.W. Roberts, printer, 1845. 20 p. N; NAuT; NjPT; NRom; PPPrHi. 45-3704

Kinglake, Alexander William, 1809-1891. Eothen or traces of travel brought home. New York: R. Craighead, 1845. 178 p. RP. 45-3705

Kinglake, Alexander William, 1809-1891. Eothen, or traces of travel brought home from the East. New York: W.H. Colyer, 1845. 93 p. DLC; LN; MBBC; P. 45-3706

Kinglake, Alexander William, 1809-1891. Eothen, or traces of travel brought home from the East. New York: Wiley and Putnam, 1845. 232 p. CtY; InGrD; OC; RJa; WvC. 45-3707

Kinglake, Alexander William, 1809-1891. Traces of travel brought home from the East. Auburn, New York: J.C. Derby and company; Geneva, New York: Derby and company, 1845. 232 p. CtHT; DLC; ICU; NcGu; PU. 45-3708

The kings of England; arranged and illustrated for the young. New York: Josiah Adams, 1845. 163 p. DLC; KWiU; ODaB; PU; WHi. 45-3709

Kingsley, George, 1811-1884. Juvenile choir; a selection of the choicest melodies from the German, Italian, French, English, and American composers, designed for public and private schools and for young classes in academies and seminaries. New York:

A.S. Barnes, 1845. 160 p. CtHC; MH; MWA; MWborHi; PU. 45-3710

Kingsley, George, 1811-1884. The sacred choir; a collection of church music, consisting of selections from the most distinguished authors... Tenth edition, corrected. New York, 1845. CtY. 45-3711

Kingsley, James Luce, 1778-1852. Life of Ezra Stiles, president of Yale College. Boston, 1845. DLC; MB: OClWHi. 45-3712

Kingsley, James Luce, 1778-1852. Lives of Ezra Stiles, John Fitch and Anne Hutchinson. Boston: Charles C. Little and James Brown, 1845. 376 p. MFi; RLa; RHi. 45-3713

Kinne, Asa. Kinne's quarterly law compendium for 1845; or digest of cases reported in the United States and Great Britain in 1843, 1844 and 1845, alphabetically arranged. Being an appendix to Kinne's law compendium... New York: Published for the author, 1845. 512 p. Ct; IaU-L; MBC; MiU-C; NRAL. 45-3714

Kip, William Ingraham, 1725-1795. Two pastoral letters, addressed to the congregation of St. Paul's Church, Albany, by their absent rector, Rev. William Ingraham Kip. Printed for private circulation. Albany: Erastus H. Pease, 1845. 12 p. CtY; MWA; NjPT. 45-3715

Kippis, Andrew, 1725-1795. A narrative of the voyage round the world, performed by Captain James Cook. With an account of his life during the previous and intervening periods. Cooperstown,

New York: H. and E. Phinney, 1845. IaDL; MB; NJost. 45-3716

Kirby, Stephen R. Sunday school spelling and reading book. Second edition. New York: G. Lane and C.B. Tippett, 1845. ScSpW. 45-3717

Kirk, Philip A. The Catholic harp, containing the morning and evening service of the Catholic Church, embracing a choice collection of masses, litanies, Psalms, sacred hymns, anthems versicles and motetts. Selected from the compositions of the first masters. Boston: D. Reilly, 1845. 112 p. DLC; MH. 45-3718

Kirkbride, Thomas S. Account of the Pennsylvania Hospital for the Insane. From the American Journal of Insanity. Extracted principally from the reports of T.S.K. [Philadelphia, 1845] NBuG. 45-3719

Kirkham, Samuel. English grammar in familiar lectures, accompanied by a compendium, embracing a new systematic order of parsing... To which are added a compendium, an appendix and a key to the exercises, designed for the use of schools and private learners. Latest edition. Cincinnati: E. Morgan and company, 1845. 228 p. InIBU; NjR. 45-3720

Kirkham, Samuel. English grammar in familiar lectures, accompanied by a compendium, embracing a new systematic order of parsing... To which are added a compendium, an appendix and a key to the exercises, designed for the use of schools and private learners. Seventieth edition, enlarged and improved. Rochester: William Alling, 1845. 228 p. MH; NNC: OCl; PSt; WU. 45-3721

Kirkham, Samuel. English grammar in familiar lectures, accompanied by a compendium, embracing a new systematic order of parsing... To which are added a compendium, an appendix and a key to the exercises, designed for the use of schools and private learners. One hundred and fifth edition. Baltimore: Cushing and brothers, 1845. 228 p. IAIS; InFtwC; MH; ScGaL; WvH. 45-3722

Kirkham, Samuel. English grammar in familiar lectures, accompanied by a compendium, embracing a new systematic order of parsing... To which are added a compendium, an appendix and a key to the exercises, designed for the use of schools and private learners. One hundred and fifth edition. Baltimore: J. Plaskitt, 1845. MH. 45-3723

Kirkham, Samuel. English grammar in familiar lectures, accompanied by a compendium, embracing a new systematic order of parsing... To which are added a compendium, an appendix and a key to the exercises, designed for the use of schools and private learners. One hundred and seventh edition. New York: Collins brothers and company, 1845. 228 p. ICU; MiU; PMA. 45-3724

Kirkham, Samuel. An essay on elocution, designed for the use of schools and private learners. Third edition, enlarged and improved. New York: Pratt, Woodford and company, 1845. 355 p. MiOC; OO; PMA. 45-3725

Kirkland, Caroline Matilda Stansbury, 1801-1864. Western clearings. New York: Wiley and Putnam, 1845. 238 p. DLC; ICHi; LU; MdHi; NjR. 45-3726

Kirkland, Hugh. Sermon on the Roman

Catholic and Protestant controversy, with strictures on the constitution of the Protestant Association of Pittsburgh and Allegheny, auxiliary to the American Protestant Association. Pittsburgh: E. Robinson, 1845. DLC; PPins. 45-3727

Kirkpatrick, John Lycan, 1813-1885. The moral tendency of the doctrine of falling from grace examined. A sermon... Mobile: Printed at the Register and Journal office, 1845. 28 p. A-Ar; CSmH; NcD; PPL; PPPrHi. 45-3728

Kitchel, Henry Denison, 1812-1895. An appeal to the people for the suppression of the spirit traffic. An address delivered at Goshen, Connecticut, October 28, 1845. Hartford: Litchfield County Temerance Society, 1845. 16 p. Ct; CtSoP; CtY; NN; OClWHi. 45-3729

Kitto, John, 1804-1854. A cyclopaedia of biblical literature edited by John Kitto. New York: Mark H. Newman, 1845. 2 v. KyDC; OMC; PV; TxGR. 45-3730

Kitto, John, 1804-1854. A cyclopaedia of biblical literature edited by John Kitto. New York: Mark H. Newman; Cincinnati: William H. Moore and company, 1845. 2 v. CV; MMh; NCaS; PCA; ScDuE. 45-3731

Kitto, John, 1804-1854. Illustrated history of Palestine from the Patriarchal age to the present time. New York: Graham, 1845. 223 p. MH; PPiW; PPLT. 45-3732

Kline, N. Journey under the ground. Boston: Saxton Pierce and company, 1845. NPV. 45-3733

Knapp, George Christian, 1753-1825.

Lectures on Christian theology. Translated by Leonard Woods, Jun. Second American edition. Reprinted from the last London edition. Philadelphia: Thomas Wardle, 1845. 572 p. GAU; GAGTh; GOgU; IaPeC; OSW. 45-3734

Knapp, Jacob, 1799-1874. The evangelical harp: a new collection of hymns and tunes, designed for revivals of religion, and for family and social worship... Utica: Bennett, Backus and Hawley, 1845. 222 p. DLC; NNUT; PCA; NRAB. 45-3735

Knickerbacker almanac for 1845. New York: T.W. Strong, [1845] MWA. 45-3736

Knickerbacker almanac for 1846. By David Young. New York: H. and S. Raynor, [1845] MWA. 45-3737

Knight, Abel F. The umbrella courtship; a comic song arranged for the pianoforte by A. F. Knight. Boston: Keith's Publishing House, 1845. 3 p. MB. 45-3738

Knight, Helen Cross, 1814-1906. Pictorial alphabet. Written for the Massachusetts Sabbath School Society, and revised by the committee of publication. Boston: Massachusetts Sabbath School Society, 1845. 36 p. DLC; MLexHi. 45-3739

Knight, Helen Cross, 1814-1906. Reuben Kent's first winter in the city. Philadelphia: American Sunday School Union, 1845. 174 p. IU; NjP; MW; NN; NNMHi. 45-3740

Knitting, netting and crochet work. A winter gift for ladies; being instructions in knitting, netting, and crochet work;

containing the newest and most fashionable patterns. From the latest London edition, revised and enlarged. By an American lady. Philadelphia: G.B. Zieber and company, 1845. 65 p. ICBB. 45-3741

Knowles, James Davis, 1798-1838. Memoir of Ann H. Judson, late missionary to Burmah; including a history of the American Baptist Mission in the Burman Empire. A new edition with a continuation of the history of the mission to the present time. Boston: Gould, Kendall and Lincoln, 1845. 392 p. IaDmD; MH-AH; MWA; NNNG; RLa. 45-3742

Knowles, James Davis, 1798-1838. Memoir of Mrs. Ann H. Judson, Boston, 1845. 345 p. MWA. 45-3743

Knowles, James Sheridan, 1784-1862. The elocutionist; a first class rhetorical reader and recitation book... and adapted to the purposes on instruction in the United States, Epes Sargent. Seventh edition. New York, 1845. 322 p. CtHWatk; NFred; RPB. 45-3744

Knowles, James Sheridan, 1784-1862. The hunchback. A play in five acts... With the author's latest corrections, all the stage business... As preformed by Mr. Knowles, Mr. and Miss Kemble, Mr. and Mrs. Charles Kean... The only unmutilated edition... New York: S. French, [1845?] [9]-82 p. CtHWatk; MH; MWA; NjR; NN. 45-3745

Knowles, James Sheridan, 1784-1862. The wife; a tale of Mantua, a play in five acts. With the stage directions, marked and corrected as played at the Park theatre by J.B. Addis, prompter. New York: William Taylor and company, 1845. 68 p. MB. 45-3746

Knowlson, John C. The complete farrier; a treatise on the diseases of horned cattle and calves... The whole being the result of seventy years extensive practice of the author. New York: Wilson and company, 1845. 64 p. DLC; OClWHi. 45-3747

Knowlton, Charles, 1800-1850. Address of Dr. Charles Knowlton, before the friends of mental liberty, at Greenfield, Massachusetts, and the constitution of the United Liberals of Franklin County, Massachusetts. Boston: J.P. Mendum, 1845. 23 p. M; NN. 45-3748

Knox, Loren L. Man's want and supply. Boston: American Pulpit, 1845. CtHC. 45-3749

Knox College, Galesburgh, Illinois. Catalogue of the corporation, officers and students of Knox College, Galesburgh, Illinois, for the year ending July 2, 1845. Peoria: S.H. Davis, printer, 1845. 12 p. IG; IGK. 45-3750

Koch, Albrecht Karl. Description of the Hydrarchos harlani: a gigantic fossil reptile: lately discovered by the author, in the state of Alabama, March, 1845. Together with some geological observations made on different formations of the rocks, during a geological tour through the eastern, western and southern parts of the United States, in the years 1844-1845. New York, 1845. CtY; DNLM; KyU; NN; PHi. 45-3751

Koch, Albrecht Karl. Description of the Hydrarchos harlani: a gigantic fossil reptile: lately discovered by the author, in the state of Alabama, March, 1845. Together with some geological observations made on different formations of the rocks, during a geological tour through the eastern, western and southern parts of the United States, in the years 1844-1845. Second edition. New York: [B. Owen, printer] 1845. 24 p. C-S; DLC; MHi; PHi; TxH. 45-3752

Kock, Charles Paul de, 1794-1871. Paul, the Profligate, or Paris as it is. A novel, translated by George Braithwaite Smith. New York: Published for the translator, 1845. CtY. 45-3753

Kohlrausch, Friedrich, 1780-1865. A history of Germany; from the earliest period to the present time. Translated from the last German edition, by James D. Haas. With a complete index, prepared expressly for the American edition. New York: D. Appleton and company; Philadelphia: G.S. Appleton, 1845. 487 p. DeWi; IaDaM; KyLoP; NGH; OC. 45-3754

Krauth, Charles Porterfield, 1823-1883. The benefits of the pastoral office; a farewell discourse. Baltimore: Printed by Sherwood and company, 1845. 8 p. PPLT. 45-3755

Krebs, Johann Philipp, 1771-1850. Guide for writing Latin; consisting of rules and examples for practice. From the German of Samuel H. Taylor. Second edition. Andover, Massachusetts: Allen Morrill and Wardwell; New York: M.H Newman, 1845. 514 p. CtMW; GDecCT NBuG; PP; VtU. 45-3756

Kriss Kringle's Christmas tree. A holiday present for boys and girls Philadelphia: E. Ferrett and company 1845. 160 p. DLC; ICN; MNF; TxSaWi 45-3757

Krummacher, Friedrich Wilhelm, 1796-1868. The martyr lamb; or Christ, the representative of his people in all ages, translated from the German of F.W. Krummacher. Fifth edition. New York: Carter, 1845. 288 p. IaMP; InCW; MeBaT; OkU. 45-3758

Kuhner, Raphael, 1802-1878. Elementary grammar of the Latin language, with a series of Latin and English exercises for translation and a collection of Latin reading lessons, with the requisite vocabularies. Translated from the German by J.T. Champlin. Boston: J. Munroe and company, 1845. 383 p. CtMW; DLC; MBAt; NNC; WyU. 45-3759

Kurtz, Benjamin, 1795-1865. Why are you a Lutheran: or a series of dissertations, of the Evangelical Lutheran Church in the United States. Baltimore: Lutheran Church printers, 1845. 227 p. MoSC. 45-3760

L

Ladd, Alexander. Letter to the subscribers for the stock in the Portsmouth and Concord Railroad Company. Portsmouth, 1845. Nh. 45-3761

The ladies album and gentleman's parlor miscellany. A magazine embracing every department of Literature... Boston, 1845-1846. MB; Mi; NjR. 45-3762

Ladies' Chinese Association of Philadelphia. First Annual report. Philadelphia, 1845. 12 p. PHi; IU; WHi. 45-3763

The ladies' scrap book... Hartford: S. Andrus and son, [845] [7]- 336 p. CoHi; DLC; MnU; NjR; RPB. 45-3764

The ladies work table book; containing clear and practical instructions in plain and fancy needlework, embroidery, knitting, netting and crochet. With numerous engravings, illustrative of the various stitches in those useful and fashionable employments. Philadelphia: G.B. Zeiber and company, 1845. 168 p. CtHT; MdBG; NH; PP; ViU. 45-3765

Ladreyt, Casimir, 1797-1877. Chrestomathie de la litterature Francaise, ou Morceaux choisis des meilleurs ecrivains Francais... Nouvelle edition. New York: W.E. Dean, 1845. 355 p. CtMW; CtY; DLC; MB; NCats. 45-3766

Lafayette, Louisiana. The ordinances and resolutions of the city of Lafayette; compiled by order of the board of council; also, the act of incorporation and amendatory acts. By A.W. Jourdan. New Orleans: Rea's Rotary Press office, 1845. 122 p. LNSCR; OClWHi. 45-3767

Lafayette College, Easton, Pennsylvania. Catalogue of the officers and students of Lafayette College for 1844-1845. Easton, Pennsylvania: Sentinel office, 1845. 20 p. NjN; PPM. 45-3768

LaGrange Female Seminary, LaGrange, Georgia. Catalogue of the instructors and pupils and patron... 1844. Hartford: Brown and Parsons, 1845. Ct. 45-3769

Laicus. A review of the Rev. William Croswell's letter to the Bishop of the diocese of Massachusetts. Boston: William A. Hall and company, 1845. 27 p. CtHT; MB; MBC; NGH; NjR. 45-3770

Laicus. The trial tried; or the bishop and the court at the bar of public opinion. New York: D. Appleton and company, 1845. 24 p. IU; MnHi; OCHP; PPL; WHi. 45-3771

Lake Champlain and Connecticut River Railroad Company. Remarks and statements of the character, feasibility of the route, and its importance to Boston trade. Boston: Eastburn's Press, 1845. 16 p. ICU; MB; MBAt; MHa; NN. 45-3772

Lamb, Charles, 1775-1834. The essays

of Elia. Second series. New York: Wiley and Putnam, 1845. 169 p. CU; MBAt; RWe; WvC. 45-3773

Lamb, Charles, 1775-1834. Specimens of English dramatic poets, who lived about the time of Shakespeare. With notes. New York: Wiley and Putnam, 1845. 2 parts. CtY; KyBC; MNBedf; NbU; RWoH. 45-3774

Lamb, Charles, 1775-1834. The works of Charles Lamb. To which are prefixed his letters, and a sketch of his life. By Thomas Noon Talfourd. New York: Harper and brothers, 1845. 2 v. AMob; CU; KyDC; RWe. 45-3775

LaMotte-Fouque, Friedrich Heinrich Karl, 1777-1843. Thiodolf, the Icelander, and Aslanga's knight, from the German of the Baron de LaMotte Fouque. New York: Wiley and Putnam, 1845. 349 p. CtY; IJI; LNH; NBuG; PRA. 45-3776

LaMotte-Fouque, Friedrich Heinrich Karl, 1777-1843. Undine and Sintram and his companions. From the German of Friedrich de LaMotte Fouque. New York: Wiley and Putnam, 1845. DLC; KHi; LN; PU; WvC. 45-3777

LaMotte-Fouque, Friedrich Heinrich Karl, 1777-1843. Undine, or the water spirit. Also, Sintram and his companions. From the German of LaMotte-Fouque. New York, 1845. 238 p. MH; NIC. 45-3778

LaMotte-Fouque, Friedrich Heinrich Karl, 1777-1843. Wild love. A romance. From the German of de LaMotte fougue. Philadelphia: E. Ferrett and company, 1845. 112 p. DLC; NN. 45-3779

Lancaster, Daniel, 1796-1880. The history of Gilmanton, embracing the proprietary, civil, literary, ecclesiastical biographical, genealogical, and miscel laneous history, from the first settlemen to the present time; including what is now Gilford, to the time it was disannexed Gilmanton, [New Hampshire] Printed by A Prescott, 1845. [13]-304 p. DLC CtSoP; MBC; RHi; WHi. 45-3780

Lancaster Academy, Lancaster, Mas sachusetts. Catalogue for 1845. Wor cester: P.L. Cox, 1845. DLC. 45-3781

Landon, Letitia Elizabeth, 1802-1838 The poetical works of Miss Landon Philadelphia: Henry F. Anners, 1845. 2 v in 1. ICU; MH; NN; OCl; PU. 45-3782

Lane, Benjamin Ingersol, 1797-1875 Midwinter's day dream. By Alquis. Troy New York: Young and Hartt, 1845. 20 p CSmH; N; NT. 45-3783

Lane, Benjamin Ingersol, 1797-1875. The mysteries of tobacco... with an intro ductory letter addressed to the Hon. John Quincy Adams, by the Rev. Samuel Hanson Cox... New York: Wiley and Put nam, 1845. 185. p. CU; DLC; DSG; LNP; NNNAM. 45-3784

Lane, Benjamin Ingersol, 1797-1875. Strictures on a letter containing some comments on a work entitled, "The refuge of lies and the covert from the storm." From the Hon. John Galbraith, of Erie, to the Rev. Henry Tullidge, by the Rev. B.I. Lane. Troy, New York: Press of J.C. Kneeland, 1845. 58 p. OU. 45-3785

Lane, Lunsford, b. 1803. The narrative of Lunsford Lane, formerly of Raleigh, orth Carolina, embracing an account of is early life, the redemption by purchase f himself and family from slavery, and is banishment from the place of his birth or the crime of wearing a colored skin. ublished by himself. Third edition. Boson: Printed for the publisher, Hewes and Vatson's print, 1845. [5]-54 p. DLC; /IBC; MPiB; Nh; Tx. 45-3786

Lang, William Bailey. Views, with round plans of the highland cottages at Roxbury [near Boston] designed and rected by William B. Lang. Boston: 'rinted by L.H. Bridgham and H.E. Felch, 1845. 2 p. MB; MWA; NNC; PPM; Vi. 45-3787

The language of love with hints on courtship. New York: Redfield, 1845. 124 p. MB; NcD; OO. 45-3788

Lanman, Charles, 1819-1895. Letters of a landscape painter. By the author of "Essays for summer hours." Boston: J. Munoe and company, 1845. 265 p. MH; NjN; PPA; RPA; VtU. 45-3789

Lanman, James Henry, 1812-1887. History of Michigan from its earliest colonization to the present time. New York: Harper, 1845. [15]-269 p. ICJ; MnU; OCX; PWW; TSewU. 45-3790

Lanner, Joseph Franz Carl, 1801-1843. The Bozwaltzes as performed at the grand Festival Park Theatre. New York: Firth and Hall, [1845?] 8 p. MB. 45-3791

Lanusse, Armand. Les cenelles. Choix de poesies indigenes... Nouvelle Orleans: Imprime par H. Lauve et compagnie, 1845. IAIS; L-M. 45-3792

Laporte, Theodore Charles. A key to

the French exercises. By Count de LaPorte. Boston: Count de LaPorte, 1845. 106 p. MoSpD. 45-3793

LaPorte, Theodore Charles. Self teaching reader of the French language. New York: Berard and Mondon, 1845. 141 p. MB; MBAt; MBr; MH; RPA. 45-3794

Laporte, Theodore Charles. Speaking exercises, for the illustration of the rules and idioms of the French language. Boston: Count de LaPorte, 1845. 14 8 p. MB; MBAt; MH; NNC; RPA. 45-3795

Laporte, Theodore Charles. Speaking exercises for the illustration of the rules and idioms of the French language. Boston: Count de LaPorte; New York: Bernard and Mondon, 1845. MB MBBC; MH; NNC; TxU-T. 45-3796

LaPorte University, Laporte, Indiana. Annual circular and catalogue of the officers and students. Session of 1844-5. Chicago: James Campbell, printer, 1845. 8 p. CSmH; In; OC. 45-3797

Lardner, Dionysius, 1793-1859. Popular lectures on science and art; delivered in the principal cities and towns of the United States. New York: Greeley and McElrath, 1845. InNd; InU; MH; MtU; NN. 45-3798

Larrabee, Charles, 1782-1863. Thoughts on peace and war; the result of twenty odd years reflection. Hartford: Press of Case, Tiffany, and Burnham, 1845. 63 p. CtHT-W; MWA; OC. 45-3799

Larry O'Gaff. A comic Irish song. Boston: Keith's Music Publishing House, 1845. 3 p. MB. 45-3800

The last awful tragedy, or conspiracy of the crowned heads exposed. From an article of the Westminister Review for September, 1844, entitled Mazzin and the ethics of politicians. New York: Houel and Macoy, 1845. ICPNA; MH-AH. 45-3801

The last of the Saxons, or the camp of refuge. A tale of the times of William the Conqueror. Philadelphia: E. Ferrett and company, 1845. 112 p. IaHi; TxComT. 45-3802

The late convention of the diocese of New York. A review of a pamphlet, by J.C. Spencer. New York, 1845. 38 p. CtY. 45-3803

Lathrop, L.E. The nature and influence of evangelical faith. Auburn: H. and J.C. Ivison. New York: Leavitt, Trow and company, 11845. 136 p. MiKL. 45-3804

Latrobe, John Hazlehurst Boneval, 1803-1891. Memoir of Benjamin Banneker, read before the Maryland Historical Society... Published under direction of the society. Baltimore: Printed by J.D. Loy, 1845. 16 p. IU; MH; NcD; OClWHi; PHi. 45-3805

The laugh of a layman at a pamphlet entitled the conspiracy against the Bishop of New York, unravelled by one of the conspirators, viz., James C. Richmond. New York: J.H. Welsh and G.F. Coachmon, 1845. 8 p. CtHT: MBC; MH; NN; WHi. 45-3806

Laurie, James. The prayer of the departing saint; a sermon, occasioned by the death of the Rev. William Hawley. Delivered February 2, 1845. Washington, 1845. 15 p. DLC; NjPT; PPPrHi. 45-3807

Laurie, Joseph, d. 1865. Homoepathi domestic medicine. Arranged as a pra tical work for students. Containing glossary of medical terms. Secon American edition, enlarged and im proved. New York: W. Radde, 1845. 26 p. MBM; MdUM; NN; OO. 45-3808

Law, William Fabian. Eulogy upon th life and character of the late Gener Charles R. Floyd pronounced... July 2 1845. Savannah, 1845. 16 p. CtY. 45-380

Lawrence, A.H. An examination o Hume's argument on the subject o miracles. Washington: Printed by J. an G.S. Gideon, 1845. 20 p. CBPSR; ICM MBC; MH; Nh. 45-3810

Lawrence, William Beach, 1800-188 German Reformed Church in the city o New York. In the court for the correctio of errors, Jacob F. Miller... argument o Mr. William Beach Lawrence... a Rochester, on September 2, 3, and 4 1845. New York: Tribune, printer, 1845 80 p. MH; MH-L; NNC; NjR. 45-3811

Lawrence Academy, Groton, Mas sachusetts. Program of commencemen exercises, November 18, 1845. Groton G.H. Brown, printer, 1845. M. 45-3812

A layman's remarks upon a letter to th Bishop of Massachusetts. By Rev. Mr Croswell, rector of the Church of the Ad vent. Boston: Dutton and Wentworth printers, 1845. 12 p. CtHT; MB; MBD MH. 45-3813

Lea, Albert Miller, 1807-1890. Addres following the prize speeches of the veral classes of East Tennessee niversity, August 5, 1845. Knoxville, ennessee: James C. Moses, 1845. 12 p. [dBD; T; TU. 45-3814

Leaman, John. An address delivered efore the students of Strasburg cademy, September 8, 1845. Lancaster: ieffer, [1845] PPPrHi. 45-3815

LeBoys des Guays, Jean Francois tienne, 1794-1864. Letters to a man of ie world, disposed to believe; translated om the French. Cincinnati: A. Peabody, 845. 225 p. CU; IEG; MdBJ; OU; PBa. 5-3816

LeBrethon, J.J.P. Guide to the French anguage, especially devised for persons ho wish to study the elements of that inguage. Second American from the eventh London edition, corrected, en-rged and improved by P. Bekeart. New ork: W.E. Dean, 1845. 388 p. KyDC; UM; PP; PV. 45-3817

LeConte, John Lawrence, 1825-1883. escription of some new and interesting isects, inhabiting the United States. 3oston, 1845] 7 p. MH-Z; PPAmE. 45-818

Lee, Charles Alfred, 1801-1872. Iuman Physiology, for the use of lementary schools. Seventh edition. ew York: W.E. Dean, 1845. 14-336 p. Rom. 45-3819

Lee, Hannah Farnham Sawyer, 1780-865. Historical sketches of the old ainters. By the author of "Three ex-eriences of living." A new edition, en-rged. Boston: E.J. Peet, 1845. 350 p. tMW; LNT; MeWa; MH; MNBedf. 45-820

Lee, Harriet, 1757-1851. Kruitzner; the German's tale. Boston: Saxton and Kelt; New York: Saxton and Miles, 1845. 211 p. MB; MdBMC; MWA; NjP. 45-3821

Lee, Henry, 1782-1867. Cultivation of cotton in connection with the currency. Boston: Dutton and Wentworth, 1845. MH. 45-3822

Lee, Henry Washington, 1815-1874. Prayers for children. Fifth edition. New York: General Protestant Episcopal Sunday School Union, 1845. 28 p. MB; RPB. 45-3823

Lee, N.K.M. The cook's own book and housekeeper's register. Being receipts for cooking of every kind of meat, fish, and fowl; and making every sort of soup, gravy, pastry, preserves and essences with a complete system of confec-tionery.... New York: Charles S. Francis, 1845. 337 p. ViRVal. 45-3824

Leeser, Isaac, 1806-1868. Catechism for younger children, designed as a familiar exposition of the Jewish religion. Second edition. Philadelphia: C. Sherman, [1845] 168 p. OCH; PPDrop. 45-3825

Legare, Hugh Swinton, 1797-1843. Writings of Hugh Swinton Legare... prefaced by a memoir of his life. Edited by his sister... Charleston, South Carolina: Burges and James; New York: D. Appleton and company, 1845-1846. 2 v. CU-Law; InCW; MB; NcU; WaS. 45-3826

Legendre, Adrien Marie. Elements of geometry and trigonometry; translated from the French by D. Brewster; revised and adapted to the course of instruction in the United States by C. Davies. New

York, 1845. 297 p. InU; MB; MCM; MH; MoS. 45-3827

Leigh, Percival, 1813-1869. The comic English grammar: a new and facetious introduction to the English tongue. Embellished with upwards of forty-five characteristic illustrations by J. Leech. New York: Wilson and company, 1845. 144 p. MH; NNC; OClWHi; PJA. 45-3828

Leighton, Robert, 1611-1684. The works of Leighton. New York: J.C. Riker, 1845. 300 p. NcAS. 45-3829

Leland, John, 1754-1841. The writings of the late elder John Leland, including some events of his life, written by himself. With additional sketches, etc., by Miss L.F. Greene, Lanesboro, Massachusetts. New York: Printed by G.W. Wood, 1845. 744 p. DLC; MPiB; NNC; PCC; TxU. 45-3830

Lemon, Mark, 1809-1870. Grandfather Whitehead. An original drama. In two acts. New York: W. Taylor; Baltimore: William Taylor and company, 1845. 38 p. AzU; MH; MPiB; NN; ViU. 45-3831

Lemon, Mark, 1809-1870. Love launched a fairy boat. Ballad. Boston: Oliver Ditson, [1845] 5 p. KU. 45-3832

Lempriere, John, 1765?-1824. Bibliotheca classica; or a dictionary of all the principal names and terms relating to the geography, topography, history, literature, and mythology of antiquity and of the ancients, with a chronological table. Fifteenth American edition, greatly enlarged in the historical department by L.L. DaPonte. New York: W.E. Dean,

1845. 803 p. AB; CS; DLC; MoK; PN 45-3833

Leonard, Charles C. Leonard's new sy tem of mathematics. Sixth editio Columbus: Tribune office, printer, 184. 104 p. OClWHi; OHi. 45-3834

Leonard, David Augustus, 1771-181! The laws of Siasconset, a ballac proposed with a pipe of tobacco, and a evening's amusement to the fishermen. [First published in 1797] New Bedfor Massachusetts: Press of Benjami Lindsey, 1845. 8 p. CtY; MH; MNBed 45-3835

Leonard, Levi Washburn, 1790?-186 The North American spelling book, cor formed to Worcester's dictionary, with progressive series of easy reading les sons. Thirtieth revised edition. Keen New Hampshire: G. Tilden, etc., etc [1845?] MH. 45-3836

The Leonard family; or the history c the Jews from the captivity to th destruction of Jerusalem... Boston: 184! [9]-136 p. RPB. 45-3837

LeSage, Alain Rene, 1668-1747. Th devil upon two sticks. Hartford: S Andrus and son, 1845. 337 p. MHa; NIC 45-3838

LeSage, Alain Rene, 1668-1747. His toire de Gil Blas de Santilland. Nouvell edition. New York: Roe Lockwood an son, 1845. 504 p. FNp; MB. 45-3839

Leslie, Charles, 1650-1722. Leslie' method with deists; wherein the truth o the Christian religion is demonstrated i a letter to a friend. New York: G. Lan

nd C.B. Tippett, 1845. 32 p. NbOP. 45-
3840

Leslie, Eliza, 1787-1858. Companion to
Miss Leslie's cookery; containing direc-
ions for laundry work, lights and fires,
emoving stains, cleaning furniture,
kitchen affairs, waiting on company,
carving, house cleaning, making up linen,
dress making... Seventh edition.
Philadelphia: Carey and Hart, 1845.
WGr. 45-3841

Leslie, Eliza, 1787-1858. Directions for
cookery in its various branches. Twentieth edition, with improvements, supplementary receipts and a new appendix.
Philadelphia: Carey and Hart, 1845. MH;
MoU. 45-3842

Leslie, Eliza, 1787-1858. Directions for
cookery in its various branches. Twenty-
third edition. With improvements, supplementary receipts and a new appendix.
Philadelphia: Carey and Hart, 1845. 511
p. CtY; RWe. 45-3843

Leslie, Eliza, 1787-1858. The house
book; or a manual of domestic economy
for town and country. Seventh edition.
Philadelphia: Carey and Hart, 1845. 436
p. WGr; WS. 45-3844

Leslie, Eliza, 1787-1858. The house
book; or a manual of domestic economy
for town and country. Eighth edition.
Philadelphia: Carey and Hart, 1845. 436
p. DNAL; FMU; MdBLC; NcAS; PHi.
45-3845

Leslie, Eliza, 1787-1858. Stories for
Helen. Philadelphia: Henry F. Anners,
[1845] 140 p. MBev; MH; NNC; RLa. 45-
3846

Lester, Charles Edwards, 1815-1890.
The artist, the merchant, and the statesman of the age of the medici, and of our
own times.... New York: Paine and Burgess, 1845. 2 v. LN; MWA; OO; RP; TxU.
45-3847

Lester, Charles Edwards, 1815-1890.
The condition and fate of England...
Second edition. New York: H.G.
Langley, 1845. 2 v. IC; MiU; NGH; NIC;
ScDuE. 45-3848

Lester, Charles Edwards, 1815-1890.
Glory and the shame of England. New
York: Harper and brothers, 1845. 2 v.
GMM; IaGG; LN; OClW; Vi. 45-3849

Letter addressed to the Hon. John C.
Calhoun, on the law relating to slaves,
free negroes, and mulattoes, by a Virginian. Published by request. Washington: J. and G.S. Gideon, printers, 1845.
13 p. DLC; MH; NN. 45-3850

Letter on the higher powers. Pittsburgh:
W. Allinder, 1845. 8 p. NcMHi. 45-3851

Letter to Rev. Jason Whitman, by a
southerner and Mr. Whitman's reply.
Boston: Office of the Christian World,
1845. 24 p. MB; MnHi. 45-3852

Letter to the Honorable James. F. Simmons. By a Rhode Island conservative on
the Rhode Island controversy. [Pro-
vidence, 1845] 8 p. CtY; PPL. 45-3853

A letter to the Rev. James C. Richmond
Presbyter of Rhode Island, and by his
own showing, principal agent of the conspirators in the recent combination to
destroy the Bishop of New York. New
York: Jones and Welsh, 1845. 24 p.

CtHT; MH-L; MiD-B; NGH; WHi. 45-3854

Letters addressed to the Philadelphia Sabbath Association regarding labor on Sunday, by the employees of the Delaware and Hudson Canal. [Philadelphia? 1845] 8 p. MnHi. 45-3855

Letters from a sick room. Written for the Massachusetts Sabbath School Society, and revised by the committee of publication. Boston: Massachusetts Sabbath School Society, 1845. 132 p. DLC. 45-3856

Lever, Charles James, 1806-1872. Charles O'Malley, the Irish Dragoon. By Harry Lorrequer. With illustrations by Phiz... Philadelphia: Carey and Hart, 1845. 2 v. in 1. CtY. 45-3857

Lever, Charles James, 1806-1872. Jack Hinton, the guardsman. Philadelphia: Carey and Hart, 1845. 400 p. NNU-W. 45-3858

Lever, Charles James, 1806-1872. O'Donoghue; a tale of Ireland fifty years ago. New York: W.F. Burgess, 1845. 136 p. InLW; InNd; PPL. 45-3859

Lever, Charles James, 1806-1872. St. Patrick's eve. New York: Harper and brothers, 1845. 38 p. DLC; LNH; NN; ViU. 45-3860

Lever, Charles James, 1806-1872. Tom Burke of "Ours." New York, 1845. PPL. 45-3861

Lever, John Charles Weaver, 1811-1858. A practical treatise on organic diseases of the uterus, being the prize essay to which the medical society of London awarded the Fothergill gold medal for 1843. Newburgh, New York: D.L. Proudfit, 1845. 240 p. CSt-L; IU-M; MBM OCIM; PPM. 45-3862

Leverett, Frederick Percival, 1803-1836. A new and copious lexicon of the Latin language; compiled chiefly from the magnum totius latinitatis lexicon of Facciolati and Forcellini, and the German works of Scheller and Luenemann Boston: J.H. Wilkins and R.B. Carter 1845. 2 v. in 1. IaPeC; MShM; OCl PPDrop; RPB. 45-3863

Leverett, Frederick Percival, 1803-1836. The new Latin tutor; or exercises in etymology, syntax and prosody: compiled chiefly from the best English works Philadelphia: Uriah Hunt and son, 1845. 350 p. GMM; MB; MH; NjP; TWcW. 45-3864

Levett, M. Observations on the best means of preserving the teeth. Indispensable to health, comfort and appearance. Founded on long and very extensive practice. New York, 1845. 24 p. MBCo; NBMS; PU-D. 45-3865

Levin, Lewis Charles, 1808-1860. Intemperance. The prelude to gambling and suicide as illustrated in the life of the Rev. C.C. Colton... Delivered at La-Fayette College, Easton, September 18, 1844, and published at their request. Philadelphia: Printed by William F. Geddes, 1845. 21 p. CtY; LU; MBAt; PHi; PPPrHi. 45-3866

Levin, Lewis Charles, 1808-1860. Speech of Mr. Levin, of Pennsylvania, on the subject of altering the naturalization laws, delivered in the House, December

18, 1845. [Washington] 1845. 15 p. DLC; MH; Vi; WHi. 45-3867

Levison, J.L. Mental culture; or the means of developing the human faculties. Boston, 1845. MH. 45-3868

Levizac, Jean Pons Victor Lecoutz de, d. 1813. A theoretical and practical grammar of the French language in which the present usage is displayed agreeably to the decisions of the French Academy... Eleventh edition. Philadelphia: Carey and Hart, 1845. 467 p. CtHT-W; IaFayU; MnU. 45-3869

Levizac, Jean Pons Victor Lecoutz de, d. 1813. A theoretical and practical grammar of the French language in which the present usage is displayed agreeably to the decisions of the French Academy... Fifteenth American edition. New York: W.E. Dean, 1845. 446 p. CoLH; DLC; T. 45-3870

Levizac, Jean Pons Victor Lecoutz de, d. 1813. A theoretical and practical grammar of the French language in which the present usage is displayed agreeably to the decisions of the French Academy... Twenty-fifth edition. Philadelphia: Carey and Hart, 1845. 294, 173 p. ArL; DLC; KWiW; MH; OrU. 45-3871

Lewis, Alonzo, 1794-1861. Love, forest flowers and sea shells. Boston: The author, 1845. [7]-127 p. MB; MLy; MWH; NcD. 45-3872

Lewis, Alonzo, 1794-1861. The picture of Nahant [Massachusetts] Lynn: Printed by J.B. Tolman, 1845. 14 p. ICN; MWA; PHi; RHi; WHi. 45-3873

Lewis, Ellis, 1798-1871. Eulogium upon the life and character of Andrew Jackson, June 26, 1845. Lancaster: J. Forsyth Carter, 1845. 16 p. PHi; RPB. 45-3874

Lewis, Enoch, 1776-1856. Observations on the militia system; addressed to the serious consideration of the citizens of Pennsylvania, and particularly those who occupy judicial or legislative stations. Philadelphia: Printed by Joseph Rakestraw, 1845. 44 p. InRchE; MHi; NjR; PPAmP; PPL. 45-3875

Lewis, F. The sinner's guide. In two books: Book I. Containing a full and ample exhortation to the pursuit of virtue; with instructions and directions on how to become virtuous. Book II. The doctrine of virtue; with necessary instructions and advice for making a man virtuous. Translated from the Spanish. Philadelphia: Henry M'Grath, 1845. 402 p. IaPeC; MdW; MiDSH; OCX; WMMU. 45-3876

Lewis, George. Impressions of America, and the American churches. From journal of the Rev. G. Lewis. New York: Harper and brothers, 1845. 432 p. CtY; DLC; IaPeC; NjR; ScU. 45-3877

Lewis, Hannah Jane Woodman, b. 1816. The language of gems, with their poetic sentiments. Boston: A. Topkins and B.B. Mussey, 1845. 160 p. MB; MnU; MWA; RPB; ViU. 45-3878

Lewis, Matthew Gregory, 1775-1818. Abellino; or the bravo of Venice. Philadelphia: E. Ferrett and company, 1845. 192 p. MS. 45-3879

Lewis, Matthew Gregory, 1775-1818. The monk, a romance. First American reprint from the tenth London edition.

New York: Moore and Jackson, 1845. DLC; MH. 45-3880

Lewis, Meriwether, 1774-1809. History of the expedition under the command of Captains Lewis and Clarke, to the sources of the Missouri, thence across the Rocky Mountains, and down the River Columbia to the Pacific Ocean; performed during the years 1804, 1805, 1806, by order of the Government of the United States. Prepared for the prefs [sic] by Paul Allen. Revised and abridged with an introduction and notes by A. M'Vickar. New York: Harper and brothers, 1845. 2 v. InCW; MB; MLaw; NcWfC; OCY. 45-3881

Lewison Falls Academy, Lewiston, Maine. The annual catalogue of Lewiston Falls Academy, for the year ending August 20, 1845. Portland: Thurston, Ilsley, and company, 1845. 16 p. MeHi. 45-3882

Lhomond, Charles Francois, 1727-1794. Elements of French grammar. Translated from the French by H.W. Longfellow, with notes and exercises. Eighth edition. Boston: James Munroe, 1845. 196 p. CtMW; MeU; MH; NNC; ViU. 45-3883

Lhomond, Charles Francois, 1727-1794. Epitome historiae sacrae, on an improved plan... Designed as a primary book. By Andrew Comstock. Philadelphia: D.H. Butler, 1845. 2 v. DLC; IaDuU. 45-3884

Lhomond, Charles Francois, 1727-1794. Epitome historiae sacrae, on an improved plan... Designed as a primary book. By Andrew Comstock. Twentieth edition. Philadelphia: Thomas, Cow-

perthwait and company, 1845. 2 v. CU IaDuU; NcMHi; PP. 45-3885

Lhomond, Charles Francois, 1727-1794. Viri Romae; with introductory exercises, intended as a first book in the study of Latin, with English notes. By F.P Leverett and Thomas G. Bradford. A lexicon has been added to this edition. Boston: Wilkins, Carter and company, 1845. 299 p. IGK; MB: MeBa; MH; MH- Ed. 45-3886

The liberty almanac... 1845... By J.N.T. Tucker... Syracuse, New York: Tucker and Kinney, [1845] MH; MWA; NUtHi. 45-3887

The liberty bell. By a friend of freedom... Boston: Massachusetts Anti-slavery fair, 1845. CoD; FNp; KHi; NjR; OkU. 45-3888

Liberty chimes. Providence: Ladies Anti-slavery Society, 1845. IEN; MWA; NIC; RWe; TNF. 45-3889

Liberty Party. National Convention. Proceedings of the great convention of Friends of Freedom in the Eastern and Middle states. Boston, October 12, 1845. Lowell, Massachusetts: Knapp, 1845. 34 p. NIC; NBuG. 45-3890

Library of oratory; embracing select speeches of celebrated orators of America, Ireland and England. Philadelphia: E.C. and J. Biddle, 1845. 4 v. GEU; IU; MiU; MoFloSS; NjNbS. 45-3891

Lieber, Francis, 1800-1872. A lecture on the origin and development of the first constituents of civilization. Columbia, South Carolina: S.C. Morgan, 1845. 18 p.

DLC; GDecCT; KyLx; ScU; TxU. 45-3892

Liebig, Justus, 1803-1873. Animal chemistry, or organic chemistry in its application to physiology and pathology. Philadelphia and New York: James M. Campbell, 1845. 111, 16 p. MAA; MoS; PHi; WMAM. 45-3893

Liebig, Justus, 1803-1873. Chemistry in its application to agriculture and physiology... Philadelphia: J.M. Campbell, 1845. 135 p. ICJ; IdU; NN; OC. 45-3894

Life and death of Cardinal Wolsey; illustrated with portraits by Holbein. Boston, 1845. 192 p. WFonBG. 45-3895

Life and exploits of Arthur Wellesley, First Duke of Wellington. Philadelphia, 1845. PPL-R. 45-3896

The life and institute of the Jesuits. Translated by C. Seager. Philadelphia: W.J. Cunningham, 1845. 180 p. MoSU. 45-3897

The life of Felix Neff. Prepared from Gillie's memoir of Felix Neff. By an American lady. New York: G. Lane and C.B. Tippett, 1845. 168 p. GAGTh; IEG. 45-3898

The life of Rev. John Campbell. Revised by the committee of publication. From the London edition. Boston: Sabbath School Society, 1845. 24 p. OClWHi. 45-3899

The life of the Rt. Rev. Dr. [James] Doyle; compiled from authentic documents. New York: D. and J. Sadlier, 1845. 288 p. CMenSP; IaDmDC; MdBS; NRSB. 45-3900

The life, trial and conversations of Robert Emmet, leader of the Irish insurrection of 1803. New York: R. Coddington, 1845. 132 p. DLC; MBC; MdBS; MH; NjP. 45-3901

Light and the truth of slavery. Aaron's history. Springfield, 1845. CtHWatk; MH-AH. 45-3902

Lightning from steam. An account of the Benjamin Franklin steam electrical machine. Philadelphia, 1845. PPL. 45-3903

Lincoln, Ensign, 1779-1832. Aids to devotion, in three parts. Including Watts' guide to prayer. Second edition. Boston: B. Perkins and company, 1845. MBC; MH; OO. 45-3904

Lincoln, Frederic Walker, 1817-1898. An address delivered before the Massachusetts Charitable Mechanic Association of its first semi-centennial anniversary and thirteenth triennial festival, October 2, 1845. Boston: Dutton and Wentworth, 1845. 64 p. MB; MBC; MH; MWA; RPB. 45-3905

Lind, Adam. The true prosperity. A sermon on the revival of religion. Elgin: Peter MacDonald, 1845. 25 p. CSansS. 45-3906

Linsley, James Harvey, 1787-1843. Catalogue of the shells of Connecticut... [New Haven, 1845] 16 p. CtY; MH-Z. 45-3907

Linwood Cemetery. Haverhill, Massachusetts. Bylaws of the Linwood Cemetery, Haverhill, Massachusetts. Haverhill: From the Essex Banner Press, 1845. 10 p. MHa; MHaHi. 45-3908

Lippard, George, 1822-1854. The Quaker city; or the monks of Monk Hall. A romance of Philadelphia life, mystery and crime. Philadelphia: T.B. Peterson and brothers, 1845. 2 v. in 1. CtHT- W; MH; RPB; TxU. 45-3909

Lipscomb, Andrew Agate, 1816-1890. Literature auxiliary to Christianity. A premium essay... Charleston, South Carolina: Printed by Walker and Burke, 1845. 16 p. TxU. 45-3910

The literary emporium; a compendium of religious, literary and philosophical knowledge. New York: J.K. Wellma, 1845-1846. 4 v. in 2. CU; ICU; MoK; MWA; RPB. 45-3911

The literary news and law intelligencer. Philadelphia, 1845. V. 1. No. 1. MHi; WaU-L. 45-3912

Little, George, b. 1791? Life on the ocean; or twenty years at sea: being the personal adventures of the author. Boston: Wait, Peirce and company, 1845. 395 p. CPg; DLCl; ICN; MdAN; RPE. 45-3913

Little, George, b. 1791? Life on the ocean; or twenty years at sea: being the personal adventures of the author. Third edition. Boston: Wait, Peirce and company, 1845. 395 p. DLC; ICU; MH; MWA; OU. 45-3914

Little, Sophia. The branded hand; a dramatic sketch commemorative of the tragedies of the South in the winter of 1844-1845. Pawtucket, Rhode Island, 1845. 46 p. NcD; NIC; RHi; RP; RPB. 45-3915

The little child's tutor; or a first book for children, in words not exceeding two syllables. A new edition. Derby [Connecticut] Mozley, 1845. 72 p. IaU. 45-3916

The little collector; or I wish to be useful in some way. Revised by the editor D.P. Kidder. New York: Lane and Tippett for the Sunday School Union of the Methodist Episcopal Church, 1845. 32 p MnU. 45-3917

Little Emma; or the beautiful foundling. Boston: H.L. Williams, 1845. 48 p RPB. 45-3918

Little Falls, New York. Academy. Catalogue of the officers and students... Little Falls, New York, 1845. NN. 45-3919

Little Fort Porcupine. Prospectus for the Little Fort Porcupine and Democratic Banner. Commencing March 4, 1845. [Waukegan: N.W. Fuller, 1845] Broadside. Graff. 45-3920

The little gift. Edited by Mrs. S. Colman. Boston: T.H. Carter and company, 1845. 94 p. MHa. 45-3921

The little gift for little folks. Philadelphia: B. Walker, 1845. 80 p. IaU; MLex. 45-3922

The little history of England. Philadelphia: Loomis and Peck, 1845. 191 p DLC. 45-3923

Little present for a good child. Greenfield: A. Phelps, 1846. 18 p. PHi; RPB. 45-3924

Little verses, for good children. Greenfield, 1845. 8 p. PHi. 45-3925

The lives of celebrated children. Boston: C. Tappan, 1845. [7]-157 p. MB; MFai; Vi; ViU. 45-3926

Livius, Titus. Historeasum liber primus et selecta quaedam capita. Edited by Caroline Folsom. Fifteenth edition. Bostoniae: Sumphtis Samuel G. Simpkins, 1845. IES; IU; MB; MdW. 45-3927

Livius, Titus. Titi Livii Patavini historiarum. Liber primus et selecta quaedam capita. Sixteenth stereotype edition. Boston: Phillips and Sampson, and S.G. Simpkins, 1845. 287 p. MeHi; NcWfc; TKimJ. 45-3928

Livre des petits enfants. New York, [1845] MB. 45-3929

Lloyd, Benjamin, 1804-1860. The primitive hymns, spiritual songs, and sacred poems. Third edition, corrected and enlarged. Published for the proprietor, and for sale by him at Wetumpka, Alabama, 1845. 290 p. NNUT; T. 45-3930

Loan Fund Life Assurance Society of London. [Prospectus] New York, 1845. 28 p. DLC. 45-3931

Locke, John, 1632-1704. Conduct of the understanding. With essays, moral, economical and political by John Locke. New York: Harper and brothers, 1845. 299 p. InCW; PMA. 45-3932

Lockwood, Peter, 1798-1882. Memoir of John D. Lockwood being reminiscenses of a son by his father. New York and Pittsburg: Robert Carter, 1845. 252 p. ICP; MH-AH; NcWfc; PHi; PPPrHi. 45-3933

The lofty and the lowly; a sermon by a presbyter of New Jersey. New York, 1845. CtHT; CtMW; MB; MH. 45-3934

Logan, James, 1794?-1872. The Scotish Gael; or celtic manners as preserved among the highlanders, being an historical and descriptive account of the inhabitants... First American edition. Hartford: S. Andrus and son, 1845. 520 p. CSmH; IEN; MiU; OCl; ScC. 45-3935

London lancet; a journal of British and foreign medical and chemical science, criticism, literature and news. In two volumes annually. Edited by Thomas Wakley and Henry Bennet. New York: Burgess, Stringer, 1845-. v. 1-. ArU-M; CoCsE; IaU; KyLxT; NjR; PP. 45-3936

Long, Catharine Walpole, d. 1867. Sir Roland Ashton; a tale of the times. New York: R. Carter, 1845. 2 v. MA; NN; PPL-R. 45-3937

Long Island Insurance Company. Report of the Long Island Insurance Company in answer to a resolution of the assembly. Albany, 1845. 3 p. WHi. 45-3938

Long Island Railroad Company. Report of the directors... to the stockholders, January 1, 1845. 14 p. MH-BA; NIC; NN; WU. 45-3939

Longfellow, Henry Wadsworth, 1807-1882. Ballads and other poems. Ninth edition. Cambridge, Massachusetts: Owen, 1845. 132 p. MH; MLin; NN; OC; RPB. 45-3940

Longfellow, Henry Wadsworth, 1807-1882. Hyperion: a romance. Boston:

Ticknor and Fields, 1845. 382 p. WaU.
45-3941

Longfellow, Henry Wadsworth, 1807-
1882. Hyperion: a romance. Second edition. Cambridge, [Massachusetts] J.
Owen, 1845. 370 p. DLC; InU; MH;
OrU; ViU. 45-3942

Longfellow, Henry Wadsworth, 1807-
1882. Kavanagh. Boston: Ticknor and
Fields, 1845. 188 p. IaK. 45-3943

Longfellow, Henry Wadsworth, 1807-
1882. Poems by Henry Wadsworth
Longfellow, with illustrations by D.
Hunt-ington, engraved by American artists. Third edition. Philadelphia: Carey
and Hart, 1846. 415 p. AMob; IaDuU;
MWHi; WU. 45-3944

Longfellow, Henry Wadsworth, 1807-
1882. The poets and poetry of Europe.
With introductions and biographical
notices. Philadelphia: Carey and Hart,
1845. 779 p. MeB; MdBP; NNP; OCad;
RPA. 45-3945

Longfellow, Henry Wadsworth, 1807-
1882. Spanish student; a play in three
acts. Cambridge, Massachusetts: Owen,
1845. 183 p. NjP; PP. 45-3946

Longfellow, Henry Wadsworth, 1807-
1882. Voices of the night. Boston: Redding and company, 1845. 32 p. CSt; IU;
MWH; PP; TxU. 45-3947

Longfellow, Henry Wadsworth, 1807-
1882. Voices of the night. Eleventh edition. Cambridge, Massachusetts: J.
Owen, 1845. 144 p. MB; MWH; OClW.
45-3948

Longfellow, Henry Wadsworth, 1807-

1882. The waif; a collection of poems
First edition. Cambridge, Massachusetts
John Owen, 1845. 144 p. MB; NN; OO
PPL-R; RPB. 45-3949

Longfellow, Henry Wadsworth, 1807
1882. The waif; a collection of poems
Second edition. Cambridge: John Owen
1845. 144 p. CtHWatk; MBAt; MH
NNC; NjR. 45-3950

Longfellow, Henry Wadsworth, 1807
1882. The waif; a collection of poems
Third edition. Cambridge: John Owen
1845. 144 p. MWH; MWo. 45-3951

Longfellow, Henry Wadsworth, 1807
1882. The waif; a collection of poems
Fourth edition Cambridge: J. Owen
1845. 144 p. MB; MsJMC; NjP; VtPifi
45-3952

Longking, Joseph. Questions on the
Gospel; the lessons in historical and
chronological order according to the arrangement of Townsend's chronological
New Testament. New York: G. Lane and
C.B. Tippett, 1845. NoLoc. 45-3953

Longstreet, Augustus Baldwin. Georgia
scenes, characters, incidents, etc., in the
first half century of the republic, by a native Georgian [pseud.] Second edition
With original illustrations. New York
Harper and brothers, 1845. 214 p. MB
MoS; ScC; TJaU; TxU. 45-3954

Longstreet, Augustus Baldwin. Letters
on the Epistle of Paul to Philemon, or the
connection of Apostolical Christianity
with slavery. Charleston, South Carolina
Printed by B. Jenkins, 1845. 47 p. KyLx
LU; ScSp. 45-3955

Loomis, D.W. A memoir of Harrie

Eliza Snow. Second edition. Boston, 1845. DLC; MH. 45-3956

Loomis' no. 12 Pittsburgh almanac... for... 1846... calculated by Sanford C. Hill, Esq., to equal, mean, or clock time for the horizon and meridian of Pittsburgh... Pittsburgh: Luke Loomis, [1845] 35 p. MnHi; MWA. 45-3957

Lord, John Chase, 1805-1877. The supernatural element of Christianity; an address before the Society of Christian Research of Hamilton College, delivered on the Sabbath evening before commencement, 1845. Clinton, 1845. 31 p. CSmH; MH; NBu; NUt; PPPrHi. 45-3958

Lord, John King, 1819-1849. The influence exerted upon our youth, and its effects. An address delivered before the senior class of Kimball Union Academy, Meriden, New Hampshire, May 5, 1845. Windsor, Vermont: Chronicle Press, 1845. 24 p. MBC; MH-AH; TxU. 45-3959

Lord, John Perkins, 1786-1877. Maine townsman; or laws for the regulation of towns; with forms and judicial decisions, adapted to the revised statutes of Maine. Portland: Sanborn and Carter, 1845. 300 p. ICN; MeB. 45-3960

Lord, John Perkins, 1786-1877. Reference book of the state of Maine, for the year of our Lord, 1845. Portland: Sanborn and Carter, 1845. 140 p. MeBa; MeWC; MHi. 45-3961

Lord, William Wilberforce, 1819-1907. Poems. New York: D. Appleton and company; Philadelphia: G.S. Appleton, 1845. 158 p. ICU; MH; NBuG; NNC; WU. 45-3962

Lord, Willis, 1809-1888. The federal character of Adam, and the imputation of his sin. Philadelphia: Presbyterian Board of Publication, 1845. 16 p. CU; DLC; MnSM; NcD; PLFM. 45-3963

Lorenzo, or the empire of religion. By a non-conformist. A convert to the Catholic faith. Translated from the French by a lady of Philadelphia. Baltimore: John Murphy, 1845. 311 p. MdB. 45-3964

Loring, Charles Greely, 1794-1867. Argument of Charles G. Loring, esq., on behalf of the Eastern Railroad Company, at a hearing on the petitions of David Pingree and others, and W.J. Valentine and others, before the railroad committee of the Massachusetts legislature, Boston, March 7, 1845. Boston: Dutton and Wentworth, 1845. 88 p. DLC; ICU; NjR; OCLaw; PPi. 45-3965

Lorner, M. Wonderful disclosure! The mystery solved! Or narrative of Dr. M. Lorner, one of the passengers of the steam ship President! New York: W.L. Knapp and E.O. Locke, 1845. 16 p. DLC; MB; Nh; NNNAM. 45-3966

Lossing, Benson J. Outline history of the fine arts, embracing a view of the rise, progress, and influence of the arts among different nations, ancient and modern, with notices of the character and works of many celebrated artists. New York: Harper and brothers, 1845. 330 p. Me; NBuCC; NjR; RPE; ScGrw. 45-3967

Lothrop, D.W. Native American's quick step. Boston: Bradke and company, 1845. MB. 45-3968

Loudon, Jane Webb, 1807-1858. Gardening for ladies; and companion to the flower garden. First American edition, edited by A.J. Downing. New York: Wiley, 1845. 430 p. ICJ; MH; NBu; NCats. 45-3969

Louisiana. Actes passes a la premiere session de la dixseptieme legislature de l'etat de la Louisiane, tenue et commencee en la ville de la Nouvelle-Orleans, le sixieme jour de Janveir. New Orleans: Magne and Weisse, 1845. 192 p. NoLoc. 45-3970

Louisiana. Acts passed at the first session of the sixteenth legislature of the state of Louisiana. New Orleans: Magne and Weisse, 1845. 187 p. LNT-L. 45-3971

Louisiana. Acts passed at the first session of the seventeenth legislature of the state of Louisiana. New Orleans: Magne and Weisse, 1845. 91 p. In-SC; Mo; Mi-L; NNLI; Nv. 45-3972

Louisiana. Journal de la convention de la Louisiane. Nouvelle Orleans: J. Bayon, 1845. 367, 11 p. MnU. 45-3973

Louisiana. Journal of the convention called for the purpose of re-adopting, amending or changing the constitution of the state of Louisiana [convened at Jackson], August 5, 1844. n.p. [1845] 72 p. DLC; IU; Nj. 45-3974

Louisiana. Journal of the proceedings of the convention of the state of Louisiana, begun and held in the city of New Orleans, on January 14, 1845. New Orleans: Besancon, Ferguson and company, 1845. 356 p. IU; LNT-L; LU; MiU-C; NN. 45-3975

Louisiana. Journal of the special committee appointed by the House... to investigate the frauds perpetrated in the state during the late presidential election. New Orleans: Magne, 1845. 43 p TxU. 45-3976

Louisiana. The new constitution of the state of Louisiana: adopted in convention on May 14, 1845, and ratified by the people of the state on November 5, 1845. With a comparative view of the old and new constitutions of the state; and a copious index. By S.F. Glenn... New Orleans: J.C. Morgan, 1845. 36 p. DLC; MH-L; NjP; OClWHi. 45-3977

Louisiana. Official report of debates in the Louisiana convention. August 5, 1844-January 17, 1845. [New Orleans? 1845?] 146 p. DLC; ICJ; MH-L; MnU; NNC. 45-3978

Louisiana. Proceedings and debates of the convention of Louisiana, which assembled in the city of New Orleans, January 14, 1844. Robert J. Ker, reporter. New Orleans: Besancon, Ferguson and company, 1845. 960 p. ICU; LNT; MiU; NN; WHi. 45-3979

Louisiana. Rapports officals des debats de la convention de la Louisiane. James Foullouze Rapporteur. New Orleans, 1845. 460 p. DLC; ICN; LU; MnU; PHi. 45-3980

Louisiana. Report on the penitentiary, by a joint committee of the Senate and House of Representatives. J. Bernard, chairman. New Orleans: Magne and Weisse, 1845. 16 p. MiGrL; NjR; OO. 45-3981

Louisiana. Special committee to investigate the frauds perpetrated in the state, during the late presidential election. New Orleans: Magne and Weisse, 1845. CSmH; LNH. 45-3982

A love gift for 1845. Boston: Saxton, Pierce and company, 1845. 144 p. ICU; MB; MWA; NBLiHi; NjR. 45-3983

Lovejoy, J.C. The robbers of Adullam; or a glance at organic sins, a sermon. Boston, 1845. 22 p. MBC; NjPT. 45-3984

Lovell, John Epy, 1795-1892. United States speaker; a copius selection of exercises in elocution, consisting of prose, poetry and dialogue... including a variety of pieces suitable for very young speakers, designed for the use of colleges and schools. New edition, enlarged. New Haven: Babcock, 1845. 504 p. DLC; OC; RP. 45-3985

Lovell, John Epy, 1795-1892. The young pupil's first book... New Haven, 1845. CtHWatk. 45-3986

Lovell, John Epy, 1795-1892. The young pupil's second book; comprising a great variety of interesting lessons, the whole progressively arranged, and beautifully illustrated, by simple and compound cuts. Fourth edition, carefully revised and corrected. New Haven: S. Babcock, 1845. 216 p. CtHWatk; NIDHi. 45-3987

Lovell, John Epy, 1795-1892. The young speaker: an introduction to the United States speaker; designed to furnish exercises in both reading and speaking, for pupils between the ages of six and fourteen. New Haven, Durrie and Peck, 1845. 300 p. CtHWatk; CtY; DLC; NIC; TxU. 45-3988

Lovering, Joseph, 1813-1892. An ac-count of the magnetic observations made at the observatory of Harvard University, Cambridge. Communicated by Joseph Lovering. n.p., [1845] 76 p. NNC; OO; WaU. 45-3989

Lowe, Enoch Louis, 1820-1892. Discourse delivered at the commemoration of the landing of the pilgrims of Maryland, celebrated May 12, 1845, at St. Mary's near Emmitsburg, Maryland. Gettysburg: Printed by H.C. Neiustedt, 1845. 37 p. MBAt; MdBP; MdBJ; NcMHi; PPPrHi. 45-3990

Lowell, Anna Cabot Jackson, 1819-1874. Olympic games; a gift for the holidays. Boston: W.D. Ticknor and company, 1845. 143 p. CtY; ICN; MB; NNU-W. 45-3991

Lowell, Charles, 1782-1861. A discourse delivered in the West Church in Boston, August 3, 1845. By Charles Lowell, one of the ministers of the West Church. Cambridge: Metcalf and company, printers, 1845. 25 p. CBPac; MDeeP; MH; NCH; WHi. 45-3992

Lowell, James Russell, 1819-1891. Conversations on some of the old poets... Cambridge, Massachusetts: J. Owen, 1845. 263 p. CSt; ICU; MB; NBuU; PPL-R. 45-3993

Lowell, James Russell, 1819-1891. Poems... Cambridge, 1845. NN; TxU. 45-3994

Lowell, John A. Considerations addressed to churchmen of the diocese of New York: By a layman. [n.p.] Printed for the author, 1845. 15 p. MiD-B. 45-3995

Lowell, Massachusetts. The first report

of the minister at large in Lowell to the missionary society connected with the South Parish. Lowell: Joel Taylor, 1845. 22 p. MB; MBC; MLow; MWA. 45-3996

Lowell, Massachusetts. Fourth Congregational Church. The importance and the means of evangelizing manufacturing cities. Lowell, 1845. 11 p. MBC. 45-3997

Lowell, Massachusetts. St. Anne's Church. The rector's library of St. Anne's Church, Lowell, Massachusetts. Boston: James B. Daw, 1845. 8 p. MB; MBD; MdBD; MH-AH. 45-3998

Lowell Missionary Society. The first report of the minister at large in Lowell to the missionary society connected with the south parish. Lowell: Joel Taylor, 1845. 22 p. MBC; MiD-B. 45-3999

Lowell offering. Mind amongst the spindles. A miscellany, wholly composed by the factory girls. Selected from the Lowell offering. With an introduction by the English editor and a letter from Harriet Martineau. Boston: Jordan, Swift and Wiley, 1845. 214 p. DLC; ICN; MB; MLow; TxU. 45-4000

Lowrie, Walter Macon, 1819-1847. The land of Sinim; or an exposition of Isaiah XLIX, 12 together with a brief account of the Jews and Christians in China. Philadelphia: W.S. Martien, 1845. 147 p. CU; KyLoP; NNMr; PWW; PU. 45-4001

Loydsville and Walholding Nurseries. Catalogue of the Loydsville and Walholding Nurseries, owned by E. Nichols and sons. St Clairsville, Ohio: Heaton and Gressinger, 1845. 24 p. PWW. 45-4002

Lucas, Fielding, 1781-1854. Plan of the city of Baltimore. Baltimore, 1845. 1 p. PHi. 45-4003

Ludlow, H.G. Submission to God; a sermon preached at the funeral of Mrs. Caroline E. Lathrop. Pittsfield, 1845. 14 p. MBC; MoSpD; NjPT. 45-4004

Lugol, J.G.A., 1786-1851. Researches on scrofulous diseases. Translated from the French, by A. Sidney Doane. New York: J.S. Redfield, 1845. 276 p. CSt-L; MeB; NNU-M; PPCP; WMAM. 45-4005

Lukens, I. The sickman's guide; or family director; compiled from the best botanic publications, with directions for using Samuel Thomson's medicines... Bridgeton, New Jersey: G.S. Harris, 1845. 189 p. NBMS; Nh-Hi; OCLloyd; WU-M. 45-4006

Lunt, George, 1803-1885. An address delivered before the Massachusetts Horticultural Society, on the dedication of Horticultural Hall, May 15, 1845. Boston: Dutton and Wentworth, 1845. 26 p. Ct; MWA; NjR; OO; WHi. 45-4007

Luther, John. An appeal for the cause of education; addressed to the people of Ohio. Columbus: S. Medary, 1845. 15 p. N; OClWHi; OO. 45-4008

Luther, Martin, 1483-1546. A commentary on Saint Paul's Epistle to the Galatians. New York and Pittsburg: Robert Carter and company, 1845. 575 p. KyDC; NbOP; OO; TxShA; VtU. 45-4009

Luther, Martin, 1483-1546. Der kleine catechismus. Philadelphia: Mentz und

Rovoudt, 1845. 144 p. PPeSchw; PSt. 45-4010

Lyell, Charles, 1797-1875. Elements of geology. Second American edition. Philadelphia: J. Kay, Jun. and brother; Pittsburgh: C.H. Kay, 1845. 316 p. MH; MiU; OkLaw; P. 45-4011

Lyell, Charles, 1797-1875. A second visit to the United States of America. n.p., 1845-1846. 2 v. RP. 45-4012

Lyell, Charles, 1797-1875. Travels in North America in the years 1841-1842; with geological observations on the United States, Canada and Nova Scotia... New York: Wiley and Putnam, 1845. 2 v. in 1. A-GS; CO; GU; NNE; PAnL. 45-4013

Lyman, Azel Storrs, b. 1815. Historical chart, containing the prominent events of the civil, religious, and literary history of the world, from the earliest times to the present day. Philadelphia: J.H. Doughty and company, 1845. CSt; DLC; ILM; MeBa; PP. 45-4014

Lyman, Azel Storrs, b. 1815. Questions designed for the use of pupils engaged in the study of Lyman's chart of universal history; with a key to the names mentioned on the chart, and a list of geographical names and ancient and middle history, with their corresponding modern names. Philadelphia: J.H. Doughty and company, 1845. 7-114 p. IEG; MH; NCH; PU; VtRut. 45-4015

Lynchburg, Virginia. Revised ordinances of the corporation. Lynchburg: Printed by Toler, Townley and Statham, 1845. 140 p. NN. 45-4016

Lyng, S.H. Address... funeral of Dr. Milnor. New York, 1845. MB. 45-4017

Lynn, Massachusetts. First Church of Christ. A catalogue of members of the church, embracing those members who were members January 1, 1845. Lynn: Kimball and Butterfield, 1845. 8 p. MH; MHi. 45-4018

Lyons, Jacques Judah, 1813-1877. Shemang Israel; Ten Commandments. Jewish creed and festivals and facts. New York, 1845. 12 p. PPDrop. 45-4019

Lytton, Edward George Earle Lytton Bulwer-Lytton, 1803-1873. The caxtons, a family picture. New York: International Book company, 1845. 2 v. in 1. NNF. 45-4020

Lytton, Edward George Earle Lytton Bulwer-Lytton, 1803-1873. Harold the last of the Saxon kings. New York: American Publishers Corporation, 1845. 191 p. MoCgSV. 45-4021

Lytton, Edward George Earle Lytton Bulwer-Lytton, 1803-1873. The lady of Lyons, or love and pride, a play in five acts. Philadelphia: Turner and Fisher, 1845. 63 p. CSmH; DLC; MB; NNC. 45-4022

Lytton, Edward George Earle Lytton Bulwer-Lytton, 1803-1873. Money; a comedy in five acts. New York: William Taylor; Baltimore: William Taylor and company, 1845. 72 p. AMob; MB; MH; NN; PLFM. 45-4023

Lytton, Edward George Earle Lytton Bulwer-Lytton, 1803-1873. Night and morning. With a frontispiece by Hablot K. Browne. New York: George Routledge and sons, 1845. 367 p. IaWav; OkEnP; REd; WEau. 45-4024

Lytton, Edward George Earle Lytton Bulwer-Lytton, 1803-1873. Pelham; adventures of a gentleman. New York: George Routledge and sons, 1845. 480 p. NNebg. 45-4025

Lytton, Edward George Earle Lytton Bulwer-Lytton, 1803-1873. Poems of Sir Edward Lytton. Collected and arranged by C. Donald MacLeod. New York: James W. Judd and company, 1845. 143 p. CtMW; MdBLC; MiD; MNe; NNUT. 45-4026

Lytton, Edward George Earle Lytton Bulwer-Lytton, 1803-1873. Zanoni. New York: John W. Lovell company, [1845] 345 p. C-S; FNo; NBuDC; TxHuT; WvWev. 45-4027

M

Mabel, the actress; or the perils of illicit love. By Baron St. Leger. Philadelphia: G.B. Zieber, 1845. 47 p. NjP. 45-4028

Mabire, J.L. The guide to French conversation. Revised and improved by Gustave Chouquet. Second edition. New York: Roe Lockwood and son, 1845. 190 p. MH; MoS. 45-4029

Macaulay, Thomas Babington Macaulay, 1800-1859. Essays, critical and miscellaneous. By T. Babington Macaulay. Philadelphia: Carey and Hart, 1845. 758 p. InID; NNC; OCY; PMA; TxAbH. 45-4030

McClernand, John Alexander, 1812-1900. Speech on the Oregon bill delivered in the House, January 30, 1845. [Washington, 1845] 8 p. CtY; OClWHi; TxHU; WHi. 45-4031

MacClintock, John, 1814-1870. Analysis of Watson's theological institutes designed for the use of students. New York: Lane and Tippett, 1845. 228 p. CtHC; InCW; KyDC; MnSH; OBerB. 45-4032

M'Crie, Thomas, 1772-1835. Life of John Knox, containing illustrations of the history of the reformation in Scotland; with biographical notices of the principal reformers, and sketches of the progress of literature in Scotland during the sixteenth century; and an appendix consisting of original papers. First complete American edition. Philadelphia: Presbyterian Board of Publication, 1845. 579 p. GMM; KyDC; NcDaD; ODa; TMC. 45-4033

M'Culloch, John Ramsay, 1789-1864. A dictionary, geographical, statistical and historical, of commerce and commercial navigation. Philadelphia: T. Wardle, 1845. 2 v. DLC; FTaSU; I; PPF; Okent-U. 45-4034

M'Culloch, John Ramsay, 1789-1864. A dictionary, practical, theoretical, and historical, of commerce and commercial navigation. Edited by Henry Vethake. Philadelphia: King and Baird, 1845. 2 v. I; MoSW; NNE; ODa; PPF. 45-4035

M'Culloch, John Ramsay, 1789-1864. M'Culloch's universal gazetteer. A dictionary, geographical, statistical and historical of the various countries, places, and principal natural objects in the world. In which the articles relating to the United States have been greatly extended... by Daniel Haskel. New York: Harper and brothers, 1845. 2 v. CtHC; LU; MH; NjP; THi. 45-4036

McCulloh, Richard Sears, 1818-1894. Letter from the secretary of the treasury, communicating a report of chemical analyses of sugars, molasses, etc., and of researches on hydrometers, made under the superintendence of Professor A.D. Bache. [Washington, 1845] 106 p. DLC; DSG; OO; RPB. 45-4037

McCulloh, Richard Sears, 1818-1894. Letters from the secretary of the treasury. [Washington, 1845] 105 p. DLC. 45-4038

McCulloh, Richard Sears, 1818-1894. Report of researches in relation to sugars, molasses, etc. and to hydrometers, etc. Washington, 1845. 106 p. PPAmP. 45-4039

McCullough, John W., d. 1868. The dead in Christ: an inquiry concerning the intermediate state, the future blessedness, and the mutual recognition... Baltimore: J. Robinson, 1845. [12]-202 p. CtMW; InID; MdBD; MdHi; WNaE. 45-4040

McCullough, John W., d. 1868. The probation of truth. A sermon, on the sufficiency of the Holy Scriptures... Wilmington, Delaware: Porter and Naff, printers, 1845. 36 p. CtHT; MdBD; NcU; NNC; PPPrHi. 45-4041

McCurdy, Dennis. First lessons in geometry, adapted, in connexion with the chart of geometry, no. 1, to the use of public schools. Philadelphia: E. Ferrett and company, 1845. [5]-60 p. DLC; NPV; TxComT; ViPo. 45-4042

McCurry, Henry D. The confession of Henry McCurry embodying particulars of his life convicted of the murder of Paul Roux, of Macon, Georgia with a sketch of his trial and sentence of death as pronounced by the Hon. Judge Brice. Baltimore: Shurtz and Wilde, 1845. 13 p. MdBB; NIC-L; PPL. 45-4043

McDermott, William. The twins or Edward and the Indian protege; a tale of

early settlement of Western New York. Syracuse, 1845. 48 p. NRU. 45-4044

McElligott, James Napoleon, 1812-1866. Manual, analytical and synthetical, of orthography and definition. New York: Van Norden and King, 1845. [9]-207 p. DLC; ICP; NjPass; PU. 45-4045

McElroy's Philadelphia directory, for 1846. Ninth edition. Philadelphia: Edward C. and John Biddle, 1845. 459 p. PPPCity. 45-4046

McFarland, Joel B. An oration before the I.O.O.F. and citizens of Lafayette, Indiana, September 10th, 1845. Lafayette: Fry and Jackson, 1845. 14 p. MH. 45-4047

McGee, Thomas D'Arcy, 1825-1868. Historical sketches of O'Connell and his friends, with a glance at the future destiny of Ireland. Boston: Donahoe and Rohan, 1845. 208 p. DLC; MBC; MWA; ODaU; PV. 45-4048

McGee, Thomas D'Arcy, 1825-1868. Historical sketches of O'Connell and his friends, with a glance at the future destiny of Ireland. Second edition. Boston: Donahoe and Rohan, 1845. 208 p. DLC; IaDuC; MdW; MWH; NjR. 45-4049

McGee, Thomas D'Arcy, 1825-1868. Historical sketches of O'Connell and his friends, with a glance at the future destiny of Ireland. Third edition. Boston: Donohue and Rohan, 1845. 208 p. IaKeos; NjN; OC; MWA; PScrS. 45-4050

MacGeoghegan, James, 1702-1763. The history of Ireland, ancient and modern, taken from the most authentic records, and dedicated to the Irish brigade. By the Abbe MacGeoghegan.

Translated from the French by Patrick O'Kelly... New York: D. and J. Sadlier, 1845. 630 p. DLC; MB; NbOP; OCX; ScU. 45-4051

Macgowan, John, 1726-1780. The dialogues of the devils, on the many vices which abound in the civil and religious world. New York: Nafis and Cornish, 1845. 284 p. IEG; OSW; TNS. 45-4052

McGuffey, Alexander Hamilton, 1816-1896. Eclectic series, newly improved. McGuffey's rhetorical guide; or fifth reader of the eclectic series. Cincinnati: Winthrop B. Smith, 1845. 480 p. CtHWatk; InI; MoKU; MsU; OS. 45-4053

Machiavelli, Niccolo, 1469-1527. The Florentine histories. Translated from the Italian edition, prepared in 1843, by G.B. Niccolini, of Florence, by C. Edward Lester. New York: Paine and Burgess, 1845. 2 v. ICN; MWA; NIC; OCl; RPA. 45-4054

McIlvaine, Abraham Robinson, 1804-1863. Speech of Mr. McIlvaine, of Pennsylvania on the annexation of Texas. Delivered in the House, January 25, 1845. [Washington, 1845] 7 p. CtY; MBAt; NBu; PHi. 45-4055

MacIntosh, Maria Jane, 1803-1878. The cousins; a tale of early life by the author of "Conquest and self-conquest." New York: Harper and brothers, 1845. 205 p. ICN IEG; MB; MWA; NNC. 45-4056

MacIntosh and Company. Descriptive catalogue of fruit and ornamental trees, flowering shrubs and roses, herbacious and green house plants, cultivated at their green house and nursery, St. Clair Street. Cleveland: Press of M.C. Youngove [sic], 1845. 60 p. OClWHi. 45-4057

McJilton, John Nelson, 1805-1875. God speaketh. A sermon, preached in St. Stephen's Church, Baltimore, in the evening of June 22, 1845, being the Sunday after the news reached the city of the decease of his Excellency, Andrew Jackson, late president of the United States. Baltimore: D. Brunner, 1845. 16 p. MdBD; MiD-B; NcU; PPM; WHi. 45-4058

McJilton, John Nelson, 1805-1875. James Martle, or the boy that went to Sunday School; a story. Baltimore: D. Brunner, 1845. 49 p. MdBD. 45-4059

McJilton, John Nelson, 1805-1875. Man's duty to the civil government and to God. A sermon preached in St. Stephen's Church, Baltimore, November 10, 1844. Baltimore: D. Brunner, 1845. 15 p. MdBP; NGH; PPL; PPM. 45-4060

McJilton, John Nelson, 1805-1875. The memorial of the just. A funeral sermon, occasioned by the death of Sarah Johnson, who died September 4th, 1845, at the advanced age of nearly one hundred and four years. Baltimore: D. Brunner, 1845. 18 p. MB; NN; PPL. 45-4061

McJilton, John Nelson, 1805-1875. Sermon on the decease of Andrew Jackson. Boston, 1845. PPL. 45-4062

Mackay, Charles, 1814-1889. Memoirs of commercial delusions; embracing historical sketches of the Mississippi scheme, and the south sea bubble. [New

York, 1845] DLC; MH; MiD; NBuG; OOxM. 45-4063

Mackeldey, Ferdinand, 1784-1834. Compendium of Modern civil law. Edited by Philip Ignatius Kaufmann... from the twelvth German edition. New York: P.I. Kaufmann, 1845. 2 v. C; IaU-L; NIC; TNP; ViU. 45-4064

Mackenzie, Alexander Slidell, 1803-1848. The life of Commodore Oliver Hazard Perry. In two volumes. New York: Harper and brothers, 1845. 2 v. IGK; MnU; OCX; PHi; ScGrw. 45-4065

Mackenzie, Alexander Slidell, 1803-1848. The life of Paul Jones. New York: Harper and brothers, 1845. 2 v. CSmH; MiU; Nh; NN; OU. 45-4066

Mackenzie, William Lyon, 1795-1861. Sketches of William L. Marcy, Jacob Barker and others. Boston, 1845. PPL-R. 45-4067

Mackenzie, William Lyon, 1803-1848. Lives and opinions of Benjamin Franklin Butler, United States District Attorney for the Southern District of New York. Boston: Cook and company, 1845. 152 p. CoU; ICHi; MWA; PPi; RP. 45-4068

Mackey, Albert Gallatin, 1807-1881. Lexicon of freemasonry; containing a definition of all its communicable terms, notices of its history, traditions and antiquities and an account of all the rites and mysteries of the ancient world. Charleston, [South Carolina] 1845. 360 p. IaCrM; MBBC; OC; PPM; ScCC. 45-4069

Mackie, John Milton, 1813-1894. Life of Godfrey William von Leibnitz. On the basis of the German work of Dr. G.E.

Gubrauer. Boston: Gould, Kendall and Lincoln, 1845. 288 p. KyDC; MBBC; NNF; PPA; RNR. 45-4070

Mackie, John Milton, 1813-1894. Life of Samuel Gordon. Boston, 1845. 411 p. MW; OClWHi; RPB. 45-4071

Macklem, O. Rates of tolls and harbor dues and compendium of the provincial, British and American tariffs. To which is added: a part of the law for the registration of British vessels. Compiled by O. Macklem, esq. Chippawa, C.W. Buffalo: Clapp and M'Credie, printers, 1845. 58 p. ArCh; CaOA; Cdn. 45-4072

McLane, Louis, 1786-1857. To Samuel C. Anderson of the House of Delegates. n.p., 1845. 10 p. CSmH; DBRE. 45-4073

Maclay, Archibald, 1778-1860. An address delivered at a public meeting, held in Hope Street Baptist Chapel. Glasgow, January, 1840. New York, 1845. 16 p. NjPT; RPB. 45-4074

McLean, John, 1785-1861. Address delivered on the consecration of the Spring Grove Cemetery, near Cincinnati, August 20, 1845. Cincinnati: Printed at the Daily Atlas office, 1845. 29 p. DLC; MWA; NjR; OCo; PPL. 45-4075

McLellan, Isaac, 1806-1899. The gold demon and the poor cobbler of Boston: a romance of the revolution. Boston: D. Ruggles, 1845. 59 p. CtY; CU; MB. 45-4076

McLeod, Alexander, 1774-1833. The life and power of true godliness described in a series of discourses. Fourth edition. New York: Robert

Carter, 1845. 280 p. GDecCT; GMM; NcSalL; PPWe. 45-4077

MacMaster, Erasmus Darwin, 1806-1866. The relations between religion and academic education: an address at the author's inauguration as president of Miami University, Ohio, August 13, 1845. [Oxford? Ohio] Printed for the university, 1845. 36 p. DLC; ICP; ICU; OClWHi; OHi. 45-4078

McMurray, A. Awful disclosure! Murders exposed; downfall of Popery; death bed confession; death bed confession and renunciation of the right Rev. Bishop McMurray. Buffalo: E. Mosher, 1845. 32 p. MH; NBu. 45-4079

MacNevin, Thomas. The history of the volunteers of 1782. New York: R. Martin and company, 1845. 124 p. DLC; ICBB; MB; MdW; OCIJC. 45-4080

Macnish, Robert, 1802-1837. The anatomy of drunkeness. From the fifth Glasgow edition. Hartford: S. Andrus and son, 1845. 96 p. CtY; MA; ODW. 45-4081

Macnish, Robert, 1802-1837. The philosoply of sleep. Hartford: S. Andrus and son, 1845. 55 p. CSansS; IaHoL; MNS; OWoC; TxU. 45-4082

M'Sparran, Archibald. The Irish legend; or M'Donnell and the Norman De Borgos; a biographical tale. Philadelphia: A. Gross, 1845. 238 p. InNd. 45-4083

Madison, Indiana. Second Presbyterian Church. Manual for the members of the Second Presbyterian Church in Madison, Indiana... Madison: Courier Office, 1845. 15 p. ICU; OCHP; WHi. 45-4084

Madison County, New York. Agricultural society. Transactions for the year 1842-1845 together with an abstract of the census of 1845 and an article on the geology of the county with a map. Hamilton: Waldron and Baker, 1845. 46 p. ICJ; NN; PPL. 45-4085

Magendie, Francois, 1783-1855. An elementary treatise on human physiology on the basis of the precis elementaire de physiologie. Par F. Magendie. Fifth edition. Translated and enlarged by John Revere. New York: Harper and brothers, 1845. [13]-539 p. CSt-L; IU-M; LNOP; NBMS; TxSaO. 45-4086

Magill, Seagrave, W. An address delivered at the temperance tea party of the Young Men's Temperance Society, Middlebury, Wednesday eveing February 26, 1845. Middlebury: J.Cobb, Jr., [1845] 16 p. MH; VtMiM; VtMidSM. 45-4087

Magill, Thomas F. Two sermons; education a national defense preached by Thomas Magill. November 3, 1844. Mansfield, Ohio: Glessner, 1845. 24 p. PPPrHi. 45-4088

The magnetic almanac for 1846... Calculations by George R. Perkins. Albany, New York: George Dexter, [1845] NjR; NSchHi. 45-4089

Magnolia, or young lady's azalia. Boston? 1845-1846. 2 v. in 1. ICN. 45-4090

Maguire, Thomas, 1792-1847. The celebrated controversial discussion between the Rev. Thomas Maguire and the

Rev. Richard T.P. Pope, which took place at the lecture room of the Dublin Institution. A full, complete, and authentic report. New York: D. and J. Sadlier and company, [1845?] 309 p. MWH. 45-4091

Mahan, Asa, 1800-1889. Doctrine of the will. New York: M.H. Newman; Oberlin, Ohio: R.E. Gillet, 1845. [9]-218 p. DLC; IEG; MPiB; NjPt; PPM. 45-4092

Mahan, Asa, 1800-1889. A system of intellectual philosophy. New York: Saxton and Miles; Boston: Waite, Pierce and compnay, and others, 1845. [13]-330 p. ICU; KSalW; MWiW; NCH; NbOM. 45-4093

Mahoney, S.I. Six years in the monasteries of Italy, and two years in the islands of the Mediterranean and in Asia Minor. Boston, 1845. DLC; ICN; MH; NNC; PPL. 45-4094

Maine. An abstract of the returns of corporations, made to the office of the secretary of state, in January 24, 1845, for the year 1844. Augusta: William T. Johnson, printer to the state, 1845. 37 p. MeHi; MeLewB; MeLR. 45-4095

Maine. An act for the supression of drinking houses and tippling shops. Augusta: William T. Johnson, printer to the state, 1845. 4 p. MeB. 45-4096

Maine. An act in addition to the sixteenth chapter of the revised statutes. Augusta: William T. Johnson, printer to the state, 1845. 10 p. MeB. 45-4097

Maine. An act in relation to the one hundred and forty eighth chapter of the revised statutes. Augusta: William T. Johnson, printer to the state, 1845. 7 p. MeB. 45-4098

Maine. An act in relation to the Steam Navigation Corporation. Augusta: William T. Johnson, printer to the state, 1845. 5 p. MeB. 45-4099

Maine. Act incorporating the Bangor Boom Company. Approved March 23, 1844. Augusta: William T. Johnson, printer to the state, 1845. 5 p. MeB. 45-4100

Maine. An act making towns liable for certain personal injuries. Augusta: William T. Johnson, printer to the state, 1845. 3 p. MeB. 45-4101

Maine. An act relating to appeals from county commissioners. Augusta: William T. Johnson, printer to the state, 1845. 5 p. MeB. 45-4102

Maine. An act to abolish the district court and additional to the ninety sixth chapter. Augusta: William T. Johnson, printer to the state, 1845. 4 p. MeB. 45-4103

Maine. An act to apportion and assess a tax on the inhabitants of this state, for the year 1845. Augusta: William T. Johnson, 1845. 23 p. MHi. 45-4104

Maine. An act to establish the Atlantic and St. Lawrence Railroad Company, Augusta: William T. Johnson, printer to the state, 1845. 11 p. MB; WU. 45-4105

Maine. An act to establish the Atlantic and St. Lawrence Railroad Company. Augusta: William T. Johnson, printer to the state, 1845. 14 p. MeB. 45-4106

Maine. An act to incorporate the Cape Telos and Webster Pond Dam and Sluiceway Company. Augusta: William T. Johnson, printer to the state, 1845. 7 p. MeBa. 45-4107

Maine. Annual report of the inspectors of the Maine State Prison. Augusta: William T. Johnson, printer to the state, 1845. 18 p. MeB. 45-4108

Maine. Annual report of the warden of the state prison. Augusta: William T. Johnson, printer to the state, 1845. 10 p. MeB. 45-4109

Maine. Documents printed by order of the Legislature of the state of Maine, during its session. Augusta: William T. Johnson, printer to the state, 1845. 308 p. MeHi; MeU. 45-4110

Maine. List of stockholders, in the banks of Maine. Augusta: William T. Johnson, printer to the state, 1845. 69 p. MeB; MeBa; MeHi; MeU. 45-4111

Maine. Memorial to the honorable, the Senate and the House, of the state of Maine, in the Legislature assembled, in January, 1845. Augusta: William T. Johnson, printer to the state, 1845. 10 p. MeB. 45-4112

Maine. Message of Governor Anderson, to both branches of the legislature of the state of Maine, May, 1846. Augusta: William T. Johnson, printer to the state, 1845. 21 p. MeB; MeBa; MeHi; MeLewB. 45-4113

Maine. Message of Governor Anderson, to both branches of the legislature of the state of Maine, May, 1846. Augusta:

William T. Johnson, printer to the state, 1845. 24 p. MeBa; MeHi. 45-4114

Maine. Report of the adjutant general of the militia of Maine, December 31, 1844. Augusta: William T. Johnson, printer to the state, 1845. 24 p. MeB; MeHi; MeU. 45-4115

Maine. Report of the committee of investigation, in relation to the claims of the state of Maine against the United States. Augusta: William T. Johnson, printer to the state, 1845. 141 p. MeB. 45-4116

Maine. Report of the committee which was referred so much of the Governor's message as relates to the annexation of Texas. Augusta: William T. Johnson, printer to the state, 1845. 5 p. MeB. 45-4117

Maine. Report of the joint select committee on the infraction of the Treaty of Washington, March 25, 1845. Augusta: William T. Johnson, printer to the state, 1845. 20 p. MHi. 45-4118

Maine. Report of the land agent of the state of Maine, December 31, 1844. Augusta: William T. Johnson, printer to the state, 1845. 27 p. MeLewB; MeLR. 45-4119

Maine. Report of the treasurer of Maine, on the state treasury, December 31, 1844. Augusta: William T. Johnson, printer to the state, 1845. 16 p. MeB; MeLewB; MeLR; MeU. 45-4120

Maine. Reports of the trustees, Steward and Treasurer, and superintendent of the insane hospital. Augusta: William T.

Johnson, printer to the state, 1845. 45 p. MeLewB. 45-4121

Maine. Reports of the trustees, Steward and Treasurer, and superintendent of the insane hospital. Augusta: William T. Johnson, printer to the state, 1845. 48 p. MeB; MeLewB. 45-4122

Maine. Resolves providing for an amendment of the constitution in relation to the election of representatives to the legislature. Augusta: William T. Johnson, printer to the state, 1845. 3 p. MeB. 45-4123

Maine. Rules and orders of the House of Representatives of the state of Maine. Augusta: William T. Johnson, printer to the state, 1845. 119 p. MeAu; MeB; MeBa; MeLewB; MeLR. 45-4124

Maine. Rules and orders of the Senate of Maine. Augusta: William T. Johnson, printer to the state, 1845. 14 p. 45-4125

Maine. Rules and orders of the state of Maine. Augusta: William T. Johnson, printer to the state, 1845. 119 p. DLC; MeBa; MeLew. 45-4126

The Maine farmer's almanac for the year of our Lord 1846... By Daniel Robinson... Hallowell: Glazier, Masters and Smith, [1845] MeLeB; MWA; WHi. 45-4127

The Maine farmer's almanac for the year of our Lord 1846... By Daniel Robinson... Portland: Hyde, Lord and Duren, [1845] MeBa; MeHi; MWA. 45-4128

Malcom, Howard, 1799-1879. Dictionary of the most important names, objects and terms, found in the holy scriptures.

Boston: Gould, Kendall and Lincoln, 1845. 305 p. GAuP. 45-4129

Malcom, Howard, 1799-1879. Travels in southeastern Asia, embracing Hindustan, Malaya, Siam, and China; with notices of numerous missionary stations, and a full account of the Burman empire. Seventh edition. Boston: Gould, Kendall and Lincoln, 1845. 2 v. LNP; WHi. 45-4130

Malden, Henry, 1800-1876. Distinguished men of modern times. New York: Harper and brothers, 1845. 2 v. IGK; MdBLC; MMen; MSher; OSW. 45-4131

Malte-Brun, Conrad, 1775-1826. A system of universal geography. Boston: Printed by Samuel Walker, 1845. 1394 p. RPaw. 45-4132

Mamma's lessons. Worcester: J. Grant, [1845] 24 p. MWA. 45-4133

Manchester, New Hampshire. Report of the superintending school committee for the town of Manchester. [Manchester: Gleaner, 1845] 16 p. CSmH. 45-4134

Manchester, New Hampshire. Second Congregational Church. Articles of faith, and form of covenant... Boston, 1845. 8 p. MBC. 45-4135

Mancur, John Henry. The palais royal. An historical romance. New York: W.H. Colyer, 1845. 252 p. CoCsUP; DLC; MH; NjP. 45-4136

Mandeville, Henry, 1804-1858. The elements of reading and oratory. Utica: R. Northway and company, printers, 1845.

443 p. DLC; NjP; NUt; OClWHi; ViU. 45-4137

Manesca, John, 1778?-1838. Oral system of teaching living languages. Sixth edition, revised. New York: R. Lockwood and son, 1845. 518 p. DLC; MoS; NjP; NN. 45-4138

Mann, Horace, 1796-1859. Answer to the rejoinder of the twenty-nine Boston schoolmasters. Part of the thirty-one who published: Remarks on the seventh annual report of the secretary... Boston: William B. Fowle and Nahum Capen, 1845. 124 p. DLC; ICJ; MeB; MWA; TNF. 45-4139

Mann, Horace, 1796-1859. Lectures on education. By Horace Mann, secretary of the Massachusetts Board of Education. Boston: William B. Fowle and N. Capen, 1845. 11-338 p. MiU; MPiB; NhPet; PU; RWe. 45-4140

Manners and customs of the Japanese, in the nineteenth century, from the accounts of recent Dutch residents in Japan and from the German works of Dr. Ph. Fr. Von Siebold. New York: Harper and brothers, 1845. 289 p. CSansS; IGK; NcD; OrU; WNaE. 45-4141

Manning, Anne, 1807-1879. Deborah's diary. Boston, [1845?] 44 p. MH. 45-4142

Manning, Henry Edward, 1808-1892. Sermons. From the third London edition. New York: J.R. Dunham, 1845. 119 p. ICU; NBuDD; PP; TSewU; WNaE. 45-4143

Mansfield, Daniel, 1807-1847. Two sermons, delivered on the second centennial anniversary of the organization of the First Church, and the settlement of the first minister in Wenham. Published by request of the church. Andover: Printed by Allen, Morrill and Wardwell, 1845. 72 p. DLC; MBC; MjPT; PHi; WHi. 45-4144

Mansfield, Edward Deering, 1801-1880. The legal rights, liabilities, and duties of women... Including the law of marriage and divorce, the social relations of husband and wife, parent and child, of guardian and ward and of employer and employed... Salem, [Massachusetts] J.P. Jewett and company; Cincinnati: W.H. Moore and company, 1845. 369 p. IaB; MBC; NhD; PPi; WHi. 45-4145

A manual for law students exhibiting courses for the study of conveyancing, of equity and common law, with questions on each course. From the London edition. Harrisburg: M'Kinley and Lescure, 1845. 50 p. DLC; MH-L; NIC-L; PPL; WaU-L. 45-4146

Manzoni, Alessandro, 1785-1873. The betrothed. [I promessi sposi] Translated from the Italian. New York: D. Appleton and company, 1845. 2 v. KyDC; MeBaT; NcU; PV; RWoH. 45-4147

Manzoni, Alessandro, 1785-1873. I promessi sposi: The betrothed. New York: Printed by Appleton, 1845. 336 p. PAlt. 45-4148

Manzoni, Alessandro, 1785-1873. I promessi sposi. The betrothed. A new translation. Reprinted entirely from the last English edition. New York: D. Appleton and company, etc., etc., 1845. 2 v. LNT; MH; PU; RWoH; ViU. 45-4149

Map of mineral lands adjacent to Lake

Superior. [Washington, 1845?] MB. 45-4150

A map of the State of New York exhibiting the situation and boundaries of the several towns, wards and counties, population, etc. prepared under the direction of the Secretary of State. Hartford: E.B. and E.C. Kellogg, [1845?] 1 p. NIC-A. 45-4151

Mapes, James Jay. Address delivered at the opening of the 18th annual fair of the American Institute at Niblo's Garden, Tuesday, October 7, 1845. New York: James Van Norden and company, 1845. 8 p. CBPSR; DLC; MWA; PPL-R. 45-4152

Mapes, James Jay. Inauguration address before the Mechanics Institute of the City of New York, January 7. New York, 1845. 23 p. DLC; MB; MBAt. 45-4153

Marblehead Female Humane Society. Rules and regulations of Marblehead Female Humane Society. Organized, 1816. Incorporated, 1845. n.p., 1845? 15 p. MHi. 45-4154

Marcet, Jane Haldemand, 1769-1858. Conversations on the natural philosophy adapted to the comprehension of young pupils. Improved by J.L. Blake. Boston: Gould, 1845. 276 p. CLCM; IaAS; KHi; MH; ViRu. 45-4155

Marion Raymond; or the wife with two husbands. A romance of the heart. Boston: H.L. Williams, 1845. 50 p. CtY; CU; MB; MH. 45-4156

Marks, Richard, 1779?-1840. Retrospect; or review of providential mercies;

with anecdotes of various characters. by Aliquis. Fourth American from seventeenth London edition. New York and Pittsburg: Robert Carter, 1845. 255 p MLow; NbOP. 45-4157

Marlborough, Massachusetts. West Parish Church. Order of services at the installation of Rev. Horatio Alger, as minister of the West Parish in Marlborough on January 22, 1845. Boston. Butts, printer, 1845. MHi. 45-4158

Marmaduke multiply. Boston: Munroe and Francis, 1845. KU; MH; MiU; MNHi; NN. 45-4159

Marrel, Mark. [pseud.] The slave of the mine; or the stolen heir. Boston: Gleason's Publishing Hall, 1845. 58 p. MB; RPB. 45-4160

Marryat, Frederick, 1792-1848. Masterman ready or the wreck of the pacific. New York: D. Appleton and company, 1845. 136 p. MeU. 45-4161

Marryat, Frederick, 1792-1848. The mission. New York: D. Appleton and company; Philadelphia: George S. Appleton, 1845. 198 p. DLC; GWay; KyBC; MNS; ScCliTO. 45-4162

Marryat, Frederick, 1792-1848. The settlers in Canada. Written for young people. New York: A. Appleton and company, [1845] 2 v. CU; MH; MWA; NN; WHi. 45-4163

Marryat, Frederick, 1792-1848. Smarleyyow, or the dog fiend. A historical novel. Philadelphia: J. Harding, 1845. 2 v. in 1. CSt. 45-4164

Marsh, Abram. Discourse; reasons for

aw, with some special references to the traffic in intoxicating liquors. Hartford: Courant, 1845. 15 p. Ct; CSmH; CtHT; In. 45-4165

Marsh, Caldwell Anne Caldwell, 1791-1894. Mount Soreloron; the heiress of de Veres. New York: Harper, 1845. 156 p. CtY; IU; MH; NRMA; PBM. 45-4166

Marsh, George Perkins, 1801-1882. Address delivered before the New England Society of the city of New York, December 24, 1844. New York: M.W. Dodd, 1845. 54 p. DLC; MB; NCH; RPB; WHi. 45-4167

Marsh, George Perkins, 1801-1882. Remarks on an address delivered before the New England Society of the City of New York, December 23, 1844. Boston: C. Stimpson, 1845. 23 p. MB; MdBD; MWA; RPB; VtU. 45-4168

Marsh, George Perkins, 1801-1882. Speech of Mr. Marsh, of Vermont, on the annexation of Texas. Delivered in the House, in committee of the whole on the state of the union, January 20, 1845. [Washington, 1845] 15 p. MBAt; MH; NBu; VtU. 45-4169

Marsh, James, 1794-1842. The remains of the Rev. James Marsh, late president and professor of moral and intellectual philosophy, in the University of Vermont, with a memoir of his life. Second edition. Burlington: Chauncy Goodrich, 1845. 642 p. ICP; MWA; OWoC; PHi; VtMidbC. 45-4170

Marsh, James, 1794-1842. The remains of the Rev. James Marsh, late president, and professor of moral and intellectual philosophy, in the University of Ver-

mont, with a memoir of his life. Second edition. New York: Mark H. Newman, 1845. 642 p. GEU; NNUT. 45-4171

Marsh, John, 1788-1868. An epitome of general ecclesiastical history, from the earliest period to the present time. With an appendix. Eighth edition. New York: J. Tilden and company, 1845. 462 p. KWiU; MB. 45-4172

Marsh, John, 1788-1868. Hannnah Hawkins, the reformed drunkard's daughter. Second edition. New York: American Temperance Union, 1845. N; ViU. 45-4173

Marsh, John, 1788-1868. Hannah Hawkins, the reformed drunkard's daughter. Fourth edition. New York: American Temperance Union, 1845. 72 p. ICN; MBNMHi. NN: NNC; MVh. 45-4174

Marsh-Caldwell, Anne Caldwell, 1791-1874. The admiral's daughter, the baronet's birde; the wedding garmet, fortune's frolics, and other select tales. Franklin library edition. New York: E. Ferrett, 1845. 110 p. ICU. 45-4175

Marsh-Caldwell, Anne Caldwell, 1791-1874. Love and duty. A novel. Philadelphia, 1845. MdBP; MH; NN. 45-4176

Marshall, Elihu F. A spelling book of the English language; or the American tutor's assistant. Concord: L. Roby, 1845. MH. 45-4177

Marshall, John. A new universal gazetteer. Boston: Phillips and Sampson, 1845. 816 p. MWarh. 45-4178

Marshall, John, 1755-1835. The life of George Washington, commander in chief of the American forces during the war which established the independence of his country. Second edition, revised and corrected by the author. Philadelphia: James Crissy and Thomas, Cowperthwait and company, 1845. 2 v. NjNBs OU; PPF. 45-4179

Marshall, Josiah T. The farmers' and emigrants' handbook; being a full and complete guide for the farmer and the emigrant, comprising the clearing of forest and prairie land, gardening. Second edition, revised. New York: D. Appleton and company, 1845. 492 p. IaHi; MiU-C; PPAmP; TxGR; WHi. 45-4180

Marshall, Leonard. The mountaineer, a song of poetry by J.H. Warland, music composed by Leonard Marshall. Boston [1845?] 7 p. MH. 45-4181

Marston, William Augustus. An address delivered before the St. Johnsbury and Lyndon chapters of the '1001.' Their anniversary, January 1, 1845. Boston: Samuel Dickinson, 1845. 27 p. DLC; MiD- B; MMeT; WHi. 45-4182

Martineau, Harriet, 1802-1876. Berkley, the banker: or bank notes and bullion; a tale for the times. Hartford, 1845. 2 v. InGrD; MSa; TxU; ViRVal. 45-4183

Martineau, Harriet, 1802-1876. The charmed sea or Polanders in Siberia; a tale for all. Hartford: S. Andrews and son, 1845. 180 p. InGrD; NUt. 45-4184

Martineau, Harriet, 1802-1876. The crofton boys. New York: D. Appleton and company, 1845. 177 p. KyDC; NjR. 45-4185

Martineau, Harriet, 1802-1876. Five years of youth, of sense and sentiment with a preface. Second American edition Boston: William Crosby and H.P Nichols, 1845. 255 p. MBAt; MWelC NcU. 45-4186

Martineau, Harriet, 1802-1876. Glen of the echoes; or Dan Mahoney and Dora Sullivan; a tale of Ireland. Hartford: S Andrews and son, 1845. 178 p. InGrD MF. 45-4187

Martineau, Harriet, 1802-1876. For each and for all; or Letitia and Maria; a tale for the reader. Hartford: Andrus, 1845. 176 p. InGrD. 45-4188

Martineau, Harriet, 1802-1876. French wines and politics; or Charles and Antoine Lucyon; a tale of the French Revolution. Hartford: Andrus and son, 1845. ICBB; OrU. 45-4189

Martineau, Harriet, 1802-1876. Hill and valley; or hands and machinery; a tale for the people. Hartford: Andrus, 1845. 182 p. InGrD; N. 45-4190

Martineau, Harriet, 1802-1876. Homes abroad; or Frank and Ellen Castle; a tale for the people. Hartford: Andrus, 1845. 172 p. InGrD. 45-4191

Martineau, Harriet, 1802-1876. Life in the sick room. Essays by Harriet Martineau with an introduction to the American edition by Eliza L. Follen. Second American edition. Boston: William Crosby, 1845. 196 p. CtHC; KyU; LN; MH; PPCP. 45-4192

Martineau, Harriet, 1802-1876. Life in the wilds; or the South African settlement; a tale for young and old. Hartford:

Andrus, 1845. 177 p. InGrD; NN. 45-4193

Martineau, Harriet, 1802-1876. Loom and lugger or weavers and smugglers. Hartford: S. Andrus and son, 1845. 174 p. InGrD; MnSH. 45-4194

Martineau, Harriet, 1802-1876. Miss Martineau's letters on mesmerism. New York: Harper and brothers, 1845. 27 p. CSansS; DLC; MB; NN; TxHuT. 45-4195

Martineau, Harriet, 1802-1876. Sowers not reapers; or Chatham and Mary Kay; a tale for the people. Hartford: S. Andrews and son, 1845. 186 p. CtY; InGrD; MF. 45-4196

Martineau, James, 1805-1900. Bible and the child; a discourse. Boston: H.B. Greene, 1845. 23 p. ICMe; MH; MMeT; NN; PPL-R. 45-4197

Marx, Jacob. History of the robe of Jesus Christ. Preserved in the Cathedral of Trives. Philadelphia: James M. Campbell, 1845. 119 p. ICU; MB; MBAt; PPL; OO. 45-4198

Mary Fisher; or the Quaker maiden and the grand Turk; with other poems. Philadelphia, [1845?] 36 p. PHC. 45-4199

Mary Gertrude. [pseud.] Philip Randolph: a tale of Virginia. New York: D. Appleton and company; Philadelphia: G.S. Appleton, 1845. 177 p. InCW; KyBC; MB; MH; ViRU. 45-4200

Mary Kale; or big thunder! Chief of the anti-renters. Boston: F. Gleason, 1845. 56 p. ICU; MBC; MnU; MWA; NN. 45-4201

Mary Wilson; a tale of New England. Boston: Waite, Peirce and company, 1845. 157 p. CtY; NNC; OU; RPB. 45-4202

Maryland. Annual circular of the faculty of the medical department. Baltimore: J. Murphy, 1845. DLC. 45-4203

Maryland. Annual message of the Executive. Annapolis: Riley and Davis, 1845. 28 p. DLC. 45-4204

Maryland. Annual message of the Executive to the General Assembly of Maryland. December session, 1845. [Annapolis: Thomas G. Pratt, 1845] 29 p. WHi. 45-4205

Maryland. Annual message of the Executive to the General Assembly of Maryland. December session, 1845. Annapolis: William M'Neir, 1845. 331 p. MdLR. 45-4206

Maryland. Journal of proceedings of the House of Delegates of the state of Maryland. December session, 1844. Annapolis: Riley and Davis, 1845? 675 p. MdHi; MdLR. 45-4207

Maryland. Journal of proceedings of the House of Delegates, of the state of Maryland, December session. Annapolis: Riley and Davis, 1845. 495 p. MdBB. 45-4208

Maryland. Journal of proceedings of the Senate of Maryland, at the December session, 1844. Annapolis: William M'Neir, 1845? 208 p. MdBB. 45-4209

Maryland. Laws made and passed by the General Assembly of the state of Maryland, at a session begun and held at

Annapolis on Monday, the 30th day of December, 1844, and ended on Monday the 10th day of March, 1845. Annapolis: M'Neir, 1845. IaU-L; MdBS; Nj; Sc; Wa-L. 45-4210

Maryland. Report on the memorial of W.J. Ross. Annapolis, 1845. PPL. 45-4211

Maryland. Select committee to visit the line of the Chesapeake and Ohio Canal and the Baltimore and Ohio Railroad. Report of the select committee. [Annapolis? 1845] 16 p. DLC. 45-4212

Maryland manual; a compendium of legal, historical and statistical information. Annapolis, 1845-. MiU. 45-4213

Mason, Augustus. The quackery of the age. A satire on the times. Boston: Printed by White, Lewis and Potter, 1845. 44 p. MBilHi; MdUM; MHi; MWA; WU-M. 45-4214

Mason, C. An address on temperance, delivered at Lancaster. Fitchburg, 1845. MLanc. 45-4215

Mason, C.C. A history of all denominations of Christians in the United States, their doctrines, usages, etc. By C.C. Mason and J. Tait. Boston, 1845. 68 p. RPB. 45-4216

Mason, Charles. The present means of suppressing intemperance. An address delivered in Fitchburg before the Washington Abstinence Society. Fitchburg: S. and C. Shepley, 1845. 22 p. MFiHi; MHi. 45-4217

Mason, Erskine, 1805-1851. Victory over death; a sermon... occasioned by the death of John E. Hyde. New York: William A. Wheeler, stationer, 1845. 24 p. ICMe; MH; NjR. 45-4218

Mason, Erskine, 1819-1840. Economy of the church. Sabbath schools. A sermon preached in the Bleecker Street Church, New York, preceding a contribution to the American Sunday School Union, June, 1845. Philadelphia: American Sunday School Union, [1845] 16 p. MBAt; MBC; NcMHi; NjR; PPPrHi. 45-4219

Mason, Henry M. The olden church: a sermon. Printed by request of the vestry. Habere jam non potest Ceum patrem qui ecclesiam ono haber matrem, St Cyprian. Baltimore: Printed by Jos Robinson, 1845. 16 p. MdBD; MdBE MdHi. 45-4220

Mason, John, 1706-1763. A treatise on self-knowledge, showing the nature and benefit of that important science. To which is added a sketch of the life of the author. Hartford: S. Andrus and son, 1845. 41 p. CSansS; MA; MBrockKC; OWoC. 45-4221

Mason, John Mitchell, 1770-1829. Essays on the Church of God; edited by Rev. Ebenezer Mason. New York: Carter, 1845. 258 p. OO. 45-4222

Mason, Lowell, 1792-1872. Book of chants; consisting mostly of selections from the Scriptures adapted to appropriate music and arranged for chanting. Boston: Wilkins, Carter and company, 1845. 180 p. MB. 45-4223

Mason, Lowell, 1792-1872. The Boston glee book; consisting of an extensive collection of glees, madrigals and rounds.

Boston: Wilkins, 1845. 264 p. DLC; MH; NNUT; OrP. 45-4224

Mason, Lowell, 1792-1872. The Boston chool song book. Original and selected. Boston: Wilkins, Carter and company, 1845. ICN; MB; MH. 45-4225

Mason, Lowell, 1792-1872. Carmina acra; or Boston collection of church music, comprising the most popular psalm and hymn tunes in general use, ogether with a great variety of new unes, chants, sentences, motetts, and anthems. Boston: Wilkins, Carter, 1845. 348 p. CBPac; MH; NCH; RPaw; WHi. 45-4226

Mason, Lowell, 1792-1872. Church psalmody; a collection of psalms and hymns adapted to public worship. Boston: Marvin, 1845. 598 p. CPasr; IU. 45-4227

Mason, Lowell, 1792-1872. Church psalmody; a collection of psalms and hymns, selected from Dr. Watts and other authors. Boston: T.R. Marvin, 1845. 598 p. MWinchr. 45-4228

Mason, Lowell, 1792-1872. The gentlemen's glee book: consisting of a selection of glees for men's voices, by the most admired German composers. Boston: Wilkins, Carter and company, 1845. 112 p. MdBJ; MdBP; MH. 45-4229

Mason, Lowell, 1792-1872. Manual of the Boston Academy of Music for instruction in the elements of vocal music on the system of Pestalozzi. Fifth edition. Boston: J.H. Wilkins and R.B. Carter, 1845. 252 p ICU; MH; MHa. 45-4230

Mason, Lowell, 1792-1872. The psal-

tery, a new collection of church music, consisting of psalm and hymn tunes, chants and athems; being one of the most complete music books for church choirs, congregations, singing schools and societies ever published. By Lowell Mason and George James Webb... Boston: Wilkins, Carter and company, 1845. 348 p. CtY; ICN; MWA; NNUT: WaU. 45-4231

Mason, Lowell, 1792-1872. The psaltery, a new collection of church music, consisting of psalm and hymn tunes, chants and athems; being one of the most complete music books for church choirs, congregations, singing schools and societies ever published. By Lowell Mason and George James Webb... Boston: Wilkins, Carter and company, 1845. 352 p. CtHWatk; ICN; MeLewB; MWA; PPPrHi. 45-4232

Mason, Lowell, 1792-1872. The sacred harp; eclectic harmony. A collection of church music. Enlarged, revised and improved edition. Cincinnati: William T. Truman, 1845. 237 p. ICP KyLxT; NcD; NcU; NRivHi. 45-4233

Mason, Lowell, 1792-1872. Vocal exercises and solfeggios, with an accompaniment for the piano forte. Adapted to the wants of private pupils, or classes in vocal music. Selected from Italian, French and German composers. Boston: Wilkins, Carter and company, 1845. 56 p. MH; NN; NBuG. 45-4234

Mason, Lowell, 1792-1872. The vocalist: consisting of short and easy glees, or songs, in parts. Arranged for soprano, alto, tenor, and bass voices. By Lowell Mason and George James Webb, professors in the Boston Academy of

Music. Boston: Wilkins, Carter and company, 1845. 200 p. CtHWatk; MH; MWA; NFri; NRES. 45-4235

Mason, Richard. The gentlemen's new pocket farrier comprising a general description of the noble and useful animal; the horse; together with the quickest and simplest mode of fattening; necessary treatment while undergoing excessive fatigue. Philadelphia: Grigg and Elliot, 1845. InPerM; TBrik; UPB. 45-4236

Mason, Samuel Louis, 1817-1853. Relations of forts and ships. Washington, 1845. PPL. 45-4237

Mason, T.B. Juvenile harp containing a large number of new and beautiful melodies. Selected and translated from the German. A simplified system of elementary principles, peculiarly adapting it to the juvenile singing schools, common schools, and Sunday schools. Boston: A.B. Kidder, 1845. 206 p. LU. 45-4238

Mason, Timothy B. The sacred harp; or beauties of church music. Volume II. A new collection of Psalm and hymn tunes, anthems, motetts, sentences and chants, derived from the highest sources of the musical talent of Europe and America. New edition enlarged and improved. Cincinnati: Truman, 1845. 352 p. ICN. 45-4239

Mason, William, 1829-1908. Works for the piano. Boston, 1845-1891. MH. 45-4240

The Masonic mirror and organ of the Grand lodge of Kentucky; a monthly magazine, devoted to masonry, litera-

ture, science and art. Edited by P.G.M Richard Apperson, Leander M. Cox Covington, Kentucky: H.B. Brown, 1845 v.1-. NNFM. 45-4241

Massachusetts. Abstract from the returns of agricultural societies in Massachusettts. Boston: Dutton and Wentworth, 1845. Ct; IaAS; MHi. 45-4242

Massachusetts. Abstract of the district attorneys reports. Boston, 1845- PPAmP. 45-4243

Massachusetts. Abstract of the Massachusetts school returns for 1844-1845 Boston: Dutton and Wentworth, printers, 1845. 48 p. NjR. 45-4244

Massachusetts. Abstract of the return of insurance companies, incorporated with specific capital: and also of Mutual Marine, and Mutual fire and Marine Insurance companies, exhibiting the condition of those institutions on the first day of December, 1844. Prepared by John G Palfrey. Boston: Dutton and Wentworth 1845. 13 p. MiD-R; NjR. 45-4245

Massachusetts. An account of the state of the treasury of the commonwealth of Massachusetts. Boston: Dutton and Wentworth, state printers, 1845. 37 p MiD-B. 45-4246

Massachusetts. An act in addition to an act incorporating the Boston and Maine Railroad. [Boston, 1846] 4 p. IU. 45-4247

Massachusetts. An act to establish the city of Cambridge. Boston, 1846. 20 p MB. 45-4248

Massachusetts. An act to establish the

anover Branch Railroad Company. Boston, 1846] 4 p. IU. 45-4249

Massachusetts. An act to establish the ewburyport Railroad company. [Boston, 1846] 5 P. IU. 45-4250

Massachusetts. Annual report of cretary, John G. Palfrey, of the expenses of the office. Boston, 1845. 14 p. MH-H. 45-4251

Massachusetts. Annual reports of the ilroad corporations, in the state of Massachusetts, for 1844. Boston: Dutton nd Wentworth, state printers, 1845. 123 MeHi; NjR. 45-4252

Massachusetts. Annual reports to the gislature, relating to the registry and turns of births, marriages, etc. Boston: utton and Wentworth, 1845. InU. 45-253

Massachusetts. Argument by C.G. oring in behalf of the Eastern Railroad ompany. Boston, 1845. 88 p. PPFrankI. 5-4254

Massachusetts. Argument on behalf of oseph Tilden and others, remonstrants, n the hearing... for a grant of... powers construct an aqueduct from Long ond to the city. By William Hubbard, sq. Boston: Press of T.R. Marvin, 1845. 4 p. MBB. 45-4255

Massachusetts. By his excellency George N. Briggs, governor of the Commonwealth of Massachusetts, a roclamation for a day of public thanksgiving and praise. n.p., 1845. roadside. CtHT. 45-4256

Massachusetts. The constitution and

bylaws of the Independent Company of Cadets. Accompanied by papers and documents. Boston, 1845. 47 p. MH; MiD-B. 45-4257

Massachusetts. Convention of delegates to take into consideration the proposed annexation of Texas. Proceedings of a convention chosen by the people of Massachusetts, without distinction of party, and assembled at Faneuil Hall in Boston. Boston: Eastburn's Press, 1845. 18 p. MHi; MnHi; NNC; OClWHi; TxU. 45-4258

Massachusetts. Documents prefered and submitted to the General Court, by the Secretary of the Commonwealth. Boston: Dutton and Wentworth, printers, 1846. DLC. 45-4259

Massachusetts. The insolvent laws of Massachusetts. With notes. By Jos. Cutter. Boston: Mussey, 1846. 108 p. MB. 45-4260

Massachusetts. Message concerning Henry Hubbard. Boston, 1845. Nh. 45-4261

Massachusetts. Message of the governor, returning the resolution, on the petition of John J. Howe and others vs. the Washington Bridge Company, with his objections. Hartford: printed by John L. Boswell, state printer, 1845. 8 p. M. 45-4262

Massachusetts. Report and resolution on international exchanges. Boston, 1845. Nh. 45-4263

Massachusetts. Report and resolutions concerning slavery. Boston, 1845. Nh. 45-4264

Massachusetts. Report and resolutions relating to the annexation of Texas. Boston, 1845. Nh. 45-4265

Massachusetts. Report of the joint special committee concerning the treatment of Samuel Hoar, by the state of South Carolina with resolves and declaration of the state of Massachusetts. [n.p., 1845] 54 p. DLC; MB: Nh; RPB. 45-4266

Massachusetts. Report of the joint special committee instructing them to consider whether any, and if any, what further measures should be taken at the present session of the General Court respecting the annexation of Texas. Boston, 1845. 6 p. MH. 45-4267

Massachusetts. Report of the special committee relating on hours of labor. [Boston, 1845?] 25 p. IU; Nh. 45-4268

Massachusetts. Report on the petition for a railroad. Boston, 1845. Nh. 45-4269

Massachusetts. Resolutions concerning Jonathan Walker. Boston, 1845. Nh. 45-4270

Massachusetts. Resolutions concerning matters to slavery. Boston, 1845. Nh. 45-4271

Massachusetts. Revised statutes of the Commonwealth of Massachusetts and additional laws to 1844... for the use of schools and families. Boston, 1845. 116 p. MHi. 45-4272

Massachusetts. Session laws, acts and resolutions passed by the General Court of Massachusetts at the legislative assemblies. Boston: State printers, 1845-. 99 v. CLSU. 45-4273

Massachusetts. Statement and review of the whole case of the Reverend Jay H Fairchild. From its commencement to i termination compiled from origina documents, with an appendix. Bosto Wright's Steam Press, 1845. 104 MdBB. 45-4274

Massachusetts. A suit in equity betwee Oliver Earle and others... Boston, 184 RPB. 45-4275

Massachusetts. Supplementary repo filling blanks, supplying omissions an making corrections in the penal code Massachusetts, reported to the legisl ture, January 27, 1844. Boston, 1845. 5 p. MBAt; NjR; RPB. 45-4276

Massachusetts. Tables of bearings, di tances, latitudes, longitudes, etc., asce tained by the astronomical an trigonometrical survey, by J.C. Palfre Boston, 1846. 38, 73 p. IaHi; MW. 4 4277

Massachusetts. Transactions of th agricultural societies in the state of Ma sachusetts for 1845-1852. Collated... Amasa Walker. Boston, 1845-[185 NcRA. 45-4278

Massachusetts and South Carolina; a examination of the controversy betwee them. By a member of Congress fro South Carolina. Washington: J. and G. Gideon, 1845. 14 p. NcD; NN; OClWH ScU; TxHU. 45-4279

The Massachusetts register, and Unite States calendar, for 1846. And othe valuable information. Boston: Jame Loring, [1845] 250 p. MBevHi; MeBa MiD; MoSpD; MTop. 45-4280

Massachusetts Sabbath School Society. t's mine. Boston: Massachusetts Sabbath School Society, 1845. 16 p. MHa. 45-4281

Massachusetts Sabbath School Society. Mothers encouraged; containing hints on their particular situation, duties, and chores. From the London edition revised by the committee of publication. Boston: Massachusetts Sabbath School Society, 1845. 124 p. GAlN. 45-4282

Massachusetts State Texas Committee. How to settle the Texas question. [Boston, 1845] CSfCW; DLC; MB. 45-4283

Masse, Joseph Nicolas, d. 1801. A pocket atlas of the descriptive anatomy of the human body. Translated from the last Paris edition and edited by Granville Sharp Pattison. New York: Harper and brothers, [1845] 112 plates. CtMW; LNT-M; MdBM; ScCMe; ViRA. 45-4284

Massillon, Jean Baptist, 1663-1742. Sermons... to which is prefixed the life of the author. From the last London edition. With an introduction by Rev. William M. Willett. Boston: Waite, Peirce and company, 1845. 581 p. ICU; LNH; OO; TxDaM; WBeloC. 45-4285

The master of Langford; or the treachous [sic] guest. New York, 1845. NoLoc. 45-4286

Mather, Cotton, 1663-1728. Essay upon the good that is to be devised and designed by those who desire good while they live. Revised. Boston: Massachusetts Sunday School Society, 1845. CtHC; IaHa; MB; MoSpD; OOxW. 45-4287

Mather, William Williams, 1804-1859. Elements of geology. Fifth edition. New York, 1845. ODW. 45-4288

Mathews, Cornelius, 1817-1889. Americanism: an address delivered before the Euclean Society of the New York University, June 30, 1845. New York: Paine and Burgess, 1845. 34 p. MH; PPM. 45-4289

Mathews, Cornelius Mathews. Big Abel, and the little Manhattan. New York: Wiley and Putnam, 1845. 93 p. DLC; ICU; MB; NjP; RPA. 45-4290

Matlack, Lucius C. Narrative of the anti-slavery experience of a minister in the Methodist Episcopal Church who was twice rejected by the Philadelphia annual conference and finally deprived of a license to preach for being an abolitionist. Philadelphia: Merrihew and Thompson, 1845. 24 p. OO; PSt. 45-4291

Matthews, Thomas. The whist player's hand-book, containing the laws as laid down by the latest authorities and concise rules for playing. From the London edition. Boston: Saxton and Kelt, 1845. 32 p. IaDaP; MB. 45-4292

Mattson, Morris, 1809-1885. American vegetable practice, or a new and improved guide to health, designed for the use of families. Second edition. Boston: Johnson, 1845. 2 v. in 1. DLC; DNLM; DSG; MB. 45-4293

Maturin, Edward, 1812-1881. Montezuma: the last of the Aztecs... New York: Paine and Burgess, 1845. 2 v. KHi; MB; MWA; NcD; WU. 45-4294

Maunder, Samuel, 1783-1848. The

treasury of history... To which is added the history of the United States, by John Inman, esq. New York: Daniel Adee, 1845. 2 v. MiD; MGos; NN; OkTohT; TxH. 45-4295

Maunsell, Henry, 1806-1879. The Dublin practice of midwifery. With notes and additions by Chandler R. Gilman. New York: W.E. Dean, 1845. [13]-292 p. CU-M; DSG; NBuU-M; NNN; ViRA. 45-4296

Maurette, Jean Jacques. Der papst und das evangelium, oder, abachied von ron. New York, 1845. NNUT; OO. 45-4297

Maurette, Jean Jacques. Le Pape l'-Evangile; on encore des adieux a Rome. New York: Publie par la Societe pour impression de livres religieux, [1845?] 76 p. NNUT. 45-4298

Maury, Matthew Fontaine, 1806-1873. A new theoretical and practical treatise on navigation; in which the auxilliary branches of mathemetics and astronomy... are treated of; also the theory and methods of finding time, latitude and longitude, etc. Philadelphia: E.C. and J. Biddle, 1845. 336 p. DLC; InCW; NIC; PU. 45-4299

Maxims of Washington. New York: D. Appleton and company, 1845. 423 p. MNBedf. 45-4300

Maxwell, N.W. Historical memories of my own time. Philadelphia, 1845. MDed. 45-4301

Maxwell, William Hamilton, 1792-1850. History of the Irish rebellion in 1798; with memoirs of the union, and Emmett's insurrections in 1803 by W.H.

Maxwell. With numerous illustration drawn and engraved by George Cruik shank. Sixth edition. New York: C. Scrib ner and company, [1845] 477 p. MiD MLanc; RNR. 45-4302

May, George. Sermon on the connec tion of the church with slavery. By George May, pastor of Wesleyar Church, Lowell, Massachusetts. Lowell W.H. Stevens, 1845. 24 p. MBNMHi MWA; NjR. 45-4303

May, Samuel Joseph, 1797-1871 Emancipation in the British West Indies August 1, 1834; an address delivered ir the First Presbyterian Church ir Syracuse, on the first of August, 1845 Syracuse: Printed by J. Barber, 1845. 2 p. CtSoP; ICMe; MBAt; NCH; WHi. 45 4304

Maygrier, Jacques Pierre. Midwifery il lustrated. With two hundred illustra tions. Fifth edition, with additiona matter and plates. New York: J.S. Red field; Philadelphia: Thomas, Cow perthwait and company; Boston: Otis Broaders and company, 1845. 180 p MdBJ-M; ScSp; TU-M. 45-4305

Mayo, Robert, 1784-1864. A synopsis o the commercial and revenue system o the United States. Washington, 1845. 12 p. DLC. 45-4306

Meade, William, 1789-1862. A brie review of the Episcopal Church in Vir ginia, from its first establishment to the present time; being part of an address o the Right Rev. William Meade, Bishop of Virginia, to the convention of the church in Fredericksburg, May 22, 1845 Richmond: Printed by William Macfar lane, 1845. 15 p. InID; OClWHi; PPL; TSewU; ViU. 45-4307

Meade, William, 1789-1862. Statement of Bishop Meade, in reply to some parts of Bishop Onderdonk's statement of facts and circumstances connected with his trial. New York: Stanford and Swords; Philadelphia: George S. Appleton, 1845. 21 p. MdBD; MH; NcD; NN; ViU. 45-4308

Meadows, F.C. A new French and English pronouncing dictionary. With many new words in general use, in two parts. Fourth American edition, corrected and improved. New York: Alexander V. Blake, 1845. 376 p. InThR; MoS; NdFM; TxBrdD; WaU. 45-4309

Meads, Orlando. What ought the diocese to do? Considerations addressed to churchmen of the diocese of New York. By a layman. New York: Printed for the author, 1845. 15 p. MB; MH; MiD-B; NjR; WHi. 45-4310

The medeatorial work of our Lord Jesus Christ. New York and Pittsburg: Robert Carter, 1845. 214 p. CtHC; KyLoP; NN. 45-4311

Medford, Massachusetts. Statements of town of Medford expenses. 1844-1845. Charlestown: Caleb Rand, [1845] 24 p. MiD-B. 45-4312

Medical Association of the District of Columbia. Regulations. Washington: Gales and Seaton, 1845. 13 p. DSG. 45-4313

Medical College of Ohio. Annual catalogue of the students of the Medical College of Ohio session 1844-5. Cincin-

nati: R.P. Brooks, 1845. 16 p. NNNAM; OC. 45-4314

Medical Institute of Philadelphia. An account of the Institute. Philadelphia: J.C. Clark, 1845. 15 p. DSG. 45-4315

Medicus, pseud. Principles applied to the preservation of health. Albany: Munsell and Tanner, 1845. 30 p. MB; NjR. 45-4316

Meetings of colporteurs and agents of the American Tract Society, at Syracuse, Detroit, Cincinnati, Pittsburgh and New York. New York: Published by the Society, 1845. 40 p. NjPT; PLT. 45-4317

Meigs, Henry, 1782-1861. An address on the subject of agriculture and horticulture, delivered in the Church of the Messiah, on October 9, 1845. New York: J. Van Norden and company, 1845. 10 p. DLC; WU-A. 45-4318

Meigs, Mary Noel Bleeker. Fanny Herbert and other stories. A holiday gift. New York: H.M. Onderdonk, 1845. 205 p. ICU; NNC; OAsht. 45-4319

Meinhold, Wilhelm. Mary Schweilder, the amber witch. The most interesting trial for witchcraft ever known, printed from an imperfect manuscript by her father, Abraham Schweilder, the pastor of Coseroe, in the Island of Usedom. New York: Wiley and Putnam, 1845. 180 p. IaMp; MH; OCY; PU; RJa. 45-4320

Melanethon, pseud. An essay on the defects of the license law as now existing. Penfield, Georgia: Benjamin Brantley, 1845. 12 p. N; NcU. 45-4321

Mellen, Greenville, 1799-1841. A book

of the United States: Exhibiting its geography, divisions, constitution and government together with a condensed history of the land, from its first discovery to the present time. Hartford: Sumner and Goodman, 1845. 846 p. SdBroSC. 45-4322

Melvill, Henry, 1798-1871. Sermons on certain of the less prominent facts and references in sacred story. New York: Stanford and Swords, 1845. 131 p. CSans-S; GDecCT; IaHol; MLow; TChU. 45-4323

The memento; a gift of friendship. Edited by C.W. Everest. New York: Wiley and Putnam, 1845. 278 p. Ct; IaB; IU; MnU; MWA. 45-4324

Memoir of Anna Mary Adams, a member of the Society of Friends. New York: American Tract Society, 1845. 8 p. MH. 45-4325

Memoir of Mrs. Susan Howard. Extracts from her journal and letters. By William Chapin, principal of the Ohio Institute for the Blind. New York: Methodist Book Concern, 1845. 138 p. IEG; LNH; NjMD; OUrC; ScOrC. 45-4326

Memoirs of General Andrew Jackson containing a full account of his Indian campaigns, and defense of New Orleans together with his veto of the bank bill; proclamation to the nullifiers; farewell address, etc. Compiled by a citizen of New York. Auburn, New York: J.C. Derby and company, 1845. 270 p. 45-4327

Memoirs of General Andrew Jackson, seventh president of the United States to which is added the eulogy of Hon. George Bancroft, citizen of western New York. Auburn, New York: James C. Derby and company, [etc., etc.] 1845 [17]-270 p. IaU; KyBgW; LNH; MB; NcAs. 45-4328

A memorial to the legislature of the state of New York, upon the effects of the passage of the trade of the western states, through the Welland and Oswego canals... Rochester: Press of E. Shepard, 1845. 24 p. DLC; Nh-Hi; NNS; OClWHi; PPL. 45-4329

Memorials of Mrs. Harriet W. Fowler, wife of Rev. Professor William C. Fowler, and daughter of the late Noah Webster, deceased March 30, 1844. 56 p. CtB; MB; NN. 45-4330

Mercantile Library Association. Boston. Address and poem delivered before the Boston Mercantile Library Association, 1845. Boston: T.P. Marvin, 1845. M; MB-FA; NCH. 45-4331

Mercer, Charles Fenton, 1778-1858. An exposition of the weakness and inefficiency of the government of the United States of North America. [?] Printed for the author, 1845. 380 p. IU; LNH; MB; OCY; TxU. 45-4332

The merchant and seaman's expeditious measurer; containing a set of tables, which show at one view the solid content of all kinds of packages and casks. New York: E. and G.W. Blunt, 1845. 195 p. LNH; MH. 45-4333

Meredith, Louisa Anne Twamley, 1812-1895. The bouquet; containing the poetry and language of flowers. Boston: Oliver L. Perkins, 1845. 128 p. MDux. 45-4334

Merle d'Aubigne, Jean Henri, 1794-1872. Confessions of the name of Christ in the sixteeth and nineteenth centuries. New York: John S. Taylor, 1845. 56 p. GDecCT; MH; OO; TChU. 45-4335

Merle d'Aubigne, Jean Henri, 1794-1872. D'Aubigne's miscellany. New York: Taylor, 1845. 5 v. in 1. KAn; MLow; MPiB; OO; PPPrHi. 45-4336

Merle d'Aubigne, John Henri, 1794-1872. History of the great reformation of the sixteenth century, in Germany, Switzerland, etc. Cooperstown: H. and E. Finney, 1845. 366 p. GOgU; KCoU; NSpepF; PMA. 45-4337

Merle d'Aubigne, John Henri, 1794-1872. History of the great reformation of the sixteenth century, in Germany, Switzerland, etc. New York and Pittsburg: Robert Carter, 1845-1846. 4 v. NcCJ; NcHil; ORav; TNS. 45-4338

Merle d'Aubigne, Jean Henri, 1794-1872. History of the great reformation of the sixteenth century in Germany, Switzerland, etc. Philadelphia: James M. Campbell; New York: Saxton and Miles, 1845. 3 v. CtW; MNt; NNS; ODaB; TWeW. 45-4339

Merle d'Aubigne, John Henri, 1794-1872. History of the great reformation of the sixteenth century; translated by H. White. Philadelphia: American Tract Society, 1845. 5 v. MNoboro; NcWfC. 45-4340

Merle d'Aubigne, Jean Henri, 1794-1872. Luther and Calvinism; or the true spirit of the reformed church. New York: Robert Carter, 1845. 91 p. CSansS; MbCrD; NjPT; OSW; PPiW. 45-4341

Merriam, George, 1803-1880. The village reader; designed for the use of schools, by the compilers of the easy primer child's guide and intelligent reader. Springfield, Massachusetts: G. and C. Merriam, 1845. 300 p. OOxM. 45-4342

Merrick, Pliny, 1794-1867. Eulogy on General Andrew Jackson, late president of the United States, delivered in Faneuil Hall, July 9, 1845. Boston: Eastburn, 1845. 32 p. MBC; NCH; RPB; TxU; WHi. 45-4343

Merrick, William Duhurst. Speech of Mr. Merrick of Maryland, on the bill to reduce the rates of postage, and to regulate the use and correct the abuse of the franking privilege; delivered in the Senate, January 27, 1845. Washington: Printed by Gales and Seaton, 1845. IU; MHi; NBu; PHi; PPL. 45-4344

Merrill, A.D. The vestry harp; a collection of hymns and tunes, appropriate for social worship. First Edition. Lowell: A.D. Merrill, 1845. 108 p. CtHWatk; KMK; MB; MLow. 45-4345

Merrill, A.P. Addresses delivered at the dedication of the Natchez Institute, July 4, 1845. Natchez, 1845. MBC. 45-4346

Messler, Abraham. The importance of cherishing domestic feeling in our church; a sermon... before the classes of New Brunswick... at Grigstown... New York: Daniel Fanshaw, printer, 1845. 40 p. NjPT; NjR; OClWHi; PLT; PPPrHi. 45-4347

Metcalf, I.N. The blind girl. A ballad. Poetry by Joshua Swan, Jr. Music composed and respectfully dedicated to Miss

Caroline Hill, by I.N. Metcalf. Boston: Henry Prentiss, 1845. 7 p. MB; MBNEC; MNe; MNF; ViU. 45-4348

The meteor of light, containing the minutes of the infidel convention, held in the city of New York, May, 1845. Boston: J.P. Mendum, 1845. 41 p. MBAt; MiD-B; MHi. 45-4349

Methodist almanac for the year of our Lord 1846... Calculated in equal clock time, for Baltimore, Cincinnati, Richmond, Nashville, etc. by David Young, Hanover, New Jersey... George Peck, editor. New York: Lane and Tippett for the Methodist Episcopal Church... [1845] KBB; MiGr; MWA; NjR; WHi. 45-4350

Methodist Episcopal Church. A collection of hymns, for the use of the Methodist Episcopal Church, principally from the collection of the Rev. John Wesley. Revised and corrected with a supplement. New York: G. Lane and C.B. Tippett, 1845. 623 p. DLC; IEG; MH; OCl; ViU. 45-4351

Methodist Episcopal Church. A collection of hymns, for the use of the Methodist Episcopal Church, principally from the collection of the Rev. John Wesley. Revised and corrected with a supplement and an index. New York: G. Lane and C.B. Tippett, 1845. 635 p. DLC; IEG; MiD. 45-4352

Methodist Episcopal Church. A collection of hymns, for the use of the Methodist Episcopal Church, principally from the collection of the Rev. John Wesley. Revised and corrected with a supplement. New York: T. Mason and G.

Lane, 1845. 616 p. CtY; DLC; MH; NNUT; OCl. 45-4353

Methodist Episcopal Church. The debates of the General Conferences of the Methodist Episcopal Church, May 1844. To which is added a review of the proceedings of said conference by Rev. Luther Lee and Rev. E. Smith. New York: O. Scott, 1845. 504 p. IEG; MoWgT; MWA; TxU; Wv. 45-4354

Methodist Episcopal Church. The doctrines and discipline of the Methodist Episcopal Church. New York: G. Lane and C.B. Tippett, for the Methodist Episcopal Church, 1845. 213 p. CoDI; CtY-D 45-4355

Methodist Episcopal Church. Hymns for the use of the Methodist Episcopal Church edited by J. Wesley. New York 1845. MiD. 45-4356

Methodist Episcopal Church. The lesser hymnal; a collection of hymns for the Sunday school and social worship Cincinnati, 1845. 274 p. IU. 45-4357

Methodist Episcopal Church. Minutes of the Troy Conference of the Methodist Episcopal Church. Held at Schenectady New York, May 7, 1845. n.p., 1845. 20 p IEG. 45-4358

Methodist Episcopal Church. South History of the organization of the Methodist Episcopal Church, South comprehending all the official proceedings of the general conference; the southern annual conferences, and the general convention.... Nashville: Compiled and published by the editors and publishers of the South Western Chrisian Advocate, 1845. 267 p. ABBS; CtMW; ICN; NcD; ODaB. 45-4359

Metropolital Catholic almanac and laity's directory for 1846. Baltimore: F. Lucas, Jr., [1845] MoKCC; MWA. 45-4360

Metropolitan Tract Society. The aposolicity of the Church. Baltimore: Metropolitan Tract Society, 1845. 22 p. MdBS. 45-4361

Miami University, Oxford, Ohio. Addresses at the inauguration of Rev. E.D. MacMaster, as president of Miami University, Ohio. August 13th 1845. Cincinnati: Printed for the University by E. Shepard, 1845. 64 p. MH-AH; NjPT; OOxM; RPB. 45-4362

Miami University, Oxford, Ohio. Twentieth annual circular; comprising the catalogue, the course of studies, etc. August, 1845. Oxford: Miami University, 1845. MeHi; MGH; OCHP; OCo. 45-4363

Michelet, Jules, 1798-1874. History of France. Translated by G.H. Smith. New York: D. Appleton and company; Philadelphia: George S. Appleton, 1845. 2 v. DeWi; LNT; MBev; RNR; Vi. 45-4364

Michelet, Jules, 1798-1874. Spiritual direction and auricular confession their history, theory and consequences; being a translation of "Du pretre de la femme, de la famille." New York: Saxton and Miles, 1845. 224 p. CtY; GEU; MH; NN. 45-4365

Michelet, Jules, 1798-1874. Spiritual direction, and auricular confession; their history, theory and consequences. Being a translation of "Du pretre, de la femme, de la familie." Philadelphia: James P. Campbell; New York: Saxton and Miles, [1845] 224 p. GDecCT; ICN; MBBC; NhD; PPL. 45-4366

Michelet, Jules, 1798-1874. The Jesuits. Translated from the French of MM. Michelet and Quinet, Professors in the College of France. Edited by C. Edwards Lester. New York: Gates and Stedman, 1845. 225 p. GDecCT; InCW; NNG; OCX; PPiW. 45-4367

Michigan. Acts of the legislature of the state of Michigan, passed at the annual session of 1845. With an appendix, containing the treasurer's annual report. Detroit: Bagg and Harmon, printers to the state, 1845. 190 p. Wa-L. 45-4368

Michigan. Reports of cases argued and determined in the court of chancery of the state of Michigan. By Henry N. Walker. Detroit: Harsha and Willcox, 1845. 587 p. Ar-SC; DLC; MH; NIC-L; Vi-L. 45-4369

Mickle, Isaac. Reminiscences of old Gloucester: or incidents in the history of the countries of Gloucester, Atlantic and Camden, New Jersey. Philadelphia: T. Ward, 1845. 98 p. IHi; MB; NjN; OC; PP. 45-4370

Middlebrook's New England almanac for 1846. By Elijah Middlebrook. Bridgeport, Connecticut: Sanford and Oakley, [1845] MWA; NCH; WHi. 45-4371

Middlebury College. Catalogue of the officers and students, 1845-6. Troy, New

York: J.C. Kneeland and company, 1845. 16 p. MeHi; PPM. 45-4372

Middlesex District Medical Society. Bylaws. Lowell: Varney, 1845. 12 p. MH-M. 45-4373

The mignonnette. A selection of prose and poetry. Boston: A. Tompkins, 1845. 106 p. MVh. 45-4374

Miles, Henry Adolphus, 1809-1895. The letters and their answers. Lowell? Taylor, 1845. 24 p. CBPac. 45-4375

Miles, Henry Adolphus, 1809-1895. Lowell, as it was, and as it is. Lowell: Powers and Bagley and N.L. Dayton, 1845. 234 p. IaHA; Me; RJa; TMeC; ViU. 45-4376

Miles, Pliny, 1818-1865. Elements of phreno-mnemotechny, or art of acquiring memory; applied to history, geography, biography, etc. Richmond, Virginia: H.K. Ellyson, printer, 1845. 40 p. DLC; ICJ; NcMHi. 45-4377

Miles, Pliny, 1818-1865. Illustrations of Prof. Fauvel-Gourand's system of Phreno-mnmostechny... Detroit: Bagg and Harson, printers, 1845. 40 p. MiD-B. 45-4378

Mill, John Stuart, 1806-1873. A system of logic. New York: Harper and brothers, 1845. 593 p. NRU. 45-4379

Millard, David, 1794-1873. Hymns and spiritual songs original and selected for the use of Christians. Eleventh edition. Union Mills, New York, 1845. 464 p. TxU. 45-4380

Miller, Edward. Report of Edward

Miller, civil engineer on the improve ment of the Schuylhill Navigation mad to the board of managers, March 1: 1845. Philadelphia: John C. Clark printer, 1845. 33 p. MB; MH-BA; NNE PPL; WHi. 45-4381

Miller, Ferdinand H. The oral gramma or ready grammarian to abridge labo refresh the memory, and prepare classe for the thorough instruction arranged ex pressly for the benefit of teachers an students. Fourth edition. Daneville, Ne York: A.R. Knox and F.H. Miller, 184! DLC; NBuG. 45-4382

Miller, George B. Harmonious actio the duty of the church. A sermon preached before the New York mini sterium of the Evangelical Luthera Church, at its semi-centennial anniver sary, at Albany, September 7, 1845. Al bany: Erastus H. Pease, 1845. 25 ꜰ MWiW; NNUT; PPLT; RPB; WHi. 45 4383

Miller, George B. A sermon before th New York Ministerium of the Evangeli cal Lutheran Church, Albany, Septem ber 7, 1845. New edition. Albany, 184! 25 p. MH-AH; ScCoT. 45-4384

Miller, Jacob F. In the court for the tria of impeachments and the correction o errors; Jacob F. Miller, et al. vs. Henr Gable et al. New York: Tribune Jol Printing Establishment, 1845. 615 p NjR. 45-4385

Miller, Jacob Welsh, 1800-1862 Speech of Mr. Miller of New Jersey against the resolution from the House c Representatives for the admission o Texas as a new state into the Union delivered in the Senate of the Unite

States on February 25, 1845. Newark: Daily Advertiser office, 1845. 20 p. CSmH; CtY; NBu; Nj. 45-4386

Miller, James, 1812-1864. The principles of surgery. Philadelphia: Lea and Blanchard, 1845. 525 p. CSt-L; GU-M; ICACS; OC; P. 45-4387

Miller, John F. A refutation of the slander and falsehoods contained in a pamphlet entitled Sally Miller with the entire evidence in the case of Sally Miller vs. L. Belmonti and al, on which the supreme court decided she was entitled to her freedom. New Orleans, 1845. 70 p. LU; MH; NcD. 45-4388

Miller, Lydia Falconor Fraser, 1811-1878. A story book of county scenes written for young children. Philadelphia: W.G. Wardle, 1845. 15 p. CtY; ScC. 45-4389

Miller, Samuel, 1769-1850. Letters on the observance of the monthly concert in prayer addressed to the members of the Presbyterian Church in the United States. Philadelphia: Presbyterian Board of Publication, [1845] 104 p. ViRut. 45-4390

Miller, Samuel, 1799-1852. The law of equitable mortgatges, treating of the liens of vendors and purchasers, of the rights and remedies of equitable mortgages by deposit of deeds and other securities, and particularly with reference to the claims of judgment creditors.... Philadelphia, 1845. 170 p. CoU; DLC; IU; MdBB; PP. 45-4391

Miller's planters' and merchants' almanac for 1846. Charleston, South Carolina: A.E. Miller, [1845] MWA. 45-4392

Miller's planters' and merchants' almanac for 1846. Third edition. Charleston, South Carolina: A.E. Miller, [1845] MH; MWA; ScHi. 45-4393

Millet, Joshua. A history of the Baptists in Maine: together with brief notices of societies and institutions and a dictionary of the labors of each minister. Portland: Printed by Charles Day and company, 1845. 472 p. Ct; PCC; PHi; PPPrHi; RPB. 45-4394

Milliary directory of both banks of the Mississippi and of Bayou Lafourcle and Tecole. St. Martinville: Laurent Courajou and company, 1845. 71 p. NcU. 45-4395

Mills, Henry. Horae Germanicae: a version of German hymns. Auburn: H. and J.C. Ivison, 1845. 274 p. CBe; ICP; MBAU; NCH; PPL. 45-4396

Mills, Robert. The American light house guide: with sailing directions, for the use of the mariner... Washington: William M. Morrison, 1845. 189 p. MFran; MSbri: NNA; MMC; PPL-R. 45-4397

Milner, John, 1752-1826. The end of religious controversy, in a friendly correspondence between a religious society of Protestants and a Roman Catholic divine. New York: D. and J. Sadlier, 1845. 352 p. MdBLC; MoSpD; TN; ViRut. 45-4398

Milner, Joseph, 1744-1797. The history of the Church of Christ. With additions and corrections, by the late Rev. Isaac

Milner, Dean of Carlisle, and president of Queen's College, Cambridge. From the last London edition. Philadelphia: James M. Campbell; New York: Saxton and Miles, 1845. 2 v. ICME; ICU; NcWsM; Nh; TJaU. 45-4399

Milnor, James, 1773-1845. A charitable judgment of the opinion and conduct of others, recommended; being the last sermon preached in St. George's Church, New York, April 6, 1845. New York: Stanford and Swords, 1845. 24 p. CtHC; LU; MB; NjR; RPB. 45-4400

Milton, John, 1608-1674. The complete poetical works of John Milton: with explanatory notes and a life of the author by Rev. H. Stebbing. To which is prefixed Dr. Channing's essay on the poetical genius of Milton. New York: Appleton, 1845. 552 p. MdAS; MoSU; NNC; TKin. 45-4401

Milton, John, 1608-1674. Paradise lost. Philadelphia: H. Altemus, 1845. 319 p. PPiU. 45-4402

Milton, John, 1608-1674. Paradise lost. A poem. In twelve books. A new edition. Boston: Phillips and Sampson, 1845. 294 p. InStmaS; MBelc; MWiW; RPB; VtCas. 45-4403

Milton, John, 1608-1674. Paradise lost. With explanatory notes, by the Rev. Henry Stebbing. New York: D. Appleton and company, 1845. 296 p. IaDuU; MH; OO. 45-4404

Milton, John, 1608-1674. The poetical works of John Milton. A new edition. Boston: Charles C. Little and Brown, 1845. 2 v. CSansS; OSW; PCC; RLa; TSewU. 45-4405

Milton, John, 1608-1674. The prose works of John Milton; with a biographical introduction by Rufus Wilmot Griswold. Philadelphia: Herman Hooker, 1845. 2 v. C-S; ICN; PPi; ScDuE; WHi. 45-4406

Milton, John, 1608-1674. Samson, an oratorio, the words by Milton, the music composed 1742 by Handel. [Boston: Marden, 1845] 8 p. MB. 45-4407

Milton, John, 1608-1674. Selections from the works by Basil Montague. First American from the Fifth London edition. New York: Wiley and Putnam, 1845. 242 p. NjHo. 45-4408

Milwaukee Horticultural Society, Milwaukee, Wisconsin. Constitution and by-laws of the Milwaukee Horticultural Society organized in 1845. [Milwaukee, 1845] Broadside. WHi. 45-4409

Mine Hill and Schuylkill Haven Railroad Company. Report of the board of managers to the stockholders of Mine Hill at their annual meeting January 13th, 1845. Philadelphia: Joseph and William Kite, 1845. 7 p. WU. 45-4410

Miner, Charles, 1780-1865. History of Wyoming, in a series of letters, from Charles Miner, to his son, William Penn Miner... Philadelphia: J. Crissy, 1845. 104 p. GEU; ICHi; MWiW; ScU; WGr. 45-4411

Miner, Ovid. Odd Fellowship, its character and tendencies: With notes of other secret societies. New York: J.K. Willman, 1845. KyDC. 45-4412

Miner, Ovid. Secret societies hostile to freedom and virtue. Odd fellowship, its character and tendencies; with notes of other secret societies. New York: J.K. Wellman, 1845. 24 p. MBC; NjR; NN. 45-4413

A minute and authentic narrative of the conduct and conversation of John B. Gough, during each day of his late absence as related by the inmates of the house where he stopped. New York: Lewis C. Donald, 1845. 16 p. MBNEH. 45-4414

The minute gun. Worcester, 1845. NoLoc. 45-4415

The miracles of Christ. Revised by the editor, D.P. Kidder. New York: G. Lane and C.B. Tippett, 1845. 265 p. TxAuPT. 45-4416

Mirror of truth. A periodical devoted to the dissemination of the doctrines of the New Jerusalem Church. Cincinnati: A. Peabody, 1845-. v. 1-. NIC; OC; PBA. 45-4417

Miss Eliza Russell. A tale of the unfortunate female. Written by a Friend. Boston: Z.D. Montague, 1845. 36 p. MNBedf; NN; RPB. 45-4418

Mitchel, Ormsby MacKnight, 1810-1862. Elementary treatise on algebra designed to facilitate the comprehension, demonstration and application of leading principles of that science. Cincinnati: Morgan, 1845. 306 p. InCW; InNd; MoS; OC; OO. 45-4419

Mitchel, Samuel Augustus. A system of modern geography, comprising a description of the present state of the world and its five great divisions. America, Europe, Asia, Africa, and Ocenia. Philadelphia: Thomas, Cowperthwait, and company, 1845. 336 p. PAtM; PPeSchw. 45-4420

Mitchell, Alexander. A letter on church government to the Rev. Joseph Claybaugh in review of his addresses to his students delivered November 10th, 1844. Cincinnati: Conahan and brother, 1845. 35 p. MdBLC. 45-4421

Mitchell, John, 1794-1870. Notes from over seas; consisting of observations made in Europe, in the years 1843 and 1844. New York: Gates and Stedman, 1845. 2 v. GHi; KyU; MDeeP; NCats; PAtM. 45-4422

Mitchell, John, 1794-1870. Practical church member, a guide to the principles and practice of the congregational churches of New England. New York: Leavitt, Trow and company, 1845. 13 p. CtSoP; MA; MiU. 45-4423

Mitchell, Samuel Augustus, 1792-1868. An accompaniment to Mitchell's map of the world, on Mercator's projection... Philadelphia: S.A. Mitchell, 1845. 572 p. LNUrs; NcA-S; PPFr. 45-4424

Mitchell, Samuel Augustus, 1792-1868. An accompaniment to Mitchell's reference and distance map of the United States containing an index of the various counties, districts, parishes, tonwships, towns, etc.... Philadelphia: S.A. Mitchell, 1845. 302 p. NN; NNC; OClWHi; WBB. 45-4425

Mitchell, Samuel Augustus, 1792-1868. An accurate synopsis of the sixth census of the United States; including every town, township, county, district, parish, territory and state... alphabetically arranged: also the aggregate amount of the different classes of the people and their pursuits... And a comparative view of the population of the Union at different periods... Philadelphia: S.A. Mitchell, 1845. [89]-208 p. CaBVaU; DLC; TU-AE. 45-4426

Mitchell, Samuel Augustus, 1792-1868. A general view of the world, comprising a physical, political, and statistical account of its grand divisions... Illustrated with upwards of nine hundred engravings... By S. Augustus Mitchell. Philadelphia: Thomas, Cowperthwait and company, 1845. 828 p. IaHA; LNB; NIC; OUrC; ViL. 45-4427

Mitchell, Samuel Augustus, 1792-1868. A general view of the world, comprising a physical, political, and statistical account of its grand divisions... Illustrated with upwards of nine hundred engravings... By S. Augustus Mitchell. Richmond, Virginia: Harrold and Murray, 1845. 828 p. NcD. 45-4428

Mitchell, Samuel Augustus, 1792-1868. Key for exercise on Mitchell's series of outline, maps, for the use of academies and schools... Hartford: Case, Tiffany and company, 1845. 118 p. CtHWatk; IC; OMC; RPB. 45-4429

Mitchell, Samuel Augustus, 1792-1868. Map of Massachusetts, Connecticut and Rhode Island, constructed from the latest authorities. Philadelphia, 1845. DLC; NCH. 45-4430

Mitchell, Samuel Augustus, 1792-1868. Map of the states of Louisiana, Mississippi, and Alabama. Philadelphia: S.A. Mitchell, 1845. LU. 45-4431

Mitchell, Samuel Augustus, 1792-1868. Map of the states of Ohio, Indiana and Illinois, with the settled parts of Michigan and Wisconsin. Philadelphia, 1845. MB. 45-4432

Mitchell, Samuel Augustus, 1792-1868. Mitchell's ancient atlas, classical and sacred, containing maps illustrating the geography of the ancient world. Philadelphia: Thomas, Cowperthwait and company, 1845. 12 p. IaU; InCW; OrU; ViU. 45-4433

Mitchell, Samuel Augustus, 1792-1868. Mitchell's ancient geography, designed for academies, schools and families. A system of classical and sacred geography... With an ancient atlas... Philadelphia: Thomas, Cowperthwait and company, 1845. 216 p. InRchE; MdAN; MH; NcD; PP. 45-4434

Mitchell, Samuel Augustus, 1792-1868. Mitchell's national map of the American republic or United States of North America; together with maps of the vicinities of thirty-two of the principal cities and towns in the union. Drawn by J.H. Young; engraved by J.H. Brightly. Philadelphia: Samuel Augustus Mitchell, 1845. Map. MoK. 45-4435

Mitchell, Samuel Augustus, 1792-1868. Mitchell's primary geography. An easy introduction to the study of geography designed for the instruction of children in schools and families. Philadelphia: Thomas, Cowperthwait, and company, 1845. MB; MH; WHi. 45-4436

Mitchell, Samuel Augustus, 1792-1868. Mitchell's school geography. A system of modern geography, comprising a description of the present state of the world, and its five great divisions. Philadelphia: Thomas, Cowperthwait and company, 1845. 336 p. ICP; MFHi; NNC; P; PAtM. 45-4437

Mitchell, Samuel Augustus, 1792-1868. Mitchell's travel guide through the United States, containing the principal cities, towns... Philadelphia: Thomas, Cowperthwait and company, 1845? 78 p. CU-B. 45-4438

Mitchell, Samuel Augustus, 1792-1868. Tourist's pocket map of the state of Virginia. Philadelphia: S.A. Mitchell, 1845. InI. 45-4439

Mitchell, Samuel Latham, 1764-1831. A chemical examination of the mineral water of Schooley's mountain springs. Morristown: J.A. Hull, 1845. 20 p. MH; NNNAM. 45-4440

Mitchell, Thomas Duche. The reciprocal obligations of professors and pupils. Lexington: Published by the medical class, Transylvania University, 1845. 16 p. KyLx; MBAt; NhD; OCHP; PPL. 45-4441

Mitchell, Thomas Duche. Letter to the medical public in regard to the writers dismissal from the Ohio Medical College with reference to the part played by Daniel Drake. n.p., 1845. 4 p. IEN-M. 45-4442

Mitchell, William H. An address delivered before Wetumpka Lodge No. 39 on the anniversary of John the Baptist, June 24, 1845. Wetumpka, Alabama: Charles Yancey, 1845. 14 p. NNFM. 45-4443

Miter, John J. The patriots duty. A dis-

course delivered in the First Congregational Church on Thanksgiving. December 12, 1844. Milwaukie [sic], 1845. 29 p. CSmH; MDeep. 45-4444

Miter, John J., 1809-1875. The patriot's duty. A discourse delivered in the First Congregational Church, Milwaukee, on the day appointed for public thanksgiving, December 12, 1844. Milwaukee, [Wisconsin] Edward Hopkins. David M. Keeler, Milwaukee Daily Sentinel Press, 1845. 29 p. CSmH; DLC; MDeeP; WHi. 45-4445

Moffat, Robert, 1795-1883. Missionary labours and scenes in Southern Africa. New York, 1845. 406 p. LN; PPi; PPPD. 45-4446

Moffat, Robert, 1795-1883. Missionary labours and scenes in Southern Africa. Third edition. New York, 1845. 406 p. PHC. 45-4447

Moffat, Robert, 1795-1883. Missionary labours and scenes in Southern Africa. Seventh edition. New York: Carter, 1845. ICMe; KWiU; PPLT; PWmpDS. 45-4448

Moffat, Robert, 1795-1883. Missionary labours and scenes in Southern Africa. Eighth edition. New York and Pittsburgh: Robert Carter, 1845. 406 p. CtMW; FTaSU; MnM; NjPT; OU. 45-4449

Moffatt, Mary Anne Ursula. An answer to six months in a convent, exposing its falsehoods and manifold absurdities. By the Lady Superior. With some preliminary remarks. Boston: J.H. Eastburn, 1845. 66 p. MH. 45-4450

Moffat's agricultural almanac. New York: W.B. Moffat, 1845. MWA. 45-4451

Moffat's medical and agricultural almanack... 1846... New York: Dr. William B. Moffat, [1845] MeHi; MWA; WHi. 45-4452

Mogridge, George, 1787-1854. The book of the Indians of North America; illustrating their manners, customs, and present state. New York: D. Appleton and company; Philadelphia: G.S. Appleton, 1845. 283 p. DLC; MiU; NcU; PU; WaSp. 45-4453

Mogridge, George, 1787-1854. The book of the Indians of North America; illustrating their manners, customs, and present state; edited by John Frost. New York: D. Appleton and company; Philadelphia: G.S. Appleton, 1845. 294 p. MH; MnHi; NcU; RPAt; TxU. 45-4454

Mogridge, George, 1787-1854. Ephraim Holding's homily hints chiefly addressed to Sunday school teachers by Old Humphrey. New York and Pittsburg: Robert Carter, 1845. 241 p. MLow; MP; NN; PU; RLa. 45-4455

Mogridge, George, 1787-1854. Old Humphrey's country strolls. New York and Pittsburg: R. Carter, 1845. 243 p. MLow; OO; PPM. 45-4456

Mogridge, George, 1787-1854. Old Humphrey's observation. Third edition. New York: Robert Carter, 1845. TxAuPT. 45-4457

Mogridge, George, 1787-1854. Old Humphrey's observation. Sixth edition.

New York: Carter, 1845. 258 p. LNP; OWoC. 45-4458

Mogridge, George, 1787-1854. Old Humphrey's walks in London and its neighborhood. Fourth edition. New York: R. Carter, 1845. 286 p. MB; MiD; MLow. 45-4459

Mogridge, George, 1787-1854. The old sea captain. By Old Humphrey. New York and Pittsburg: Robert Carter, 1845. 252 p. CLU. 45-4460

Mogridge, George, 1787-1854. Thoughts for the thoughtful. Fifth edition. New York and Pittsburg: Robert Carter, 1845. 240 p. IaOt; MLow. 45-4461

Mogridge, Joseph. Comprehensive summary of universal history. Philadelphia: Grubb and Reazor, 1845. MdW. 45-4462

Monell, Gilbert Chichester, 1816-1881. Rheumatism, acute and chronic. A prize essay. [Published by order of the Orange County Medical Society] New York: H.G. Langley, 1845. 144 p. CSt-L; MB; NbU-M; NNN; OO. 45-4463

Mongomery, George Washington, 1804-1841. Novelas espanolas y coplas de manrique, con algunos passages de Don Quijote, etc. Brunswick: J. Griffin, 1845. MeBa; MeLeB; MH; ViU. 45-4464

Monsalvatge, Ramon. The life of Ramon Monsalvatge, a converted Spanish monk, of the order of the Capuchins. With an introduction by Robert Baird. New York: J.F. Trow and company, 1845. 170 p. MiD; MWiW; NjR; OkTu; PPM. 45-4465

Montagu, Basil, 1770-1851. Selections from the works of Taylor, Latimer, Hall. First American from the fifth London edition. New York: Wiley and Putnam, 1845. 242 p. CtHC; IaG; MeBat; NbU; PPL- R. 45-4466

Monteith, Alexander H. The course of lessons in the French language on the Robertson method; intended for the use of persons studying the language without a teacher. Fifteenth American from the eighth Brussels edition. New York: Wilson and company, 1845. 80 p. CtHT; LStBA; MdBP; NCaS; OCU. 45-4467

Montgomery, James, 1771-1854. Poems. New York: Hurst and company; Philadelphia: Sorin and Hill, 1845. 2 v. MdW. 45-4468

Montgomery, James, 1771-1854. Poetical works of James Montgomery. With a memoir of the author, by the Rev. Rufus W. Griswold. Philadelphia: Sorin and Ball, 1845. 2 v. CtNb; KyBC; LNH; MoSU; TN. 45-4469

Montgomery, James E. Report of survey for the Tyrone, Clearfield, and Erie Railroad by James E. Montgomery, civil engineer. Clearfield, Pennsylvania: Moore and Wilson, 1845. 16 p. NNE; PHi. 45-4470

Montgomery, New York. Presbyterian Church. Articles of faith and covenant... with a list of the members. Goshen, New York: Mead, 1845. PPPrHi. 45-4471

The monthly rose, a periodical conducted by the present and former members of the Albany Female Academy. Albany: E.H. Pease and W.C. Little, 1845. 188 p. MB; TxU. 45-4472

Monticello Female Seminary. Catalogue of the officers and members for the year ending March, 1845. Alton: Telegraph office, 1845. 16 p. IHi. 45-4473

Moody, Paul. A practical plan of book keeping, by double entry. Adapted to a large or small business, with or without cash or other auxiliary books to daily journal and ledger. Philadelphia: J.B. Lippincott and company, 1845. DLC; MB; USlC. 45-4474

Mooney, Thomas. A history of Ireland, from its first settlement to the present time. Boston: Published by the author, 1845. 2 v. InNd; MB; MWH; NIC; ViU. 45-4475

Moore, George, 1803-1880. The power of the soul over the body, considered in relation to health and morals. New York: Harper and brothers, 1845. 6, 270 p. GEU-T; ICU; MH-AH; RPaw; ViRu. 45-4476

Moore, Henry, 1751-1844. The life of the Rev. Henry Moore including his autobiography; and a combination written from his own papers. New York: Lane and Tippett, 1845. 432 p. CtY; IaHi; NcD; NNUT; TxU. 45-4477

Moore, Henry, 1751-1844. A system of Latin prosody, with many useful exercises. Philadelphia: H. Hooker, 1845. 111 p. OClJC; VtNofN. 45-4478

Moore, Horatio Newton, 1814-1859. Life and services of Gen. Anthony Wayne. Founded on documentary and other evidence, furnished by his son, Col. Isaac Wayne. Philadelphia: John B. Perry, 1845. 210 p. DLC; NOnei; OC; PPM; PWmpDS. 45-4479

Moore, Horatio Newton, 1814-1859. Life and services of Gen. Anthony Wayne. Founded on documentary and other evidence, published by his son, Col. Isaac Wayne. Philadelphia: Leary, Getz, and company, 1845. 210 p. CLU; ICN; MiGr; NCH. 45-4480

Moore, Horatio Newton, 1814-1859. The life and times of Gen. Francis Marion with an appendix. Philadelphia: J.B. Perry, [1845] MdBE; MMal; NcU; TxU; Vi. 45-4481

Moore, Horatio Newton, 1814-1859. The life and times of Gen. Francis Marion with an appendix. Philadelphia: Leary, Getz and company, [1845] 210 p. MdBJ; NN; OC; OClWHi; ScCliP. 45-4482

Moore, Horatio Newton, 1814-1859. Mary Morris and other tales. Philadelphia: G.B. Zieber and company, 1845. 161 p. CU; ICU; NNC. 45-4483

Moore, John Weeks, 1807-1889. The musician's lexicon or encyclopedistical treasury of musical knowledge. Bellows Falls, Vermont: J.W. Moore, 1845-1846. DLC; VtHi. 45-4484

Moore, Lindley Murray. An address on the encroachments of the slave power, delivered at an anti-slavery meeting at the court house in Rochester. Rochester: Warren, 1845. 12 p. MB; MBAt; PHi; PPPrHi. 45-4485

Moore, Thomas, 1779-1852. Come sing me that sweet air again. Philadelphia; New York: E. Ferrett, 1845. 13 p. ViU. 45-4486

Moore, Thomas, 1779-1852. Lalla Rookh. An original romance. A new edition. New York: C.S. Francis; Boston: Jos. H. Francis, 1845. 278 p. MB. 45-4487

Moore, Thomas, 1779-1852. The poetical works of Thomas Moore including his melodies, ballads, etc. Philadelphia: J. Crissy, 1845. 431 p. GOgU; Mi; NNG; PBm; ViU. 45-4488

The moral almanac for... 1846... Philadelphia: Tract Association of Friends... Joseph Rakestraw, printer, [1845] MWA; NcGU; PPM. 45-4489

Mordecai, Alfred, 1804-1887. Report of experiments on gunpowder, made at Washington Arsenal, in 1843 and 1844. Washington: Printed by J. and G.S. Gideon, 1845. 328 p. ICJ; LN; MnHi; PPAmP; Vi. 45-4490

More, Hannah, 1745-1833. The book of private devotion, a series of prayers and meditations; with an introductory essay on prayer, chiefly from the writings of Hannah More; revised and enlarged. Hartford: Brown and Parsons, 1845. WKen. 45-4491

More, Hannah, 1745-1833. The book of private devotion, a series of prayers and meditations; with an introductory essay on prayer, chiefly from the writings of Hannah More. Revised and enlarged. New York: William Robinson, 1845. 252 p. FLh; MBNMHi; OO; PMA. 45-4492

More, Hannah, 1745-1833. Rural tales; portraying social life. New York: D. Appleton, 1845. 180 p. NcHy. 45-4493

Morgan, J.M. Speech on the bill to submit the constitution to the people. Iowa

City, Iowa: Printed by Williams and Palmer, 1845. 14 p. IaHi. 45-4494

Morgan, William Ferdinand, 1817-1888. The chief labor of life. A discourse preached at the funeral of Mr. William Henry Nash, January 9, 1845 in St. James' Church, Poquetanock. Norwich: G.W. Concklin, 1845. 11 p. Ct; CtHT. 45-4495

Morgan, William Ferdinand, 1817-1888. A letter addressed to the members of the parish of Christ Church, Norwich. [Norwich, 1845] 8 p. CBCDS; CtHT; MiD-B. 45-4496

Morison, John Hopkins, 1808-1896. Life of the Hon. Jeremiah Smith, member of Congress during Washington's administration... Boston: C.C. Little and J. Brown, 1845. 516 p. ICHi; Nh-Hi; PPA; RPA; VtU. 45-4497

Morning watch, January 2, 1845. New York, 1845. MBAt. 45-4498

Morrell, Luke A. The American sheep, with their breeds, management and diseases. New York: Harper and brothers, 1845. KNK; LU; OUrC; PPL-R; WU-A. 45-4499

Morris, Robert D. Slavery its nature, evils and remedy. A sermon preached to the congregation of the Presbyterian church, Newton, Pennsylvania. On sabbath morning, July 27, 1845. Published by request. Philadelphia: Printed by William S. Martien, 1845. 31 p. ICN; MBC; PHi; PPM; PPPrHi. 45-4500

Morris, Thomas Asbury, 1794-1874. Sermons on various subjects. Cincinnati: L. Swormstedt and J.T. Mitchell, 1845.

355 p. ArL; IaOskJF; IRA; M; TxU. 45-4501

Morris and Canal Banking Company. Copy of the contract, entered between the Morris Canal and Banking Company and the Society for Establishing Useful Manufactures, February 17, 1836. Paterson, New Jersey: T. Warren, printer, 1845. 7 p. DLC. 45-4502

Morris Canal and Banking Company. Charter of the Morris Canal and Banking Company, and the several acts of the legislature in relation thereto, 1845. DBRE; NNE. 45-4503

Morrison, Rederick N. Speech... in assembly... on the constitutional amendments. Albany: C. Van Benthuysen and company, 1845. 13 p. NN. 45-4504

Morse, Sidney Edwards, 1794-1871. The cerographic atlas of the United States. By Sidney E. Morse and Samuel Breese. New York: S.E. Morse and company, 1845. 20 p. Ct; NIC. 45-4505

Morse, Sidney Edwards, 1794-1871. The cerographic Bible altas. New York: S.E. Morse and company, 1845. Ct; CrHC; DLC; IU; MH-AH 45-4506

Morse, Sidney Edwards, 1794-1871. The geographical atlas of the United States; no. 3. New York: Morse, 1845. OO. 45-4507

Morse, Sidney Edwards, 1794-1871. Morse's North American atlas. New York, 1845. NN. 45-4508

Morse, Sidney Edwards, 1794-1871. A system of geography, for the use of schools. Illustrated with more than fifty geographic maps, and numerous wood cut engravings. New York: Harper and brothers, 1845. 72 p. Ct; MeLew; MH; OClWHi; WBeloC. 45-4509

Mortimer, G.W. The phyrotechnist's companion, familiar system of recreative fire. Philadelphia, 1845. PPL-R. 45-4510

Morton, John Madison, 1811-1891. The corporal's wedding; or a kiss from the bride; a farce in one act. New York: Samuel French, [1845] 27 p. OCl. 45-4511

The Morton family. By a young lady. Boston: James Munroe and company, 1845. 71 p. DLC; OU; ViU. 45-4512

Mosheim, Johann Lorenz, 1694?-1755. Institutes of ecclesiastical history, ancient and modern. In four books, much corrected, enlarged and improved, from the primary authorities. A new and literal translation from the original Latin, with copious additional notes, original and selected. Second edition revised and enlarged. New York: Harper and brothers, 1845. GMM; IaStac; KEmC; MoSpD; NbCrD. 45-4513

Mosheim, Johann Lorenz, 1694?-1755. Institutes of ecclesiastical history, ancient and modern, in four books, much corrected, enlarged and improved from the primary authorities. Third edition revised and enlarged. New York: Harper and brothers, 1845. 3 v. CoU; MoMM; OSW; OUr. 45-4514

The moss rose, or an annual gift. New York: Nafis and Cornish, [1845?] 348 p. MH; WU. 45-4515

The mother's new primer; or the infant's library. New York: Richard Marsh, 1845. 16 p. RPB. 45-4516

The mother's primer to teach her child its letters and how to read. Hartford: Belknap and Hamersley, 1845. 45 p. MH. 45-4517

Mott, Valentine, 1785-1865. Travels in Europe and the East in the years 1834-1841. New York: Harper and brothers, 1845. 452 p. IEG; NICLA; NNCoCi; OMC; ScC. 45-4518

Moulton, Elizabeth Anne. Young pastor's wife. Memoir of Elizabeth Anne Moulton; containing her biography, diary, letters, etc. Boston: Waite, Peirce and company, 1845. 275 p. DLC. 45-4519

Mount Hebron Cemetery Company, Winchester, Virginia. Dedication of Mount Hebron Cemetery in Winchester, Virginia, June 22, 1844. Winchester: Republican office, 1845. 31 p. NcD; ViU. 45-4520

Mount Lucas Orphan and Guardian Institute, Princeton, New Jersey. First annual report of the trustees. Princeton: John T. Robinson, 1845. 20 p. MHi; NjP. 45-4521

Mount Pleasant, Ohio. High school. Catalogue of teachers and student in the Mount Pleasant High School for the year ending ninth month, 1845. Mount Pleasant, Ohio: E. Harris, Jr., 1845. 8 p. CSmH; OClWHi. 45-4522

Mount Vernon, New Hampshire. Congregational Church. Articles of faith and covenant. Amherst, 1845. 8 p. Nh-Hi. 45-4523

Mr. Major refuted by himself; being an answer to his reasons for acknowledging the Holy Roman See by a priest of the Church in Pennsylvania. Philadelphia: King, 1845. PPPrHi. 45-4524

Mr. Moffat's visit to the children of Manchester and letter to children on missions. From the London edition. Revised by the committee of publication. Boston: Massachusetts Sabbath School Society, 1845. 48 p. NcD; OO. 45-4525

Mulder, Gerardus Johannes, 1802-1880. The chemistry of vegetable and animal physiology. First American edition with notes and corrections by B. Sillman, Jr. New York: Wiley and Putnam, 1845. 78 p. DLC; MWA; NjR; PPC; ViU. 45-4526

Munchausen, English. The curious and entertaining adventures and travels by sea and land of the renowned Baron Munchausen. Including a tour through the United States in the year 1803. New York: Farmer and Daggers, 1845. 56 p. DLC; NN; OFH. 45-4527

Munger, Sendol Barnes. The conquest of India by the church. By Rev. S.B. Munger, missionary at Ahmednugger. Boston: Massachusetts Sabbath School Society, 1845. [7]-376 p. KWiU; MiOC; NNNr; OO; TWcW. 45-4528

Munger, Sendol Barnes. The conquest of India by the church. Written for the Massachusetts Sabbath School Society and revised by the Committee of Publication. Boston: The society, 1845. ICN; MA; NR. 45-4529

Murdoch, James Edward, 1811-1893. Orthophony, or vocal culture in elocu-

tion a manual of elementary exercises adapted to Dr. Rush's philosophy of the human voice and designed as an introduction to Russell's American elocutionist. Boston: W.D. Ticknor and company, 1845. 336 p. IaDuU; MoSpD; OO; PU. 45-4530

Murdock, William David Clark. Our true title to Oregon. Georgetown: John T. Crow, 1845. 12 p. CU-B; MnHi; NN; OrP. 45-4531

Murray, Charles Augustus, 1806-1895. The prairie bird. A novel. New York: Harper and brothers, 1845. MH. 45-4532

Murray, Hugh, 1779-1846. An historical and descriptive account of British America. New York: Harper and brothers, 1845. 2 v. LN; OSW; PPGi; PWW; RPE; WaU. 45-4533

Murray, Hugh, 1779-1846. The encyclopaedia of geography: comprising a complete description of the earth, physical, statistical, civil, and political... Philadelphia: Lea and Blanchard, 1845. 3 v. IaDm; IU; MH; NNC; THi. 45-4534

Murray, James, 1732-1782. Sermons to asses. Portland: William Hyde, 1845. 261 p. NRivHi. 45-4535

Murray, Joseph Alexander, 1815-1889. Reasons for gratitude. A sermon preached in the Presbyterian Church, Petersburg, Pennsylvania, on Thursday, November 27, 1845. Gettysburg: H.C. Neinstadt, 1845. 19 p. PPPrHi; PWCHi. 45-4536

Murray, Lindley, 1745-1826. English grammer; adapted to the different classes of learners, with an appendix.

Philadelphia: Joseph McDowell, 1845. 306 p. NPee. 45-4537

Murray, Lindley, 1745-1826. English grammar, adapted to the different classes of learners, with an appendix, containing rules and observations for assisting the more advanced student to write with perspicuity and accuracy. Claremont, New Hampshire: Claremont Manufacturing company, 1845. 228 p. CSmH; WU. 45-4538

Murray, Lindley, 1745-1826. English grammar, adapted to the different classes of learners, with an appendix, containing rules and observations for assisting the more advanced student to write with perspicuity and accuracy. New London and New York, 1845. CtY; PPL; TxU-T. 45-4539

Murray, Lindley, 1745-1826. English grammar adapted the different classes of learners. With an appendix containing rules and observations for assisting the more advanced students to write with perspicuity and accuracy. Newark: Benjamin Olds, 1845. 310 p. MdBMC; NBu; NjN; OClWHi. 45-4540

Murray, Lindley, 1745-1826. The English reader, or pieces in prose and poetry, selected from the best writers. Cooperstown: H. and E. Phinney, 1845. 252 pl. KaStB; PClWHi. 45-4541

Murray, Lindley, 1745-1826. The English reader, or pieces in prose and poetry, selected from the best writers with a few preliminary observations on the principles of good reading. Philadelphia: Uriah Hunt and company, 1845. 252 p. NcGuG; NjR; PSC-Hi. 45-4542

Murray, Lindley, 1745-1826. The English reader; or pieces in prose and verse from the best writers; designed to assist young persons to read with propriety and effect. New London: Bolles and Williams; New York: Collins, Brother and company, 1845. 252 p. MH; NbOM; NjR; RPB. 45-4543

Murray, Lindley, 1745-1826. Sequel to the English reader; or elegant selections in prose and poetry. New York: Collins Brother and company, 1845. 299 p. NNF. 45-4544

Muse, J.E. Address to the agricultural society, of New Castle County at the 10th annual meeting assembled at Wilmington, Delaware on September 18, 1845. Wilmington: Evans and Vernon, 1845. 17 p. DeWi. 45-4545

Musical counting room almanac. By H.W. Day. Boston: J.B. Page, 1845. Broadside. MWA. 45-4546

Mutual Benefit Life Insurance Company. Death losses and matured endowments paid since organization. Newark, 1845-1880. 206 p. MBC. 45-4547

Mutual Fire and Marine Insurance Company. An act to incorporate the Mutual Fire and Marine Insurance Company of Baltimore. Baltimore: Robert Neilson, 1845. 11 p. MdHi. 45-4548

Muzzey, Artemus Bowers, 1802-1892. Christ our head. Printed for the American Unitarian Association. Boston: James Munroe and company, 1845. 14 p. ICMe; MBC; MeB; MHi; RP. 45-4549

Muzzey, Artemas Bowers, 1802-1892.

A plea for the christian spirit. A sermon... Boston: William Crosby and H.P. Nichols, 1845. 12 p. ICMe; MBC; MiD-B; MWA; RPB. 45-4550

Muzzey, Artemas Bowers, 1802-1892. A sermon of nature... from the Monthly Religious Magazine. Boston: Crosby and Nichols, 1845. 10 p. ICMe; MBAt; Md-CatS; MH; MNe. 45-4551

Muzzey, Artemas Bowers, 1802-1882. The young maiden. Boston: W. Crosby and H.P. Nichols, 1845. 264 p. MiU; PMA. 45-4552

My early home, and other tales. Designed to promote the welfare and happiness of the family. Boston: Waite, Peirce, and company, 1845. 14 p. ICN; InU; MBevHi; NN; ViU. 45-4553

N

Napoleon I. Emperor of the French, 1769-1821. Napoleon's maxims of war. Translated from the French by Colonel D'Aguilar. New York: J.S. Redfield, 1845. 212 p. CU; MB; NBuG; OO; ViLxW. 45-4554

Napoleon I. Emperor of the French, 1769-1821. Sketches from his history adapted for the young. Philadelphia: American Sunday School Union, 1845. 124 p. ArBaA; DLC. 45-4555

A narrative of facts, collected by a tract visitor in connection with the life and death of Jane Brown, Brooklyn, 1845. 8 p. MWA. 45-4556

A narrative of Griswold, the African youth from the Mission school at Cape Palmas who died in Boston, May 16, 1844. Boston: Published by a Friend of Missions, 1845. 16 p. MB; MBNEH; WHi. 45-4557

Narrative of the capture and providential escape of Misses Frances and Almira Hall. Also a particular account of the war with Black Hawk. Portland: S.H. Cotesworthy, 1845. 24 p. CtY; MH. 45-4558

The Nashua and Nashville directory by Murray and Kimball. Nashua: Printed by the Publishers, 1845. 99 p. MBNEH; NhD. 45-4559

Nashua Manufacturing Company. The act of incorporation and by laws of the

Nashual Manufacturing Company. Nashville: Printed by Albin Beard, 1845. 21 p. MHi; Nh. 45-4560

Nashville and Chattanooga Railroad Company. Charter, passed December 11, 1845. [Nashville] Union Press, J.G. Shepard, printer, [1845] 15 p. T. 45-4561

Natalia, Aslauga's knight and other tales. Edited by a lady. Boston: Jordan and Wiley, 1845. 96 p. MH; NN. 45-4562

National Association of Inventors. Preamble, constitution and bylaws of Inventors with the officers and committees; with an appendix containing the call and proceedings of a National Convention of Inventors, the address of its president, etc. New York: Padney, Hooker and Russel, 1845. 16 p. MH-BA; NIC. 45-4563

National clay almanac for 1845. Philadelphia: Desilver and Muir, 1845. MWA; PHi. 45-4564

National Convention of Farmers and Gardeners, and Friends of Agriculture, New York, 1844. Proceedings of the the National Convention of Farmers and Gardeners, and Friends of Agriculture, held at the American Institute... New York: J. Van Norden and company, printers, 1845. 51 p. MBHo; MH; MiGr; NBuG; NSyHi. 45-4565

National Fire Insurance Company.

Report of the National Fire Insurance Company, in answer to a resolution of the assembly. [transmitting statement of premium received and taxes paid for the years 1842, 1843 and 1844] [Albany, 1845] 3 p. WHi. 45-4566

National Institute for the Promotion of Science, Washington. National institute. Memorial of the institute, soliciting the aid of congress in its behalf. [Washington: Blair and Rives, printers, 1845] DLC. 45-4567

National Loan Fund Life Assurance Society of London. Prospectus. New York: G.F. Nesbitt, 1845. 31 p. DLC; MH-BA; MHi. 45-4568

National Lord's day convention, Baltimore, Maryland. Abstract of the proceedings of the national Lord's day convention held in the city of Baltimore on the 27th and 28 November, 1844. Baltimore: Printed at the Publication rooms of the Evangelical Lutheran Church, [1845?] 82 p. GEU-T; MdBP OO; PLT; TxDaM. 45-4569

National police gazette. New York, 1845. v.1-. MH; PSt. 45-4570

National Reform Association. Young America, principles and objects of the National Reform Association or Agrerian League, by a member. New York, 1845. PHi. 45-4571

Native almanac for 1846. Lexington, 1775; Kensington, 1844; Philadelphia, 1845. 24 p. WHi. 45-4572

Native American Convention, Philadelphia, 1845. Declaration of principles, comprised in the address and resolutions of the Native American convention, assembled at Philadelphia, July 4, 1845. New York: Whitney, 1845. 14 p. NNC. 45-4573

Naumkeag Steam Cotton Company. Salem, Massachusetts. By laws... in Salem. Salem: Ives and Pease, printers, 1845. 8 p. NjR. 45-4574

Nautical almanac for 1848. [sic] Blunt's edition. New York: E. and G.W. Blunt, 1845. MWA. 45-4575

Neal, Joseph Clay, 1807-1847. Charcoal sketches; or scenes in a metropolis. With illustrations by David C. Johnston. New edition. Philadelphia, Carey and Hart, 1845. 222 p. DLC; MLow; NcAS; PLFM. 45-4576

Neale, Samuel, 1729-1792. Some account of the lives and religious labours of Samuel Neale and Mary Neale. Philadelphia, [1845] 267 p. CtY; NIC; NRAB; OClWHi; PHC. 45-4577

Neale, William Johnson, 1812-1893. History of the mutiny at Spithead and the Nore; with an inquiry into its origin and treatment and suggestions for the prevention of future discontent in the royal navy. Philadelphia: G.B. Zieber and company, 1845. 239 p. LNHT; NIC; NNS; PPL-R; RPA. 45-4578

Neff, Jacob K. The army and navy of America: containing a view of the heroic adventures, battles, naval engagements, remarkable incidents and glorious achievements in the cause of freedom, from the period of the French and Indian wars to the close of the Florida war; independent of an account of warlike operations on land and sea... Philadelphia: J.H. Pearson and company, 1845. 9-624 p. ICHi; MB; NN; OAl; TxGR. 45-4579

Neill, John, 1819-1880. Outlines of the arteries with short descriptions. Designed for the use of medical students. Philadelphia: Ed. Barrington and George D. Haswell, 1845. 30 p. CSt-L; DLC; MH-M; PU; WU-M. 45-4580

Neill, John, 1819-1880. Outlines of the nerves with short descriptions. Designed for the use of medical students. Philadelphia: E. Barrington and George D. Haswell, 1845. 30 p. CSt-L; ICJ; IU-M; OCo; PBa. 45-4581

Nelson, John, 1786-1871. A sermon, delivered in Rutland, July 14, 1845, at the funeral of Rev. Josiah Clark. Worcester: Printed by Thomas W. Butterfield, 1845. 15 p. MBC; RPB. 45-4582

Nepos, Cornelius. De vita excellentium imperatorum; ex editions quarta, J.H. Bremi; accedunt notae Anglicae atque index historicus et geograhicus. Second edition. Philadelphia: Hunt, 1845. ArL; MB; MH; MnSS; OClJC. 45-4583

Nesmith, John, 1793-1869. The case of John Nesmith and another versus Francis A. Calvert and others, in Chancery in the circuit court of the United States for the First Circuit District of Massachusetts. Boston: Freeman and Bolles, 1845. 136 p. MB. 45-4584

The nest. Revised by D.P. Kidder. New York: G. Lane and C.B. Tippett, 1845. 37 p. DLC. 45-4585

Nettleton, Asahel, 1783-1844. Memoir of the life and character of Rev. Asahel

Nettleton. By Bennet Tyler, president and professor of Christian theology in the Theological Institute of Connecticut. Second edition. Hartford: Robins and Smith, 1845. 367, 16 p. CtEhad; DLC; MBAt; OkU; ViRuT. 45-4586

Nettleton, Asahel, 1783-1844. Remains of the late Rev. Asahel Nettleton... consisting of sermons, outlines and plans of sermons, brief observations on texts of scripture, and miscellaneous remarks. Compiled and prepared for the press by Bennet Tyler... Hartford: Robins and Smith, 1845. 408 p. GDecCT; MoSpD; NCH; TxH; VtU. 45-4587

Nettleton, Asahel, 1783-1844. Village hymns for social worship, selected and original, designed as a supplement to the psalms and hymns of Dr. Watts. Hartford: Brown and Parsons, 1845. 488 p. CtHT; CtHWatk; MGlHi; MWHi. 45-4588

Neue Americanische Landwirthschafts calender, 1846. Von Carl F. Egelmann. Reading, Pennsylvania: Johann Ritter und company, [1845] MWA. 45-4589

Neuer calender fur bauern und handwerker. Philadelphia: Mentz und Rovaudt, 1845. PPeSchw. 45-4590

Neuer calender fur die bauern und handwerker, 1846. Von Carl F. Egelmann. Philadelphia: Mentz und Rovoudt, [1845] MWA. 45-4591

Neuer calender fur die vereingten staaten auf das Jahr 1846. Philadelphia: R. Wilson Desilva, [1845] MWA. 45-4592

Neuer Deutscher Americanis cher

volkskalender, 1845. Von Gust Nieritz. New York: Wilhelm Radde, 1845. MWA. 45-4593

Neuer Gemeinnutziger Pennsylvanischer calender, 1846. Lancaster, Pennsylvania: Johann Bar; [1845] MWA. 45-4594

Neuman, Henry. Dictionary of the Spanish and English languages; wherein the words are correctly explained, agreeably to their different meanings and a great variety of terms, relating to the arts, sciences, manufactures, merchandise, navigation, and trade, elucidated. Boston: Wilkins Carter and company, 1845. IP; KyLoS; LNX; MdAS. 45-4595

Neuman, Henry. A pocket dictionary of the Spanish and English languages. From the last improved edition of Neuman and Baretti. Philadelphia: S. Wakeling, 1845. 714 p. CoU; MBNEC; NjP. 45-4596

Neville, Edmund. Autumn lessons; or the leaf an emblem of man. A sermon preached in St. Philip's Church, Philadelphia, November 23, 1845. Published by request. Philadelphia: George S. Appleton, 1845. 23 p. CtHC; ICMe; MH; MiD-B; PPFHi. 45-4597

Nevin, John Williamson. A baccalaureate address: spoken, September 10, 1845, to the graduating class of Marshall College, by the president of the institution. Chambersburg: Office of publication of the German Reformed Church, 1845. 18 p. MdBD; PLERC-Hi; PPL; PPM. 45-4598

Nevins, William. Select remains of the Rev. William Nevins, with a memoir. Third edition revised and corrected. New York: John S. Taylor and company, 1845. 398 p. ArCH; CSansS; ICP; MnHi; TNV. 45-4599

Nevins, William, 1797-1835. I will give liberally. Park Hill, Oklahoma: Cherokee Nation, Mission Press, 1845. DLC; ICN. 45-4600

The new American pocket farrier and farmer's guide in the choice and management of horses, meat cattle, sheep and swine; including a description of their internal structure, their digestive system, the diseases to which they are liable, with their causes, symptoms, and most approved methods of cure, from the writings of Youatt, etc. To which is added a variety of agricultural and miscellaneous receipts. Philadelphia: Leary and Getz, 1845. 284 p. DNAL; LNH; MH; PPL; PU. 45-4601

The New American singer's own book; a choice selection of the most popular sentimental, patriotic, naval and comic songs. To which is added a collection of useful letters on various subjects. Philadelphia: J.B. Perry, 1845. 192 p. NRES. 45-4602

New Bedford, Massachusetts. Bylaws and ordinances of the Town of New Bedford with certain municipal regulation of police. New Bedford: Press of Benjamin Lindsey, 1845. 20 p. MHi; MNBedf. 45-4603

New Bedford, Massachusetts. Rules of the school committee and regulations of the public schools of the town of New Bedford. n.p., [1845?] 16 p. ICN; MB; MNBedf. 45-4604

The New Bedford directory; containing

the names of the inhabitants, their occupations, places of business and dwelling houses and the town register, with lists of the streets and wharves and other useful information to which is added the by-laws and ordinances of the town. New Bedford: B. Lindsey, 1845. 190 p. Ct; ICN; MNBedf. 45-4605

The new birth. A Euklant vita. Park Hill, Oklahoma: Mission Press, 1845. 16 p. ICN; MBAt. 45-4606

The New England almanac and farmer's friend for 1846. By Nathan Daboll. New London: Bolles and Williams, [1845] ICMcHi; NjR; WHi. 45-4607

New England almanack. By Nathan Daboll. New London: Bolles and Williams, 1845. MWA. 45-4608

New England almanack for 1846. By Nathan Daboll. New London, Connecticut: Bolles and Williams, [1845] MWA; WHi. 45-4609

New England almanack for 1846. By Nathan Daboll. Norwich: L. and E. Edwards, 1845. MWA. 45-4610

New England almanack for 1846. By Nathan Daboll. Norwich: T. Robinson, 1845. MWA. 45-4611

The New England family magazine; for the diffusion of useful knowledge. Robert L. Wade, editor. Boston: Bradbury, Soden, and company, 1845-. v.1-. CtY; DLC; MB; MH. 45-4612

The New England farmer. Boston, 1845-. v.1-. OCl. 45-4613

New England Farmer's almanac for 1846. By Dudley Leavitt. Concord, New Hampshire: John F. Brown, 1845. 48 p. RNR. 45-4614

New England farmer's almanac for 1846. Truman W. Abell. Claremont, New Hampshire: Claremont Manufacturing Company, [1845] MWA. 45-4615

New England farmer's almanac. By T.W. Abell. Claremont, New Hampshire: Claremont Bookstore, 1845. MWA; PHi; WHi. 45-4616

The New England farmer's almanack, on an improved plan for the year 1846. By Dudley Leavitt... Concord, New Hampshire: John F. Brown, [1845] 24 l. MiD-B; MWA; NhHi; RNR; WHi. 45-4617

The New England Historical and Genealogical Register. Boston: Samuel G. Drake, 1845-1848. 3 v. in 1. MeHi; MH; Nj; NP; OClWHi. 45-4618

New England Mutual Life Insurance Company. Exposition of the objects of the institution. Boston: Samuel N. Dickinson, 1845. 32 p. MH-BA; NNIns; WHi. 45-4619

New England odd fellow's almanac for 1846. By Chadbourn and Sampson. Exeter, New Hampshire: C.C. Dearborn, [1845] MWA. 45-4620

The New England primer; or an easy and pleasant guide to the art of reading to which is added the catechism. Boston: Sabbath School Society, 1845. PPPrHi. 45-4621

New England Society of Cincinnati,

Ohio. Charter Constitution and bylaws together with the names of the members. Organized January 14, 1845. Cincinnati: Shepard and company, 1845. 37 p. OC; OCHP. 45-4622

New English-German and German-English dictionary. Compiled from the dictionaries of Lloyd, Nonden and Sporschil. Philadelphia: Metz and Rovoudt, 1845. 498 p. CtHT; IJT; MB; MH-AH; NIC. 45-4623

New Hagerstown Academy. New Hagerstown Ohio. Catalogue of the officers and students of the New Hagerstown Academy, New Hagerstown, Carroll County, Ohio. From July 1844 to July, 1845. Cadiz, Ohio: L. Harper, 1845. 12 p. PWW. 45-4624

New Hampshire. Journal of the Honorable Senate of the state of New Hampshire at their session held at the capitol in Concord, commencing Wednesday, November 20, 1844. Concord: Carroll and Baker, 1845. 145 p. KWiU. 45-4625

New Hampshire. Journal of the Honorable Senate. Journal of the House of Representatives, of the state of New Hampshire. Concord: Carroll and Baker, 1845. 422 p. IaHi; KWiU; Mi. 45-4626

New Hampshire. Journal of the House of Representatives of the state of New Hampshire at their session held at the Capitol in Concord, commencing Wednesday, June 4, 1845. Concord: Carroll and Baker, 1845. 435 p. IaHi. 45-4627

New Hampshire. Laws of the state of New Hampshire. Passed at June session.

Concord: Carroll and Baker, 1845. 70 p. Ky; Nv. 45-4628

New Hampshire. Laws of the state of New Hampshire passed November session, 1844, published by authority. Concord: Carroll and Baker, 1845. 220 p. Ky; Nv; W. 45-4629

New Hampshire. Message of his excellency, the governor, to both branches of the General court of New Hampshire. June session, 1845. Concord: Carroll and Baker, 1845. 12 p. Nh; Nh-Hi; NNC. 45-4630

New Hampshire. Message of the Governor J.H. Steele to the general court June session, 1845. Concord, 1845. 12 p. MHi. 45-4631

New Hampshire. Statistical report of the Boston, Concord and Montreal Railroad from Concord to Haverhill, New Hampshire. Haverhill? 1845. NhDO. 45-4632

The New Hampshire annual register and United States calendar for the year 1846. Concord: G. Parker Lyon, [1845] 143 p. MnHi. 45-4633

New Hampshire Patriot. Annexation, an American question, February 24, 1845. Concord, New Hampshire, 1845. 2 p. CtY. 45-4634

The New Hampshire register and United States Calendar for 1846. By G. Parker Lyon. Concord: Parker Lyon, [1845] 143 p. MWA; NhHi. 45-4635

The New Hampshire, Texas and Oregon resolution of the Legislature of

New Hampshire. Washington: Blair and Rives, 1845. 2 p. MH 45-4636

New Haven, Connecticut. Chapel Street Congregational Church. The standing rules, confession of faith, covenant, and catalogue of the officers and members of the Chapel Street Congregational Church in New Haven. New Haven: J. Hall Benham, 1845. 22 p. Ct. 45-4637

New Haven, Connecticut. Howe Street Church. Catalogue of the Howe Street Church, in New Haven. New Haven: William Storer, printers, 1845. 12 p. MiD-B. 45-4638

New Haven almanac for 1846. By Charles Prindle. New Haven, Connecticut: Durrie and peck and S. Babcock, [1845] MWA. 45-4639

New Haven and Northampton Company. Engineers report on the survey from New Haven up the canal to Plainville. New Haven: Hitchcock and Stafford, 1845. 24 p. CtSoP; CtY; DBRE; MB; MiD-B. 45-4640

New Haven as it is. Embellished with a map of the city and several engravings. New Haven: Willim Storer, 1845. 24 p. Ct; MB. 45-4641

New Haven Company. Consociation of the Western District. Summary of the constitution adopted. New Haven: Storer, 1845. CtHC. 45-4642

New Jersey. Acts of the sixty-ninth legislature of the state of New Jersey, and first session under the new constitution. Trenton: Phillips and Boswell, 1845. 310 p. CU; In-SC; MdBB; Ms; T. 45-4643

New Jersey. Annual report of the trustees of the school fund of the state of New Jersey. Trenton: Sherman and Harron, 1845. 35 p. NjR. 45-4644

New Jersey. Journal of the proceedings of the first Senate of the state of New Jersey convened at Trenton being the sixty-ninth session. Morristown, New Jersey: S.P. Hull, 1845. 900 p. Mi; N; NcU; Nj. 45-4645

New Jersey. Message from the governor of New Jersey to both houses of the sixty-ninth legislature at the commencement of the session. Trenton: Sherman and Harron, 1845. 26 p. NjP; NjR. NNC. 45-4646

New Jersey. Message from the governor of New Jersey, to both houses of the sixty-ninth legislature at the commencement of the session. Trenton: Sherman and Harron, 1845. 50 p. MdBJ; MiD-B. 45-4647

New Jersey. Minutes of the proceedings of the joint meeting of the Senate and General Assembly of New Jersey, 1845. n.p., 1845. N. 45-4648

New Jersey. New constitution of the state of New Jersey. Newark: J.L. Agens, 1845. 45 p. NjR. 45-4649

New Jersey. Report of the joint committee on the state prison accounts. Trenton: Sherman and Harron, 1845. 26 p. Nj; NN. 45-4650

New Jersey. Report of the joint committee relative to an asylum for lunatics read February 25, 1845. Trenton: Sherman and Harron, 1845. 9 p. CSmH; Nj. 45-4651

New Jersey. Report of the minority of the Senate committee on the subject of lotteries. Trenton: Sherman and Harron, 1845. 21 p. NjR. 45-4652

New Jersey. Reports of the inspectors of the state prison and of the keeper and physician, to the legislature. Trenton: Sherman and Harron, 1845. 18 p. Nj. 45-4653

New Jersey. Rules for the government of the General Assembly of the state of New Jersey; adapted to their proceedings on business of legislation. Trenton: Sherman and Harron, 1845. 10 p. DLC. 45-4654

New Jersey. To the Senate and General Assembly of New Jersey, relative to care of the insane. Trenton: n.p., [1845] NjR. 45-4655

The New Jersey annual register and general calendar for the year 1846. By Samuel Lloyd. Trenton: R. Gosman, 1845. 143 p. MH; Nj; NjR; NjT. 45-4656

New Jersey Historical Society. Constitution and bylaws... With the circular of the executive committee. [Newark] New Jersey: Press of the Historical Society, 1845. 23 p. DLC; MH; PU; RHi. 45-4657

New Jersey Historical Society. Proceedings, a magazine of history, biography, and notes on families. First series. n.p.: The Society, 1845-. v. 1-. CoD; KHi; NBLiHi; Nh-Hi; OO. 45-4658

The new library of law and equity, edited by Francis J. Troubat. Harrisburg, Pennsylvania: McKinely and Lescure, 1845-1849. 15 v. in 14. DLC; MH; NjR; NNU; OU. 45-4659

New library of standard novels. New York, 1845. DLC. 45-4660

New London Academy. Catalogue of the officers and students of New London Academy, Chester County, Pennsylvania. Baltimore: John Murphy, 1845. 16 p. IaHA. 45-4661

New Orleans, Louisiana. Annual reports of the council of municipality number two, of the City of New Orleans, on the conditions of its public schools. New Orleans, Office of the Picayune, 1845. 39 p. TxU. 45-4662

New Orleans, Louisiana. Chamber of Commerce. Report to the New Orleans Chamber of Commerce in reply to the questions propounded by the Hon. Secretary of the treasury on the subject of the tariff and warehouse system. New Orleans: Daily Tropic, 1845. 20 p. LNT; MH-BA; NjR; PPL. 45-4663

New Orleans, Louisiana. A digest of the ordinances of the city. New Orleans: J. Bayon, 1845. 109 p. DLC; LU; NCD; NN. 45-4664

New Orleans, Louisiana. Digeste des ordonnaces et resolutions du Conseil general de la ville de la Nouvelle-Orleans. Nouvelle-Orleans, 1845. 109 p. LNX. 45-4665

New Orleans, Louisiana. Presbytery. Memorial to the member of the presbytery of New Orleans. n.p., 1845. PPPr-Hi. 45-4666

New Orleans, Louisiana. Proceedings and debates of the convention of New Orleans, which assembled at the city of New Orleans, January 14, 1844. Robert J. Ker, reporter. New Orleans: Besconcon, Ferguson and company, 1845. 960 p. LNT. 45-4667

New Orleans, Louisiana. Rules and regulations for the government of the public schools, within the second municipality. [New Orleans] 1845. CtHT-W. 45-4668

New Orleans annual and commercial register for 1846. Containing the names, residences and professions of all the heads of families and persons in business of the city and suburbs, Algiers and Lafayette. New Orleans: E.A. Michel and company, 1845. 610, 58 p. DLC; ICU; IU; LU. 45-4669

The new pictorial family magazine. Established for the diffusion of useful knowledge. New York: Robert Sears, 1846. CtHWatk; IaU; ICN; ODaB. 45-4670

The new world; a game of American history, by a yankee. New York: Josiah Adams, 1845. 48 p. NjR; RPB. 45-4671

New York [City] Annual statement of the funds of the corporation of the city of New York, for the year ending December 31, 1844. By the comptroller of the city of New York. New York, 1845. 45-4672

New York [City] Association for improving the condition of the poor. New York, 1845-. v. 1-. MB. 45-4673

New York [City] Bylaws and ordinances

of the Mayor, aldermen and commonalty of the city of New York. Revised 1845. Published by authority of the common council. New York: William Osborn, printer, 1845. 668 p. IU; MiD NNLI. 45-4674

New York [City] Committee of arrangements of the common council of the city of New York upon the funeral ceremonies in commemoration of the death of General Jackson. New York 1845. TxU. 45-4675

New York [City] Houston Street Presbyterian Church. Manual for the use of the members of the Presbyterian Church, in the city of New York. New York: Lambert and Lane, 1845. 36 p. NNUT. 45-4676

New York [City] List of conveyances made by Charles Henry Hall and recorded in the office of the register of the city and county of New York. New York: A.S. Gould, 1845. 55 p. NNMuCN. 45-4677

New York [City] Map of New York Bay and Harbor and the environs. Washington, 1845. 6 sheets. PHi. 45-4678

New York [City] Mechanics Institute. Constitution of the institute adopted April, 1845. Incorporated by an act of the legislature, April 24, 1833. New York: Printed for the institute by J. Windt, 1845. 8 p. Mh. 45-4679

New York [City] National Academy of Design. Catalogues of the 19th annual exibition, 1844. New York [1845] 29 p. MB. 45-4680

New York [City] New Jerusalem

Society. Rules of order of the New Jerusalem Society of the City of New York. New York, 1845. PBa. 45-4681

New York [City] Plan of instruction for the board of trustees of the public schools. [New York, 1845?] MB. 45-4682

New York [City] Report of the committee of arrangements of the common council of the city of New York, upon the funeral ceremonies in commemoration of the death of Gen. Andrew Jackson. New York: Printed by order of the board, 1845. 303 p. NNMuCN; T. 45-4683

New York [City] Report of the joint special committee on the subject of the fire in New Street, July 19, 1845. [New York, 1845] MH. 45-4684

New York [City] St. George's Church. Report of the board of directors of the Association of St. George's Church, New York, for the promotion of christianity, presented and approved at the annual meeting of the association, on the evening of Friday, March 28, 1845. New York: George F. Bunce, 1845. 15 p. NNG. 45-4685

New York [City] University. Annual announcement of lectures, session, 1845-1846. New York: Joseph H. Jennings, printers, 1845. 16 p. OC. 45-4686

New York [City] University. Catalogue of the officers and students of the University of the city of New York. New York: J.H. Jennings, 1845-1846. OClWHi. 45-4687

New York: J.A. Fraetas, printer, 1845. 30 p. M. 45-4688

New York [State] Annual report of abstracts of convictions for criminal offences, and of returns of sheriffs respecting the persons convicted. [Albany, 1845] MH. 45-4689

New York [State] Annual report of the Prison Association Female Department. New York, 1845-. WHi. 45-4690

New York [State] Annual report of the secretary of state relative to railroad statistics. [Albany, 1845] 45 p. IaHi; NRU. 45-4691

New York [State] Anti-rent state convention. Proceedings of the Anti-rent state convention. [Albany, 1845] 15 p. MiD-B. 45-4692

New York [State] Communication from Martin Van Buren, delineating the appointment of regent of the University. [Albany, 1845] 1 p. WHi. 45-4693

New York [State] Communication from the adjutant general, relative to the troops at Hudson. [Albany, 1845] 1 p. WHi. 45-4694

New York [State] Communication transmitting the final report of [J.R. Brodhead] on documents in Europe relative to the colonial history of this state. [Albany, 1845] 374 p. NNC. 45-4695

New York [State] Concurrent resolutions in relation to the proceedings of the legislature of South Carolina, in the case of the Hon. Samuel Hoar, the agent of the state of Massachusetts. [Albany, 1845] 4 p. WHi. 45-4696

New York [State] Concurrent resolutions [protesting against the annexation of Texas] [Albany, 1845] 1 p. WHi. 45-4697

New York [State] Court for the correction of errors. The Mohawk and Hudson Railroad Company, Appellants, vs. John Costigan, respondent. Albany: C. Wendell's printers, 1845. 101 p. NN. 45-4698

New York [State] Hospital, Utica. First annual report. Albany, 1845-. R. 45-4699

New York [State] Laws of the state of New York, passed at the sixty-eighth session of the legislature, begun and held in the city of Albany, January 7, 1845. Albany: Printed by C. Van Benthuysen and company, 1845. 447 p. MdBB. 45-4700

New York [State] Library. Annual report of the trustees of the state library. Second edition. [Albany] 1845. 55 p. WaU. 45-4701

New York [State] Manual for the use of the legislature of the state of New York, for the year 1845. Prepared by the Secretary of State. Albany: C. Van Benthuysen and company, 1845. 364 p. NNS. 45-4702

New York [State] Memorial of Henry Foster, relative to the report of the committee on claims, in regard to him as a former member of the senate, [relative to charges against him in connection with the Erie Canal enlargement, through the village of Rome] [Albany, 1845] 50 p. WHi. 45-4703

New York [State] Memorial remonstrating against altering the charter of the

New York and Erie Railroad company so as to allow them to run their road into Pennsylvania. [Albany, 1845] 3 p. WHi 45-4704

New York [State] Message from the governor, in answer to a resolution of the assembly inquiring whether the sum of ten thousand dollars has not been set apart for this state from the United States Land Fund. [Albany, 1845] 2 p. WHi. 45-4705

New York [State] Message from the governor transmitting a memorial from the pilots of New York, on the subject of the state and federal laws regulating pilotage. [Albany, 1845] 24 p. WHi. 45-4706

New York [State] Message from the governor transmitting Carroll and Cook's contract for the printing and binding of the geological survey of the state. [Albany, 1845] 4 p. MB; WHi. 45-4707

New York [State] Message from the governor [Silas Wright] January 7, 1845 [Albany, 1845] 52 p. MHi; WHi. 45-4708

New York [State] Message of the governor, returning with his objections, the bill in relation to the canals. [Albany, 1845] 31 p. WHi. 45-4709

New York [State] Petition of the inhabitants of Western New York, praying that the tolls upon the canal between Oswego and Albany, be the same as between Buffalo and Albany. [Albany, 1845] 7 p. WHi. 45-4710

New York [State] A plan of instruction

or the New York public schools. [New York, 1845] 16 p. WHi. 45-4711

New York [State] Report in relation to weights and measures. [Albany, 1845] MB. 45-4712

New York [State] Report of Messrs. Comstock, McKey, Soger and Pierce, from the select committee of one from each senate district, to which was referred Mr. Crain's bill relative to a convention. [Albany, 1845] 13 p. WHi. 45-4713

New York [State] Report of the agent appointed to procure and transcribe documents in Europe, relative to the colonial history of the state. Albany, 1845. 375 p. MBC. 45-4714

New York [State] Report of the attorney general in answer to a resolution of the assembly in relation to the New York and Erie Railroad Company. [Albany, 1845] 16 p. WHi. 45-4715

New York [State] Report of the attorney general in answer to a resolution of the assembly, referring the petition of John Roof, deceased in compensation for lands taken by the state. [Albany, 1845] 23 p. WHi. 45-4716

New York [State] Report of the attorney general in answer to a resolution of the assembly, [relating to corporations] [Albany, 1845] 4 p. WHi. 45-4717

New York [State] Report of the bill to amend the act for the relief of Ira Pearsons, for damages sustained in the construction of section 27 of the Genesee Valley Canal. [Albany, 1845] 2 p. WHi. 45-4718

New York [State] Report of the canal appraisers on the petition of John Watkins, relating to damages due to the construction of the Seneca Canal. [Albany, 1845] 3 p. WHi. 45-4719

New York [State] Report of the canal appraisers, upon the petition of Joseph Demont, Orin Tyler, and Edward Mynderse for canal damages. [Albany, 1845] 2 p. WHi. 45-4720

New York [State] Report of the commissioners of the land office, on the petition of Eleazer Williams, [praying for the passage of a law] to confirm two conveyances of land from his grant of the Oneida Indian lands. [Albany, 1845] 2 p. WHi. 45-4721

New York [State] Report of the commissioners of the land office, on the petition of Peter Bain and others, purchasers of lands in the Oneida Purchase of 1840; and the petition of William Page and others, purchasers in the New Stockbridge purchases of 1825, 1830 and 1834. [Albany, 1845] 7 p. WHi. 45-4722

New York [State] Report of the committee of claims on the petition of Asa T. Smith for relief, [relating to contract for building bridges on the Black River Canal] [Albany, 1845] 2 p. WHi. 45-4723

New York [State] Report of the committee of claims on the petition of Marcus Brown, for relief, [for property taken for the use of the army in 1781, from Conradt Brown, a revolutionary soldier] [Albany, 1845] 4 p. WHi. 45-4724

New York [State] Report of the committee on agriculture on so much of the governor's message as relates to agriculture. [Albany, 1845] 15 p. WHi. 45-4725

New York [State] Report of the committee on banks and insurance companies on the memorial of insurance companies of the cities of New York and Brooklyn. [Albany, 1845] 10, 8 p. WHi. 45-4726

New York [State] Report of the committee on canals on the petition of Charles Shepperd and others, to connect a slip and basin with the Dansville sidecut of the Genesee Valley Canal. [Albany, 1845] 7 p. WHi. 45-4727

New York [State] Report of the committee on canals to whom was referred numerous petitions praying for a repeal of the act granting the right to railroads to carry freight. [Albany, 1845] 35 p. WHi. 45-4728

New York [State] Report of the committee on canals, in the case of Homer Caswell, [relating to claims for work done on Steel's aqueducts, on the Erie Canal enlargement] [Albany, 1845] 2 p. WHi. 45-4729

New York [State] Report of the committee on canals, on numerous memorials, praying that the locks on the canals may be closed on Sunday. [Albany, 1845] 9 p. WHi. 45-4730

New York [State] Report of the committee on canals, on so much of the governor's message as relates to canals, and numerous petitions and resolutions in relation to canals. [Albany, 1845] 15 p. WHi. 45-4731

New York [State] Report of the committee on canals, on the petition of certain canal contractors. [Albany, 1845] 2 p WHi. 45-4732

New York [State] Report of the committee on canals, to whom was referred both the bill "to provide for the removal of cases decided by the canal board, to the supreme court by certiorari." [Albany, 1845] 5 p. WHi. 45-4733

New York [State] Report of the committee on canals, to whom was referred the petition of Isaac I. Yates, praying for compensation for work on the Erie Canal enlargement, since the suspension act of 1842. [Albany, 1845] 3 p. WHi. 45-4734

New York [State] Report of the committee on charitable and religious societies, on the petition of the monogers of the New York Institution for the blind, praying for relief. [Albany, 1845] 2 p. WHi. 45-4735

New York [State] Report of the committee on charitable and religious societies, on the petition of the New York Institution for the Instruction of the Deaf and Dumb. [Albany, 1845] 2 p. WHi. 45-4736

New York [State] Report of the committee on charitable and religious societies, on the petition of the prison association of New York for an act of incorporation. [Albany, 1845] 2 p. WHi. 45-4737

New York [State] Report of the committee on "colonial agency." Albany, 1845. MB. 45-4738

New York [State] Report of the committee on claims in the matter of the claim of Sage, Walrath, and Dunham, [relating to the construction of locks 18, 19 and 20 for the northern division of the Chenango Canal] [Albany, 1845] 9 p. WHi. 45-4739

New York [State] Report of the committee on claims of the petition of Asaph Seymour, William Coffin, Richard Savage and William S. Harrison for relief, [in relation to a contract for iron valve gates for locks on the Chenong Canal] [Albany, 1845] 5 p. WHi. 45-4740

New York [State] Report of the committee on claims of the petition of John Merriam and others, for relief for damages sustained on a contract [for the enlargement of the Erie Canal] [Albany, 1845] 3 p. WHi. 45-4741

New York [State] Report of the committee on claims on the petition of Ferdinand Mongin and Asenath Mongin for relief, [relating to land escheated to the state] [Albany, 1845] 2 p. WHi. 45-4742

New York [State] Report of the committee on claims, on the petition of Henry Rector for relief, for services rendered by him as architect in the building of the new state hall. [Albany, 1845] 3 p. WHi. 45-4743

New York [State] Report of the committee on claims, on the petition of John M. Stitt and Elizabeth, his wife, praying for relief to the heirs of Thomas Mott, a revolutionary soldier. [Albany, 1845] 8 p. WHi. 45-4744

New York [State] Report of the committee on claims, on the petition of Mary Murray and others for relief for damages sustained by the erecting of a dam across

the Genesee River, at Mount Morris. [Albany, 1845] 3 p. WHi. 45-4745

New York [State] Report of the committee on claims, to which was referred the petition of Aaron Barnes and John E. Henman, for damages, [sustained by a break in the agreement of the Erie Canal near Yorkville in 1840] [Albany, 1845] 2 p. WHi. 45-4746

New York [State] Report of the committee on colleges, academies and common schools, on the bill to increase the capital of the common school fund. [Albany, 1845] 4 p. WHi. 45-4747

New York [State] Report of the committee on colleges, academies and common school. [relating to the common schools of the state] [Albany, 1845] 23 p. WHi. 45-4748

New York [State] Report of the committee on grievances on the petition of A.M. Adsit for relief for damage to his boat and goods in transportation through Lock no. 3 of the Erie Canal. [Albany, 1845] 3 p. WHi. 45-4749

New York [State] Report of the committee on grievances on the petition of Abel Chandler for relief, [for damages sustained by the division of the waters of the Otselic Creek into the Chenango and Erie Canals] [Albany, 1845] 2 p. WHi. 45-4750

New York [State] Report of the committee on grievances on the petition of Patrick Fitzsimmons and James Brady for relief, [for extra work in the construction of sections 8 and 9 of the enlargement of the Erie Canal] [Albany, 1845] 2 p. WHi. 45-4751

New York [State] Report of the committee on grievances on the petition of William Smith for relief, [for loss of water power through the Chenago Canal] [Albany, 1845] 5 p. WHi. 45-4752

New York [State] Report of the committee on grievances on the petition of Yates and Vandebogart, [relating to contracts for the Erie Canal enlargement] [Albany, 1845] 2 p. WHi. 45-4753

New York [State] Report of the committee on Indian affairs on the assembly bill in relation to the Seneca Indians. [Albany, 1845] 13 p. WHi. 45-4754

New York [State] Report of the committee on medical colleges and societies, on the petition of the College of Physicians and Surgeons of the City of New York. [Albany, 1845] 2 p. WHi. 45-4755

New York [State] Report of the committee on medical societies and colleges, on the several petitions of citizens of the city of New York for aid to the dispensaries of that city. [Albany, 1845] 32 p. WHi. 45-4756

New York [State] Report of the committee on privileges and elections, on the case of J.H. Dayton, of Suffolk, [Appointed United States collector of customs] [Albany, 1845] 3 p. WHi. 45-4757

New York [State] Report of the committee on privileges and elections, on the petition of sundry inhabitants of the city of New York, praying for the passage of a law to prevent naturalized citizens from voting until after one years residence in the state and six months after naturalization. [Albany, 1845] 2 p. WHi. 45-4758

New York [State] Report of the committee on privileges and elections, on the prayer of Abraham Aher [that he may be permitted to take his seat as a member of the House in place of George J.J. Barber] [Albany, 1845] 3 p. WHi. 45-4759

New York [State] Report of the committee on public lands, to whom was recommitted the bill from the assembly, authorizing the surveyor general to lease a certain lot of land belonging to the state in the St. Regis Reservation, together with the amendment proposed thereto by the Senate. [Albany, 1845] 4 p. WHi. 45-4760

New York [State] Report of the committee on railroads, in relation to the construction of the New York and Erie Railroad. [Albany, 1845] 6 p. CSt. 45-4761

New York [State] Report of the committee on railroads, on sundry memorials praying for a reduction of fare, and the appointment of a railroad commissioner. [Albany, 1845] 12 p. WHi. 45-4762

New York [State] Report of the committee on railroads, on the bill to incorporate the Troy and Greenbush Railroad Association. [Albany, 1845] 40 p. WHi. 45-4763

New York [State] Report of the committee on railroads, on the interrogatories, offered by Mr. Bailey, relative to the Long Island Railroad Company. [Albany, 1845] 9 p. WHi. 45-4764

New York [State] Report of the committee on railroads, on the petition of the New York and Harlem Railroad Comany for an alteration of their charter. Albany, 1845] 5 p. WHi. 45-4765

New York [State] Report of the committee on railroads, on the petition praying for a surrender of the lien of the state upon the New York and Erie Railroad. Albany, 1845] 7 p. WHi. 45-4766

New York [State] Report of the committee on the erection and division of owns and counties, on the senate bill for he erection of a new town from parts of he towns of Broome and Blenheim, Schoharie County [to be called Gilboa] Albany, 1845] 3 p. WHi. 45-4767

New York [State] Report of the committee on the Judiciary, on the governor's message respecting the laws regulating pilots and pilotage by the way of Sandy Hook. [Albany, 1845] 2 p. WHi. 45-4768

New York [State] Report of the committee on the judiciary, on the petition of Jacob Scramling for a divorce. [Albany, 1845] 2 p. WHi. 45-4769

New York [State] Report of the committee on the judiciary on the petition of sundry inhabitants of Sullivan County, relative to the naturalization of foreigners. [Albany, 1845] 4 p. WHi. 45-4770

New York [State] Report of the committee on the militia and public defence, on the bill entitled "An act to pay the guard of one hundred enlisted men, for the protection of the jail in the city of Hudson." [Albany, 1845] 15 p. WHi. 45-4771

New York [State] Report of the committee on the militia and public defence,

on the bill to provide for the payment of troops called into service in December of 1844 and January of 1845, [in the war with Mexico] [Albany, 1845] 3 p. WHi. 45-4772

New York [State] Report of the committee on the militia and public defence, on the petition and affidavit of John Whitehead, [revolutionary soldier] [Albany, 1845] 5 p. WHi. 45-4773

New York [State] Report of the committee on the militia and public defence, on the senate bill for the erection of a flag staff on the capital. [Albany, 1845] 3 p. WHi. 45-4774

New York [State] Report of the committee on trade and manufactures, relative to renewing and continuing the charter of the American Atlantic Steam Navigation Company. [Albany, 1845] 5 p. WHi. 45-4775

New York [State] Report of the committee to whom was referred the concurrent resolution in regard to the New York and Erie Railroad. [Albany, 1845] 2 p. WHi. 45-4776

New York [State] Report of the comptroller, in answer to a resolution, February 7, 1845, respecting the resolution of real estate, and the government. [Albany, 1845] 2 p. WHi. 45-4777

New York [State] Report of the comptroller, in answer to a resolution, February 14, 1845, relative to the issue to the banks of registered notes in the place of the outstanding old emission. [Albany, 1845] 9 p. WHi. 45-4778

New York [State] Report of the comptroller, in answer to a resolution, in relation to the Delaware and Hudson Canal Company. [Albany, 1845] 3 p. WHi. 45-4779

New York [State] Report of the comptroller, in answer to a resolution of the assembly of February 5, last, relative a deposit received from the United States. [Albany, 1845] 2 p. WHi. 45-4780

New York [State] Report of the judiciary committee, on the bill relative to the Chenango Bridge. [Albany, 1845] 7 p. WHi. 45-4781

New York [State] Report of the majority and minority of the committee on charitable and religious societies, on the petition of sundry persons asking for the incorporation of the American and Foreign Bible Society. [Albany, 1845] 5 p. WHi. 45-4782

New York [State] Report of the majority [and minority] of the committee on claims, on the petition of John I. Walrath and Daniel Walrath, [relating to damages sustained by diverting the waters of the Chittenango Creek for the use of the Erie Canal] [Albany, 1845] 2, 4 p. WHi. 45-4783

New York [State] Report of the majority and the minority of the select committee on the remonstraces against the annexation of Texas. [Albany, 1845] 3, 7 p. WHi. 45-4784

New York [State] Report of the majority of the committee on canals relative to discriminating tolls on the Erie and Oswego Canals. [Albany, 1845] 9 p. WHi. 45-4785

New York [State] Report of the majority of the committee on roads and bridges, on the application for a bridge across the Hudson at Albany. [Albany, 1845] WHi. 45-4786

New York [State] Report of the majority of the committee on the petition of aliens, relative to the Leake and Watt's Orphan House, and others. [Albany, 1845] 8 p. WHi. 45-4787

New York [State] Report of the majority of the judiciary committee on the case of John H. Dayton. [Albany, 1845] 3 p. WHi. 45-4788

New York [State] Report of the majority of the select committee on numerous petitions from man or tenants in several counties in the state for relief. [Albany, 1845] 17 p. WHi. 45-4789

New York [State] Report of the minority of the committee on banks and insurance companies, in favor of increasing the tax on foreign agencies. [Albany, 1845] 7 p. WHi. 45-4790

New York [State] Report of the minority of the committee on canals relative to discriminating tolls on the Erie and Osenego Canals. [Albany, 1845] 66 p. WHi. 45-4791

New York [State] Report of the minority of the committee on roads and bridges, on the application for a bridge across the Hudson and Albany. [Albany, 1845] 4 p. WHi. 45-4792

New York [State] Report of the minority of the committee on the erection and division of towns and counties, on the petitions and remonstrances on he subject of erecting a new county, with he seat of justice either at Bainbridge or Jnadilla. [Albany, 1845] 3 p. WHi. 45-4793

New York [State] Report of the minority of the committee on the erection and division of towns and counties, relating to the erection of a new county from parts of Delaware, Otsego and Chenango, to be called Undilla County. Albany, 1845] 7 p. WHi. 45-4794

New York [State] Report of the minority of the committee on the erection of towns and counties on the senate bill to erect the town of Gilboa. [Albany, 1845] 2 p. WHi. 45-4795

New York [State] Report of the minority of the committee on the militia and public defence, in relation to a modification of the militia laws. [Albany, 1845] 7 p. WHi. 45-4796

New York [State] Report of the minority of the committee on 2/3 bills, on the bill relative to the Long Island Railroad Company. [Albany, 1845] 6 p. WHi. 45-4797

New York [State] Report of the minority of the judiciary committee on the case of John H. Dayton. Albany, 1845. 9 p. WHi. 45-4798

New York [State] Report of the minority of the select committee on landlord and tenant. [Albany, 1845] 7 p. WHi. 45-4799

New York [State] Report of the New York Bowery Insurance Company, in answer to a resolution of the assembly transmitting statement of the premiums received and taxes paid during the years 1842, 1843 and 1844] [Albany] 1845. 3 p. WHi. 45-4800

New York [State] Report of the New York Contributionship Insurance Company, in answer to a resolution of the assembly, [transmitting statement of premiums received and taken and paid from January 1, 1842 to December 31, 1844] [Albany, 1845] 3 p. WHi. 45-4801

New York [State] Report of the regents of the University on a petition of the trustees of the St. Lawrence Academy, referred to them by the assembly. [Albany, 1845] 6 p. WHi. 45-4802

New York [State] Report of the secretary of state and surveyor general, relative to a tract of land purchased from the Indians By William Smith, Jr. and others in 1761. [Albany, 1845] 5 p. WHi. 45-4803

New York [State] Report of the secretary of state, in relation to repairs made to the standards of weights and measures in assembly. [Albany, 1845] 4 p. WHi. 45-4804

New York [State] Report of the secretary of state pursuant to the resolution of the senate in relating to civil officers whose appointments are vested in the governor, with the consent of the Senate. [Albany, 1845] 58 p. WHi. 45-4805

New York [State] Report of the secretary of state, relative to the proposed amendments to the constitution, relating to the state debt and to the judiciary. [Albany, 1845] 9 p. WHi. 45-4806

New York [State] Report of the select committee appointed to investigate and examine the different charges of abuse made by the county superintendent, and other matter past and present, connected with the subject of common school education during the existence of the present board. [New York? 1845?] MH. 45-4807

New York [State] Report of the select committee in relation to the natural history of the state. [Albany, 1845] 15 p. MB; WHi. 45-4808

New York [State] Report of the select committee of the senate, appointed to investigate the cause and circumstances of the fatal disaster of the steamboat Swallow, on the Hudson River, April 7, 1845. [Albany, 1845] 23 p. WHi. 45-4809

New York [State] Report of the select committee on lawyer's fees and costs in courts of law. [Albany, 1845] 3 p. WHi. 45-4810

New York [State] Report of the select committee on the petition of 200 democrats of Madison County, in relation to the case of Thomas W. Dorr. [Albany, 1845] 9 p. WHi. 45-4811

New York [State] Report of the select committee on the petitions to abolish capital punishment. [Albany, 1845] 7 p. WHi. 45-4812

New York [State] Report of the select committee on the proposed amendments to the constitution. [Albany, 1845] 4 p. WHi. 45-4813

New York [State] Report of the select committee on the subject of licentiousness. [Albany, 1845] 8 p. WHi. 45-4814

New York [State] Report of the select committee to which were referred numerous petitions, praying for a modification of the excise law. [Albany, 1845] 13 p. WHi. 45-4815

New York [State] Report of the select committee to whom was referred, an act for ascertaining by proper proofs, the citizens who shall be entitled to the right of sufferage in the city and county of New York. [Albany, 1845] 5 p. WHi. 45-4816

New York [State] Report of the select committee to whom was referred the memorial of the city of New York, relative to the landing of alien passengers. [Albany, 1845] 5 p. WHi. 45-4817

New York [State] Report of the trustees of the state library on the expediency of purchasing for the use of the state, the library of David B. Warden of Paris, consisting of books relating to America. [Albany, 1845] 11 p. WHi. 45-4818

New York [State] Several acts relative to the Seneca Road Company, compiled by a committee of the board, for that purpose. March 12, 1845. Utica: R.W Roberts, 1845. 36 p. N. 45-4819

New York [State] Statement of the commissary general, in answer to the resolution of the assembly, relative to expenses incurred by the troops ordered to Hudson. [Albany, 1845] 2 p. WHi. 45-4820

New York [State] Statement of the conditions of the banks of the state of New

York, August 1, 1845. [Albany, 1845] MH. 45-4821

New York [State] Testimony taken before the railroad committee, in the matter of the Troy and Greenbush Railroad Association. [Albany, 1845] 10 p. WHi. 45-4822

New York [State] Titles of acts passed by the legislature of the state of New York at the 68th session, thereof. [Albany, 1845] 23 p. WHi. 45-4823

New York [State] University. Instructions from the regents to the several colleges, academies... prescribing the requisites and forms for reports, applications... Albany, 1845. 112 p. MBC; NLew; NNNAM. 45-4824

New York, Albany, and Buffalo Electro Magnetic Telegraph Company. Articles of association for the creation of the... Utica: R.W. Roberts, printers, 1845. 12 p. NNE. 45-4825

New York and Brooklyn directory, 1845-46. New York: Groot and Elston, 1845. 487 p. Mi. 45-4826

New York and Erie Railroad Company. Address of the directors of the New York and Erie Railroad Company to the public, September 2, 1845. [New York, 1845] 7 p. DLC; DBRE; MB; PU. 45-4827

New York and Erie Railroad Company. Historical notices respecting the origin and proceedings of the New York and Erie Railroad Company. New York: Houel and Macoy, printers, 1845. 25 p. CSt; DBRE; N; NNC. 45-4828

New York and Erie Railroad Company. Memorial remonstrating against altering the charter of the New York and Erie Railroad Company so as to allow them to run their road into Pennsylvania. [Albany, 1845] 3 p. CSt. 45-4829

New York and Erie Railroad Company. Opinions and decisions on the question whether the bill for conditionally releasing the New York and Erie Railroad Company from the state loan is a majority bill. Albany, 1845. 19 p. CSt. 45-4830

New York and Erie Railroad Company. Statements in relation to the cost of this road, its connection with tributory works and its probable productiveness. [New York? 1845?] 11 p. CSt. 45-4831

New York and Hartford Railroad Company. Report of the executive committee upon the statistics of business and of the engineer upon the survey of the several routes for the contemplated New York and Hartford Railroad, via Danbury. Hartford: Press of Case, Tiffany, and Burnham, 1845. 119 p. CSt; ICJ; MH-AH; NcD; NN. 45-4832

New York and New Haven Railroad Company. Engineer's report on the survey and primary location. New Haven: Hitchcock and Stafford, printer, 1845. 39 p. DBRE; MH-BA. 45-4833

The New York annual register for the year of our Lord, 1845, containing an almanac, civil and judicial list, political, statistical and other information respecting the state of New York and the United States. By Edwin Williams. New York: Turner and Hayden, 1845. 283 p. Mi; MiD-B; NjR; NNLI. 45-4834

New York Association for Improving the Condition of the Poor. The first annual report. New York: John F. Trow and company, 1845. 45 p. CU; MiD-B; KyU; PSt; WaS. 45-4835

New York City directory for 1845 and 1846. Fourth publication. New York: John Diggett, Junior, 1845. 430 p. MoSU; NNA; PPL. 45-4836

New York City Mariner's Family Industrial Society. First Annual report. New York, 1845. 45-4837

New York City O'Connel Club. Preamble, constitution, and bylaws of the O'Connell Club. New York: Published for the Association by Casserly and Sons, 1845. 12 p. M; MBAt; PPL; WHi. 45-4838

New York College of Physicians and Surgeons, New York. Catalogue of the officers and students of the College and annual announcement of lectures. Session of 1845-6. New York: Daniel Ades, 1845. 12 p. NNC. 45-4839

New York College of Physicians and Surgeons, New York. Charter, by-laws and regulations. New York: William Jennings, 1845. 16 p. NNUT. 45-4840

New York Fire Insurance Company. Report in answer to a resolution of the assembly. [Transmitting a statement of the amount of premiums received during the years 1842, 1843, 1844] [Albany, 1845] 3 p. WHi. 45-4841

New York form book and interest tables; containing complete forms for the transaction of all the routine of business between man and man, requiring the ex-
ecution of papers, together with the statutory provisions relating thereto; also complete interest tables, discount tables, scantling and timber measure, cubical contents of square timber, etc. Buffalo: Oliver G. Steele, 1845. 132 p. NBuHi; NT. 45-4842

New York Guardian Insurance Company. Report, in answer to a resolution of the assembly, [transmitting a statement of the amount of premiums received and taxes paid during the years 1842, 1843 and 1844] [Albany, 1845] 3 p. WHi. 45-4843

New York Historical Society. Report of the aboriginal names and geographical terminology of the state of New York. Part I. Valley of the Hudson. By Henry R. Schoolcraft, chairman. New York: The society, 1845. 43 p. DLC; MiU; NBu; PPAmP; RHi. 45-4844

New York Historical Society. Report of the committee of the New York Historical Society on a national name. March 31, 1845. New York, 1845. 8 p. DLC; MB; MWA; NRU; RHi. 45-4845

New York Hospital. A catalogue of the books belonging to the library of the New York Hospital, arranged alphabetically and analytically, and the regulations for the use of the same. New York: R. Craighead, printer, 1845. 194 p. CSt-L; DLC; MBM; MnU; NNC. 45-4846

New York Hospital. Catalogue of the books belonging to the New York Hospital Library, arranged alphabetically and analytically, and the regulations for the use of the same. Supplementary catalogue, 1-5. New York, 1845-1880. 6 v. MH-M. 45-4847

New York Institution for the Education of the Blind. Acts of incorporation, bylaws and general rules of the New York institution for the blind. New York, 1845. 38 p. IU; MB; NRU; OO; PHi. 45-4848

New York Institution for the Instruction of the Deaf and Dumb. Bylaws of the directors of the New York institution for the instruction of the deaf and dumb; with the act of incorporation, and other legislative acts. New York: Egbert, Hovey and King, 1845. 24 p. DLC. 45-4849

New York Institution for the Instruction of the Deaf and Dumb. Report on the institutions for the deaf and dumb in central and western Europe in the year 1844, to the board of directors of the New York institution... New York: Egbert, Hovey and King, printers, 1845. 79-223 p. ICU; MHi. 45-4850

New York journal of commerce. Review of the tract controversy. New York: Leavitt, Trow and company, 1845. 62 p. Ct. 45-4851

New York journal of education. New York, 1845-. v. 1-. MH. 45-4852

New York medical and surgical reporter. v. 1- 1845-. New York: Wiley and Putnam, 1845-1846. MH-M. 45-4853

The New York medical and surgical reporter; edited by Clarkson T. Collins. New York: Piercy and Reed, 1845-1847. 84 p. CtY; DNLM; MH-M; NBCP. 45-4854

The New York pictorial almanac for 1846. Rochester, New York: M. Miller; Rochester: Mark H. Newman, [1845] MWA; NUt; NUtHi. 45-4855

New York, Providence and Boston Railroad Company. Reports of the directors. New York: Francis Hart, 1845-1854. MH-BA. 45-4856

The New York reader. New York: Samuel S. and William Wood, 1845. MH. 45-4857

New York recorder. New York, 1845-. DLC; ICRL; ICU. 45-4858

New York State Natural History Survey. Natural history of New York. Agriculture by Ebenezer Emmons. Albany, 1845. In. 45-4859

The New York state register for 1845; containing an almanac for 1845-6. With political, statistical, and other information relating to the state of New York and the United States. Also a complete list of county officers, attorneys, etc. Edited by O.L. Holley. New York: J. Disturnell, 1845. CU; ICJ; MBC; NHem; PHi. 45-4860

The New York state statistical almanac for 1846. Rochester: E. Shepard, [1845] MWA. 45-4861

The New York traveller; containing railroad, steamboat, canal packet, and stage routes through the state of New York. Also, other information useful to travellers. New York: J. Disturnell, 1845. DLC; ICN; MB; RPJCB. 45-4862

New York Weekly Herald. New York, 1845-. v. 1-. PP. 45-4863

Newcomb, Harvey, 1803-1863. History

of the Waldenses; with a sketch of the general state of the church in the thirteenth century; being the tenth volume of the Sabbath School church history. Third edition. Boston: Sabbath School Society, 1845. 240 p. InEvW; MBC; MH; WPri. 45-4864

Newcomb, Harvey, 1803-1863. Scripture questions on the book of Job. Boston: Sabbath School Society, 1845. MH. 45-4865

Newcomb, Harvey, 1803-1863. Scripture questions on the Gospels in Harmony. Revised edition. Boston, 1845. IEG. 45-4866

Newcomb, Harvey, 1803-1863. The Wea mission: a conversation between a mother and her children. Boston, 1845. MBC. 45-4867

Newcomb, Harvey, 1803-1863. The young lady's guide to the harmonious development of Christian character. Sixth edition enlarged and revised. Boston: Phillips and Sampson, 1845. 323 p. CBPSR. 45-4868

Newcomb, Richard English, 1770-1849. Recollections and retrospect of forty years; an address delivered before the temperance society at Ashfield, Massachusetts, in 1838. Greenfield: L. Merriam, 1845. 14 p. MH; NN; RP. 45-4869

Newell, William, 1804-1881. A discourse occasioned by the death of the Hon. Joseph Story, delivered in the church of the First Parish in Cambridge, on September 14, 1845. Cambridge: Metcalf and company, 1845. 23 p. ICMe; MB; MH; NNG; TxU. 45-4870

Newhall, James Robinson, 1809-1893. Lectures on the occult sciences; embracing some account of the New England Witchcraft. Salem: G.W. and E. Crafts, 1845. 36 p. CtHWatk; IEN-M; MB; OMC; PHi. 45-4871

Newman, John Henry, 1801-1890. Apostacy. Documents relating to the apostacy of the Rev. John Henry Newman to the Romish Church. New York: Burgess, Stringer and company, 1845. 24 p. IEG; MH-AH; NBuDD; PPM; PPPr-Hi. 45-4872

Newman, John Henry, 1801-1890. An essay on the development of christian doctrine. New York: D. Appleton and company, 1845? 206 p. CtHT; ICU; MiU; NNG; WNaE. 45-4873

Newnham, William, 1790-1865. Human magnetism; its claims to dispassionate inquiry, being an attempt to show the utility of its application for the relief of human suffering. New York: Wiley and Putnam, 1845. 396 p. ICP; OCY; PPA; RJa; ViW. 45-4874

Newstead, Robert. Rules for holy living with questions for self examination. New York: Lane, 1845. 48 p. OO. 45-4875

Newton, Israel. A new method of ascertaining interest and discount at various rates, both simple and compound, and of interest and endorsements; also a few magic squares of a singular quality. Montpelier: E.P. Walton and sons, 1845. 16 p. MWA. 45-4876

Newton, John, 1725-1807. The letters of the Rev. John Newton to which are prefixed memoirs of his life, etc., by the Rev. Richard Cecil. New York: Robert

Carter, 1845. 380 p. ArBaA; EEG; NjMD; NNUT; PPP. 45-4877

Newton, Willoughby, 1802-1874. Letter of Willoughby Newton of Virginia, addressed to his constituents, chiefly in explanation and defence of the joint resolutions, passed by the House of Representatives, for the admission of Texas into the Union. Washington: J. and G.S. Gideon, 1845. 16 p. CtY; ICN; MdBP; TxU; Vi. 45-4878

Nicholls, Benjamin Elliott. Lessons on the morning and evening services of the church for Sunday schools. Philadelphia: Herman Hooker, 1845. 82 p. DLC; MB; MdBD; NNG. 45-4879

Nichols, Thomas L. Lecture on immigration and the right of naturalization. New York: Burgess, Stringer and company, 1845. 34 p. MdBLC; NjR; NNC. 45-4880

Nichols, Thomas Low. Raffle for a wife. New York: Burgess, Stringer and company, 1845. 72 p. CtY; MH. 45-4881

Nicholson, Peter. Mechanic's companion or the elements and practice of carpentry, joinery, bricklaying, masonry... Philadelphia, 1845. MdBP. 45-4882

Nicollet, Joseph Nicolas, 1786-1843. Report intended to illustrate a map of the hydro-geographical basin of the upper Mississippi River. Made by J.N. Nicollet, while in employ under the bureau of the corps of topographical engineers. Washington: Blair and Rives, 1845. 170 p. InU; MnHi; NNA; OrHi; RPB. 45-4883

Niles, John Milton, 1787-1856. Speech on the post office bill, delivered in the Senate... January 16, 1845. Washington, 1845. 8 p. NNC. 45-4884

Noah, Mordecai Manuel, 1785-1851. Discourse on the restoration of the Jews; delivered at the tabernacle, October 28 and December 2, 1844. With a map of the land of Israel. New York: Harper, 1845. 55 p. CBPSR; MBC; MdBP; NjR; PPL. 45-4885

Noah, Mordecai Manuel, 1785-1851. Gleanings from a gathered harvest. New York: C. Wells, 1845. 216 p. MB; MiD; MnU; NPStA. 45-4886

Noble, Samuel, 1799-1853. An appeal in behalf of the views of the eternal world and state, and the doctrine of faith and life held by the body of Christians who believe that a new church is signified [in the Revelation, chapter xxi] by the New Jerusalem, embracing answers to all principal objections. Second edition. Boston: T.H. Carter and company, and Otis Clapp, 1845. 540 p. IaDmD; InI; GMM; ViU; WHi. 45-4887

Noel, M. Nouvelle grammaire Francaise, sur un plan tres methodique, avec de nombreus exercises D'Orthographe, desyntaxe et de Ponctiation, tires de nos Meilleurs auteurs.... Philadelphia: Carey and Hart, 1845. 394 p. ScCMu. 45-4888

Nordheimer, Isaac, 1809-1842. A critical grammar of the Hebrew language. Second edition. New York, 1845. 2 v. MH-AH. 45-4889

Norfolk, Virginia. The ordinances of the borough of Norfolk; to which are prefixed the charter of the borough and a collection of acts and parts of acts of assembly, relating to the corporation. Published by authority of the common council, 1845. Norfolk: Printed by T.G. Broughton and company, 1845. 325 p. ICU; IU; NN; Vi; ViU. 45-4890

Norman, Benjamin Moore, 1809-1860. Norman's New Orleans and environs... presenting a complete guide to... the southern metropolis... New Orleans: B.M. Norman; New York: D. Appleton and company, 1845. 223 p. IaK; LU; MiD-B; RNR; TxU. 45-4891

Norman, Benjamin Moore, 1809-1860. Rambles by land and water, or notes of travel in Cuba and Mexico: including a canoe voyage up the river Panuco and researches among the ruins of Tamaulipas... New York: Paine and Burgess; New Orleans: B.M. Norman, 1845. 21-216 p. AzU; CSt; KHi; MnU; OkU. 45-4892

Norman, Benjamin Moore, 1809-1860. Rambles in Yucatan; or notes of travel through the peninsula including a visit to the remarkable ruins of Chi-Chen, Kabah, Zavi, and Uxmal. Third edition. New York: J. and H.G. Langley; Philadelphia: Thomas, Cowperthwait, 1845. 304 p. WBeloC. 45-4893

Norman, Edward. Supremacy of the Pope. The Catholic doctrine on the above subject examined and asserted in a lecture delivered at Kingscourt, County Cavan, April 7, 1841. Boston: C.B. Ewer, 1845. 32 p. MBNMHi. 45-4894

Norris, George Washington. Table showing the mortality following the operation of typing the subclavian artery. Philadelphia, 1845. PPCP. 45-4895

Norris, Moses, 1799-1855. Speech of Mr. Norris on the annexation of Texas delivered in the House. Washington: Globe office, printer, 1845. 20 p. Nh; Nh-Hi; NjR; PHi. 45-4896

North, Ralph, 1814-1883. A treatise on the law and practice of the probabe court of Mississippi: comprising a compilation of the statutes of the state on the subject of the probate courts, last wills and testaments, estates and decedents. Philadelphia: Thomas, Cowperthwait and company, 1845. 531 p. IChaw; Ms; MsU; TxU-L. 45-4897

North Ashburnham, Massachusetts. Union Church. Constitution. Fitchburg, 1845. 8 p. MBC. 45-4898

North Branch Canal Company. North Branch Canal Company, its prospects and its laws of incorporation. Philadelphia, 1845. 45 p. MB; MH-AH; NNC; PHi; PPL. 45-4899

North Carolina. Act to consolidate and amend the acts heretofore passed on the subject of common schools. Raleigh: Gales, 1845. 15 p. NcU. 45-4900

North Carolina. A bill more effectually to prevent the imprisonments of honest debtors, 1844. Raleigh, 1845. 1 p. Nc. 45-4901

North Carolina. Journals of the Senate and the House of Commons, of the General Assembly of the state of North Carolina at its session in 1844-1845. Raleigh: Weston P. Gales, 1845. 778 p. Nc; NcU. 45-4902

North Carolina. The laws of the state of North Carolina passed by the General

Assembly at the session of 1844-1845. Raleigh: Thomas J. Lemay, printer, 1845. 228 p. Ar-SC; In-SC; L; Ms; Nj; T. 45-4903

North Carolina. Notes of a few decisions, superior court, North Carolina, and circuit court, United States for North Carolina district, 1778-1797. Second edition. By W.H. Battle. Raleigh, 1845. PU-L. 45-4904

North Carolina. Reports of the school for the blind. 1845-. Raleigh, 1845-. MWatP. 45-4905

North Carolina. Resolutions in relation to the fourth installment, 1845. Raleigh, 1845. Nc. 45-4906

North Carolina. University. Catalogue of the University of North Carolina, 1845-1846. Raleigh: Weston R. Gales, 1845. 20 p. MeHi. 45-4907

North Carolina. University. First report of the historical soceity of the University of North Carolina, June 4, 1845. Hillsborough: D. Heartt, 1845. 8 p. MeHi; NcAS; NN; OClWHi; RPB. 45-4908

North River Insurance Company. Report in answer to a resolution of the assembly [transmitting a statement of premiums received and taxes paid. Albany, 1845] 3 p. WHi. 45-4909

North Yarmouth Classical and English Academy. Catalogue of officers and students. Portland: F.A. and A.F. Garrish, printers, 1845. 16 p. MeHi; MHi. 45-4910

Northend, Charles, 1814-1895. The common school book keeping; being a simple and practical system, by single entry; and adapted to the wants of mechanics, farmers, and retail merchants. By Charles Northend, principal of the Epes School, Salem, Massachusetts. Boston: William J. Reynolds, 1845. 8, 6 p. ICU; MH; MLy; NNC; OO. 45-4911

Northend, Charles, 1814-1895. Obstacles to the greater success of common schools. Boston: Ticknor, 1845. 42 p. CtHT-W. 45-4912

Northern Kentucky Temperance Union. Proceedings of the eighth annual convention of the Northern Kentucky Temperance Union held at Flem-ingsburg, 4th and 5th June, 1845. n.p., 1845. PPPrHi. 45-4913

Northern Railroad Company. Act of incorporation and bylaws. Concord, 1845. 16 p. MH; MH-BA. 45-4914

Northern Railroad Company. Address... to the friends of internal improvement in New Hampshire. Hanover, 1845. 15 p. DLC; ICU; MH; N. 45-4915

Northrop, Claudian Bird, 1812-1865. Mr. C.B. Northrop's exposition of controversy between, Dr. George Washington Taylor and himself. Charleston, South Carolina, 1845. 48 p. DLC; ScU. 45-4916

Northwestern liberty almanac for 1846. By Z. Eastman. Chicago, Illinois: Eastman and Davidson, [1845?] 40 p. MWA; WWauHi. 45-4917

Norton, Caroline Sheridan. The dream and other poems. New York: C.S. Francis, 1845. 260 p. LN; MB; OCo; RPA; TxU. 45-4918

Norton, Herman, 1799-1850. Signs of danger and promise. Duties of American Protestants at the present crisis. New York: Leavitt, 1845. 72 p. CtHC; DLC; MBC; VtMidSM. 45-4919

Norton, William Augustus, 1810-1883. Elementary treatise of astronomy: in four parts... New York: Wiley and Putnam, 1845; Philadelphia: Thomas, Cowperthwait and company; Boston: C.C. Little and company, 1845. 367, 112 p. IEG; GEU; MH; PPAmP; NGH. 45-4920

The Norwich almanac, directory and business advertiser, for 1846. Norwich: L. and E. Edwards, [1845] 108 p. Ct. 45-4921

Norwich and Worcester Railroad Company. Statement of facts concerning the intended railroad from Worcester to Nashua. Worcester: Henry J. Howland, 1845. 28 p. MH-BA. 45-4922

Norwich University, Northfield, Vermont. Catalogue, 1844-5. Hanover: Dartmouth Press, 1845. 16 p. MiD-B. 45-4923

Nott, Samuel. Map showing the railroad routes in the vicinity of Portsmouth, N.H. compiled from Carrigan's map and various surveys. Boston, 1845. Nh-Hi. 45-4924

Nott, Samuel, 1788-1869. Sixteen years preaching and procedure at Wareham, Massachusetts, with a reprint of the memorial, legal opinion, and result of ex-parte council, laid before the mutual council, September 23, 1845. Boston: Charles Tappan, 1845. 192 p. Ct; MB; MH; MiD-B; RPB. 45-4925

Noye, William, 1577-1634. The principal grounds and maxims, with an analysis of the laws of England. Third American from the ninth London edition by William Waller Hening. Burlington, Vermont: Chauncey Goodrich, 1845. 219 p. CtY; DLC; NIC; Vi. 45-4926

Noye, William, 1577-1634. The principal grounds and maxims, with an analysis of the laws of England. Third American from the ninth London edition with references to modern authorities, both British and American. Philadelphia: T. and J.W. Johnson, 1845. 219 p. NNC-L. 45-4927

Nugent, Thomas, 1700-1772. A new pocket dictionary of the French and English languages. The fifth American from the last London Edition. Philadelphia: Carey and Hart, 1845. 452 p. KyU. 45-4928

Nuttall, William. Wayside flowers of poesy and sentiment. Philadelphia: James K. Simon, 1845. 82 p. PU. 45-4929

O

Oak Hall, or the glory of Boston, a poem. By a young gentleman of Boston. Fifth edition. Boston: Printed by Mead and Beal, 1845. 34 p. MAbD; MHi; MiD-B. 45-4930

O'Brien's Philadelphia, wholesale business directory and United States and South America, and West India circular for 1845. Philadelphia, 1845. 259 p. PHi. 45-4931

O'Callaghan, Edmund Bailey, 1797-1880. History of the New Netherlands; or New York under the Dutch. New York: D. Appleton and company, 1845. 2 v. C-S; InNd; NNUT; OC; OCY. 45-4932

O'Connell, James F., b. 1808. The life and adventures of James F. O'Connell, the tattooed man. During a residence of eleven years in New Holland and the Caroline Islands. New York: W. Applegate, printer, 1845. 29 p. DLC; MH. 45-4933

Odd Fellows, Independent Order of. Connecticut. Constitution and bylaws of the Charter Oak Lodge, No. 2, adopted as amended April 29, 1845. Hartford: Sprague, 1845. 35 p. Ct. 45-4934

Odd Fellows, Independent Order of. Iowa. Constitution, bylaws and rules of order of the Muscatine Lodge, No. 4. Bloomington, [Iowa] Printed at the Herald office, 1845. 40 p. IaHi. 45-4935

Odd Fellows, Independent Order of. Kentucky. Constitution, bylaws and rules of order of the Grand Lodge of Kentucky, revised and adopted August, 1845. Louisville, Kentucky: Morton, 1845. KyLo. 45-4936

Odd Fellows, Independent Order of. Massachusetts. Constitution and bylaws of the Essex Lodge, No. 24. Salem: C.W. and E. Crafts, 1845. 42 p. OClWHi. 45-4937

Odd Fellows, Independent Order of. Massachusetts. Constitution, bylaws and rules of Groton Lodge, No. VI. Instituted at Groton, May 28, 1845. Boston: Printed by Brother Alfred Mudge, 1845. 38 p. MH; WHi. 45-4938

Odd Fellows, Independent Order of. Massachusetts. Constitution, bylaws and rules of Pocoptuck Lodge, No. 67, instituted at Greenfield, May 6, 1845. Greenfield: Merriam, 1845. 36 p. Ct. 45-4939

Odd Fellows, Independent Order of. Massachusetts. Proceedings of the right worthy grand lodge of the state of Massachusetts, at its quarterly session held at Covenant Hall, in the city of Boston. Boston: T. Prince, printer, 1845-. No. 1-. MH; MLy; MWA. 45-4940

Odd Fellows, Independent Order of. New Hampshire. Constitution and bylaws of the Grand Lodge of the state of New Hampshire. Concord, New Hampshire: Printed by Morrill, Silsby and company, 1845. 36 p. WHi. 45-4941

Odd Fellows, Independent Order of. New York. Constitution and bylaws of Magnolia Lodge, No. 166, of the state of New York. Brooklyn, 1845. 31 p. NBLi-Hi. 45-4942

Odd Fellows, Independent Order of. New York. Constitution and bylaws of Montague Lodge, No. 153, of the state of New York. Brooklyn, 1845. 32 p. NBLi-Hi. 45-4943

Odd Fellows, Independent Order of. New York. Constitution and bylaws of Tuckahannock Lodge, No. 132 of the state of New York. Ithaca, New York: Wells and Selkreg, printers, 1845. 24 p. NjR. 45-4944

Odd Fellows, Independent Order of. New York. Constitution, bylaws and rules of order of the Right Worthy Grand Lodge. New York, 1845. 60 p. NNC. 45-4945

Odd fellow's almanac and general directory for 1846. By Bro. Thomas Prince. Boston: T. Prince, [1845] MHi; MWA. 45-4946

The odd fellow's gem, containing sentiments of friendship, love and truth. Edited by a lady... Springfield: Benjamin F. Brown, 1845. 156 p. Ct; MB; NBLiHi; RHi; WLacT. 45-4947

The odd fellow's gift; a holiday present for 1845. Edited by George Hatch. Containing a variety of articles in prose and verse. New York: Daniel Adee, 1845. 216 p. NjR. 45-4948

The odd fellows' offering for 1845. Edited by Paschal Donaldson. New York: McGowan, 1845. 288 p. CtMW; MB; MLy; MWA. 45-4949

Odd Fellowship exposed. Exeter: Printed for the publisher, 1845. 12 p. MWHi. 45-4950

Odin, John. Report of a committee of the Association of Masters... on a letter. Boston, 1845. 18 p. MBC. 45-4951

An officer in the late army. Complete History of the Marquis de Lafayette, Major General in the army of the United States of America. By an officer in the late army. Hartford: S. Andrews and son, 1845. 504 p. ICLoy; MB; MLow. 45-4952

The officer's guide and western manual; containing a comprehensive collection of judicial, ministerial and business forms... with reference to the latest Indiana laws and court decisions. Revised and enlarged by J.H. Bradley. Fourth edition. Indianapolis: Turner and Jenison, 1845. InU; In-SC. 45-4953

Ogden, Elias Dayton. Tariff, or rates of duties payable on goods... imported into the United States of America, from and after December 1, 1846. New York: Rich and Soutrel, 1845. MiU. 45-4954

Ogden, Louisa W. Reasons for joining the New Jerusalem Church. New York: John Douglass, 1845. 153 p. ICMe; MCNC; MH; MH-AH. 45-4955

Ohio. An act to incorporate the State Bank of Ohio and other banking companies. Columbus: Samuel Medary, 1845. 32 p. MH-BA; NN. 45-4956

Ohio. An act to incorporate the Central Ohio Railroad. [Columbus, 1845] 12 p. MH-BA. 45-4957

Ohio. Acts of a general nature, passed by the forty-third General Assembly of the state of Ohio, begun and held in the city of Columbus, December 4, 1844. Columbus: Samuel Medary, 1845. 163 p. Nj; NNLI. 45-4958

Ohio. Acts of a local nature passed by the forty-third General Assembly of the state of Ohio, begun and held in the city of Columbus, December 2, 1844 and in the forty-third year of said state. Columbus: Samuel Medary, 1845. Nj; NNLI. 45-4959

Ohio. Acts passed by the General Assembly of the state of Ohio. Columbus: Samuel Medary, 1845. 514 p. Nv. 45-4960

Ohio. Annual report of the auditor of state. Columbus, 1845-. MiU. 45-4961

Ohio. Bylaws of the State Bank of Ohio. Columbus: Charles Scott and company, 1845. 14 p. OClWHi. 45-4962

Ohio. Commissioners to examine the books of the board of public works. Report. Columbus, 1845. 574 p. OCHP. 45-4963

Ohio. Journal of proceedings of the grand council of royal and select masters, of the state of Ohio. Columbus: C. Scott and company, 1845. 20 p. NNFM. 45-4964

Ohio. Journal of the House of Repre-

sentatives of the state of Ohio. Columbus, 1845. OAU. 45-4965

Ohio. Journal of the Senate of the state of Ohio being the first session of the forty-third General Assembly held in the city of Columbus, commencing on Monday, December 2, 1844. Columbus: Samuel Medary, 1845. 213 p. O-LR. 45-4966

Ohio. Laws of the state of Ohio, relating to the Miami Bridge Company at Hamilton. Rossville, Ohio: J.M. Christy, 1845. 114 p. OClWHi. 45-4967

Ohio. Re-evaluation of the lands of the Ohio University, with the proceedings of the legislature on that subject and the act by University in the town of Athens. Athens: N.H. Van Vorhes, 1845. 84 p. NoLoc. 45-4968

Ohio. Report of a majority of the select committee, proposing to repeal all laws creating distinctions on account of color commonly called black laws. [Columbus, 1845] 8 p. WHi. 45-4969

Ohio. Report of the board of commissioners, to examine the books and accounts of the board of canal fund commissioners. [Columbus? 1845?] 244 p. MH-BA. 45-4970

Ohio. Report of the minority of the select committee upon the subject of the laws relative to people of color. [Columbus, 1845] 11 p. WHi. 45-4971

Ohio. Resolutions of the legislature of Ohio, remonstrating against the annexation of Texas to the United States. January 22, 1845. Read and committed to the committee of the whole house on the state of the Union. [Washington] Blair and Rives, [1845] 2 p. TxU. 45-4972

Ohio Baptist Book and Tract Society. Claims of the Ohio Baptist Book and Tract Society presented in an address to the denomination, with its constitution, a list of its officers, stockholders, etc. Zanesville, Ohio: Edwin C. Church, 1845. 16 p. WHi. 45-4973

The Ohio cultivator. A semimonthly journal devoted to the improvement of agriculture and horticulture, and the promotion of domestic industry. Columbus: M.B. Bateham, 1845-. v. 1-. CU; DLC; ICJ; OSW; Vi. 45-4974

Ohio Mutual Fire Insurance Company. The life assurance department of the company, containing a prospectus of the principles and useful application of the mutual system. Also the terms and conditions of insurance. Second edition. Columbus: O.C.C. and G.R. Hazewell, 1845. 18 p. DLC; OClWHi. 45-4975

Old American Comic almanac for 1846. Boston: Printed by S.N. Dickinson and company, [1845] 29 p. MHi. 45-4976

Old American Comic almanack for 1846. Boston: Thomas Groom and company, [1845] MWA. 45-4977

Old American Comic almanack for 1846. Boston: William J. Reynolds, [1845] MWA. 45-4978

The old farmer's almanac, calculated on a new and improved plan for the year of our lord, 1845. By Robert B. Thomas... Boston: Jenks and Palmer, 1845. 48 p. MoK; MOrl; MoU. 45-4979

The old farmer's almanack for the year of our Lord, 1846. By Robert B. Thomas. Woburn: Printed by William White, [1845] MWo. 45-4980

Old oaken bucket almanac for 1846. By David Young, Philom. New York: Baker, Crane and Day, [1845] MWA. 45-4981

Olden times of Albany and Schenectady. First known dicovers of America. Schenectady, 1845. 16 p. MeHi; MWA. 45-4982

Oliphant's western farmer's almanac for 1846; being the seventieth and seventy-first year of American independence. Calculated for the western part of New York, and will serve for the western part of Pennsylvania and Northern part of Ohio, Michigan, Upper Canada, etc. Calculations by Horace Martin. Auburn, New York: H. Oliphant, 1845. 32 p. NAuCM; NAuHi; NCH. 45-4983

Oliver, Benjamin Lynde, 1788-1843. Practical conveyancing, a selection of forms of general utility, with notes interspersed. Fourth edition, corrected and enlarged by Peter Oliver. Hallowell, [Maine] Glazier, Masters and Smith, 1845. 622 p. CSt; In-SC; MBAt; PU-L; VtU. 45-4984

Ollendorff, Heinrich Gottfried, 1803-1865. A key to the exercises in Ollendorff's new method of learning to read, write and speak the German language. New York: American Book company, 1845. 182 p. PSC. 45-4985

Ollendorff, Heinrich Gottfried, 1803-1865. New method of learning to write and speak the German language. New York: American Book Publishing company, 1845. 510 p. InNd; KyLoPM; MdU; PSC; WRao. 45-4986

Olmsted, Denison, 1791-1859. Beau ideal of the perfect teacher; a lecture before the American Institute of Instruction, Hartford, August, 1845. Boston: William D. Ticknor and company, 1845. 29 p. Ct; DLC; MHi; MWA; RPB. 45-4987

Olmsted, Denison, 1791-1859. A compendium of astronomy; containing the elements of science, familiarly explained and illustrated with the latest discoveries. Designed for schools and academies and the general reader. New York: Collins, Brother and company, 1845. 276 p. CSt; IaFayU; ICU. 45-4988

Olmsted, Denison, 1791-1859. A compendium of natural philosophy; adopted to the use of the general reader, and to schools... To which is now added a supplement... with copious list of experiments. New Haven: S. Babcock, 1845. 420 p. CEu; MBevHi; MH; OS; TxU-T. 45-4989

Olmsted, Denison, 1791-1859. An introduction to natural philosophy designed as a text book, for the use of the students in Yale College. Compiled from various authorities. Stereotype edition. New York: Collins, Brother and company, 1845. 529 p. InU; PU; TxU; ViRU; WBeloC. 45-4990

Olmsted, Denison, 1791-1859. Rudiments of Natural philosophy and astronomy: Designed for the younger classes in academies and common schools. Stereotype edition. Cincinnati: William H. Moore and company, 1845.

288 p. InGrD; IP; KyU; NIC; OMC. 45-4991

Olney, Jesse, 1798-1872. An improved system of arithmetic, for the use of families, schools and academies. By J. Olney and P. Gallup. Hartford: Robins and Smith, 1845. 312 p. Ct; MoK. 45-4992

Olney, Jesse, 1798-1872. The national preceptor; or selections in prose and poetry; consisting of narrative, descriptive, argumentative, didactic, pathetic and humorous pieces. Twentieth edition. New York: Pratt, Woodford and company, 1845. 336 p. CtHwatk; ICU; MH. 45-4993

Olney, Jesse, 1798-1872. A practical system of modern geography; or a view of the present state of the world. Simplified and adapted to the capacity of youth. Revised and illustrated by a new and enlarged atlas, by J. Olney. Forty-seventh edition. New York: Pratt, Woodford and company, 1845. 292 p. MsJMC; NcU; OClWHi; WaU. 45-4994

Olney, Jesse, 1798-1872. A practical system of modern geography; or a view of the present state of the world. Simplified and adapted to the capacity of youth. Revised and illustrated by a new and enlarged atlas, by J. Olney. Forty-eighth edition. New York: Pratt, Woodford and company, 1845. 294 p. McKCM; OSW; PP. 45-4995

Olney, Jesse, 1798-1872. A practical system of modern geography; or a view of the present state of the world. Simplified and adapted to the capacity of youth. Revised and illustrated by a new and enlarged atlas, by J. Olney. Forty-ninth edition. New York: Pratt, Woodford and company, 1845. 298 p. CStclU; MHolliHi; MNoberoHi. 45-4996

Onderdonk, Benjamin Tredwell, 1791-1861. Bishop Onderdonk's statement. A statement of facts and circumstances connected with the recent trial of the Bishop of New York. New York: H.M. Onderdonk; Philadelphia: G.S. Appleton, 1845. 31 p. KHi; NcD; OClWHi; PPP; RPB. 45-4997

Onderdonk, Benjamin Tredwell, 1791-1861. The proceedings of the court convened under the third canon of 1844, in the city of New York... New York: D. Appleton and company; Philadelphia: G.S. Appleton, 1845. 333 p. IEN; MWA; NcU; PJA; TxDaM. 45-4998

Onondaga Academy. Catalogue of the officers and students of the Onondaga Academy at Onondaga Hollow. Syracuse: Religious Recorder office, 1845. 16 p. NSyHi. 45-4999

Onondaga County, New York Teachers' Institute. Proceedings of the Onondaga Teachers' Institute. Spring term, 1845. Syracuse: Tucker and Kinney, 1845. 34 p. MH. 45-5000

Ontario Agricultural Society. Premiums for 1845. Rules and regulations. Canandaigua: T.B. Hahn, 1845. Broadside. NCanHi. 45-5001

Ontario Teachers Institute. Catalogue of the county and town superintendents and teachers who attended the Ontario Teacher's Institute. By Miss Luvina R. Colson. Canandaigua: George L. Whitney, 1845. 12 p. NCanHi. 45-5002

Opie, Amelia Alderson, 1769-1853.

The stage coach and other tales on lying. Boston, 1845. 93 p. MH. 45-5003

Opie, Amelia Alderson, 1769-1853. Tale of trials; told to my children. Boston: Saxton and Kelt, 1845. MH. 45-5004

Opie, Amelia Alderson, 1769-1853. White lies. A tale. Boston: Saxton and Kelt: New York: Saxton and Miles, 1845. 100 p. MBeHi; MHi; PU. 45-5005

Opinions of thirty-two scientific gentlemen on the invention of Muzio Muzzi; in English and Italian. [New York: Herald Book and Job Printing office, 1845] 14 p. CtY; DLC; ICRL; WU-E. 45-5006

Order of United Americans. Constitutions of the O. of U.A. and bylaws of the Alpha chapter. New York: R.C. Root, 1845. 22 p. MiD-B. 45-5007

Oregon. Journal of the House of Representatives, 1845-1870. Salem, 1845-1870. 16 v. WaU. 45-5008

An original and thrilling sketch from the diary of a Methodist traveling preacher. New York: Anderson and company, 1845. 40 p. MBC; MBNMHi. 45-5009

Original letter writer; on friendship, love, marriage, and business. Lowell: L. Dayton, 1845. 147 p. CtY; Nh-Hi. 45-5010

Orleans High School, New Orleans, Louisiana. Statutes and regulations of the Orleans High School. New Orleans: Jerome Bayon, 1845. 22 p. LU. 45-5011

Ormsby, Robert McKinley, 1814-1881.

The American reader; or exercises in reading with introductory exercises in the principles of articulation, pronunciation. Bradford Vermont: Low, 1845. 190 p. CtHWatk; DLC; VtBrad; VtU. 45-5012

Orr, Hector. The native American; a gift for the people. Philadelphia: H. Orr, 1845. 199 p. ICN; MiU; NNC; TNP; WHi. 45-5013

Orr, John William, 1815-1887. Pictorial guide of the falls of Niagara... giving an account of this stupendous natural wonder... with every historical incident of interest; maps, charts... Buffalo: Press of Salisbury and Clapp, 1845. 232 p. DLC; MPeHi; MWA. 45-5014

Osborn, Laughton, 1809-1878. Handbook of young artists and amateurs in oil painting, being chiefly a condensed compilation from the celebrated manual of Bouvier. New York: Wiley and Putnam, 1845. 398 p. MH; OO; PPL-R; RPA; WGr. 45-5015

Osgood, Frances Sargent Locke, 1811-1850. Poems. New York, 1845. 252 p. RHi. 45-5016

Osbourn, James. Spiritual gleanings, or celestial fruit from the tree of life. Intended for the use and benefit of sin-sick souls. Baltimore: John D. Toy, 1845. 116 p. MdBD; MdBP. 45-5017

Osgood, Charles, 1808-1881. Causes, treatment and cure of fever and ague, and other diseases of bilious climates. Seventh edition. New York: The author, 1845. 14 p. MH-M. 45-5018

Osgood, Frances Sargent Locke, 1811-1850. The poetry of flowers and flowers of poetry; to which are added, a simple treatise on botany, with familiar examples, and a copious floral dictionary. Edited by Frances S. Osgood. New York: J.C. Riker, 1845. 276 p. GMM; OO. 45-5019

Osgood, Jason C. In the court for the correction of errors, Jason C. Osgood vs. George Harp. Error book. Case made by the plaintiff in error. Utica: H.H. Curtis, printer, 1845. 16 p. NSyCA. 45-5020

Ossoli, Sarah Margaret Fuller. Woman in the the nineteenth century. New York: Greeley and McElrath, 1845. 201 p. CL; ICMe; MdBP; MHi; RPaw. 45-5021

O'Sullivan, Mortimer, 1791?-1859. The Nevilles of Garretstown. A tale of 1760 by the author of Harry Lorrequer, Charles O'Malley, etc. New York: Harper and brothers, 1845. 170 p. MeLewB; MH; NjR. 45-5022

Oswald, John, 1804-1867. An etymological dictionary of the English language, on a plan entirely new. Revised and improved, by J.M. Keagy. Philadelphia: E.C. and J. Biddle, 1845. InU. 45-5023

Oswego County Teacher's Institute. Catalogue of the institute held at Mexico, October, 1845. Pulaski: Tallmadge, 1845. 16 p. CtHT-W. 45-5024

Otey, James Hervey, 1800-1863. The Unity of the church; the ministry; the apostolical succession: Three discourses... New York: Daniel Dana, Jr., 1845. 86 p. MBC; MdBD; NNC; TSewU; VtMidSM. 45-5025

Otheman, Edward Brenton, 1833-1888. Memoirs and writings of Mrs. Hannah Maynard Pickard, late wife of Rev. Humphrey Pickard, principal of the Wesleyan Academy at Mount Allison, Sackville. Boston: David H. ELa, 1845. 311 p. ICHi; MeBa; MH; MNe; NjMD. 45-5026

Ouseley, Gideon, 1762-1839. Old christianity against papal novelties, including a review of Dr. Milner's "End of controversy." Fourth American from the fifth Dublin edition. Philadelphia: Sorin and Ball, 1845. 406 p. NNMHi; IaPeC. 45-5027

Outlines of American history; from the first discovery to the present time. For families and schools. With numerous engravings and questions for the examination of pupils. Philadelphia: Thomas, Cowperthwait and company and Carey and Hart, 1845. 191 p. ICU; DLC; KyLoS; MNBedf; NcAS. 45-5028

Outlines of Roman history; for families and schools, with numerous engravings. Published under the direction of the Committee of General Literature and Education, appointed by the Society for Promoting Christian Knowledge. From the ninth London edition, with additions and questions. Philadelphia: Thomas, Cowperthwait and company and Carey and Hart, 1845. CtHT; DLC; MiThr; PPL; TxU-T. 45-5029

Outlines of the history of England for families and schools, with numerous engravings from the fourteenth London edition. Philadelphia: Thomas, Cowperthwait and company and Carey and Hart, 1845. 168 p. MAnHi; MB; MdBLC; RKi. 45-5030

Ovidius Naso, Publius. Excerpl ex scriptis Publius Ovidius Naso, accedunt notulae anglicas et questiones, in usum scholae, Bostoniensis, Cura B.A. Gould. Boston: Benjamin B. Mussey, 1845. 237 p. TxCsA; ViRut. 45-5031

Ovidius Naso, Publius. Selections from the Metamorphoses and Heroides of Ovid, with notes, grammatical references, and exercises in scanning. By E.A. Andrews. Boston: Crocker and Brewster, 1845. 264 p. IaDuTM; MBrigStJ; NNC; ScCliTO. 45-5032

Owen, David Dale, 1807-1860. Mineral lands of the United States. Message from the president of the United States, in reply to a resolution of the House on February 6, [1839] concerning the mineral lands of the United States. Washington: Government Printing office, 1845. 161 p. CU; ICHi; MiU; NIC; OO. 45-5033

Owen, Robert. The book of the new moral world, containing the rational system of society, founded on demonstrable facts, developing the constitution and laws of human nature and of society. First American edition. New York: G. Vale, 1845. 264 p. ICN; KyLoS; MdBJ; MiD; PU. 45-5034

Owen, Robert. Robert Owen's letter to the Senate of the 28th congress of the United States, requesting permission to deliver a course of lectures in its chamber, on an entirely new state of human existence, also Robert Owen's letter to the public... Washington: Printed at the Globe, 1845. 7 p. DNLM; ICU; MBAt; PReaHi; TxHU. 45-5035

P

Paalzow, Henriette Wach von, 1788-1847. The citizens of Prague. [New York: Harper and brothers, 1845] MH. 45-5036

Paalzow, Henriette Wach von, 1788-1847. Thyrnau, the Bohemian conspirator; or the days of Maria Theresa. A historical romance. Translated from the German by G.C. Hebbe... and C.B. Burkhardt, esq. New York: W. Taylor, 1845. 290 p. IC; NN. 45-5037

Page, David Perkins, 1810-1848. Advancement in the means and methods of public instruction; a lecture. Boston: William D. Ticknor and company, 1845. 38 p. NjR. 45-5038

Page, Frederic Benjamin. Prairiedom; rambles and scrambles in Texas or Estremadura. By a suthron. New York: Paine and Burgess, 1845. 166 p. CtHT; ICHi; MiD; TxD-W; WM. 45-5039

Page, Joseph Rusling, 1816 or 1817-1884. Nature and importance of revivals of religion. Discourse delivered on Thanksgiving Day, 1844. Perry, New York: Mitchell, 1845. 12 p. OO. 45-5040

Paige, Elbridge Gerry, 1816-1859. Short patent sermons, by Dow, Jr. [pseud.] Originally published in the New York Sunday Mercury. New York: Paige, Nichols and Krauth, 1845. 2 v. DLC; ICN; MH; OkentU; OO. 45-5041

Paine, David. The social minstrel, a collection of songs, etc. from the best European authors. Boston: Crocker and Brewster, 1845. CtHWatk; MB; MLanc; NjP. 45-5042

Paine, Martyn, 1794-1877. A lecture on the philosophy of medicine, delivered before the medical class of the University of New York, at the session of 1845-1846. New York: Printed for the medical class of the University, 1845-1846. 19 p. MdBM; MH; MHi; NNNAM; OMC. 45-5043

Paine, Thomas, 1737-1809. Theological works of Thomas Paine. To which are added the profession of faith of Savoyard Vicar. By J.J. Rosseau, and other miscellaneous pieces. Boston: Printed and published at the Boston Investigator office, by J.P. Mendun, 1845. 384 p. MB; NLag; ViU. 45-5044

Paley, William, 1743-1805. Natural theology: or evidences of the existence and attributes of the Deity, collected from the appearances of nature. Illustrated by the plates, and by a selection from the notes of James Paxton. With additional notes, original and selected, for this edition. And a vocabulary of scientific terms. Boston: Gould, Kendall and Lincoln, 1845. 2 v. InCW; LN; MiU; NjP; OCX. 45-5045

Paley, William, 1743-1805. Paley's moral and political philosophy. As condensed by A.J. Valpy. To which are added notes from popular authors; embracing present opinions in ethical science, and an exposition of our own political institutions. Philadelphia: U. Hunt and son, 1845. 298 p. GEU; ICJ; OCl; TxU; ViU. 45-5046

Paley, William, 1743-1805. Paley's natural theology, with illustrative notes, etc. By Henry Lord Brougham and Sir Charles Bell. With numerous woodcuts. To which are added, preliminary observations and notes. By A. Potter. New York: Harper and brothers, 1845. 2 v. InCW; MsU; NcRP; WM. 45-5047

Paley, William, 1743-1805. Paley's view of the evidences of christianity. In three parts. With a memoir. Philadelphia: James Kay, Jun. and brother; Pittsburgh: C.H. Kay and company, 1845. 264 p. DLC; MiU; KyLoP; OClW. 45-5048

Paley, William, 1743-1805. The principles of moral and political philosophy. Boston: N.H. Whitaker, 1845. 2 v. in 1. NjR; ScU. 45-5049

Palfrey, John Gorham, 1796-1881. A discource on the life and character of the Rev. Henry Ware. Pronounced in the First Church in Cambridge, September 28, 1845. Cambridge, [Massachusetts] J. Owen, 1845. 37 p. CtY-D; IU; MWA; NcD; RPB. 45-5050

Palmer, Aaron. A key to the endless, self-computing scale. New York: William Waters, 1845. 72 p.NNE. 45-5051

Palmer, Aaron. Palmer's pocket scale, with rules for its use in solving arithmetical and geometrical problems. Boston: Aaron Palmer, 1845. 48 p. IU; MBC; MiHi; OClWHi; TxU-T. 45-5052

Palmer, Benjamin Morgan, 1818-1902. Influence of religions upon national character. An oration delivered before the Demosthenian and Phi Kappa Societies, of the University of Georgia, August 7, 1845. Athens: Printed at the Banner office, 1845. 30 p. A-Ar; GU- De; PPL; ScSp; TxU. 45-5053

Palmer, Phoebe Worrell, 1807-1874. Recollections and gathered fragments of Mrs. Lydia N. Cox, of Williamsburg, Long Island. New York: Piercy and Reed, printers, 1845. 231 p. NjMD; NjR; NSmb. 45-5054

Palmer, Phoebe Worrell, 1807-1874. The way of holiness, with notes by the way; being a narrative of religious experiences resulting from a determination to be a Bible christian. New York: G. Lane and B. Tippett, 1845. 288 p. CtMW; KyBC; NcD; NN. 45-5055

The Palmis [sic]; a new collection of hymns for the use of the Baptist churches. By Baron Stow and S.F. Smith. Boston: Gould, Kendall, and Lincoln; Philadelphia: American Baptist Publication and Sabbath Sunday School Society; New York: Lewis Colby; Utica: Bennett, Backus and Hawley; Hartford: Robins and Smith, 1845. 720 p. MBoy. 45-5056

Pancoast, Joseph, 1805-1882. Introductory lecture to the course of general descriptive and surgical anatomy, in Jefferson Medical College, delivered November 5, 1845. Philadelphia: Merrihew and Thompson, printers, 1845. 23 p. IEN; MeB; MH-AH; PHi; PPM. 45-5057

Parish, M.P. The green mountain temperance songster. Selected and aranged by M.P. Parish. Burlington: Goodrich, 1845. 48 p. RPB; VtU. 45-058

Park, Edwards Amasa, 1808-1900. The preacher and pastor. Edited and accompanied with an introductory essay by Edwards A. Park. Andover: Allen, Morrill and Wardwell, 1845. CtHC; CU; IaB; NbCrD; RPA. 45-5059

Park, Mungo, 1771-1806. The life and travels of Mungo Park. With the account of his death from the journal of Isaaco, the substance of later discoveries relative to his lamented fate, and the termination of the Niger. New York: Harper and brothers, 1845. MLow; MsU; NcElon, WNaE. 45-5060

Parke, Peter W. Protest of Peter W. Parke executed for murder, in which he declared his innocence to the last moment of life. New York, 1845. 24 p. NjR; NNU-L; PPL. 45-5061

Parke, Uriah. Farmers and mechanics practical arithmetic... use of schools and men of business and adapted to federal money of the United States. Zanesville: Merrick, 1845. 178 p. OO. 45-5062

Parker, [Alderman] Address to Alderman Parker to the city council, January 3, 1845. Boston, 1845. 7 p. MHi. 45-5063

Parker, George A. Survey of a railroad route from Shirley, through Townsend Harbor, Centre and West Village, to the line of New Hampshire at Mason, January, 1845. Boston: Press of the Bunker Hill Aurora, 1845. 10 p. DBRE; MB; MHi; NN. 45-5064

Parker, J.W. The history, philosophy

and uses of human magnetism, or mesmerism; with practical instructions on how to apply the power in curing pains and diseases, being a brief compilation of the most important knowledge on this subject. Salem, Ohio: J.H. Painter, 1845. 48 p. MiDM-W. 45-5065

Parker, Joel, 1795-1875. Courtship and marriage. Moral principles illustrated in their application to courtship and marriage. Philadelphia: Perkins, 1845. 179 p. IGK; MBC; PPM; PPPrHi. 45-5066

Parker, Richard Green, 1798-1869. Aids to English composition, prepared for students of all grades; embracing specimens and examples of school and college exercises and most of the higher departments of English composition, both in prose and verse. A new edition, with additions and improvements. New York: Harper and brothers, 1845. 429 p. InRch; PHi; TNP. 45-5067

Parker, Richard Green, 1798-1869. The Boston school compendium of natural and experimental philosophy. Fifteenth edition, stereotyped. Boston: Jordan, Swift and Wiley, 1845. 237 p. MeHi; MH; MPeHi; NNC; PV. 45-5068

Parker, Richard Green, 1798-1869. Progressive exercises in English composition. Forty-fifth stereotype edition. Boston: Robert S. Davis; New York: Pratt, Woodford and company, and Collins, brothers and company; Philadelphia: Thomas, Cowperthwait and company; Baltimore: Cushing and brothers, 1845. 107 p. ICBB; LU; MH; OClWHi; WaPS. 45-5069

Parker, Richard Green, 1798-1869. Progressive exercises in English grammar. Eleventh edition. Boston: Crocker and Brewster, 1845. 96 p. NNC. 45-5070

Parker, Theodore, 1810-1860. Excellence of goodness. A sermon preached in Boston, January 26, 1845. Boston: B.H. Greene, 1845. 16 p. CtHT; MB; NNC; OO; RPaw. 45-5071

Parker, Theodore, 1810-1860. A letter to the Boston Association of Congregational Ministers. By Theodore Parker, minister of the Second Church in Roxbury. Boston: Charles C. Little and James Brown, 1845. 20 p. CBPac; MH; MiD-B; MWey; PPL. 45-5072

Parker, Theodore, 1810-1860. A letter to the Boston Association of Congregational Ministers, touching certain matters of their theology. Second edition. Boston: Little and Brown, 1845. CtHC; ICN; MBAt; NcU; OCHP. 45-5073

Parker, Theodore, 1810-1860. The relation of Jesus to his age and the ages. A sermon preached at the Thursday lecture, in Boston, December 26, 1844. Boston: Charles C. Little and James Brown, 1845. 18 p. CBPac; ICN; MHi; PPL-R; OO. 45-5074

Parker, Theodore, 1810-1860. A sermon preached in the church of the disciples in Boston. By Theodore Parker, minister of the Second Church in Roxbury. Boston: Benjamin H. Greene, 1845. 16 p. MdCatS; MBD; PHi. 45-5075

Parkman, Samuel, 1816-1854. Introductory lecture to the spring session of lectures in Castleton Medical College. Whitehall, New York: Printed by Southmayd and Watkins, 1845. 15 p. CSmH; DNLM; MeB; NNNAM. 45-5076

Parmalee, S.N. An analysis and index o the revised statutes and laws of the stat of Vermont, which are not in force. Bur lington: Chauncey Goodrich, 1845. 24 p Ia; In-SC; MdBB; Nj; Nv. 45-5077

Parrish, Isaac, 1811-1852. Biographica memoir, of John C. Otto, late vice presi dent of the College of Physicians, rea before the college by appointment March 4, 1845. Printed by order of the college. Philadelphia: W.F. Geddes printer, 1845. 20 p. ICJ; MHi; NjP OCLloyd; PPCP. 45-5078

Parry, William Edward, 1790-1855 Three voyages for the discovery of a north-west passage from the Atlantic to the Pacific, and narrative of an attempt to reach the North Pole. New York: Harper, 1845. 2 v. InCW; MNF; MB-FA NBuCC; OSW. 45-5079

Parsons, Charles Booth. Oration delivered before the Grand Lodge of Kentucky of I.O.O.F. on the occasion of their celebration at Louisville, May 10, 1845. Published by request of the order. Louisville, Kentucky: C.C. Hull and brothers, printers, 1845. 16 p. ICU; NNG. 45-5080

Parsons, Robert, 1546-1610. A christian directory guiding men to their eternal salvation. New York: D. Murphy and son, 1845. 342, 258 p. CoDR; MBBC; MnSS; OCX; PV. 45-5081

Parsons, Theophilus, 1797-1882. Essays. Boston: Otis Clapp, 1845. 7-228 p. KyWa; MH; NjP; MPiB; WHi. 45-5082

Parsons and Company, Flushing, Long Island. Catalogue of fruit and ornamental trees, shrubs, vines and plants. Cultivated and for sale at their commercial garden and nursery. Flushing, 1845. 42, 2 p. MHi; N. 45-5083

Pasteur, Thomas A. Masonic address delivered before the members of Huntington Lodge. Jackson: M'Clanahan and Day, printers, 1845. 16 p. NNFM. 45-5084

Pastoral life of the ancients. The history of silk, cotton, linen, wool and other fibrous substances; including observations in spinning, dyeing and weaving, also an account of the ancients, their social state and attainments in the domestic arts. New York: Harper and brothers, 1845. 464 p. MNF. 45-5085

Paterson, Thomas J. Speech on the post office reform and the reduction of the rates of postage; in the House, March 1, 1845. Washington, 1845. 14 p. MBAt; MHi; MiD-B. 45-5086

Patten, Ruth Wheelock. Interesting family letters of the late Mrs. Ruth Patten of Hartford, Connecticut. Hartford: D.B. Mosely, 1845. 306 p. CtHC; MBC; Nh-Hi. 45-5087

Patten's New Haven directory for the years 1845-1846. New Haven, 1845. No. 6. 124 p. MHi. 45-5088

Patten's New Haven directory for the years 1845-6, by James Patten. New Haven: J.H. Benham, 1845. 132 p. CtHC; CtY; MiD-B. 45-5089

Patterson, Henry Stuart, 1815-1854. Lecture introductory to the course of materia medica and pharmacy in the medical department of Pennsylvania College, Philadelphia, for the session 1844-1845; delivered November 9, 1844. Philadelphia: Published by the members of the class, 1845. 24 p. NNNAM; PHi; PPLT; PPPrHi; ViU. 45-5090

Paul, Henry H. The book of chemical amusement, a complete encyclopedia of experiments in various branches of chemistry. Philadelphia: Getz and Smith, 1845. 172 p. CtY; KU; OClWHi. 45-5091

Paulding, James Kirke, 1778-1860. The Dutchman's fireside. Fifth edition. New York: Harper and brothers, 1845. 2 v. MB; NN. 45-5092

Paulding, James Kirke, 1778-1860. A life of Washington. New York: Harper and brothers, 1845. 2 v. IGK; NcD; ODa PSew; WM. 45-5093

Paulding, James Kirke, 1778-1860. Westward ho! New York: Harper and brothers, 1845. 2 v. CtY; NN; ViU. 45-5094

Paxton, W.E. The briganad; or a tale of the west. By Orlando [pseud.] Georgetown, Kentucky, 1845. 38 p. ICU. 45-5095

Payne, Robert. A funeral discourse, on the life and history of Andrew Jackson, delivered at Courtland, Alabama, on July 4, 1845. Huntsville: Democrat office, printer, 1845. 16 p. NN; T. 45-5096

El payo de Nuevo Mejico. Periodico del gobierno del departamento... [Santa Fe: Imprenta del gobierno a cargo de J.M.B. Ano de 1845] 2 l. CSmH; CU-B; DLC. 45-5097

Peabody, Andrew Preston, 1811-1893. Anti-supernaturalism. A sermon preached before the senior class of the divinity school in Harvard University, July 13, 1845. Cambridge, [Massachusetts] John Owen, 1845. 26 p. CBPac; ICMe; MHi; NjR; RPB. 45-5098

Peabody, Andrew Preston, 1811-1893. The connection between science and religion. An oration delivered before the Phi Beta Kappa Society of Harvard University. Boston: C.C. Little and J. Brown, 1845. 29 p. MAnP; MBAt; MH-AH; MiD-B; OO. 45-5099

Peabody, Ephraim. A scripture catechism; containing the principles of the Christian religion stated in the words of the Bible. For the use of Sunday schools. Boston: William Crosby and H.P. Nichols, 1845. 56 p. MBrZ; MH-AH; MWA; NNUT. 45-5100

The peace almanac for 1845. New York: Collins, brother and company, [1845?] 30 p. RNHi. 45-5101

The peace almanac for 1846. New York: Collins, brother and company, 1845. MWA. 45-5102

The peace almanack. New York: Collins, brother and company, 1845. MWA; RNHi. 45-5103

Peacock, Thomas Love, 1785-1866. Headlong Hall and Nightmare Abbey. First American edition. New York: Wiley and Putnam, 1845. 172 p. InGrD; LNH; MeSaco; MoSW; OCl. 45-5104

Peale, Rembrandt, 1778-1860. Graphics, the art of accurate delineation; a system of school exercise, for the education of the eye and the training of the hand, as auxiliary to writing geog-

raphy and drawing. Philadelphia: E.C Biddle, [1845] 132 p. DLC; NjP; PHi; Pl PU. 45-5105

The pearl offering; a compendium religious, literary and philosophica knowledge. New York: T.L. Magagna [1845?] NBuG. 45-5106

Pearson, John, 1613-1686. An expos tion of the creed. With an appendix, cor taining the principal Greek and Lati creeds. Revised by the Rev. W.S. Dot son. New York: D. Appleton and con pany; Philadelphia: George S. Appleto [1845] 616, 16 p. CoDI. 45-5107

Pease, John, 1797-1868. Address c John Pease to Friends in America. Ne York: Egbert, Hovey and King, 1845. 1 p. InRchE; MiD-Bp; NjR; OClWH PHi. 45-5108

Pease, John, 1797-1868. Address t Friends of the Yearly Meeting of Ne York and in North America generally [Dates at Boston. Seventh month 1s 1845. Philadelphia, 1845?] 4 p. MH PHC. 45-5109

Peck, George, 1797-1876. The answe to the question, why are you a Wesleya Methodist. New York: Lane and Tippet 1845. TxDaM. 45-5110

Peck, George, 1797-1876. Christian ex ertion; or the duty of private members o the Church of Christ to labor for the soul of men explained and enforced. Nev York: Lane and Tippett, 1845. 160 p CtMW; GEU-T; IaFayU; NNMHi ScOrC. 45-5111

Peck, George, 1797-1876. The scriptur doctrine of Christian perfection state and defended. Abridged from the author's larger work. New York: Lane and Tippett, for the Methodist Episcopal Church, 1845. 332 p. IEG; KyBC; MoS; OberB; PPM. 45-5112

Peck, George, 1797-1876. Slavery and the episcopacy: being an examination of Dr. Bascom's review of the reply of the majority to the protest of the minority of the late general conference of the Methodist Episcopal Church, in the case of Bishop Andrew. New York: G. Lane and C.B. Tippett, 1845. 139 p. A-Ar; CtMW; ICN; PPL; RPB. 45-5113

Peck, Jesse T. Essential element of divine character. Boston: American Pulpit, 1845. CtHC. 45-5114

Peck, John, 1780-1849. Two discourses; the former presenting a history of the First Baptist Church, Cazenvia, New York. The latter presenting a history of the Baptist Church, Cazenovia Village, New York. Utica: Bennett, Backus and Hawley, 1845. 40 p. N; NCH-S; RPB. 45-5115

Peck's tourist's companion to Niagara Falls, Saratoga Springs, the lakes, Canada... Buffalo: W.B. and C.E. Peck, 1845. 194 p. CSmH; DLC; MWA; PHi; RPA. 45-5116

A peep into the sanctuary, being a succinct examination of the Right Rev. B.T. Onderdonk, Bishop of New York. Boston, 1845. 32 p. NoLoc. 45-5117

Peet, Elijah. General business directory of the city of Cleveland, for the years 1845-1846, together with a historical and statistical account. Second year of publication. Cleveland: Smead, 1845-1846. 2 v. DLC; ICN; OClW; OO. 45-5118

Peet, Harvey Prindle, 1794-1873. Course of instruction for the deaf and dumb. New York, 1845. MH; MiU. 45-5119

Peet, Harvey Prindle, 1794-1878. Mr. Peet's tour through central and western New York, in the summer of 1844, with a select number of deaf mute pupils. [n.p., 1845] MH. 45-5120

Peirce, Benjamin, 1809-1880. An elementary treatise on plane and spherical trigonometry with their applications to navigation, surveying, heights and distances and spherical astronomy, and particularly adapted to explaining the construction of Bowditch's navigation, and the nautical almanac. Third edition, with additions. Boston: J. Munroe and company, 1845. 449 p. LNP; MBAt; MsU; NNC; OO. 45-5121

Peirce, Benjamin, 1809-1880. An elementary treatise on algebra: to which are added exponential equations and logarithms. Fifth edition. Boston: James Munroe and company; New York: Collins, brother and company; Philadelphia: Thomas, Cowperthwait and company; Philadelphia: Thomas, Cowperthwait and company, 1845. ViLxW. 45-5122

Peirce, Bradford Kinney, 1819-1889. One talent improved; or the life and labors of Miss Susan G. Bowler. Revised by the editor, D.P. Kidder. New York: G. Lane and C.B. Tippett, 1845. 197 p. DLC; ODW; TNT. 45-5123

Peirce, Bradford Kinney, 1819-1889. Sabbath school teachers manual, or the important office and necessary qualifications and studies of the teacher. Boston: Waite, Peirce and company, etc., 1845. IEG; MH. 45-5124

Peirson, Lydia Jane Wheeler, 1802-1862. Forest leaves. Philadelphia: Lindsay and Blakiston, 1845. [13]-264 p. CtSoP; ICN; MoSM; OC; PAtM. 45-5125

Pelby, Rosalie French, 1793-1857. Grand exhibition of [wax] statuary. Descriptive catalogue. Boston: D. Hooton, 1845. 16 p. MHi; NN. 45-5126

Penfeather, Amabel [pseud.] Elinor Wylls; or the young folk at Longbridge. A tale. Edited by James Fenimore Cooper. Philadelphia: Carey and Hart, 1845. 2 v. DLC; MWA; PPL-R. 45-5127

Penington, Isaac, 1616-1679. Some deep considerations on the state of Israel. New Bedford: [Registry Press] 1845. 12 p. MNBedf. 45-5128

Peninsula Mining Company. Articles of association. New York, 1845. 8 p. 45-5129

Penn, William, 1644-1718. No cross, no crown. A discourse, showing the nature and discipline of the holy cross of Christ... New York: Collins, brother and company: New Bedford: William C. Taber and son, 1845. 323 p. CMary; IaHi; NBF; PSC-Hi; RWe. 45-5130

Penn, William, 1644-1718. No cross, no crown. A discourse, showing the nature and discipline of the holy cross of Christ... Philadelphia: [J. Kite and company, printers] 1845. 408 p. CBB; KKcBT; MB; RPaw; ScC. 45-5131

Penna Company for Insurance on Lives and Granting Annuities. Proposals and rates... Philadelphia: United States Book and Job Printing office, 1845. 22 p. MH-BA; PHi; PPCP. 45-5132

Pennington, James W.C. A two year absence; or a farewell sermon. Hartford: H.T. Wells, 1845. 31 p. CSmH; CtY; MNF; NN-Sc. 45-5133

Pennsylvania. An act to incorporate the Philadelphia Mutual Insurance Company, passed February 24, 1845. Philadelphia: John C. Clark, 1845. 20 p. MH-BA. 45-5134

Pennsylvania. Laws of the General Assembly of the commonwealth of Pennsylvania, passed at the session of 1845 in the sixty-ninth year of independence, including seven acts passed by both branches of the Legislature. Harrisburg: J.M.G. Lescure, 1845. 558 p. Wa-L. 45-5135

Pennsylvania. A tabular statement relating to common school appropriation, for the school years 1841 to 1844. Communicated by the superintendent. Harrisburg: J.M.G. Lescure, 1845. 12 p. MH;OSW. 45-5136

Pennsylvania. University. Address on the occasion of their biennial celebration, May 23rd, 1845, by H.D. Gilpin. Philadelphia: King, 1845. 30 p. PU. 45-5137

Pennsylvania. University. Announcements of various schools and departments, 1845. Philadelphia, 1845-. PP; PPUG; PPUnC. 45-5138

Pennsylvania. University. General catalogue of the medical graduates of the

University of Pennsylvania with an historical sketch of the origin, progress, and present state of the Medical department. Third edition. Philadelphia: L.R. Bailey, 1845. 119 p. MH; MoS; NcD; PU; ViU. 45-5139

Pennsylvania Academy of the Fine Arts. Philadelphia. Address on its destruction by fire. Philadelphia, 1845. PPL. 45-5140

Pennsylvania Academy of the Fine Arts, Philadelphia. Exhibition of paintings, statues and casts. Philadelphia: Collins, 1845. 16 p. PU. 45-5141

Pennsylvania almanac for 1846. Calculated by John Ward. Philadelphia: Thomas Davis, [1845] MWA. 45-5142

Pennsylvania and New Jersey almanac for 1846. By Joseph Faulke. Philadelphia: Thomas L. Bonsal, [1845] MWA. 45-5143

Pennsylvania Artillery. Jackson Artillery. Constitution of the volunteer company of Jackson Artillery. Philadelphia: Barrett and Jones, 1845. NWM. 45-5144

Pennsylvania Historical Society. Bulletin. Philadelphia, 1845-1847. V. 1. No.1-. 45-5145

The Pennsylvania journal of prison discipline and philanthropy. Published under the direction of the Philadelphia Society for the Alleviation of the Miseries of Public Prison. Philadelphia, 1845-. MB; PPCP; PSC-Hi; PU. 45-5146

Pennsylvania Seamen's Friend Society. Address of the Pennsylvania Seamen's Friend Society to the citizens of Philadelphia, with the constitution and officers, 1845. Philadelphia, 1845. 16 p. PHi; PPL. 45-5147

The penny library, for school children, W.B. Fowle, editor. Boston: Fowle and Capen, 1845. V. 1. No. 1-10. DLC; MH; RPB. 45-5148

People's almanac for 1846 and 1847. Calculations by David Young. New York: Piercy and Reed, [1845] MWA. 45-5149

Pepperell, Massachusetts. Church of Christ. Articles of faith and covenant of the Church of Christ in Pepperell, Massachusetts, adopted August 11, 1842. Groton, [Massachusetts] Brown, 1845. 8 p. CtHC; MBC; MH; WHi. 45-5150

Percy, Thomas, 1729-1811. The hermit of Warkworth. And the two captains, by the author of 'Undine,' etc. Edited by a lady. Boston: Jordan and Wiley, 1845. 98 p. MH. 45-5151

The Percy anecdotes. Revised edition. To which is added, a valuable collection of American anecdotes. Original and select... New York: Harper and brothers, 1845. 400 p. MB; MdHi; MWinchr; NcAS. 45-5152

Perdicaris, G.A. The Greece of the Greeks. By G.A. Perdicaris, late council of the United States at Athens. New York: Paine and Burgess, 1845. 2 v. GHi; NBu; PU; RP; WM. 45-5153

Perkins, George Roberts, 1812-1876. An elementary arithmetic, designed for academies and schools; also serving as an introduction to the higher arithmetic. Third revised edition. Utica: Bennett,

Backus and Hawley, 1845. MH; NSyU; NUtHi. 45-5154

Perkins, George Roberts, 1812-1876. The elements of Algebra, designed for the use of common schools... Utica: Morrell, 1845. 254 p. DLC; MH; NUt; NUtHi. 45-5155

Perkins, Samuel, 1767-1850. The world as it is. Eighth edition. New Haven: T. Belknap, 1845. [13], 483 p. MeBa; MiD; WGr. 45-5156

Perkins, William L. An address delivered before the Geauga County Teacher's Institute, October 30, 1845. Chardon, Ohio: White's Press, [1845] 6 p. OClWHi. 45-5157

Perrin, Jean Baptiste, fl. 1786. A selection of one hundred of Perrin's fables accompanied with a key; containing the text, a literal and a free translation, arranged in such a manner as to point out the difference between the French and the English idiom. New edition. Philadelphia: Lea and Blanchard, 1845. 181 p. DLC; LN; NjP; MH; WU. 45-5158

Perrin, Jean Paul. History of the old waldenses anterior to the reformation. With illustrative notes, from modern historians and theologians. Philadelphia: Griffith and Simon, 1845. 475 p. CSfCW; MW; PPL. 45-5159

Perry, J.H. Consideration. Boston: American Pulpit, 1845. CtHC. 45-5160

Peters, John R. Guide to, or descriptive catalogue of the Chinese museum, in the Marlboro Chapel, Boston, with miscellaneous remarks upon the government, history, religions, literature, agriculture, arts, trades, manners and customs of the Chinese. Boston: Eatburn's Press, 1845. 152 p. CtHC; ICJ; MBC; PPM. 45-5161

Peters, John R. Miscellaneous remarks upon the government, history, religions, literature, agriculture, arts, trades, manners and customs of the Chinese. Boston: Eastburn's Press, 1845. 182 p. CSansS; ICJ; MH-AH; Nh; PU. 45-5162

Peterson, Edward, 1796-1855. Facts on congregational intolerance and ecclesiastical Depotism. Providence, Rhode Island. Providence: B.F. Moore, printer, 1845. 16 p. ICN; RHi RP; RPB. 45-5163

Petition for a charter for a Charles River Aqueduct Company. Boston, 1845. MCM. 45-5164

Pettibone, Philo C. The kingdom come. A sermon preached October 16, 1844 at the dedication of the Trinitarian Church. Fitchburg, 1845. 4-32 p. ICT; MBC; MPiHi; RPB; WHi. 45-5165

Petzholdt, Alexander, 1810-1889. Lectures to farmers on agricultural chemistry. New York: Greeley and McElrath, 1845. MB. 45-5166

Phases of life; or the mysteries of Catskill. Catskill, 1845. 2 v. CtHWatk; RPB. 45-5167

Phelps, Almira Lincoln, 1793-1884. Botany for beginners; an introduction to Mrs. Lincoln's lectures on botany for the use of common schools and the younger pupils of higher schools and academies. Twelfth edition. New York: Huntington and Savage, 1845. 216 p. DLC; InI; MB; MPiB; NPalk. 45-5168

Phelps, Almira Hart Lincoln, 1793-1884. Chemistry for beginners; designed for common schools, and younger pupils of higher schools and academies. New York: Huntingdon and Savage, 1845. 216 p. MH; MiU; PPF. 45-5169

Phelps, Almira Hart Lincoln, 1793-1884. Chemistry for schools, families and private students. New edition, revised and corrected. New York: Huntington and Savage, 1845. 336 p. IaDaM; NElmC; RPB. 45-5170

Phelps, Almira Hart Lincoln, 1793-1884. Familiar lectures on botany, practical elementary and physiological, with a new and full description of the plants of the United States, and cultivated exotics, etc. For use of seminaries, private students, and practical botanists. New edition, revised and enlarged. New York: Huntington and Savage; Cincinnati: H.W. Derby and company, [1845] [9]-246, 220 p. CS; IU; MNe; PSC-Hi; TxU. 45-5171

Phelps, Humphrey. Map of the city of New York, with the adjacent cities of Brooklyn and Jersey City and the village of Williamsburg. New York, 1845. MB. 45-5172

Phelps, Noah Amherst, 1788-1872. History of Simsbury, Granby and Canton, Connecticut from 1642-1845. Hartford: Case, Tiffany and Burnham, 1845. 176 p. CtB; MnHi; NNS; OFS; RHi. 45-5173

Phelps, Noah Amherst, 1788-1872. A history of the copper mines and Newgate Prison, at Granby, Connecticut. Also of the captivity of Daniel Hayes, of Granby, by the indians, in 1707. Hartford: Press of Case, Tiffany and Burnham, 1845. 4-34 p.

CtHC; ICN; MMal; OClWHi; WHi. 45-5174

Phelps, Samuel Shethar, 1793-1855. Mr. Phelp's appeal to the people of Vermont, in vindication of himself against the charges made against him [by W. Slade] upon the occasion of his re-election to the senate of the United States, in relation to his course as a senator. Middlebury, 1845. 43 p. DLC; NIC; NN; VtHi; VtMidbC. 45-5175

Phelps, Sophia Emilia Lyon Linsley. Memoir of the Rev. James H. Linsley. Hartford: Robins and Smith, 1845. 178 p. CtSoP; IEG; MH; NN; PPPrHi. 45-5176

Phelps and Ensigns' travellers guide through the United States; containing stage, steamboat, canal and railroad routes, with the distances from place to place. New York: Phelps and Ensigns, 1845. 53 p. MoSW; PHi. 45-5177

Philadelphia, Pennsylvania. Erste Deutsche Bischoefliche Methodist Kirche. Jubilaeum der Ersten Deutschen Bischoeflichen Methodisten Kirche zu. Philadelphia, 1845-. PPG. 45-5178

Philadelphia, Pennsylvania. Rules and regulations of the Board of Engineers of the Middle Fire District. Revised 1845 with the ordinance. Philadelphia, 1845. 18 p. PHi. 45-5179

Philadelphia, Pennsylvania. First Unitarian Church. Description of a concert of sacred music at the First Unitarian Church. Philadelphia, 1845. PPL. 45-5180

Philadelphia, Pennsylvania. Ronaldson's Cemetery. Deed of trust. Philadelphia, 1845. PPL. 45-5181

Philadelphia and Reading Railroad Company. Report of the president and managers of the Philadelphia and Reading Railroad Company to the stockholders. January 13, 1845. Philadelphia: Isaac M. Moss, 1845. 20 p. LU; MdHi; NjR. 45-5182

Philadelphia as it is; the stranger's guide to the public buildings, institutions, and other objects worthy of attention in the city of Philadelphia and its environs. Philadelphia, 1845. 113 p. DLC; MB; NhHi; PPFHi. 45-5183

Philadelphia Athenaeum. Circulars on building. Philadelphia, 1845. 1 p. PHi. 45-5184

Philadelphia Athenaeum. Report on the erection of a suitable building. Philadelphia, 1845. 2 p. PHi. 45-5185

Philadelphia Cemetery. Copy of the deeds of trust, charter, bylaws, and list of lot-holders: with an account of the cemetery. Philadelphia: Mifflin and Parry, 1845. 43 p. DLC; DNLM; PHi; PPN; WHi. 45-5186

Philadelphia County Volunteers. Regulations by the standing committee of companies A.B. and C. Adopted June 8th, 1845. Philadelphia, 1845. 4 p. NoLoc. 45-5187

Philadelphia Gas Works. Report to the trustees of the Philadelphia Gas Works by J.C. Cresson, superintendent. Philadelphia: Bailey, 1845. 15 p. M; PPAmP. 45-5188

Philadelphia Hospital. Philadelphia, Pennsylvania. Appeal for means to enlarge the institution. Philadelphia, 1845. PPL. 45-5189

Philadelphia Mutual Insurance Company. Act to incorporate the Philadelphia Mutual Insurance Company, passed February 24, 1845, being a supplement to the charter of the Delaware Insurance Company of Philadelphia. Philadelphia: John C. Clark, printer, 1845. 20 p. PHi; PHInsLib. 45-5190

Philadelphia medical advertiser published by Pleasants and Maris, and distributed gratuitously to the druggists and physicians of the United States. Philadelphia, 1845. PPCP. 45-5191

Philadelphia pocket diary and almanac for 1846. Philadelphia: R. Wilson Desilver, [1845] MWA. 45-5192

Philip, Robert, 1791-1858. Manly piety in its principles. Hartford: Robins and Smith, 1845. 130 p. NbOM; OrPWB. 45-5193

Philips, Lloyd C. The new birth; showing its necessity. A discourse upon heaven and hell, and one upon friends knowing each other in heaven. Cincinnati: Printed for the author by Shepard and company, 1845. 618 p. ArPb; TxAuPT. 45-5194

Phillips, Benjamin, 1805-1861. Scrofula; its nature, its causes, its prevalence and the principles of treatment. Philadelphia: Lea, 1845. 350 p. PPCP. 45-5195

Phillips, C.E. I'll not forget thee. Arranged for the guitar by James Flint. Boston: Bradlee and company, 1845. 2 p. MB. 45-5196

Phillips, Charles, 1787-1859. Speeches of Charles Phillips, esq., delivered at the bar and on various public occasions in Ireland and England. To which is added a letter to George IV. Philadelphia, 1845. MDeeP. 45-5197

Phillips, G.P. A glimpse into the world to come. Boston, 1845. MA. 45-5198

Phillips, Richard, 1767-1840. Geographical view of the world, embracing the manners, customs and pursuits of every nation founded on the best authorities. Eighth American edition revised, corrected and improved by James G. Percival. New York: Robinson, Pratt and company, 1845. 406 p. CtY; ICN; KyWA; NE; ODW. 45-5199

Phillips, Stephen C. Sunday school service book. Boston, 1845. 213 p. RPB. 45-5200

Phillips, Stephen Clarendon, 1801-1857. An address on the annexation of Texas, and the aspect of slavery in the United States, in connection therewith: delivered in Boston, November 14 and 18, 1845. Boston: W. Crosby and H.P. Nichols, 1845. 56 p. IaHi; KHi; MHi; PPPrHi; TNF. 45-5201

Phillips, Wendell, 1811-1884. Can abolitionists vote or take office under the United States constitution. New York: American Anti-slavery Society, 1845. 39 p. A-Ar; CtY; MHi; NcD; PHi. 45-5202

Phillips, Wendell, 1811-1884. The constitution, a pro-slavery compact; or selections from the Madison papers... Second

edition, enlarged. New York: American Anti-slavery Society, 1845. 131 p. DLC; ICU; MiU; NIC; OO. 45-5203

The philopoena; a perennial gift. Edited by Paschal Donaldson. New York: Printed by J. Levison, 1845. 144 p. MNF; NN; RPB. 45-5204

Phinney's calendar, or western almanack for 1846. By George R. Perkins. Cooperstown, New York: H. and E. Phinney, [1845] DLC; ICHi; MWA; NN; NUtHi. 45-5205

The phrenological almanac and physiological guide. By Orson Squire and L.N. Fowler. New York: O.S. Fowler, 1845. MS; MWA; NSyHi. 45-5206

The phrenological almanac for 1846. [By Orson Squire Fowler and Lorenzo Niles Fowler] New York, [1845] 72 p. MB; MHi. 45-5207

Phrenological and physiological almanac for 1846. By O.S. and L.N. Fowler. New York: Fowler and Wells, [1845] MWA; MWHi; WHi 45-5208

A phrenological guide. Designed for students of their own character. New York: Fowler and Wells, 1845. 54 p. NN; NRHi; OO; PPL. 45-5209

Pickering, Ellen, d. 1843. Agnes Serle, a novel. New York: E. Ferrett and company, 1845. 151 p. CtY; MH; OrU; ScC; WU. 45-5210

Pickering, Ellen, d. 1843. The expectant. A novel. New York: F. Ferrett and company, 1845. 112 p. MMel; NjR; NRMA; OrU; RPA. 45-5211

Pickering, Ellen, d. 1843. The fright. New York: E. Ferrett and company, 1845. 120 p. CtY; NjRp ScU; WU. 45-5212

Pickering, Ellen, d. 1843. The grumbler, a novel. New York: Harper and brothers, 1845. CtY; MdRo. 45-5213

Pickering, Ellen, d. 1843. The heiress, a novel. New York: E. Ferrett and company, 1845. 160 p. MH; NjR; OrU; WU. 45-5214

Pickering, Ellen, d. 1843. The heiress, a novel. New York and Philadelphia: E. Ferrett and company, 1845. 45-5215

Pickering, Ellen, d. 1843. The merchant's daughter. New York and Philadelphia: E. Ferrett and company, 1845. 117 p. NRMA; WU. 45-5216

Pickering, Ellen, d. 1843. The prince and the pedler; or the siege of Bristol. New York and Philadelphia: E. Ferrett and company, 1845. 110 p. NjR; NRMA. 45-5217

Pickering, Ellen, d. 1843. The quiet husband. Philadelphia and New York, 1845? CtY. 45-5218

Pickering, Ellen, d. 1843. The secret foe. An historical novel. Philadelphia, 1845. 128 p. CtY; NjP; NN. 45-5219

Pickering, Ellen, d. 1843. Select works. New York: E. Ferrett and company, 1845. InU. 45-5220

Pickering, Ellen, d. 1843. The squire, a novel. New York: E. Ferrett and company, 1845. 109 p. CtY; NjP; NRMA; ScC; WU. 45-5221

Pickering, Ellen, d. 1843. Who shall be heir? New York and Philadelphia, [1845?] CtY. 45-5222

Pickering, John, 1777-1846. Memoir on the language and inhabitants of Lord North's Island. Cambridge: Metcalf and company, 1845. 247 p. CtHWatk; DLC; LNH; MB; PPAN. 45-5223

Picket, Albert, 1771-1850. Introduction to Picket's expositor. By A. Picket and John W. Picket. Cincinnati: U.P. James, 1845. MH. 45-5224

Picket, Albert, 1777-1850. The normal teacher; being an introduction to Picket's introduction; containing an improved system of illustrative teaching... Cincinnati: J. Ernst, 1845. 190 p. DLC. 45-5225

Pickett, A.J. A reply to the objections urged against a prohibitory law in relation to the introduction of negroes. By A.J. Pickett, of Montgomery. Wetumpka: Printed by Charles Yancery, 1845. 12 p. A-Ar. 45-5226

Picknan, C. Gayton. An address delivered before the East Cambridge Temperance Society, December 22, 1835. Also an address delivered before the Ladies Benevolent Society at Cambridge, December 18, 1836. Boston: C.C. Little and J. Brown, 1845. 31 p. A-Ar; MDeeP; MiD-B; RPB. 45-5227

Picot, Charles, 1789-1852. First lessons in French; consisting of rules and directions for the attainment of a just pronunciation. Second improved edition. Philadelphia: Thomas, Cowperthwait and company, 1845. 132, 18 p. MoS; NbOM; NIC-L; NjR. 45-5228

Picot, Charles, 1789-1852. Fleurs du Parnasse Francais; or elegant extracts from the most approved productions of the best French poets. Philadelphia: Thomas, Cowperthwait and company, 1845. 252 p. ICN; MB; MLy; NjR; TxU. 45-5229

Picot, Charles, 1789-1852. The French student's assistant; being a recapitulation of the most important grammatical examples and facts of the French language; with a key to pronunciation. Second improved edition. Philadelphia: Thomas, Cowperthwait and company, 1845. 48 p. GDu; MdBE; NbOM; NjR; PPL. 45-5230

Picot, Charles, 1789-1852. Historical narrations in French; consisting of interesting historical pieces, intended for reading, translation, and particularly for narration. Philadelphia: Thomas, Cowperthwait and company, 1845. 252 p. ArBaA; CtHWatk; MPiB; NjR; PPL. 45-5231

Picot, Charles, 1789-1852. Interesting narrations in French; consisting of interesting tales, fables and anecdotes, intended for reading... Philadelphia: Thomas, Cowperthwait and company, 1845. 180 p. ICMCHi; MH; PHi; RPB; TNP. 45-5232

Picot, Charles, 1789-1852. Scientific narrations, etc., in French; consisting of instructive pieces, relating chiefly to scientific and to other interesting subjects, intended for reading... carefully selected and arranged for American schools and private students. Philadelphia: Thomas, Cowperthwait and company, 1845. 396 p. NbOM; OO. 45-5233

Pictet, Benedict, 1655-1724. Christian theology; translated from the Latin of Benedict Pictet. Philadelphia: Presbyterian board of publication, 1845? 434 p. ICN; KyLoS; NNUT; ODaB; PPM. 45-5234

Pictorial almanac for 1846. New York: Baker, Crane and Day, [1845] MB; MWA. 45-5235

Picture riddler. Boston: Munrow and Francis, 1845. NPV. 45-5236

Picture riddler. Boston: G.W. Cottrell, [1845?] 120 p. NN. 45-5237

Pictures and poems. Providence, Rhode Island: George P. Daniels, 1845. 16 p. RPB. 45-5238

Pictures and stories about birds. Worcester: J. Grout, Jr., [1845] 16 p. MWA. 45-5239

Pierce, George Edmund, 1794-1871. A plea for stability and permanence in institutions of learning; delivered before the trustees, officers and students of the Cleveland Medical College, February 26, 1845. Cleveland: Younglove's Steam Power Press, 1845. 16 p. DLC; MH; NNNAM; OClWHi; WU-M. 45-5240

Pierce, Willard, 1790-1860. A discourse, preached at the dedication of the meeting house of the Union Church and Society, East Bridgewater, Massachusetts, January 1, 1845. By W. Pierce, Pastor of the North Church, Abington. Published by request. Boston: Press of T.R. Marvin, 1845. 20 p. MAnP; MiD-B; MWA; OO; RPB. 45-5241

Pierpont, John, 1785-1866. The

American first class book, or exercises in reading and recitation. Selected principally from modern authors of Great Britain and America. Thirtieth edition. New York: G.F. Cooledge, [1845?] MH. 45-5242

Pierpont, John, 1785-1866. National reader. Twenty-eighth edition. New York: G.F. Cooledge, [1845?] MH. 45-5243

Pierpont, John, 1785-1866. Young reader. Twentieth edition. New York: G.F. Cooledge, [1845] AU; MH; MnU; NcU. 45-5244

Pike, John Gregory, 1784-1854. The divine origin of christianity. New York: R. Carter and brother, 1845. 176 p. ICP. 45-5245

Pike, Robert. Mnemonics; the analytical basis of classification, and the system of chronics. Boston: Pike, Hilborn and company, 1845. 34 p. MWA; NbHi. 45-5246

Pike, Stephen. The teachers' assistant; or a system of practical arithmetic; wherein the several rules of that useful science are illustrated by a variety of examples. A new edition, with corrections and additions by the author. Philadelphia: Thomas Davies, 1845. 198 p. MH; MiU. 45-5247

Pillsbury, J.D. Annual public address... Middlesex District Medical Society, at Lowell, May 23, 1845. Lowell: Nathaniel L. Dayton, 1845. 27 p. MH-M; MLow; NBMS. 45-5248

Pilsbury, Amos, 1805-1875. Memorial of Amos Pilsbury, late warden of the state prison, to the general assembly, May session, 1845. Together with his report for the nine months ending December 31, 1844. Hartford: Press of Alfred E. Burr, 1845. 33 p. Ct; CtSoP; MWA. 45-5249

Pinamonti, F. Hell opened to Christians; to caution them from entering into it; or considerations on the infernal pains, proposed to our meditations to avoid them and distributed for every day in the week written in Italian by F. Pinamonti. Philadelphia: Henry McGrath, [1845] 122 p. CoDR; MdW; MeSU; NcBe; OCX. 45-5250

Pinckney, Henry Laurens, 1794-1863. A memoir of the late Robert L. Hayne, of South Carolina. Charleston: Burges and James, 1845. CU. 45-5251

Pinckney, Henry Laurens, 1794-1863. The necessity of popular enlightenment to the honor and welfare of the state. An oration delivered before the literary societies of the South Carolina College, on December 3, 1844. Columbia, South Carolina: Issued from I.C. Morgan's Letter Press, 1845. 28 p. A-Ar; ICU; GDec-Ct; ScC; TSewU. 45-5252

Pingree, Enoch Merrill, 1817-1849. A debate in the doctrine of universal salvation; held in Cincinnati, Ohio, from March 24, to April 1, 1845, between Rev. E.M. Pingree and Rev. N.L. Rice. Taken down by a reporter, and revised by the parties. Cincinnati: J.A. James; New York: J.S. Redfield, 1845. [13]-429 p. CU; IaMp; KyLoP; NbOP; PPL. 45-5253

Pingree, Enoch Merrill, 1817-1849. A debate on universalism: held in Warsaw, Kentucky, May, 1844, between Rev. E.M. Pingree... and Rev. John L.

Walker... Reported by a stenographer, and revised by the disputants. Cincinnati: W.L. Mendenhall, printer, 1845. [5]-357 p. ICU; KyLoS; LNB; TxU. 45-5254

Pinkerton Academy, Derry, H.H. [sic] Catalogue of the officers and students. Andover, 1845-1847. PU. 45-5255

Pinkney, W. An address delivered before the Rockville and Bladensburg Lyceums. Published by request. Baltimore: Printed by Joseph Robinson, 1845. 16 p. MdBD. 45-5256

Piratical and tragical almanac for 1846. Philadelphia: John B. Perry, [1845] MWA. 45-5257

Pise, Charles Constantine, 1802-1866. Lectures on the invocation of saints, veneration of sacred images and purgatory. New York: H.G. Daggers, 1845. 67 p. IaHi; MWA; NjR; PPL; ViRut. 45-5258

Pise, Charles Constantine, 1802-1866. Saint Ignatius and his first companions. New York: Ed. Dunnigan, 1845. [15]-361 p. GDecCT; IEG; MdW; NNUT; OCX. 45-5259

Pise, Charles Constantine, 1802-1866. Zenosius; or the pilgrim convert. New York: Edward Dunigan, 1845. 279 p. CU; MiU; KEmT; LN; MdBLC. 45-5260

Pitcairn, David, d. 1870. Perfect peace letters. Memorial of the late John Warren Howell. New York: Robert Carter, 1845. 175 p. GDecCT; MBC; PU 45-5261

Pitcher, William. Grace; a series of discourses delivered to the people of his charge, in the Reformed Protestant

Dutch Church of the Boght, 1844-1845. Published by consistory at their request. Albany: Erastus H. Pease, 1845. 176 p. NRSB. 45-5262

Pitt, William, 1708-1778. Celebrated speeches of Chatham, Burke and Erskine to which is added the argument of Mr. Mackintosh in the case of Peltier. Selected by a member of the Philadelphia Bar. Philadelphia: E.C. and J. Biddle, 1845. 538 p. NBu; NN; NNF; MoFloSS. 45-5263

Pittsburgh, Pennsylvania. Digest of the ordinances of the corporation of the city of Pittsburgh, and of the acts of assembly relating thereto. Pittsburgh: Whitney, 1845. PPi; PU. 45-5264

Pittsfield, Massachusetts. Reports of committees... to examine the House of correction... Pittsfield: Phinehas Allen and son, 1845. 23 p. MnHi 45-5265

Planche, James Robinson, 1796-1880. Somebody also; a farce, in one act. New York: Samuel French, [1845] InU; MB; MH; NIC-L; OCl. 45-5266

Plato. Contra Atheos. Plato against the atheists; or the tenth book of the dialogue on laws, accompanied with critical notes, and followed by extended dissertations on some of the main points of the Platonic philosophy and theology, especially as compared with the Holy Scriptures. By Tayler Lewis. New York: Harper and brothers, 1845. 378 p. CtMW; ICU; MeBat; NBuG; PPPrHi. 45-5267

Playfair, John, 1748-1819. Elements of geometry: containing the first six books of Euclid, with a supplement on the quadrature of the circle, and the geometry of solids. From the last London edition, enlarged. New York: W.E. Dean, 1845. 317 p. MnAn; MSaP; NbOM; PEaL; TxGR. 45-5268

Plow boy's almanac for 1845. By Robinson and Jones. Cincinnati: 1845? OCHP. 45-5269

Plutarchus. Plutarch's lives of the most select and illustrious characters of antiquity translated from the original Greek with notes, historical and critical by John Langhorn and William Langhorn and others. Ithaca: Mack, Andrus and company, 1845. 432 p. C; FU. 45-5270

Plutarchus. Plutarch's lives translated from the original Greek; with notes, critical and historical and a life of Plutarch. By John Langhorne and William Langhorne. New York: Harper brothers, 1845. 688 p. IaMp; LN. 45-5271

Plymouth almanac, directory and business advertiser for 1846. Plymouth, Massachusetts: Timothy Berry, [1845] MWA. 45-5272

Pocket almanack. Boston: T. Groom and company, 1845. MWA. 45-5273

The pocket classical dictionary and chronological companion; being a guide to the study of mythology, ancient history and ancient geography. Philadelphia: G. Bell, 1845. 266 p. IEG; MB; MH; PMA. 45-5274

The pocket lawyer and family conveyancer. Comprising a selection of forms necessary in all mercantile and money transactions. Compiled by a gentleman of the bar. Philadelphia:

Charles Bell, 1845. 142 p. DLC; ICBB; MH-L; MWauHi; MBevHi.Poe, 45-5275

Poco Mas, pseud. Scenes and adventures in Spain. Philadelphia, 1845. MB; PPL-R. 45-5276

Poe, Edgar Allen, 1809-1849. The conchologist's first book; or a system of testaceous malacology, arranged expressly for the use of schools in which the animals, according to Cuvier, are given with the shells, and a great number of new species added. Philadelphia: Harrington ad Haswell, 1845. 166 p. CSt; IaDaM; ICU; MnSJ; NbU. 45-5277

Poe, Edgar Allen, 1809-1849. The raven. Boston: Richard G. Badger and company, [1845] 36 p. MdCatS. 45-5278

Poe, Edgar Allen, 1809-1849. The raven and other poems. New York: Little Leather Library Corporation, 1845. 160 p. MnSM. 45-5279

Poe, Edgar Allen, 1809-1849. The raven and other poems. New York: Wiley and Putnam, 1845. 91 p. MeBat; NBuG; RPA; TxSaO; ViU. 45-5280

Poe, Edgar Allan, 1809-1849. Tales... First edition. New York: Wiley and Putnam, 1845. 228 p. CSmH; MB: MeBat; NN; PU. 45-5281

The poetical works of Milton, Young, Gray, Beattie and Collins. Philadelphia: Grigg and Elliot, 1845. 5 pts. in 1 v. IU; OCU; OrCS; ViU. 45-5282

The poetical works of Rogers, Campbell, J. Montgomery, Lamb and Kirke White. Philadelphia: Grigg and Elliot, 1845. GA; IaMu; LNX; MWal; NRU. 45-5283

The poetry of the sentiments. Edited by R.W. Griswold. Philadelphia: John Locken, 1845. 320 p. LNH. 45-5284

Poinsett, Joel Roberts, 1779-1851. Oration on the life and character of Andrew Jackson, delivered on July 4, 1845. [Greenville, South Carolina, 1845] 8 p. DLC; PPL. 45-5285

Pollard, Andrew, 1814-1886. The sanctuary, the design of its services, and the requisites to their acceptableness and efficiency. A discourse... in Barnstable, October 15, 1845. Boston: Hallworth, 1845. 23 p. CtHC; IaPeC; NHC-S; OO; RPB. 45-5286

Pollok, Robert, 1798-1827. The course of time, a poem, in ten books... with a sketch of the life of the author. New York: Kearny, 1845. 248 p. CBPac; ICart-C; PLFM; TxAu. 45-5287

Pollok, Robert, 1798-1827. Helen of the glen; a tale of the Scotch covenanters. New York: Robert Carter, 1845. 113 p. CSmH. 45-5288

Pollock, Robert, 1798-1827. Tales of the Scottish Covenanters. New York: Robert Carter; Pittsburgh, Thomas Carter, 1845. 103 p. ScCoB. 45-5289

Polo, Marco, 1254-1323? The travels of Marco Polo, greatly amended and enlarged from valuable early manuscripts recently published by the French Society of Geography, and in Italy by Count Baldelli Boni. New York: Harper and brothers, 1845. 326 p. InCW; NCaS; OSW; PAnL; PPA. 45-5290

Pomey, Francois Antoine, 1618-1673. Tooke's pantheon of the Heathen Gods, and illustrious heroes. Revised for a classical course of education, and adapted for the use of students of every age and of either sex. Baltimore: Cushing and brother, 1845. 305 p. IJ; IU; LStBA. 45-5291

Pomroy, John N. A defence of our naturalization laws, with a friendly warning to members of the Native American Party. Second edition. Norristown, Pennsylvania: A Slemmer, printer, 1845. 22 p. DLC; ICN; IU; PHi. 45-5292

Poncelet, Jean Victor, 1788-1867. Sustaining walls; geometrical constructions to determine their thickness under various circumstances, derived chiefly from a memoir of M. Poncelet with modifications and extensions by D.P. Woodbury. Washington: W.Q. Force, 1845. 36 p. MB; MH; WU-En. 45-5293

Pond, Enoch, 1791-1882. The world's salutation. Boston: Massachusetts Sabbath School Society, 1845. 414 p. ArCH; IEG; MiOC; NbCrD; OWoC. 45-5294

Popular directions for the prevention and cure of the headache. Philadelphia, 1845. PPL. 45-5295

Poole, John. The comic miscellany for 1845. By John Poole, Esq. New York: William H. Colyer, 1845. 80 p. LNH; NN. 45-5296

Poole, Sophia Lane. The Englishwoman in Egypt; letters from Cairo, written during a residence there in 1842 with E.W. Lane. By his sister. Philadelphia: G.B. Zieber and company, 1845. 247 p. MoK; MWA; NNC; NP; RP. 45-5297

Poor will's almanac for the year 1846: being the second after leap year... Philadelphia: Joseph M. Dowell, [1845] MWA; Nj. 45-5298

Pope, Alexander. The essay on man; in four epistles to Henry St. John, Lord Bolingbroke; by Alexander Pope. To which are added notes, grammatical and explanatory; adapting it to the use of schools. Claremont, New Hampshire: Manufacturing company, 1845. 60 p. MB; MBC; NNC. 45-5299

Pope, R.S. A sermon delivered in Hyannis, on October 19, 1845. Barnstable, 1845. 15 p. MMeT. 45-5300

The pope and the Presbyterians, a review of the warning of Jefferson. Respecting the dangers to be apprehended to our civil and religious liberties, from Presbyterianism. By an American citizen, author of "A voice from Rome answered." Philadelphia: James M. Campbell; New York: Saxton and Miles, 1845. 72 p. KyLoP; MBC; NjR; PPPrHi; ViRut. 45-5301

Popery in the Protestant churches; by Francis Hawley, pastor of the Church of Christ in Cazenovia. Syracuse: Tucker and Kinney, 1845. 12 p. DLC; N. 45-5302

The pope's journey to heaven; a poem. Philadelphia, 1845. 32 p. PHi; RPB. 45-5303

The popular national songster, and Lucy Neal and Dan Tucker's delight, containing a choice collection of the most admired, patriotic, comic, Irish, negro and sentimental songs. Philadelphia: J.B. Perry, 1845. NbU; NcD. 45-5304

Porter, Benjamin Faneuil, 1808-1868. Odd fellowship, and its purposes. The substance of a discourse delivered before the Tuscaloosa Lodge... and other citizens of Tuscaloosa. Tuscaloosa: Printed by M.D.J. Slade, 1845. 22 p. NcD. 45-5305

Porter, Benjamin Faneuil, 1808-1868. The past and the present. A discourse delivered before the Erosophic Society of the University of Alabama. Tuscaloosa: Printed by M.P.J. Slade, 1845. 39 p. AB; CU; OCHP; TxU; ViU. 45-5306

Porter, Ebenezer, 1772-1834. The rhetorical reader; consisting of instructions for regulating the voice, with a rhetorical notation, illustrating inflection... Two hundred and thirtieth edition. Cincinnati: William H. Moore and company, 1845. InGrD. 45-5307

Porter, Elbert Stothoff, 1819-1888. A sermon occasioned by the death of Mrs. Barrent Van Buren. Hudson: Bryan and Moore, printers, 1845. 12 p. NjR. 45-5308

Porter, James, 1808-1888. Modern infidelity, alias come-out-ism, as taught by ultra non-resistants, transcendentalists, garrisonians, and other revolutionists; in three lectures. Second edition. Boston: David H. Ela, 1845. 56 p. IEG; MB; MBNMHi; MH. 45-5309

Porter, James H. A new system of arithmetic and mathematics. Fourth edition. New York: Piercy and Reed, printers, 1845. 240 p. MH; MoSpD; NNC. 45-5310

Porter, Jane, 1776-1850. Sir Edward Seaward's narrative of his shipwreck, and consequent discovery of certain islands in the Caribbean Sea. Edited by Miss

Jane Porter. New York: Harper and brothers, 1845. InU; RPE; ScGrw. 45-5311

Porter, Jane, 1776-1850. The Scottish chiefs. A romance. Newark, New Jersey: B. Olds, 1845. 3 v. CL. 45-5312

Porter, Jane, 1776-1850. Thaddeus of Warsaw. New and revised edition. Chicago: Donohue, Hennsberry and company, [1845] 2 v. MH. 45-5313

Porter, Jane, 1776-1850. Thaddeus of Warsaw. New and revised edition. Hartford: A. Andrus and son, 1845. 2 v. MH. 45-5314

Porter, Jane, 1776-1850. Thaddeus of Warsaw. New and revised edition. New York: A. Cogswell, [1845?] NjP. 45-5315

Porter, Jane, 1776-1850. Thaddeus of Warsaw. New and revised edition. New York: George Routledge, [1845?] 459 p. CFrT; CSansS; ViU. 45-5316

Porter, Jane, 1776-1850. Thaddeus of Warsaw. New and revised edition. New York: Hurst, [1845?] 461 p. IaU; MH; NcU; NN; OO. 45-5317

Porter, Jane, 1776-1850. Thaddeus of Warsaw. New and revised edition. New York: J.W. Lovell, [1845?] 459 p. CoFtm; NNC. 45-5318

Porter, Jane, 1776-1850. Thaddeus of Warsaw. New and revised edition. Philadelphia: Porter and Coates, 1845. 536 p. PSt. 45-5319

Porter, William Henry, 1817-1861. Proverbs arranged in alphabetical order in two parts... Boston: James Munroe and company, 1845. 10-280 p. CtHC; MBC; NhPet; RPA. 45-5320

Porter, William S. Life of Rowland Hill. New York: Lewis Colby, 1845. 376 p. KyPr. 45-5321

Porter, William Trotter. The big bear of the Arkansas, and other sketches, illustrative of characters and incidents in the South and Southwest. Edited by William T. Porter. Philadelphia: Carey and Hart, 1845. 181 p. ICN; MoS; MoSHi; NcAS; NcD. 45-5322

Porteus, Beilly. Summary of the principal evidences for the truth and divine origin of the Christian revelation. Philadelphia: Henry Longstreth, 1845. 96 p. PHi; PWaybu. 45-5323

Potter, Alonzo, 1800-1865. A discourse, pronounced at Schenectady, July 22, 1845, on the fiftieth anniversary of the foundation of Union College. Schenectady: I. Riggs, printer, 1845. 29 p. CtHT; ICMe; MB; PPAmP; WHi. 45-5324

Potter, Alonzo, 1800-1865. Handbook for readers and students, intended as a help to individuals, associations, school districts and seminaries of learning, in the selection of works for reading, investigation or professional study. New York: Harper and brothers, 1845. 330 p. MH; MsU; OCo; PP; RWe. 45-5325

Potter, Andrew P. 1822-1846. Trial and confession of Andrew P. Potter, for the murder of Lucius P. Osborn; together with the judge's charge to the jury and sentence... New Haven, 1845. 32 p. Ct; MH-L; PP. 45-5326

Potter, Horatio, 1802-1887. Remarks in

favor of free churches; being part of an address delivered on the occasion of laying the cornerstone of a free church at Fort Edward, Washington County, New York. Albany, 1845. 12 p. MB; MHi; NNG; WHi. 45-5327

Potter, Lewis. An appeal to the law and to the testimony in behalf of the Methodist Episcopal Church. Middlebury: Justus Cobb, printer, 1845. 24 p. MB; PPPrHi; VtMiS; VtMidSM. 45-5328

Potter, Reuben Marmaduke, 1802-1890. A prophetic article published in the Galveston Civilian. n.p., 1845. 12 p. DLC; TxH. 45-5329

Poughkeepsie almanac for 1846. Poughkeepsie, New York: George Magell, [1845] MWA. 45-5330

Pound, Jesse. The echo of truth to the voice of slander: or John B. Gough's early history by his foster father. New York: Stanford Swords, 1845. 20 p. MB; MWA; NGH; NjR; PPPrHi. 45-5331

Powell, Thomas. An essay on apostolic succession; being a defense of genuine Protestant ministry. New York: T. Lane and C.B. Tippett for the Methodist Episcopal Church, 1845. 354 p. C-S; OU; PReaAT; TNT; WHi. 45-5332

Power, Thomas. Solo and chorus. Written expressly for the festival of the Massachusetts Horticultural Society, September 19, 1845. Boston, 1845. MH. 45-5333

Powers, Daniel. A grammar, on an entirely new system. West Brookfield, 1845.

12-188 p. CtHWatk; NNC; OSW; RP; WU. 45-5334

Powers, J.A. Mathematical tables for practical men; comprising several new and useful tables adopted to the wants of surveyors, engineers and navigators, New York: C. Wells, 1845. 59 p. DLC; MB. 45-5335

Powers, Pike. Address delivered before the Sons of Temperance, in Staunton, July 4, 1845. Staunton: Printed at the Spectator office, 1845. 15 p. ViRU. 45-5336

Practical morality or a guide to man and mariners, consisting of Lord Chesterfield advice to his son. Hartford: S. Andrews and son, 1845. MH. 45-5337

Practical trigonometry, mensuration and surveying, for the use of students in Rensselaer Institute. Troy: Printed at the Budget office, 1845. 12 p. NjR. 45-5338

The practice of christian graces; or the whole duty of man, laid down, a plain and familiar way, for the use of all. With private devotions for several occasions. Philadelphia: T. Wardle, 1845. 336 p. LU; MA; OrPD; PPLT; TChU. 45-5339

Prairie farmer almanac for 1846. Chicago, Illinois: W.W. Barlow and company, [1845] MWA. 45-5340

Pratt, John Henry, 1809-1871. The mathematical principles of Mechanical philosophy, and their application to elementary mechanics and architecture, but chiefly to the theory of universal gravitation. Second edition, revised and improved. Cambridge, Massachusetts:

Barclay and Macmillan, 1845. 620 p. CtY; MoFayC; NN; PPF; ViU. 45-5341

Pratt, Stillman, 1804-1862. Glory and downfall of Edom, written for the Massachusetts Sabbath School Society, and revised by the committee of publication. Boston: Sabbath School Society, 1845. 54 p. NoLoc. 45-5342

Pratt, Zadock, 1790-1871. Address delivered at the fair of the Greene County Agricultural Society, September 25, 1845. Catskill, Maine, 1845. 8 p. NCH; NjR; NN; WU-A. 45-5343

Pratt, Zadock, 1798-1871. Address of Mr. Zadock, of New York, to his constituents. [Washington, 1845?] 6 p. OClWHi. 45-5344

Pray, Lewis G. The Boston Sunday school hymn book, with devotional exercises. Approved by the Boston Sunday School Society. Revised edition. Boston: Benjamin H. Greene, 1845. 180 p. ICCB; PMA. 45-5345

Presbuteros, pseud. The Bible against the gallows. New York, 1845. MB. 45-5346

Presbuteros, pseud. The Bible against the gallows; an essay on capitol punishment. New York, 1845. 88, 20 p. MBLi-Hi; WU. 45-5347

A presbyter of New Jersey. A homily for the times; the lofty and the lowly; a sermon for the eleventh Sunday after Trinity. New York: Stanford and Swords, 1845. 28 p. MNF. 45-5348

The Presbyterian almanac adapted for the use in every part of the United States, for the year of our Lord and Jesus Christ. 1845... Philadelphia: Presbyterian board of Publication, Paul I. Jones, Publishing Agent, 1845. 48 p. IaDaP; NCH; OdW. 45-5349

Presbyterian Church in the United States of America. Church manual for the use of the churches under the care of the presbytery of Montrose. Prepared by order of the presbytery and adopted by them, April, 1845. New York: J.F. Trow and company, 1845. 24 p. ICP; NNUT. 45-5350

Presbyterian Church in the United States of America. Synod of Buffalo. Alleged relations of the American board of C.F. missions to slavery examined. By a committee of the Presbytery of Buffalo. [Buffalo, 1845?] 52 p. PPPrHi; WBeloC. 45-5351

Presbyterian Church in the United States of America. Synod of New York and New Jersey. Proceedings of the Synod of New York and New Jersey, at their late session, in reference to the publications of the American Tract Society, together with an abstract of the report of the Synod's committee upon the same. Originally reported for the New York Evangelist. New York: R. Lockwood and son, 1845. 30 p. CBPSR; ICU; MBC; NjR; PHi. 45-5352

Presbyterian reporter. Alton, Illinois, 1845-. v. 1-. PHi; PPPrHi. 45-5353

Prescott, J.H. Valuable receipts; or the mystery of wealth; containing the lady's cook book, together with several hundred very rare receipts and patents, to be found in no other work. Boston:

Printed at the office of Mead and Beal, 1845. 48 p. MB; MPeHi; Nh-Hi. 45-5354

Prescott, William Hickling, 1796-1859. Biographical and critical miscellanies. New York: Harper and brothers, 1845. 638 p. ArL; KyLx; NUt; ScDuE; ViRut. 45-5355

Prescott, William Hickling, 1796-1859. The complete works of William H. Prescott. Biographical and critical miscellaneous. New York: Thomas Y. Crowell and company, 1845. 464 p. WvU. 45-5356

Prescott, William Hickling, 1796-1859. History of the conquest of Mexico, with a preliminary view of the ancient Mexican civilization and the life of the conqueror, Hernando Cortes. New York: Harper and brothers, 1845. 3 v. CtHT; IUr; MCR; NcMHi; TxGR. 45-5357

Prescott, William Hickling, 1796-1859. History of the reign of Ferdinand and Isabella, the Catholic. Tenth edition. New York: Harper and brothers, 1845. 3 v. AzU; ICMe; MdBD; PV; ScDuE. 45-5358

Present for the young. First American from the eighth London edition. Philadelphia: W.G. Wardle, 1845. 180 p. CtY; PU. 45-5359

A present for the young. Second from the London edition. Boston: Massachusetts Sunday School Society, 1845. 162 p. GAlN. 45-5360

A present to the rumsellers of New Haven and Boston. [Boston? 1845?] Broadside. NN. 45-5361

Preston, Lyman, b. 1795. Treatise on book keeping; a common sense guide to a common sense mind. In two parts. New York: Collins, brother and company, 1845. 224 p. MH; NhD. 45-5362

Prevost, Antoine Francois, 1697-1763. Manon Lescaut. By the Abbe Prevost. Boston: Dwight Ruggles, 1845. 144 p. CtY; DLC; OFH. 45-5363

Price, William, 1794-1868. Letter to the Hon. John G. Chapman, speaker of the House of Delegates of Maryland. n.p., 1845. 15 p. MdBJ. 45-5364

Priest, Josiah, 1788-1851. Slavery, as it relates to the negro, or African race, examined in the light of circumstances, history and the Holy Scriptures: with an account of the origin of the black man's color, causes of his state of servitude and traces of his character as well in ancient as in modern times: with strictures on abolitionism. Albany, New York: C. Van Benthuysen and company, 1845. 340 p. MH; MnU; OU. 45-5365

Prime, Nathaniel Scudder, 1785-1856. A history of Long Island, from its first settlement by Europeans, to the year 1845, with special reference to its ecclesiastical concerns... New York and Pittsburg: R. Carter, 1845. 420 p. CtMW; NHem; OClWHi; PU; TxH. 45-5366

Prime, Samuel Ireneus, 1812-1885. Elizabeth Thornton; or the flower and fruit of female piety. Second edition. New York: M.W. Dodd, 1845. 211 p. CSdNHM; NNUT. 45-5367

Prince, John. Rural lays and sketches and other poems. Essex, [Massachusetts]

Printed by the author, 1845. [7]-83 p. ICU; MH; MPeHi; RPB. 45-5368

Princeton Theological Seminary. Catalogue of the officers and students of the theological seminary of the Presbyterian Church. Princeton, 1845-6. 16 p. MB; MBC; MH-AH; NjP; OClWHi. 45-5369

Princeton University. Catalogue of the American Whig Society, instituted in the college of New Jersey, 1769. Princeton: Published by order of the society, 1845. 63 p. DHEW; ICN; MdBP; NN; OClWHi. 45-5370

Princeton University. Catalogue of the Cliosophic Society, instituted in the college of New Jersey, 1765. Princeton: John T. Robinson, 1845. 48 p. KyDC; OClWHi. 45-5371

Princeton University. Catalogue of the officers and students of the college of New Jersey, for 1844-1845. Princeton: John T. Robinson, 1845. 24 p. M; NBLi-Hi; OCHP; OClWHi. 45-5372

Princeton University. Catalogus Collegii neo-caesariensis. Rerumpublicarum foederatarum Americae summae potestatis anno LXX. Princetoniae: Typis J.T. Robinson, 1845. 73 p. MH; NN; Nj; OCHP. 45-5373

Prindle's almanac for 1846. By Charles Prindle. Branford, Connecticut: E.F. Rogers, [1845] CtMW; MWA. 45-5374

Prindle's almanac for 1846. By Charles Prindle. New Haven, Connecticut: A.H. Maltby and company, [1845] MWA 45-5375

Prison Association of New York. Annual report. Albany: [etc., 1845?] 1st-. CU; ICJ; MdBJ; MH; OCl. 45-5376

Pritts, Joseph. The farmer's book and family instructor, embracing the most important of the recent scientific discoveries connected with practical agriculture. Carefully compiled from the best sources. Chambersburg, Pennsylvania: Printed for purchasers, 1845. 609 p. GMiloC; IU; MoInRC; PP. 45-5377

The prize story book; consisting chiefly of tales translated from the German, French and Italian, together with select tales from the English. Philadelphia: George S. Appleton, 1845. 280 p. FTU; LNH; PPL. 45-5378

Proceedings of a convention held at Carthage in Hancock County, Ill., on Tuesday and Wednesday, October 1st and 2nd, 1846. Published by order of the convention under the superintendence of the military committee of Quincy, Ill. [Quincy, 1845] 9 p. ICHi; MH; MoKU. 45-5379

Proceedings of a public meeting in behalf of the society for the promotion of collegiate and theological education at the west, held in Park Street Church, Boston, May 28, 1845. New York: J.F. Trow and company, 1845. 16 p. TxHuT. 45-5380

Proclamation to the Church of Jesus Christ of Latter Day Saints. New York, 1845. 16 p. USlC. 45-5381

Proctor, John Waters, 1791-1874. Address to the Essex Agricultural Society, September 25, 1844. Salem: Printed at the Gazette office, 1845. 46 p. MBAt; MH; MHi; MPeHi. 45-5382

Promovide por el Sor. Toserero departamental en averiguacion de los efectes del Sor. [Monterey? 1845?] 13 p. CU-B. 45-5383

The prophetic almanac for 1846. By Orson Pratt. New York: Messenger office, [1845] DLC. 45-5384

Protest against American slavery by Unitarian ministers. Medford? 1845. 20 p. MnHi; NIC. 45-5385

Protest of some free men, states and presses against the Texas rebellion, against the law of nature and of nations. Anti-Texas Legion. Sold at the Patriot office. Albany, 1845. 72 p. MB. 45-5386

Protestant Episcopal Church in the United States of America. Journal of the proceedings of the bishops, clergy and laity of the Protestant Episcopal Church in the United States of America. New York: James A. Sparks, 1845. MBD; NBuDD; NGH; RNR. 45-5387

Protestant Episcopal Church in the United States of America. Journal of the seventh annual convention of the Portestant Episcopal Church in the diocese of Louisiana, held in St. Johns Church West Baton Rouge on April 3, and 4th, 1845. New Orleans: T. Rea, printer, 1845. 28 p. NcU. 45-5388

Protestant Episcopal Church in the United States of America. Tract on industry; being one of the homilies of the church; to which is added a sermon on the same subject, preached and published in the year 1838, Bishop

Meade. Alexandria: Printed at the office of the Son Churchman, 1845. 24 p. MdBD; MdBJ. 45-5389

Protestant Episcopal Church in the United States of America. Book of Common Prayer. The book of common prayer and administration of the sacraments, and other rites and ceremonies of the church according to the use of the Protestant Episcopal Church, together with the psalter or Psalms of David. Buffalo: Oliver Steele, 1845. 288 p. MBrigStJ; MSwan; NRU. 45-5390

Protestant Episcopal Church in the United States of America. Book of Common Prayer. The book of common prayer and administration of the sacraments, and other rites and ceremonies of the church according to the use of the Protestant Episcopal Church, together with the psalter or Psalms of David. Buffalo: W.B.and C.E. Peck, 1845. 286, 124 p. IaSlB; DLC; MB; OAlM. 45-5391

Protestant Episcopal Church in the United States of America. Book of Common Prayer. The book of common prayer and administration of the sacraments, and other rites and ceremonies of the church according to the use of the Protestant Episcopal Church, together with the psalter or Psalms of David. Canandaigua: George W. Bemis, [1845] NCanHi. 45-5392

Protestant Episcopal Church in the United States of America. Book of Common Prayer. The book of common prayer and administration of the sacraments, and other rites and ceremonies of the church according to the use of the Protestant Episcopal Church, together with the psalter or Psalms of David. Hartford: S.

Andrus and son, 1845. MH; MPeHi; NBuDD. 45-5393

Protestant Episcopal Church in the United States of America. Book of Common Prayer. The book of common prayer and administration of the sacraments, and other rites and ceremonies of the church according to the use of the Protestant Episcopal Church, together with the psalter or Psalms of David. New York and Philadelphia: D. Appleton and company, 1845. 277 p. ScCliP. 45-5394

Protestant Episcopal Church in the United States of America. Book of Common Prayer. The book of common prayer and administration of the sacraments, and other rites and ceremonies of the church according to the use of the Protestant Episcopal Church, together with the psalter or Psalms of David. New York: Appleton, 1845. 402 p. OrP. 45-5395

Protestant Episcopal Church in the United States of America. Book of Common Prayer. The book of common prayer and administration of the sacraments, and other rites and ceremonies of the church according to the use of the Protestant Episcopal Church, together with the psalter or Psalms of David. New York: Appleton, 1845. 670 p. MB; MH; NRU; OrP; WMFM. 45-5396

Protestant Episcopal Church in the United States of America. Book of Common Prayer. The book of common prayer and administration of the sacraments, and other rites and ceremonies of the church according to the use of the Protestant Episcopal Church, together with the psalter or Psalms of David. New York: D. Appleton and company, 1845. 546, 275 p. NBuDD; NN; NRU; PAtM. 45-5397

Protestant Episcopal Church in the United States of America. Book of Common Prayer. The book of common prayer and administration of the sacraments, and other rites and ceremonies of the church according to the use of the Protestant Episcopal Church, together with the psalter or Psalms of David. New York: D. Appleton and company, 1845. 906 p. NSyHi; ViPet. 45-5398

Protestant Episcopal Church in the United States of America. Book of Common Prayer. The book of common prayer and administration of the sacraments, and other rites and ceremonies of the church according to the use of the Protestant Episcopal Church, together with the psalter or Psalms of David. New York: Harper, 1845. 304, 96 p. NRCR; ViU. 45-5399

Protestant Episcopal Church in the United States of America. Book of Common Prayer. The book of common prayer and administration of the sacraments, and other rites and ceremonies of the church according to the use of the Protestant Episcopal Church, together with the psalter or Psalms of David. New York: Harper, [1845] 580 p. MB. 45-5400

Protestant Episcopal Church in the United States of America. Book of Common Prayer. The book of common prayer and administration of the sacraments, and other rites and ceremonies of the church according to the use of the Protestant Episcopal Church, together with the psalter or Psalms of David. New York: Harper and brothers, 1845. 267 p. DLC; MH; OO; RPB. 45-5401

Protestant Episcopal Church in the United States of America. Book of Common Prayer. The book of common prayer and administration of the sacraments, and other rites and ceremonies of the church according to the use of the Protestant Episcopal Church, together with the psalter or Psalms of David. New York: Harper and brothers, 1845. 394 p. NN; OO. 45-5402

Protestant Episcopal Church in the United States of America. Book of Common Prayer. The book of common prayer and administration of the sacraments, and other rites and ceremonies of the church according to the use of the Protestant Episcopal Church, together with the psalter or Psalms of David. New York: New York Bible and Common Prayer Book Society, 1845. 308 p. OrPD. 45-5403

Protestant Episcopal Church in the United States of America. Book of Common Prayer. The book of common prayer and administration of the sacraments, and other rites and ceremonies of the church according to the use of the Protestant Episcopal Church, together with the psalter or Psalms of David. New York and Philadelphia: D. Appleton and company, 1845. 277 p. ScCliP. 45-5404

Protestant Episcopal Church in the United States of America. Book of Common Prayer. The book of common prayer and administration of the sacraments, and other rites and ceremonies of the church according to the use of the Protestant Episcopal Church, together with the psalter or Psalms of David. Philadelphia, [1845] 327, 159 p. MWA. 45-5405

Protestant Episcopal Church in the United States of America. Book of Common Prayer. The book of common prayer and administration of the sacraments, and other rites and ceremonies of the church according to the use of the Protestant Episcopal Church, together with the psalter or Psalms of David. Philadelphia: George and Wayne, 1845. 673 p. MdBJ; NN; PPPD; ViU; WaWW. 45-5406

Protestant Episcopal Church in the United States of America. Book of Common Prayer. The book of common prayer and administration of the sacraments, and other rites and ceremonies of the church according to the use of the Protestant Episcopal Church, together with the psalter or Psalms of David. Philadelphia: J.B. Lippincott and company, 1845. 460 p. KWiU; OCU. 45-5407

Protestant Episcopal Church in the United States of America. Diocese of Georgia. Journal of the proceedings of the twenty-third annual convention of the Protestant Episcopal Church in the Diocese of Georgia held in St. Stephen's Church, Milledgeville, commending on the 8th of May, 1845. Savannah, 1845. 36 p. MiD-B; NcWsM; WHi. 45-5408

Protestant Episcopal Church in the United States of America. House of Bishops. Pastoral letters, from the House of Bishops, to the clergy and members of the church. Philadelphia: Edward C. Biddle, 1845. 273 p. DLC; IU; NjR; RPB; WNaE. 45-5409

Protestant Episcopal Church in the United States of America. Hymnal. Hymns suited to the feasts and fasts of the church, and other occasions of public worship. New York: D. Appleton and company, 1845. 275 p. NBuG; NNG; TxU. 45-5410

Protestant Episcopal Church in the United States of America. Hymnal. Hymns suited to the feasts and fasts of the church, and other occasions of public worship. Philadelphia: J.B. Lippincott, 1846. 126 p. NBuDD. 45-5411

Protestant Episcopal Church in the United States of America. Hymnal. Hymns... as authorized by the general convention. With additional selections by the Rev. C.W. Andrews... Philadelphia: H. Hooker, 1845. 234 p. CBB; DLC; GEU; NNUT; WNaE. 45-5412

The Protestant's objections to points of Catholic Doctrine; or the Protestant's trial in controverted points of faith, by the written word. Philadelphia: M. Fithian, 1845. 208 p. MdBS; MdW; MeSU; MiDSH. 45-5413

Providence almanac and business directory for 1845. Providence: Benjamin J. Moore, 1845. 149 p. RPB. 45-5414

Providence and Worcester Railroad Company. Charters... with the bylaws. Providence: Knowles and Vose, 1845. 35 p. N; NjP. 45-5415

Providence and Worcester Railroad Company. Facts and estimates relative to the business on the route of the contemplated Providence and Worcester Railroad. Providence: Knowles and Vose, printers, 1845. 31 p. DBRE; DLC. 45-5416

Providence Franklin Society. Catalogue of plants, collected by the botanical department of Providence Franklin Society, principally in Rhode Island in 1844. Arranged by S.T. Olney. Providence: Knowles and Vose, 1845. 8 p. DLC; MBtlo; NcD; NIC. 45-5417

The psalmist: a new collection of hymns for the use of the Baptist churches. By Baron Stow and S.F. Smith. Boston: Gould, Kendall and Lincoln, 1845. [64], 656 p. ICU; MB; MBC; Nh-Hi; PCA. 45-5418

Public School Society of New York. A manual of the system of discipline and instruction. New York: Egbert, Hovey and King, printer, 1845. 30 p. M; NGH. 45-5419

Pulpit sketches on the dreams of a pew holder. Albany: Printed by Munsell and Tannen, 1845. 36 p. MB; NAl; NjR; NN; PPPrHi. 45-5420

Pulte, Joseph Hippolyt, 1811-1884. Organon der Weltgeschichte. Cincinnati: Carl Friedrich Schmidt, 1845. 123 p. DLC; MB; MiU; OC; PPAN. 45-5421

Punch, pseud. Compete letter writer. Philadelphia, 1845. 65 p. MH; PU. 45-5422

Punch, pseud. Heathen mythology. Philadelphia: Carey and Hart, 1845. 71 p. Mi; PHi; PWW; TxDa; Vil. 45-5423

Punch, pseud. The labours of Hercules. Philadelphia: Carey and Hart, 1845. 56 p. LNHT; MH; MoSU; NNP; RPA. 45-5424

Punch, pseud. A peep into London society. Philadelphia: Carey and Hart, 1845. 54 p. MH; NT; PPL. 45-5425

Punch, pseud. The physiology of the London medical student and curiosities of medical experience. Philadelphia: Carey and Hart, 1845. 2 v. MdBM; MH; ViL. 45-5426

Punchiana; or selections from the London Charivari. With ten humorous illustrations by Leech and others. Philadelphia: Carey and Hart, 1845. 72 p. MH; TxU; ViU. 45-5427

Punch's Dossay portraits. Engraved by Duval. Philadelphia, 1845. 17 p. MH; MWA. 45-5428

Puss in boots and the Marquis of Carabas. A pure translation from the original German. New York: D. Appleton, 1845. 62 p. MHi; MH- L; MnDu; WaPS. 45-5429

Putnam, George, 1807-1878. Remarks upon an oration delivered by Charles Sumner before authorities of the city of Boston, July 4th, 1845. By a citizen of Boston. Boston: W. Crosby and H.P. Nichols, 1845. 31 p. MB; MBAt; MH; MiD-B; WHi. 45-5430

Putnam, George Palmer. American facts. Notes and statistics in government, resources, engagements, manufactures, commerce, religion, education, literature, fine arts, manners and customs of the United States of America. New York: Wiley and Putnam, 1845. 292 p. CoFcS; MiCW; PHi; PPL-R; PU. 45-5431

Putnam, John Milton. Historical sketch of the Congregational Church in Dunbarton, New Hampshire, November, 1845. 16 p. MBC; Nh; RPB. 45-5432

Pycroft, James, 1813-1895. A course of English reading, adapted to every taste and capacity; with anecdotes of men of genius. With additions by J.G. Coggswell. New York: Wiley and Putnam, 1845. CU; MH; PPL; ScC; TxU-T. 45-5433

Q-R

Quain, Jones, 1796-1865. A series of anatomical plates; with references and physiological comments... Third edition, revised, with additional notes by Joseph Pancoast... Philadelphia: Carey and Hart, 1845. 445 p. GU; IU-P; MnU; NNC-M; ViU. 45-5434

The queen's own. A quick step, performed with great applause at the reception of Her Majesty, Victoria, in German. Boston: C. Bradlee and company, 1845. 2 p. MBNEC; MH; MH-Mu. 45-5435

Queenston, a tale of the Niagara frontier. Buffalo: Steele's Press, 1845. 156 p. CSfCW; DLC; MBuHi; NBu; OHi. 45-5436

Quinby, George Washington, 1810-1884. Fifteen sermons from fifteen universalist clergymen of Maine. Rev. G.W. Quinby, editor. Portland and Saco: S.H. Colesworthy, 1845. 352 p. MeB; MMeT-Hi; NCaS; ViW. 45-5437

Quincy, Josiah, 1772-1864. Address delivered at the annual exhibition of the New York State Agricultural Society; at Utica, September 18, 1845. Albany: C. Van Benthuysen and company, 1845. 30 p. MHi; MoS; NN; RPB. 45-5438

Quincy, Josiah, 1772-1864. Memoir of James Grahame, LL.D. author of "The history of the United States of North America". Boston: Published by Charles

C. Little and James Brown, 1845. 51 p. ICMe; MBAt; MBC; MH-L; RPB. 45-5439

Quincy, Josiah, 1772-1864. Speech of Josiah Quincy, president of Harvard University, before the board of overseers of that institution, February 25, 1845, on the minority report of the committee of visitation, presented to that board by George Bancroft, February 6, 1845. Boston: C.C. Little and J. Brown, 1845. 64 p. ICMe; MDeeP; NN; OO; RPB. 45-5440

Quincy, Josiah, 1772-1864. Speech of Josiah Quincy, president of Harvard University, before the board of overseers of that institution, February 25, 1845 on the minority report of the committee of visitation, presented to that board by George Bancroft, February 6, 1845. Second edition. Boston: Charles C. Little and James Brown, 1845. 64 p. GDecCT; MeB; ViU. 45-5441

Quincy, Massachusetts. Quincy Savings Bank. Act of incorporation and bylaws. Quincy: John A. Green, printer, 1845. 20 p. MH-BA. 45-5442

Quincy, Massachusetts. Rules and regulations with extracts from the laws of the commonwealth relating to public schools. July 3d, 1845. [Quincy, John A. Green, 1845] MHi. 45-5443

Quinet, Edward, 1803-1875. The Roman church and modern society.

Translated from the French of E. Quinet. New York: Gates and Stedman, 1845. 198 p. GDecCT; MnU; NBuG; PBA; TChU. 45-5444

The railroad traveller and general express. Boston: Haliburton and Dudley, 1845. v.1-. MH-BA. 45-5445

Ramsay, Martha Laurens, 1759-1811. Memoirs of Martha Laurens Ramsay who died in Charleston, South Carolina on the 10th of June, 1811 in the 52d year of her age with extracts from her diary, letters and other private papers. Revised by the committee of publication of the American Sunday School Union. Philadelphia: American Sunday School Union, 1845. 262 p. DLC; MA; MB; Or; PHi. 45-5446

Ramsbotham, Francis Henry, 1800-1868. The principles and practice of obstetric medicine and surgery. In reference to the process of parturition. Illustrated by one hundred and forty eight figures. A new edition from the enlarged and revised London edition. Philadelphia: Lea and Blanchard, 1845. 519 p. ArU-M; InU-M; KyLxT; MdUM; PPi. 45-5447

Ramsey, W.R. An address delivered at Woodstock, Vermont at the anniversary of the Vermont Medical College, 11th of June, 1845. Woodstock Vermont: Mercury, 1845. 16 p. IEN-M. 45-5448

Ramsey, William, 1803-1858. The drunkard's doom. Philadelphia, 1845. 102 p. NPV; PPPrHi; RPB. 45-5449

Ramsey, William. Ebenezer: A sermon embracing the history of the Cedar Street Presbyterian Church, to the close of the year 1844. Philadelphia: Printed at the office of the Christian Observer, 1845. 29 p. MNBedf; PPPrHi; PWW; ViRut. 45-5450

Randall, Samuel Sidwell, 1809-1881. An educational reader; containing selections from a variety of standard English and American authors in prose and poetry; adapted to family and school reading. Albany: E.H. Bender; New York: A.V. Blake, 1845. 313 p. CtHWatk; DLC. 45-5451

Randolph County, Illinois. Notice. Ordered by the county commissioners court, that no allowance will be made to any person... [for services rendered the poor except in poorhouse, unless the person has certificate from a judge of the court or the overseer of the poor. Kaskaskia: Parsons Percy, printer, 1845] Broadside. CSmH. 45-5452

Ranke, Leopold von, 1795-1886. The history of the popes, their church and state, in the sixteenth and seventeenth centuries. Translated from the last edition of the German by Walter Keating Kelly, esq., New York: W.H. Colyer, 1845. 519 p. ICMe; MdBJ; NbOM; OO; WvW. 45-5453

Ranke, Leopold von, 1795-1886. The Ottoman and the Spanish empires in the sixteenth and seventeenth centuries by Leopold Ranke. Philadelphia: Lea and Blanchard, 1845. 138 p. MWA; NNUT; PHC; ScSoH. 45-5454

Ranney, Waitstill R. b. 1791. An address delivered at Woodstock, Vermont, on the anniversary of Vermont Medical College, June 11, 1845. Woodstock: Office of Vermont Mercury, 1845. DLC; DNLM; ICJ. 45-5455

The ransomed child and little letters from Beersheba, South Africa. From the London edition. Boston: Massachusetts Sabbath School Society, 1845. 48 p. MeBa. 45-5456

Ranyard, Ellen Henrietta White, 1810-1879. The book and its story; a narrative for the young. Philadelphia, 1845. 463 p. PPAmS. 45-5457

Rapp, Adam William. A complete system of scientific penmanship without ruling, and pen-making; by which method any number of pens may be used to correspond with each other... New York, 1845. PHi; PP. 45-5458

Rathbone, Hannah Mary Reynolds, 1798-1878. So much of the diary of Lady Willoughby, as relates to her domestic history, and to the eventful period of the reign of Charles the First. New York: Wiley and Putnam, 1845. 100 p. IU; MAnP; MH; PPL-R; ViU. 45-5459

Rathbun, George. Speech of Mr. Rathbun, of New York, on the annexation of Texas, delivered in the House, January 22, 1845. [Washington, 1845] NcD. 45-5460

Raumer, Friedrich Ludwig Georg von, 1781-1873. America and the American people translated from the German by William W. Turner. New York: Langley and Astor House, 1845. 501 p. AB; DLC; MWA; PHi; ViU. 45-5461

Ravignan, Gustave Francois Xavier de Lacroix de, 1795-1858. On the life and institute of the Jesuits by the Rev. Father

de Ravignan of the company of Jesus. Carefully translated from the fourth edition of the French by Charles Seager. Philadelphia: W.J. Cunningham, 1845. 180 p. CSanS; MdBN; MWA; ODaU; PPL. 45-5462

Rawlings, Thomas. Imigration; an address to the clergy of England, Ireland and Wales on the condition of the working classes, with a few suggestions as to their future welfare. New York: G. Trehern, 1845. 31 p. NN; NNC. 45-5463

Ray, Joseph, 1807-1855. Ray's arithmetical key. Containing solutions to the questions in Ray's third book. Cincinnati: Van Antwerp, Bragg and company, 1845. 220 p. IaOskJF; MoCgS; TNT. 45-5464

Ray, Joseph, 1807-1855. Ray's arithmetical key, containing solutions to the questions in Ray's third book. New York: Clark, Austin and Smith; Cincinnati: Winthrop B. Smith and company, [1845] 336 p. CSt; DLC; OClWHi. 45-5465

Rayer, Pierre Francois Olive, 1793-1867. A theoretical and practical treatise of the diseases of the skin. Second edition. Remodelled. Philadelphia: Carey and Hart, 1845. 494 p. MdBLC; MeB; MNF; NRU-M; PP. 45-5466

Rayer, Pierre Francois Olive, 1793-1867. A theoretical and practical treatise on the diseases of the skin. From the second edition, entirely remodelled. With notes and other additions by John Bell. Philadelphia: Carey and Hart for G.N. Loomis, 1845. GEU-M; IU-M; MB; NbU-M; OCo. 45-5467

Raymond, Daniel, 1786-1849. The elements of constitutional law. First stereotype edition. Cincinnati: J.A. James, 1845. 120 p. Ct; MH; OClWHi; OCHP; PU. 45-5468

Rayner, Kenneth. Speeches of Mr. Rayner of North Carolina on the question of Texas annexation... also the bill making appropriation for improvement of harbors and rivers. In the House... Prefaced by an address to his constituents, declining a re-election. Washington: J. and G.S. Gideon, 1845. 32 p. MBAt; NBu; NcAS; PHi; Tx. 45-5469

Read, Daniel, 1805-1878. Oration, commemorative of the life and services of General Andrew Jackson, delivered in compliance with the request of the citizens of Monroe County, at the celebration of the funeral solemnities in honor of his memory, at Bloomington, Indiana, August 8, 1845. Bloomington: Printed at the Christian Record office, 1845. 31 p. CSmH; DLC; In; MH; WHi. 45-5470

Read, Nathan, 1759-1849. An essay on creation and annihilation, the future existence and final state of all sentient beings. Belfast, Maine: C. Giles, 1845. 14 p. MB; MH. 45-5471

Read, Thomas Buchanan, 1822-1872. Paul Redding: A tale of the Brandywine... Boston: A. Tompkins and B.B. Mussey, 1845. 136 p. CU; MBAt; MWA; PHi; RPB. 45-5472

Read, Thomas Buchanan, 1822-1872. Paul Redding: A tale of the Brandywine... Second edition. New York: E. Ferrett and company, 1845. 136 p. CU; DLC; ICU. 45-5473

Reade, Thomas Shaw Bancroft. The christian experience. As displayed in the life and writings of Saint Paul, by the author of christian retirement. New York: Robert Carter, 1845. 2 p. CtHC; FH; LNB; NIC; OU. 45-5474

Reade, Thomas Shaw Bancroft. Christian retirement or spiritual exercises of the heart by the author of "Christian experience as displayed in the life and writings of St. Paul". From the fourteenth London edition. New York and Pittsburg: Robert Carter, 1845. 476 p. RJa; WvHuC. 45-5475

Recollections of the United States army. A series of thrilling tales and sketches by an American soldier. Written during a period in the service since 1830. Boston: James Munroe and company, 1845. 167 p. CtY; DLC; ICN; MH; PHi. 45-5476

Recollections of the United States army. A series of thrilling tales and sketches. By an American soldier. Second edition. Boston: J. Munroe and company, 1845. 167 p. ICN; MiD-B; NhHi; OkU; ViU. 45-5477

Record of the Berkshire County Jubilee of Pittsfield, Massachusetts. Albany, 1845. 244 p. MWA. 45-5478

The red squirrel. Greenfield, 1845. 8 p. PHi. 45-5479

Redburn: or the schoolmaster of a morning. New York: W.M. Christy, 1845. 71 p. ICN; IU; MB; MH; NNC. 45-5480

Redfield, W.C. On the drift ice and currents of the North Atlantic with a chart showing the observed positions of the ice at various times. New Haven: B.L. Hamlen, 1845. CtY; DLC; MB; NN. 45-5481

Reed, Henry, 1808-1854. Introductory lectures on modern history. Delivered in Lent Term 1844, with the inaugural lecture. Boston: D. Appleton and company, 1845. 428 p. MMonsA; PReaA. 45-5482

Reed, John, 1777-1845. The peace of Jerusalem. A sermon addressed to the Parish of Christ Church, Poughkeepsie. Poughkeepsie: Platt and Schram, 1845. [7]-31 p. NCH; NNG; NP. 45-5483

Rees, James, 1802-1885. The dramatic authors of America. Philadelphia: G.B. Zieber and company, 1845. [13]-144 p. C-S; IEN; MH; PPiHi; RPA. 45-5484

Reese, David Meridith, 1800-1861. Address in behalf of the Bible in the schools; delivered in the Broadway Tabernacle on Christmas afternoon, December 25, 1844. New York: J.F. Trow and company, 1845. 16 p. DLC; MWA; NN. 45-5485

Reese, David Meredith, 1800-1861. Inaugural address before the Teachers Institution of the city and county of New York... delivered in the Broadway Tabernacle, April 19, 1845. New York: Marks and Craft, printers, 1845. 16 p. CtHC; M; MnHi; WHi. 45-5486

Reese, David Meredith, 1800-1861. Medical lexicon of modern terminology; being a complete vocabulary of definitions including all the technical terms employed by writers and teachers of medical science at the present day. New York: H.G. Langley, 1845. 240 p. MB; MBM; NbU-M; NNN; PPCP. 45-5487

Reformed Church in America. The acts

and proceedings of the General Synod of the Reformed Protestant Dutch Church in North America at New Brunswick, June, 1845. New York: J. Post, 1845. 122 p. IaPeC. 45-5488

Reformed Church in America. The acts and proceedings of the synod of the German Reformed Church in the United States at York County, Pennsylvania, October 1845. Chambersburg, Pennsylvania: Printed at the publication office of the German Reformed Church, 1845. 161 p. MoWgT. 45-5489

Reformed Church in America. Extracts from the minutes of the proceeding of the Associate Reformed Synod of New York held at Senica. Newburgh, New York: David L. Proudfit, 1845. 30 p. NjR. 45-5490

Reformed Church in America. Proceedings of the convention of Reformed Churches. Session seven. Philadelphia, May, 1845, extracted from the minutes. Cincinnati: William L. Mendenhall, 1845. 32 p. NcMHi. 45-5491

Reformed Church in America. Psalms and hymns, with a catechism, confession of faith, and liturgy, of the Reformed Dutch Church in North America... Philadelphia: Mentz and Rovoudt, 1845. 599 p. NN; NNUT. 45-5492

Reformed Church in the United States. Psalms and hymns for the use of the German Reformed Church, in the United States of America. Sixteenth edition. Chambersburg, Pennsylvania: German Reformed Church, 1845. 602 p. NIC; NNUT. 45-5493

Reformed Church of North America.

Verhandlungen der Synode der Hoch-deutschen Reformirten Kirche in den Vereinigten Staaten von Nord Amerika. Gehalten in York, York County, Pennsylvania, October, 1845. Chambersburg, Pennsylvania: In der Druckerei der Hochdeutsch-Reformirten Kirche, 1845. 151 p. PLERCHi. 45-5494

Reformed Presbyterian Church. Oregon Synod. An address on a scriptural education by the Synod of the Reformed Presbyterian Church. Newburgh: J.D. Spaulding, 1845. 15 p. NcMHi. 45-5495

A refutation of the charge of abolitionism brought by David Henshaw and his partisans against the Hon. Marcus Morton. Boston: Felch's Press, 1845. 32 p. LNH; MiD-B; MWA; NcD; OClWHi; WHi. 45-5496

The regenerator. A free paper for the promotion of universal inquiry and progressive improvements. Orson S. Murray. Fruit Hills, Ohio, 1845. v. 1-. OClWHi. 45-5497

Register of the West Presbyterian Church. New York: John Post's Press, 1845. 24 p. IaB. 45-5498

Reid, Adam, 1808-1878. A historical address before the Congregational Church in Salisbury, Connecticut, at their first Centennial celebration, November 20, 1844. Hartford: Elihu Geer, 1845. 63 p. IaHA; MPiB; MnHi; OClWHi; WHi. 45-5499

Reid, Alexander, 1802-1860. A dictionary of the English language, containing the pronunciation, etymology, and explanation of all words authorized by

eminent writers. New York: D. Appleton and company; Philadelphia: G.S. Appleton, 1845. 564 p. CtHT; DLC; MH; MsEj; NNG. 45-5500

Reid, John S. Gulzar; or the rose bower: a tale of Persia. Indianapolis: S. Turner; [etc., etc.] 1845. 212 p. DLC; In; InCW; InU; RPB. 45-5501

Reid, Marion Kirkland. A plea for women: being a vindication of the importance and extent of her natural sphere of action. With remarks on recent works on the subject... With an introduction, By Mrs. C.M. Kirkland. New York: Farmer and Daggers, 1845. 156 p. ICJ; MiGr; MLow; MS. 45-5502

Religion as seen through the church. New York: Stanford and Swords, 1845. 168 p. InID; NNS; VtMidSM. 45-5503

Religious consolation. Eighth edition. Boston: Joseph Dowe, 1845. 16 p. CtHC. 45-5504

The religious souvenirs; a Christmas, New Year's and birthday present. Hartford: S. Andrus and son, 1845. 288 p. FDU; MB; MnS; ScRhW; WU. 45-5505

The religious telescope. Devoted to the interests of morality, useful knowledge and religion in the private, social or public circle from December 10, 1845. to July 22, 1846. Circleville, Ohio: U.B. Publishing House, 1845-1846. 420 p. ODaUB; OWervO. 45-5506

Religious Tract Society, London. Journeys of the children of Israel; and their settlement in the promised land. Revised by the editor, D.P. Kidder. New York: G.

Lane and C.B. Tippett, 1845. 253 p. NNMHi; OO. 45-5507

Remarks on odd fellowship addressed to the members of the Methodist Episcopal Church by an old watchman. New York, 1845. 16 p. TxDaM. 45-5508

Remarks on the scarcity of American seamen; and the remedy; the naval apprenticeship system; a home squadron, etc. By a gentleman connected with the New York Press. New York: Herald office, 1845. 36 p. DLC; MH; NBu; NN; PPL. 45-5509

Remarks upon the controversy between the commonwealth of Massachusetts and the state of South Carolina. Boston: William Crosby and H.P. Nichols, 1845. 21 p. ICU; MiD-B; NjR; RP; WHi. 45-5510

Remington, S. Lowell. Love of Christ the cause of Christian love. Boston: American Pulpit, 1845. CtHC. 45-5511

Rennie, James, 1787-1867. Natural history of birds. Their architecture, habits, and faculties. With numerous engravings. New York: Harper and brothers, 1845. 308 p. MsU; NBuB; OSW; PP. 45-5512

Rensselaer Polytechnic Institute, Troy, New York. Rensselaer Institute; established especially to instruct students in the application of experimental chemistry, mathematics, philosophy and natural history to agriculture, domestic economy.... Troy: Press of N. Tuttle, 1845. 12 p. MH. 45-5513

Renwick, Henry Brevoort, 1817-1895. Lives of John Jay and Alexander Hamilton. New York: Harper, 1845. 341 p.

CtHC; IGK; MnU; MoRM; OCY. 45-5514

Renwick, James, 1790-1863. First principles of chemistry; being a familiar introduction to the study of that science. For the use of schools, academies and lower classes of colleges. New York: Harper and brothers, 1845. 444 p. CSt; NNN; OrSaW; TSewU. 45-5515

Renwick, James, 1790-1863. Life of De-Witt Clinton. New York: Harper and brothers, 1845. 334 p. IGK; MoSM; NNC; OSW; PMA. 45-5516

Renwick, James, 1790-1863. Lives of Count Rumford [by Henry Renwick] Zebulon Montgomery Pike [By Henry Whiting] and Samuel Groton [by John M. Mackie] Boston: Charles C. Little and James Brown, 1845. CSmH; ICN. 45-5517

Renwick, James, 1790-1863. Treatise on the steam engine... to which is added an appendix, being an analysis of a new theory of the steam engine. New York, 1845. 327 p. DN-Ob. 45-5518

Reply to an article in the March number of the Democratic Review entitled The late acting president. New York, 1845. 14 p. NNC. 45-5519

A reply to hints on the reorganization of the Navy. [New York?] 1845. 40 p. DLC; NN. 45-5520

Report of the Committee appointed to consider the sentence upon the Right Reverend Benjamin T. Onderdonk, and the effect thereof upon the powers and duties of the standing committee of the Diocese of New York. New York: Stanford and Swords, [1845] MdBP; MnHi; PPL. 45-5521

Report of the committee appointed to investigate the relative difference of the cost of the motive power of water and steam, as applicable to manufacturing. Utica: R.W. Roberts, 1845. 15 p. DLC; NUtHi; OClWHi. 45-5522

Report of the committee on horticulture in conjunction with the Agricultural Board of the American Institute. New York, 1845. PPL-R. 45-5523

Report on the business and surveys of the contemplated New York and Hartford Railroad via Danbury. Hartford: Press of Case, Tiffany and Burnham, 1845. 119 p. Nh; NNE; NRom. 45-5524

Republic, a magazine for the defence of civil and religious liberty, August, 1845. Philadelphia, 1845-. v. 1-. PU. 45-5525

Resurrection past. Boston, A. Mudge, 1845. 35 p. MMeT. 45-5526

A retrospective and prospective glance at the political condition of the United States of America, as affected by the present bearing of our naturalization laws. Written by a young member of the Nashville bar. Cincinnati: Daily Atlas office, 1845. NN; T. 45-5527

A review of a pamphlet by the Hon. John C. Spencer by a lay delegate. New York: John R. Winser, 1845. 38 p. MiD-B. 45-5528

Review of Dr. Sparrow's sermon entitled love among Christians urged. From the Churchman of August 23, 1845. New York: James A. Sparks, 1845. 13 p. CtHT; MdBD; MiD-B; NNG; OCHP. 45-5529

Review of the elementary spelling book compiled by Aaron Ely, and published under the name of Noah Webster. Extracted principally from Cobb's critical review. New York, 1845. 32 p. CtHWatk. 45-5530

Review of the tracer controversy; being substantially a reprint of an editorial article in the New York Journal of Commerce, April 19, 22, 24, 1845. New York: Leavitt, 1845. PPPrHi. 45-5531

The revival system and the paraclete. A series of articles from the Church Journal. Claremont: Claremont Manufacturing company, [1845] NH. 45-5532

Reybaud, Henriette Etiennette Fanny Arnoud, 1802-1871. Les deux Marguerite. New York: F. Gailledet, 1845. PPM. 45-5533

Reynolds, H.H. Observations on the best means of preserving the health, beauty, and durability of the teeth. Buffalo: Faxon and company, 1845. DLC. 45-5534

Reynolds, J.N. Voyage of the Potomac during the circumnavigation of the globe. New York: Harper, 1845. 560 p. PWW. 45-5535

Reynolds, O. A brief treatise on the physiology, anatomy, etc. of the bee. Rochester: Daily Advertiser Book and Job office, 1846. 39 p. CoDU; DLC; LNH; NRU. 45-5536

Reynolds, William Morton. American literature, an address delivered before the philomathanean and phrenahosmian Societies of Pennsylvania College. Getysburg, Pennsylvania: Printed by H.C. Neinestedt, 1845. 32 p. CSdNHM; MBAt; NcU; OSW; PHi. 45-5537

Rhett, Robert Barnwell, 1800-1876. Speech of Mr. Rhett, of South Carolina, on the annexation of Texas to the United States, delivered in the House, January 21, 1845, [Washington, 1845] 8 p. NcWfc; P; ScC. 45-5538

Rhoads, Samuel. Consideration on the use of the productions of slavery, addressed to the Religious Society of Friends. Second edition. Philadelphia: Merrihew and Thompson, 1845. 36 p. CtSoP; ICN; MB; NB; OClWHi. 45-5539

Rhode Island. Interference of the Executive in the affairs of Rhode Island. [Washington, 1845] 1075 p. M; MHi; MiD-B; NN. 45-5540

Rhode Island. Proceedings in the Rhode Island legislature on sundry resolutions of the state of Maine. Providence: Knowles and Vose, 1845. 27 p. Me; MH-L. 45-5541

Rhode Island. Report from the minority of the select committee of Congress. Washington, 1845. DLC. 45-5542

Rhode Island almanac for 1845. Providence: H.H. Brown, [1845] 24 p. RPE. 45-5543

Rhode Island Medical Society. Fiske fund prize dissertation. No. 10. Boston, 1845. 48 p. DLC. 45-5544

Rhode Island Society for the Encouragement of Domestic Industry. The

charter and bylaws with a list of its members. Providence: Knowles, 1845. 16 p. CtHWatk. 45-5545

Rice, Nathan Lewis, 1807-1877. Address... before the Miami Union Literary Society of the Miami University at its twentieth anniversary, Oxford, Ohio. Cincinnati: Daily Atlas office, 1845. 24 p. CSmH; NjR; OCHP; OOxM; PPPrHi. 45-5546

Rice, Nathan Lewis, 1807-1877. Lecture on slavery, delivered in the First Presbyterian Church, Cincinnati, July 1st and 3rd, 1845. Cincinnati: J.A. James, 1845. 72 p. DLC; OC; PHC; PPPrHi. 45-5547

Rich, Ezekiel. Thirty six rules to aid in the education of children and youth in the general concerns of Christian morals and worldly wisdom in the form of a blank epistle from a parent, teacher, or friend, to be filled or not, at pleasure. Rochester, New York, 1845. 32 p. MiHi. 45-5548

Richard White, or One Eyed Dick of Massachusetts. A tale for the young. Second edition. Boston, 1845. 107 p. CSmH; MHi; MWA; PMA; WHi. 45-5549

Richardson, Nathaniel Smith, 1810-1883. The churchman's reasons for his faith and practice. New York: James A. Sparks, 1845. 324 p. GMM; PPL-R; ScCoB; TChU; ViAl. 45-5550

Richardson, Nathaniel Smith, 1810-1883. Historical sketch of Watertown [Connecticut] from its original settlement; with the record of its mortality, from March, 1741, to January, 1854...

New Haven: S. Babcock, 1845. 48 p. CtB; DLC; MdHi; MWA; NBuG. 45-5551

Richardson's Virginia and North Carolina almanacs for the year of our Lord, 1845. Calculated by David Richardson, of Louisa County, Virginia. Richmond, Virginia: Drinker and Morris, [1845] 26 p. ViRVal. 45-5552

Richmond, James Cook. The conspiracy against the late Bishop of New York unravelled by one of the conspirators, viz: James C. Richmond... New York: J.C. Richmond, 1845. 16 p. CSmH; MB; NNC; PHi; RPB. 45-5553

Richmond, James Cook. A defence of the ladies and others against the bishop of Maryland. New York: Burgess, Stringer and company, 1845. 16 p. DLC; MB; NNG; PPL. 45-5554

Richmond, James Cook. Mr. Richmond's reply to the statement of the late Bishop of New York... New York: Burgess, Stringer and company, 1845. 16 p. DLC; MHi; NN; PPM; RPB. 45-5555

Richmond, Indiana. Revised ordinances, passed by the Common Council of the city of Richmond. Richmond, 1845. 40 p. In. 45-5556

Richmond, Virginia. St. Paul's Church. Report of the building committee of St. Paul's Church adapted at a meeting held October 22, 1845. Richmond, 1845. CSmH. 45-5557

Richmond's pamphlets reviewed; or the priest of Cedar Grove called to order, by a South Carolinian. New York: Jones and Welsh, 1845. 24 p. MiD-B. 45-5558

Richter, Johann Paul Friedrich, 1763-1825. Flower, fruit and thorn pieces, or the married life, death and wedding of the advocate of the poor, Firmian Stanislaus Siebenkas... translated from the German by Edward Henry Noel. Boston: J. Monroe and company, 1845. 2 v. KWiU; MH; OAU; PPL; ViU. 45-5559

Ricord, Philippe, 1800-1889. A practical treatise on venereal diseases or critical and experimental researches on inoculation applied to the study of these affections with a therapeutical summary and special formulary. Translated from the French by Henry Pilkington Drummond. Second American edition. Philadelphia: Lea Blanchard, 1845. 256 p. MdBM; NBMS; OrU-M; PPCP; PPiU-M. 45-5560

Riddell, John Leonard, 1807-1867. A monograph of the silver dollar good and bad. New Orleans: Norman; New York: Wiley and Putnam, 1845. 178 p. AU; ICJ; MB; OCU; PU. 45-5561

Riddle, David Hunter, 1805-1888. The nation's true glory: the annual address to the senior class of Jefferson College, delivered in Providence Hall. Pittsburgh: George Parkin, 1845. 21 p. MMUT; OClWHi; PPL; PPPrHi; PWW. 45-5562

Rider, Nathaniel. A description of the improved truss bridge, invented by Nathaniel Rider, patented, October 1845. New York, 1845-1846. DLC; ICJ; MH; NNC. 45-5563

Ridgeley, James Lot, 1807-1881. Oration delivered in Faneuil Hall before the Independent Order of Odd Fellows, at their celebration in Boston on the 19th of June, 1845, together with a description of the banners carried in the procession, etc. Boston, 1845. IaCrM; MH. 45-5564

Ries, Ferdinand, 1784-1838. The morning; a cantata in four vocal parts. Boston: A.B. Kidder, 1845. 23 p. MiU. 45-5565

The rights of the free states subverted; or an enumeration of some of the most prominent instances in which the federal constitution has been violated by our national government, for the benefit of slavery. By a member of congress. [Washington? 1845?] 16 p. CtHC; DLC; ICN; MH; TNF. 45-5566

Ring, David. Three thousand exercises in arithmetic. Second edition revised and corrected. Philadelphia: Edward C. Biddle, 1845. 72 p. ICBB. 45-5567

Ripsnorter comic almanac for 1846. New York: Elton, [1845] MWA. 45-5568

Ritchie, Anna Cora Ogden Mowatt, 1819-1870. Evelyn; or a heart unmasked; a tale of domestic life. Philadelphia: G.B. Zieber and company, 1845. MdBP; MH; MWA; NN; ODaB. 45-5569

Ritchie, Anna Cora Ogden Mowatt, 1819-1870. Fashion; or life in New York, a comedy in five acts. New York [1845] 62 p. DLC. 45-5570

Ritchie, Leitch, 1800-1865. The robber of the Rhine. Philadelphia: E. Ferrett and company, 1845. 111 p. CtY; MeB; NN. 45-5571

Rivers, Henry Wheaton. Accidents; popular directions for their immediate treatment... Boston: Thomas H. Webb and company, 1845. 108 p. Mlaw; MoSpD; NBMS; PPCP; RPB. 45-5572

Rivers, Henry Wheaton. Accidents; popular directions for their immediate treatment... New York: J. and H.G. Langley, 1845. CU-M; MBM; MH; PPiU. 45-5573

Rives, William Cabell, 1793-1869. Discourse on the character and services of John Hampden, and the great struggle for popular and constitutional liberty in his time. Delivered before the trustees, faculty and students of Hampton-Sydney College, November 12, 1845. Richmond: Printed by Shepard and Colin, 1845. 68 p. A-Ar; CSmH; MH; PHi; ViU. 45-5574

Rives, William Cabell, 1793-1868. Speech of the Hon. William C. Rives, of Virginia, on the resolution for the annexation of Texas. In the Senate, February 15, 1845. [Washington, 1845] CU; DLC; KHi; MiD-B; NBu; 45-5575

Robbins, Chandler, 1810-1882. Our pastors' offering. A compilation from the writings of the pastors of the Second church. For the Ladies' fair to assist in furnishing the new church edifice. Boston: G. Coolidge, 1845. 126 p. CtMW; ICN; MB; NNUT; RPB. 45-5576

Robbins, Chandler, 1810-1882. A sermon delivered before the proprietors of the Second Church, September 17, 1845. at the dedication of their new house of Worship. Boston, Isaac Butts, 1845. 40 p. ICN; MWA; NN; PPL; RPB. 45-5577

Robbins, Chandler, 1810-1882. Two sermons delivered before the Second Chruch and Society March 10, 1844 on the occasion of taking down their ancient place of worship. Boston, 1845. 76 p. MB; MCon. 45-5578

Robbins, Eliza, 1786-1853. Biography for schools or good examples for young persons. Philadelphia: Uriah Hunt and son, 1845. 256 p. NCoxhi; RBr. 45-5579

Robbins, Eliza, 1786-1853. Elements of mythology; or classical fables of the Greeks and Romans. Fourth edition improved. Philadelphia: Hogan and Thompson, 1845. 272 p. IaK; MDB. 45-5580

Robbins, Gilbert. Death and blessing to the righteous. A funeral discourse delivered at the residence of the Hon. Josiah Quincy, of Romney, New Hampshire, on the death of Mary G. Quincy, his wife, December 9, 1844. By G. Robbins, pastor of the Romney Baptist Church. Concord: Charles Young, printer, 1845. 16 p. IaPeC; MH; Nh; NhHi. 45-5581

Robbins, Royal, 1788-1861. Outlines of ancient and modern history. Hartford: Belknap and Hammersly, 1845. 2 v. in 1. ICP; KHi; MH; ScAnC; TNL. 45-5582

Roberts, Solomon White. Report to the board of managers of the Schuylkill Navigation Company on the improvement of the Schuylkill navigation. Philadelphia: Joseph and William Kits, 1845. 24 p. MH-BA; NNE; PPAmP; PPM. 45-5583

Roberts, William, 1767-1849. Life, memoirs and correspondence of Mrs. Hannah More. New York: Harper and brothers, 1845. 2 v. NP. 45-5584

Roberts, William, 1767-1849. Memoirs on the life and correspondence of Mrs. Hannah More. New York: Harper and brothers, 1845 [-1851] 2 v. CU; IdDmD; MnHi; OrU; TJoV. 45-5585

Roberts, William, 1767-1849. Treatise on the construction of the statutes, 13 Eliz C. 5 and 27 Eliz C 4 relating to voluntary and fraudulent conveyances in the courts of law and equity. Third American from last English edition. Burlington, 1845. 675 p. CSmH; InHuP; MsU; NN; OCLaw. 45-5586

Robertson, Alexander H. Address at the opening of the June communication. New York, 1845? 7 p. NN. 45-5587

Robertson, George. The true issue, and the property question; being a statement of the real matter in controversy between the North and the South in the Methodist Episcopal Church. Lexington, Kentucky: Observer and reporter, 1845. 39 p. ICU; MoS; OCHP. 45-5588

Robertson, William, 1721-1793. The history of the reign of the Emperor Charles V with a view of the progress of society in Europe; from the subversion of the Roman empire, to the beginning of the sixteenth century. New York: Harper and brothers, 1845. 643 p. LShC; MB; NbOC; ScDue; ViU. 45-5589

Robins, Thomas E. Address relative to the bonds of Mississippi. Vicksburg, 1845. PPL. 45-5590

Robinson, Edward, 1794-1863. A dictionary of the Holy Bible for the use of schools and young persons, by Edward Robinson. Fourth edition. Boston: Crocker and Brewster, 1845. 361 p. CSto; CtHWatk; DLC. 45-5591

Robinson, Horatio Nelson, 1806-1867.

A new practical and theoretical arithmetic. Cincinnati: E. Morgan and company, 1845. 288 p. NdFM; OMC; OO; PPi. 45-5592

Robinson, Thomas, 1790-1873. The last days of Bishop Heber. New York, 1845. 273 p. IU; NNUT. 45-5593

Rocchietti, Joseph. Why a national literature cannot flourish in the United States of North America. New York: Printed by J.W. Kelley, 1845. 84 p. LNH; MBAt; MWA; NN; PreaHi. 45-5594

Rock River Seminary, Mount Morris, Illinois. Rock River Seminary, Mount Morris, Ogle County, Illinois. Rev. James C. Finley, Principal. [Grand Detour, Illinois? John W. Sweetland, 1845] 2 p. WHi. 45-5595

Rockwell, John Arnold, 1803-1861. Remarks of Mr. Rockwell. [Washington] J. and G.S. Gideon, 1845. 7 p. Ct; CtY; DLC; MBAt. 45-5596

Rockwell, Julius, 1805-1888. Speech of Mr. Julius Rockwell, of Massachusetts, upon the question of the admission of Texas as a state into the Union. Delivered in the House of Representatives. Washington: J. and G.S. Gideon, 1845. 16 p. CU-B. 45-5597

Rockwell and Stone's New York circus, 1845. Games of Greece, or the reformation of man! A poem in six cantos with a prologue and epilogue. Boston: J.H. and F.F. Farwell, [1845] 16 p. MH; RPB. 45-5598

Roddey, R.L. Address on origin, design and duty of Freemasonry. Forsyth, Georgia: S. Harris, 1845. 15 p. MBFM. 45-5599

Rodman, William Blount. Eulogy on Andrew Jackson; delivered in the Presbyterian Church at Washington, North Carolina on the 26th day of June, 1845. Tarboro: Howard, 1845. 8 p. NcU. 45-5600

Rogers, George, fl. 1838. Memoranda of the experiences, labors and travels of a Universalist preacher. Cincinnati: J.A. Gurley, 1845. 400 p. CSt; KyU; MoU; PPL; RPB. 45-5601

Rogers, George W. The shipwrights own book together with useful rules and tables of measurement. Pittsburgh: J. M'Millin, 1845. 128 p. MoKU; NNE; PPQ. 45-5602

Rogers, Henry Bromfield. Remarks on the present project of the city government, for supplying the inhabitants of Boston with pure soft water. Boston: Dickinson and company, printers, 1845. 39 p. DLC; IU; LNH; MWA; NNC. 45-5603

Rogers, Henry J. Telegraph dictionary and seamen's signal book adapted to signals by flags or other semaphores and arranged for secret correspondence through Morse's electro-magnetic telegraph for the use of commanders of vessels, merchants. Baltimore: Lucas, 1845. 334 p. IU; MB; MH; PPFrankI. 45-5604

Rokitausky, Karl von, 1804-1878. A treatise on pathological anatomy. Translated from the German with additions on diagnosis from Schoenlein, Skoda, and others. New York: W. Radde, 1845. 164 p. CtY; DLC; MH-M; NBMS. 45-5605

Rollin, Charles, 1661-1741. The ancient history of the Egyptians, Carthaginians, Assyrians, Babylonians, Medes, and Persians, Grecians, and Macedonians; including a history of the arts and sciences of the ancients. With a life of the author by James Bell. Cincinnati: G. Conclin, 1845. 2 v. MsCliM; OCU; PAtM; TNP. 45-5606

Rollin, Charles, 1661-1741. The ancient history of the Egyptians, Carthaginians, Assyrians, Babylonians, Medes, and Persians, Macedonians and Grecians. From the latest London edition carefully revised and corrected. New York: Nafis and Cornish; Philadelphia: John B. Perry, 1845. 4 v. KyLoS; LN; MH; MWA; PH. 45-5607

Romaine, William, 1714-1795. Letters on the most important subjects during a correspondence of twenty years. New York: R. Carter, 1845. 225 p. NNUT; OO; PPLT. 45-5608

Romaine, William, 1714-1795. Treatises upon the life, walk and triumph of faith. New York: Robert Carter, 1845. [9]-392, 12 p. InU; KMK; MBC; OO; ViAl. 45-5609

The Roman pontiffs or a sketch of the lives of the supreme heads of the Roman Catholic Church translated from an original and very popular work just published in France. New York: H.G. Daggers, 1845. 40 p. DLC; MH; NN; NNG; PPM. 45-5610

Ronge, John. The holy coat of Treves.

New York: Harper, 1845. DLC; OClW; OM; OUrC. 45-5611

Root, David, 1790-1873. A tract for the times and for the churches: being the substance of a discourse delivered at South Boston, June, 1845. Boston: A.J. Wright, printer, [1845] 16 p. MBC; NN; OClWHi; OO. 45-5612

Rose, Jacob Servoss. The reformed practice of medicine based upon the principles of the chronothermal system practised by the celebrated Dr. Dickinson of London. Philadelphia: J. Pennington; New York: W.H. Graham, 1845. 268 p. MdB; MH; PPCP; PPL-R; PU. 45-5613

The rose; or affections gifts, for 1845. Edited by Emily Marshall. New York: Appleton, 1845. 252 p. Ia; NcD; WU. 45-5614

Rosewood, Emma. Alford and Selina; or the mystery disclosed and the reputed orphan restored to a father's embrace. A tale of real life. Boston: Dow and Jackson, 1845. 30 p. DLC; MB; MH; MWA; NjR. 45-5615

Rosewood, Emma. The virtuous wife or the libertine detected. A tale of Boston and vicinity. Containing a warning to girls from the country and an example for city ladies. Boston: Dow and Jackson, 1845. CU; NN. 45-5616

Ross, A.F. The duties of an American citizen. An address, delivered before the literary societies of Bethany College, February 22, 1845. Bethany, Virginia: Printed by A. Campbell, 1845. 27 p. DLC; MB; NcD; OClWHi; TxU. 45-5617

Ross, James, 1744-1827. A Latin grammar, comprising all the rules and observations necessary to an accurate knowledge of the Latin classics. Philadelphia: Thomas, Cowperthwait and company, 1845. 211 p. CtY; KyLoS; TWcW. 45-5618

Ross, Joel H. Remarks on hot air and vapour bathing, etc. New York, 1845. 8 p. DNLM; DSG. 45-5619

Rossini, Gioacchino Antonio, 1792-1868. Guillaume Tell, opera poeme de M.M. de Jouy et H. Bis. New York, 1845. MBAt. 45-5620

Rossini, Gioacchino Antonio, 1792-1868. Semiramide di gaetano Rossi. Semiranis. A tragico dramatic opera in two acts. New York: Houel and Macoy, 1845. 60 p. MH; RPB. 45-5621

Rost, Pierre Adolphe, 1797-1868. Oration delivered before the Agricultural and Mechanics' Association of Louisiana on the 12th of May, 1845 by Judge P.A. Rost. Philadelphia: J.Van Court, 1845. 16 p. MH; MHi; NCH; PPAmP; PPL. 45-5622

Roussel, Napoleon. Patriarchal scenes. From the French of Napoleon Roussel. Translated from the Massachusetts Sabbath School Society and revised by the Committee of Publication. Boston: Massachusetts Sabbath School Society, 1845. 264 p. DLC; MA. 45-5623

Rowan, Frederica Maclean, 1814-1882. History of the French revolution, its causes and consequences. New York: D. Appleton and company; Philadelphia: G.S. Appleton, 1845. 2 v. in 1. DLC; LNMus; NNS; PPL-R; RPA. 45-5624

Rowson, Susanna Haswell. Charlotte Temple, a tale of truth. Boston: Skinner and Blanchard, 1845. 60 p. MH; MWA. 45-5625

Roxbury, Massachusetts. Laws regulating the fire department in the town of Roxbury. Roxbury: Printed by order of the town, Joseph G. Tarrey, printer, 1845. 36 p. MB; MBC; MHi. 45-5626

Roxbury, Massachusetts. Report on the subject of an application to the Legislature for a city charter. n.p., [1845] M. 45-5627

Roxbury, Massachusetts. School committee of the town of Roxbury presented to the town, March 3, 1845. Roxbury, 1845. 15 p. KHi; MBC; MB-FA; WHi. 45-5628

The royal oak and other stories. By a western teacher. Boston: Waite, Peirce and company, 1845. 144 p. MH; PPe-Schw. 45-5629

The Royston, Samuel Watson. The enemy conquered or love triumphant. New Haven: T.H. Pease, 1845. 31 p. CtY; MB; MH; ViU. 45-5630

Rudy, Johann, 1791-1842. Thut die thore auf! Einweihungs predigt... Chambersburg, Pennsylvania: Druckerei der reformirten kirche, 1845. 12 p. CSmH. 45-5631

Rules for playing the game of chess for four persons. New York: T.J. Crowen, 1845. 8 p. OCl. 45-5632

Rules of the rosary of the blessed Virgin Mary, also of the scapular. Revised by Rt. Rev. John Hughes. Bishop of New

York. New York: Patrick Kavanaugh, 1845. 254 p. GMM; KWish; MBrigCC; PPL-R. 45-5633

Rundell, Samuel. Observations on the commencement and progress of the work of vital religion in the soul; on divine worship; and on the partaking of the flesh and blood of our Lord Jesus Christ... Third edition. Manchester: Harrison, 1845. 52 p. MH; OO; PHC. 45-5634

Ruoff, A. Joseph Fridericus. Repertory of homoeopathic medicine nosologically arranged, translated from the German by A.H. Okie, with additions and improvements by Gideon Humphrey. Second American edition. New York: Radde, 1845. 251 p. CSt-L; CU-M; NBMS; NNN; PPiAM. 45-5635

Rupp, Israel Daniel, 1803-1878. History and topography of Northumberland, Lehigh, Monroe, Carbon and Schuylkill counties; containing a brief history of the first settlers, topography of townships... Harrisburg: Hickok and Cantine, printers, 1845. 568 p. DLC; MWA; NN; OO; PHC. 45-5636

Rupp, Israel Daniel, 1803-1878. History of Lancaster and York Counties from the earliest settlements made within them; in the former, from 1709; in the latter from 1719, to the present time, with an appendix. Lancaster, Pennsylvania: G. Hills, 1845. 750 p. KHi; MdHi; PHi; PLT; WHi. 45-5637

Rupp, Israel Daniel, 1803-1878. History of Northampton, Lehigh, Monroe, Carbon, and Schuylkill Counties: containing a brief history of the first settlers... composed from various authentic sources. Harrisburg: G. Hills, 1845. 568 p. Mi-L; MNBedf; NjP; ODaB; PP. 45-5638

Rupp, Israel Daniel, 1803-1878. History of York County, from one thousand seven hundred and nineteen to the present time. Lancaster, Pennsylvania: Gilbert Hills, 1845. 750 p. DeWi; MiD-B; OCHP; WHi. 45-5639

Ruschenberger, William Samuel Waithman, 1807-1895. Elements of anatomy and physiology; prepared for the use of schools and colleges. Fifth edition. Philadelphia: Grigg and Elliot, 1845. 120 p. IEG; MH; NcU; OO; PU. 45-5640

Ruschenberger, William Samuel Waithman, 1807-1895. Elements of botany. Prepared for the use of schools and colleges. From the text of Milne Edwards and Achille Comte. Philadelphia: Grigg and Elliot, 1845. 159 p. CtW; In; OO; PHi; RPB. 45-5641

Ruschenberger, William Samuel Waithman, 1807-1895. Elements of conchology: prepared for the use of schools and colleges. From the text of Milne Edwards and Achille Comte. Philadelphia: Grigg and Elliot, 1845. 114 p. CtY; LU; MH; NBuG; OO. 45-5642

Ruschenberger, William Samuel Waithman, 1807-1895. Elements of entomology, prepared for the use of schools and colleges. From the text of Milne Edwards and Achille Comte. Philadelphia: Grigg and Elliot, 1845. 145 p. DLC; FU; MoU; NcD; PPAmE. 45-5643

Ruschenberger, William Samuel Waithman, 1807-1895. Elements of geology: prepared for the use of schools and colleges. From the text of F.S. Bendant, Milne Edwards and Achille Comte. With three hundred engravings. Philadelphia: Grigg and Elliot, 1845. 11-235 p. ArL; IaCli; InNd; NcGC. 45-5644

Ruschenberger, William Samuel Waithman, 1807-1895. Elements of herpetology, and of ichthyology; prepared for the use of schools and college from the text of Milne Edwards and Achille Comte. Philadelphia: T.K. and P.G. Collins, 1845. [21]-145 p. DLC; MH; NRU; OClW; PPAN. 45-5645

Ruschenberger, William Samuel Waithman, 1807-1895. Elements of mammalogy. Prepared for the use of schools and colleges. Philadelphia: Grigg and Elliot, 1845. 151 p. MiU; MPB; NcU; OMC; OO. 45-5646

Ruschenberger, William Samuel Waithman, 1807-1895. Elements of ornithology. Prepared for the use of schools and colleges. Philadelphia: Grigg and Elliot, 1845. 125 p. Ct; IaDuU; M; NcU; OO. 45-5647

Ruschenberger, William Samuel Waithman, 1807-1895. Naval. Examination of a reply to hints on the reorganization of the navy. New York: Wiley and Putnam, 1845. 38 p. DLC; MB; MdAN; PPAmP; PPL. 45-5648

Ruschenberger, William Samuel Waithman, 1807-1895. The navy, hints on the reorganization of the navy including an examination of the claims of its civil officers to an equality of rights. New York: Wiley and Putnam, 1845. 71 p. MB; MdAN; PHi; PPL-R. 45-5649

Rush, James, 1786-1869. The philo-sophy of the human voice: embracing its physiological history: Together with a system of principles, by which criticism in the art of elocution may be rendered intelligible, and instruction, definite and comprehensive. Two which is added a brief analysis of song and recitative. Third edition enlarged. Philadelphia: J. Crissy, printer, 1845. [43]-499 p. DLC; GAU; IJI; MeB; PPl-R. 45-5650

Rush, Richard, 1780-1859. Memoranda of a residence at the court of London, comprising incidents official and personal from 1819-1825. Including negotiations on the Oregon question, and other unsettled questions between the United States and Great Britain. By Richard Rush, envoy extraordinary and minister plenipotentiary from the United States, from 1817-1825. Philadelphia: Lea and Blanchard, 1845. 640 p. CSt; CoD; OrHi; NjR; WaU. 45-5651

Rush Medical College. Chicago, Illinois. Annual announcements and catalogues... [n.p.] 1845-. PPCP. 45-5652

Rush Medical College. Chicago, Illinois. Third annual announcement and catalogue of the Rush Medical College... Session of 1844-1845. Chicago, Illinois: Ellis and Fergus, printers, 1845. 13 p. MB. 45-5653

Rush Medical College. Chicago, Illinois. Third annual announcement and catalogue of the Rush Medical College... Session of 1844-1845. Chicago, Illinois: Ellis and Fergus, printers, 1845. 7 p. MB. 45-5654

Russell, Anna U. The young ladies' elocutionary reader; containing a selection of reading lessons. Boston: James

Munroe and company, 1845. 480 p. InNd; MH; MnSM; NNC; RP-PPB. 45-5655

Russell, B.A. Robin red breast. A new juvenile singing book. New York, 1845. IEG. 45-5656

Russell, John Archibald, 1816-1899. A treatise on the laws relating to factors and brokers. Philadelphia: T. and J.W. Johnson, 1845. [15]-228 p. CU; In-SC; MdBB; PP; RPL. 45-5657

Russell, Michael, 1781-1848. Nubia and Abyssinia: comprehending their civil history, antiquities, arts, religion, literature and natural history... Illustrated by a map and several engravings. New York: Harper and brothers, 1845. 331 p. MB; MdAN; OO; RWe; ViRU. 45-5658

Russell, Michael, 1781-1848. Polynesia; or an historical account of the principal islands in the South Sea, including New Zealand. New York: Harper and brothers, 1845. 362 p. InRch; MdW; OCX; RWe; WM. 45-5659

Russell, William, 1741-1793. History of modern Europe; with a view of the progress of society from the rise of the modern kingdoms to the peace of Paris in 1763; and a continuance to the present time by William Jones. New York: Harper, 1845. 3 v. IaFd; MB; MLaw; OrP. 45-5660

Russell, William, 1798-1873. The American elocutionist; comprising lessons in enunciation, exercises in elocution, and rudiments of gesture; with a selection of new pieces for practice in reading and declamation; and engraved illustrations in attitude and action. Second edition. Boston: Jenks and Palmer, 1845. 380 p. MB; MH; NjP; OO. 45-5661

Russell, William, 1798-1873. The American elocutionist; comprising lessons in enunciation, exercises in elocution, and rudiments of gesture; with a selection of new pieces for practice in reading and declamation; and engraved illustrations in attitude and action. Third edition. Boston: Jenks and Palmer, 1845. 380 p. MH. 45-5662

Russell, William, 1798-1873. The American elocutionist; comprising lessons in enunciation, exercises in elocution, and rudiments of gesture; with a selection of new pieces for practice in reading and declamation; and engraved illustrations in attitude and action. Fourth edition. Boston: Jenks and Palmer, 1845. 380 p. InU; MH. 45-5663

Russell, William, 1798-1873. Elements of musical articulation. With illustrations in vocal music. Boston: Wilkins, Carter and company, 1845. 79 p. DLC; MB; MH; MLanc; MMedHi. 45-5664

Russell, William, 1798-1873. Introduction to the American common school reader and speaker; comprising selections in prose and verse; with elementary rules and exercises in pronounciation. Boston: Charles Tappan, 1845. 288 p. DLC; MB; MPiB; RPB. 45-5665

Russell, William, 1798-1873. Introduction to the young ladies elocutionary reader: containing a selection of reading lessons; together with rudiments of elocution. Boston: J. Munroe and company, 1845. 252 p. CtSoP; DLC; InCW; MH; NCH. 45-5666

Russell, William, 1798-1873. Lessons in enunciation; comprising a course of elementary exercises, and a statement of common errors in articulation, with the rules of correct usage in pronouncing. To which is added an appendix. Boston: C.J. Hendee and Jenks and Palmer, 1845. 81 p. MH; MW; RPB. 45-5667

Russell, William, 1798-1873. Orthophony, on the cultivation of the voice in elocution; a manual of elementary exercises adapted to Dr. Rush's philosophy of human voice and the system of vocal culture introduced by James E. Murdoch. Tenth edition. Boston: Ticknor and Fields, 1845. 300 p. NNG; WaU; WWauHi. 45-5668

Russell, William, 1798-1873. Spelling book: or second course of lessons in spelling and reading. Boston: Charles Tappan, 1845. 160 p. CtHWatk; DLC; MH; MLow; NNC. 45-5669

Russell, William Oldnall, 1785-1833. A treatise on crimes and misdemeanors. Fifth American from the third London edition with the notes and references contained in the former American editions by Daniel Davis. Philadelphia: T. and J.W. Johnson, 1845. 2 v. DLC; NcU; OrU-L; PPB; TMeB. 45-5670

Rutgers University. Catalogue of the corporation, officers and students of Rutgers College, New Brunswick, New Jersey, 1845-6. New Brunswick: J. Terhune, 1845. 23 p. MBC; MeHi; NcU. 45-5671

Rutgers University. Statutes of Rutgers College in the city of New Brunswick, New Jersey, August, 1845. New Brunswick: J. Terhune's Press, 1845. 16 p. CSmH; MH; NjP; NjR. 45-5672

Rutland and Burlington Railroad Company. Remarks and statements respecting the character, feasibility and productiveness of the route and its importance to the trade of Boston. Boston: Eastburns Press, 1845. 16 p. MH; Nh. 45-5673

Ryan, James, 1748-1819. Elementary treatise on algebra, theoretical and practical, adapted to the instruction of youth in schools and colleges. Sixth edition. New York: Langley, 1845. 391 p. LNT; NIC; OO. 45-5674

Ryder, William, b. 1805. The superannuate: or anecdotes, incidents, and sketches of the life and experience of William Ryder, a worn out preacher of the Troy Conference of the Methodist Episcopal Church. Related by himself. George Peck, editor. New York: G. Lane and C.B. Tippett, for the Methodist Episcopal Church, 1845. 160 p. CtY-D; DLC; ILM; MoSM; NNMHi. 45-5675

S

The sabbath question. Review of the report of the national convention of the Lord's day, held in Baltimore, December 28th and 29th, 1844. The assemblys shorter catechism... Wheeling, Virginia: J.E. Wharton, printer, 1845. 24 p. OCHP; Vi. 45-5676

Sadler, L.L. A sermon. Secession from social alliance. Portland: Thurston, Ilsley, and company, 1845. 16 p. MeHi; MMeT. 45-5677

Safford, Truman Henry, 1836-1901. Astronomical calculations for the young mathematical almanac, etc. n.p., [1845] MH. 45-5678

Sailor's almanac. New York, 1845. MWA. 45-5679

Saint Andrew's Society of Baltimore. Constitution. Baltimore, 1845. PPL. 45-5680

St. Charles College, Grand Coteau, Louisiana. Catalogue of the professors, officers, and students of the St. Charles College, Grand Coteau, Louisiana. Prospectus of the College, July, 1845. St Martinsville: Attakapas Gazette, 1845. 10 p. MoSU. 45-5681

St. James College, Hagerstown, Maryland. Register of the College of St. James near Hagerstown, Maryland, containing the names of the trustees, faculty and students together with the course of studies, rules, discipline, etc. Baltimore: J. Robinson, 1845. 23 p. MdBD; MdHi. 45-5682

Saint John, Samuel. An introductory lecture delivered before the Medical Department of the Western Reserve College. Cleveland: Younglove's Steam Power Press, 1845. 16 p. CtY; DNLM; NN; OClWHi; PPHa. 45-5683

Saint Mary's Hall, New Jersey. Catalogue and prospectus for 1845. Burlington, 1845-. MdBD; PHi. 45-5684

The Saint Nicholas gift for little boys and girls. Boston: T.H. Carter and company, 1845. 96 p. ICN; ICU; RPB. 45-5685

St. Pierre, Jacques Henri Bernardin de, 1737-1814. Paul et Virginie, suivi de la Chaumiere indienne, du Cafe de Surate. Nouvelle edition, ornee de vignettes. New York: R. Lockwood and son, 1845. 356 p. NN. 45-5686

Saintine, Joseph Xavier Boniface, 1798-1865. Picciola, par X. B. Saintine, precede de quelques recherches dur L'emploi du temps dans les prisons d'etat par Paul L. Jacob, bibliophile. Nouv. ed. rev. et cor. Boston: Otis, Broaders, et compagnie, 1845. 252 p. CtHWatk; FCor; NN; OZaN; ViU. 45-5687

Salazar, Francisco, 1559-1599. The sinner's conversion, reduced to principles. Arranged according to the method of the spiritual exercises of St. Ignatius, of Loyola. Stereotyped from the second Dublin edition. Philadelphia: William J. Cunningham, 1845. 227 p. MdBLC; MdW; MoSU; ViU. 45-5688

Salem, Massachusetts. Address of the Mayor, upon the organization of the city government, March 24, 1845. Salem, 1845. 34 p. DLC; MiD-B. 45-5689

Salem, Massachusetts. Rules and orders of the common council of the city of Salem; with the city charter, and city ordinances; etc., etc. Salem: Printed at the Observer office, 1845. [4]-82 p. DLC; M; MH; MPeaHi; NjR. 45-5690

Salem, Ohio. Presbyterian Church. A review of the report adopted by the general assembly of the Presbyterian Church, in 1845, on the subject of slavery. Greenfield, Ohio: Printed by J.F. Wright, 1845. 16 p. MA; NNUT; PPPrHi; WHi. 45-5691

Salem Seamen's Orphan and Children Friend Society. Salem Massachusetts. Constitution... with the fifth annual report and a list of the members. Salem, 1845. 18 p. MBC; MHi; WHi. 45-5692

Salems Sonntagschul-Gesellschaft in den Nordlichen Freiheiten von Philadelphia. Sonntagsschul-Gesangbuchlein. Herausgegeben von der Salems-Sonntagsschul-Gesellschaft in den nordlichen Frieheiten von Philadelphia. Philadelphia: D. Wyeth, 1845. MH. 45-5693

Salisbury, Samuel, 1806-1850. Descriptive, historical, chemical and therapeutical analysis of the Avon Sulpher Springs,

Livingston County, New York, with directions for their use. Rochester: Dewey, 1845. MB; MBM; NBu; PPCP; WHi. 45-5694

Salisbury and Sloan. Daily and weekly report. Syracuse, 1845. CtHWatk. 45-5695

Sallustius Crispus, Caius. Jugurthine war and conspiracy of Catiline with an English commentary and geographical and historical indexes. Ninth edition, corrected and enlarged. New York: Harper and brothers, 1845. 332 p. FStan; MH; MiD; ScU. 45-5696

Sallustius Crispus, Caius. Sallust's history of the war against Jugurtha, and of the conspiracy of Catiline; with a dictionary and notes. Philadelphia: Smith and Peck; Boston: Crocker and Brewster; New Haven: Durrie and Peck, 1845. 336 p. CtSoP; IaDuU; MB; MH; NNCP. 45-5697

Sallustius Crispus, Caius. Sallust's history of the war against Jugurtha, and of the conspiracy of Catiline. With a dictionary and notes by Prof. E.A. Andrews. Third edition. Philadelphia: Loomis and Peck; Boston: Crocker and Brewster, 1845. 336 p. IaDuU; MB; MH. 45-5698

Samaritan Association, Washington, D.C. Constitution of the Samaritans for the relief of the poor of the city of Washington. Washington, 1845. DLC. 45-5699

Samory, C. The merchant's expeditious calculator containing a set of tables by means of which can be ascertained the product of any given quantity at any given rate.... New Orleans: J.L. Sollee, 1845. 100 p. DLC; LNT; LNHT. 45-5700

Sample, Samuel Caldwell, 1796-1855. Speech of Mr. Sample, of Indiana, on the annexation of Texas. Delivered in the House, January 10, 1845. [Washington, 1845] 8 p. CtHWatk; MBAt; MH; MHi; MMal. 45-5701

Sanborn, Peter E. The family doctor or sick man's friend, showing the medical properties and use of the most valuable medical roots and herbs, and how to apply them... Fifth edition. Boston: New England Book and Periodical company, 1845. 35 p. DNLM; DSG; MBCo. 45-5702

Sand, George, 1804-1876. Consuelo. Translated by Francis G. Shaw. New York: R. Lockwood and son, 1845.4 v. DLC; ICU. 45-5703

Sand, George, 1804-1876. The Mosaic workers; a tale of Venice. Translated from the French of George Sand. Philadelphia: E. Ferrett and company, 1845. 216 p. DLC; MeB. 45-5704

Sand, George, 1804-1876. The uscoque. [New York, 1845?] DLC; U. 45-5705

Sanders, Charles Walton, 1805-1889. The primary school primer. New York: M.M. Newman, 1845. 48 p. CLU. 45-5706

Sanders, Charles Walton, 1805-1889. A school reader. Third book. Rochester, New York: Sage and brother, 1845. 252 p. WRichM. 45-5707

Sanders, Charles Walton, 1805-1889. A school reader. Third book. Thirtieth edition. New York: M.H. Newman; Cincinnati: W.H. Moore and company, 1845. 250 p. CtY; IaHi; MBiB; NCanHi. 45-5708

Sanders, Charles Walton, 1805-1889. A school reader. Fourth book. Rochester, New York: Sage and brother, 1845. 304 p. NRU. 45-5709

Sanders, Charles Walton, 1805-1889. Spelling book. New York: Ivison, Phinney, Blakeman and company; Chicago: S.C. Griggs and company, [1845] 168 p. NRU-W; OAsht; PPM; PReaHi. 45-5710

Sanders, Charles Walton, 1805-1889. Spelling book; containing a minute and comprehensive system of introductory orthography. New York: M.H. Newman and company, [1845] MH; NBuG; KyHi; MiHi; NhD. 45-5711

Sanders, Charles Walton, 1805-1889. Spelling book: containing a minute and comprehensive system of introductory orthography: A new easy and practical scheme. Appropriate reading lessons, abbreviations, names of counties, towns, rivers... Rochester, New York: Sage and brothers, 1845. 168 p. NRHi; OOxM. 45-5712

Sanders, Charles Walton, 1805-1889. Spelling book: introductory orthography: designed to teach a system of orthography and orthoepy in accordance with that of Dr. Webster. Cazenovia: Charles Crandall, [1845] MH; MID-B; MiToC; OClWHi; PU. 45-5713

Sanders, Elizabeth Elkins, 1762-1851. Tract on missions to expose the injurious effect of foreign missions. Salem:

Gazette office, 1845. 21 p. DLC; PPL. 45-5714

Sanders, John, 1810-1858. Memoirs on the military resources of the valley of the Ohio, as applicable to operations on the Gulf of Mexico... Pittsburgh: Whitney, Dumars and Wright, 1845. 19 p. DLC; Nh. 45-5715

Sanders, John, 1810-1858. Memoirs on the military resources of the valley of the Ohio, as applicable to operations on the Gulf of Mexico; and on a system for the common defence of the United States... Published by authority of the war department. Washington: C. Alexander, printer, 1845. 24 p. DLC; MH; NjR; OClWHi; WHi. 45-5716

Sanders, R. A call from God to the American churches, being the substance of a sermon delivered to the First Congregational Church in Vernon Centre, July 25, 1845. Published by request. Utica, New York: H.H. Curtiss, printer, 1845. 19 p. MH; MHi. 45-5717

Sandford, Lewis Halsey, 1807-1852. Opinion upon charitable uses for religious tenets. New York, 1845. NN. 45-5718

Sandwich Collegiate Institute. A boarding school for boys and misses. [Prospectus] Boston: Printed by S.N. Dickinson and company, 1845. 8 p. MAM; MB; MH. 45-5719

Sargent, John Turner, 1808-1877. The ministry at Suffolk Street Chapel under the charge of the Benevolent Fraternity of Churches. Boston: Printed by Benjamin H. Greene, 1845. 40 p. ICN; MBC; MHi; MnHi; RPB. 45-5720

Sargent, John Turner, 1808-1877. Obstacles to the truth. A sermon preached in Hollis Street Church, on December 8, 1844. Published by request of the society. Boston: Dickinson, 1845. 20 p. CBPac; ICMe; MBAU; MHi; RPB. 45-5721

Sargent, John Turner, 1808-1877. Obstacles to the truth. A sermon preached in Hollis Street Church, on December 8, 1844. Published by request of the society. Second edition. Boston: Dickinson, 1845. MB. 45-5722

Sargent, John Turner, 1808-1877. The true position of Theodore Parker, being a review of R.C. Waterston's letter in the fourth quarterly report of the Benevolent Fraternity of Churches. Boston: Andrews, Prentiss and Studley, 1845. 22 p. CtY; MB; MWA; NcD; OO. 45-5723

Savage, Eleazer. Manual of church discipline. Second edition. Rochester: Sage and brothers, 1845. 119 p. ICNBT; ICU; NHC-S. 45-5724

Sawyer, Leicester Ambrose, 1807-1898. Elements of moral philosophy, on the basis of the ten comandments. New York: Mark H. Newman, 1845. 335 p. CBe; IaScM; KMK; OBerB; PWW. 45-5725

Sawyer, Thomas Jefferson, 1804-1899. Endless punishment; its origin and grounds examined; with other discourses. New York: C.L. Stickney, 1845. 252 p. InU; LNB; NCaS; MH; MMeT-Hi. 45-5726

Saxton, N.S. A lecture on the elements of physiology, May, 1845. New York:

Daniel Adee, printer, 1845. 23 p. NNNAM. 45-5727

Say, Jean Baptiste, 1767-1832. A treatise on political economy; or the production, distribution, and consumption of wealth. Translated from the fourth edition of the French by C.R. Prinsep. New American edition. Philadelphia: Grigg and Elliot, 1845. 488 p. CoU; MnSM; NB; IGK; TWcW. 45-5728

Sayers, Edward. A manual on the cultivation of live fences, with a practical treatise on the cultivation of evergreens, ornamental trees, etc. Cincinnati: Elyand Campbell, 1845. 108 p. MBHo; MH; NN; OCHP. 45-5729

Schaff, Philip, 1819-1893. Princip des protestantismus. Dargestellt von Philip Schaff... Chambersburg: In der Druckerei der Hochdeutsch Reformirten Kirche, 1845. [9]-180 p. MoWgT; NNUT; PHi; PPLT; WU. 45-5730

Schaff, Philip, 1819-1893. The principle of protestantinsm as related to the present state of the church. Translated from the German with an introduction by John W. Nevin. Chambersburg: German Reformed Church, 1845. ICMe; MB; PPiW; OClWHi; TSewU. 45-5731

Schaumburg, James W. Statement relative to his right to be restored to the army. Washington: J.E. Dow and company, 1845. 32 p. DLC; PHi; PPL. 45-5732

Schenectady, New York. Catalogue of books belonging to the district school library of Schenectady. Schenectady: I. Riggs, 1845. 45 p. CSmH; NSchHi. 45-5733

Schiller, Johann Christoph Friedrich von, 1759-1805. The aesthetic letters, essays, and the philosophical letters of Schiller; translated with an introduction, by J. Weiss. Boston: C.C. Little and J. Brown, 1845. 379 p. CtHT; IaGG; MWiW; NjP; OCY. 45-5734

Schiller, Johann Christoph Friedrich von, 1759-1805. Correspondence between Schiller and Goethe, from 1794 to 1805; translated by George H. Calvert. New York: Wiley and Putnam, 1845. IaGG; MPiB; MWA; PPA; RPB. 45-5735

Schiller, Johann Christoph Friedrich von, 1759-1805. Schiller; the aesthetic letters, essays, and the philosophical letters of. Translated with an introduction by J. Weiss. Boston: C.C. Little and J. Brown, 1845. 379 p. MB; MNF. 45-5736

Schiller, Johann Christoph Friedrich von, 1759-1805. The visionary; from the papers of the Count de O---. New York and Philadelphia: E. Ferrett and company, 1845. DLC; MdBP; MH; NN. 45-5737

Schlegel, Friedrich von, 1772-1829. Lectures on the history of literature, ancient and modern, from the German of Frederick Schlegel. New York: J. and H.G. Langley, 1845. 392 p. CtHT; IGK; MBC; RWe; ScCMu. 45-5738

Schmid, Christoph von, 1768-1854. Biblische geschichten des alten und neuen bundes. Cincinnati: Gedruct und in Verlag Bei Louis Meyer und company, 1845. 142 p. MoWgT. 45-5739

Schmid, Christoph von, 1768-1654. Rosa of Linden Castle or Trilia affection.

Philadelphia: Perkins, 1845. CtY; MeBaT. 45-5740

Schmidt, Henry. Immanuel, 1806-1889. Education. New York: Harper and brothers, 1845. 340 p. DLC; OClW. 45-5741

Schmucker, John George, 1771-1854. Prophetic history of Christian religion explained or brief exposition of the revelation of St. John. Baltimore: Evangelical Lutheran Church, 1845. 2 v. in 1. OO; ViRut. 45-5742

Schmucker, Samuel Simon, 1799-1873. Dissertation on capital punishment. Third edition. Philadelphia: Perkins and Purves, 1845. 31 p. ICJ; MB; OCLaw; PPL; WHi. 45-5743

Schmucker, Samuel Simon, 1799-1873. Elements of popular theology; with occasional reference to the doctrines of the reformation, as avowed before the Diet at Augsburg in 1530, designed chiefly for private Christians and theological students. Edition five with numerous additions. Philadelphia: S. S. Miles, 1845. 512 p. GMM; KKC; OCl; OCoC; ScNC. 45-5744

Schmucker, Samuel Simon, 1799-1873. The papal hierarchy, viewed in the light of prophecy and history. Being a discourse delivered in the English Lutheran Church, Gettysburg, February 2, 1845. Second edition. Gettysburg: H.C. Neinstedt, 1845. 32 p. CSansS; DLC; ICN; MBC; PCA. 45-5745

Schmucker, Samuel Simon, 1799-1873. The patriarchs of American Lutheranism, being a discourse, delivered before the historical society of the Lutheran

Church in the United States... Baltimore: Printed at the publication rooms, 1845. 55 p. ICN; MdHi; PPLT; WHi. 45-5746

Schmucker, Samuel Simon, 1799-1873. Psychology or elements of a new system of mental philosophy on the basis of consciousness and common sense. Second edition much enlarged. New York: Harper and brothers, 1845. 329 p. MH; TxBrdH. 45-5747

Schneck, Benjamin Shroder, 1806-1874. Der Deutche Kanzel: Eine sammlung auserlesener predigten der neuesten Zeit. Auf. 2. Chambersburg, Pennsylvania: in Der Druckerei Der Hochdeutch Reformirten Kirche, 1845. 560 p. DLC; MBC; MH-AH; PSt. 45-5748

Scholfield, Nathan. Elements of plane geometry and mensuration; being the first part of a series on elementary and higher geometry, trigonometry and mensuration. New York: Collins, 1845. 288 p. CtHT; DLC; MLow; OO; PPFrankI. 45-5749

Scholfield, Nathan. Elements of solid geometry and mensuration. New York: Collins, brother and company, 1845. 148 p. CtHT; DLC; OO; PEaL. 45-5750

Scholfield, Nathan. Higher geometry and trigonometry: being the third part of a series on elementary and higher geometry, trigonometry, and mensuration... New York: Collins, brother and company, 1845. 250, 10 p. CSt; IU; MB; MH; OO. 45-5751

Scholfield, Nathan. A series on elementary and higher geometry, trigonometry, and mensuration, containing many valuable discoveries and improvements in mathematical science. New York: Collins, brother and company, 1845. 4 v. in 2. DLC; CtHT; MiU; RPB; TxGR. 45-5752

The school cabinet. Published every Saturday morning for the pupils of the Boston school. Boston, 1845. v. 1-. MH. 45-5753

The school friend or lessons in prose and verse. By the author of American popular lessons. Second edition. New York: W.E. Dean, 1845. 252 p. MLow. 45-5754

The school girl in France or Protestant girl in a French nunnery. First American from the Last London edition. Philadelphia: James M. Campbell, 1845. 272 p. CStcr; MiTo; NjR. 45-5755

The school girl in France or the snares of popery; a warning to protestants against education in Catholic seminaries. New York: J.K. Wellman, 1845. 248 p. IAlS. 45-5756

Schoolcraft, Henry Rowe, 1793-1864. The aboriginal names and geographical terminology of the state of New York... New York: Printed for the society, 1845. 43 p. MB; MdBJ; N. 45-5757

Schoolcraft, Henry Rowe, 1793-1864. An address, delivered before the Was-ah-Ho-de-son-ne or New Confederacy of the Iroquois at its third annual council, August 14, 1845. Rochester: Published by the confederacy, printed by Jerome and brother, 1845. 48 p. PPRF. 45-5758

Schoolcraft, Henry Rowe, 1793-1864. Oneota, or characteristics of the red race of America. From original notes and manuscripts... New York and London: Wiley and Putnam, 1845. [5]-512 p. AzT; IaK; OZam; MiU; NNS. 45-5759

Schott, James, d. 1860. A statement in relation to the duel between James Schott, Jr. and Pierce Butler. Philadelphia, 1845. MB; PPL-R. 45-5760

Schumann, C.A. The culture of the grape. Cincinnati: Robinson and Jones, 1845. 24 p. DLC; MB; OCHP; OCl; TxD-W. 45-5761

Scientific American, the advocate of industry and enterprise and journal of mechanical and other improvements. New York: Mann and company, 1845-. v. 1-. ICJ; MiU; OO; PPL; ScU. 45-5762

Scituate, Massachusetts. First Trinitarian Congregational Church. Review of a pamphlet entitled "A second series of letters concerning the history of the first parish in Scituate, Massachusetts." Boston, 1845. 36 p. MH. 45-5763

Scituate, Massachusetts. First Trinitarian Congregational Church. A series of letters... Boston, 1845. 84 p. MH. 45-5764

Scofield, A. Qualifications of rulers. Sermon. Hamilton, 1845. 12 p. MBC. 45-5765

Scoresby, William. American factories and their female operatives; with an appeal on behalf of the British factory population. Boston: W.D. Ticknor and company, 1845. 136 p. ICN; IU; MdBP; MLow; OMC. 45-5766

Scott, John Williamson. A statement of the causes which led to the recent changes in the Miami University. [Oxford, Ohio, 1845] 23 p. OClWHi. 45-5767

Scott, Thomas, 1747-1832. The Bible, revelation from God being the preface to his family Bible. Philadelphia, 1845. 44 p. IaDuU- S. 45-5768

Scott, Thomas, 1747-1832. Practical observations on the New Testament. By the Rev. Thomas Scott. Arranged for family worship with an introduction by A. Alexander. Philadelphia: Griffin and Simon, 1845. 532 p. CBPac; CtHC; PPPrHi. 45-5769

Scott, Walter, 1771-1832. The abbot, being a sequel to the monastery. Parker's edition. Boston: Samuel H. Parker, 1845. 2 v. MCli; MDeeP. 45-5770

Scott, Walter, 1771-1832. Anne of Geirestein; or the maiden of the mist. Parker's edition. Boston: Samuel H. Parker, 1845. 2 v. NjPLC. 45-5771

Scott, Walter, 1771-1832. The antiquary. Boston: Samuel H. Parker, 1845. 2 v. in 1. MnM; NPlak. 45-5772

Scott, Walter, 1771-1832. Bride of Lammermoor; also legend of Montrose. Boston, 1845. MCli; MDeeP. 45-5773

Scott, Walter, 1771-1832. Chronicles of the Conongate. Parker's edition revised and corrected. Boston: S.H. Parker, 1845. 21 v. in 1. FG; MBur; MCli; NRU; RP; WM. 45-5774

Scott, Walter, 1771-1832. Count Robert of Paris. Boston, 1845. MCli. 45-5775

Scott, Walter, 1771-1832. Count Robert of Paris. Philadelphia, 1845. MDeeP. 45-5776

Scott, Walter, 1771-1832. Fair maid of Perth. Philadelphia, 1845. MDeeP. 45-5777

Scott, Walter, 1771-1832. The fortunes of Nigel. Parker's edition. Boston: Samuel E. Parker, 1845. 2 v. FG; MCli. 45-5778

Scott, Walter, 1771-1832. Guy Mannering; or the astrologer. Parker's edition. Boston: Samuel E. Parker, 1845. 2 v. FG; MCLi. 45-5779

Scott, Walter, 1771-1832. Harold the dauntless and dramatic poems. A new edition with the author's latest corrections. New York: C.S. Francis and company; Boston: J.H. Francis, 1845. 383 p. MWwo. 45-5780

Scott, Walter, 1771-1832. Highland widow. Philadelphia, 1845. MCli; MDeeP. 45-5781

Scott, Walter, 1771-1832. The history of Scotland. New York: Harper and brothers, 1845. 2 v. GNe; IGK; NcWsS; RPE; ScDuE. 45-5782

Scott, Walter, 1771-1832. Kenilworth. Parker's edition corrected and revised. Boston: Samuel E. Parker, 1845. 2 v. MCli; PLebYMC. 45-5783

Scott, Walter, 1771-1832. The lady of the lake; a poem in six cantos by Sir Walter Scott. New York: D. Appleton and company; Philadelphia: George S. Appleton, 1845. 133 p. MB; MBBC; NcBe; NGlf. 45-5784

Scott, Walter, 1771-1832. Lay of the last minstrel with ballads, songs and miscellaneous poems. New edition with the author's latest corrections. New York, 1845. 412 p. NNC; NStonr; OCX. 45-5785

Scott, Walter, 1771-1832. Letters on demonology and witchcraft; addressed to J.G. Lockhart. New York: Harper and brothers, 1845. 338 p. ICJ; OCY; PCC; ScCC; WM. 45-5786

Scott, Walter, 1771-1832. The lord of the isles, the field of Waterloo, and other poems. A new edition, with the author's latest corrections. New York: Francis, 1845. 396 p. NN; NNF; OClW. 45-5787

Scott, Walter, 1771-1832. Marmon. A tale of flodden field and occasional poems. New York: C.S. Francis and company; Boston: J.H. Francis, 1845. 359 p. ICMundC; WoSht. 45-5788

Scott, Walter, 1771-1832. Monastery. Philadelphia, 1845. MCli; MDeeP. 45-5789

Scott, Walter, 1771-1832. Poetical works... New York: D. Appleton, 1845. 624 p. MH; ViU. 45-5790

Scott, Walter, 1771-1832. Poetical works... A new edition. New York: C.S. Francis and company; Boston: Joseph H. Francis, 1845. 2 v. OkBacC; ScU. 45-5791

Scott, Walter, 1771-1832. Redgauntlet. A tale of the eighteenth century. Parker's edition revised and corrected. Boston: Samuel H. Parker; Philadelphia: Thomas, Cowperthwait and company; New York: C.S. Francis; Baltimore: Cushing and sons, 1845. 260 p. FG; MCli; NvVc. 45-5792

Scott, Walter, 1771-1832. Rob Roy. Parker's edition revised and corrected with a general preface as introduction to each novel and notes, historical and illustrative by the author. Boston: Samuel H. Parker; Philadelphia: Thomas, Cowperthwait and company; New York; C.S. Francis; Baltimore: Cushing and sons, 1845. 2 v. MCli; TNB. 45-5793

Scott, Walter, 1771-1832. St. Roman's well. Boston: Samuel H. Parker, 1845. 2 v. in 1. FG; MCli; MnM. 45-5794

Scott, Walter, 1771-1832. Surgeon's daughter. Philadelphia, 1845. MDeeP. 45-5795

Scott, Walter, 1771-1832. Tales of a grandfather; being stories taken from Scottish history. Humbly inscribed to Hugh Littlejohn. First series. Boston: Samuel H. Parker; Philadelphia: Thomas, Cowperthwait, and company, 1845. 3 v. LNL. 45-5796

Scott, Walter, 1771-1832. Tales of a grandfather; being stories taken from Scottish history. Second series. Boston: Parker, 1845. 2 v. in 1. MMarm; NRU. 45-5797

Scott, Walter, 1771-1832. Tales of a grandfather; being stories taken from Scottish history. Third series. Boston: Samuel H. Parker, 1845. 2 v. FG; NRU. 45-5798

Scott, Walter, 1771-1832. Tales of a grandfather; fourth series in two volumes. Boston: Samuel H. Parker,

1845. 2 v. FG; LNL; MMe; RWe; TNB. 45-5799

Scott, Walter, 1771-1832. Tales of my landlord, fourth and last series. Castle dangerous complete in one volume. Parker's edition revised and corrected. Boston: Samuel H. Parker, 1845. 2 v. MBur; NNUT; PLebYMC; TNB. 45-5800

Scott, Walter, 1771-1832. Tales of the Crusaders. The betrothed. Parker's edition. Boston: Samuel H. Parker, 1845. 2 v. FG; MB. 45-5801

Scott, Walter, 1771-1832. Waverley novels, with the author's last corrections and additions. Philadelphia: Carey and Hart, 1845. 5 v. OCU. 45-5802

Scott, Walter, 1771-1832. Waverley novels. Parker's edition, revised and corrected, with a general preference... Boston: S.H. Parker, 1845. 54 v. in 27. MB. 45-5803

Scott, Walter, 1771-1832. Waverly or; Tis sixty years since. Philadelphia: Porter and Coates, 1845. 389 p. IaPeC; MBBcHS. 45-5804

Scott, Walter, 1771-1832. Woodstock; or the cavalier in two volumes. Boston: Samuel H. Parker, 1845. 2 v. LNB; MCli; TNB. 45-5805

Scott, Walter, 1771-1832. Works complete in 19 volumes. Philadelphia: Carey and Hart, 1845? 10 v. NjR. 45-5806

Scott, William Anderson, 1813-1885. Documents relating to certain calumnies against the Hon. Henry Clay, and ascribed to the Rev. W.A. Scott of this city with a review thereof, by a member of his congregation. New Orleans, 1845. 107 p. PPPrHi; TxWB. 45-5807

Scott, William Anderson, 1813-1885. The education we want. A discourse pronounced on November 23, 1844, before the board of directors of the public schools, of municipality no. 2... At the dedication of Franklin's school-house. New Orleans: Printed by Besancom, Ferguson and company, 1845. [7]-28 p. CSansS; MH; PPPrHi; RP; TNP. 45-5808

Scott, William Anderson, 1813-1885. The house of God: a discourse delivered at the request of the officers of the Second Presbyterian Church of the city of Mobile, Alabama. New Orleans: William H. Troy, printer, 1845. 40 p. A-Ar; CSansS; MWA; NcD; PPPrHi. 45-5809

Scribner, J.M. Scribner's engineers' and mechanics' companion; comprising United States' weights and measures; mensuration of superficies and solids. The mechanical powers. Second edition revised, enlarged and improved. New York: Huntington and Savage, 1845. 240 p. DLC; ICU; LNH; MH; NCH. 45-5810

A scriptural catechism of the Christian religion. Boston, 1845. DLC. 45-5811

The Scripture natural history containing a description of birds, reptiles, fishes, trees, precious stones, and metals, mentioned in the Scriptures reprinted from the edition of the London Religious Tract Society. Philadelphia: Presbyterian Board of Publication, 1845. 268 p. CtHC; IaMp; MWiW; NdU; PPPrHi. 45-5812

The Scripture natural history containing a description of quadrupeds, birds, reptiles, amphibia, fishes, insects, maluscous animals mentioned in the holy scriptures. Philadelphia: Presbyterian Board of Publication, 1845. 8, 268 p. P. 45-5813

Scudder, John, 1798-1855. Sermon to children on the condition of the heathen. Revised by the committee of publication. Boston: Massachusetts Sabbath School Society, 1845. 120 p. IaMP; MH. 45-5814

Seabury, Samuel. A sermon... in reference to the trial of the Rt. Rev. Benjamin T. Onderdonk... [New York: J.A. Sparks, 1845] 7 p. DLC; MHi; MiD-B; NN; NNG. 45-5815

Sealsfield, Charles, 1793-1864. The cabin book or sketches of life in Texas. Philadelphia: Colon and Adriance, 1845. 3 parts. CtY; DLC. 45-5816

Sealsfield, Charles, 1793-1864. Life in Texas. In three parts. Translated from the German by Prof. Charles F. Mersch. Philadelphia: Colon and Adriance, 1845. 155 p. DLC. 45-5817

Sealsfield, Charles, 1793-1864. Rambleton; a romance of fashionable life in New York during the great speculation of 1836. Translated from the German. New York: W. Taylor, [1845?] 285 p. NN. 45-5818

Sealsfield, Charles, 1793-1864. Tokeah; or the white rose. An Indian tale. Second edition. Philadelphia: Lea and Blanchard, 1845. 98 p. CLSM; ICN; MB; RPB; WHi. 45-5819

Seamen's Orphan and Children's Friend Society, Salem, Massachusetts. Constitution of the Salem Seamen's Orphan and Children's Friend Society; with the fifth annual report; and a list of the members. Salem: Ives and Pease, 1845. 18 p. MH. 45-5820

Sears, Barnas, 1802-1880. The ciceronian; or the Prussian method of teaching the elements of the Latin language. Boston: Gould, Kendall and Lincoln, 1845. 184 p. CLSU; DLC; NPV; OCl. 45-5821

Sears, Barnas, 1802-1880. Essays on ancient literature and art. Boston, 1845. NNebg. 45-5822

Sears, Edmund Hamilton, 1810-1876. Voices of the past. A discourse preached at Lancaster, the last Sabbath in the year, December 29, 1844. Boston, 1845. 16 p. ICMe; ICU; MBC; MeU; MH-AH. 45-5823

Sears, Robert, 1810-1892. Bible biography; or the lives and characters of the principal personages recorded in the sacred writings. Fourteenth edition. New York: Redfield and Savage, 1845. 491 p. GDecCT; MNe; MHi. 45-5824

Sears, Robert, 1810-1892. The guide to knowledge forming a complete library of entertaining information in the several departments of science, literature, and arts. Tenth edition. New York: E. Walker and company, 1845. 484 p. CtY; MHi; NHem; RJa; WU. 45-5825

Sears, Robert, 1810-1892. A new and complete history of the Bible as contained in Old and New Testaments with numerous engravings. New York: Sears and Walker, 1845. 2 v. in 1. GDec; IaCli; MNe; PNt. 45-5826

Sears, Robert, 1810-1892. New and complete history of the Holy Bible, as contained in the Old and New Testaments. Fourth edition. New York: Sears and Walker, 1845. 2 v. in 1. CtHC; MHi. 45-5827

Sears, Robert, 1810-1892. Pictorial history of the American revolution; with a sketch of the early history of the country, the constitution of the United States, and a chronological index. New York: R. Sears; Boston: Redding and company, 1845. 432 p. InNd; LNH; NcDaD; RPB; ViU. 45-5828

Sears, Robert, 1810-1892. Pictorial illustrations of the Holy Bible. New York: Sears and Walker, 1845. 383 p. IGK; MiCw; NNUT; OkEnS; PLor. 45-5829

Sears, Robert, 1810-1892. Wonders of the world, in nature, art and mind. Eighth edition. New York: Edward Walker, 1845. 528 p. IaGG; IaPeC; MiKL; PP. 45-5830

Seaton, Oneida. It is all for the best; or Clarke the baker. A tale for youth. Boston: D. Ticknor and company, 1845. DLC; MB. 45-5831

Sechs verschiedene gesprache qwischen einem Reformirten Vorsteher, und einem Evangelischen Klassfuhrer. Doylestown, 1845. 24 p. PHi. 45-5832

A second letter to the public in relation to the New York and Erie Railroad Company. [New York] W.G. Boggs, [1845?] 14 p. NN. 45-5833

Second part of the tract on mission. Salem: Printed at the Gazette office, 1845. 21 p. MBC; MeB; MWA; NjR; WHi. 45-5834

Second series of questions in geography compiled for the use of Mr. and Mrs. Hamilton's Seminary for Young Ladies. Baltimore: John D. Toy, 1845. 48 p. MdHi. 45-5835

Sedgwick, Catharine Maria, 1784-1867. Letters from abroad to kindred at home. New York: Harper and brothers, 1845. 2 v. MB; MeAu; MWel; OM; WM. 45-5836

Sedgwick, Catharine Maria, 1789-1867. The poor rich man, and the rich poor man. New York: Harper and brothers, 1845. 186 p. MoSpD; MSher. 45-5837

Sedgwick, Catharine Maria, 1789-1867. Means and ends or self training. Second edition. New York: Harper and brothers, 1845. 278 p. MShM; NSYU. 45-5838

Sedgwick, Catharine Maria, 1789-1867. Settlers from abroad to kindred at home. New York: Harper and brothers, 1845. 2 v. in 1. LNP. 45-5839

Sedgwick, Catharine Maria, 1789-1867. Wilton Harvey. New York: Harper, 1845. NoLoc. 45-5840

Sedgwick, Elizabeth Buckminster. Moral tales, for young people; lessons without books. Boston: Crosby and Nichols, 1845. 216 p. DLC; MB; MeBa; NN; TNP. 45-5841

Sedgwick, Susan Anne Livingston Ridley. Louisa and her cousin. Boston: Crosby and Nichols, 1845. 244 p. MBSi; NN. 45-5842

Sedley, William Henry, 1806-1872. The drunkard, or the fallen saved. A moral domestic drama in five acts. New York: William Taylor and company; Baltimore: William and Henry Taylor, [1845?] NBuG. 45-5843

Seely, W.A. A lecture on the philosophy of vegetation, read at the organization of the American Agricultural Association at the University in the city of New York, the 10th February, 1845. New York: Wiley and Putnam, 1845. 25 p. CtY; NjR; NNC. 45-5844

Segur, Phillippe Paul, 1780-1873. History of the expedition to Russia, undertaken by the Emperor Napoleon in the year 1812. New York: Harper and brothers, 1845. 2 v. NeWfC; OCY; PSeW; RWe. 45-5845

Seiss, Joseph Augustus. Ravages of intemperance. An address... Baltimore: Publishing rooms of the Evangelical Lutheran Church, 1845. 20 p. DLC; OSW; PPLT. 45-5846

The select manual almanac of useful and entertaining knowledge, for 1846. By Aaron Maynard. [Boston? 1845] MH; MWA. 45-5847

Select novels. New York: Harper and brothers, 1845. 560 p. IU; MB; MnU. 45-5848

Selma, Alabama. Dallas Academy. Catalogue of the officers, faculty, and pupils. Tuscaloosa, Alabama, 1845. v. 1- GEU. 45-5849

The semi-colon. Cincinnati: E. Morgan and company, 1845. n.p., 1845-. v. 1-. CSmH; MH; PPL-R. 45-5850

Seneca, Lucius Annaeus. Hercules Furens, a tragedy of Seneca. Edited by Charles Beck... Boston: James Munroe and company, 1845. 94 p. CtMW; IGK; MoS; OO; ViU. 45-5851

Seneca, Lucius Annaeus. Seneca's morals. By way of abstract. To which is added, a discourse, under the title of an after thought. Sixth American edition. Philadelphia: Grigg and Elliot, 1845. 359 p. ILM; KyU; OU. 45-5852

Seneca Nation. To the Congress of the United States of America. The memorial of the undersigned chiefs of the Seneca Nation assembled in public council on the Chattaraugus Reservation, on the 3d day of December, 1845. n.p., 1845? 8 p. DLC; WHi. 45-5853

Sequoya, Cherokee Indian, 1770-1843. Cherokee alphabet. Cherokee Baptist Mission. [n.p.] H. Upham, printer, [1845?] NoLoc. 45-5854

Seton, Samuel Worthington, 1789-1869. Plan of instruction for the New York public schools. [New York, 1845?] NN. 45-5855

Seven letters from a gentelman who had been a Protestant clergyman to his brother, explaining the motives of his conversion to the Roman Catholic and Apostolic faith. Jersey City, New Jersey; James Walsh, [1845] 63 p. MoFloSS. 45-5856

Sewall, Henry Devereux. A collection of psalms and hymns. Revised edition with supplment. New York: C.S. Francis, 1845. 520 p. DLC; NNUT. 45-5857

Sewall, Henry Devereux. A collection

of psalms and hymns for social and private worship. Revised edition with supplement. New York: Francis, 1845. 519 p. CBPac; DLC; GAGTh; IEG; MBUPH. 45-5858

Seward, William Henry. In the Supreme Court of the United States. On a certificate of division of opinion from the Circuit Court of the United States for the Northern District of New York. James G. Wilson vs. Lewis Rousseau and Charles Easton... Auburn: Printed by Henry Oliphant, 1845. MBS. 45-5859

Sewell, Elizabeth Missing, 1815-1906. Amy Herbert. Edited by Rev. W. Sewell. New York: Harper brothers, 1845. 133 p. MWiW; NN. 45-5860

Sewell, Elizabeth Missing, 1815-1906. Gertrude. Edited by the Rev. W. Sewell. New York: D. Appleton and company, 1845. 332 p. CtY; LNT; MdBP; MwiW; PPL. 45-5861

Sexton's monitor and cemetery memorial, Dorchester, Massachusetts. Third edition. Boston, 1845. 36 p. DLC; MPlyP; MWA; NSy. 45-5862

Seybold, Carl Friedrich. Die historie vom ervaler jacob und seiner ziwolf Sohnen, etc. Lancaster: J. Bar, 1845. 68 p. DLC; PHi. 45-5863

Seymour, David L. Speech of Mr. Seymour on the annexation of Texas. Delivered in the House, January 23, 1845. Washington, 1845. DLC; NBu; RP. 45-5864

Shakers. Sacred hymns for spiritual worship of believers in Christ's second appearing... Canterbury, New Hampshire, 1845. 180 p. MWiW; NNUT. 45-5865

Shakers. To the Senate of the state of New York: The memorial of Stanton Buckingham, Stephen Wells, Justice Harwood and Chauncey Copley, trustees of the United Society of Believers called Shakers, residing at Watervelist in the county of Albany. [Watervelist, 1845] DLC; OClWHi. 45-5866

Shakespeare, William, 1564-1616. Dramatic works and poems with notes, original and selected and introductory remarks to each play, by Samuel Weller, singer and a life of the poet by Charles Symmons. New York: Harper and brothers, 1845. 2 v. CoU; IaFd. 45-5867

Shakespeare, William, 1564-1616. The dramatic works of William Shakespeare, from the text of the corrected copies of Stevens and Malone, with a life of the poet. Hartford: S. Andrus and son, 1845. 844 p. CoU; IaFd; MNBedf; OWoC. 45-5868

Shakespeare, William, 1564-1616. Hamlet. A tragedy, in five acts. New York: S. French, 1845. 77 p. MB; MH. 45-5869

Shakespeare, William, 1564-1616. Hamlet; Prince of Denmark. A tragedy, in five acts. New York: Turner and Fisher, 1845. 86 p. NN. 45-5870

Shakespeare, William, 1564-1616. Much ado about nothing; a comedy in five acts. New York: S. French, 1845. 61 p. MH; NNC. 45-5871

Shand, Peter J. Address at the laying of the corner stone of the new Episcopal

Church, Columbia, S.C. November 26, 1845 by the Rector. Columbia: J.C. Morgan's Letter Press, 1845. 9 p. ScSp. 45-5872

Shattuck, Lemuel. Letter from Lemuel Shattuck, in answer to interrogatories of J. Preston, in relation to the introduction of water into the city of Boston. Boston: Samuel N. Dickinson, printer, 1845. 40 p. MiD-B; MWA; NjR; PPL; WHi. 45-5873

Shaw, Edward, B.L. Medical remembrancer, or book of emergencies; in which are concisely pointed out the immediate remedies to be adopted in the first moments of danger from poisoning, etc. Revised and improved by an American physician. New York: Wood, 1845. 112 p. DWLM; MnU; NNN; OC; PPCP. 45-5874

Shaw, Edward, B.L. Medical remembrancer, or book of emergencies. Second edition. New York: Samuel S. and William Wood, 1845. 112 p. JeffMedC. 45-5875

Shaw, Elijah, b. 1771. A short sketch of the life of Elijah Shaw, who served for twenty-one years in the United States navy, taking an active part in four different wars between the United States and foreign powers... Third edition. Rochester: E. Shepard, 1845. [5]-63 p. CSmH; DLC; ICN; MBAt; NN. 45-5876

Shaw, James, 1806-1875. Farewell sermon to the Presbyterian Church at Middlebury, Ohio. Hudson: Observer office, 1845. 16 p. MBC; OClW. 45-5877

Shaw, Lemuel, 1781-1861. An address delivered at the opening of the new court house in Worcester, September 30, 1845.

By the Hon. Lemuel Shaw, chief Justice of the Supreme Judicial Court of Massachusetts. Worcester: Printed by Henry J. Howland, 1845. 14 p. ICN; MB; MeHi; NNC; OClWHi. 45-5878

Shaw, R. A cabinet of genius, etc., for virtue and piety. Albany, 1845. MB. 45-5879

Shaw, Robert. An exposition of the confession of faith of the Westminister Assembly of Divines. Revised by the committee of publication. Philadelphia: Presbyterian Board of Publication, 1845. 360 p. CtHC; CSt; MiDMCh; PPPrHi. 45-5880

Shea, John Augustus, 1802-1845. A poem, delivered at the tenth anniversary of the Caliopean Society, Suffield, Connecticut on August 5, 1845. New York: W.H. Graham, 1845. 13 p. CtWHatk; MBuG; RPB. 45-5881

Shea, John H., 1800?-1855. Bookkeeping by single and double entry. Third addition. Baltimore: John Murphy, printer, 1845. 184 p. CU; IU; NcD; NNAIA. 45-5882

Shedd, William Greenough Thayer, 1820-1894. Method and influence of theological studies. Discourse pronounced at Burlington, before the literary societies of the University of Vermont, August 5, 1845. Burlington: University Press, 1845. 52 p. CtHC; IaB; KWiU; MAnP; VtU. 45-5883

Sheldon and Company's business or advertising directory; containing the cards, circulars, and advertisements of the principal firms of the cities of New York, Boston, Philadelphia, Baltimore, etc. New

York: J.F. Trow and company, 1845. 176 p. ICU; N. 45-5884

Shelley, Mary Wollstonecroft Goodwin, 1797-1851. Frankenstein or the modern Prometheus. New York: H.G. Daggers, 1845. 114 p. CSf. 45-5885

Shelley, Percy Bysshe, 1792-1822. Poetical works. Boston: Crosby and Raines, 1845. 246. IaIndianS. 45-5886

Shelley, Percy Bysshe, 1792-1822. The poetical works of Percy Bysshe Shelley. First American edition with some remarks on the poetic faculty and its influences. New York: J.S. Redfield, 1845. 750 p. IU; MdBJ; MH; PBL. 45-5887

Shepard, Samuel, 1772-1846. All things earthly, changing and transitory; a sermon preached in Lenox, Massachusetts, April 30, 1845, at the celebration of the fiftieth anniversary of his ordination to the work of the gospel ministry in said town. Together with the address of Mr. Todd. Lenox: J.G. Stanley, 1845. 32 p. MBC; MiD-B; MWA; OO; RPB. 45-5888

Shepard, W.A. Rejoinder to the second section of the reply of Hon. H. Mann. [Boston, 1845] 56 p. MB. 45-5889

Sheperdstown, Maryland. Trinity Church. A historic sketch of Trinity Church. To which is added an address to the ladies' benevolent association of this Church. Baltimore: Joseph Robinson, 1845. 13 p. MdBD. 45-5890

Shepherd, T.J. Spiritual destitutions of Maryland: a sermon preached, by appointment, before the Presbytery of the District of Columbia, in the Fifth Presbyterian Church, Baltimore, October 15, 1845, and published by request of the presbytery. Washington, 1845. 16 p. MBC; MiD-B; PPL; PPPrHi. 45-5891

Shepley, Charles. The mysteries of Fitchburg. Fitchburg: Published by the author, 1845. 28 p. MFiHi. 45-5892

Shepley, David, 1804-1881. Convictions essential to missionary exertions. A sermon delivered in Fryeburg, June 25, 1845 before the Maine Missionary Society at its thirty-eighth anniversary. Portland: Thurston, Ilsley and company, 1845. 48 p. CBPSR; KyDC; Me; MeBaT; MH. 45-5893

Sheppard, J.H. A practical treatise on the use of Peruvian and Ichaboe African guano. First American from the second London edition. New York, 1845. 60 p. WU-A. 45-5894

Sheridan, Richard Brinsley Butler, 1751-1816. The school for scandal; a comedy in five acts. With the stage directions, costumes, etc. New York: W. Taylor; Baltimore: W. Taylor and company, 1845. 86 p. DLC; MH; MWA; NjP; VtU. 45-5895

Sherman and Smith. The world of Mercator's projection, showing the latest explorations throughout the globe. New York, 1845. MB. 45-5896

Sherrill, Hunting, 1783-1866. A manual of homeopathic prescriptions with a full and improved repertory in which diseases are alphabetically arranged with the remedy for them connected. New York: W. Raddie, 1845. 181 p. DLC; ICJ. 45-5897

Sherwin, Thomas, 1799-1869. Common school algebra. Boston: Phillips and Sampson, 1845. 238 p. DLC; MH; NIC; PU; RPB. 45-5898

Sherwin, Thomas, 1799-1869. An elementary treatise on algebra, for the use of students in high schools and colleges. Second edition. Boston: Benjamin B. Mussey, 1845. 300 p. NhD; RPB. 45-5899

Sherwood, Adiel, 1791-1879. The true and spurious churches contrasted. Philadelphia: King and Baird, 1845. 36 p. PPM. 45-5900

Sherwood, Henry Hall. Manual for magnetizing with the rotary and vibrating magnetic machine in the duodynamic treatment of diseases. Sixth edition, enlarged. New York: Wiley and Putnam, 1845. 219 p. CtY; DLC; DNLM; MB; PU. 45-5901

Sherwood, Henry Hall. A manual for magnetizing with the rotary and vibrating magnetic machine, in the duodynamic treatment of diseases. Seventh edition. New York: Wiley and Putnam, 1845. 219 p. MeB. 45-5902

Sherwood, Mary Martha Butt, 1775-1851. Duty is safety; or troublesome Tom. Philadelphia: George S. Appleton, 1845. 64 p. ICartC. 45-5903

Sherwood, Mary Martha Butt, 1775-1851. Lady of the manor; being a series of conversations on the subject of confirmation. Intended for the use of the middle and higher ranks of young females. New York: Harper and brothers, 1845. 586 p. ViU. 45-5904

Sherwood, Reuben. Workmen, and their work, in God's building; sermon at the opening of the annual convention of the Protestant Episcopal Church in the diocese of New York, September 24, 1845. New York: Henry Onderdonk and company, 1845. 23 p. MH; MWA; NNC. 45-5905

Shew, Joel, 1816-1855. Hydropathy; or the water cure: its principles, modes of treatment, etc... Second edition. New York: Wiley and Putnam, 1845. [15]-360 p. CU; MnHi; NbCrD; NNN; OC. 45-5906

Shindler, Mary Stanley Bunce Dana, 1810-1883. Letters addressed to relatives and friends, chiefly in reply to arguments in support of the doctrine of the Trinity. Boston: James Munroe and company, 1845. 318 p. LNH; MWA; NbOP; OHi; TxGR. 45-5907

Shindler, Mary Stanley Bunce Dana, 1810-1883. The northern harp, consisting of original sacred and moral songs, adapted to the most popular melodies, for the pianoforte and guitar. Fifth edition. New York: Mark H. Newman, 1845. 99 p. MnU; NRU; OO. 45-5908

Shipman, Thomas Leffingwell. Future blessedness of the righteous. A sermon delivered December 30, 1844, at the funeral of Joseph Punderson Tyler. Norwich, Connecticut: Dunham's Press, 1845. 16 p. CtHC; CtSoP; MBC; RPB. 45-5909

Shippingport and Portland directory for 1845-1846. Containing a list of civil and military officers. Louisville: The office of the Louisville Journal, 1845. 295 p. KyLoF. 45-5910

Shoberl, Frederic, 1775-1853. Persia; containing a description of the country with an account of its government, laws and religion, etc. Philadelphia: Grigg and Elliott, 1845. 181 p. MB; PP; PPM. 45-5911

Short, Charles Wilkins, 1794-1863. Duties of medical students during attendance on lectures. An introductory address, delivered at the opening of the session of 1845-1846, in the Medical Institute of Louisville, November 3, 1845. Louisville, Kentucky: Printed by Morton and Griswold, 1845. 24 p. ICJ; ICU; KyLoF; MoS; WU. 45-5912

Short, Milton. A condensed system of geography; exhibiting the different countries of the globe, with their capitals, governments, society, religion, bodies of water, rivers, capes, mountains, etc. adapted to the forty second edition of Olney's geography. Springville, Indiana, 1845. 16 p. In. 45-5913

A short history of the public debt of Maryland and of the causes which produce it. By a citizen of Maryland. Baltimore: Printed by Bull and Tuttle, 1845. 95 p. MB; MdBJ; MdHi; Vi; WHi. 45-5914

Shurtleff, J.B. The governmental instructor; or a brief and comprehensive view of the government of the United States, and of the state governments, in easy lessons, designed for the use of schools. New York: Collins, brother and company, 1845. [5]-183 p. Ct; FMF; NcG; OOxM; PU. 45-5915

Shurtleff, J.S. Der kleine staatsmann; oder, eine kurze und umfassende uebersicht der regierung der Versinigten Staaten und der staaten-regienungen. New York: Radde, 1845. 183 p. PPG; PPGi; PU. 45-5916

Shurtleff College. Annual catalogue of the officers and students. Alton, 1845-. 3 v. in 1. MoS. 45-5917

Shute, James M. Specimen of modern printing types, cast at the letter foundry of the Boston type and stereotype company, Minot's building. Boston: White, Lewis and Potter, 1845. 266 p. TNDL; TNL. 45-5918

Siborne, William, 1797-1849. History of the war in France and Belgium, in 1815; containing minute details of the battles of Quatre-Bras, Ligny, Wavre and Waterloo. First American from the second London edition. Philadelphia: Lea and Blanchard, 1845. 2 v. GMWa; In; KyLx; MdBP; RPA. 45-5919

Siddons, Joachim Hayward, 1801?-1885. The object of interest. A farce. In one act. By J.H. Stocqueler, pseud. New York: Samuel French, [1845] 17 p. OCl. 45-5920

Sigourney, Lydia Howard Huntley, 1791-1865. The boy's book; consisting of original articles in prose and poetry. New York: Turner, Hughes and Hayden, etc., etc., 1845. 247 p. CtHWatk; MH; MWA; OO; ViU. 45-5921

Sigourney, Lydia Howard Huntley, 1791-1865. The girl's reading book. Fourteenth edition. New York: Turner, Hughes and Hayden; Raleigh: Turner and Hughes, 1845. 243 p. NGos. 45-5922

Sigourney, Lydia Howard Huntley, 1791-1865. Letters to mothers. New

York: Harper and brothers, 1845. MB; MWA; OO. 45-5923

Sigourney, Lydia Howard Huntley, 1791-1865. Letters to mothers. Sixth edition. New York: Harper and brothers, 1845. [9]-297 p. CtHC; KyLoS; LN; NbOM; OO. 45-5924

Sigourney, Lydia Howard Huntley, 1791-1865. Letters to young ladies. Fourteenth edition. New York: Harper and brothers, 1845. 295 p. ICMcC; ICP; IEdS; MChi. 45-5925

Sigourney, Lydia Howard Huntley, 1791-1865. The lovely sisters, Margaret and Henrietta. Hartford: H.S. Parsons and company, 1845. 100 p. CtHT; CtHWatk; MnU. 45-5926

Sigourney, Lydia Howard Huntley, 1791-1865. Poetry for seamen. Boston: J. Munroe and company, 1845. 63 p. CtHT; MB; NNUT; RPB; TxU. 45-5927

Sigourney, Lydia Howard Huntley, 1791-1865. Scenes in my native land. Boston: J. Munroe and company, 1845 319 p. CtSoP; DeWi; MH; NBuDD; OrP. 45-5928

Sigourney, Lydia Howard Huntley, 1791-1865. Select poems. Philadelphia: E.C. and J. Biddle, 1845. 338 p. IaFair; MnSJ; MoS; NNC; VtMiC. 45-5929

Sigourney, Lydia Howard Huntley, 1791-1865. The stockbridge bowl. A poem read by Hon. Ezekiel Bacon at the Berkshire Jubilee. Albany: Weare C. Little; Pittsfield: E.P. Little, 1845. 4 p. MPiB. 45-5930

Silliman, Benjamin, 1779-1864. Report of the cause of the explosion at the fire in Broad Street, New York. New York: Bryant and company, printers, 1845. 29 p. IEN-M; MB; MH; NBLIHI; WHi. 45-5931

Silliman, Benjamin, 1779-1864. Report on the analysis of the waters. New Haven: Yale College Laboratory, 1845. 11 p. LNH. 45-5932

Silliman, Benjamin, 1816-1885. Report on the chemical examination of several waters for the city of Boston. Boston, 1845. 32 p. CtY; DLC; MBC; Nh; PPAN. 45-5933

Silver, Joseph S. The philosophy of evil. Showing its uses and its unavoidable necessity; by illustrations drawn from philosophical examination of the most startling evils of life. Philadelphia: G.B. Zieber and company, 1845. 2 v. in 1. IEG; IU; MH; MWA; PU. 45-5934

Simeon, Charles, 1759-1836. The offices of the Holy Spirit; four sermons preached before the University of Cambridge in the month of November, 1831. New York: Stanford, 1845. 103 p. InID; KNeo; NCH. 45-5935

Simmons, Charles, 1798-1856. A scripture manual, alphabetically and systematically arranged designed to facilitate the finding of proof texts. Stereotype edition enlarged and revised. New York: M.W. Dodd; Boston: Crocker and Brewster, 1845. KyBC; PCA; ScCoB; ViRut; WAsN. 45-5936

Simmons, James Fowler, 1795-1864. Remarks of Mr. Simmons, of Rhode Island in support of his proposition to reduce postages to a uniform rate of five cents for a single letter, for all distances... In the Senate... February 6, 1845. Washington: J. and G.S. Gideon, 1845. 13 p. IU; MHi; NNC; OClWHi; WHi. 45-5937

Simms, Jeptha Root, 1807-1883. History of Schoharie County, and border wars of New York: containing also a sketch of the causes which led to the American revolution; and interesting memoranda of the Mohawk Valley... Albany: Munsell and Tanner, 1845. 20-672 p. CSt; ICN; MnHi; NjR; PPA. 45-5938

Simms, William Gilmore, 1806-1870. Castle dismal; or the bachelor's Christmas. A domestic legend... New York: Burgess, Stringer and company, 1845. 192 p. MiU; NN; TxU. 45-5939

Simms, William Gilmore, 1806-1870. The Charleston book; a miscellany in prose and verse. Charleston: Samuel Hart, 1845. 404 p. AB; MnHi; NcAS; PHi; RPB. 45-5940

Simms, William Gilmore, 1806-1870. Count Julian; or the last days of the Goth. A historical romance. Baltimore: W. Taylor and company; New York, New York: W. Taylor, 1845. 201 p. MdBP; MH; NcD; ScU; RPB. 45-5941

Simms, William Gilmore, 1806-1870. Grouped thoughts and scattered fancies; a collection of sonnets... Richmond, Virginia: Printed by W. Macfarland, 1845. 61 p. AU; MH; NcD; NN; PU. 45-5942

Simms, William Gilmore, 1806-1870. Helen Halsey; or the swamp state of Conelachita. A tale of the borders... New York: Burgess, Stringer and company, 1845. 216 p. CSmH; DLC; OClW; ScU; WU. 45-5943

Simms, William Gilmore, 1806-1870. The life of Francis Marion... New York: Henry G. Langley, 1845. 347, 24 p. IU; KHi; MMal; NN; PHi. 45-5944

Simms, William Gilmore, 1806-1870. Views and reviews in American literature, history and fiction. New York: Wiley and Putnam, 1845. 2 v. ICU; PAtM; ScCC; Vi; WHi. 45-5945

Simms, William Gilmore, 1806-1870. The wigwam and the cabin. First and second series. First edition. New York: Wiley and Putnam, 1845. 2 v. CSt; ICU; MBAt; RPA; TxWB. 45-5946

Simon, Johann Franz, 1807-1843. The chemistry of man... Translated by Thomas E. Day, Philadelphia, 1845. PPAN. 45-5947

Simonde de Sismondi, Jean Charles Leonard, 1773-1842. History of the crusades against the Albigenses in the 13th century. Philadelphia: Wilson, 1845. 156 p. OO. 45-5948

Simonds, William, 1822-1859. Sinners' friend or disease of sin, its consequences and the remedy. Boston: Massachusetts Sabbath School Society, 1845. 360 p. CBPSR; MoSpD; MTop; UU. 45-5949

The sin and danger of neglecting the Savior. Philadelphia, 1845. 16 p. IaDuUS; OO; WHi. 45-5950

The sinner saved; or the divine law and saving faith by the author of "Child assisted in giving his heart to God." Boston:

Massachusetts Sabbath School Society, 1845. 90 p. DLC; MTop; ViU. 45-5951

Sister Lucy's recreations. Tales for the young. Philadelphia: Walker and Gillis, 1845. MH. 45-5952

Sketch of the commercial intercourse of the world, with China. New York: Hunts' Merchants' Magazine, 1845. 342 p. MFiHi; MS. 45-5953

A sketch of the life of Solomon, the last King of Israel. Philadelphia, 1845. 204 p. TxH. 45-5954

Skinner, Dolphus. Address at Syracuse Lodge, no. 102 at dedication and installation of officers, March 18. Syracuse: Tucker and Kinney, 1845. 16 p. MBFM. 45-5955

Skinner, H.B. The family doctor; or guide to health; containing a brief description of the general causes, symptons and cure of diseases. Forty-second edition. Boston: J.K. Wellman, 1845. 56 p. NN. 45-5956

Skinner, John Stuart, 1788-1851. Address delivered before the Agricultural Society of Newcastle County, Delaware, at the annual meeting held September 11, 1844. n.p.: Published for distribution by order of the society, 1845. 28 p. DLC; MBH; MH; NcD. 45-5957

Skinner, John Stuart, 1788-1851. The dog and the sportsman. Embracing the uses, breeding, training, diseases, etc. of dogs and an account of the different kind of game, and their habits... Philadelphia: Lea and Blanchard, 1845. [17]-223 p. CtHT; MnDu; MNF; PPL-R; RPA. 45-5958

Skinner, Thomas Harvey, 1791-1871. A discourse delivered in the Mercer Street Church, October 19, 1845, ten years after its organization. New York: Leavitt Trow and company, 1845. 24 p. CtHC; ICP; KyDC; MWA; PPPrHi. 45-5959

Slack, David B. An essay on the human color, in three parts. Providence: J.F. Moore, 1845. 100 p. DLC; MiU-C; MNBedf; NN-Sc. 45-5960

Sleepes, John Sherburne, 1794-1878. Tales of the ocean, and essays for the forecastle. Boston, 1845. CtHWatk. 45-5961

Smellie, William, 1740-1795. The philosophy of natural history. With an introduction and various additions and alterations, intended to adapt it to the present state of knowledge. Boston: William J. Reynolds, 1845. 344 p. IaFayU; MB; MeB; MH; OO. 45-5962

Smiley, Thomas Tucker, d. 1879. A complete key to Smiley's new federal calculator; or scholar's assistant. Philadelphia: Grigg and Elliott, 1845. InU. 45-5963

Smiley, Thomas Tucker, d. 1879. The new federal calculater, of scholar's assistant. For the use of schools and counting houses. Philadelphia: Grigg and Elliot, 1845. 180 p. CoU; PAtM. 45-5964

Smith, Albert Richard, 1816-1860. The adventures of Jack Holiday, with something about his sister. New York: C. Shepard, [1845?] 28 p. MH. 45-5965

Smith, Albert Richard, 1816-1860. Beauty and the beast. New York: Burgess, Stringer, and company, [1845?] 64 p. DLC; NN. 45-5966

Smith, Alexander. Aleck, the last of the mutineers, or the history of Pitcairn's Island. Amherst: J.S. and C. Adams, 1845. 162 p. MAJ; MNF; MWA; NN. 45-5967

Smith, Alexander. Aleck, the last of the mutineers, or the history of Pitcairn's Island. Second edition. Philadelphia: E.C. Biddle, 1845. 162 p. MNF; MWA; NN; NYPL; TxH. 45-5968

Smith, Alexander. Aleck, the last of the mutineers, or the history of Pitcairn's Island. Third edition. Philadelphia: E.C. Biddle, 1845. MH. 45-5969

Smith, Azariah, 1817-1851. Ruins of Nineveh; description of the discoveries made in 1843 and 1844. [New Haven, 1845] 14 p. MH; VtU. 45-5970

Smith, Caleb Blood, 1808-1864. Speech of Mr. Smith, of Indiana, on the annexation of Texas. Delivered in the House, January 8, 1845. Washington: J. and G.S. Gideon, printers, 1845. 15 p. CtHWatk; MWA; PPL; RP; Tx. 45-5971

Smith, Charles Billings, d. 1890. Education of young men. An address delivered before the Pythagarean Institute of Chicago. Chicago: Ellis and Fergus, 1845. 16 p. NCHi. 45-5972

Smith, Charles Billings, d. 1890. True greatness. An address delivered before the Cleosophic Society of Yates Academy, March 4, 1845. Lockport, [New York] Printed by J. A. Harrison, 1845. ICHi. 45-5973

Smith, Daniel, 1806-1852. Natural his-

tory. For Sunday Schools. Prepared by Rev. Daniel Smith. New York: G. Lane and C.B. Tippett for the Sunday School Union of the Methodist Episcopal Church, 1845. 188 p. MPeHi. 45-5974

Smith, Elizabeth Oakes Prince, 1806-1893. The poetical writings of Elizabeth Oakes Smith. First complete edition. New York: J.S. Redfield, 1845. 204 p. MB; MeHi; MnU; NN; TxU. 45-5975

Smith, Elizabeth Oakes Prince, 1806-1893. The true child. Boston: Saxton and Kelt, 1845. 160 p. DLC; MBoy; MHa; NBLiHi; NN. 45-5976

Smith, Francis Henney, 1812-1890. The American statistical arithmetic; designed for academies and schools. Philadelphia: Thomas, Cowperthwait and company, 1845. 282 p. CtHT; DLC; NjR; OO; ViU. 45-5977

Smith, Francis Ormond Jonathan, 1806-1876. The secret corresponding vocabulary; adapted for use to Morse's electro-magnetic telegraph... Portland, Maine: Thurston, Ilsley and company, 1845. 230 p. MB; MdBP; NIC; Vi; VtU. 45-5978

Smith, Gerrit, 1797-1874. Letter to William H. Seward. Peterboro: Sinclair Tousey, 1845. 3 p. MiU-C; NSyU. 45-5979

Smith, Gerrit, 1797-1874. Open letter to Hon. F. Whittlesey of Rochester. Peterboro: American News company, 1845. 3 p. DLC; NSyU. 45-5980

Smith, Gerrit, 1797-1874. To those ministers in the county of Madison who refuse to preach politics. [Peterboro, 1845] 3 p. NIC; NSyU; WHi. 45-5981

Smith, Gibson. Lectures on clairmativeness: or human magnetism. With an appendix. New York: Printed by Searing and Prall, 1845. 40 p. CSt; MBAt; MWA; OCGHM; NNNAM. 45-5982

Smith, Gideon B. Silk culture in the United States. Baltimore, 1845. 4 p. MeB. 45-5983

Smith, Henry Hollingsworth, 1815-1890. Anatomical atlas, illustrative of the structure of the human body. Under the supervision of William E. Horner. Philadelphia: Lea and Blanchard, 1845. 200 p. CSt-L; GU-M; LNOP; NNNAM; OCIM. 45-5984

Smith, Henry I. Education; Part 1. History of education, ancient and modern. Part 11. A plan of culture and instruction, based on Christian principles and designed to aid in the right education of youth... New York: Harper and brothers, 1845. [12]-340 p. LU; PAtM; OSW; ScCoB; WHi. 45-5985

Smith, I. Mary Dalton or wealth and worth. A tale of New York life. New York: W. Taylor, 1845. 36 p. MnU. 45-5986

Smith, James. The book that will suit you or a word for every one. Third edition. New York: M.W. Dodd, 1845. 349 p. IEG; PCA. 45-5987

Smith, Jerome Van Crowinshield, 1800-1879. Memoirs of Andrew Jackson, late Major-General and commander in chief of the southern division of the army of the United States. Philadelphia: T.K. and P.O. Collins, printers, 1845. MH. 45-5988

Smith, John C. Divine faithfulness; sermon, death of Dr. Phinenas Bradley, March 8, 1845. Washington: J. and G.S. Gideon, 1845. 16 p. RPB. 45-5989

Smith, John Calvin. Guide through Ohio, Michigan, Indiana, Illinois, Missouri, Wisconsin and Iowa showing the township lines of the United States surveys. New York: Colton, 1845. In. 45-5990

Smith, John Calvin. Map of the state of New York, showing the boundaries of counties and townships, the location of cities, towns, and villages the courses of railroads, canals, and stage roads. New York: J. Disturnell, 1845. Map. ICN; MB; MWA; TCU. 45-5991

Smith, John Calvin. Map of the United States of America, Canada, and a large portion of Texas. New York: Sherman and Smith, 1845. Map. ICU; MiU; VtU; WaSp. 45-5992

Smith, Joseph Few, 1816-1888. American Lutheran mission with an appeal in its behalf: Being an address delivered at the meeting of the General Synod of the Evangelical Lutheran Church, at Philadelphia, May 16, 1845. Albany: E.H. Pease, 1845. 50 p. MWA; NNMr; OSW; ScCoT; Vi. 45-5993

Smith, Joseph, 1805-1844. The doctrine and covenants of the Church of Latter Day Saints, carefully selected from the revelations of God. Third American edition. Nauvoo, Illinois: Printed by John Taylor, 1845. 448 p. C-S; DLC; IU; NNUT; UU. 45-5994

Smith, Josiah William, 1816-1887. An original view of executory interests in real and personal property, comprising the points deducible from the cases stated in the treatise of Fearne... Philadelphia: Printed by William S. Martien, 1845. 492 p. C; Ia; Ky; PPB; OrSC. 45-5995

Smith, Matthew Hale, 1810-1879. Impiety in high places, and sympathy with crime, a curse to any people; sermon in Nashua, New Hampshire, April 20, 1845. Boston: S.N. Dickinson and company, printers, 1845. 32 p. CtHC; MWA; NhHi; PPL; RPB. 45-5996

Smith, Matthew Hale, 1810-1879. Textbook of Universalism; comprising the origin of the system, a biography of its founders; its system of doctrine; an examination of its prominent arguments... Salem: John P. Jewett and company, 1845. 67 p. CtHC; ICU; MBC; OClWHi; PPPrHi. 45-5997

Smith, Richard McAllister, 1819-1870. A new system of modern geography, for the use of schools, academies, etc. Particularly designed for the South and West. Philadelphia: Grigg and Elliot, 1846. 168 p. MoS; PBL; Vi. 45-5998

Smith, Richard Penn, 1798-1834. Col. Crockett's exploits and adventures in Texas wherein is contained a full account of his journey from Tennessee to the Red River and Natchitoches and thence across Texas to San Antonio. Written by himself. New York: Nafis and Cornish; Philadelphia: John B. Perry, 1845. 216 p. MiU; MsOK; MWA; NP; RP. 45-5999

Smith, Robert. The scourge; devoted to the mental and moral improvement of Rev. John A. Gurley, E.M. Pingree, and the Connecticut Convention of Universalists. Prepared and applied by Elders Robert Smith and J.J. Moss. Covington, Kentucky: The authors, 1845. CSmH; PPPrHi. 45-6000

Smith, Robert, 1802-1867. Speech of Mr. Smith, of Illinois, on the harbor and river bill. Delivered in the House, February 26, 1845. Washington: Printed at the Globe office, 1845. 7 p. IHi; LU; NBu; WHi. 45-6001

Smith, Robert, 1802-1867. Speech of Mr. Smith, of Illinois, on the harbor and river bill. Delivered in the House, February 26, 1845. Washington: Printed at the Globe office, 1845. 8 p. MiD-B; NBu; WHi. 45-6002

Smith, Roswell Chamberlain, 1797-1875. Arithmetic on the productive system. Accompanied by a key and cubical blocks. New York: Paine and Burgess, 1845. 311 p. CtY. 45-6003

Smith, Roswell Chamberlain, 1797-1875. English grammar on the productive system. Cincinnati: W.T. Truman, 1845. MH. 45-6004

Smith, Roswell Chamberlain, 1797-1875. English grammar on the productive system; a method of instruction recently adopted in Germany and Switzerland, designed for schools and academies. Philadelphia: Butler and Williams, 1845. 192 p. MH; MnHi; NjR. 45-6005

Smith, Roswell Chamberlain, 1797-1875. Key to Smith's new arithmetic... designed to lessen the burden on teachers. New York: Paine and Burgess, 1845. MH. 45-6006

Smith, Roswell Chamberlain, 1797-1875. Practical and mental arithmetic. To which is added a practical system of bookkeeping. Auburn: H. and J.C. Ivison, 1845. MDeeP; MPiB; NIC; Tx-BrdD. 45-6007

Smith, Roswell Chamberlain, 1797-1875. Smith's atlas, designed to accompany the geography. New York: Paine and Burgess, 1845. 22 leaves. MH; NNC. 45-6008

Smith, Roswell Chamberlain, 1797-1875. Smith's geography. Geography on the productive system: for schools, academies and families. Revised and improved. New York: Paine and Burgess, 1845. 312 p. CSt; CtHwatk; DLC; Lu; MH. 45-6009

Smith, Roswell Chamberlain, 1797-1875. Smith's new grammar. English grammar on the productive system; a method of instruction recently adopted in Germany and Switzerland. Philadelphia: E.H. Butler and company, 1845. 192 p. DLC; MB; MH; NNC; PRB. 45-6010

Smith, Samuel Francis, 1808-1895. Lyric gems; a collection of original and select sacred poetry. Boston: Gould, Kendall and Lincoln, 1845. 128 p. DLC; OU; TxU. 45-6011

Smith, Seba, 1792-1868. Jack Downings letters, by Major Jack Downing. [pseud.] Philadelphia: T.B. Peterson, [1845?] 119 p. DLC; ICU; NNC; PU; TU. 45-6012

Smith, Seba, 1792-1868. May day in

New York. New York: Burgess, Stringer and company, 1845. 120 p. ICN; MeB; NBuG; OO; RPB; 45-6013

Smith, Sydney, 1771-1845. A fragment on the Irish Roman Catholic Church. Boston: Redding and company, 1845. 32 p. ICMe; MBBC; MiD-B; MWA; RPB. 45-6014

Smith, Sydney, 1771-1845. Memoir of the Rev. Sidney Smith. New York: Harper, 1845. 2 v. InThE. 45-6015

Smith, Sydney, 1771-1845. The works of the Rev. Sidney Smith. Philadelphia: Carey, 1845. 3 v. in 1. ArL; CoU; FTa; MdBJ; RWe. 45-6016

Smith, Thomas. The rule for Christians as to the possession and the use of property. Cincinnati, 1845. 60 p. MBC. 45-6017

Smith, Thomas. Speech of Mr. Smith, of Indiana, on the public land bill. Delivered in the House, January 2, 1845. Washington: Printed at the Globe office, 1845. 8 p. NNC; WHi. 45-6018

Smith, Thomas Marshall. A review of the opinion of the Hon. George Robertson on the constitution and organization of the Methodist Episcopal Church and on the right of the property of the Church within the slaveholding states and the bounds of the Church South now being organized. Louisville, 1845. 32 p. NIC; ODW. 45-6019

Smith, William Rudolph, 1787-1868. Address on the consecration and installation of the officers of Olive Branch Lodge, Iowa County, Wisconsin Territory. Mineral Point, 1845. 15 p. IaCrM; NNFM; WHi. 45-6020

Smith's weekly volume. A select circulating library for town and country containing the best popular literature. Philadelphia: L.P. Smith, 1845-6. 3 v. in 1. CU; DLC; NcD; OrP; PP. 45-6021

Smock, David V., 1808?-1878. Systematic benevolence; a sermon delivered at Greensburgh, Iowa, September, 1844. Before the Presbytery of Indianapolis. Indianapolis: S.V.B. Noel, 1845. 24 p. CSmH; In; OCHP. 45-6022

Smull, D.B. and Company, Baltimore, Maryland. The patent portable tubular steam generator. Manufactured by D.B. Smull and Company. Baltimore, 1845. 8 p. PHi. 45-6023

Smyth, Thomas, 1808-1873. The name, nature and functions of ruling elders, wherein is shown from the testimony of scripture, the fathers, and the reformers, that ruling elders are not presbyters or bishops; and that as representatives of the people their office ought to be temporary. With an appendix... New York: Mark H. Newman, 1845. 186 p. CSansS; InCW; KyLo; NbOP; ScU. 45-6024

Smyth, Thomas, 1808-1873. The Romish and prelatical rite of confirmation examined, and proved to be contrary to the scriptures, and the practice of all the earliest and purest churches, both Oriental and Western, with an appendix on the duty of requiring a public profession of religion. New York: Mark H. Newman et al., 1845. [13] 213 p. CoD; GDecCT; NjP; ScU; WHi. 45-6025

Smythies, Harriet Maria Gordon. The jilt. New York, 1845. MBr. 45-6026

Snelling, William Joseph, 1804-1848. The lover's chase. Boston, 1845. 47 p. NjR. 45-6027

Snethen, W.G. Address delivered before the Grand Lodge of Kentucky in the Unitarian Church in the city of Louisville, on Tuesday, September, 1st, 1835. By W.G. Snethen. Frankfort, Kentucky: Albert G. Hodges, 1845. 15 p. NNFM. 45-6028

Snodgrass, William Davis, 1796-1886. An address delivered before the alumni association of Washington College, September 23, 1845. New York: Printed by H. Ludwig, 1845. 32 p. MH-AH; NjR; NN; OClWHi; PWW. 45-6029

Society for the Promotion of Collegiate and Theological Education at the west. Proceedings of a public meeting in behalf of the Society for the promotion of collegiate and theological education at the West. New York: J.F. Trow and company, 1845. 16 p. CBPSR; ICT; MH; NNUT. 45-6030

Society of the friendly sons of St. Patrick of Philadelphia for the relief of emigrants from Ireland. Act of incorporation, bylaws, etc of the Hibernian Society for the Relief of Emigrants from Ireland. Philadelphia: Severus and Magill, 1845. 28 p. RPB. 45-6031

Society of the New York Hospital. Charter of the Society of the New York Hospital and the laws relating thereto with the bylaws and regulations of the institution and those of the Bloomingdale

Asylum for the Insane. New York: J.R. M'Gown, 1845. 104 p. MH; PU. 45-6032

Somervill, M. An exposition of the administration of Maine state prison with such reflections as the subject and facts have suggested. Portland: Published by the Author, 1845. 32 p. NHi. 45-6033

Somerville, Massachusetts. First Congregational Society. Order of services at the dedication of the first house of public worship, erected by the First Congregational Society, in Somerville, September 3, 1845. Broadside. MHi. 45-6034

The Song bird. Revised by D.P. Kidder. New York: G. Lane and C.B. Tippett, 1845. 34 p. DLC. 45-6035

Songs of the quilt or tea party offering. Written by the multitude. New London, 1845. 16 p. CtHWatk; NBuG. 45-6036

Songs of the Washingtonians composed and confirmed by Mrs. V.R.A. New York: F.D. Allen, Jr., 1845. 60 p. DLC. 45-6037

Sonntageschul gesanbuchl ein. Herausgegeben von der Salems sonntagsschul gesellschaft in den nordlichen freiheiten von Philadelphia. Second enlarged edition. Philadelphia: Douglas Wyeth, 1845. 284 p. OBerB; MH; PNazMHi. 45-6038

Sons of Temperance of North America. Bylaws... instituted October 28, 1845. [Fayetteville, North Carolina? 1845?] 4 p. NcU. 45-6039

Sons of Temperance of North America. Bylaws, rules of order, and principles of discipline, adopted by the grand division of the Sons of Temperance of the state of Pennsylvania, at an adjourned session, held September 20, 1845. Philadelphia: William F. Geddes, 1845. 14 p. PHi. 45-6040

Sons of Temperance of North America. Constitution and bylaws of Excelsior Division, No. 16 of the Sons of Temperance of Boston, state of Massachusetts. Instituted August 22, 1845. Boston: White, Lewis, Cotter, 1845. 13 p. MB. 45-6041

Sons of Temperance of North America. Constitution and bylaws of Rock Spring Division, no. 12 of Humphreyville, Connecticut. Adopted January 17, 1845. New Haven: Printed by J.H. Benham, 1845. 33 p. CtY. 45-6042

Sons of Temperance of North America. Constitution and bylaws of the Grand Division of Connecticut. New York: J. Oliver, printer, 1845. 30 p. MH. 45-6043

Sons of Temperance of North America. Constitution and bylaws of Tomochichi Division, no. 1, Macom, Georgia. Instituted December 29, 1845. Macon, Georgia: Printed at the Telegraph office, 1845. 15 p. GU. 45-6044

Sons of Temperance of North America. Constitution, bylaws and rules of order of Delaware Division, no. 22 of the Sons of Temperance of the state of Pennsylvania located at New Hope. Philadelphia: A. Scott, 1845. 32 p. PHi. 45-6045

Sons of Temperance of North America. Constitution, bylaws and rules of order of Neptune Division, no. 64 of the Sons of Temperance of the state of Pennsylvania. Philadelphia: William Higgs, 1845. 24 p. PHi. 45-6046

Sons of Temperance of North America. Constitution, bylaws and rules of order of Hope Division, no. 3 of the Sons of Temperance of Pennsylvania, organized March 26, 1844. Philadelphia: William F. Geddes, 1845. 40 p. PHi. 45-6047

Sons of Temperance of North America. Constitution, bylaws and rules of order of Niagara Division, no. 14 of the Sons of Temperance, of the state of Pennsylvania. Philadelphia: Barrett and Jones, 1845. 30 p. PHi. 45-6048

Sons of Temperance of North America. Constitution, bylaws and rules of order of the Grand Division of Pennsylvania, Lancaster Division. Lancaster, Pennsylvania: Pearsol, 1845. 22 p. PLF. 45-6049

Sons of Temperance of North America. Constitution, bylaws and rules of order of the Grand Division of Pennsylvania, Siloam Branch. Philadelphia: Scott, 1845. 21 p. PPAmP. 45-6050

Sons of Temperance of North America. Constitution, bylaws, and rules of the Grand Division of Pennsylvania No. 22. Philadelphia, 1845. 32 p. PHi. 45-6051

Sons of Temperance of North America. Constitutions of the order of the Sons of Temperance. Revised by the national division of the United States at its second annual session, June, 1845. [New York, 1845] 27 p. ICU. 45-6052

Sons of Temperance of North America. Constitution, bylaws and rules of order of Friendship Division, no. 19. Philadelphia: Barrett, 1845. PPPrHi. 45-6053

Sons of Temperance of North America.

History, objects and principles of the order. Philadelphia, 1845. PPL. 45-6054

Sons of Temperance of North America. Journal of proceedings from the formation of the order, September 29, 1842 to October, 1844. Together with statistical tables, showing the progress of the order. By Luke Hassert. New York: Piercy and Reed, 1845. MH. 45-6055

Sons of Temperance of North America. Journal of proceedings of the Grand Division of the Sons of Temperance of the state of New York and jurisdiction thereunto belonging from the formation of the order, September 29, 1842 to the close of the annual session of October 1844 by Luke Hassert. New York: Piercy and Reed, 1845. MHi. 45-6056

Sons of Temperance of North America. Journal of proceedings of the Grand Division of the Sons of Temperance of the state of New York from the formation of the order, September 29, 1842 to the close of the annual session of October, 1844. By L. Hassert. New York, 1845. 282 p. MHi; NNC; NSy; WHi. 45-6057

Sons of Temperance of North America. Minutes of the Grand Division of the state of Virginia at its session, January 29, 1845. [Richmond, 1845-] NcU; PPL; PPPrHi; Vi; ViU. 45-6058

Sons of Temperance of North America. Report on by laws of order and principles of discipline; read in the Grand Division of the Sons of Temperance of the state of Pennsylvania, which was ordered to be printed and distributed among the members for their examination; and to be regarded by each as document entrusted to him in the strictest confidence, until the injunction of secrecy shall be removed from the same. Philadelphia, 1845. 15 p. PHi. 45-6059

Sophocles, Evangelinus Apostolides, 1807-1883. Greek exercises, followed by an English and Greek vocabulary. Third edition. Hartford: H. Huntington, 1845. MBC; MH. 45-6060

Sophocles, Evangelinus Apostolides, 1807-1883. A Greek grammar, for the use of learners. Eleventh edition. Hartford: H. Huntington, Jr., 1845. 284 p. ICU; MeHi; MLy; NNC; OClW. 45-6061

Sophocles, Evangelinus Apostolides, 1807-1883. Greek lessons, adapted to the author's Greek grammar. Hartford: H. Huntington, 1845. 116 p. ICU; MB; MH; NNC. 45-6062

Sophocles, Evangelinus Apostolides, 1807-1883. Greek lessons. Eleventh edition. Hartford: H. Huntington, 1845. MH. 45-6063

Sotter, Paruclete. The clerk and magistrate's assistant. n.p.: William Wilson Poughkeepsie, 1845. 383 p. MdBB. 45-6064

Soule, Henry Birdsall. Biography of Rev. W.H. Griswold. Utica: A. Walker, 1845. 102 p. MMeT; NCaS; NHi; OClWHi. 45-6065

Soulie, Frederic, 1800-1847. Eulaile Pontois; or the stolen will. A novel. Translated from the French. New York: E. Winchester, 1845. 48 p. NjR. 45-6066

Soulie, Frederic, 1800-1847. Il etait temps, on a quelque chose malheur est bon. New York: F. Gaillardet, 1845. PPM. 45-6067

South, Robert, 1634-1716. Sermons preached upon several occasions. A new edition in four volumes including the posthumous discourses. Philadelphia: Sorin and Ball, 1845. 4 v. IaPeC; IEG; MdBP; PPLT. 45-6068

South Carolina. Acts of the general assembly of the state of South Carolina, passed in December, 1844. Columbia: A.H. Pemberton, 1845. 204 p. T. 45-6069

South Carolina. Acts of the general assembly of the state of South Carolina, passed in December, 1844. Columbia: A.H. Pemberton, 1845. 75 p. L. 45-6070

South Carolina. Journal of the House of Representatives, of the state of South Carolina. Columbia: A.G. Summer, 1845. 174 p. In- SC; Ms; PP; SC; T. 45-6071

South Carolina. Journal of the Senate of the state of South Carolina. Columbia: A.G. Summer, 1845. 160 p. Sc; T. 45-6072

South Carolina. The militia and patrol laws of South Carolina, December 1844. Columbia: A.H. Pemberton, 1845. 80 p. NcWfC; NHi. 45-6073

South Carolina. Reports and resolutions of the general assembly of South Carolina, passed at its regular session of 1845. Columbia: A.G. Sumner, 1845. 221 p. In-SC; Ms; Or; Sc. 45-6074

South Carolina. Reports of cases at law argued and determined in the court of appeals and court of errors of South

Carolina, by J.S.G. Richardson, state reporter. Columbia: A.S. Johnston, 1845. 15 v. NCH; OClW; PU-L; RPL; TMeB. 45-6075

South Carolina Railroad Company and South Western Railroad Bank. Proceedings of the stockholders... at their annual meeting... on February 11-13, 1845. Charleston, 1845. 46 p. IU; NjR; NNC; ScU; WU. 45-6076

South Carolina State Agricultural Society. Columbia, August 15, 1846. n.p., 1845. Broadside. NcHiC. 45-6077

South Cove Corporation. Catalogue of 132 lots of land... to be sold at auction... Boston: Crocker and Brewster, 1845. 8 p. MB; MH-BA. 45-6078

South Weymouth, Massachusetts. Union Congregational Church. The confession of faith and covenant of the Union Congregational Church, in South Weymouth, Massachusetts. Organized November, 1842. Boston: S.N. Dickinson, printer, 1845. 7 p. MBC; MWA. 45-6079

Southern almanac by Robert Grier. Americus, Georgia: T.P. Ashmore, [1845] MWA. 45-6080

Southern and Western Liberty Convention, Cincinnati, 1845. Principles and measures of true democracy; the address of the Southern and Western Liberty Convention, held at Cincinnati, June 11, 1845, to the people of the United States. Also the letter of Elihu Burritt to the convention. Cincinnati, 1845. 15 p. DLC; MB; MdHi; WHi. 45-6081

Southern and Western Liberty Conven-

tion. Address to the people of the United States at the Southern and Western Liberty Convention held at Cincinnati, June 11 and 12, 1845. With notes by a citizen of Pennsylvania. New York, [1845] 15 p. PHi. 45-6082

Southern and Western Liberty Convention, Cincinnati. The address of the Southern and Western Liberty Convention held at Cincinnati, June 11 and 12, 1845. With notes by a citizen of Pennsylvania. Second edition. [Philadelphia, 1845] 15 p. MH. 45-6083

Southern and Western Liberty Convention, Cincinnati. The address of the Southern and Western Liberty Convention held at Cincinnati, June 11 and 12, 1845. With notes by a citizen of Pennsylvania. Third edition. [New York, 1845] 15 p. MH. 45-6084

Southern and Western Liberty Convention, Cincinnati. The address of the Southern and Western Liberty Convention, to the people of the United States; the proceedings and resolutions of the convention; the letters of Elihu Burrit, William H. Seward and others. Cincinnati, 1845. 24 p. DLC; KHi; MH; MiD-B; NN. 45-6085

The Southern and western monthly magazine and review; edited by W. Gilmore Simms. Charleston: Burges and James, 1845-. v. 1-. MH; NcD; NN. 45-6086

The Southern Christian Home Missionary Society. Constitution of the Southern Christian Home Missionary Society and the report of a committtee on the organization and conduct of a house of industry. Philadelphia: Merrihew and Thompson, 1845. 12 p. PHi. 45-6087

The southern first spelling book. In two parts. Second edition with additions and improvements. Charleston: Babcock and company, 1845. 180 p. ScCMu. 45-6088

The southern first spelling book. Second edition with additions and improvements. Richmond: Drinker and Morris, 1845. MH. 45-6089

Southern medical reformer. Edited by H.M. Price. Forsyth, Georgia, 1845-. PPC; PPCP; ViW. 45-6090

The southern reader; or child's second reader book. Containing simple reading lessons, progressively arranged. Second edition. Charleston: William R. Babcock, 1845. 252 p. ICN; NcD. 45-6091

The southern warbler; a new collection of patriotic, national, naval, martial, professional, convivial, humorous, pathetic, sentimental, old and new songs. Charleston: Babcock, 1845. 320 p. IC; MH; NjP; ScU; TxU. 45-6092

Southey, Caroline Anne Bowles, 1786-1854. Autumn flowers. First American edition. [n.p., 1845?] 16 p. IU; MB. 45-6093

Southey, Caroline Anne Bowles, 1786-1854. Autumn flowers and other poems. Third edition. Boston, 1845. MB. 45-6094

Southey, Caroline Anne Bowles, 1786-1854. The birthday; a poem in three parts. New York: Wiley and Putnam, 1845. DLC; MB; MH; NNUT; OT. 45-6095

Southey, Robert, 1774-1843. Life of Oliver Cromwell. New York: D. Appleton and company; Philadelphia: George S. Appleton, 1845. 158 p. InID; LNB; NjR; RJa; WNaE. 45-6096

Southgate, Horatio, 1812-1894. A letter to a friend, in reply to a recent pamphlet, from the missionaries of the American Board of Commissioners for Foreign Missions at Constantinople. New York: D. Appleton and company; Philadelphia: George S. Appleton, 1845. 43 p. CtHT; IEG; MeB; NGH; RPB. 45-6097

Southwell, Charles, 1814-1860. Two pennyworth of truth about Owenism and Owenites. [Pentonville: W. Baker, 1845.] 12 p. MH. 45-6098

Southwestern Convention. Memphis, Tennessee. Journal of the proceedings of the Southwestern convention, began and held at the city of Memphis on the 12th November, 1845. Memphis, 1845. 127 p. ICU; MoSM; PPL; RPB; TNN. 45-6099

Southworth, Tertius Dunning, 1801-1864. Man's hope destroyed by the death of the young; sermon on the death of Miss Susan M. Thayer. Boston: S.N. Dickinson, 1845. 16 p. MBC; MH; MWA; NBuG; RPB. 45-6100

Southworth, Tertius Dunning, 1801-1864. Memorial of unassuming piety; sermon, burial of Mrs. Melita Richardson, Franklin, September 22, 1844. Boston: Printed by Samuel N. Dickinson, 1845. 16 p. MBC; MH; NHi; RPB. 45-6101

Spalding, Henry Harmon, 1803-1874. Shapahitamenash suyapu timtki. Clear

Water: Mission Press, 1845. 24 p. CSmH. 45-6102

Spalding, William, 1809-1859. Italy and the Italian islands, from the earliest ages to the present time. New York: Harper and brothers, 1845. 3 v. IGK; MeAu; NOg; OCo; PMA. 45-6103

Sparks, Jared, 1789-1866. The library of American biography. Conducted by Jared Sparks. Second series. Boston: Charles C. Little and James Brown, 1845. 15 v. PPF; ViU; WvW. 45-6104

Sparks, Jared, 1789-1866. Life of George Washington. Boston: Charles Tappan, 1845. 562 p. CoU; InRchE; MNe; PEaL. 45-6105

Sparks, Jared, 1789-1866. Lives of John Ribault, Sebastian Rale and William Palfrey. Boston: Little and Brown, 1845. 448 p. CSmH; DLC; MHoly; OO; PP. 45-6106

Sparks, Quartus S., 1816?-1891. Priestcraft exposed; false religion unmasked, derided and slain; hypocrisy unveiled; truth vindicated, sectaries mad and Babylon falling! Hartford: Printed for the publisher, 1845. 37 p. CU-B. 45-6107

Sparrow, William, 1801-1874. A sermon preached in St. George's Church. Fredricksburg, Virginia, May 23, 1845. Alexander: Printed at the Southern Churchman office, 1845. 20 p. NNG; PPPrHi; TxU; ViU; WHi. 45-6108

Spear, Charles, 1801-1863. Essays on the punishment of death. Tenth edition. Boston: The author, 1845. 237 p. IU; LU; MNBedf; TNM. 45-6109

Spear, Charles, 1801-1863. Essays on the punishment of death. Eleventh edition. Boston: Published by the author, 1845. 237 p. Ct; MH; MMilf; NN. 45-6110

Spear, Charles, 1801-1863. Essays on the punishment of death. Twelfth edition. Boston: Published by the author, 1845. 237 p. IaE; IaOskJF; NN. 45-6111

Spear, Matthew P. The teacher's manual of English grammar: consisting of three parts in one volume. Boston: William D. Ticknor and company; New Bedford: William C. Taber, 1845. 116 p. CtHWatk; NN; NNC; WU. 45-6112

Spear, Samuel Thayer, 1812-1891. The politico-social foundations of our republic; a sermon preached on Thanksgiving day, December 12, 1844. New York: Saxton, 1845. 21 p. CtHWatk; NCH; NcMHi; NN; PPPrHi. 45-6113

Spectral visitants, or journal of a fever; by a convalescent. Portland: S.H. Colesworthy, 1845. 75 p. MH. 45-6114

Speed, J.J. Opinion of council on the election of the Susquehanna Canal Company of the 12th May, 1845. [Baltimore, 1845] MdBP. 45-6115

Speed, Joseph J. A letter to a landholder of Baltimore County, on the subject of resumption of the payment of the debts of Maryland. Baltimore: J. Lucas, 1845. 11 p. MdBE; MdBJ; MdHi; PPL; WHi. 45-6116

Speed the plough. An essay, showing the effects of protective and prohibitory duties and the operation of the present tariff. By a Georgia planter. Athens,

Georgia: Southern Banner office, 1845. 21 p. CSmH; GHi; MH-AH; NcD. 45-6117

Spelling and thinking combined; or the spelling book made a medium of thought; the sequel to my first school book. Boston: T.R. Marvin, 1845. 144 p. MPeHi. 45-6118

Spencer, George, d. 1856. Latin lessons, with exercises in parsing; introductory to Bullion's Latin grammar and Latin reader. Second edition. New York: Pratt, Woodford and company, 1845. [9]-196 p. ICN; MiOC; NCH; OO; ScCliTO. 45-6119

Spencer, James, 1816-1893. Christian forberance. A sermon, preached in the Second Baptist Church, Solon, New York. Requested to be published by the society. Courtland Village: S. Haight, 1845. 16 p. NRAB; PCA. 45-6120

Spencer, Thomas, 1793-1857. Argument to the Court for the Correction of Errors. The medical institution of Geneva College, plaintiff in error: vs. Oliver S. Patterson; defendent in error. To prove that the institution is a corporation... Geneva: I. and S.H. Parker, Printers, 1845. 149 p. WHi. 45-6121

Spencer, Thomas, 1793-1857. Vital chemistry. Lectures on animal heat. Geneva, New York: Ira and Stephen H. Parker, printers, 1845. 114 p. CtY; DLC; NBuU-M; PPAN; WU-M. 45-6122

Spenser, Edmund, 1552?-1599. The poetical works of Edmund Spencer. First American edition. With introductory observations on the Faerie Queene, and notes by the editor. Boston: Charles C.

Little and James Brown, 1845. 5 v. CtHC; GOgU; NcGA; PPiW; ScDuE. 45-6123

Sperry, H.T. Country love vs. city flirtation. New York: Carleton, The New York Printing company, 1845. 90 p. MeLewB. 45-6124

Spies, William A. Rude veins of a poetic conformation. The Heavens. New York: Henry Ludwig, 1845. 179 p. 12 p. MP. 45-6125

Spofford's United States farmer's almanac for 1846. Boston: Thomas Groom and company, [1845] 29 p. MHi; MWHi. 45-6126

Spofford's United States Farmer's almanac, for the year of our Lord and Saviour, 1846. By Thomas Spofford. Boston: Thomas Groom and company, [1845. 28] p. MHi; MPeHi; MWA; WHi. 45-6127

Spooner, Lysander, 1808-1887. The unconstitutionality of slavery. Boston: Bela Marsh, 1845. 156 p. A-Ar; CtHC; IaHi; MH; PHi. 45-6128

Sprague, William Buell, 1795-1876. An address delivered April 11, 1845, on occasion of the internment of Mr. William Davis, Misses Lucinda and Anna Wood and Miss Mary Ann Torrey, who perished in the wreck of the steamboat, Swallow. Albany: Erastus H. Pease, 1845. 30 p. IEN-M: MHi: NAl: NjR; OMC. 45-6129

Sprague, William Buell, 1795-1876. A discourse on Sabbath evening, August 17, 1845, before the Mills Society of Inquiry, and the Theological Society, of Williams College. Albany: Printed by C.

Van Benthuysen and company, 1845. 58 p. CU; MPiB; MWiW; NjR; RPB. 45-6130

Sprague, William Buell, 1795-1876. A discourse on the ruling passion. New York, November 16, 1845. [Albany? 1845?] 32 p. MBC; MH-AH. 45-6131

Sprague, William Buell, 1795-1876. A sermon at the installation of M.N. McLaren, as pastor of the First Presbyterian Church, in Rochester. Albany: Charles Van Benthuysen and company, 1845. MWA; MWiW; NRHi; PHi; RPB. 45-6132

Sprague, William Buell, 1795-1876. A sermon delivered April 22, 1845, at the opening of the new church, erected by the First Presbyterian Congregation, Lansingburgh. Lansingburgh: Pelatiah Bliss, 1845. 44 p. MBC; MH; NN; PPPrHi; WHi. 45-6133

Sprague, William Buell, 1795-1876. A sermon preached in the Second Presbyterian Church, Albany, February 9, 1845, the Sabbath immediately succeeding the death of Mrs. O.S. Strong... Albany, 1845. 32 p. MBC; PPPrHi; RHi. 45-6134

Spring, Gardiner, 1785-1873. The attraction of the cross; designed to illustrate the leading truths, obligations and hopes of Christianity. New York: M.W. Dodd, 1845. 413 p. ICNBT; MChiA; Sc; TxShA; ViRut. 45-6135

Spring, Gardiner, 1785-1873. The obligations of the world to the Bible. A series of lectures to young men. New York: John S. Taylor and company, 1845. 404 p. CSt; GHi; ICP; MeAu; ScCoT. 45-6136

Spxnud, X.L. [pseud.] Cryptograhical table, for secret correspondence by magnetic telegraph or otherwise with telegraphic alphabet. Buffalo: O.G. Steele, [1845?] DLC. 45-6137

Stael-Holstein, Anne Louise Germaine Necker, 1766-1817. The influence of literature upon society, to which is prefixed a memoir of the life and writings of the author. Hartford: S. Andrus and son, [1845?] 112 p. CSansS; IaHoL; MA; MBrockKS; OWoC. 45-6138

Stamp Act Congress, New York. Journal of the first congress of the American colonies in opposition to the tyrannical acts of the British Parliament. New York: Winchester, 1845. 59 p. ArU; CtSoP; InU; MB; MeBa. 45-6139

Stanhope, Philip Henry Stanhope, 1805-1875. The life of Louis, Prince of Conde, Surnamed the Great. New York: Wiley and Putnam, 1845. 2 v. in 1. CU; IEG; MH; ODa; ScU. 45-6140

Stanley, Arthur Penrhyn, 1815-1881. The life and correspondence of Thomas Arnold. First American from the third English edition. New York: D. Appleton and company; Philadelphia: George S. Appleton, 1845. 516 p. DeWi; KWiU; LNB; PPA; ScU. 45-6141

Staples, William Read, 1798-1868. The documentary history of the destruction of the Gaspee. comp. for the Providence Journal. Providence: Knowles, Vose and Anthony, 1845. 56 p. CtHWatk; MB; NIC; NWM; PSt. 45-6142

Stapp, William Preston. The prisoners of Perote: containing a journal kept by the author, who was captured by the Mexicans at Mier, December 25, 1842, and released from Perote, May 16, 1844. Philadelphia: G.B. Zieber and company, 1845. [13]-164 p. CtW; MnHi; OHi; PU; TxW. 45-6143

Statistical companion for 1846. By Edwin Williams. New York, New York: Homans and Ellis, [1845] MWA. 45-6144

Stearns, Oliver, 1807-1885. The duty of moral reflection with particular reference to the Texas question. A sermon preached to the third Congregational Society of Hingham, on Sunday, November 16, 1845. Hingham: Farmer, 1845. 21 p. CBPac; MB; MBAt; Tx; TxU. 45-6145

Steele's Albany almanack for 1846. Albany, New York: Steele and Durrie, [1845] MWA. 45-6146

Stephen, Henry John, 1787-1864. A treatise on the principles of pleading in civil actions; comprising a summary view of the whole proceedings at a suit at law. Fifth American edition with notes; and additions from the first London edition. Philadelphia: R.H. Small, 1845. 453 p. MH-L; NcD; OCo; PU-L; ViU. 45-6147

Stephens, Alexander Hamilton, 1812-1883. Speech on the joint resolution for the annexation of Texas. Delivered in the House, January 25, 1845. Washington, 1845. 22 p. MHi; NBu; PHi. 45-6148

Stephens, John Lloyd, 1805-1852. Incidents of travel in Egypt, Arabia Petrea and the Holy Land. By an American. Tenth edition with additions. New York:

Harper and brothers, 1845. 2 v. MeAu; NNA; OO; ScDuE; WU. 45-6149

Stephens, John Lloyd, 1805-1852. Incidents of travel in Greece, Turkey, Russia, and Poland. Seventh edition. New York: Harper and brothers, 1845. 2. v. MH; NNC; OSW; OWoC; PHC. 45-6150

Stetson, Samuel. Speech of Mr. Stetson, of New York, on the annexation of Texas. Delivered in the House, January 7, 1845. Washington: Printed at the Globe office, 1845. 7 p. CtY; MHi; NBu; NjMD. 45-6151

Stevens, Abel, 1815-1897. The pastor's stories. Moral sketches for youth. Boston: Waite, Peirce and company, 1845. 176 p. MNF. 45-6152

Stevenson, John, d. 1893. Christ on the cross. First American from the Tenth London editon. New York: Robert Carter, 1845. 345 p. MoS; NjPT. 45-6153

Stevenson, John, d. 1893. The Lord our shepherd: an exposition of the twenty-third psalm. New York: Robert Carter, 1845. 239 p. DLC; KyDC; NCH; RPB; TWcW. 45-6154

Stewart, Alvan, 1790-1849. A legal argument before the Supreme Court of the state of New Jersey, at the May term, 1845, at Trenton, for the deliverance of four thousand persons of bondage... New York: Finch and Weed, 1845. 52 p. ICN; MH-AH; NbCrD; PU; RPB. 45-6155

Stewart, Andrew, 1792-1872. Speech of Mr. Stewart, of Pennsylvania, on the portion of the President's message and treasury report relating to the tariff. Delivered in the House, December 9,

1845. [Washington] J. and G.S. Gideon, printers, 1845. 16 p. KyLx; MiD-B; MiGr; NbU; RPB. 45-6156

Stewart, James, 1799-1864. A practical treatise on the diseases of children; including an introductory chapter on the management of infants in health. Third edition. New York: Harper and brothers, 1845. 544 p. MdBJ; MsU; PPCP; TNV; ViRMC. 45-6157

Stewart, John. Stable economy; a treatise on the management of horses, in relation to stabling, grooming, feeding, watering and working... From the third English edition, with notes and additions adapting it to American food and climate, by A.B. Allen... New York: D. Appleton and company; [etc., etc.] 1845. CU; IaGG; MDBP; NBuG; RPA. 45-6158

Still, Peter. The cottar's Sunday, and other poems, chiefly in the Scottish dialect. Philadelphia: Henry Longstreth, 1845. 216 p. MNBedf; NNC; PPL-R; PPWa; RPB. 45-6159

Stille, Alfred. An address, delivered before the class of the Philadelphia Medical Association, at the close of the session of 1845... Philadelphia: J.C. Clark, printer, 1845. 16 p. MdBJ; MH-M; NNNAM; PPAN; PPCP. 45-6160

Stimpson's Boston directory, containing the names of the inhabitants. Their occupations, places of business and dwelling houses and the city register with lists.... Boston, 1845. 550 p. MHi; WHi. 45-6161

Stimson, Alexander Lovett. Poor Caroline, the Indianman's daughter; or all's well that ends well. A tale of Boston and our own times. Boston: The author, 1845. 64 p. DLC; MB; MWA; TNF. 45-6162

Stockton, John. Report from the secretary of war, communicating a report of J. Stockton, superintendent of the mineral lands on Lake Superior, March 19, 1845. [Washington, 1845] 22 p. DI-GS; MiU; OO. 45-6163

Stokes, William, 1804-1878. Lectures on the theory and practice of physics. Third edition, enlarged and improved. Philadelphia: E. Barrington and G.D. Haswell, 1845. 2 v. CU-M; MBM; MnU; NcU; RPM. 45-6164

Stone, John Seely, 1795-1882. Sermons on death of James Milnor; April 11-13, 1845. New York, 1845. 66 p. PHi. 45-6165

Stone, Marsena. A sermon for the times, before the Baptist Missionary Convention at Trumansbury, October 15, 1845. Homer: R.A. Reed, 1845. 16 p. NHCS; RPB. 45-6166

Stone, William Leete, 1792-1844. Border wars of the American revolution. New York: Harper and brothers, 1845. 2 v. CS; InRch; LNH; OU; ViU. 45-6167

Stone, William Leete, 1792-1844. Life of Joseph Brant, [Thayendanegea] including the border wars of the American revolution, and sketches of the Indian Campaigns of Generals Harmar, St. Clair, and Wayne and other matters connected with the Indian relations of the United States and Great Britain, from the peace of 1783 to the Indian peace of 1795. Cooperstown: Phinney, 1845. 2 v. IaBo; MB; MiD-B; NGH; NjP. 45-6168

Stories of voyages. Being authentic narratives of the most celebrated voyages from Columbus to Parry with accounts of remarkable shipwrecks and naval adventures. Dayton: D.W. Noble, 1845. 283 p. LNH. 45-6169

Storrs, Richard Salter, 1787-1873. The importance of religiously instructing the young; a sermon, preached at the request of the American Sunday School Union, at Philadelphia, May 18, 1845. Philadelphia: American Sunday School Union, 1845. 35 p. CSansS; MeB; MWiW; PPL; RPB. 45-6170

Storrs, Richard Salter, 1787-1873. The ministry strong in the grace of Christ. A sermon, preached at the ordination of Mr. Richard S. Storrs, Jr... October 22, 2845. By Richard Storrs. Boston: Press of T.R. Marvin, 1845. 30 p. CtHC; MB; MiD-B; NCH; RPB. 45-6171

Storrs, Richard Salter, 1787-1873. The necessity and benefits of early religious training. A sermon at the request of the American Sunday School Union. Philadelphia, New York, 1845. 23 p. MH-AH; NbCrD; NjR. 45-6172

Story, Joseph, 1779-1845. Commentaries on the law of promissory notes, and guaranties of notes and checks on banks and bankers. With illustrations from the commerical law of the nations of continental Europe. Boston: C.C. Little and J. Brown, 1845. 675 p. CLSU; IaU-L; PP; TxWB-L; WLac. 45-6173

A story of Charles. Greenfield: A. Phelps, 1845. 8 p. MH; PHi. 45-6174

Stoughton's western farmer's almanac, for 1846... Calculations by Horace Martin. Syracuse: C.H. Stoughton, [1845] NCanHi. 45-6175

Stout, Z. Barton. Address delivered before the Ontario Agricultural Society, at its annual meeting, October, 1845. Canandaigua: George L. Whitney, 1845. 12 p. N. 45-6176

Stow, Baron, 1801-1869. Daily manna for Christian pilgrims. Boston: Gould, Kendall and Lincoln, 1845. 128 p. MBevHi; MH; Nh. 45-6177

Stow, Baron, 1801-1869. The whole family in heaven and earth. Boston: Gould, Kendall and Lincoln, 1845. 52 p. MBevHi; Nh; NHC- S. 45-6178

Stowell, Hugh, 1799-1865. The life of the Right Reverend Thomas Wilson. From the third London edition... New York: James R. Dunham, 1845. 108 p. CtHT; MBrZ; NBuDD; PP; TSewU. 45-6179

Strauss, David Friedrich, 1808-1878. The life of Christ or a critical examination of his history... Translated from the German, and reprinted from an English edition. Second American edition. New York: G. Vale, 1845. 284 p. MoS; NcCJ; OO; PPL; PU. 45-6180

Street, Alfred Billings, 1811-1881. The poems of Alfred B. Street. Complete edition. Boston: Clark and Austin, 1845. [6], 319 p. LN; NBuG; OWoC; RPB; TxU. 45-6181

Strickland, William Peter. Oration delivered in the Wesley Chapel on the occasion of laying the cornerstone of the new Masonic hall edifice, Cincinnati, June 4, 1845. Cincinnati: R.P. Donogh and company, 1845. 24 p. DLC; OClWHi; OCM. 45-6182

Stuart, Issac William, 1809-1861. Address before the Hartford County Agricultural Society, October 3, 1845... Together with the reports of the committees and the transactions of the society. Hartford: E. Gleason, 1845. 83 p. Ct; MiD-B; NcD; NNUT; PPL-R. 45-6183

Stuart, James Park. Reasons for leaving the Presbyterian ministry, and adopting the principles of the New Jerusalem Church; being a letter to the Knox Presbytery, and the substance of an address read before the Western New Church Convention, at Cincinnati, May, 1845. Cincinnati: A. Peabody, 1845. 48 p. MB; PBa; OCHP; OUrC; PPPrHi. 45-6184

Stuart, Moses, 1780-1852. A commentary on the Apocalypse. Andover: Allen, Morrill and Wardwell, 1845. 2 v. CBPSR; IaMp; MBC; NCaS; RPA; ViRU. 45-6185

Stuart, Moses, 1780-1852. Critical history and defence of the Old Testament canon. Andover: Allen, Morrill and Wardwell; New York: Mark H. Newman, 1845. 452 p. CBPSR; IEG; OkU; PPWe. 45-6186

Stuart, Moses, 1780-1852. Sermon at the ordination of the Rev. William G. Shauffler, as missionary to the Jews, preached at Park Street Church, Boston on the evening of November 14, 1831. [Third edition] Boston: Press of Crocker and Brewster, 1845. [3]-35 p. ICU; MH-AH; PPPrHi; WHi. 45-6187

Stubbs, Stephen. Agnes; or the power of love. A tale of Missouri, founded on fact.

Boston: Gleason's Publishing Hall, 1845. 46 p. CtY; IGK; ViU. 45-6188

Sturges, Joshua, d. 1813. Sturges' guide to the game of draughts; in which the whole theory and practice of that scientific recreation are clearly illustrated; including one hundred and fifty critical positions. First American from the last London edition. New York: Burgess, Stringer and company; Philadelphia: Zuber and company; Boston: Jordan and Wiley, 1845. 119 p. IaFairP; MW; OC. 45-6189

Sturgis, William, 1782-1863. Oregon question; substance of a lecture before the Mercantile Library Association, Delivered January 22, 1845. Boston: Jordan, 1845. 32 p. CtHC; ICN; MiD-B; OrP; WaS. 45-6190

Sturtevant, Julian Monson, 1805-1886. American colleges. An address delivered by J.M. Sturtevant, at his inauguration as president of Illinois College, June 25, 1845. Jacksonville, [Ill.] W.C. Swett, printer, 1845. 32 p. CtHC; IaB; MH-AH; MWiW; PPPrHi. 45-6191

Suberwick, Mne. The mysteries of the inquisition and other secret societies of Spain. By M.V. de Fereal, with historical notes, by M. Manuel de Cuendias. Translated from the French. Philadelphia: J.B. Lippincott and company, 1845. 354 p. MB; NdToH; MeBat; NcMHi. 45-6192

The subjection of the world to come. By a clergyman of the Church of England. Boston: H.B. Pratt, 1845. 95 p. MH; MH-AH. 45-6193

Suddards, William, b. 1805. The British pulpit: consisting of discourses by the most eminent living divines, in England, Scotland and Ireland... Seventh edition. New York: Robert Carter [etc.] 1845. 2 v. CU; InID; NbCrD; PAnL; TKC. 45-6194

Sue, Eugene, 1804-1857. Der ewige Jude, von Eugen Sue. 1. Amerikanisch-deutsche ausg... Philadelphia: L.A. Wollenweber, 1846. 2 v. in 1. AFIT; DLC; NIC; OWorP; PPG. 45-6195

Sue, Eugene, 1804-1857. The godolphin Arabian; or the history of a thorough-bred. New York: E. Winchester, New World Press, 1845. 32 p. InU; NjP; NjR; NN. 45-6196

Sue, Eugene, 1804-1857. The hotel Lambert, or the engraver's daughter; a tale of love and intrigue. Translated from the French by a lady of Boston. New York: E. Winchester, 1845. 102 p. CtY; MH; NN. 45-6197

Sue, Eugene, 1804-1857. Latreaumont; or the court conspirator. Translation by Thomas Williams. New York, 1845. PPL. 45-6198

Sue, Eugene, 1804-1857. Matilda; or the orphan. A novel. By Eugene Sue. Translated from the French by Henry William Herbert. Baltimore: Taylor Wild, 1845. 418 p. ScU. 45-6199

Sue, Eugene, 1804-1857. The mysteries of Paris, a novel by Eugene Sue. Translated from the French, by Charles H. Town. Boston: C.T. Brainard, [1845?] 3 v. OKentU. 45-6200

Sue, Eugene, 1804-1857. De Rohan; or the court conspirator. New York: Harper and brothers, 1845. 152 p. MBilHi; MNF; NjP. 45-6201

Sue, Eugene, 1804-1857. The temptation or the watch tower of Koat Ven; a romantic tale. Translated from the French. New York, 1845. 128 p. MdBP; NjP. 45-6202

Sue, Eugene, 1804-1857. The wandering Jew, complete edition, in one volume with illustrations by Gavarni and Girardet. New York: George Routledge sons, limited, 1845. 847 p. CoGrS; CoPu; NNopo; OClW; RJa. 45-6203

Sullivan, William. The political class book; intended to instruct the higher classes in schools in the origin, nature, and use of political power... New edition with amendments and additions. Boston: Charles J. Hendee and Jenks and Palmer, 1845. [7]-157 p. LNL; MiU; MStow. 45-6204

Summerfield, John, 1798-1825. Sermons and sketches of sermons... late a preacher in the Methodist Episcopal Church. New York: Harper and brothers, 1845. 437 p. DLC; GAM-R; MiU; ODaB; OMC. 45-6205

Sumner, Charles, 1811-1874. The true grandeur of nations; an oration delivered before the authorities of the city of Boston, July 4, 1845. Boston: William D. Ticknor and company, 1845. 104 p. CtY; DLC; NN; OO; WaU. 45-6206

Sumner, Charles, 1811-1874. The true grandeur of nations; an oration delivered before the authorities of the city of Boston, July 4, 1845. Second edition. Boston: American Peace Society, 1845. 96 p. IC; MH; NjR; PHi; TN. 45-6207

Sumner, George. Memoirs of the Pilgrims at Leyden. Cambridge: Metcalf and company, 1845. 35 p. MH; Nh-Hi; NIC; RHi. 45-6208

Sumner, Thomas Hubbard. A new and accurate method of finding a ship's position at sea, by projection on Mercator's chart. Second edition. Boston: T. Groom, 1845. 88 p. MeHi; MH; MSaP; PPL-R. 45-6209

Sunday school conversations on some of the interesting subjects recorded in the New Testament. By the author of "The factory girl," etc. Boston: William Crosby, 1845. 124 p. KWiF. 45-6210

The Sunday school teacher and Bible class guide. By Rev. Bradford K. Pierce. Boston: Reid and Rand, 1845. MAtt. 45-6211

Sunderland, LaRoy, 1802-1885. Confessions of a magnetiser exposed; exhibiting the folly and falsehood of a recent pamphlet with the above title. Boston: Redding and company, 1845. 47 p. CBPSR; DLC; ICN; MH-AH; Nh. 45-6212

Super Annuted Fund Society. Constitution and acts of incorporation. Baltimore: Sherwood and company, 1845. MdBMP; MdHi. 45-6213

Supp, John Henry. The celebrated love not quick step... arranged for the pianoforte. Boston: Keith, 1845. 4 p. MB. 45-6214

Susan Harvey. Confirmation. New York: General Protestant Episcopal Sunday School Union, 1845. 69 p. CtHC. 45-6215

Swan, Joseph Rockwell, 1802-1884. The practice in civil actions and proceedings at law, in Ohio, and precedents in pleading, with practical notes; together with the forms of process and clerks and entries. Columbus: Isaac N. Whiting, 1845-1850. 2 v. DLC; MH- L; OClW; OFH; OO. 45-6216

Swan, William Draper, 1809-1864. The district school reader; or exercises in reading and speaking; designed for the highest classes in public and private schools. Boston: Charles C. Little and James Brown, 1845. 468 p. DLC; MB; MH; OClW. 45-6217

Swan, William Draper, 1809-1864. A grammar school reader; consisting of selections in prose and poetry with exercises in articulation. Part third. Boston: Charles E. Little and James Brown, 1845. 248 p. MB; MH; MNan. 45-6218

Swan, William Draper, 1809-1864. A primary school reader. Three parts by William D. Swan. Boston: Charles C. Little and James Brown, 1845. 3 v. MH; NNC; NH; OCl. 45-6219

Sweetser, Henry Washington, 1809-1846. The progress of passion; a poem in four books. New York: C. Shepard, 1845. 71 p. MH; NBuG; NBLiHi. 45-6220

Sweetser, Seth, 1807-1878. Living to do good. A sermon occasioned by the death of the Hon. Daniel Waldo; preached on Sunday July 13, 1845 by the pastor of the Centre Church, Worchester. Worcester? E.R. Fiske and company, 1845. 15 p. CBPac; ICMe; NjR; OClWHi; WHi. 45-6221

Swift, Elisha Pope, 1792-1865. The

calamity of Pittsburgh. A sermon, delivered in the First Presbyterian Church, Allegheny City, April 24, 1845; Being the day appointed by the mayor of said city, as a season of fasting, humiliation and prayer, in consequence of the appalling conflagration of a large portion of Pittsburgh, on the tenth of that month. Allegheny, [Pennsylvania] Kennedy and brother, 1845. 27 p. DLC; MiD-B; OClWHi; PPPrHi; PWCHi. 45-6222

Swift, Mary A. First lessons on natural philosophy for children. Part Second. Stereotyped edition. Hartford: Belknap and Hamersley, 1845. 176 p. CtHWatk; MDeeP; MH; PU. 45-6223

Sword's pocket almanack and annual register of the Protestant Episcopal Church in the United States, 1846. New York: Stanford and Swords, 1845. 127 p. MWA. 45-6224

Sword's pocket almanack, churchman's calendar and ecclesiastical register for 1845-1856. Also the constitutions and canons of the Protestant Episcopal Church in the United States. New York: 1845- 1856. 3 v. RPB. 45-6225

Swords' pocket almanack for 1846. New York: Stanford and Swords, [1845] MWA; NNS. 45-6226

T

Talbot, J.W. Outlines of phrenology. Examined by J.W. Talbot. Springfield, Massachusetts: Printed by Wood and Rupp, 1845. 40 p. MB. 45-6227

Talbott, John L. Practical arithmetic containing a great variety of exercises, particularly adapted to the currency of the United States. Cincinnati: E. Morgan and company, 1845. IdHi. 45-6228

Talbott, John L. The western practical arithmetic, wherein the rules are illustrated, and their principles explained. Containing a great variety of exercises particularly adapted to the currency of the United States. With an appendix. Designed for the use of schools and private students compiled by John Talbott. Cincinnati, Ohio: E. Morgan and company, 1845. 240 p. MH; OOxM. 45-6229

Talfourd, Thomas Noon, 1795-1854. Ion: a tragedy in five acts. New York: W. Taylor and company, [1845?] MH; MWA; MnSS; NNC. 45-6230

A talk about birds and Audubon. Boston, 1845. 45-6231

Tallmadge, James, 1778-1853. Address delivered at the close of the eighteenth annual fair of the American Institute, of the city of New York, at Niblo's saloon, October 24, 1845. New York: J. Van Norden and company, printers, 1845. 16 p. CtY; DLC; MdBP; PPL. 45-6232

Tallmadge, James, 1778-1853. Address delivered at the close of the eighteenth annual fair of the American Institute, of the city of New York, at Niblo's saloon, October 24, 1845. Second edition. New York: J. Van Norden and company, printers, 1845. 16 p. DLC. 45-6233

Tallmadge, James, 1778-1853. Address delivered at the close of the eighteenth annual fair of the American Institute, of the city of New York, at Niblo's saloon, October 24, 1845. Third edition. New York: J. Van Norden and company, printers, 1845. 16 p. IU; PHi. 45-6234

Tannehill, Wilkins, 1787-1858. The master mason's manual; or illustrations of the degrees of entered apprentice, fellow craft and master mason, with ancient ceremonies. Nashville: William T. Berry, and Wilkins F. Tannehill, 1845. 292 p. IaCrM; T; TMeC; TNV. 45-6235

Tanner, Henry Schenck, 1786-1858. Map of Connecticut. [Philadelphia] 1845. MBAt. 45-6236

Tanner, Henry Schenck, 1786-1858. A new general atlas, comprising a complete set of maps, representing the grand divisions of the globe, together with the several empires, kingdoms, and states in the world. New York: Tanner's Geographical Establishment, 1845. 2 l. ICN; PU. 45-6237

Tanner, Henry Schenck, 1786-1858. A

new map of Maryland and Delaware, with their canals, roads and distances. Philadelphia, 1845. 1 p. PHi. 45-6238

Tanner, Henry Schenck, 1786-1858. A new universal atlas containing maps of the various empires, kingdoms, states and republics of the world. With a special map of each of the United States. Philadelphia: Carey and Hart, 1845. 77 p. FDeS; NN; PHi; PPL; Vi. 45-6239

Tanner, Henry Schenck, 1786-1858. Stranger's guide to the city of New York and its environs... together with a description of each of the neighboring towns... New York: T.R. Tanner, [1845] 36 p. ICU. 45-6240

Tanner, Henry Schenck, 1786-1858. The travellers' hand book for the state of New York, the province of Canada, and parts of the ajoining states; the whole arranged on a new plan. Third edition. New York: Published at the geographical establishment, 1845. MH; NN; NRCR. 45-6241

Tansill, Robert. Letters to the Honorable, the secretary of the navy. Washington, 1845. 83 p. DLC. 45-6242

Tappan, Charles. How to do things well and cheap. Boston: Charles Tappan, 1845. 66 p. MWinchrHi. 45-6243

Tariff or rates of duties payable on goods, wares, and merchandise imported into the United States of America, on and after August 30, 1842. Revised and corrected by E.D. Ogden. New York: Rich and Loutrel, 1845. 38, 20 p. MSaP; Nh. 45-6244

Tasso, Torquato, 1544-1595. Godfrey of

Bulloigne; or the recovery of Jerusalem: done into English heroic verse from the Italian of Tasso; by Edward Fairfax... To which are prefixed an introductory essay, by Leigh Hunt, and the lives of Tasso and Fairfax, by Charles Knight. New York: Wiley and Putnam, 1845- 1846. 2 v. in 1. KyDC; MNF; NBu; PPL; ScCh. 45-6245

Tate, Benjamin. The American form book, containing legally approved precedents for agreements, arbitrations, assignments, bonds, bills of exchange, promisory notes... and other matters of importance, with a complete index to the whole. Richmond, Virginia: Drinker and Morris, [etc., etc.] 1845. 261 p. MWCL; NcDaD; NhD; ViPet; ViU. 45-6246

Tayler, Charles Benjamin, 1797-1875. The records of a good man's life. New York: Stanford and Swords, 1845. 298 p. NcD; NN. 45-6247

Tayler, Thomas. The law glossary, being a selection of the Greek, Latin, Saxon, French, Norman and Italian sentences, phrases and maxims, found in the leading English and American reports, and elementary works, with historical and explanatory notes... Third edition, revised and corrected. New York: Gould, Banks and company; Albany: William and A. Gould and company, 1845. 482 p. LNT-L; MoS; PWbO; MsU; TxSaSM-L. 45-6248

Taylor, Alfred Swaine, 1806-1880. Manual of medical jurisprudence. First American edition. Philadelphia: Lea, 1845-. DNLM. 45-6249

Taylor, Alfred Swaine, 1806-1880. Medical jurisprudence. Edited with notes and additions by R. Egglesfield

Griffith. Philadelphia: Lea and Blanchard, 1845. 539 p. CSt-L; IU-M; MH-L PU; ScCMeS. 45-6250

Taylor, C.B. Allgemeine Geshichte der Vereingten Staaten von Amerika. Hartford: E. Strong, 1845. 612 p. MiU; NN; WHi. 45-6251

Taylor, C.B. A universal history of the United States of America, embracing the whole period, from the earliest discoveries down to the present time. Giving a description of the western country. Hartford, 1845. 606 p. OClWHi. 45-6252

Taylor, Fitch Waterman, 1803-1865. A voyage round the world, and visits to various foreign countries, in the United States frigate Columbia... Fifth edition. New Haven: H. Mansfield; New York: D. Appleton and company, 1845. 2 v. in 1. CU-B; MSaP; NCH; OMC; TxH. 45-6253

Taylor, Isaac, 1787-1865. Memoirs of Jane Taylor. New edition. Boston: T.H. Carter and company, 1845. 96 p. MB; MBC; WHi. 45-6254

Taylor, James Wickes, 1819-1893. Address delivered before the Erodelphian Society of Miami University, Oxford, Ohio, at their late anniversary, August 12, 1845. Published by request of the society. Cincinnati: Printed at the Daily Atlas office, 1845. 26 p. InU; MHi; OHi; OOxM; PHi. 45-6255

Taylor, Jane, 1783-1824. Original poems for infant minds. Boston: Munroe, 1845. 208 p. PP. 45-6256

Taylor, Jane, 1783-1824. Physiology for children. Boston: Saxton and Huntington, 1845. 91 p. CtHWatk; DLC; NPalk. 45-6257

Taylor, Jane, 1783-1824. Poetical remains and correspondences of the late Jane Taylor. A new edition. Boston, 1845. 144 p. WHi. 45-6258

Taylor, Jane, 1783-1824. Rural scenes; or a peep into the country. For children. First American edition. Philadelphia: W.G. Wardle, 1845. 136 p. NNC. 45-6259

Taylor, Jane, 1783-1824. Selections from the writings of Jane Taylor. Philadelphia: Joseph Rakestraw, printer, 1845. 40 p. N; PAtM. 45-6260

Taylor, Jefferys, 1792-1853. The forest; or rambles in the woodland. From the London edition, revised by the editors. New York: Lane and Tippett, 1845. MiU. 45-6261

Taylor, Jeremy, 1613-1667. Selections from the works of Jeremy Taylor, by Basil Montague, esq. First American from fifth London edition. New York: Wiley and Putnam, 1845. 91 p. RNR. 45-6262

Taylor, Jeremy, 1613-1667. The sermons of the Right Rev. Jeremy Taylor, comprising a course for the whole year, and a supplement of sermons on various subjects and occasions. Philadelphia: H. Hooker, 1845. 565 p. IU; MiD; PMA; VtU; WHi. 45-6263

Taylor, Richard Cowling, 1789-1851. On the anthracite and bituminous coal fields in China; the system of mining, etc. Philadelphia, 1845. 6 p. MH-Z; PHi; PPAmP; PPAN. 45-6264

Taylor, Richard Cowling, 1789-1851. Reports on the Washington Silver Mine in Davidson County, North Carolina... Philadelphia: E.G. Dorsey, 1845. 40 p. DLC; ICJ; MH; NcU; PPL. 45-6265

Taylor, Timothy Alden, 1809-1858. Afflictions. Worchester: Henry J. Howland, 1845. DLC. 45-6266

Taylor, William Cooke, 1800-1849. A manual of ancient and modern history. With questions adapted for schools and colleges. New York: D. Appleton and company, 1845. MdW; MeLewB; NNG; TxH; WU. 45-6267

Taylor, William Cooke, 1800-1849. A manual of ancient and modern history. Revised, with a chapter on the history of the United States, by C.S. Henry. Second edition. New York: D. Appleton and company, 1845. 797 p. CtHC; MH; NNS; TNP; ViU. 45-6268

Taylor, William Cooke, 1800-1849. A manual of ancient and modern history. Revised, with a chapter on the history of the United States, by C.S. Henry. Third edition. New York: D. Appleton and company, 1845. 797 p. IEG; MB; NR; PPA. 45-6269

Taylor, William Cooke, 1800-1849. A manual of ancient and modern history. Revised, with a chapter on the history of the United States, by C.S. Henry. Fifth edition. New York: D. Appleton and company, 1845. 797 p. ScU. 45-6270

Taylor, William Cooke, 1800-1849. A manual of ancient and modern history. Revised, with a chapter on the history of the United States, by C.S. Henry. Sixth

edition. New York: D. Appleton and company, 1845. 797 p. PPA. 45-6271

Taylor, William Cooke, 1800-1849. A manual of ancient and modern history. Revised, with a chapter on the history of the United States, by C.S. Henry. Eighth edition. New York: D. Appleton and company, 1845. 797 p. MB; MWA; PPA. 45-6272

Taylor, William Cooke, 1800-1849. A manual of ancient history; containing the political history, geographical position, and social state of the principal nations of antiquity, carefully revised from the ancient writers. New York: D. Appleton and company; Philadelphia: G.S. Appleton, 1845. 323 p. ViU. 45-6273

Taylor, William Cooke, 1800-1849. Outlines of sacred history; from the creation of the world to the destruction of Jerusalem. With questions for examinations. Intended for the use of schools an families. New edition, enlarged and improved. Philadelphia: Edward C. Biddle, 1845. 269 p. MBD; NcWsM. 45-6274

Taylor, William W. The centurion; or scenes in Rome, in the early days of Christianity. New York: M.W. Dodd, 1845. 108 p. CSfA; MB; MBUPH; Tx-Sani. 45-6275

Teacher's advocate. A weekly paper estab-lished by the New York State Teacher's Association. Syracuse: L.W. Hall, 1845-1846. DLC. 45-6276

Teacher's and parent's assistant; or thirteen lessons conveying to uninformed minds the first idea of God and his attributes. By an American Jewess.

Philadelphia, 1845. 35 p. DLC; NN; PPDrop; PU; WHi. 45-6277

Teacher's Institute, Sandusky City. Catalogue of the instructors and students. Organized in September, 1845. Sandusky City, Ohio: Printed by Mills and Ross, 1845. OClWHi. 45-6278

The teacher's manual. First edition. Moulmain, 1845. 17 p. MH. 45-6279

The teachings of nature. Or the songs of earth... Written for the Massachusetts Sabbath School Society, and revised by the committee of publication. Boston: Sabbath School Society, 1845. 84 p. DLC; RPB. 45-6280

Teeth almanac for 1846. Boston: Haliburton and company, [1845] MWA. 45-6281

Tefft, Benjamin Franklin, 1813-1885. The far west, its present, past and future; an inaugural address delivered to the trustees of the Indiana Asbury University, at the annual commencement, August 20, 1845. Indianapolis: Printed by E. Chamberlain, 1845. 38 p. CBPSR; IEG; In; MiD-B; OMC. 45-6282

Tefft, Benjamin Franklin, 1813-1885. Inequality in the condition of man inevitable. A sabbath evening lecture, delivered before the... Indiana Asbury University... Greencastle: Press of the Western Visitor, 1845. 16 p. CSmH; MnHi; NN; NNG. 45-6283

Temperance: address before the crew of the United States frigate Cumberland. Boston, 1845. 8 p. MBC. 45-6284

Temperance addresses at various temperance meetings in Boston, with an account of the grand simultaneous anniversary. Boston, 1845. 48 p. MBC. 45-6285

The temperance almanac... 1845. Published under the direction of the Executive Committee of the New York State Temperance Society, [1845] MeHi; MWA. 45-6286

Temperance almanac of the Massachusetts Temperance Union, for the year of our Lord, 1845... Boston: Massachusetts Temperance Union, [1845?] WaSp. 45-6287

Temperance Mass meeting at Mt. Morris, September 3, and 4, 1845. Mt. Morris, 1845. MB. 45-6288

The temperance offering. Salem, Massachusetts, 1845. v. 1. DLC; MBC; MHi; RPB. 45-6289

Templeton's musical entertainment, embracing the words of his first and second series entitled the rose, shamrock and thistle. Boston: Dutton, 1845. 24 p. CoU; MB. 45-6290

Tennessee. Governor's message, delivered in the Senate and House of Representatives on the 10th October, 1845. Nashville: W.F. Bang and company, 1845. 12 p. T. 45-6291

Tennessee. Message of Governor Jones to the General Assembly of the state of Tennessee. [Nashville, 1845] 8 p. T. 45-6292

Tennessee. Message of the Hon. A.V. Brown, governor of Tennessee to the General Assembly, November, 1845.

Nashville: J.G. Shepard, 1845. 14 p. THi.
45-6293

Tennessee. Message of the Hon. Aaron
V. Brown, governor of Tennessee to the
General Assembly, November 7th, 1845.
Nashville: B.R. M'Kennie and company,
1845. 15 p. T. 45-6294

Tennessee. Report of the committee on
banks in the Senate of the legislature of
Tennessee, delivered November 13th,
1845. Nashville: W.F. Bang and company, 1845. 10 p. ICU; TU; TxL-Mc;
TxU. 45-6295

Tennessee. Report of the internal improvement committee, appointed by the
twenty-fifth General Assembly of the
state of Tennessee to investigate the affairs of, and settle with the respective internal improvement companies in which
the state is a stockholder. Nashville: J.G.
Sheppard, 1845. 55 p. TxU. 45-6296

Tennessee. Report of the keeper of the
penitentiary, delivered in both houses of
the General Assembly of Tennesse, 13th
October, 1845. Nashville: W.F. Bang and
company, 1845. 19 p. T. 45-6297

Tennessee. Report of the president of
the Bank of Tennessee delivered to the
Senate, October 11th, 1845. Nashville:
B.R. M'Kennie and company, 1845. 47 p.
MH-BA; THi; TU; TxL-Mc. 45-6298

Tennessee. East Tennessee University.
Catalogue of the officers and students of
East Tennessee University for the
academic year, 1845-1846. Knoxville,
Tennessee: James C. Moses, 1845.
MeHi; T; TU. 45-6299

Tennessee. Tennessee Institution for

the Education of the Deaf and Dumb.
The first biennial report of the board of
trustees of the Tennessee Institution for
the Education of the Deaf and Dumb, to
the legislature of the state of Tennessee,
for 1844-1845. Nashville: W.F. Bang and
company, 1845. 30 p. T. 45-6300

Tennessee Boundary Commission.
Report of the Commissioners appointed
by the Governors of Tennessee and Kentucky to run and remark certain portions
of the boundary line between said states.
November 8, 1845. [Frankfort, Kentucky, 1845] 4 p. WHi. 45-6301

Tennessee Conference Female Institute. Catalogue of the officers and students of the Tennessee Conference
Female Institute for the year 1844 and
1845. Athens, Alabama, 1845. 15 p. T;
TxU. 45-6302

Tennessee Medical Society. Proceedings of the medical society of the state of
Tennessee, at the sixteenth annual meeting, held in the city hall, Nashville, May,
1845. Nashville: Cameron and Fall, 1845.
15 p. T; W. 45-6303

Tennessee School for the Blind, Nash-
ville. Report of the trustees, principal,
etc., of the Tennessee Institution for the
Instruction of the Blind to the General
Assembly of Tennessee. Nashville: B.R.
M'Kennie and company, 1845. 22 p. T;
TxU. 45-6304

Terre Haute, Indiana, Canal Convention. Proceedings of the canal convention; assembled at Terre Haute, May 22,
1845, for the purpose of considering the
best mode of applying the proceeds of
the liberal grant of land by the general
government, towards extending the

Wabash and Erie Canal to the Ohio River, at Evansville. Terre Haute, Indiana, 1845. 15 p. In. 45-6305

Teschemacher, James Englebert, 1790-1853. Essay on guano; describing its properties and the best methods of its application is agriculture and horticulture; with the value of importations from different localities; founded on actual analyses, and on personal experiments upon numerous kinds of trees, vegetables, flowers, and insects in this climate. Boston: A.D. Phelps, 1845. 51 p. ICJ; MB; N; PPL; WU-A. 45-6306

The test. Or the way to distinguish tinsel from gold and pearl from pottery; being a critical notice of "Poems by Amelia." By a lady. Louisville, Kentucky: Printed at the office of the Morning Courier, 1845. 35 p. DLC; PPL. 45-6307

Test tested. Louisville, 1845. PPL-R. 45-6308

Testamentary counsels, and hints to christians on the right distribution of their property by will, by a retired solicitor, carefully revised by a member of the American bar. First American edition. Troy, New York: W. and H. Merriam, 1845. 108 p. ICP; InGrD; MiD; MWA; NNUT. 45-6309

A testimonial of gratitude and affection to Henry Clay. The proceedings of the Whigs of Philadelphia assembled in town meeting on December 19, 1844. Philadelphia: Carey and Hart, 1845. 236 p. Ct; KyLx; MB; NNC; PPA. 45-6310

Texas. Appendix to the journals of the ninth congress of the Republic of Texas.

Washington: Miller and Cushney, 1845. 91 p. Tx; TxWFM. 45-6311

Texas. Communication from the commissioner of the General Land Office, in reply to a resolution of the convention of August 4. Austin: Printed at the office of the "New Era," [1845] TxU. 45-6312

Texas. Constitucion del estado de Tejas adoptada en convencion en la cuidad de Austin, 1845. Austin: Impreso en la oficina de la Nueva era, 8145. 34 p. Tx. 45-6313

Texas. Constitution of the state of Texas adopted unanimously in convention, at the city of Austin, 1845. An ordinance assenting to the proposals of the United States Congress for the annexation of Texas. Houston, 1845. 32 p. CSmH; ICT; PU; TxU; WaU. 45-6314

Texas. Correspondence relating to a treaty of peace between Mexico and Texas, upon the basis of an acknowledgment of the independence of the latter. Washington: National Register Printer, [1845] 8 p. TxU. 45-6315

Texas. Election proclamation of Anson Jones, November 10, 1845. n.p., 1845. 2 p. Tx. 45-6316

Texas. Ein handbuch fur deutsche auswaner, mit besonderer rucksicht auf diejenigen, welch ihre ueberfahrt und ansiedlung durch hilfe des vereins zum schutze deutscher einwanderer in Texas bewirken wollen. Bremen: A.D. Geisler, 1845. 141 p. NcD; NjP. 45-6317

Texas. Journals of the convention, assembled at the city of Austin on the fourth of July, 1845, for the purpose of framing a constitution for the state of Texas. Austin: Miner and Cruger, 1845. 378 p. Ct; GEU; Ia; NcD; Tx. 45-6318

Texas. Journals of the House of Representatives of the extra session, ninth congress of the Republic of Texas. Washington: Miller and Cushney, 1845. 94 p. TxSaA. 45-6319

Texas. Journals of the House of Representatives of the ninth congress of the Republic of Texas. Washington: Miller and Cushney, 1845. 395 p. Tx. 45-6320

Texas. Journals of the Senate of the extra session, Ninth Congress, of the Republic of Texas. Washington: Miller and Cushney, public printers, 1845. DLC; M; NN; Tx. 45-6321

Texas. Report of the committee on foreign relations, in the Senate of the Republic of Texas, on the subject of annexation with the correspondence between the secretary of state and Major Donaldson, the United States' charge d' affairs. Washington: Vindicator office, 1845. 20 p. TxWFM. 45-6322

Texas committee for Massachusetts. Circular. Boston, October 10, 1845. TxU. 45-6323

Texas in 1840, or the emigrants guide to the new republic. New York: Nafis, 1845. 275 p. P. 45-6324

Thackeray, William Makepeace, 1811-1863. The Paris sketch book of Mr. M.A. Titmarsh and eastern sketches, a journey from Cornhill to Cairo, the Irish sketch book and character sketches by W.M. Thackeray. New York: F.M. Lupton Publishing company, 1845. 451 p. GBar; KAr; LU; McDarN; WyLu. 45-6325

Thackeray, William Makepeace, 1811-1863. The Paris sketch book of Mr. M.A. Titmarsh; The Irish sketch book and notes of a journey from Cornhill to Grand Cairo. New York: Hurst and company, [1845] 511 p. MoCg; OkMu. 45-6326

Thanksgiving anthem. Boston, 1845. 7 p. MWA. 45-6327

Thatcher, Benjamin Bussey, 1809-1840. Indian biography or an historical account of those individuals who have been distinguished among the North American natives as orators, warriors, statesmen and other remarkable characters. New York: Harper and brothers, 1845. 3-320 p. InI; OCl; MB; RWe; ScGrw. 45-6328

Thayer, John Quincy Adams. Review of the report of the special committee of the legislature of Massachusetts. On the petition relating hours of labor... Boston: J.N. Bang, 1845. 32 p. MiD-B; MMeT; NN. 45-6329

Theodore and Matilda; or the fatal plot and foul deeds detected: on which are displayed the triumphs of virtue and the punishments of vice. Boston: Dow and Jackson, 1845. 29 p. CU; DLC; N; NNC. 45-6330

Theological sketch book, or skeletons or sermons; carefully arranged in systematic order so as to constitute a complete body of divinity. Baltimore: Printed at the publication rooms, Robert Carter, 1845. 3 v. MdBLF; MoBolS. 45-6331

Thierry, Augustin, 1795-1856. The historical essays, published under the title of "Dix ans d'etudes historiques," and narratives of the Merovingian era; or scenes of the sixth century. With an autobiographical preface... Philadelphia: Carey and Hart, 1845. [25]-204 p. CS; ICP; MMal; MCaS; RNR. 45-6332

Thiers, Adolphe, 1797-1877. History of the consulate and empire of France under Napoleon. Translated from the French by D.F. Campbell and H.W. Herbert with notes and additions. Philadelphia: Carey and Hart, 1845. 2 v. MBC; KyHi; NjR; OCl. 45-6333

Thiers, Adolphe, 1797-1877. History of the consulate and empire of France under Napoleon. Translated from the French by D.F. Campbell and H.W. Herbert with notes and additions. Philadelphia: Carey and Hart, 1845-1849. MH; PPFr. 45-6334

Thiers, Adolphe, 1797-1877. The history of the French revolution. Translated with notes and illustrations from the most authentic sources. Third American edition. Philadelphia: Carey and Hart, 1845. 3 v. DeU; IaNh; MoSpD; OrU; RWe. 45-6335

Thiers, Adolphe, 1797-1877. The history of the French revolution. Translated with notes and illustrations from the most authentic sources. Third American edition. Philadelphia: Carey and Hart, 1845. 4 v. KMK; MdBLC; OWoC; PMA; RWe. 45-6336

Third general epistle of Peter, to the rulers of the visible church. Fourth edition. Indianapolis: Printed for the publisher by W. Thompson Hatch, 1845. 16 p. PSC-Hi. 45-6337

Thirlwall, Connop, 1797-1875. A history of Greece. New York: Harper and brothers, 1845. 592 p. CtMW; GAuY; MAnP; RPB; TU. 45-6338

Thirlwall, Connop, 1797-1875. A history of Greece. New York: Harper and brothers, 1845-1848. 2 v. McGU; NjP; OO; TSewU. 45-6339

Thirty-one schoolmasters: penitential tears: or a cry from the dust by the thirty-one prostrated and pulverized by the hand of Horace Mann. Boston, 1845. 59 p. MNtCA. 45-6340

Thomas, Abel Charles, 1807-1880. A discussion on the important question, do the scriptures teach the doctrine of the final holiness and happiness of all mankind? In a series of letters between Rev. Abel C. Thomas and Rev. Luther Lee. Terre Haute, Indiana: E. Manford, 1845. 154 p. In; InHi. 45-6341

Thomas, Benjamin Franklin. The town officer. A digest of the laws of Massachusetts in relation to the powers, duties and liabilities of towns and of town officers; with the necessary forms. Worcester: Warren Lazell, 1845. 392 p. MBoy; MBS; MH-L; MWA; WaU. 45-6342

Thomas, Francis. Statement... Monteone, Frederick County, Maryland, 1845. 52 p. MB; NN; OClWHi; PPL; Vi. 45-6343

Thomas, John. The things of the spirit of God; an essay illustrative of the unscriptural character, and heathen origin, of the popular traditions of the age, concerning immortality, heaven and hell: and setting forth the truth respecting these things. Richmond, 1845. MWA. 45-6344

Thomas, R. The glory of America; comprising memoirs of the lives and glorious exploits of some of the distinguished officers engaged in the late war with Great Britain. New York: Ezra Strong, 1845. 574 p. CaNSWA; NcD; OFH. 45-6345

Thomas, R. History of the American wars: comprising the war of the revolution and the war of 1812. Being a complete history of the United States, from the year 1775 to 1815. With a historical introduction. Hartford: House and Brown, 1845. 380 p. Ct. 45-6346

Thomas, R. A pictorial history of the United States of America, from the earliest discoveries, by the Northmen, in the tenth century, to the present time. Hartford: E. Strong, 1845. 755 p. InPerM; KyLx; NPV. 45-6347

Thompson, Augustus Charles, 1812-1901. Songs in the night; or hymns for the sick and sufferings. Boston: B. Perkins, 1845. 271 p. CtHC; MBC; MeBat; OO; PPPrHi. 45-6348

Thompson, Jacob. Speech of Mr. Thompson, of Mississippi, on the Oregon bill, delivered in the House, January 30, 1845. [Washington? 1845?] 7 p. CU-B; WaU; WHi. 45-6349

Thompson, Joseph Parrish, 1819-1879. Lewdness and murder. A discourse suggested by the late murder; delivered in the Chapel Street Congregational Church, on March 9, 1845; and repeated in the Center Churches of New Haven and Hartford. New Haven: J.H. Benham,

1845. 24 p. CtY; ICU; MWA; NN. 45-6350

Thompson, Joseph Parrish, 1819-1879. Lewdness and murder. A discourse suggested by the late murder; delivered in the Chapel Street Congregational Church, on March 9, 1845; and repeated in the Center Churches of New Haven and Hartford. Second edition. New Haven: J.H. Benham, 1845. 24 p. CtY; MeLewB; MH; MHi; MnHi. 45-6351

Thompson, Joseph Parrish, 1819-1879. Lewdness and murder. A discourse suggested by the late murder; delivered in the Chapel Street Congregational Church, on March 9, 1845; and repeated in the Center Churches of New Haven and Hartford. Third edition. New Haven: J.H. Benham, 1845. 24 p. Ct; CtY; CtMHHi; MH-AH. 45-6352

Thompson, Joseph Parrish, 1819-1879. Lewdness and murder. A discourse suggested by the late murder; delivered in the Chapel Street Congregational Church, on March 9, 1845; and repeated in the Center Churches of New Haven and Hartford. Fourth edition. New Haven: J.H. Benham, 1845. 24 p. CtSoP; MB; MBC; MWA; OCl. 45-6353

Thompson, Leander, 1812-1896. A nations increase; not a nations joy. A discourse in the South Congregational Church, South Hadley, Annual fast, April 3, 1845. Springfield: Printed by Horace S. Taylor, 1845. 4-11 p. CtHC; MLy; MWo. 45-6354

Thompson, Matthew LaRue Perrine. Religious sectarianism: a discourse delivered in the First Presbyterian Church of Philadelphia. Philadelphia:

William F. Geddes, printer, 1845. 23 p. ICP; MH-AH; NjR; PHi; PPPrHi. 45-6355

Thompson, William Tappan, 1812-1882. Chronicles of Pineville; embracing sketches of Georgia scenes, incidents and characters. With twelve original engravings by Darley. Philadelphia: Carey and Hart, 1845. 186 p. IU; LNHT; MH; NcD. 45-6356

Thompson, Zadock. Guide to Lake George, Lake Champlain, Montreal and Quebec, with maps and tables of routes and distances from Albany, Burlington and Montreal. Burlington: Chauncey Goodrich, 1845. 48 p. LNH; MBC; Nh-Hi; PHi; Vt. 45-6357

Thompsons Island, Boston. Farm and Trades School. Report, act of incorporation, bylaws and general rules and regulations. Boston: S.N. Dickinson and company, 1845. 40 p. ICU; MB; MiD-B; WHi. 45-6358

Thompsonville, Connecticut. First Presbyterian Church. Particulars of the controversy, relating to the Presbyterian Church at Thompsonville, September, 1845. Report of the committee opposed to music in the church, and a reply to the report. New York, 1845. 10 p. MBC; MHi; PPPrHi. 45-6359

Thomson, Anthony Todd, 1778-1849. A conspectus of the pharmacopoeias of the Edinburgh and Dunlin Colleges of Physicians and of the United States pharmacopoeia... Third American edition, edited by Charles A. Lee. New York: H.G. Langley, 1845. 313 p. MBP; MnRM; NNN; OClM; PPAN. 45-6360

Thomson, Anthony Todd, 1778-1849. The domestic management of the sick room, necessary, in aid of medical treatment, for the cure of diseases. First American, from the second London edition. Philadelphia: Lea and Blanchard, 1845. 353 p. KWiU; MdBP; NBMS; PP; RPB. 45-6361

Thomson, Charles West, 1798-1879. The love of home and other poems. Philadelphia: P. Thomson, 1845. 120 p. CtY; DeU; MH; PHi; RPB. 45-6362

Thomson, James, 1700-1748. The seasons. A new edition. Boston: Phillips and Sampson, 1845. 154 p. InNd; KyBC; KWiF; MH. 45-6363

Thomson, James, 1700-1748. The seasons. To which are added notes, grammatical and explanatory; adapting the work for use in schools, by Josiah Swett. Claremont, New Hampshire: Manufacturing company, 1845. 199 p. ICU; Matt; MH; VtU. 45-6364

Thomson, James Bates. 1808-1883. Elements of algebra, being an abridgement of Day's algebra, adapted to the capacities of the young, and the method of instruction in schools and academies. Sixth edition. New Haven: Durrie and Peck, 1845. 252 p. CtY; MH. 45-6365

Thomson, James Bates, 1808-1883. Practical arithmetic, uniting the inductive with the synthetic mode of instruction; also illustrating the principles of cancellation. New York: Newman, 1845. ICU; NRMA. 45-6366

Thomson, Samuel Harrison, 1813-1882. A review of Mr. MacMaster's speech before the Synod of Indiana, October 4,

1844. Madison: Jones and Lodge, printers, 1845. 16 p. DLC; InU; InHi. 45-6367

Thorburn, Grant, 1773-1863. Fifty year's reminiscences of New York, or flowers from the garden of Laurie Todd: being a collection of fugitive pieces which appeared in the newspapers and periodicals of the day... New York: Daniel Fanshaw, 1845. 287 p. MB; NbU; OClW; PP; RPA. 45-6368

Thornton, Henry, 1760-1815. Family prayers and prayers on the ten commandments. New York: Stanford and swords, 1845. 354 p. ICP. 45-6369

Thornton, Phineas. Southern gardener and receipt book containing a collection of valuable receipts for cookery, the preservation of fruits and other articles of household consumption, and for the cure of diseases. Second edition, improved and enlarged. Newark, New Jersey: A.L. Dennis, for the author, 1845. 403 p. KyLo; MWA; NcFay; ScU. 45-6370

Thornwell, James Henley, 1812-1862. The arguments of Romanists from the infallibility of the church and the testimony of the fathers in behalf of the Apocrypha, discussed and refuted... New York: Leavitt, Trow and company; Boston: C. Tappan, [etc., etc.] 1845. 417 p. MH; O; PPPrHi; ScSp; WNaE. 45-6371

Thornwell, James Henley, 1812-1862. The necessity of the atonement. A sermon, preached in the chapel of the South Carolina College, on December 1, 1845. Columbia: Printed by Samuel Weir at the Southern Chronicle office, 1845. 72 p.

ICP; MAnP; MH-AH; N; PPPrHi. 45-6372

Thoughts on the effects of our railroads, on the business and prosperity of Portsmouth, and on a remedy for the evils, by a citizen. [Portsmouth] 1845. 10 p. CSmH; Nh; WU. 45-6373

Three nights in a lifetime. A domestic tale. New York: E. Ferrett and Jones, 1845. 84 p. MB; MdBP; NjR; ScU. 45-6374

Thrilling and romantic story of Sarah Smith and the Hessian, an original tale of the American revolution. To which is added, female heroism exemplified. An interesting story founded on fact; together with an essay on industry. Philadelphia, 1845. 32 p. Ct; ICU; MB; PU. 45-6375

Thucydides. History of the Peloponnesian war, translated from the Greek of Thucydides. By William Smith, rector of the Holy Trinity Church and chaplain to the Rt. Hon. the Earl of Derby. A new edition. Philadelphia: Thomas Wardle, 1845. LNL; Mi-L; OCY; NCaS; ViU. 45-6376

Tibbatts, John W. Speech of Mr. Tibbatts, on the reannexation of Texas... in the House, January 13, 1845. Washington: Globe office, 1845. 14 p. MH; NBu; OCHP; Vi. 45-6377

Ticknor, Almon, d. 1796. The columbian calculator; being a practical and concise system of decimal arithmetic. Second edition. Easton, Pennsylvania: Sentinel office for the author, 1845. 256 p. PLFM; PPT. 45-6378

Tinker, Reuben, 1799-1854. The book of God. An address delivered before the Lake Company Bible Society, and the Painesville Female Bible Society, August 31, 1844. Chardon: Printed by David T. Bruce, 1845. 16 p. MWA. 45-6379

Tioga County Teachers Institute, Tioga County, New York. Catalogue of officers, teachers and students. Ithaca, New York, October 1845. MH. 45-6380

To emigrants; John Almy, state agent. 1845. New York, 1845. 7 p. N. 45-6381

To the members of the legislature of Maryland. Evil effects of the pilot law: its opposition to the agricultural interests of Maryland, and its deleterious effects upon the commercial prosperity of Baltimore. Baltimore: John W. Woods, printer, 1845. 12 p. WHi. 45-6382

To the people of Pennsylvania. Read! Pause! Reflect! n.p., 1845? 15 p. DLC. 45-6383

To the whigs of the ninth congressional district. Richmond: P.D. Bernard, printer, 1845. 8 p. NcU. 45-6384

Tobin, John, 1770-1804. The honeymoon, a play in five acts. New York: William Taylor; Baltimore: Taylor, Wilde and company, 1845. 63 p. MB. 45-6385

Tocqueville, Alexis Charles Henri Maurice Clerel de, 1805-1859. Democracy in America by Henry Reeve. New York: Henry G. Langley, 1845. 494 p. LU; OO; PPRF; PU; ViU. 45-6386

Tocqueville, Alexis Charles Henri Maurice Clerel de, 1805-1859. Democracy in American. With an original preface and notes by John C. Spencer. Fourth edition, revised and corrected from the eighth Paris edition. New York: H.G. Langley, 1845. 2 v. CSansS; OO; PU; ScU; ViU. 45-6387

Todd, John, 1800-1873. Hafed's dream. Edited by J. Brace Jr. Pittsfield, Massachusetts: E.P. Little, 1845. 124 p. LNT; MH; MNF. 45-6388

Todd, John, 1800-1873. Long Lake, by John Todd, edited by J. Brace, Jr. Pittsfield, Massachusetts: E.P. Little, 1845. 100 p. CtMW; ICN; MPiB; NN; OClWHi. 45-6389

Todd, John, 1800-1873. Simple sketches. Edited by J. Brace, Jr. Pittsfield, Massachusetts: E.P. Little, 1845. 2 v. MNF; NN; OMC; OO; WMHi. 45-6390

Todd, John, 1800-1873. The student's manual; designed, by specific directions, to aid in forming and strengthening the intellectual and moral character and habits of the students. Thirteenth edition. Northampton: J.H. Butler, 1845. 392 p. IaAt; MH; OClW; OCY; ViU. 45-6391

Todd, John, 1800-1873. The young man. Hints addressed to the young men of the United States. Second edition. Northampton: J.H. Butler; Buffalo: J. H. Butler and company, 1845. 355 p. CtHT; MB; MH; MPiB; PCC. 45-6392

Todd, Lewis C. b. 1794. Moral justice of universalism. To which is prefixed a brief sketch of the author's life. Erie: J.M. Sterrett, 1845. 192 p. MH; MMeT-Hi; OAsht; OClWHi; OO. 45-6393

Todd, Robert S. Mr. Todd's reply to Mr. Wickliffe. Lexington, Kentucky: Observer and Reporter, printer, 1845. 7 p. CSmH; KyDC; PPL; PPL-R; OC. 45-6394

The token; or affection's gift; a Christmas and New Year's present. Edited by S.G. Goodrich. New York: A. Edwards, [1845] CU; IaU; NN; ViU. 45-6395

Tomlinson, Russell, 1808-1878. Orthodoxy as it is; or its mental influence and practical inefficiency and effects illustrated by philosophy and facts. Boston: A. Tompkins, 1845. 234 p. IaMp; MFiHi; MiU; MMeT-Hi; NCaS. 45-6396

Tompkins Teachers Institute, Ithaca, New York. Catalogue of the instructors and students of Tompkins Teachers Institute, spring term, April, 1845. Ithaca: Mack, 1845. 12 p. NCH. 45-6397

Tonna, Charlotte Elizabeth Browne, 1790-1846. The church visible in all ages. By Charlotte Elizabeth [pseud.] New York: J.S. Taylor and company, 1845. ArCH; ICBB; KyLx; MH; MoSpD; NN; PPL-R. 45-6398

Tonna, Charlotte Elizabeth Browne, 1790-1846. Conformity. New York: M.W. Dodd, 1845. ICBB. 45-6399

Tonna, Charlotte Elizabeth Browne, 1790-1846. The convent bell: and other poems. New York: J.S. Taylor and company, 1845. 78, 121, 146 p. ICN; ICU; MB; MLow; PPL-R. 45-6400

Tonna, Charlotte Elizabeth Browne, 1790-1846. The deserter. New York: M.W. Dodd, 1845. 239 p. CtY; LLafS; MPiB; PPL-R. 45-6401

Tonna, Charlotte Elizabeth Browne, 1790-1846. The flower of innocence or Rachel. A true narrative, with other tales. New York: J.S. Taylor, 1845. 174 p. NN. 45-6402

Tonna, Charlotte Elizabeth Browne, 1790-1846. Izram; a Mexican tale. New York: John S. Taylor and company, 1845. 3-121 p. ICU; KyBC; KLaw; MAnP; MPiB. 45-6403

Tonna, Charlotte Elizabeth Browne, 1790-1846. Judah's lion. New York: S. Taylor and company, 1845. 335 p. ICN; MWA. 45-6404

Tonna, Charlotte Elizabeth Browne, 1790-1846. Kindness to animals. New York: G. Lane and C.B. Tippett, 1845. 128 p. NjMD. 45-6405

Tonna, Charlotte Elizabeth Browne, 1790-1846. Osric, a missionary tale: with the garden and other poems. Fourth edition. Boston: John S. Taylor and company, 1845. 146, 32 p. ICU; MH; MLow; NN; PP. 45-6406

Tonna, Charlotte Elizabeth Browne, 1790-1846. Osric, a missionary tale: with the garden and other poems. Fourth edition. New York: Baker and Scribner, 1846. 146 p. CtHC; NBu; PPM. 45-6407

Tonna, Charlotte Elizabeth Browne, 1790-1846. Personal recollections. By Charlotte Elizabeth [pseud.] From the London edition. New York: J.S. Taylor and company, 1845. 357 p. ICN; NAnge; ViU; VtU. 45-6408

Tonna, Charlotte Elizabeth Browne, 1790-1846. Principalities and powers in heavenly places. With an introduction by the Rev. Edward Bickersteth. New York: John S.Taylor and company, 1845. 298 p. IAlS. 45-6409

Tonna, Charlotte Elizabeth Browne, 1790-1846. Principalities and powers in heavenly places. With an introduction by the Rev. Edward Bickersteth. New York: John S.Taylor and company, 1845. 351 p. LLafs; OO; RLa. 45-6410

Tonna, Charlotte Elizabeth Browne, 1790-1846. The siege of Derry: or sufferings of the Protestants: A tale of the revolution. New York: Taylor, 1845. 322 p. PP; TWcW. 45-6411

Tonna, Charlotte Elizabeth Browne, 1790-1846. The simple flower and other tales. New York: John S. Taylor and company, 1845. 166 p. ICU; MBiB; NNC. 45-6412

Tonna, Charlotte Elizabeth Browne, 1790-1846. Works of Charlotte Elizabeth; with an introduction by H.B. Stowe. Second edition. New York: Dodd, 1845. 3 v. FOA; IaFd; WMMD. 45-6413

Tonna, Charlotte Elizabeth Browne, 1790-1846. The wrongs of woman. New York: M.W. Dodd, 1845. 141 p. N; RWe. 45-6414

Torrey, Charles Turner, 1813-1846. Home! or the pilgrims faith revived. Salem: John P. Jewett and company; Cincinnati: G.L. Weed, 1845. 256 p. ICN; MBC; MWHi; NbCrD; OO. 45-6415

Torrey, Charles Turner, 1813-1846. Home! or the pilgrims faith revived.

Second edition. Salem: John P. Jewett and company; Cincinnati: G.L. Weed, 1845. 256 p. MiOC; MTop; OClWHi. 45-6416

Torrey, Henry Warren, 1814-1893. English Latin lexicon, prepared to accompany Leaverett's Latin-English Lexicon. Boston: Wilkins: Carter and company, 1845. 318 p. CtHWatk; NBuCC. 45-6417

Torrey, Jesse. The moral instructor, and guide to virtue; being a compendium of moral philosophy; with practical rules for the conduct of life. Philadelphia: Grigg and Elliot, 1845. 300 p. IaB; LNL; ScU; TU. 45-6418

Torrey, Jesse. The pleasing companion; or second reader, designed for the use of common schools and families, 1845. 142 p. NcD; NjP. 45-6419

Tower, David Bates, 1808-1868. A complete key to Tower's intellectual algebra, for common schools... New York: Paine and Burgess; Boston: B.B. Mussey, 1845. 100 p. CtHWatk; MH; NNC; OC; RPB. 45-6420

Tower, David Bates, 1808-1868. Gradual primer. Part I. New York: Paine and Burgess, etc., etc., 1845. CtHWatk; IEG; MH. 45-6421

Tower, David Bates, 1808-1868. The gradual reader. First step, or exercises in articulation. Enlarged and improved edition. Boston: Charles Stimpson, 1845. 168 p. MB; MLow; PU-Penn; RPB. 45-6422

Tower, David Bates, 1808-1868.

Gradual speller. Boston: Crosby and Nichols, [1845] 150 p. MoSpD. 45-6423

Tower, David Bates, 1808-1868. The gradual speller and complete enunciator; showing the orthography and orthoepy of all words in common use. Eleventh edition. New York: D. Burgess, [1845] MH. 45-6424

Tower, David Bates, 1808-1868. The gradual speller and complete enunciator; showing the orthography and orthoepy of all words in common use. Fourteenth edition. New York: D. Burgess, [1845] IEG; MH. 45-6425

Tower, David Bates, 1808-1868. Intellectual algebra, or oral exercises in algebra... New York: Paine and Burgess; Boston: B.B. Mussey, [1845] 208 p. CtHT; ICU; MB; NNC; OClWHi. 45-6426

Tower, David Bates, 1808-1868. North American second class reader. New York, 1845. MWbor. 45-6427

Tower, Fayette Bartholomew. Illustrations of the Croton Aqueduct. New York: Wiley, 1845. NjP; NRom; NSchU; PWW. 45-6428

The town and American punch. New York: Andrews, Beaumont and company, 1845. DLC; IU. 45-6429

Town, Ithiel, 1784-1844. Catalogues of his library. New York, 1845. NN. 45-6430

Town, Salem, 1779-1864. An analysis of the derivative words in the English language. Twenty-first edition, carefully revised, enlarged and adapted to schools of all grades. Auburn, New York: Mer-

rell and Hollett, 1845. 164 p. CtMW. 45-6431

Town, Salem, 1779-1864. An analysis of the derivative words in the English language. Twenty-first edition, carefully revised, enlarged and adapted to schools of all grades. Rochester: Fisher and company, 1845. 164 p. NRHi; NRU. 45-6432

Town, Salem, 1779-1864. The child's first book; being a series of easy lessons prepared in strict accordance with the view; of practical teachers. New York: R.V. Root and company, 1845. 72 p. N. 45-6433

Town, Salem, 1779-1864. The little thinker comprising reading lessons so arranged as to exhibit the obvious sense of words. New York: R.C. Root and company, 1845. 64, 63 p. NN. 45-6434

Town, Salem, 1779-1864. Town's first reader. Cooperstown: H. and E. Phinney, 1845. 128 p. NN. 45-6435

Town, Salem, 1779-1864. Town's first reader, to be used with any speller... Rochester: Fisher and company, 1845. [9[-128 p. CtHWatk; NRU; WRichM. 45-6436

Town, Salem, 1779-1864. Town's second reader; or the speller's companion. Portland, 1845. CtHWatk. 45-6437

Town, Salem, 1779-1864. Town's third reader: containing a selection of lessons exclusively from American authors. New York: R.C. Root and company, 1845. 288 p. CtHWatk; NBuG; OClWHi. 45-6438

Town, Salem, 1779-1864. Town's fourth

reader, containing a selection of lessons, exclusively from American authors. Cincinnati: Derby, Bradley and company, 1845. 288 p. ICBB; NjP. 45-6439

Town, Salem, 1779-1864. Town's second reader; or the speller's companion. New York: R.C. Root and company, 1845. 11-239 p. NoLoc. 45-6440

Town, Salem, 1779-1864. Town's spelling and defining book: containing rules for designating the accented syllable in most words in the language; being an introduction to Town's analysis. One hundredth edition. Critically revised and corrected. Rochester: Fisher and company, 1845. 167 p. CtHT-W; DLC; NRHi; OOxM; RPB. 45-6441

The town. New York, 1845. v. 1. No. 1. MB. 45-6442

Townes, George. Elementary chemistry. Theoretical and practical... with numerous illustrations. Edited with additions, Robert Bridges. Philadelphia: Lea and Blanchard, 1845. 460 p. MChiA; NBuU-M; NTRPI; TxBrdD. 45-6443

A tract for the day. How to conquer Texas before Texas conquers us. Boston: Redding and company, 1845. 16 p. CSmH; DLC; MHi; Tx; TxU. 45-6444

Tracts for the churches. No. 1. Bethany, Virginia: W.F.M. Arny, 1845. 4-12 p. KyLx. 45-6445

Tracy, Calvin. A new system of arithmetic in which is explained and applied to practical purposes. Fourth edition. New York: M.H. Newman, 1845. 288 p. CtHWatk; MiU; NRU-W. 45-6446

Tracy, Ebenezer Carter, 1796-1862. Memoir of the life of Jeremiah Evarts... late corresponding secretary of the American Board of Commissioners for Foreign Missions. Boston: Crocker and Brewster, 1845. 448 p. IaB; KWiU; NNC; TxGR; VtU. 45-6447

Tracy, Henry. Chart of Long Pond. Boston, [1845] MB. 45-6448

Tracy, Henry. Map of the vicinity of Boston, showing the sources of water for supplying the city. Boston, 1845. DLC; MB. 45-6449

Tracy, Joseph, 1793?-1874. Colonization and missions. A historical examination of the state of society in western Africa, as formed by Paganism and Muhammedanism, slavery, the slave trade and piracy, and of the remedial influence of colonization and missions... Second edition. Boston: Press of T.R. Marvin, 1845. 40 p. InU; NjR; OC; OClWHi; TNF. 45-6450

Tracy, Joseph, 1793?-1874. Colonization and Missions. A historical examination of the state of society in Western Africa. Third edition. Boston: T.R. Marvin, 1845. 40 p. CtSoP; M; MBBC; OClWHi; WHi. 45-6451

Tracy, Joseph, 1793?-1874. Colonization and Missions. A historical examination of the state of society in Western Africa. Published by the board of managers. Fourth edition. Boston: T.R. Marvin, 1845. 40 p. CtY-D; LU; MiU-C. 45-6452

Tracy, Joseph, 1793?-1874. The great awakening. A history of the revival of religion in the time of Edwards and

Whitefield. Boston: Charles Tappan; New York: Dayton and Newman; Philadelphia: Henry Perkins, 1845. 433 p. MnHi; NNUT; PPP; TxH; VtB. 45-6453

Tracy, Joseph, 1793?-1874. The great awakening. A history of the revival of religion in the time of Edwards and Whitefield. Boston: Crocker and Brewster, 1845. 433 p. MBNMHi; ODefC. 45-6454

Tragic almanac for 1846. New York: T.W. Strong, 1845. MWA. 45-6455

Tragical calendar and pirate's own almanac for 1846. New York: Turner and Fisher, [1845] MWA. 45-6456

Trajetta, Philip, 1777-1854. Eight small progressive choruses, on sacred words, with an accompaniment for the pianoforte and violin. Philadelphia: King and Baird, 1845. 20 p. PPM. 45-6457

Trajetta, Philip, 1777-1854. Six sacred hymns, with an accompaniment for the organ, to which are added an overture and five ricercarios, making a cantata entitled, "The day of rest". Philadelphia: King and Baird, 1845. 36 p. NN; PPM. 45-6458

Trall, Russell Thacher, 1812-1877. The philosophy of the temperance reformation; or the relations of alchohol and the human organism, chemically, physiologically considered. A prize essay. [New York? 1845?] 12 p. CtY; DLC; MBC; NN. 45-6459

The transcript to the electors of Rhode Island. Providence, 1845. MB. 45-6460

Trapier, Paul, 1806-1872. Narrative of facts which lead to the presentment of the Rt. Rev. Benjamin T. Onderdonk. New York: Stanford and Swords, 1845. 22 p. ICU; MBC; NjR; PPL; RNR. 45-6461

The traveller: an entirely original weekly book of surpassing interest. New York: The traveller, 1845-. v. 1-. TxU. 45-6462

The traveller; containing railroad, steamboat, canal packet and stage routes, through the state of New York. Also other information useful to travellers. New York: J. Disturnell, 1845. 48 p. M. 45-6463

Treadwell, Daniel, 1791-1872. Account of an improved cannon. Cambridge, Massachusetts, 1845. MB. 45-6464

Treadwell, Daniel, 1791-1872. Papers and memoirs concerning the improvement of cannon, published between the years 1845 and 1862. Cambridge, Massachusetts, 1845-1864. ICJ; RP. 45-6465

Treadwell, Daniel, 1791-1872. Papers on cannon. Cambridge, Massachusetts, 1845-1861. 6 v. RPB. 45-6466

Treadwell, Daniel, 1791-1872. A short account of an improved cannon, and of the machinery and processes employed in its manufacture. Cambridge: Metcalf and company, printers to the university, 1845. 23 p. MH; MHi; MWA; NIC. 45-6467

Treadwell, Francis C. Conspiracy to defeat the liberation of Governor Dorr or the Hunkers and Algerines identified and their policy unveiled. New York:

John Windt, 1845. 47 p. CtSoP; IaU; MBAt; MiD-B; PHi. 45-6468

Trego, Charles B. 1794-1874. A geography of Pennsylvania. Philadelphia, 1845. PPAN. 45-6469

Tremayne, Edwards. Tremayne's table of post offices in the state of Pennsylvania. Philadelphia: Thomas, Cowperthwait, 1845. 26 p. DLC; PHi. 45-6470

Trench, Richard Chenevix, 1807-1886. The fitness of holy Scripture for unfolding the spiritual life of men; being the Hulean lectures for the year 1845. Cambridge, Massachusetts: Macmillan, Barclay, and MacMillan, 1845. 168 p. GDecCT; IaDuU. 45-6471

Trimmer, Sarah Kirby, 1741-1810. The ladder to learning: a collection of fables arranged progressively in words of one, two, and three syllables, with original morals. Third American from the thirteenth London edition. Boston: Carter, 1845. 171 p. OC. 45-6472

Trimmer, Sarah Kirby, 1741-1810. A natural history of the most remarkable quadrapeds, birds, fishes, reptiles and insects. Boston: Simpkins, 1845. 233 p. CtHWatk; DSI; MB. 45-6473

Trimmer, Sarah Kirby, 1741-1810. The robins; or domestic life among the birds. With anecdotes of other animals. Boston: J.H. Francis, 1845. 194 p. MNBedf. 45-6474

Trimmer, Sarah Kirby, 1741-1810. The robins; or domestic life among the birds. With anecdotes of other animals. A new edition, revised. New York, 1845. 199 p. MHi. 45-6475

Trinity College, Hartford, Connecticut. Catalogue of the officers and graduates of Trinity College, from its foundation in 1823. Published by the House of Convocation. Hartford: Press of Case, Tiffany and company, 1845. 49 p. CtHT; MBD; RP. 45-6476

Trinity College, Hartford, Connecticut. Catalogue of the officers and students for the academic year 1844-1845. Hartford: Press of Case and Burnham, 1845. 23 p. Ct. 45-6477

Trinity College, Hartford, Connecticut. Catalogue of the officers and students for the academic year 1845-1846. Published by the students. Hartford: Press of William Faxon, [1845] 16 p. CtHT; RP. 45-6478

Trinity College, Hartford, Connecticut. Statutes adopted by the trustees, 1845. Hartford: William Faxon, 1845. CtHT; RP. 45-6479

Troy almanac for 1846. Troy, New York: George Redfield, [1845] MWA. 45-6480

Troy, New York. Memorial of the mayor, recorder, alderman and commonality of the city of Troy, in relation to a bridge across the Hudson at Albany. In assemby, February 12, 1845. [Albany, 1845] 11 p. WHi. 45-6481

Troy almanac for 1846. Troy, New York: Young and Hartt, [1845] MWA. 45-6482

Troy and Greenbush Railroad Association. Report in compliance of the resolutions of the assemby. In assemby,

February 10, 1845. [Albany, 1845] 40 p. WHi. 45-6483

Troy Young Men's Association, Troy, New York. Catalogue of the library of the Troy Young Men's Association, of the city of Troy, 1845. 32 p. DLC; NjR. 45-6484

True, Charles Kittredge, 1809-1878. Shawmut; or the settlement of Boston. By the Puritan pilgrims... Boston: Waite, Peirce and company, 1845. [5]-136 p. CoD; MB; MNBedf; MoS; WHi. 45-6485

True, Charles Kittredge, 1809-1878. Tri-mountain; or the early history of Boston. Boston: Heath and Graves, [1845] 136 p. DLC; MB; MBAt; MWA; PP. 45-6486

A true account of the initiation of J-B-into the S.S. Society for the discouragemet of artistical saps.] New York: C.Smith, 1845. 19 p. MB; NN. 45-6487

True American. Devoted to universal liberty. Lexington, Kentucky, 1845-. v. 1-CtY; VtBrt. 45-6488

Trumbull, David, 1819-1889. The death of Captain Nathan Hale. A drama in five acts. Written by David Trumbull... Hartford: Press of E. Geer, 1845. 32 p. CtSoP; ICU; MHi; MI; NN. 45-6489

Trust Fire Insurance Company. Report of the Trust Fire Insurance Company in answer to a resolution of the assembly. [Albany, 1845] 3 p. WHi. 45-6490

Tucker, George, 1775-1861. Memoir of the life and character of John P. Emmet. Delivered before the visitors, faculty, and alumni of the University of Virginia. Philadelphia: C. Sherman, printer, 1845. 31 p. DLC; MBAt; PHi; PPAmP; ViU. 45-6491

Tucker, Joshua T. Dying scenes; being the last days of the life of Mrs. Mary Orland Tucker, wife of Rev. Joshua T. Tucker of Missouri, who died August 31, 1844 at the age of 29 years. By her husband. Boston: Massachusetts Sabbath School Society, 1845. 24 p. MBC; MHolliHi. 45-6492

Tucker, Mark, 1795-1875. Centennial sermon... Beneficent Congregational Church and Society, in Providence, Rhode Island, March 19, 1843. Together with the articles of faith, covenant, etc., and a list of the members. Providence: Knowles and Vose, printers, 1845. 84 p. CtY-D; MBs; MnU; MWA; RP. 45-6493

Tucker, Nathaniel Beverley, 1784-1851. A series of lectures on the science of government; intended to prepare the student for the study of the constitution of the United States. Philadelphia: Carey and Hart, 1845. 464 p. ICU; NcD; LU; MiD; NCH. 45-6494

Tuckerman, Edward, 1817-1886. An enumeration of North American lichens... To which is prefixed an essay on the natural systems of Oken, Fries and Endlicher. Cambridge, [Massachusetts] John Owen, 1845. 59 p. ICJ; CtHT; KMK; MDeeP; NcU; ScCC. 45-6495

Tupper, Martin Farquhar, 1810-1889. The crock of gold, a rural novel... New York: Wiley and Putnam, 1845. 192 p. MnS; NGH; OClW; PU; RPB. 45-6496

Tupper, Martin Farquhar, 1810-1889.

Heart: a social novel. New York: Wiley and Putnam, 1845. 100 p. MdBP; MeB; PPLiR; OCW; WU. 45-6497

Tupper, Martin Farquhar, 1810-1889. Proverbial philosophy: a book of thoughts and arguments, originally treated. New York: Wiley and Putnam, 1845. 2 v. AzT; CtMW; LN; MWA; NBuG. 45-6498

Tupper, Martin Farquhar, 1810-1889. Proverbial philosophy: a book of thoughts and arguments, originally treated. Second American from the fifth London edition. Philadelphia: Herman Hooker, 1845. 289 p. PP; T; ViU. 45-6499

Tupper, Martin Farquhar, 1810-1889. The twins: a domestic novel. New York: Wiley, and Putnam, 1845. 110 p. CtY; MeBat; OClW; PPL- R; WU. 45-6500

Turford, Hugh. The grounds of a holy life... To which is added, Paul's speech to Titus, called the first Bishop of Crete, and also, a true touchstone, or trial of Christianity. Revised edition. Byberry: John Comley, 1845. 118 p. IaOSleW; IU; NBF; PHC; PSC-Hi. 45-6501

Turner, George. Case of Thomas W. Dorr [convicted of an offence under the act entitled an act in relation to offences against the sovereign power of the state of Rhode Island] explained. Washington? 1845. 11 p. MH; NNC. 45-6502

Turner, John Bryant, 1786-1849. An ecclesiastical controversy: containing the correspondence between Hon. John B. Turner, member of the First Parish, and Rev. Daniel Wight, Jr., Pastor of the First Church in Scituate, Massachusetts. Boston: Samuel N. Dickinson, printer, 1845. 78 p. CBPac; MB; MH; OCLaw; RPB. 45-6503

Turner, John Bryant, 1786-1849. A second series of letters concerning the history of the First Parish in Scituate. Boston: Munroe, 1845. 84 p. CBPac; MB; MH; MWA. 45-6504

Turner, Joseph W. The freed bird; or speed away! speed away. A quartette. Boston: Keith, 1845. 4 p. MB. 45-6505

Turner, Joseph W. Mary of the wild moor. A song adapted for the piano forte. Boston: Keith, 1845. 2 p. MB. 45-6506

Turner, Samuel Hulbeart, 1790-1861. Essay on our Lord's discourse at Copernaum: recorded in the sixth chapter of St. John, By S. Turner... New York: Harper and brothers, 1845. 149 p. MBC; NCH; PU; ScCC; VtU. 45-6507

Turner, Samuel Hulbeart, 1790-1861. Remarks on a late editorial article in the Churchman, entitled "Results of the general convention, theological seminary," and on certain other articles formerly published in that journal. New York: Harper and brothers, 1845. 24 p. CtHT; MB; MdBD; MWA; NNC. 45-6508

Turner, Ulysses. Address to the Woodford County Bible Society. Frankfort, Kentucky, 1846. 14 p. ICU. 45-6509

Turner and Hughes North Carolina almanac for the year of our Lord, 1846. Carefully calculated for the horizon and meridian of Raleigh. Raleigh: Turner and Hughes, [1845] 36 p. NcD. 45-6510

Turner's comic almanac, 1846. New

York: Turner and Fisher, [1845] [36] p. WHi. 45-6511

Turner's comic almanack for 1846. Boston: James Fisher, [1845] MWA. 45-6512

Turner's comick almanack for 1846. New York: Turner and Fisher, 1845. MWA. 45-6513

Turner's improved almanac for 1846. New York and Philadelphia: Turner and Fisher, [1845] MWHi. 45-6514

Turner's improved housekeeper's almanac for 1846. New York: Turner and Fisher, [1845] MWA. 45-6515

Turner's longitude tables for correcting the observed distance of the moon and sun, or moon and star, for the effects of parallax and refraction, etc. New Bedford: W.C. Taber and son, 1845. MH; MNBedf; Nh. 45-6516

Turner's Lowell directory. Lowell, 1845. 182 p. MHi. 45-6517

Turney, Edmund. The prospect of death. An incentive to Christian constancy and faithfulness. A discourse delivered on occasion of the death of Rev. Jonathan Going, president of Granville College. With a sketch of his life. By E. Turney, pastor of the First Baptist Church of Granville, Ohio. Hartford: Robins and Smith, 1845. 22 p. MA; MBC; MWelC; NCH-S; RPB. 45-6518

Turnip vs. Tator; an original exposition of the code of procedure. Albany: Published according to an act of Congress, 1845. 10 p. WHi. 45-6519

Tustin, Josiah Phillips, 1817-1887. A discourse delivered at the dedication of the new church edifice of the Baptist church and society... Providence: H.H. Brown, 1845. 9-193, [5]-125 p. MnF; MnHi; MoSM; NBuG; R. 45-6520

Tuthill, Louisa Caroline Huggins, 1798-1879. The boy of spirit; a story for the young. Fifteenth edition. Boston: Crosby, Nichols and company, 1845. KyBgW. 45-6521

Tuthill, Louisa Caroline Huggins, 1798-1879. I will be a gentleman; a book for boys. Boston: William Crosby and H.P. Nichols, 1845. 148 p. MNF. 45-6522

Tuthill, Louisa Caroline Huggins, 1798-1879. I will be a gentleman; a book for boys. Second edition. Boston: William Crosby and H.P. Nichols, 1845. 148 p. ICU; NN; MB; NNC. 45-6523

Tuthill, Louisa Caroline Huggins, 1798-1879. I will be a gentleman; a book for boys. Third edition. Boston: William Crosby and H.P. Nichols, 1845. 148 p. MH. 45-6524

Tuthill, Louisa Caroline Huggins, 1798-1879. I will be a gentleman; a book for boys. Fifth edition. Boston: William Crosby and H.P. Nichols, 1845. 148 p. MHa. 45-6525

Tuthill, Louisa Caroline Huggins, 1798-1879. I will be a lady: a book for girls... Fourth edition. Boston: W. Crosby and H.P. Nichols, 1845. 167 p. CtY; NjR. 45-6526

Tuthill, Louisa Caroline Huggins, 1798-1879. Onward! Right onward! Boston: William Crosby and H.P. Nichols, 1845. 169 p. DLC; ViU. 45-6527

Tuthill, Louisa Caroline Huggins, 1798-1879. Onward! Right onward! Second edition. Boston: William Crosby and H.P. Nichols, 1845. 169 p. CU; NNC. 45-6528

Tuttle, George, 1804-1872. The little keepsake story book. By Thomas Teller, [pseud.] New Haven: Babcock, 1845. 64 p. CtY; IU; NjP. 45-6529

Tuttle, George, 1804-1872. The mischievious boy; a tale of tricks and troubles. New Haven: S. Babcock, [1845] CtY; MNS; PPL. 45-6530

Tuttle, George, 1804-1872. A parent's offering; or my mother's story of her own home and childhood. By Thomas Teller [pseud.] New Haven: S. Babcock, 1845. 64 p. CtY; MBev; MHad; MHi; OCl. 45-6531

Tuttle, George, 1804-1872. The pleasant journey; and scenes in town and country. By Thomas Teller, pseud. New Haven: S. Babcock, 1845. 64 p. CoBo; DLC; NcD; NjN; NjP. 45-6532

Tuttle, George, 1804-1872. Stories about whale catching. New Haven: S. Babcock, [1845] 64 p. CtY; DLC; MH; MnU; MWA. 45-6533

Tuttle, George, 1804-1872. Tales for all seasons; or stories and dialogues for little folks. By Thomas Teller. New Haven: S. Babcock, [1845?] 64 p. CtY; DLC. 45-6534

Tuttle, George, 1804-1872. Teller's amusing, instructive and entertaining tales. New Haven: S. Babcock, [1845-1849] CtY. 45-6535

Tuttle, George, 1804-1872. The two friends; or a visit to the seashore in monosyllables. New Haven: S. Babcock, [1845] 64 p. CLU; CtY ICU; NNC. 45-6536

Twing, Alvi Tabor, 1811-1882. Parental responsibility. Two sermons, preached in Trinity Church, Lansingburgh, January 12, and 19, 1845. Troy, New York: Press of N. Tuttle, 1845. 30 p. CtHT. 45-6537

Tyler, Bennet, 1783-1858. Memoir of the life and character of Asahel Nettleton. Second edition. Hartford: Robins and Smith, 1845. CtHC; NcWfc; OMC. 45-6538

Tyler, John, 1819-1896. Address delivered before the Democratic Association of Portsmouth, Virginia, during the canvass of 1844. Washington: Printed by J.E. Dow and company, [1845] 21 p. PPL; Vi. 45-6539

Tyler, Royall, 1757-1826. A book of forms, with occasional notes. Brattleboro, Vermont: J. Steen, 1845. 96 p. MH; MH-L; PU-Penn; TxU; VtHi. 45-6540

Tyng, Stephen Higginson, 1800-1885. The address at the funeral of the Rev. Dr. Milnor; and the funeral sermon of Dr. Stone; with the proceedings of various religious bodies, occasioned by his death. New York: Stanford and Swords, 1845. 66 p. LU; MH; MnHi; NNG; PHi. 45-6541

Tyng, Stephen Higginson, 1800-1885. Bible companion. Third American edition from the last London edition. Baltimore: Cook, 1845. 149 p. PU. 45-6542

Tyng, Stephen Higginson, 1800-1885. The Israel of God: a series of practical sermons. Third edition. New York: Carter, 1845. CtHC; IaDa; NcCJ; OCo; PU. 45-6543

Tyngsborough, Massachusetts. First Congregational Church. Order of exercises at the installation of Rev. William Morse, as pastor of the First Congregational Church and Society in Tyngsborough, September 24, 1845. Lowell, 1845. Broadside. MHi. 45-6544

Tyson, J. Washington. An atlas of ancient and modern history; presented in a chronological series, the rise, progress, revolutions, decline and fall of the principal states and empires of the world; conprising details of the most important events; with notices of eminent characters... for the use of schools and families. Philadelphia: S. Augustus Mitchell, 1845. IEG; MB; NCH; OO; VtU. 45-6545

Tyson, Job Robert, 1803-1858. Discourse on the two hundredth anniversary of the birth of William Penn. Delivered in the Independence Hall at Philadelphia, on October 24, 1844, before the Historical Society of Pennsylvania. Philadelphia: John Penington, 1845. 40 p. LNHT; MdBP; OCHP; PPL; Vi. 45-6546

Tytler, Margaret Fraser. Hymns and sketches in verse. Philadelphia: W.G. Wardle, 1845. 224 p. NNUT. 45-6547

Tytler, Margaret Fraser. My boy's first book. Philadelphia: W.G. Wardle, 1845. 199 p. MBAt; NN. 45-6548

Tytler, Margaret Fraser. My boy's second book. Philadelphia: W.G. Wardle, 1845. MH. 45-6549

Tytler, Margaret Fraser. Tales of the great and the brave. Philadelphia: R.S.H. George, 1847. 192 p. ICU. 45-6550

Tytler, Margaret Fraser. Tales of the great and the brave. Philadelphia: W.G. Wardle, 1845. 232 p. DLC; N; OO; PU. 45-6551

U

Underhill, Daniel G. Underhill's new table book; or tables of arithmetic made easier. A new edition, revised, enlarged and improved. New York: Collins, [1845] MA. 45-6552

Union hymns. Philadelphia, 1845. 352 p. CtY; PHi; PPLT; PU. 45-6553

Union hymns. Revised by the committee of publication of the American Sunday School Union. Philadelphia: American Sunday School Union, 1845. 345 p. CtSoP; IEG; NIC; OCoC; TxU. 45-6554

Union Theological Seminary. Catalogue. New York: Joseph H. Jennings, printer, 1845. 16 p. DLC; MWHi. 45-6555

Union University. Schenectady. Catalogue of the officers and students in Union College, September, 1845. Schenectady: Isaac Riggs, printer, 1845. 28 p. MeB; OCHP. 45-6556

Union University. Schenectady. First semi-centennial anniversary of Union College, celebrated July 22, 1845. Albany: W.C. Little and company; Schenectady: I. Riggs, printer, 1845. 186 p. DLC; MB; MnHi; NN; PHi. 45-6557

Union University. Schenectady. Order of commencement at the first semi-centennial celebration, July 22, 1845. n.p. [1845] 4 p. NN. 45-6558

Union University. Schenectady. Order of exercises at the first semi-centennial celebration, July 22, 1845. n.p. [1845] 8 p. NN; WHi. 45-6559

Union Water Convention. Boston. Proceedings of the Union Water Convention, concerning the conflagration at South Boston on September 19, 1845. Boston, 1845. 8 p. DNLM; DSG; MHi. 45-6560

The Unitarian annual register, for 1846-1847. Boston: W. Crosby and H.P. Nicols, 1845-1846. 2 v. in 1. CBPac; NNG. 45-6561

Unitarian Congregational Churches. The year book of the Unitarian Congregational Churches. Boston, 1845. 47 v. MBL. 45-6562

United American Free Will Baptist Church. North Carolina. Minutes. Tarboro: [Tarboro Press, 1845] 4 p. NcU. 45-6563

United Brethren in Christ. Origin, doctrine, constitution and discipline of the United Brethren in Christ. Seventh edition. Circleville, Ohio: Conference office, 1845. ODaB; ODaUB; NjPT. 45-6564

United Presbyterian Church of North America. The confession and testimony, as adopted by the convention of reformed churches, and submitted in overture to the churches represented in it. Philadelphia: Merihew and Thompson, printers, 1845. 22 p. NcD; PHi; PPPrHi. 45-6565

United States almanac; 1843-1845. By John Downes. Philadelphia, 1845. 3 v. PHi. 45-6566

United States almanac, and political manual for the year 1846. New York: J. Disturnell, [1845] MWA. 45-6567

United States almanac for 1846. New York: J. Disturnell, [1845] MWA; NCH. 45-6568

United States almanac for 1846. By Charles Frederick Egelmann. Philadelphia: Mentz and Rovoudt, [1845] MWA. 45-6569

United States almanac for 1846. By Seth Smith. Philadelphia: Hogan and Thompson, [1845] 34 p. NjR. 45-6570

United States almanac for 1846. By Seth Smith. Philadelphia: R. Wilson Desilver, [1845] MWA. 45-6571

United States almanac for 1846. By Seth Smith. Philadelphia: Uriah Hunt and son, [1845] MWA. 45-6572

The United States almanac; or complete ephemeris, for the year 1845. By John Downes. Philadelphia: B. Walker, etc., etc., etc., 1845. 378 p. NGH; WHi. 45-6573

The United States almanac, or complete ephemeris, for the year 1845. By John Downes. Also numerous statistics... By John Montgomery. Philadelphia: B. Walker, 1845. 199 p. NjR. 45-6574

United States annual digest for the years 1845-1868, being a digest of the decisions of the Courts of Common Law, equity and admiralty. By John Phelps Putnam. Boston: Little, Brown and company, 1845-1871. 22 v. MoKB. 45-6575

The United States at one view. New York: Humphrey Phelps, 1845. MHi; OCl; WHi. 45-6576

United States constitution almanac. New York, 1845. 45-6577

United States farmers almanac. By Thomas Spofford. New York: David Felt and company, 1845. MWA. 45-6578

United States form book; containing every variety of conveyancing, commercial and other precedents, with directions for executing the same, also a complete guide to custom house transactions, together with much other information useful in every branch of business. By a member of the New York bar. New York: Charles Wells, 1845. 384 p. CL; DLC; LNT-L; MH-L; OCLaw. 45-6579

United States liberty almanac. By W.B. Jarvis. Columbus, Ohio: Thrall and Glorce, [sic] 1845. MWA. 45-6580

United States liberty almanac for 1845. Columbus, Ohio, [1845] OCHP. 45-6581

The United States nautical magazine. New York, 1845. v. 1. no. 1. DLC; MB; MHi. 45-6582

United States practical receipt book: or complete book of reference, for the manufacturer, tradesman, agriculturist or housekeeper; containing many thousand valuable receipts, in all the useful and domestic arts, by a practical chemist. Philadelphia: Lindsay and Blakiston, 1845. 359 p. DLC; DNLM; MB. 45-6583

United States statistical and chronological almanac for 1845, carefully compiled by M. Miller. Rochester, New York: M. Miller and company, 1845. [60] p. NUtHi. 45-6584

United States statistical and chronological almanac for 1846. Rochester, New York: M. and J. Miller, [1845] MWA; OCHP; PHi. 45-6585

The universalist companion, with an almanac and register, containing the statistics of the denomination, for 1846. A.B. Grosh, editor and proprietor. Calculations for the almanac by G.R. Perkins. Utica: A. Walker, [1845] 60 p. MeB; MMeT-Hi; MWA; WHi. 45-6586

Upfold, George, 1796-1872. The last hundred years. A lecture delivered in the hall of the Western University of Pennsylvania... February 4, 1845. Pittsburgh: Printed by G. Perkins, 1845. 62 p. CtHT; In; MH; NGH; NNG; PHi. 45-6587

Upham, Albert Gookin, 1819-1847. Family history. Notices of the life of John Upham, the first inhabitant of New England who bore that name... Concord, New Hampshire: Printed by A. McFarland, 1845. 92 p. AzMe; Ct; MeBa; MHi; NhD. 45-6588

Upham, Thomas Cogswell, 1798-1872. Domestic and religious offering. Illustrative of American scenery, rural life and historical incidents, and also religious feelings. Boston: Waite, Peirce and company, 1845. 321 p. Nh. 45-6589

Upham, Thomas Cogswell, 1799-1872. Domestic and religious offering. Illustrative of American scenery, rural life and historical incidents, and also of religious feelings. Second edition. With addition by the author. Boston: Waite, Peirce and company, 1845. 3-321 p. DLC. 45-6590

Upham, Thomas Cogswell, 1799-1872. Elements of mental philosophy, embracing the two departments of the intellect and the sensibilities. New York: Harper and brothers, 1845. 2 v. CU; GMM; IaCrC; ScDuE; ViU. 45-6591

Upham, Thomas Cogswell, 1799-1872. The life of faith, in three parts; embracing some of the scriptural principles or doctrines of faith, the power of effects of faith in the regulation of man's inward nature, and the relation of faith to the divine guidance. Boston: Waite, Peirce and company, 1845. 480 p. CtHC; DLC; KBB; MH-AH; RPA. 45-6592

Upham, Thomas Cogswell, 1799-1872. The life of faith; in three parts; embracing some of the scriptural principles of doctrines of faith, the power or effects of faith in the regulation of man's inward nature, and the relation of faith to the divine guidance. New York: Harper, 1845. 480 p. CSto. 45-6593

Upham, Thomas Cogswell, 1799-1872. Life of Madame Catharina Adorna. Including some leading facts and traits in her religious experience. Together with explanations and remarks, tending to illustrate the doctrine of Holiness. Boston: Waite, Peirce and company, 1845. 268 p. IU; MeBa; MWH; OO; RPB. 45-6594

Upham, Thomas Cogswell, 1799-1872. A philosophical treatise on the will.

forming the third volume of a system of mental philosophy. New York: Harper and brothers, 1845. 26-411 p. MH-AH; NR; OMC; PU; TxShA. 45-6595

Upham, Thomas Cogswell, 1799-1872. Principles of the interior or hidden life. Designed particularly for the consideration of those who are seeking assurance of faith and perfect love. Third edition. Boston: Waite, Peirce and company, 1845. 396 p. KyLoP; LNB; MiOC; VtU; WHi. 45-6596

Upham, Thomas Cogswell, 1799-1872. Principles of the interior or hidden life. Designed particularly for the consideration of those who are seeking assurance of faith and perfect love. Fourth edition. Boston: Waite, Peirce and company, 1845. 396 p. IaDaSA; IaUp; GEU-T; MShr; TN. 45-6597

Ure, Andrew, 1778-1857. A dictionary of arts, manufactures and mines; containing a clear exposition of their principles and practice. From the third London edition, corrected. New York: D. Appleton and company; Philadelphia: George S. Appleton, 1845. 1340 p. DLC; MB; MeU; PPWa; TWcW. 45-6598

Ure, Andrew, 1778-1857. Recent improvements in arts, manufactures, and mines; being a supplement to his dictionary. Illustrated with one hundred and ninety engravings. New York: D. Appleton and company; Philadelphia: G.S. Appleton, 1845. 304, 190 p. ICJ; MH; NBMS; PU; WMAM. 45-6599

Useful almanac for 1846. By David Young. New York, New York: Elton, [1845] MWA. 45-6600

Useful trades; or how to work. A book for week day reading. Designed to mingle religious instructions with useful knowledge. New York: G. Lane and C.B. Tippett, 1845. 172 p. NNC; VtMidSM. 45-6601

Utica, New York. Female Academy. Circular and catalogue of the Utica Female Academy, for 1845-1846. Utica: Bennett, Backus and Hawley, 1845. 16 p. MH. 45-6602

Utica and oneida almanac for 1846. By George R. Perkins. Utica, New York: R.W. Roberts, [1845] MWA; NUtHi. 45-6603

The Utica city directory, for 1845-1846. Compiled by Bildad Merrell, Jr. Utica, New York: H.H. Curtiss, printer, 1845. 168 p. NUt; NUtHi; NUtSC. 45-6604

V

Vail, Alfred, 1807-1859. The American electro-magnetic telegraph: with the reports of Congress, and a description of all telegraphs known, employing electricity or galvanism illustrated, by eighty-one wood engravings. Philadelphia: Lea and Blanchard, 1845. [9]- 208 p. LNHT; MnU; NNG; PU; RPA. 45-6605

Vail, Alfred, 1807-1859. Description of the American electro-magnetic telegraph: now in operation between the cities of Washington and Baltimore. Washington: Printed by J. and G.S. Gideon, 1845. 24 p. CtHT; ICU; Nh-Hi; VtU; WHi. 45-6606

Van Amringe, Henry Hamlin. Association and christianity exhibiting the anti-moral and anti-christian character of the churches and the social relations in present christendom, and urging the necessity of industrial association founded on christian brotherhood and unity. Pittsburgh, 1845. 122 p. DLC; IU; NNC; OMC; WHi. 45-6607

Van Ingen, John Visger, 1806-1877. The preacher, an ordained witness of revealed truth. A sermon preached at the opening of the eighth annual convention of the diocese of Western New York. Rochester, [New York] printed by Canfield and Warren, 1845. 20 p. CSmH; IEG; MdBD; NBuDD; NGH. 45-6608

Van Santvoord, George, 1819-1863.

Eulogy on the life, character and public services of Andrew Jackson, delivered at Lafayette, Indiana, June 28, 1845. Lafayette: Fry and Jackson, 1845. 23 p. CSmH; IaU; In; NN; RPB. 45-6609

Van Santvoord, George, 1819-1863. The Indiana justice; a treatise on jurisdiction, authority and duty of justices of the peace in the state of Indiana in civil and criminal cases. Lafayette: Fry and Jackson, 1845. 548 p. InBrk; InU; N-L; OOxM. 45-6610

Van Santvoord, Staats, 1790-1882. A discourse delivered at the dedication of the Reformed Dutch Church of Salem, January 20, 1845. New York, 1845. 16 p. MBAt; N. 45-6611

Vandenhoff, George. A plain system of elocution; or logical and musical reading and declamation with exercises in prose and verse. Second edition. New York: C. Shepard, 1845. 327 p. MH; MoS; NbCrD; NNG; PU. 45-6612

Vane, Florence, pseud? Are we almost there? A touching ballad written and composed by Florence Vane. Boston, [1845?] 5 p. ICN; MH; ViU. 45-6613

Velde, Karl Franz van der, 1779-1824. Christina and her court. A true tale taken from the last half of the seventeenth century. New York: E. Winchester, 1845. 52 p. KyLoU. 45-6614

Velpeau, Alfred Armand Louis Marie, 1795-1867. An elementary treatise on midwifery; or principles of tokology and embryology. Translated from the French by Charles D. Meigs. Third American edition. With notes and additions by William Harris. Philadelphia: Lindsay and Blakiston, 1845. 600 p. ICJ; MeB; MnU; PPCP. 45-6615

Velpeau, Alfred Armand Louis Marie, 1795-1867. New elements of operative surgery: augmented with a treatise on minor surgery. Accompanied with an atlas in quarto of 22 plates. Translated by P.S. Townsend. New York: Henry G. Langly, 1845-1847. 3 v. GEU-M; MoU; NhD; PPCP; RPM. 45-6616

Venning, Ralph. Milk and honey or a miscellaneous collection of many Christian sentences. Arranged for daily use. Revised by the editor, D.P. Kidder. New York: Lane and Tippett for the Sunday School Union of the Methodist Episcopal Church, 1845. 109 p. MWat. 45-6617

Der Vereinigten Staaten Calender. Philadelphia: Edmund Y. Schelly, 1845. MWA; PPeSchw. 45-6618

Vergilius Marco, Publius. Publis Virgilii Maronis opera; or the works of Virgil with copious notes compiled from the best commentators to which is added a table of reference by the Rev. J.G. Cooper. Ninth stereotyped edition. New York: Pratt, Woodford and company, 1845. MDeeP; MnLer; NcU; PU; ViAl. 45-6619

Verhandlungen 98 venammlung des a lull-M--- terums. Sumnytaun, Pennsylvania, 1845. PPeSchw. 45-6620

Vericour, Louis Raymond de, d. 1879. Modern French literature. Boston, 1845. MB. 45-6621

Vermont. An act to incorporate the Vermont Central Railroad Company. Passed by the Legislature of Vermont, October session, 1843. Charleston, Massachusetts, 1845. 12 p. MHi. 45-6622

Vermont. The acts and resolutions passed by the Legislature of the state of Vermont, at their October session, 1845. Burlington: Chauncey Goodrich, 1845. 95 p. Az; In-SC; MdBB; Nv; TxU-L. 45-6623

Vermont. Circular of the state superintendent of common schools to the county superintendents and an address to the teachers of common schools in the state of Vermont. St. Albans: Messinger Printing, 1845. VtMidbC. 45-6624

Vermont. A digest of all the cases decided in the supreme court of the state of Vermont, as reported in N. Chipman's, Tyler's, Brayton's, D. Chipman's and Aiken's reports, and the first fifteen volumes of the Vermont reports. Together with manuscript cases not hitherto reported. By Peter T. Washburn, counselor at law. Woodstock: Haskell and Palmer, 1845. 2 v. IaUL; MMAnP; MdBB; MeBa; Tx-SC. 45-6625

Vermont. First annual report of the state superintendent of common schools made to the Legislature. October 18, 1846. Montpelier: Eastman and Danforth, 1845-1846. MiU. 45-6626

Vermont. First annual report on the geology of the state of Vermont. Burlington: C. Goodrich, 1845. C; Ia; NPV; OO; VtB. 45-6627

Vermont. Journal of the House of Representatives of the state of Vermont, October session, 1844. Montpelier: E.P. Walton and sons, 1845. 289 p. ICU; M; MH; MnU; NhD. 45-6628

Vermont. The journal of the Senate of the state of Vermont. Montpelier: E.P. Walton and sons, 1845. 136 p. CSmH; M; MB; MH; Mi; WHi. 45-6629

Vermont. Message to the General Assembly of Vermont from the governor. October, 1845. Montpelier, 1845. 22 p. ICJ; NhD. 45-6630

Vermont. Reports of the majority and the minority of the select committee of the state of Vermont on the subject of Texas to the United States, 1845. Windsor, Vermont: Bishop and Tracy, 1845. 15 p. IaHi; MH-L. 45-6631

The Vermont almanac, pocket memorandum and statistical register for the year 1845. Woodstock, Vermont: Haskell and Palmer, 1845. 144 p. MiD. 45-6632

Vermont and Massachusetts Railroad. Address to the stockholders. Greenfield, 1845. MB. 45-6633

Vermont and Massachusetts Railroad. First annual report of the directors made to the stockholders. Boston: White, Lewis and Potter, 1845. 10 p. IU; M; MH-BA. 45-6634

Vermont and Massachusetts Railroad. Report of the directors. Lowell: Stone and Huse, etc, 1845-. M. 45-6635

Vermont Central Railroad Company. Report of the engineer on the route surveyed for the Vermont Central Railroad, from Connecticut River, at Hartford, Vermont to Lake Champlain, at Burlington. Boston: S.N. Dickinson, printer, 1845. 12 p. ICU; MCM; Mh-BA; Nh; WU. 45-6636

Vermont year book. Astronomical calculations by Zadock Thompson. Montpelier: E.P. Walton and sons, [1845] 128 p. DLC; MHi; Nh-Hi. 45-6637

The Vicksburg almanac for the year 1845... Vicksburg: O.O. Woodman, 1845. 47 p. MsJS. 45-6638

Viereck, John Conrad. L'acceptance. Du valse. Arrangee pour le piano et dediee a Mademoiselle Charlotte Barnes. Philadelphia: Perring, 1845. PPL. 45-6639

Vieth, Isaac. A book of reference, shewing the location of each lot of land in the village of Williamburgh, together with the old and new assessment and farm numbers attached to each lot. New York: McLoughlin, 1845. 54 p. NBLiHi; NJQ; WHi. 45-6640

Views from the Bunker Hill Monument; being directions to find the principal objects to be seen from its summit. Boston: J.L. Hallworth, 1845. 8 p. MB; MMal; NBuG. 45-6641

Views of war and peace. Boston, 1845. RP. 45-6642

Vinet, Alexander Rudolphe, 1787-1847. Vital Christianity. Essays and discourses on the religion of man and the religion of God. Translated with an introduction by Robert Turnbull. Boston: Gould, Kindall and Lincoln, 1845. 355 p. FDeS; GDecCt; NbOP; OWoC; PPL-R. 45-6643

Vinton, Alexander Hamilton, 1807-1881. A discourse delivered before the ancient and honorable artillery company, on their CCVIIth anniversary. By the rector of St. Paul's Church, Boston. Boston: Printed by Dutton and Wentworth, 1845. 25 p. ICU; MWA; Nh-Hi; OClWHi; PHi. 45-6644

Vinton, Francis, 1809-1872. A thanksgiving sermon... New York: A.V. Blake, 1845. 17 p. MdBD; NBLiHi; NjR; NNG. 45-6645

Vinton, Samuel Finley, 1792-1862. Speech of Samuel Vinton, of Ohio, on the bill to admit the states of Iowa and Florida into the union. Washington: Printed by J. and G.S. Gideon, 1845. 15 p. DLC; ICN; NUtHi; PHi; WHi. 45-6646

Vinton, Samuel Finley, 1792-1862. Substance of an argument for the defendants in the case of the commonwealth of Virginia vs. Peter McGarner and others for an alleged abduction of certain slaves, delivered before the general court of Virginia at its December term. [n.p.?] 1845. KyHi; NIC; OCl; OCraD; PU. 45-6647

Virginia. Acts of the general assembly, passed at the session commencing December 2, 1844, and ending February 22, 1845, in the sixty-ninth year of the commonwealth. Richmond: Samuel Sheperd. printer, 1845. 157 p. IaU-L; Ky; MdBB; Nj; WvW-L. 45-6648

Virginia. Journal of the House. Session 1845-1846... Richmond: Printed by Samuel Shepherd, 1845. MBNEH; Vi. 45-6649

Virginia. Journal of the Senate. Richmond: Printed by John Warrock, 1845. Vi. 45-6650

Virginia. Reports of cases decided in the supreme court of appeals, and in the general court. By Peachy R. Grattan. April 1, 1844, to April 1, 1845. Richmond: Printed by Shepherd and Colin, 1845. 578 p. In-SC; MdBB; ODaL; Tx-SC; W. 45-6651

Virginia. University. Address of the society of alumni of the University of Virginia, through their committee. Charlottesville: Noel and Saunders, 1845. 20 p. NNNAM; RPB. 45-6652

Virginia Institution for Education of the Deaf and Dumb and of the Blind. A list of the officers, a copy of the act of the legislature... bylaws... Staunton: Harper, 1845. 15 p. PPPrHi. 45-6653

Virginia Military Institute. Lexington, Virginia. Regulations. New York: Wiley and Putman, 1845. 42 p. CSmH; Vi. 45-6654

Virginia Military Institute. Lexington, Virginia. Regulations of the Virginia Military Institute at Lexington. New York: Wiley and Putnam, 1845. 43 p. MdBD. 45-6655

The Virginia warbler: new collection of patriotic, national, naval, martial, professional, convivial, humurous, pathetic, sentimental, old and new songs... Richmond: J.W. Randolph and company, 1845. 320 p. MH; ViU. 45-6656

Vodges, William, 1802-1886. The United States arithmetic, designed for academies and schools. Philadelphia: E.C. and J. Biddle, 1845. 45-6657

The voice of truth; or an examination of the proceedings on the presentment, trial and sentence of the Right Rev. Benjamin T. Onderdonk, Bishop of the Protestant Episcopal Church in the diocese of New York. New York, 1845. 225 p. MH; MiD; NcD; NN; PPL. 45-6658

The voice of truth; or an examination of the proceedings on the presentment, trial and sentence of the Right Rev. Benjamin T. Onderdonk, Bishop of the Protestant Episcopal Church in the diocese of New York. [New York? 1845-1846?] 6 v. in 1. IEG; MB; N. 45-6659

Volksfreund und Hagerstauner Calender, 1845. Hagerstown, Maryland: Johann Gruber, [1845] MWA. 45-6660

Volney, Constantin Francois Chasseboeuf, comte de, 1757-1820. Volney's ruinen; oder, betrachtungen uber die umwalzungen der reiche. Aus dem franzosischen ubersetzt. Philadelphia, 1845. 220 p. CL; PPT. 45-6661

Volney, Constantin Francois Chasseboeuf, comte de, 1757-1820. Volney's ruins; or meditation of the revolutions of empires. Translated under the immediate inspection of the author, from the latest Paris edition, with his notes of illustration. To which is added the law of nature, and a short biographical notice, by Count Daru. New York: G. Vale, 1845. 220 p. MPiB; Or; OU; TMeSC; TxU. 45-6662

Vorhees, Philip Falkerson, 1792-1862. Defence before a general naval court martial, upon charges preferred against him by the Secretary of the Navy, relative to the re-encounter between the United States frigate Congress and the Argentine Squadron. Washington, 1845. DLC; MdBP; MH; NjR. 45-6663

Voltaire, Francois Marie Arouet de, 1694-1778. Histoire de Charles XII, Roi de Suede. Nouvelle dition revue et corrigee, par j. et P. Mouls. New York: W.E. Dean, 1845. 287 p. KyU; MBAt; MH-L; NN; NbK. 45-6664

Vrangel, Ferdinand, 1796-1870. Narrative of an expedition to the polar sea, in the years 1820, 1822, and 1823. Commanded by Lieutenant, now Admiral Ferdinand Wrangell, of the Russian Imperial Navy. New York: Harper and brothers, 1845. 302 p. InCW; Me; OCY; ODa; RWe. 45-6665

W

Waage, Friedrich. De todtenfeier des helden; eine rede zum gedachtniss Andreas Jackson's. New York: W. Radda, 1845. PPG. 45-6666

Waage, Friedrich. De todtenfeier des helden; eine rede zum gedachtniss Andreas Jackson's. Philadelphia: Rademacher: Hamburg, Herold, 1845. MH-AH; PPeSchw; PPG. 45-6667

Wabash and Erie Canal. Rates of tolls for the Wabash and Erie Canal, in Indiana, as established by the general superintendent of said canal. [Logansport, Pharos Press, 1845] 6 p. In. 45-6668

Wabash and Erie Canal. Report of the engineer of the survey and location of the contemplated canal from Terre Haute to Evansville. Indianapolis, 1845. 12 p. WHi. 45-6669

Wabash and Erie Canal. Report of the engineer of the survey and location of the contemplated canal from Terre Haute to Evansville, and copies of accounts and vouchers of the expenses attending the same. Indianapolis, 1845. 9 p. WHi. 45-6670

Wabash and Erie Canal. Report of the general superintendent... in reply to a resolution of the Senate, December 28, 1844. Indianapolis: J.P. Chapman, 1845. InU. 45-6671

Wabash and Erie Canal. Report of the superintendent... to the General Assembly. Indianapolis: J.P. Chapman, 1845. In; InU; WHi. 45-6672

Wabash College. Catalogue of the officers and students of Wabash College, November 12, 1845. Lafayette: John B. Semans, printer, 1845. 16 p. IN; MH. 45-6673

Waddington, John. Hebrew martyrs. Boston: Sabbath School Society, 1845. 108 p. LN. 45-6674

Wade, William, fl. 1854-1857. Panorama of the Hudson River from New York to Albany. New York: William Wade, 1845. DeU; KEmT; NPV. 45-6675

Wadsworth, Alexander, 1806-1898. Plan of Woodview Vale, in Newton, belonging to William Kenrick. Boston, 1845. MB. 45-6676

Wagner, Richard. Tannhauser and the tournament of song at Wartburg, romantic opera in three acts; written and composed by R. Wagner; edited and translated into English by Natalia Mac-Farren. New York: G. Schirmer, 1845. 343 p. MnS; NbCrD. 45-6677

Wagner, Rudolph, 1805-1864. Elements of comparative anatomy of the vertebrate animals; designed especially for the use of students. Edited from the German by Alfred Tulk... New York: J.S.

Redfield, 1845. 264 p. CU; OU; PU; RPB; ScCC. 45-6678

Wagoner, George. Plan for abolishing war and all military and naval establishments, and establishing peace in all nations. Pittsburgh: Allinder, printer, 1845. 64 p. DLC; P. 45-6679

Wagstaff, William R. A history of the Society of Friends: compiled from its standard records, and other authentic sources. New York: Wiley and Putnam, [etc.] 1845. MWiW; NBuG; PSC-Hi; RWe; WHi. 45-6680

Wainwright, Jonathan Mayhew, 1792-1854. No church without a bishop or a peep into the sanctuary. Being a succinct examination of the Rt. Rev. B.T. Onderdonk by a high churchman. Boston: H.L. Williams, 1845. 32 p. MDB; MHi; NBu; NNG; VtU. 45-6681

Wainwright, Jonathan Mayhew, 1792-1854. An order of family prayer for every day of the week, and for the commemoration of the holy days and seasons of the Church. Selected and arranged for the Bible, the Liturgy, and various books of devotion. New York: Stanford and Swords, 1845. MdBD; MH; MSyU; ScRhW. 45-6682

Wainwright, Jonathan Mayhew, 1792-1854. Responsibilities and duties of the clergy, an exhortation in Christ Church, Hartford, at an ordination by Rev. T.C. Brownell. Hartford: Henry S. Parsons and company, 1845. CtHC; MB; N; NBuDD; NNG. 45-6683

Wakefield, Samuel, 1799-1895. Minstrel of glory; a book of religious songs... with appropriate music. Philadelphia: Sain, 1845. 216 p. OO. 45-6684

Waldgrove; or the fortunes of Bertram. A tale of 1746. Brighton: Folthorp, 1845. MB. 45-6685

Walker, Alexander. The anthropological works of Alexander Walker. A new edition. New York: Henry G. Langley, 1845. 3 v. ArCH; MB; Nh; NPV; OClMN. 45-6686

Walker, Alexander. Beauty; illustrated chiefly by analysis and classification of beauty in women. New York: Henry G. Langley, 1845. 390 p. LNH; MB; NBMS; NhD; OMC. 45-6687

Walker, Alexander. Woman physiologically considered, as to mind, morals, marriage, matrimonial slavery, infidelity and divorce. New edition. New York: J. and H.G. Langley, 1845. 432 p. MdB. 45-6688

Walker, Amosa, 1799-1874. Cheap postage and how to get it. Boston, 1845. MBAt. 45-6689

Walker, Charles Edward. The warlock of the glen. A melodrama in two acts. New York and London: Samuel French, [1845] 20 p. CoU; OCl. 45-6690

Walker, James Barr, 1805-1887. Philosophy of the plan of salvation, a book for the times, by an American citizen, with an introductory essay by C.E. Stowe. Cincinnati: Weed, etc., 1845. NRCR; PPLT. 45-6691

Walker, James Barr, 1805-1887. Philosophy of the plan of salvation, a book for the times, by an American citizen, with an introductory essay by

C.E. Stowe. Salem: J.P. Jewett and company, 1845. 239 p. ICU; NN; OO. 45-6692

Walker, Jesse, 1810-1852. Fort Niagara, a tale of the Niagara frontier. Buffalo: Steele's Press, 1845. 156 p. DLC; IU; OClWHi; OHi; PRB. 45-6693

Walker, Jesse, 1810-1852. Queenston, a tale of the Niagara frontier. Buffalo: Steele's Press, 1845. 151 p. InU; NBuG; NBuHi; NN; NNC. 45-6694

Walker, Jesse, 1810-1852. Tales of the Niagara frontier. Buffalo: Steele's Press, 1845. 2 v. DLC; MiDW; InU; ViU. 45-6695

Walker, John, 1732-1807. A critical pronouncing dictionary and expositor of the English language: in which not only the meaning of every word is explained and the sound of every syllable distinctly shown, but where words are not subject to different pronunciations, the reasons for each are duly considered... First Boston Pocket edition, Boston: Joshua V. Pierce, 1845. 336 p. CU- A; MH; NN; TxU. 45-6696

Walker, John, 1732-1807. A key to the classical pronunciation of Greek, Latin and scripture proper names; in which the words are accented and divided into syllables exactly as they ought to be pronounced, according to rules drawn from analogy and the best usage. New York: Harper and brothers, 1845. 1079 p. NN; TNP. 45-6697

Walker, John, 1732-1807. Walker's critical pronouncing dictionary and expositor of the English language. Abridged by the Rev. Thomas Smith...

Cooperstown, New York: H. and E. Phinney, 1845. 400 p. IU. 45-6698

Walker, John, 1732-1807. Walker's critical pronouncing dictionary and expositor of the English language. Abridged and adapted to the use of citizens of the United States. New York: George and H. Miller, [1845] 505 p. NN. 45-6699

Walker, John, 1732-1807. Walker's critical pronouncing dictionary and expositor of the English language. Abridged for the use of schools, by an American citizen. Philadelphia: Printed by Griggs and company, 1845. 416 p. DLC; TxU. 45-6700

Walker, Jonathan, 1799-1878. Trial and imprisonment of Jonathan Walker at Pensacola, Florida, for aiding slaves to escape from bondage, with an appendix containing a sketch of his life. Boston: Anti-slavery office, 1845. GAU; ICHi; NcU; PHi; RP. 45-6701

Walker, Robert James, 1801-1869. Introductory address of the Hon. R.J. Walker, of Mississippi, delivered before the National Institute at its April meeting, 1844. Washington: Printed by W.Q. Force, 1845. 14 p. LNH; MBAt; MH; PHi; PPM. 45-6702

Walker, William Johnson, 1789-1865. An essay on the treatment of compound and complicated fractures; being the annual address before the Massachusetts Medical Society, May 28, 1845. Boston: Crocker and Brewster, 1845. 46 p. IEN- M; KyLxT; MH; MWiW; NNN. 45-6703

Wallace, James A. Diligence and preseverance: a sermon delivered in the chapel of Davidson College, October 26, 1845. Salisbury, North Carolina: Printed at the Watchman office, 1845. 20 p. KyLoS; NcD; PPPrHi. 45-6704

Wallace, John William, 1815-1884. Reporters chronologically arranged: with occasional remarks upon their respective merits. Second edition, revised. Philadelphia: T. and J.W. Johnson, 1845. 103 p. DLC; MH; PP; ViU-L; WaU-L. 45-6705

Wallace, John William, 1815-1884. Walker's court rules; the rules at law and in equity which regulate the practice of the... courts of the United States. Philadelphia: Walker, 1845. 219 p. PP; PU- L, 45-6706

Walpole, Horace, 1717-1797. Memoirs of the reign of King George the Third. Now first published from the original manuscript; edited with notes, by Dennis LeMarchant. Philadelphia: Lea and Blanchard, 1845. 2 v. DeWi; GEU; OO; PPA; TNP. 45-6707

Walton, William, 1784-1857. The alpaca; its naturalization in the British Isles considered as a national benefit, and as an object of immediate utility to the farmer and manufacturer. New York: Office of the New York Farmer and Mechanic, 1845. MiU; NNC. 45-6708

Warburton, Eliot, 1810-1852. The crescent and the cross; or romance and realities of eastern travel. New York: Wiley, 1845. 2 v. IaMp; KWiU; OWoC; PU; RNR. 45-6709

Ward, James Harmon, 1806-1861. An elementary course of instruction on ordnance and gunnery prepared for the use of the midshipmen at the naval school, Philadelphia, together with a concise treatise on steam, adapted especially to the use of those engaged in steam navigation. Philadelphia: Carey and Hart, 1845. 109, 59 p. MdAS; PHi; PPL-R. 45-6710

Ward, Thomas, 1652-1708. England's reformation: a poem in four cantos. To which is added, publisher's preface, life of the author, notes to justify the facts related, and several additions faithfully extracted from the author's manuscript... New York: D. and J. Sadlier, 1845. 486 p. IU; MoK; WMMU; WStfSF. 45-6711

Ward, Thomas, 1652-1708. Errata of the Protestant Bible; or the truth of the English translation examined. New York: D. and J. Sadlier, 1845. 118 p. NN; NNF; OSW. 45-6712

Wardwell, S.S. Child's sabbath lessons. Boston: Massachusetts Sabbath School Society, 1845. 54 p. NNUT. 45-6713

Ware, Henry, 1794-1843. On the formation of the christian character addressed to those who are seeking to lead a religious life. Twelfth edition. Boston: James Munroe and company, 1845. 176 p. ICJ; MB; MBAt; MHing; MWA. 45-6714

Ware, William, 1797-1852. Righteousness before doctrine. Two sermons preached on March 16, 1845. Boston: Little and Brown, 1845. 31 p. CBPac; ICMe; MBAU; MB-AH; RPB. 45-6715

Ware, William, 1797-1852. Two sermons preached on March 16, 1845. Boston: Charles C. Little and James Brown, 1845. 31 p. MdCatS. 45-6716

Warfield, Catherine Ann Ware, 1816-1877. The wife of Leon, and other poems. By Catherine Ann Warfield and Mrs. Eleanor Percy Lee... Second edition, revised. Cincinnati: E. Morgan and company, 1845. 268 p. KyLx; MsU; NcAS; OCY; TxU. 45-6717

Warland, John Henry, d. 1872. The mountaineer; a song. Poetry by J.H. Warland, music composed by Leonard Marshall. Boston, [1845] 7 p. MH-Mu. 45-6718

Warner, James Franklin, 1802-1864. Rudimental lessons in music; containing the primary instruction requisite for all beginners in the art, whether vocal or instrumental. New York: D. Appleton and company; Philadelphia: G.S. Appleton, 1845. 240 p. MBAt; MLanc; NjP; ViU; WBeloC. 45-6719

Warren, Charles J. The temperance harp; original and selected music, for both juvenile and adult temperance meetings. New York, 1845. 34 p. NBuG; RPB; TxU. 45-6720

Warren, John Collins, 1778-1856. The mastodon giganteus of North America. Boston: John Wilson and son, 1845. 260 p. MoSW. 45-6721

Warren, Samuel, 1807-1877. Passages from the diary of a late physician. From the fifth London edition. New York: Harper and brothers, 1845. 3 v. DLC; KyDC; MdUM; NjP. 45-6722

Warren, Samuel, 1807-1877. A popular and practical introduction to law studies, and to every department of the legal profession, civil, criminal, and ecclesiastical: with an account of the state of the law in Ireland, Scotland and occasional illustrations from American law. Second edition. Boston: C.C. Little and J. Brown, 1845. 944 p. CLSU; CtY; IU; MdBJ; OC. 45-6723

Warren, Samuel, 1807-1877. Ten thousand a year. Boston: Little, Brown and company, 1845. 3 v. CtY; MB; NRU; PBm; ViU. 45-6724

Warren Ladies Seminary. Catalogue of the trustees, instructors, and pupils of the Warren Ladies Seminary, for the academical year ending December, 1844. With an outline of the course of study. Boston: Printed by George Coolidge, 1845. 12 p. RHi. 45-6725

Warrock's Virginia and North Carolina Almanack for 1846. Calculated by David Richardson. Richmond, Virginia: John Warrock, [1845] MWA. 45-6726

Washburne and Woodman. Catalogue of valuable real estate, situated in the Wisconsin land district, for sale by Washburne and Woodman, land agents, Mineral Point, Iowa County, Wisconsin Territory. Galena, Illinois, 1845. 8 p. WHi. 45-6727

Washington, George, 1732-1799. Writings, edited by Jared Sparks. Boston, 1845. 12 v. NNer; NPtc. 45-6728

Washington almanac. New York: E. Kearney, 1845. MWA. 45-6729

The Washington almanac. Philadelphia: King and Baird, 1845. ODa; PPeSchw. 45-6730

Washington almanack for 1846. By Seth

Smith. Baltimore, Maryland: Joseph N. Lewis, [1845] MWA. 45-6731

Washington almanack for 1846. By Seth Smith. Philadelphia, Pennsylvania: King and Baird, printers, [1845] MWA. 45-6732

Washington College. Washington, Pennsylvania. Catalogue of the officers and students for 1844-1845. Washington: John Buasman, 1845. 24 p. MeHi; NbOP; PWCHi; PWW. 45-6733

Washington Female Seminary, Pennsylvania. Catalogue of the officers and members for the year ending September 30, 1845. Also various particulars concerning the institution. Washington, Pennsylvania: Printed by Grayson and Ruple, 1845. 11 p. PWW. 45-6734

Washington, D.C. Laws of the corporation of the city of Washington, passed by the forty-second council. Printed by order of the council. Washington, [D.C.] Printed by John T. Towers, 1845. 232 p. IaU-L. 45-6735

Washingtonian Massachusetts Convention. Proceedings and address of the Washingtonian Massachusetts convention, held in the city of Boston at Tremont Temple, Tuesday, May 29, 1845. Boston: New England Washingtonian office, 1845. 16 p. A-Ar; MBC; MiD-B; MNBedf; MWA. 45-6736

Waterhouse, Charles. The mental elements of arithmetic; for beginners. Portland: Waterhouse and company, 1845. 36 p. MeHi. 45-6737

Waterston, Robert Cassie, 1812-1893. A discourse on the life and character of Hon. Joseph Story... delivered on the Sunday following his death, September 14, 1845... Boston: W. Crosby and H.P. Nichols, 1845. 14 p. ICMe; MBAt; Nh-Hi; OCLaw; WHi. 45-6738

Waterston, Robert Cassie, 1812-1893. A poem, delivered before the Mercentile Library Association, at their twenty-fifth anniversary, October 15, 1845. Boston: Press of T.R. Marvin, 1845. 20 p. ICMe; MBAU; OClWHi; TxU; Whi. 45-6739

Waterville College. Catalogue... 1845-1846. Portland: F.A. and A.F. Gerrish, printers, 1845. 21 p. MeHi. 45-6740

Watkins, J.B. The child's pictorial history of the Bible. Boston: J.V. Pierce, 1845. 48 p. DLC; MH; MMeT; NNC. 45-6741

Watson, Alexander. A lecture delivered April 2, 1845, before the members of the Albany Female Academy, at the close of the annual course on astronomy. Albany: Erastus H. Pease, 1845. 30 p. Ct; MBAt; MHi; NN; OMC. 45-6742

Watson, John Fanning, 1779-1860. Annals of Philadelphia and Pennsylvania in the olden time. Philadelphia: Carey and Hart, 1845. 2 v. IES; MBNEH; MdBE; NPV; PSC-Hi. 45-6743

Watson, John Fanning, 1779-1860. Annals of Philadelphia and Pennsylvania in the olden time. Second edition. Philadelphia: Published by the author, 1845. 2 v. NSyU; PPiHi. 45-6744

Watson, Richard, 1737-1816. An apology for the Bible. In a series of letters addressed to Thomas Paine. New York: G.

Lane and C.B. Tippett, 1845. 187 p. GCuA; IaScW; ICRL; WHi. 45-6745

Watson, Richard, 1781-1833. Sermons and sketches of sermons. New York: Printed by G. Lane and C.B. Tippett, 1845-1848. 2 v. GCuA; IaMpI; NcD; OCl. 45-6746

Watson, Richard, 1781-1833. Theological institutes; or a view of the evidences, doctrines, morals and institutions of christianity. New York: G. Lane and C.B. Tippett for the Methodist Episcopal Church, 1845. 2 v. KyLxT; MiKC; MeLewB; NBuCC; OWof. 45-6747

Watson, Thomas, 1792-1882. Lectures on the principles and practice of physics; delivered at Kings College, London. Second American from the second London edition. Revised with additions by D. Francis Condie. Philadelphia: Lea and Blanchard, 1845. 1026 p. CU; MH-M; OCo; ViRA. 45-6748

Watts, Isaac, 1674-1748. Divine and moral songs for children. Boston: Sabbath School Society, 1845. MH. 45-6749

Watts, Isaac, 1674-1748. Psalms, hymns, and spiritual songs of Isaac Watts. To which are added select hymns, from other authors; and directions for musical expression... Boston: Crocker and Brewster, 1845. 776 p. CU; MH-AH; MWA; NbCrD; NNUT. 45-6750

Watts, Isaac, 1674-1748. Songs, divine and moral, for the use of children. New York, 1845. 96 p. MWA. 45-6751

Watts, Isaac, 1674-1748. Songs, divine and moral, for the use of children. Wor-

cester: C. Harris, 1845. 72 p. MWHi; NNC. 45-6752

Wayland, Francis, 1796-1865. The elements of moral science. Boston: Gould, Kendall and Lincoln, 1845. MH. 45-6753

Wayland, Francis, 1796-1865. The elements of moral science. Twenty-fifth thousand. Boston: Gould, Kendall and Lincoln, 1845. 398 p. CoGrS; KBiS; MB; OCan; TNT. 45-6754

Wayland, Francis, 1796-1865. The elements of political economy. Tenth thousand. Boston: Gould, Kendall and Lincoln, 1845. [15]- 406 p. ArL; MiEalC; MWH; TxU; ViU. 45-6755

Wayland, John. The promotion of literary taste, a duty binding upon educated men: an address delivered before the Hernean Society of Geneva College, August 6, 1845. Geneva: Ira Merrell, printer, 1845. 18 p. CtY; MH; N; NCH; NGH. 45-6756

Waylen, Edward. A history of Prince George's Parish, Montgomery County. With a preliminary glance at the rise and establishment of the Episcopal Church in Maryland. Rockville: Printed by John W. Spates, 1845. 26 p. MdBD; NNG. 45-6757

Weaver, John W., b. 1823. The life of Husti-coluc-chee, a Seminole missionary as delivered by him in the several churches of the cities of Pittsburgh and Allegheny in December, 1845. Pittsburgh: Printed by Victor Scriba, [1845] 16 p. MiD-B; OClWHi; PHi; PWW. 45-6758

Webb, J.N. Memoir of Miss Charity Richards, or grace reigning and triumphing under complicated and protracted sufferings. New York: J.C. Hatch, printer, 1845. 105 p. NoLoc. 45-6759

Weber, Karl Maria, 1786-1826. Der freischutz; a grand opera in three acts. Words by Friedrich Kind. Translated by C.B. Burkhardt. New York, 1845. 17 p. DLC; MH; MH-Mu. 45-6760

Webster, Chauncey, 1799-1880. Divine and human rights, or the Westminster confession and the constitution of the United States tested by the Holy Scripture. Philadelphia: W.S. Young, 1845. 119 p. DLC; MB; MH-AH; OCLaw; PPPrHi. 45-6761

Webster, Daniel, 1782-1852. Argument of Hon. Daniel Webster, on behalf of the Boston and Lowell Railroad Company, at a hearing on the petitions of William Livingston and others, and Robert Clark and others, before the railroad committee of the Massachusetts legislature. Boston: Dutton and Wentworth, printers, 1845. 31 p. OClWHi; MdBJ; NNE; WHi; WU. 45-6762

Webster, Daniel, 1782-1852. Argument of the Hon. Daniel Webster, and the Hon. J. Macpherson Berrien, and opinion of the Hon. George M. Dallas, in the case of Charles F. Sibbald against the United States. Philadelphia, 1845. 45, 5 p. DLC. 45-6763

Webster, Daniel, 1782-1852. Mr. Webster's remarks at the meeting of the Suffolk Bar, on moving the resolutions occasioned by the death of the Hon. Mr. Justice Story. Boston: James Munroe and company, 1845. 14 p. ICMe; MH; Nh; RPB; WHi. 45-6764

Webster, Daniel, 1782-1852. Speeches and forensic arguments. Boston: Charles Tappan, 1846. 3 v. ICN; NIC; OO; ViRU. 45-6765

Webster, Delia Ann. Kentucky jurisprudence. A history of the trial of Miss Delia A. Webster. At Lexington, Kentucky, December 17-21, 1844, before the Hon. Richard Buckner on a charge of aiding slaves to escape from that commonwealth. Vergennes: D.W. Blaisdell, 1845. 84 p. MdHi; OO; PHC; TxU; VtVe. 45-6766

Webster, Noah, 1758-1843. American dictionary of the English language. First edition in Octavo, containing the whole vocabulary of the quarto. Springfield, Massachusetts: George and Charles Merriam, 1845. 2 v. CoDR; IU; LNB; MB; WU. 45-6767

Webster, Noah, 1758-1843. American dictionary of the English language; abridged from the quarto edition of the author to which are added a synopsis of words, differently pronounced... and Walker's key to the classical pronunciation of Greek, Latin and scripture proper names. Revised edition with an appendix. New York: Harper and brothers, 1845. 1072 p. InPerM; NeWmtn; WHi. 45-6768

Webster, Noah, 1758-1843. Dictionary of the English language; abridged from the American dictionary, for the use of primary schools and the counting house. New York, 1845. MH. 45-6769

Webster, Noah, 1758-1843. The elementary spelling book. New Brunswick, New Jersey, [1845?] NN. 45-6770

Webster, Noah, 1758-1843. The elementary spelling book. Portland, Maine, 1845. MH; NN. 45-6771

Webster, Noah, 1758-1843. The elementary spelling book. Rochester: Clarendon Morse, 1845. 168 p. MA. 45-6772

Webster, Noah, 1758-1843. The elementary spelling book; being an improvement on the American spelling book. New York: G.F. Cooledge and brother, [1845] MH; MWHi; NNC; OClWHi. 45-6773

Webster, Noah, 1758-1843. The elementary spelling book; being an improvement on the American spelling book. Watertown, New York: Knowlton and Rice, [1845] 164 p. NNC. 45-6774

Webster, Thomas. Encyclopedia of domestic economy comprising such subjects as are most immediately connected with housekeeping... assisted by the late Mrs. Parkes. New York: Harper, 1845. 1238 p. KyBC; MnM; NNNAM; OCHP; RNR. 45-6775

Webster, William Greenleaf, 1805-1869. A sequel to Webster's elementary spelling book: or a speller and definer: containing a selection of 12,000 of the most useful words in the English language, with their definitions: intended to be used as a spelling book and a dictionary by W.G. Webster. Sixtieth thousand. New York: George Cooledge and brother, 1845. 172 p. A- Ar; MH; OkGoP; OOxM; TxDaM. 45-6776

Webster, William Greenleaf, 1805-1869. A sequel to Webster's elementary spelling book: or a speller and definer:

containing a selection of 12,000 of the most useful words in the English language, with their definitions: intended to be used as a spelling book and a dictionary by W.G. Webster. Six hundredth thousand. Louisville: Morton, 1845. 172 p. LNT; KyLx; NcAS; PHi. 45-6777

Webster, William Greenleaf, 1805-1869. A speller and definer; containing a selection of 12,000 of the most useful words in the English language, with their definitions... Third edition, revised and greatly improved. New York: George F. Cooledge and brother, [1845] 166 p. IEG; MnS; NcRSh; NSyU; UPB. 45-6778

Webster's calendar, or the Albany almanac for 1846. Albany, New York: Printed by J. Munsell, [1845] [36] p. MeHi; MWA; NN; WHi. 45-6779

Webster's calendar, or the Albany almanack for 1846. Albany, New York: E.H. Bender, [1845] MWA. 45-6780

Webster's calendar, or the Albany almanack for 1846. Albany, New York: E.H. Pease, [1845] MWA. 45-6781

Webster's calendar, or the Albany almanack for 1846. Albany, New York: Steele and Durrie, [1845] MWA. 45-6782

Webster's calendar, or the Albany almanack for 1846. Catskill, New York: James H. Van Gorden, [1845] MWA. 45-6783

Webster's calendar, or the Albany almanack. Albany, New York: James Henry, 1845. MWA. 45-6784

Webster's calendar, or the Albany almanack. Albany, New York: W.C. Little, 1845. MWA. 45-6785

Wedgwood, William. Revised statutes of Indiana and additional laws to 1845, reduced to questions and answers for the use of schools and families. Second edition. Indianapolis: Chamberlain and Spann, 1845. In; InU; InVi. 45-6786

Wedgwood, William. Revised statutes of Indiana and additional laws to 1845, reduced to questions and answers for the use of schools and families. Third edition. Indianapolis, 1845. In; InHi; InThT; InU. 45-6787

Weed, Henry Rowland, 1789-1870. Questions on the confession of faith and form of government of the Presbyterian Church. Philadelphia, 1845. 103 p. OUrC. 45-6788

Weems, Mason Locke, 1759-1825. Hymen's recruiting sergeant. Hartford: S. Andrus and son, 1845. 52 p. MH; NN; RPB. 45-6789

Weems, Mason Locke, 1759-1825. The life of Benjamin Franklin; with many choice anecdotes and admirable sayings of this great man, never before published by any of his biographers. Philadelphia: Uriah Hunt and son, 1845. 239 p. DeWI; KWiU; NjP; PU; WaT. 45-6790

Weems, Mason Locke, 1759-1825. The life of General Francis Marion, a celebrated partisan officer in the revolutionary war. Philadelphia: J. Allen, 1845. 251 p. DLC; KyHi; PHi; TNP; ViU. 45-6791

Weems, Mason Locke, 1759-1825. The life of William Penn, the settler of Pennsylvania, the founder of Philadelphia, and one of the first law givers in the colonies, now the United States, in 1682. Philadelphia: Uriah Hunt and son, 1845. 282 p. CtHT; IaU; KHi; NBF; OC. 45-6792

Weiss, John, 1818-1879. Our private and public stewardship. A discourse preached before the First Congregational Society in Watertown. Cambridge: John Owen, 1845. 15 p. ICMe; MB; MH-AH; RPB; WHi. 45-6793

Welby, Amelia Coppuck. Poems. Boston: A. Tomkins, 1845. 259 p. IGK; KyRE; MiD; MWH; OCX; WHi. 45-6794

Weld, Allen Hayden, 1812-1882. Latin lessons and reader, with exercises for the writing of Latin; introductory to Andrews and Stoddard's and Bullions Latin grammars, and also to Nepos or Caesar, Kreb's guide. Revised edition, enlarged. Portland: Sanborn and Carter, 1845. 7-258 p. IU; MB; OO; PHi; TxU-T. 45-6795

Weld, Allen Hayden, 1812-1882. Latin lessons and reader, with exercises for the writing of Latin; introductory to Andrews and Stoddard's and Bullions Latin grammars, and also to Nepos or Caesar, Kreb's guide. Revised edition, enlarged. Second edition, enlarged. Andover: Allen, Morrill and Wardell; New York: Mark H. Newman, 1845. ICU; MB; MH; TxU-T. 45-6796

Weld, Horatio Hastings, 1811-1888. Jonce Smiley, the yankee boy who had no friends. By Ezekiel Jones, esq. [Pseud.] Edited by H. Hastings Weld. New York:

E. Ferrett and company, 1845. 75 p. N; PU; ViU. 45-6797

Weld, Horatio Hastings, 1811-1888. Life of George Washington; embracing anecdotes illustrative of his character. Philadelphia: Lindsay and Blakiston, [1845] 222 p. DLC; IU; MoU; NcD; OkentU. 45-6798

Weld, Horatio Hastings, 1811-1888. Pictorial life of George Washington: embracing anecdotes, illustrative of his character. For the young people of the nation he founded. Philadephia: Lindsay and Blakiston, 1845. 222 p. CoU; NcD; OClW; PHi; ViU. 45-6799

Weller, John B., 1812-1875. Speech of Mr. Weller, of Ohio, on the annexation of Texas; delivered in the House, January 9, 1845. Washington: Printed at the Globe office, 1845. 7 p. CU; OClWHi; TxU. 45-6800

Welles, Albert. Things new and old for the glory of God, or old revelations and prophecies. By a Descendant from one of the early puritanic governors. Portland, William Hyde, 1845. LNH; MNan; MNe; NIC. 45-6801

Wellman's American statistical almanack for 1846. By J.K. Wellman. New York, S.W. Benedict, [1845] MWA. 45-6802

Wells, Horatio Nelson, 1808-1858. Message purporting to by by His Excellency, the governor of the people; delivered in the House, February 12, 1845. [Madison, 1845] 8 p. NN. 45-6803

Wells, Lucy K. A mother's plea for the sabbath: in a series of letters to an absent son, illustrated by facts. Second edition. Portland: Hyde, Lord and Duren, 1845. 144 p. KWiU; MeB; NN. 45-6804

Wentworth, John, 1815-1888. Remarks on Mr. Wentworth, of Illinois, on the Oregon Bill: delivered in the House, January 27, 1845. [Washington, 1845] 6 p. CU-B; TxHU; WaU. 45-6805

Wesley, John 1703-1891. A collection of hymns. New York: G. Lane and C.B. Tippett, 1845. 623 p. MdBAHi. 45-6806

Wesley, John, 1703-1791. A plain account of christian perfection, as believed and taught by the Rev. John Wesley, from the year 1725, to the year 1777. New York: Lane and Tippett, 1845. 175 p. MBCT; TMeSC. 45-6807

Wesley, John, 1703-1791. Sermons on several occasions. By John Wesley, sometime fellow of Lincoln College, Oxford. New York: G. Lane and C.B. Tippett, 1845. 2 v. IEG; InGr; MnSH; PPTU; TxGeoS. 45-6808

Wesley, John, 1703-1791. Wesleyana: a selection of the most important passages in the writings of the late Rev. John Wesley, arranged to form a complete body of divinity, with a biographical sketch. From a London edition. New York: O. Scott for the Wesleyan Methodist Connection of America, 1845. 228 p. CtMW; NNMHi; OO; VtMidb; VtMidSM. 45-6809

The Wesleyan Methodist Connection of America. A discipline of the Wesleyan Methodist Connection of America. Stereotype edition. New York: O. Scott, 1845. 128 p. IEG; MBNMHi; OO; TxHuT; WFtaHi. 45-6810

Wesleyan Methodist Connection of America. A discipline of the Wesleyan Methodist Connection of America. Stereotype edition. New York: O. Scott, 1845. 94 p. CCSC. 45-6811

West, Francis Athow. Memoir of Jonathan Saville, of Halifax, England, including his autobiography. From the London edition. New York: G. Lane and C.B. Tippett, 1845. 90 p. NjMD; NNG; NNMHi. 45-6812

West, Robert A. Records of the proceedings and debates at the sixty-first annual convention of the Protestant Episcopal Church in the diocese of New York. New York: Stanford and Swords, 1845. 148 p. CtHT; MBD; MiD-B; Nj; RPB. 45-6813

Western almanac. Cincinnati: A. Randall, 1845. MWA. 45-6814

Western almanac and Franklin calendar for 1846. Buffalo, New York: W.B. and C.E. Peck, [1845] MWA. 45-6815

Western almanac and Franklin calendar for 1846. Rochester, New York: M. and J. Miller, [1845] MWA. 45-6816

The western almanac and Franklin calendar for 1846. Rochester, New York: Samuel Hamilton, [1845] MWA; NCH; NRHi. 45-6817

Western and oneida almanac for 1846. By George R. Perkins. Utica, New York: R.W. Roberts, 1845. MWA; NElm; NUtHi. 45-6818

The western Baptist review. Edited by John L. Walker. Frankfort, Kentucky,

1845?. v. 1-. CSmH; ICRL; KyU; MnU. 45-6819

Western farmers' almanac. By Horace Martin. Syracuse: J.R. Gilmer, 1845. MWA; NCH. 45-6820

Western farmer's almanac for 1845... By Horace Martin. Auburn: H. Oliphant, 1845. 32 p. NCanHi. 45-6821

Western farmer's comprehensive almanac, for the year of our Lord, 1845... Lexington, Kentucky: Chipley, Bodley and company, 1845. 48 p. OC. 45-6822

Western farmer's comprehensive almanac, for the year of our Lord, 1846... Louisville, Kentucky: Morton and Griswold, 1846. 48 p. OC. 45-6823

Western literary journal and monthly review. Cincinnati: Robinson and Jones, 1845. v. 1. InU; IGK; IU; OClWHi; OMC. 45-6824

Western patriot and Canton almanack for 1846. By Charles F. Egelmann. Canton, Ohio: Peter Kaufmann and company, [1845] MWA; OLis. 45-6825

Western people's almanac for 1846. By H.N. Robinson. Cincinnati, Ohio: J.A. James, [1845] MWA. 45-6826

Western Railroad Corporation. Circular letter to the stockholders, upon the fares and income of 1845. By a committee of directors. Springfield: Printed by H.S. Taylor, 1845. 12 p. ICU; MB; MeHi; MH-BA; NjR. 45-6827

Western Railroad Corporation. Union of the Western and Worcester Railroad Corporation. Report of a joint committee of the stockholders of the Western and Boston and Worcester Railroad Corporations, on the subject of uniting the two companies under one charter; presented the Western Railroad Corporation, December 18, 1845. 12 p. CSt; DBRE; MH; NjR. 45-6828

Western reserve magazine of agriculture and horticulture. Cleveland: M.C. Younglove, 1845-1846. OClW. 45-6829

Western Reserve Teachers' Seminary, Kirtland, Ohio. Catalogue... for the year ending October 21, 1845. Kirtland, Lake County, Ohio. Cleveland: Younglove's Power Press, 1845. NN. 45-6830

Western Reserve University. Catalogue of the officers and students of the Western Reserve College, 1845-1846. Hudson, Ohio: Printed at the office of the Ohio Observer, 1845. 28 p. MeHi; PB; PWW; WBeloC. 45-6831

Western star. Jacksonville, Illinois: Alvin Bailey, 1845-. v. 1-. PCA. 45-6832

Western Theological Seminary, Allegheny, Pennsylvania. Triennial catalogue... February, 1845. Pittsburgh: Printed at the Franklin office, 1845. 24 p. CSansS; OClWHi; PPPrHi; PPM. 45-6833

Western Vermont Railroad Company. An act to incorporate the Western Vermont Railroad Company. [n.p.] 1845. 8 p. DBRE. 45-6834

Westervelt, Harmon C. American progress. An address delivered at the 18th annual fair ot the American Institute, on October 8, 1845, at Niblo's Garden. New York: James Van Norden

and company, 1845. 8 p. CBPSR; DLC; MB; NNMuCN; PPL-R. 45-6835

Westminster Assembly of Divines. Shorter catechism explained by way of question and answer. Part I and II. What man is to believe concerning God. By several ministers of the gospel. Philadelphia: William S. Young, 1845. 215, 264 p. CSansS. 45-6836

Wetherill cash book. 1845-. PHi; PPHi. 45-6837

Weymouth, Massachusetts. A schedule of expenses of the town of Weymouth, from March, 1844, to March, 1845. Quincy: John A. Green, printer, 1845. 27 p. MWey. 45-6838

What fairy like music; a gondola duet. Words by Mrs. C.B. Wilson. Music by J. de Pinna. Boston, [1845?] 3 p. MH. 45-6839

What is to become of the slaves in the United States? [From the Lexington, Kentucky True American, August 12, 1845. Lexington, 1845?] 7 p. MdHi; MH; WHi. 45-6840

Whately, Richard, 1787-1863. Easy lessons on reasoning. First American from the second London edition. Boston: James Munroe and company, 1845. 4-180 p. FMR; ICP; MPiB; NNS; RPB. 45-6841

Whately, Richard, 1787-1863. Elements of logic, comprising the substance of the article in the encyclopaedia metropolitana; with additions... Boston: J. Munroe and company; New York: Collins, Keese and company, 1845. 359 p. FDef; MH; NbU; OCoC; ViU. 45-6842

Whately, Richard, 1787-1863. Elements of logic, comprising the substance of the article in the encyclopaedia metropolitana; with additions... The only complete American edition from the 8th London edition revised. New York: W.H. Colyer; Boston: Phillips and Sampson, 1845. ICJ; LNH; MH; NNUT. 45-6843

Whately, Richard, 1787-1863. Elements of rhetoric, comprising the substance of the article in the encyclopedia metropolitana, with additions. Boston: James Munroe and company, 1845. 347 p. ICU; MBBC; MiU; PPWa; ScDuE. 45-6844

Whately, Richard, 1787-1863. The kingdom of Christ delineated in two essays on our Lord's own account of his person and of the nature of his kingdom. From the last London edition. Philadelphia: James M. Campbell and company, 1845. 93 p. CSansS; VtNofN. 45-6845

Whately, Richard, 1787-1863. The sabbath question. Boston, 1845. 36 p. ICMe; LNH; MBrZ; MHi; MNBedf. 45-6846

Wheat, James S. An argument on behalf of the city of Wheeling before the committee on roads and internal navigation, upon the memorial of the Baltimore and Ohio Railroad Company. Richmond: Printed by Shepherd and Colins, 1845. 61 p. MdBP; P. 45-6847

Wheatley, Charles Moore, 1822-1882. Catalogue of the shells of the United States, with their localities. [Second edition] New York: [Washington: Printed by J.T. Towers] 1845. 35 p. ICJ; MBC; NNM; PPWe; TNN. 45-6848

Wheaton, Henry, 1785-1848. History of the law of nations in Europe and America: from the earliest times to the treaty of Washington, 1842. New York: Gould, Banks and company, 1845. 797 p. CtHT; IaU-L; PU; RPA; WaU. 45-6849

Wheeler, Alfred, 1822-1903. The age: a satire, pronounced as a valedictory poem, before the New York Society of Literature at its second anniversary, January 23, 1845. New York: C. Shepard, 1845. 24 p. ICU; MnU; NjR; PPM; WU. 45-6850

Wheeler, Amos Dean. Jesus and his disciples in the Jewish synagogues. Boston: James Munroe and company, 1845. 14 p. ICMe; IEG; MeB; MH; MMeT-Hi. 45-6851

Wheeler, Clark. The Apiarian's directory; or practical remarks on the economical, advantageous, easy, and profitable management of bees; to accompany and explain the New York hive. Buffalo: Press of Charles E. Young, 1845. 64 p. NBuHi. 45-6852

Wheeler, Gervase. Rural Homes; or sketches of houses suited to American Country life, with original plans, designs, etc. New York: Charles Scribner, 1845. 11-298 p. MdBMC. 45-6853

Wheeler, N. The phrenological characters and talents of Henry Clay, Daniel Webster, John Quincy Adams, William Henry Harrison and Andrew Jackson. Boston: Dow and Jackson, 1845. 36 p. IaHi; Nh; PPL; WHi. 45-6854

Wheeling, West Virginia. Merchants and Mechanics Bank. Condition of the Merchants and Mechanics Bank of

Wheeling. Executive department, January 28, 1846... Richmond: Samuel Shepherd, printer, 1845. 2 p. WHi. 45-6855

Whelpley, Samuel. A compend of history, from the earliest times; comprehending a general view of the present state of the world, with respect to civilization, religion and government. Twelfth edition. New York: Collins, brother and company, 1845. 218, 284, 69 p. InPerM; KHi; NcMHi; OS; OWoC. 45-6856

Whewell, William, 1794-1866. The elements of morality, including polity. New York: Harper and brothers, 1845. 2 v. CoGrS; IaDmU; NGH; OCY; ViRut. 45-6857

Whewell, William, 1794-1866. Indications of the Creator. By William Whewell, Master of Trinity College, and Professor of Moral Philosophy in the University of Cambridge. Philadelphia: Carey and Hart, 1845. [13]-86 p. ICBB; KyLx; MdBJ; NjR; ScU. 45-6858

Whicher, Hiram. Christian baptism, a minister of the Free Baptist Denomination, Rochester, New York. Rochester: Erastus Shepard, printer, 1845. 16 p. OO. 45-6859

The whig almanac and politician's register for 1846. New York: Greeley and McElrath, [1845] 64 p. MiD-B; NjR; OrPr; RP; WHi. 45-6860

The whig almanac and United States register for 1845. New York: Greeley and McElrath, 1845. 64 p. MiD-B; MiHi; MWHi. 45-6861

Whitby, Daniel, 1638-1726. Commen-

tary on the gospels and epistles of the New Testament; Revolation of St. John by Moses Lowman. [Philadelphia: Carey and Hart, 1845] CtHC; MB; PU. 45-6862

White, Charles, 1795-1861. A pure and sound literature: a baccalaureate address, delivered July 22, 1845. Indianapolis: Printed by Morrison and Spann, 1845. 33 p. CSmH; DLC; MBC; NNUT; OCHP. 45-6863

White, Edward L. Love not, arranged with variations for the pianoforte by E. White. Boston: Oliver Ditson, 1845. 5 p. IG; WHi. 45-6864

White, Edward Little, 1809-1851. The Sunday school singing book: being a collection of hymns with appropriate music. Third edition. Boston: William Crosby and H.P. Nichols, 1845. 112 p. MeHi. 45-6865

White, Henry, 1790-1858. The early history of New England, illustrated by numerous interesting incidents. Ninth edition. Concord, New Hampshire: I.S. Boyd, 1845. 428 p. CtMW; MdCatS; MH; NR. 45-6866

White, Henry, 1812-1880. Elements of universal history, on a new and systematic plan; from the earliest times to the treaty of Vienna. To which is added a summary of the leading events since that period. For the use of schools and private students. Fifth American edition, with additions and questions, by John S. Hart. Philadelphia: Lea and Blanchard, 1845. 525 p. KMK; MoS; NcBe; TNJU. 45-6867

White, Hugh. Meditations and addresses on the subject of prayer. Fifth

American from the tenth English edition. New York: Robert Carter and brothers, 1845. CtHC. 45-6868

White, William Augustus, 1821-1898. Following Jesus and other poems. Philadelphia: George and Wayne, King and Baird, 1845. 84 p. MdBD; MdHi; MH; NNUT. 45-6869

White's farmer's and mechanic's almanack for 1846. Painesville, Ohio: Thomas J. White, [1845] MWA. 45-6870

Whitecross, John. The assembly's shorter catechism illustrated by appropriate anecdotes; chiefly designed to assist parents and Sabbath school teachers in the instruction of youth. New edition. New York: Robert Carter, 1845. 180 p. CBPSR; CLO; IaB; NNUT; PPM. 45-6871

Whitehead, John, 1740-1804. The life of the Rev. John Wesley, some time fellow of Lincoln College, Oxford. Collected from his private papers and printed works; and written at the request of his executors... Philadelphia, 1845. DeWI; ICP; MdBD; TxDaM; ViAL. 45-6872

Whiting, Henry, 1788-1851. Life of Zebulon Montgomery Pike. Boston: C.C. Little and J. Brown, 1845. DLC; OCLWHi; PPAmP. 45-6873

Whitman, Jason, 1799-1848. We live for heaven when we live for duty. Boston: James Munroe and company, 1845. 22 p. CBPac; ICMe; MeBat; MMeT-Hi; RP. 45-6874

Whitman, Jason, 1799-1848. The young lady's aid, to usefulness and happiness. Third edition. Portland: S.H. Coleswor-

thy; Boston: Abel Tompkins, 1845. 283 p. MeHi; MH. 45-6875

Whitney, Asa, 1797-1872. Atlantic and Pacific Railroad. A. Whitney's reply to Hon. S.A. Douglass. [Washington, 1845] 4 p. DBRE; MH-BA; OrHi; WaU. 45-6876

Whitney, Asa, 1797-1872. To the people of the United States. A plan to construct a railroad from Lake Michigan to the Pacific. [New York, 1845] 12 p. MH; MH-BA; OClWHi. 45-6877

Whitney, Thomas Richard, 1804-1858. The ambuscade. An historical poem... New York: J.S. Redfield, 1845. 83 p. DLC; FSaW; MH; NBuG; OMC; TxU. 45-6878

Whiton, John Milton, 1797-1872. Sermon on temperance, delivered at Antrim, New Hampshire, on Lords day, September 28, 1845. Boston: B.B. Mussey, 1845. 16 p. MB; Nh; NNUT. 45-6879

Whittemore, Thomas, 1800-1861. The plain guide to Universalism. Boston, 1846. 408 p. PHi. 45-6880

Whittier, John Greenleaf, 1807-1892. The stranger in Lowell. Boston: Waite, Peirce, 1845. 156 p. CO; ICU; MB; PHi; TxU. 45-6881

Whittlesey, Charles, 1808-1886. Dissertation upon the origin of mineral coal... Cleveland: Printed by M.C. Younglove, 1845. 24 p. CSt; KyLx; NjR; OCX; RPB. 45-6882

Whittlesey, Charles, 1808-1886. Justice to the memory of John Fitch; who in 1785 invented a steam engine and steam boat... Cincinnati: Printed at the Daily Atlas office, 1845. 12 p. MBAt; NN; OClWHi; PHi; WHi. 45-6883

Whittlesey, Charles, 1808-1886. Life of John Fitch. Boston: C.C. Little and J. Brown, 1845. 166 p. OClWHi; PHi. 45-6884

Whittlesey, John. Authenic account of the persecutions and trials of the Rev. John Whittlesey, of Salem, Connecticut, late ordained elder of the Methodist Episcopal Church.... New York, 1845. 72 p. Ct; MBNMHi; PP. 45-6885

Whittock, Nathaniel. The Oxford drawing book; or the art of drawing and the theory and practice of perspective, in a series of letters containing progressive information on sketching, drawing and colouring landscape scenery, animals and the human figure... for the use of teachers or self instruction. New York: Collins, brothers, 1846. 159 p. DLC; MSbri; NNC; OClStM. 45-6886

Wickens, Stephen B. Fulfillment of scripture prophecy, as exhibited in ancient history and modern travels. Third thousand. New York: G. Lane and C.B. Tippett, 1845. 352 p. IEG; ICP; ILM; NcD; ScCoT. 45-6887

Wickens, Stephen B. The life of John Bunyan, author of Pilgrim's progress. Second edition. New York: G. Lane and C.B. Tippett, 1845. 544 p. CtY; DLC; OrSaW; PPM; TxDaM. 45-6888

Wickens, Stephen B. The life of Rev. Richard Watson. Second edition. New York: Lane and Tippett, for the Methodist Episcopal Church, 1845. 312 p. ViU. 45-6889

Wickliffe, Robert, 1775-1859. To the freemen of the county of Fayette. Lexington: Kentucky Gazette print, 1845. 22 p. DLC; OCl; PPL. 45-6890

Wilberforce, Samuel, 1805-1873. History of the Protestant Episcopal Church. New York: Stanford, 1845. MWiW. 45-6891

Wilberforce, Samuel, 1805-1873. A manual for communicants; or the order for administering the Holy Communion, conveniently arranged; with meditations and prayers from old English divines, being the Eucharistica, adapted to the American service. New York: D. Appleton and company, 1845. 240 p. ICRL; IU. 45-6892

Wilberforce, Samuel, 1805-1873. A manual for communicants; or the order for administering the Holy Communion, conveniently arranged; with meditations and prayers from old English divines, being the Eucharistica, adapted to the American service. Philadelphia, 1845. 240 p. WHi. 45-6893

Wilbur, John, 1774-1856. A narrative and exposition of the late proceedings of New England Yearly meeting; with some of the subordinate meetings and their committees, in relation to the doctrinal controversy now existing in the Society of Friends. New York: Piercy and Reed, printers, 1845. 352 p. AAP; DLC; MiU; PSC; RPB. 45-6894

Wilcox, Gustavus H. Discourse in commemoration of the life and public services of Andrew Jackson, at Fayette, June 30, 1845. Natchez: Printed at the Free Trader office, 1845. 20 p. MiD; NN. 45-6895

Wiley, Calvin Henderson, 1819-1887. Address delivered before the two literary societies of Wake Forest College... Raleigh: Standard, 1845. 27 p. NcU; NcWfc. 45-6896

Wiley and Putnam, publishers. New and valuable books, published by Wiley and Putnam. New York, 1845. 14 p. MeAu. 45-6897

Wiley and Putnam, publishers. New books now ready and in preparation. New York: Wiley and Putnam, 1845. 218 p. LNT. 45-6898

Wilkes, Charles, 1798-1877. Columbia River to the Sacramento, Oakland, California: Biobooks, 1845. 140 p. WaT. 45-6899

Wilkes, Charles, 1798-1877. Narrative of the United States exploring expedition during the years, 1838-1842. Atlas. New York: Putnam, 1845. PU. 45-6900

Wilkes, Charles, 1798-1877. Narrative of the United States exploring expedition. During the years 1838-1842. Philadelphia: Lea and Blanchard, 1845. MH-P; NbU; PP; WHi. 45-6901

Wilkes, Charles, 1798-1877. Narrative of the United States exploring expedition during the years, 1838, 1839, 1840, 1841, 1842. With illustrations and maps. Philadelphia: Lea and Blanchard, 1845. 5 v. ArHa; FOA; KU; OrU. PU. 45-6902

Wilkes, George, 1820-1885. The history of Oregon, geographical and political... embracing an analysis of the old Spanish claims, the British pretensions, the United States title... a thorough examination of the project of a national railroad, from the Atlantic to the Pacific Ocean... New York: W.H. Colyer, 1845. 127 p. CSt; MH; OrHi; PPL; WHi. 45-6903

Wilkes, George, 1820-1885. Project of a national railroad from the Atlantic to the Pacific Ocean for the purpose of obtaining a short route to Oregon and the Indies. Second edition. Republished from "The history of Oregon," by the same author. New York: The author, 1845. 23 p. CU; MdBP; NcD; NjR; PPWa. 45-6904

Wilkes, William C. Common school education; an oration, delivered before the Ciceronian Society, or Mercer University, at its first anniversary celebration. Penfield, Georgia: Printed by B. Brantly, 1845. 14 p. MH. 45-6905

Wilkins, John Hubbard, 1794-1861. Arguments and statements addressed to the members of the legislature, in relation to the petition of the city of Boston for power to bring into the city the water of Long Pond. By a remonstrant. Boston: Printed by Freeman and Bolles, 1845. 25 p. DLC. 45-6906

Wilkins, John Hubbard, 1794-1861. Further remarks on supplying the city of Boston with pure water, in answer mainly to inquiry into the best mode of supplying the city of Boston with water for domestic purposes, etc. Boston: Charles C. Little and James Brown, 1845. 68 p. ICU. MBB; MH; MiD-B; WHi. 45-6907

Wilkins, John Hubbard, 1794-1861. Further remarks on supplying the city of Boston with pure water. Second edition, with additions. Boston: Charles C. Little and James Brown, 1845. 47 p. DLC; M; MHi; MMal. 45-6908

522   Wilkins, John Hubbard.

Wilkins, John Hubbard, 1794-1861. Remarks on supplying the city of Boston with pure water. Boston: Charles C. Little and James Brown, 1845. 32 p. LNH; MBAt; MBB; MiD-B; MnU. 45-6909

Wilkinson, G.E. Wilkinson's botanico-medical practice... Cincinnati: M. Swank, 1845. [13]-432 p. CSt-L; MiDW-M; NBMS; OC; WvBe. 45-6910

Wilks, Thomas. Reasons by the Rev. T. Wilks renouncing his former views and embracing the doctrines of the New Jerusalem Church... to which is appended a letter... Manchester: New Jerusalem Church Tract Society, Cave and Sever, 1845. 24 p. PBa. 45-6911

Wilks, Thomas. Reasons by the Rev. T. Wilks renouncing his former views and embracing the doctrines of the New Jerusalem Church... to which is appended a letter... Second edition. Manchester: New Jerusalem Church Tract Society, Cave and Sever, 1845. 24 p. PBa. 45-6912

Willard, Emma Hart, 1787-1870. Abridged history of the United States: or, Republic of America. New York: A.S. Barnes, 1845. 336 p. KyBU; OClWHi; TxSaD. 45-6913

Willard, Emma Hart, 1787-1870. Ancient geography, as connected with chronology, and preparatory to ancient history; accompanied with an atlas. Revised edition. Hartford: Belknap and Hamersley, 1845. 96 p. CtHWatk; MeHi; MH; MoS; NNC. 45-6914

Willard, Emma Hart, 1787-1870. History of the United States, or Republic of America. New York: A.S. Barnes and

company, 1845. 443 p. ICBB; KyRE; MeB; NH; WvEW. 45-6915

Willard, Emma, Hart, 1787-1870. Universal history in perspective. New York: A.S. Barnes and company, 1845. 494 p. MFiHi. 45-6916

Willard, Emma Hart, 1787-1870. Universal history, in perspective. Second edition. Philadelphia: A.S. Barnes and company, 1845. 33-494 p. Ct; ICU; KyHe; MNS; OClW. 45-6917

William and Mary College, Williamsburg, Virginia. Catalogue of the officers and students of William and Mary College. Session of 1844-1845. Richmond: Printed by Shepperd and Colin, 1845. 23 p. ViRVal. 45-6918

William Prince and Company. Periodical pamphlet, 1845 and 1846. Prince's descriptive catalogue of fruit and ornamental trees. Twenty fourth edition. New York, 1845. 109 p. MHi. 45-6919

Williams, Charles James Blasius, 1805-1889. A practical treatise on the diseases of the respiratory organs: including diseases of the larynx, trachea, lungs and pleura. Philadelphia: Lea and Blanchard, 1845. 508 p. CU-M; ICU-R; LNOP; MH-M; PU. 45-6920

Williams, Henry, 1805-1887. Speech of Mr. Williams, of Massachusetts, in vindication of the right of the people of Rhode Island to amend their form of government. Washington, 1845. 14 p. MiD-B; R; RHi; RP. 45-6921

Williams, Henry, 1805-1887. Speech of Mr. Williams, of Massachusetts, on the Rhode Island controversy; delivered in the House, February 28, 1845. Washington: Globe office, 1845. 14 p. OClWHi. 45-6922

Williams, Isaac, 1802-1865. Hymns on the catechism, by Rev. Isaac Williams. New York: Alexander V. Blake, 1845. 130 p. NGH; NNG. 45-6923

Williams, John, 1817-1899. Ancient hymns of holy church. Hartford: H.S. Parson, 1845. 127 p. CtHT; ICU; MB; NNG; PPPrHi. 45-6924

Williams, John Bickerton, 1792-1855. Memoirs of the life and character of Mrs. Sarah Savage, eldest daughter of the Rev. Philip Henry by Sir J.B. William with a recommendatory preface by the Rev. William Jay of Bath.... Philadelphia: Presbyterian Board of Publication, 1845. 360 p. ICMeHi; MBC; NRom; P; PPL. 45-6925

Williams, John H. A brief history of the rise and progress of the Independent Order of Odd Fellows in the United States. Boston: Haliburton and Dudley, 1845. 32 p. CtHT; MiD-B; WHi. 45-6926

Williams, Joshua, 1813-1881. Principles of the law of real property. American edition. Philadelphia, 1845. PU-L. 45-6927

Williams, Nathaniel. The memorial of Nathaniel Williams, complaining of an exercise of power by the then judges of Baltimore county court, and praying that an act may pass declaratory of the law concerning contempts of court. [Baltimore, 1845] 3 p. MdBE. 45-6928

Williams, Samuel Wells, 1812-1884. Middle kingdom, a survey of the geography, government, literature, social life,

arts and history of the Chinese Empire and its inhabitants. New York: Wiley, 1845. 2 v. In. 45-6929

Williams, Stephen West, 1790-1855. American medical biography: or memoirs of eminent physicians, embracing principally those who have died since the publication of Dr. Thacher's work on the same subject. Greenfield, Massachusetts: L. Merriam and company, printers, 1845. [17]-664 p. CSt-L; IEN-M; NGH; RPB; WHi. 45-6930

Williams, William R., 1804-1885. The church of Christ; the home and hope of the free; a discourse, at the recognition of the South Baptist Church, in the city of Brooklyn, on July 13, 1845. New York: L. Colby, 1845. 41 p. 45-6931

Williams College, Williamstown, Massachusetts. Catalogue of the officers and students of Williams College, 1845-1846. Troy, New York: Press of J.C. Kneeland and company, 1845. 20 p. MeHi; NNC; PPPrHi; PU. 45-6932

Williamsburgh. Book of reference, showing the location of each lot, with farm numbers, etc. Prepared by Isaac Vieth. New York, 1845. NBLiHi. 45-6933

Willis, Nathaniel Parker, 1806-1867. Dashes at life, with a free pencil. New York: Burgess, Stringer and company, 1845. 4 pts. in 1 v. AU; DLC; LNH; NBuG; TxSa. 45-6934

Willis, Nathaniel Parker, 1806-1867. Dashes at life, with a free pencil. Third edition. New York: J.S. Redfield, 1845. 4 pts. in 1 v. CU; DLC; MoK; NcAS; PPL. 45-6935

Willis, Nathaniel Parker, 1806-1867. The poems, sacred, passionate, and humorous. Complete edition. New York: Clark and Austin, 1845. 331 p. PLFM. 45-6936

Willis, Nathaniel Parker, 1806-1857. The poems, sacred, passionate, and humorous. Third edition. New York: Clark and Austin, 1845. 331 p. RPA. 45-6937

Willis, Nathaniel Parker, 1806-1857. The poems, sacred, passionate, and humorous. Fifth edition. New York: Clark and Austin, 1845. 331 p. CtMW; MB; MWiW; NhPet; ViNew. 45-6938

Willis, Nathaniel Parker, 1806-1857. The poems, sacred, passionate, and humorous. Sixth edition. New York: Clark and Austin, 1845. 331 p. IU; MeHi; MH; NRMA; ViU. 45-6939

Williston Seminary, East Hampton. Constitution of Williston Seminary, at East Hampton, Massachusetts. Northampton: Printed by John Metcalf, 1845. MA; MHi. 45-6940

Willoughby University. Annual catalogue and circular of the Willoughby University. Painesville, Ohio: Printed by Charles B. Smythe, 1845. 16 p. OC. 45-6941

Willson, Marcius, 1813-1905. Accompaniment to the "Comprehensive chart of American history." Designed to aid in learning the outlines of the history, and in lecturing from the chart. New York: C. Bartlett, 1845. 12 p. DLC; MB. 45-6942

Willson, Marcius, 1813-1905. A critical review of American common school his-

tories: as embraced in a report submitted to the "New Jersey Society of Teachers and Friends of Education" at a quarterly meeting held March 7, 1845. n.p. [1845] 32 p. OClWHi; NjR; NRAB; RP. 45-6943

Willson, Marcius, 1813-1905. History of the United States. New York: Mark H. Newman and company, 1845. 376 p. FLh; NGrp; OTifH; RPB; TxD-T. 45-6944

Willson, Marcius, 1813-1905. A treatise on civil polity and politcal economy; with an appendix containing a brief account of the powers, duties and salaries of national, state, county and town officers. For the use of schools and academies. New York: W.K. Cornwell, 1845. 299 p. DLC; OMC. 45-6945

Wilmington Boarding School for Girls. Circular of the institution, and catalogue of teachers and pupils. Wilmington, Delaware, 1845. 23 p. PPM. 45-6946

Wilson, Caroline Fry, 1787-1846. Sabbath musings. New York: Carter, 1845. 248 p. CtY; OC; PPL. 45-6947

Wilson, Daniel, 1778-1858. The evidences of christianity; stated in a popular and practical manner, in a course of lectures, delivered in the parish church of St. Mary, Islington. Fifth edition, revised. Boston: Crocker and Brewster; New York: J. Leavitt, 1845. 2 v. MB; MiGr; NNUT; ODW; OO. 45-6948

Wilson, Daniel, 1778-1858. The inspiration of the Holy Scriptures extracted from the evidences of Christianity. Boston: Tract Committee of the Diocese of Massachusetts, 1845. 28 p. IEG; MB; RPB. 45-6949

Wilson, John, 1785-1854. Foresters; a tale of domestic life. Boston: Saxton and Kelt, 1845. 282 p. InCW; KEmC; MB; Nh; WMMD. 45-6950

Wilson, John, 1785-1854. The genius and character of Burns. New York: Wiley and Putnam, 1845. 222 p. CU; IaDu; LNH; NhD; RJa. 45-6951

Wilson, John, 1785-1854. Lights and shadows of Scottish life. New York, 1845. MH. 45-6952

Wilson, John, 1785-1854. The trials of Margaret Lyndsay. Boston: Saxton and Kelt; New York: Saxton and Miles, 1845. 4, 264 p. InEvW; MB; MHi; Nh; MWey. 45-6953

Wilson, John, 1802-1868. The concessions of trinitarians. Being a selection of extracts from the writings of the most eminent biblical critics and commentators. Boston: Munroe and company, 1845. 614 p. CBPac; DLC; MNoanNP. 45-6954

Wilson, John Lyde, 1784-1849. The code of honor... in dwelling. Charleston: Printed by S.S. Miller, 1845. CSmH; DLC; GU; MiU-C; NBu. 45-6955

Wilson, Joshua Lacy, 1774-1846. A sermon on witchcraft, delivered in the First Presbyterian Church, Cincinnati, November 9, 1845. Cincinnati: Ben Franklin Printing House, 1845. 23 p. ICP; MH-AH; MHi; OMC; PPPrHi. 45-6956

Wilson, Thomas, Sacra privata: the private meditations, devotions, and prayers of the Rt. Rev. Thomas Wilson, Lord Bishop of Sodor and Man, accommodated to general use. New York:

Henry M. Oderdonk, 1845. 134 p. PU-S; WGr. 45-6957

Wiltbank, John, 1804-1860. Valedictory address to the graduating class of the medical department of Pennsylvania College, for the session of 1844-1845. Philadelphia: Printed by Getz and Smith, 1845. 15, [1] p. DLC; N; MH-AH; PLT; PPHa. 45-6958

Wimer's canadisches burmmittel. Fin rasches, sicheres und wirksames mittel gegen. New York, [1845] TxU. 45-6959

Windham, William, 1750-1810. Select speeches of the right honourable William Windham and the Right Honourable William Huskisson: with preliminary biographical sketches. Edited by Robert Walsh. Philadelphia: E.C. and J. Biddle, 1845. 616 p. MiDU; NB; ScNC; ViRu; WHi. 45-6960

Windham County Association of Congregational Ministers. Windham County, Connecticut. A letter from the associated ministers of the county of Windham, to the people in the several societies in said county. Boston: N.E. Printed by J. Draper, 1845. 52 p. DLC. 45-6961

Winer, Georg Benedikt, 1789-1858. Grammar of the Chaldee language, as contained in the Bible and the Targuana... Translated from the German by H.B. Hacket... Andover: Allen Morrill, and Wardwell; New York: M.H. Newman, 1845. 152 p. IEG; MAnP; OO; PPP; ViRut. 45-6962

Wing, C.P. Strength of character, an address before the literary societies of Jackson College, Columbia, Tennessee, August 13, 1845. Columbia: Printed by

Rosboroughs and Kidd, 1845. 23 p. T. 45-6963

Wing, Joel A. An address before the Medical Society of the state of New York. Albany: Printed by Munsell and Tanner, 1845. 34 p. N; DNLM; NjR. 45-6964

Winnisimmet Company. Communications between a meeting of citizens in Chelsea and the directors of the Winnisimmet Company, relative to the ferry. Boston: S.N. Dickinson and company, 1845. 36 p. MBNEH. 45-6965

Winslow, Forbes Benignus, 1810-1874. Physics and physicians; a medical sketch book, exhibiting the public and private life of the most celebrated medical men of former days; with memoirs of eminent living London physicians and surgeons. Philadelphia: G.B. Zieber and company, 1845. 2 v. in 1. CSt-L; ICU; LN; NjP; OClW. 45-6966

Winthrop, Robert Charles, 1809-1894. An address delivered before the Boston Mercantile Library Association, on the occasion of their twenty-fifth anniversary, October 15, 1845. Boston: Marvin, 1845. 38 p. IEN-M; MdHi; MWiW; PHi; RPB. 45-6967

Winthrop, Robert Charles, 1809-1894. Speech of Mr. Winthrop, of Massachusetts, on the annexation of Texas, delivered in the House, January 6, 1845. Washington, 1845. 16 p. ICU; MBAt; MHi; NjR; WHi. 45-6968

Winthrop, Robert Charles, 1809-1894. Speech of Mr. Winthrop, of Massachusetts, on the Oregon question. Delivered in the House, February 1,

1845. Washington: J. and G.S. Gideon, printers, 1845. 16 p. CU; IaGG; MH; NjR; PHi. 45-6969

Wirt, William, 1772-1834. Sketches of the life and character of Patrick Henry. Hartford: S. Andrus and son, 1845. 468 p. OCLaw; ODay; NjMD. 45-6970

Wirt, William, 1772-1834. Sketches of the life and character of Patrick Henry. Revised edition. Ithaca, New York: Mack, Andrus and company, 1845. IU; MNe; MTop; NIDHi; ViU. 45-6971

Wirt, William, 1772-1834. Sketches of the life and character of Patrick Henry. Ninth edition, corrected by the author. Philadelphia: Thomas, Cowperthwait and company, 1845. 19-468 p. MoKiW; NjP; ODa; ScRhW; ViU. 45-6972

Wirt, William, 1772-1834. Sketches of the life and character of Patrick Henry. Tenth edition, corrected by the author. Hartford: S. Andrus and son, 1845. 19-468 p. ICLaw; IU; MiU; NJost; WOsh. 45-6973

Wisconsin. Annual report of the register and receiver of the Milwaukee and Rock River Canal. [Madison, 1845] 3 p. WHi. 45-6974

Wisconsin. Communication from the governor on the subject of university lands. In council, February 13, 1845. [Madison, 1845] 8 p. WHi. 45-6975

Wisconsin. Communication from the secretary of the territory, January 31, 1845, [relating to the money appropriated by congress for the expenses of the territory] [Madison, 1845] 2 p. WHi; WM. 45-6976

Wisconsin. Communication of Mortimer M. Jackson, attorney general of the territory, in relation to the Bank of Wisconsin. [Madison, 1845] 2 p. WHi; WM. 45-6977

Wisconsin. Journal of the council. Third annual session of the fourth legislative assembly, of the territory of Wisconsin, held in Madison. Madison: Simon Mills, printer, 1845. 438 p. ICU; IN; MH; WBeloC; WGr; WHi. 45-6978

Wisconsin. Journal of the House, of the fourth legislative assembly of the Wisconsin Territory, being the third session, begun and held at Madison, on January 6, 1845. Madison: W.T. Simeon Mills, Territorial printer, 1845. 480 p. ICU; IU; In; WGr; WHi. 45-6979

Wisconsin. Laws of the Wisconsin Territory, passed by the fourth legislative assembly. Madison: W.T. Simeon Mills, 1845. 133 p. In-SC; KU; MWCL; R; WMMU-L. 45-6980

Wisconsin. Message [purporting to be by] His Excellency, the governor of the people, delivered in the House, at Madison, February 12, 1845. [Madison, 1845] 8 p. WHi. 45-6981

Wisconsin. Report of Joshua Hathaway, special agent to receive and disburse the distributive share of Wisconsin in the net proceeds of public lands, under joint resolution of April 17, 1843. [December 31, 1844] House, January 10, 1845. [Madison, 1845] 3 p. WHi; WM. 45-6982

Wisconsin. Report of superintendent of territorial property. Wisconsin Territory,

House, January 10, 1845. [Madison: Argus office, 1845] 15 p. WHi. 45-6983

Wisconsin. Report of the adjutant general for the year 1844. [Madison, 1845] 3 p. WHi. 45-6984

Wisconsin. Report of the auditor of the territory. Register of claims against the territory as per act of the legislative assembly approved January 31, 1844. [Madison, 1845] 10 p. WHi; WM. 45-6985

Wisconsin. Report of the committee appointed to examine the accounts of the treasurer of the territory, and to cancel evidences of debts redeemed by and in his hands. Reported in council and ordered to be printed, February 6, 1845. [Madison, 1845] 5 p. WHi. 45-6986

Wisconsin. Report of the committee of the judiciary on the message of the governor, in closing the communication of the commissioner of Indian affairs. House, January 15, 1845. [Madison, 1845] 3 p. WHi. 45-6987

Wisconsin. Report of the committee on incorporations to whom was referred a memorial from the president, directors, and company of the Bank of Milwaukee. In council, February 5, 1845. [Madison, 1845] 5 p. WHi; WM. 45-6988

Wisconsin. Report of the committee on internal improvements, [relative to the sale of canal lands] House, February 6, 1845. 5 p. WHi. 45-6989

Wisconsin. Report of the committee on internal improvements under a resolution of the House, passed January 21, 1845, [relating to the Milwaukee and

Rock River Canal] House, February 1, 1845. [Madison, 1845] 29 p. WHi. 45-6990

Wisconsin. Report of the committee on roads, upon that part of the governor's message relative to roads, which was referred to them; and also, upon the petition of citizens of Racine County for the incorporation of a company to construct a turnpike or plank road from Southport to Beloit. In council, February 6, 1845. [Madison, 1845] 9 p. WHi. 45-6991

Wisconsin. Report of the committee on territorial affairs, relative to the formation of a new county from the counties of Jefferson and Dodge. In council, February 15, 1845. [Madison, 1845] 2 p. WHi. 45-6992

Wisconsin. Report of the committee on territorial expenditures relative to the petition of supervisors of Walworth County. [Madison, 1845] 3 p. WHi; WM. 45-6993

Wisconsin. Report of the committee on the judiciary of the Mississippi Marine and Fire Insurance Company. [Madison, 1845] 8 p. WHi. 45-6994

Wisconsin. Report of the minority of the committee on corporations, to which was referred a resolution concerning the Wisconsin Marine and Fire Insurance Company. By Mr. Ellis. [Madison, 1845] 33 p. WHi. 45-6995

Wisconsin. Report of the secretary of Wisconsin. [Madison, 1845] 8 p. WHi; WM. 45-6996

Wisconsin. Report of the select committee appointed to ascertain the ex-pediency and practicability of constructing a railroad from Milwaukee to Potosi. In council, February 12, 1845. [Madison, 1845] 3 p. WHi. 45-6997

Wisconsin. Report of the select committee on the subject of a penitentiary, House, February 6, 1845. [Madison, 1845] 2 p. WHi. 45-6998

Wisconsin. Report of the superintendent of territorial property. [For the year 1844] [Madison, 1845] 15 p. WHi. 45-6999

Wisconsin. Report of the treasurer of the territory of Wisconsin. [Madison, 1845] 8 p. WHi; WM. 45-7000

Wisconsin. Rules for the government of the council, of the Wisconsin Territory. Adopted at a session of the legislature commenced January 6, 1845. Madison: Printed tha the Wisconsin Argus office, 1845. 11 p. WHi. 45-7001

Wise, Daniel, 1813-1898. The cottage on the moor; or the evils of pride. By a Methodist preacher. New York: Lane and Tippett, 1845. 126 p. DLC; NN. 45-7002

Wise, Daniel, 1813-1898. The infant teacher's manual; for the use of Sunday schools and families. Containing fifty-two scripture lessons for infants, with hymns. New York: Carlton and Porter, [1845] 229 p. IEG; OCamb; OSW. 45-7003

Wise, Daniel, 1813-1898. The M'Gregor family. By a Methodist preacher. Revised by the editor, D.P. Kidder. New York: G. Lane and C.B.

Tippett, 1845. 119 p. NN; NNMHi. 45-7004

Wise, Daniel, 1813-1898. Personal effort explained and enforced. Fourth edition, enlarged. New York: Lane and Tippett, 1845. 96 p. CtY-D; IEG. 45-7005

Withington, Leonard. Penitential tears; or a cry from the dust, by the thirty-one, prostrated and pulverized by the hand of Horace Mann. Boston: S. Stimpton, 1845. 59 p. ICU; MB; NIC; PU; RPB. 45-7006

Woburn, Massachusetts. Order of exercises at the consecration of the Woburn Cemetery. [Woburn, Massachusetts] Printed by William White, NN. 45-7007

Wolff, Joseph, 1795-1862. Narrative of a mission to Bokhara, in the years 1843-1845, to ascertain the fate of Colonel Stoddart and Captain Conolly. New York: Harper and brothers, 1845. 24-384 p. IaDa; KyDC; MdBP; PPAN; WM. 45-7008

Wolley, Charles. A two years journal in New York and part of its territories in America. New York: W. Gowan, 1845. 97 p. CLU. 45-7009

Woman of Sychar Jesus and the woman of Sychar. Written for the Massachusetts Sabbath School Society, and revised by the committee of publication, 1845. 54 p. NoLoc. 45-7010

Wood, Alphonso, 1810-1881. A class book of botany, designed for colleges, academies, and other seminaries where the science is taught. In two parts. Part 1. The elements of botanical science. Part 2. The natural orders... Boston: Crocker

and Brewster, 1845. 124, 474 p. CtMW; GU; MBAt; NjP; RPB. 45-7011

Wood, Alphonso, 1810-1881. A class book of botany, designed for colleges, academies, and other seminaries where the science is taught. In two parts. Part 1. The elements of botanical science. Part 2. The natural orders... Boston: Crocker and Brewster, 1845. 645 p. PBa; PPHa; VtU. 45-7012

Wood, George Bacon, 1797-1879. Introductory lecture to the course of materia medica in the University of Pennsylvania, delivered November 3, 1845. Philadelphia: Printed by John Young, 1845. 21 p. CSt-L; NNNAM; PHi; PPL; PPM; PU. 45-7013

Wood, James, 1799-1867. Old and new theology, or an exhibition of those differences with regard to scripture, doctrines, which have recently agitated and now divided the Prebyterian Church. Philadelphia, Presbyterian board of publication, 1845. 343 p. DLC; ICP; NCH; PWW; ScU. 45-7014

Wood, James, 1799-1867. Old and new theology, or an exhibition of those differences with regard to scripture, doctrines, which have recently agitated and now divided the Prebyterian Church. Second edition. Philadelphia, Presbyterian board of publication, 1845. 343 p. CSt; NcMHi; P; PPPrHi; PPL. 45-7015

Wood, James, 1799-1867. Old and new theology, or an exhibition of those differences with regard to scripture, doctrines, which have recently agitated and now divided the Prebyterian Church. Second edition. Philadelphia, Presbyterian board of publication, 1845. 343, 95 p. CSt; P; TxHR. 45-7016

Wood, John N.B. The rights of infants to christian baptism. A sermon preached in the Methodist Episcopal Church, Tarrytown. New York: Piercy and Reed, printers, 1845. 24 p. LNB. 45-7017

Woodbridge, William Channing, 1794-1845. He hoikehonua, he mea ia e hoakaka'i i ke ano o ka honua nei, a me na mea maluna iho. Oahu: Mea pai palapala a na misionari, 1845. 197 p. CtY; ICN; MiU; MH; NN. 45-7018

Woodbridge, William Channing, 1794-1845. Modern school geography, on the plan of comparison and classification; with an atlas. With improvements and additions. Second edition. Hartford: Belknap and Hamersley, 1845. [26]-350 p. ICU; MB; NNC; RPB; TxU-T. 45-7019

Woodbridge, William Channing, 1794-1845. System of modern geography, on the principles of comparison and classification and accompanied by an atlas. Improved edition. Hartford: Belknap and Hamersley, 1845. 474 p. CtHWatk; MeHi; MoS; MoSpD; MsJS. 45-7020

Woodbury, Isaac Baker, 1819-1858. The elements of musical composition and thorough bass... Boston: Charles H. Keith, 1845. 139 p. MeBat; NNUT; RP. 45-7021

Woodbury, Levi, 1789-1851. The annual address delivered before the National Institute, in the hall of the House... Washington: J. and G.S. Gideon, printers, 1845. 35 p. Ct; LNH; MdHi; NCH; PPL. 45-7022

Woodbury, Levi, 1789-1851. Eulogy on the life and character of General Andrew Jackson, pronounced by L. Woodbury, in the Universal Church. Portsmouth, New Hampshire, on July 2, 1845. Portsmouth: Printed at the Portsmouth Mercury office, 1845. 11 p. MW; Nh-Hi; P. 45-7023

Woodbury, Levi, 1789-1851. Speech of Mr. Woodbury of New Hampshire, on the annexation of Texas: delivered in the Senate of the United States, February 17, 1845. Washington: Printed at the Globe office, 1845. 13 p. Nh; Nh-Hi; P. 45-7024

Woodlands Cemetery Company, Philadelphia. The charter, bylaws and regulations of the Woodlands Cemetery Company. Philadelphia: Printed by T. and G. Town, 1845. 8 p. MH; PHi; PPM. 45-7025

Woodruff, George Catlin, 1805-1885. History of the town of Litchfield, Connecticut. Litchfield: C. Adams, 1845. 64 p. CtSoP; ICN; MH; PHi; RPB. 45-7026

Wooler, John Pratt, 1824-1868. A man without a head: a farce, in one act. New York: Samuel French, [1845?] 16 p. NjP; OCl. 45-7027

Woollen manufactories in the United States, statistics. By the proprietor of the condensing cards. New York, 1845. NNA. 45-7028

Woolman, John, 1720-1772. A journal of the life, gospel labours and Christian experiences, of that faithful minister of Jesus Christ, John Woolman, to which are added, his last epistle, and other writings. New York: Collins, brother and company; New Bedford: W.C. Taber and son, 1845. 309 p. KKcBT; MH; MoS; NBF; OO. 45-7029

Woolman, John, 1720-1772. A journal of the life, gospel labours and Christian experiences, of that faithful minister of Jesus Christ, John Woolman, to which are added, his last epistle, and other writings. Philadelphia, 1845. 372 p. InRchE; MiU; NNUT; PSC-Hi; TxH. 45-7030

Woolsey, Elijah. The supernumerary; or lights and shadows of itinerancy. Compiled from papers of Elijah Woolsey by Rev. G. Coles. New York: Lane and Tippett, 1845. 164 p. IEG; NjMD; NNMHi; OrSaW; PPM. 45-7031

The wooly bear. Revised by the editor, D.P. Kidder. New York: Lane and Tippett, 1845. 8 p. CtY. 45-7032

Worcester, Joseph Emerson, 1784-1865. Ancient, classical and scripture altas. Improved edition. Boston: Phillips and Sampson, [1845?] DLC. 45-7033

Worcester, Joseph Emerson, 1784-1865. Comprehensive pronouncing and explanatory dictionary of the English language; with pronouncing vocabularies of classical, scripture, and modern geographical names. Carefully revised and enlarged. Boston: Jenks and Palmer, 1845. 424 p. MiU; MnCollS; NNC. 45-7034

Worcester, Joseph Emerson, 1784-1865. An elementary dictionary for common schools; with pronouncing vocabularies of classical, scripture, and modern geographical names. Boston: Jenks and Palmer, 1845. 324 p. CtHWatk; LU; MB; MW; NcAS. 45-7035

Worcester, Joseph Emerson, 1784-1865. Elements of history, ancient and modern, with historical charts. Boston: W.J. Reynolds, 1845. 386 p. ICU; MH; NN; ScCMu; ViU. 45-7036

Worcester, Joseph Emerson, 1784-1865. Worcester's modern atlas. Boston: Phillips and Sampson, [1845] MH. 45-7037

Worcester, Noah, 1812-1847. A synopsis of the symptoms, diagnosis and treatment of the more common and important diseases of the skin. Philadelphia: Thomas, Cowperthwait and company; Boston: Little and Brown; Cincinnati: Desilver and Burr, 1845. 290 P. CSt-L; Gu-M; NNN; ScSp; TU-M. 45-7038

Worcester, Samuel, 1793-1844. The fourth book of lessons for reading, with rules and instructions. Stereotype edition. Boston: C.J. Hendee and Jenks and Palmer, 1845. 408 p. CtHWatk; MH; MLaw; Nh-Hi; OO. 45-7039

Worcester, Samuel, 1793-1844. An introduction to the third book for reading and spelling. Boston: Charles J. Hendee, and Jenks and Palmer, 1845. 216 p. MH; NNC. 45-7040

Worcester, Samuel, 1793-1844. The second book for reading and spelling. New edition. Boston: Jenks and Palmer, 1845. 142 p. CtHWatk; MH; MLow; NNC. 45-7041

Worcester, Samuel, 1793-1844. The third book for reading and spelling, with simple rules and instructions for avoiding common errors... One hundred and seventh edition. Boston: Charles J. Hendee, and Jenks and Palmer, 1845. 246 p. MBoy; MH; MLow; MPeHi. 45-7042

Worcester, Samuel, 1793-1844. Third book of lessons for reading. Boston, 1845. CtHWatk. 45-7043

Worcester, Samuel H. A letter to the receivers of the heavenly doctrines of the New Jerusalem. Boston: Otis Clapp, 1845. 21 p. MCNC. 45-7044

Worcester, Samuel Thomas, 1804-1882. Sequel to the spelling book. Eighth edition. Boston: J. Munroe and company, 1845. CtHWatk; MH. 45-7045

A word in season to all churchmen in the diocese of New York who love the church and depricate schism. n.p. [1845] 8 p. N. 45-7046

Worcester, Massachusetts. Bylaws of the Worcester Guards. Revised, May, 1845. Worcester: Printed by Joseph Richards, 1845. 8 p. MWHi. 45-7047

Worcester, Massachusetts. First Church. Members of the church. [n.p.] 1845. 4 p. MW. 45-7048

Worcester, Massachusetts. Reports submitted to the town of Worcester at an annual March meeting, 1845: and the bylaws of the town. Worcester: Printed by Henry J. Howland, 1845. 22 p. MWHi. 45-7049

Worcester, Massachusetts. Rules and regulations for the government and discipline of the schools of Worcester. Adopted, 1845. Worcester, [1845] 15 p. DHEW; RPB. 45-7050

Worcester Agricultural Society.

Premiums, rules and regulations. Worcester: Printed by Thomas W. Butterfield, 1845. 16 p. MWHi. 45-7051

Worcester Agricultural Society. Premiums, rules and regulations. New edition. Worcester: printed by Thomas W. Butterfield, 1845. 16 p. MH. 45-7052

Worcester and Nashua Railroad Company. Report of surveys of railroad routes, between Worcester and Nashua. Boston: Eastburn's Press, 1845. 57 p. DBRE. 45-7053

Worcester and Nashua Railroad Company. Statement of facts concerning the sources of business of the intended railroad from Worcester, Massachusetts to Nashua, New Hampshire, and an estimate of its probable cost. [Signed by T.W. Bancroft and Edwin Conant] Worcester: H.J. Howland, 1845. 28 p. IU; MB. 45-7054

Worcester Association of Ministers, Worcester, Massachusetts. A catechism in three parts. Compiled and recommended by the ministers of the association. Twelfth edition. Boston: S.G. Simpkins, 1845. 54 p. MH. 45-7055

Wraxall, Nathaniel William, 1751-1831. Historical memoirs of my own time. Philadelphia: Lea and Blanchard, 1845. 524 p. DLC; GU; NjR; OrU; PPL. 45-7056

Wraxall, Nathaniel William, 1751-1831. Posthumous memoirs of his own time. From the second London edition. Philadelphia: Lea and Blanchard, 1845. 5-419 p. MdBJ; OO; PHi; RPaw; Vi. 45-7057

The wreath, a selection of elegant poems from the best authors. New York: Printed by Collier and company, 1845. 188 p. NRU. 45-7058

Wrentham, Massachusetts. Original Congregational Church. Historical sketch, articles of faith and covenants of the original congregational Church in Wrentham. With a catalogue of its officers and present members. April 13, 1845. Boston: Dickinson, 1845. 24 p. ICN; MH; MWA; NN; WHi. 45-7059

Wrentham, Massachusetts. Original Congregational Church. Manual. Boston, 1845. 24 p. MBC. 45-7060

Wright, Albert D. Elements of the English language; or analytical orthography. Designed to teach the philosophy of orthography and orthoepy adapted to schools. Fourth edition enlarged and improved. Cazenovia, New York: Henry Hitchcock and company, 1845. 126 p. MH; MoKU; OO; RPB; WHi. 45-7061

Wright, Asher, 1803-1875. Historia de los limites del rio de la plata, islas martin Garcia y Timoteo Dominguez... Cattaraugus Reservation: New York, 1845? CtY. 45-7062

Wright, Asher, 1803-1875. Non da dyu e gi gaa nab. Do syo wah ga nok da yah, Tgaisda ni yont, nis ah 24th, 1845. Donation hymn. [Seneca Mission, 1845] Broadside. ICN. 45-7063

Wright, Caleb. A lecture on the condition of women in pagan and Mohometan countries... Troy, New York, 1845. 28 p. IaJ; MBC; MoS; NN; OClWHi. 45-7064

Wright, Daniel. Correspondence between Rev. Daniel Wright, Jr. and Hon. John B. Turner. Boston, 1845. 78 p. MBC. 45-7065

Wright, David, 1806-1877. The executor's administrator's and guardian's guide. Being a collection of... together with various decisions bearing upon the management of estates, and forms of deeds, bonds, orders, etc. Compiled by a clerk of the Court of Ordinary. Columbus, Georgia: Enquirer office, 1845. 102 p. DLC; MH-L; N; NHuntL. 45-7066

Wright, Elizur, 1804-1885. A poem before the Phi Beta Kappa Society in Yale College, August 20, 1845. New Haven, 1845. 20 p. MH; MHi; NBuG; OO. 45-7067

Wright, Elizur, 1804-1885. Total abstinence life insurance. Sir: your attention is respectfully invited to the following remarks, the subject of which may be of interest to some of your friends, if not to yourself. [Boston? 1845?] 4 p. MiU-C. 45-7068

Wright, J. Hall. Ocean work, ancient and modern; or evenings on sea and land. New York: D. Appleton and company; Philadelphia: George S. Appleton; Cincinnati: H.W. Derby and company, 1845. 168 p. ICP; MLow; MNBedf; PPFrankI. 45-7069

Wright, Marmaduke Burr, 1803-1879. A lecture on drunkedness and insanity... Cincinnati, 1845. 20 p. MBMS; N; OCHP; OClWHi; WU-M. 45-7070

Wright, William Henry, 1813?-1845. Brief practical treatise on mortars; with an account of the processes employed at the public works in Boston Harbor. Boston: William D. Ticknor and company, 1845. 148 p. CoD; Ia; MB; MoSM; NjR. 45-7071

Wyatt, William Edward, 1789-1864. Morning visits to the rector's study. On baptism. New York, [1845?] 32 p. NNG. 45-7072

Wyatt, William Edward, 1789-1864. The parting spirit's address to his mother. Second edition. Baltimore: Carey, Hart and company, 1845. 27 p. MdBD. 45-7073

Wyatt, William Edward, 1789-1864. The parting spirit's address to his mother. Fourth edition. New York: Stanford and Swords, 1845. 28 p. MdBD; NN. 45-7074

Wylie, Andrew, 1789-1851. Baccalaureate... president of Indiana University, address to the senior class, at the late commencement, September, 1845. Bloomington, Indiana: C. Davisson, printer, 1845. 18 p. ICMe; InU; PPPrHi. 45-7075

Wylie, Samuel B. Memorial of professor of languages in the University of Pennsylvania. Philadelphia, 1845. Broadside. PPL. 45-7076

Wyman, Morrill, 1812-1903. A practical treatise on ventilation. Boston: J. Munroe, 1845. DLC; ICJ; MH; NN; WaU. 45-7077

Wyoming. A tale. New York: Harper and brothers, 1845. 123 p. MB; MH; MnU; NjR; NN. 45-7078

Wythe, Joseph Henry, 1822-1901. Sketch of a sermon on temperance. Philadelphia, 1845. 12 p. PPPrHi. 45-7079

X-Y-Z

Xenophon. Anabasis. Translated by Edward Spelman. New York: Harper and brothers, 1845. 2 v. LN. 45-7080

Xenophon. Anabasis of Xenophon; chiefly according to the text of L. Dindorf; with notes; for the use of schools and colleges. By John J. Owen. Fifth edition. New York: Leavitt, Trow and company, 1845. 368 p. CoU; MnSM; NNC; ODa; TxU. 45-7081

Xenophon. The Cyropaedia, translated by the Hon. Maurice Ashly Cooper. New York: Harper, 1845. 2 v. CtHT; LShC; ODa. 45-7082

Xenophon. Expedition of Cyrus, with English notes, prepared for the use of schools and colleges, with a life of the author, by Charles Dexter Cleveland. Boston: Mussey, 1845. 306 p. GU; MeB; MH; MoKCC. 45-7083

Xenophon. The whole works of Xenophon, translated by Ashley Cooper, Spelman, Smith, Fielding and others. Philadelphia: T. Wardle, 1845. 758 p. CU; DLC; NcU; OOxM; PPA. 45-7084

Xenophon. Works translated by Edward Spelman. New York: Harper and brothers, 1845. 2 v. KOtU; NN; ViU. 45-7085

Yale University. Catalogue of the officers and students, 1845. New Haven, 1845. PPC; PPCP. 45-7086

Yale University. Catalogue of the officers and students in Yale College, 1845-1846. New Haven: Printed by B.L. Hamlin, 1845. 40 p. Ct; KHi; MeHi; MoS; ViU. 45-7087

Yale University. A poem, by Guy Bigelow Day; and the valedictory oration by Thomas Kirby Davis, before the senior class of Yale College. New Haven: Printed by B.L. Hamlen, 1845. 40 p. CtY. 45-7088

Yancey, William Lowndes, 1814-1865. Oration on the life and character of Andrew Jackson, delivered at their request before the citizens, of Wetumpka, Alabama, on July 11, 1845. Wetumpka: Printed by B.B. Moore, 1845. 16 p. NN; PPL; RPB. 45-7089

Yancey, William Lowndes, 1814-1865. Speech on the annexation of Texas to the United States in the House. n.p.: Harris and Heart, printers, 1845. 14 p. A-Ar; ICN; MdBJ; NjR; TxD-T. 45-7090

The Yankees in Fairfax County, Virginia. By a Virginian. Republished from the Richmond Virginia Whig. Baltimore: Snodgrass and Wehrly, 1845. 24 p. MdBJ; MdHi; MoSM. 45-7091

Yellott, George. Letter to a tax payer [of Hartford County] in relation to the completion of the Chesapeake and Ohio Canal. Baltimore, 1845. MdBP. 45-7092

Youatt, William, 1776-1847. The horse. A new edition. With numerous illustrations together with a general history of the horse... Philadelphia: Porter and Coates, [1845] CtW; IaDam; MdBP; TxU; ViU. 45-7093

Young, Alexander, 1800-1854. A discourse on the sins of the tongue, delivered in the church on Church Green. Boston: Charles C. Little and James Brown, 1845. 32 p. ICMe; MWA; PPL. 45-7094

Young, Alexander, 1800-1854. A discourse on the sins of the tongue, delivered in the church on Church Green. Second edition. Boston: Charles C. Little and James Brown, 1845. 29 p. MH-AH; MWA. 45-7095

Young, Alexander, 1800-1854. A discourse on the sins of the tongue, delivered in the church on Church Green. Third edition. Boston: Charles C. Little and James Brown, 1845. 32 p. MBAU; MiD-B; MWA; NNG. 45-7096

Young, Alexander, 1800-1854. A discourse on the twentieth anniversary of his ordination. Delivered in the church on Church Green. Boston: Charles C. Little and James Brown, 1845. 32 p. CtSoP; ICMe; MB; OClWHi; RPB. 45-7097

Young, Alexander, 1800-1854. Discourses on various occasions. Boston: C. Little and J. Brown, 1845. MH; MNan; RPB. 45-7098

Young, Alexander, 1800-1854. The good merchant. A discourse occasioned by the death of William Parsons, delivered in the church on Church

Green, March 26, 1837. Boston: Little and Brown, 1845. 30 p. ICN; ICMe; MB. 45-7099

Young, Alexander, 1800-1854. The good merchant. A discourse occasioned by the death of William Parsons, delivered in the church on Church Green, March 26, 1837. Second edition. Boston: Little and Brown, 1845. ICN; MeB; MH; NNC; OClWHi. 45-7100

Young, Andrew White, 1802-1877. First lessons in civil government; including a comprehensive view of the government of the state of New York, and an abstract of the laws, with an outline of the government of the United States. Fourth edition. Auburn, 1845. CtHWatk. 45-7101

Young, Andrew White, 1802-1877. First lessons in civil government; including a comprehensive view of the government of the state of New York, and an abstract of the laws, with an outline of the government of the United States. [Fifth edition] Auburn: H. and J.C. Ivison, 1845. MH; NWatt. 45-7102

Young, Andrew White, 1802-1877. First lessons in civil government; including a comprehensive view of the government of the state of New York, and an abstract of the laws, with an outline of the government of the United States. Sixth edition. Auburn: H. and J.C. Ivison, 1845. O; ViRu. 45-7103

Young, Andrew White, 1802-1877. First lessons in civil government; including a comprehensive view of the government of the state of New York, and an abstract of the laws, with an outline of the government of the United States. Eighth edition. Auburn: H. and J.C. Ivison, 1845. 235 p. DLC. 45-7104

Young, Andrew White, 1802-1877. Introduction of the science of government, and compend of the constitutional and civil jurisprudence of the United States, with a brief treatise on political economy. Thirteenth edition. Rochester: William Alling, 1845. 336 p. CLO; TCSPr; TChFPr. 45-7105

Young, Andrew White, 1802-1877. The young American statesman: a political history, exhibiting the origin, nature and practical operation of constitutional government in the United States. New York: Derby and Jackson, 1845. 1018 p. MiSH. 45-7106

Young, Augustus. Unity of purpose; being a treatise designed to elicit investigation, with the view to eradicate and expel from science certain popular errors... [Johnson, Vermont: The author, 1845] 16 p. DLC. 45-7107

Young, David. The Whig almanack and politician's register, for 1845. By David Young. Canandaigua: H.O. Hayes and company, 1845. 64 p. NCanHi. 45-7108

Young, Edward, 1683-1765. The complaint and consolation, or night thoughts. life, death, and immortality. To which is added, the force of religion. Boston: Phillips and Sampson, 1845. 288 p. MoCgSV; NN. 45-7109

Young, Edward, 1683-1765. The complaint: or night thoughts. Concord, New Hampshire: Morrill, 1845. 200 p. CtHT; MiOC. 45-7110

Young, Edward, 1683-1765. The complaint: or night thoughts. Hartford: Andrus and son, 1845. 324 p. AAP; C-S; DLC; NcD; OCl. 45-7111

Young, Edward, 1683-1765. The complaint: or night thoughts. Philadelphia: Uriah Hunt and son, 1845. 326 p. IaAS; LNT; NN; OClWHi; ViU. 45-7112

Young, James, of New Jersey. A general view of the use of wine in the last passover and the atonement and suffering of Jesus. Paterson, New Jersey: T. Warren, printer, 1845. 50 p. N; NN. 45-7113

Young, James Hamilton, b. 1793. Tourist's pocket map of Pennsylvania. Philadelphia: S. Augustus Mitchell, 1845. 1 p. PHi. 45-7114

Young, James Hamilton, b. 1793. Tourist's pocket map of the state of Kentucky, exhibiting its internal improvements, roads, distances, etc. Philadelphia: Mitchell, 1845. 1 p. PHi; PU. 45-7115

Young, John. The pulpit and platform, being discourses, arguments and orations. Lexington, Kentucky: A.W. Elder, printer, 1845. 233 p. NcWilA. 45-7116

Young, L.H. Historical cabinet. Hartford: Ezra Strong, [1845] 516 p. OkPo. 45-7117

Young, Narragansett, pseud. Hon. Elisha R. Potter. An address to the people of Rhode Island upon the course of the Hon. Elisha R. Potter in the House of Representatives of the United States upon the question of the annexation of Texas; with an outline of the proceedings of the convention at which he was nominated for re-election. [Washington? 1845?] 8 p. CU-B. 45-7118

Young, Samuel, b. 1821. The smoky city: a tale of crime... Pittsburgh: Printed by A.A. Anderson, 1845. 204 p. DLC; KEmT; NNC. 45-7119

Young, William B. An arithmetical dictionary, or book of reference: comprising a system of practical tables. Likewise embracing a system of practical arithmetic. Second edition. New York: Casper C. Childs, 1845. 224 p. IaFayU. 45-7120

Young American's library. No. 1. The Primer. New York: Wiley and Putnam, 1845. 54 p. NNC. 45-7121

Young forester; a narrative of the early life of a christian missionary. Boston: Massachusetts Sunday School Society, 1845. VtMidbC. 45-7122

Young Ladies Institute, Pittsfield, Massachusetts. Fourth annual catalogue of the instructors and pupils... August, 1845. Pittsfield, Massachusetts: Charles Montague, 1845. 12 p. NRivHi. 45-7123

The young lady's own book. A manual of intellectual improvement and moral deportment. Philadelphia: Uriah Hunt and son, 1845. 320 p. CLSU; MdU; NcGU; NIC; PHi. 45-7124

Young man, or guide to knowledge, virtue and happiness. Lowell: Dayton, 1845. 224 p. MH; OO. 45-7125

The young man's own book: a manual of politeness, intellectual improvement, and moral deportment, calculated to form the character on a solid basis, and to insure respectability and success in life. Philadelphia: Uriah Hunt and son,

1845. 320 p. MPeHI; OO; PWaybu. 45-7126

Youth's almanac, for the year 1846, astronomical calculations by Truman H. Safford, Jr. Bradford, Vermont: Published by A. Low, [1845] 48 p. MBC; MH; MWA; VtHi; VtMidbC. 45-7127

Youth's keepsake. A christmas and new year's gift for young people. Boston: Carter and Hendee, 1845. LU. 45-7128

Zeugnusse, alter und neuer lehrer der Lutherischen kirche, von dem geistlichen priesterthum. Buffalo, New York: Gedruckt bei A.E. Krause, 1845. MoSC. 45-7129

Zeuner, Charles, 1795-1857. The ancient lyre; a collection of old, new and original church music under the approbation of the professional music society in Boston. Arranged and composed by Charles Zeuner. Boston: Crocker and Brewster, 1845. 362 p. KWiU; LNH. 45-7130

Zion's watchman. In four parts. By several clergymen. [Hartford, 1845] 48 p. N; NjR. 45-7131

Zschokke, Heinrich, 1771-1848. The fool of the 19th century, and other tales. Translated from the German of Zschokke. New York: D. Appleton and company, 1845. 373 p. DLC; NcU; PPL-R. 45-7132

Zschokke, Heinrich, 1771-1848. The goldmakers' village, translated from the German of H. Zschakke. New York: D. Appleton and company, 1845. 180 p. KWiU; MH; NcD; OASht; RPA. 45-7133

Zschokke, Heinrich, 1771-1848. Tales from the German of Heinrich Zschokke, by Parke Godwin. Part 1. New York: Wiley and Putnam, 1845. 2 v. IaGG; MB; MNe; PPL; WaS. 45-7134

Zschokke, Heinrich, 1771-1848. Veronica; or, the free court of Aarau. Translated from the German of Zschokke, by the author of "Giafur al Barmeki." New York: Harper and brothers, 1845. 111 p. IU; MNF; PBm. 45-7135

Zumpt, Karl Gottlob, 1792-1849. A grammar of the Latin language. From the ninth edition of the original, adapted to the use of English students. Corrected and enlarged by Charles Anthon. New York: Harper and brothers, 1845. CSfCW; CtY; MH; PU; ViU. 45-7136

Zumpt, Karl Gottlob, 1792-1849. Latin grammar. New York: Harper and brothers, 1845? 594 p. CSfCW. 45-7137

ABOUT THE AUTHORS

SCOTT BRUNTJEN (B.A., University of Iowa; M.A., University of Iowa; M.A. Shippensburg University of Pennsylvania; D.A. Simmons College) is the Executive Vice President of Acquisitions Management Corporation of Colorado. Prior to this he served for twenty years in various library capacities from reference librarian to creator and then Director of the Iowa Locator, the first CD-ROM based statewide library computer database. Dr. Bruntjen began work on The *Checklist of American Imprints* project in 1972 and has been active in its development for the past twenty-three years. In the late 1970's he co-directed an HEA Title IIc project to bring initial control to the then unorganized WPA files which form the basis of the *Checklist*. He has more than forty publications to his credit ranging from the basic text on preparing library data for computer input (*Data Conversion*) to a bio-bibliography of Douglas C. McMurtrie (*Douglas C. McMurtrie, Bibliographer and Historian of Printing*).

CAROL R. RINDERKNECHT is a graduate of Shippensburg University of Pennsylvania. She is currently the President of Acquisitions Management Corporation of Colorado which owns and operates several smaller resort properties along the Front Range of The Rocky Mountains. She has worked on the American Imprints project since 1972 and in that capacity has published sixteen volumes in the *Checklist* series. She co-directed an HEA Title IIc project in the late 1970's at Rutgers University which brought order to the basic WPA files used in the production of the *Checklist*.